SOURCEBOOK OF AMERICAN METHODISM

Edited by
Frederick A. Norwood

Abingdon
Nashville

SOURCEBOOK OF AMERICAN METHODISM

Library of Congress Cataloging in Publication Data

Main entry under title:

Sourcebook of American Methodism.

   1. Methodist Church—United States—History—Sources.
I. Norwood, Frederick Abbott.
BX8235.S68   287'.673   82-11381

ISBN 0-687-39140-7 (pbk.)

Acknowledgment is made to the following copyright holders for permission to
reprint these materials:

Methodist History and the General Commission on History and Archives of
The United Methodist Church for the article by John Langford on p. 523; the
article by James K. Stein on p. 655; the article by Willis J. King on p. 636; the
article by Alfredo Nanez on p. 624; and for material from *Hands on the Ark* by
Robert W. Sledge on p. 570.

Christian Century Foundation for the article by Donald W. Dayton (p. 648),
copyright 1975 Christian Century Foundation, reprinted by permission from
the Feb. 26, 1975 issue of *The Christian Century*; and the article by Winifred
L. Chappel (p. 599), copyright 1926 by Christian Century Foundation,
reprinted by permission from May 6, 1926 issue of *The Christian Century*.

Excerpts from *I Was Made a Minister* by Edwin W. Hughes, copyright
renewal © 1970 by Mrs. Caroline Hughes Crummey and Mrs. William H.
Remy, is used by permission of the publisher, Abingdon Press.

MANUFACTURED BY THE PARTHENON PRESS AT
NASHVILLE, TENNESSEE, UNITED STATES OF AMERICA

DATE DUE

NOV 16 1998		
FEB 06 1999		
9-17-06		
		Printed in USA

SOURCEBOOK OF AMERICAN METHODISM

In Memory of
Florence L. Norwood

CONTENTS

FOREWORD

This volume by Frederick A. Norwood is the second in a series of scholarly publications, endorsed by the Division of Ordained Ministry and the Board of Higher Education and Ministry as part of the Bicentennial Observance of American Methodism. Gerald O. McCulloh's Ministerial Education in the American Methodist Movement has already appeared.

Recognizing the dire need for a documentary history of Methodism, and deeming it appropriate to stimulate and sponsor such a history as part of the Bicentennial, the Bicentennial Observances Steering Committee of the Division of Ordained Ministry rejoiced to discover that the dean of Methodist historians had such a volume in progress. Dr. Frederick A. Norwood graciously offered to include this volume, which he had projected as a companion to his Story of American Methodism.

Dr. Norwood is, indeed, the ideal and obvious historian to select, arrange, and interpret the documents through which Methodism is to be understood historically. He has decisively shaped our understanding of American Methodism. His Story of American Methodism is now the standard one-volume treatment. He was a contributor to and a member of the editorial board of both The History of American Methodism and The Encyclopedia of World Methodism. He contributed the article on "Methodism" to the Encyclopaedia Britannica and articles on aspects of Methodist history to various scholarly journals. He has been a member of the editorial board of Methodist History and a member of the General Commission for the Methodist Bicentennial.

As noted, the present volume is conceived as a companion to The Story of American Methodism, a fact which should enhance the value and usefulness of both. Organized on the same format, sharing general and most chapter headings with the narrative, this documentary account will move the general reader, as well as the student, quickly and readily into the stuff of Methodist history, the evidence upon which Dr. Norwood based his narrative account. Where Dr. Norwood does diverge from the earlier format, he does so to take account of historical trends that have come more fully into focus in the last decade. For instance, additional materials are devoted to the roles of women and of minorities in the church.

This volume should enjoy a long and useful life.

Russell E. Richey
Drew University

ACKNOWLEDGEMENTS

In any work of scholarship an invisible host of laborers in the academic vineyard makes any kind of harvest possible. Without them an author would be driven back to the Middle Ages, painfully scrawling his one hand-scriven copy.

My appreciation goes to the administration of Garrett-Evangelical Theological Seminary, whose continuing encouragement of scholarly activities provided the needed financial support. Of course one acknowledges the publisher and his legions of editors and technicians and designers and setters and proofreaders and all the rest, whose assigned duty it is to keep the author humble. But they have a sort of vicarious reward in direct creation of the final product.

I have in mind especially two groups of participants, who usually remain totally invisible. The first are the librarians. The materials in the present collection came from several locations. The heaviest contribution, however, came naturally from resources of this school, whose holdings in Methodistica, gathered over thirteen decades by the diligence and care of many persons who all loved the Methodist heritage, provide rich hunting ground. A salute, then, to all of them, from the early times of the Deering-Jackson Collection to most recent years, including that major addition of materials from former Evangelical Theological Seminary, especially strong for the Evangelical United Brethren.

And then finally there are the really indispensable ones, whose combination of skill and unending patience brought into being the manuscript you see in photocopy before you. Here are their names: Kathi Douglas and Dolores Roessler. In a unique way _they_ made this book.

INTRODUCTION

One of the best approaches to the study of any historical tradition is to go to the sources, by which are meant records which belong to the times they describe. They possess an immediacy and vibrancy no second-hand accounts from a later time can claim. Although they are subject to the limitations of any historical record—incomplete at best—, they are free from the further limitations imposed on secondary materials by the unavoidable time-lapse biases and distortions to which even the most honest historians of a later era are subject. An example is the altered views of the American Revolution as seen in writings of the early twentieth century, the mid-decades, and the Bicentennial of 1976-1983.

The same inherent value of original sources applies to the study of American Methodism. These materials are vast and widely scattered. Three or four of the libraries of Methodist-related theological seminaries, as well as that of the General Commission on Archives and History, possess extensive collections. But these are not easily available except in those particular localities. Furthermore, many of the older items are now in poor condition or extremely rare.

This collection aims to provide representative source readings gathered together in one substantial but compact book useful along with a textbook in either classes or independent study. There is no substitute for digging—or at least browsing—in original sources, some of which make the mind tingle as they help history come alive. A few secondary materials have been included where no primary resources are suitable.

This collection is comprehensive. It uses many kinds of record, including informal types. In fact selections from official documents, usually available elsewhere, have been restricted. It includes materials from the major chronological periods. It covers regional development and geographical expansion. It deals with institutional growth and organization and with the inevitable political forces. It takes account of economic and social factors on the one hand and of theological concerns on the other. It includes not only United Methodism and its immediate antecedents, but also the other Methodisms, Wesleyan, Free, Nazarene, etc. It deals with black, Asian, Hispanic, and Native American themes and forms. It recognizes the importance of women, the story of which is only now being vigorously recovered. One caution: Although the Table of Contents provides a general outline, additional materials beyond those given under chapter headings will be found scattered throughout. For example, women are referred to on pages 22, 31, 49, 248, 394, 482, 567-70, 650-51, 669-72, etc; Negro churches and black themes occur on pages 31, 39, 41, 46, 47, 49, 148-49, 196, 247, 248, 325, 326, 335, 336-41, 478-80, 509-23, 574-75, 576-78, 665-66, 681-83, etc. There are other references to United Brethren and Evangelical Association beyond the titled chapters.

Only one important facet has been intentionally excluded, solely for reasons of length: the organized global missions of the church, which would require another thick volume to comprehend. This book, except for introductory attention to the principal founder, John Wesley, remains,

albeit reluctantly, firmly within the continental United States. Certain other important materials, such as printed official journals and the auto-biography of Peter Cartwright, have been left out because of their general availability.

Now for a few practical matters. The readings have been organized into chapters, for each of which a succinct introduction provides the environment and significance for the individual selections. Scholarly notes on names and places have been avoided unless necessary for context and connection. Although every effort has been made to provide self-sufficient segments, sometimes rather ruthless editing and excising have been necessary. Methodists have been no freer from prolixity than other human beings. In no way can these readings, alone, serve as a basis for serious research. The scholar must herself dig and delve in the originals. On the other hand, the original text has been obediently followed, with minimal tinkering with spelling and punctuation. Deletions from the text are shown by . . . for brief and by *   *   * for longer omissions. Editorial additions to the text are marked by [brackets].

Here is a chance for the historical student to cut loose for a season from formal surveys and to make acquaintance with the performers themselves-- at least insofar as they have left written records. And that is the only way the honest historian has, beyond one generation, of getting back to the way it really was.

I

ANCESTRAL HERITAGE, 1725-1784

1. THE WESLEYAN SOURCE

Because readings from the writings of John and Charles Wesley, as well as older and more recent editions of their works, are readily available, only materials which specifically relate to the American scene are included in this collection. These have to do principally with the expedition to Georgia and the ordinations of 1784.

As a starter, however, Wesley is introduced by a famous historian, who later was elected President of the United States, Woodrow Wilson. Symbolic of the whole Evangelical Revival of the eighteenth century in England and the subsequent Methodist movement throughout the world is the person of John Wesley, who, together with his brother Charles, spurred his followers in and out of the Church of England to a peak of religious revival that spread its influence far beyond those churches which directly claim his heritage. How many other key figures of church history may be presented effectively by such a historian as Woodrow Wilson, then president of Princeton University? The occasion is described in a centennial volume published by Wesleyan University in Middletown, Connecticut:

> *On the evening of Tuesday a very large audience gathered, this time in the North Congregational Church, kindly tendered for the occasion by the officers of that society, to listen to the address of President Woodrow Wilson of Princeton University. The presiding officer of the evening was His Excellency Abiram Chamberlain, Governor of Connecticut, and about him on the platform were seated Governor Bates of Massachusetts, Hon. Martin A. Knapp, '68, of the Interstate Commerce Commission, Hon. Leslie M. Shaw, Secretary of the Treasury of the United States, President Buckham of the University of Vermont, President Tucker of Dartmouth College, President Remsen of Johns Hopkins University, President Eliot of Harvard University, Bishop E.R. Hendrix, '67, of the Methodist Episcopal Church, South, and other gentlemen prominent in school or church or state. President Wilson, who for two years occupied the chair of history in Wesleyan, has a host of friends among the Alumni of the College and the citizens of Middletown; and the interest which his admirable address on "John Wesley's*

3

*Place in History" commanded was heightened, in many
of his hearers, by their warm personal regard for
the speaker. (Wesley Bicentennial, 1703-1903
(Middletown, Conn., 1904), 12.*

One always wonders why so cloistered a scholar would forsake
his intellectual environment to fare forth on an unpromising missionary journey to as yet undeveloped Georgia. Wesley himself was
driven to seek understanding of why he went. His letter to Dr.
John Burton, friend and one of the trustees of the new colony, is
perceptive and revealing.

After his arrival in Savannah Wesley embarked in typical
fashion on his task with a carefully drawn plan in accordance with
the standards of the Church of England. No matter there was no
church structure nor the parishioners only rude settlers. The
Second Savannah Journal states his intention succinctly.

This young man's entanglement with Sophia (Sophey) Hopkey
finds frequent attention in the diaries and journal (especially,
for those interested, Journal, I, 290-94). The unhappy outcome is
illustrated by a brief journal entry.

After discouraging struggles on several fronts Wesley in due
course returned to England with a spiritual load indicated by a
journal entry near the end of Volume I. Like John Bunyan's Pilgrim
at the Wayside Cross, his burden was in large part removed at the
renowned Aldersgate experience, 24 May 1738.

¶   Address by Woodrow Wilson, "John Wesley's Place in History."

    (Taken from *Wesley Bicentennial, 1703-1903* (Wesleyan
    University, 1904), 157-170.)

John Wesley lived and wrought while the Georges reigned. He
was born but a year after Anne became queen, a year before the
battle of Blenheim was fought; while England was still caught in
the toils of the wars into which her great constitutional revolution had drawn her; when Marlborough was in the field, and the
armies afoot which were to make the ancient realm free to go her
own way without dictation from any prince in Europe. But when he
came to manhood, and to the days in which his work was to begin,
all things had fallen quiet again. Wars were over and the pipes
of peace breathed soothing strains. The day of change had passed
and gone, and bluff Sir Robert Walpole ruled the land, holding it
quiet, aloof from excitement, to the steady humdrum course of bus—

iness, in which questions of the treasury and of the routine of administration were talked about, not questions of constitutional right or any matter of deep conviction. The first of the dull Georges had come suitably into the play at the centre of the slow plot, bringing with him the vulgar airs of the provincial court of obscure Hanover, and views that put statesmanship out of the question.

The real eighteenth century had set in, whose annals even its own historians have pronounced to be tedious, unheroic, without noble or moving plot, though they would fain make what they can of the story. They have found it dull because it lacked dramatic unity. Its wars were fought for mere political advantage,—because politicians had intrigued and thrones fallen vacant; for the adjustment of the balance of power or the aggrandizement of dynasties; and represented neither the growth of empires nor the progress of political ideals. All religion, they say, had cooled and philanthropy had not been born. The thinkers of the day had as little elevation of thought as the statesmen, the preachers as little ardor as the atheistical wits, whose unbelief they scarcely troubled themselves to challenge. The poor were unspeakably degraded and the rich had flung morals to the winds. There was no adventure of mind or conscience that seemed worth risking a fall for.

But the historians who paint this sombre picture look too little upon individuals, upon details, upon the life that plays outside the field of politics and of philosophical thinking. They are in search of policies, movements, great and serious combinations of men, events that alter the course of history, or letters that cry a challenge to the spirits. Forget statecraft, forego seeking the materials for systematic narrative, and look upon the eighteenth century as you would look upon your own day, as a period of human life whose details are its real substance, and you will find enough and to spare of human interest. The literary annals of a time, when Swift and Addison and Berkeley and Butler and Pope and Gray and Defoe and Richardson and Fielding and Smollett and Sterne and Samuel Johnson and Goldsmith and Burke and Hume and Gibbon and Cowper and Burns wrote, and in which Wordsworth, Coleridge, Byron, Shelley, and Keats were born, cannot be called barren or without spiritual significance.

No doubt the wits of Queen Anne's time courted a muse too prim, too precise, too much without passion to seem to us worthy to stand with the great spirit of letters that speaks in the noble poetry with which the next century was ushered in; but there was here a very sweet relief from the ungoverned passions of the Restoration, the licentious force of men who knew the restraints neither of purity nor of taste; and he must need strong spices in his food who

finds Swift insipid. No doubt Fielding is coarse, and Richardson
prolix and sentimental, Sterne prurient and without true tonic for
the mind, but the world which these men uncovered will always stand
real and vivid before our eyes. It is a crowded and lively stage
with living persons upon it; the eighteenth century can never seem
a time vague and distant after we have read those pages of intimate
revelation. No doubt Dr. Johnson failed to speak any vital philosophy of life and uttered only common sense, and the talk at the
Turk's Head Tavern ran upon preserving the English Constitution
rather than upon improving it; but it is noteworthy that Mr. Goldsmith, who was of that company, was born of the same century that
produced Laurence Sterne, and that "She Stoops to Conquer" and the
"Vicar of Wakefield," with their sweet savor of purity and modesty
and grace, no less than "Tristram Shandy" and "Tom Jones," with
their pungent odor, blossomed in the unweeded garden of that careless age. Burns sang with clear throat and an unschooled rapture
at the North, and the bards were born who were to bring the next
age in with strains that rule our spirits still.

A deep pulse beat in that uneventful century. All things were
making ready for a great change. When the century began it was
the morrow of a great struggle, from whose passionate endeavors men
rested with a certain lassitude, with a great weariness and longing
for peace. The travail of the civil wars had not ended with the
mastery of Cromwell, the Restoration of Charles, and the ousting of
James; it had ended only with the constitutional revolution which
followed 1688, and with the triumphs of the Prince of Orange. It
had been compounded of every element that can excite or subdue the
spirits of men. Questions of politics had sprung out of questions
of religion, and men had found their souls staked upon the issue.
The wits of the Restoration tried to laugh the ardor off, but it
burned persistent until its work was done and the liberties of
England spread to every field of thought or action.

No wonder the days of Queen Anne seemed dull and thought less
after such an age; and yet no wonder there was a sharp reaction.
No wonder questions of religion were avoided, minor questions of
reform postponed. No wonder Sir Robert sought to cool the body
politic and calm men's minds for business. But other forces were
gathering head as hot as those which had but just subsided. This
long age of apparent reaction was in fact an age of preparation
also; was not merely the morrow of one revolution, but was also the
eve of another, more tremendous still, which was to shake the whole
fabric of society. England had no direct part in bringing the
French Revolution on, but she drank with the rest of the wine of the
age which produced it, and before it came had had her own rude awakening in the revolt of her American colonies.

6

Great industrial changes were in progress, too. This century, so dull to the political historian, was the century in which the world of our own day was born, the century of that industrial revolution which made political ambition thenceforth an instrument of material achievement, of commerce and manufacture. These were the days in which canals began to be built in England, to open her inland markets to the world and shorten and multiply her routes of trade; when the spinning jenny was invented and the steam engine and the spinning machine and the weaver's mule; when cities which had slept since the middle ages waked of a sudden to new life and new cities sprang up where only hamlets had been. Peasants crowded into the towns for work; the countrysides saw their life upset, unsettled; idlers thronged the highways and the marts, their old life at the plow or in the village given up, no settled new life found; there were not police enough to check or hinder vagrancy, and sturdy beggars were all too ready to turn their hands to crime and riot. The old order was breaking up, and men did not readily find their places in the new.

The new age found its philosophy in Adam Smith's "Wealth of Nations," the philosophy of self-interest, and men thought too constantly upon these things to think deeply on any others. An industrial age, an age of industrial beginnings, offers new adventures to the mind, and men turn their energies into the channels of material power. It is no time for speculations concerning another world; the immediate task is to fill this world with wealth and fortune and all the enginery of material success. It is no time to regard men as living souls; they must be thought of rather as tools, as workmen, as producers of wealth, the builders of industry, and the captains of soldiers of fortune. Men must talk of fiscal problems, of the laws of commerce, of the raw materials and the processes of manufacture, of the facilitation of exchange. Politics centres in the budget, and the freedom men think of is rather the freedom of the market than the freedom of the hustings or of the voting booth.

And yet there are here great energies let loose which have not wrought their full effect upon the minds of men in the mere doing of their daily tasks or the mere planning of their fortunes. Men must think and long as well as toil; the wider the world upon which they spend themselves the wider the sweep of their thoughts, the restless, unceasing excursions of their hope. The mind of England did not lie quiet through those unquiet days. All things were making and to be made, new thoughts of life as well as new ways of living. Masters and laborers alike were sharing in the new birth of society. And in the midst of these scenes, this shifting of the forces of the world, this passing of old things and birth of new,

7

stood John Wesley, the child, the contemporary, the spiritual pro-
tagonist of the eighteenth century. Born before Blenheim had been
fought, he lived until the fires of the French Revolution were a-
blaze. He was as much the child of his age as Bolingbroke was, or
Robert Burns. We ought long ago to have perceived that no century
yields a single type. There are countrysides the land over which
know nothing of London town. The Vicar of Wakefield rules his
parish as no rollicking, free-thinking fellow can who sups with
Laurence Sterne. Sir Roger de Coverley is as truly a gentleman of
his age as Squire Western. Quiet homes breed their own sons. The
Scots country at the North has its own free race of poets and thinkers, men, some of them, as stern as puritans in the midst of the
loose age. Many a quiet village church in England hears preaching
which has no likeness at all to the cool rationalistic discourse of
vicars and curates whom the spiritual blight of the age has touched,
and witnesses in its vicarage a life as simple, as grave, as elevated above the vain pursuits of the world as any household of
puritan days had seen. England was steadied in that day, as always,
by her great pervasive middle class, whose affections did not veer
amidst the heady gusts even of that time of change, when the world
was in transformation; whose life held to the same standards, whose
thoughts travelled old accustomed ways. The indifference of the
church did not destroy their religion. They did not lose their
prepossessions for the orderly manners and morals that kept life
pure.

It was no anomaly, therefore, that the son of Samuel and Susanna Wesley should come from the Epworth rectory to preach forth
righteousness and judgment to come to the men of the eighteenth
century. Epworth, in quiet Lincolnshire, was typical English land
and lay remote from the follies and fashions of the age. There was
sober thinking and plain living,--there where low monotonous levels
ran flat to the spreading Humber and the coasts of the sea. The
children of that vicarage, swarming a little host about its hearth,
were bred in love and fear, love of rectitude and fear of sin,
their imagination filled with the ancient sanctions of the religion
of the prophets and the martyrs, their lives drilled to right action
and the studious service of God. Some things in the intercourse and
discipline of that household strike us with a sort of awe, some with
repulsion. Those children lived too much in the presence of things
unseen; the inflexible consciences of the parents who ruled them
brought them under a rigid discipline which disturbed their spirits
as much as it enlightened them. But, though gaiety and lightness of
heart were there shut out, love was not, nor sweetness. No one can
read Susanna Wesley's rules for the instruction and development of
her children without seeing the tender heart of the true woman,
whose children were the light of her eyes. This mother was a true
counsellor and her children resorted to her as to a sort of provi-

8

dence, feeling safe when she approved. For the stronger spirits among them the regime of that household was a keen and wholesome tonic.

And John Wesley was certainly one of the stronger spirits. He came out of the hands of his mother with the temper of a piece of fine steel. All that was executive and fit for mastery in the discipline of belief seemed to come to perfection in him. He dealt with the spirits of other men with the unerring capacity of a man of affairs,--a sort of spiritual statesman, a politician of God, speaking the policy of a kingdom unseen, but real and destined to prevail over all kingdoms else.

He did not deem himself a reformer; he deemed himself merely a minister and servant of the church and the faith in which he had been bred, and meant that no man should avoid him upon his errand though it were necessary to search the by-ways and beat the hedges to find those whom he sought. He did not spring to his mission like a man who had seen a vision and conceived the plan of his life beforehand, whole, and with its goal marked upon it as upon a map. He learned what it was to be from day to day, as other men do. He did not halt or hesitate, not because his vision went forward to the end, but because his will was sound, unfailing, sure of its immediate purpose. His "Journal" is as notable a record of common sense and sound practical judgment as Benjamin Franklin's "Auto-biography" or the letters of Washington. It is his clear knowledge of his duty and mission from day to day that is remarkable, and the effieiency with which he moved from purpose to purpose. It was a very simple thing that he did, taking it in its main outlines and conceptions. Conceiving religion vitally, as it had been conceived in his own home, he preached it with with a vigor, an explicitness, a directness of phrase and particularity of application which shocked the sober decorum of his fellow ministers of the church so much that he was more and more shut out from their pulpits. He got no church of his own; probably no single parish would have satisfied his ardor had a living been found for him. He would not sit still. The conviction of the truth was upon him; he was a messenger of God, and if he could not preach in the churches, where it seemed to him the duty of every man who loved the order and dignity of divine service to stand if he would deliver the word of God, he must, as God's man of affairs, stand in the fields as Mr. Whitefield did and proclaim it to all who could come within the sound of his voice.

And so he made the whole kingdom his parish, took horse like a courier and carried his news along every highway. Slowly, with no premeditated plan, going now here, now there, as some call of counsel or opportunity directed him, he moved as if from stage to stage of a journey; and as he went did his errand as if instinctively. No stranger at an inn, no traveller met upon the road left him

9

without hearing of his business. Those he could not come to a natural parley with he waylaid. The language of his "Journal" is sometimes almost that of the highwayman. "At Gerard's Cross," he says, "I plainly declared to those whom God gave into my hands the faith as it is in Jesus: as I did the next day to a young man I overtook on the road." The sober passion of the task grew upon him as it unfolded itself under his hand from month to month, from year to year. He was more and more upon the highways; his journeys lengthened, carried him into regions where preachers had never gone before, to the collieries, to the tin mines, to the fishing villages of the coast, and made him familiar with every countryside of the kingdom, his slight and sturdy figure and shrewd, kind face known everywhere. It was not long before he was in the saddle from year's end to year's end, always going forward as if upon an enterprise, but never hurried, always ready to stop and talk upon the one thing that absorbed him, making conversation and discourse his business, seizing upon a handful of listeners no less eagerly than upon a multitude.

The news got carried abroad as he travelled that he was coming, and he was expected with a sort of excitement. Some feared him. His kind had never been known in England since the wandering friars of the middle ages fell quiet and were gone. And no friar had ever spoken as this man spoke. He was not like Mr. Whitefield; his errand seemed hardly the same. Mr. Whitefield swayed men with a power known time out of mind, the power of the consummate orator whose words possess the mind and rule the spirit while he speaks. There was no magic of oratory in Mr. Wesley's tone or presence. There was something more singular, more intimate, more searching. He commanded so quietly, wore so subtle an air of gentle majesty, attached men to himself so like a party leader, whose coming draws together a company of partisans, and whose going leaves an organized band of adherents, that cautious men were uneasy and suspicious concerning him. He seemed a sort of revolutionist, left no community as he found it, set men by the ears. It was hard to believe that he had no covert errand, that he meant nothing more than to preach the peaceable riches of Christ. "The spirit of the Lord is upon me, because he hath anointed me to preach the gospel to the poor; he hath sent me to heal the broken-hearted; to preach deliverance to the captives, and recovery of sight to the blind; to set at liberty them that are bruised, to proclaim the acceptable year of the lord,"--this had been the text from which he preached his first sermon by the highway, standing upon a little eminence just outside the town of Bristol. It described his mission,--but not to his enemies. The churches had been shut against him, not because he preached, but because he preached with so disturbing a force and directness, as if he had come to take the peace of the church away and stir men to a great spiritual revolution; and un-

10

easy questionings arose about him. Why was he so busy? Why did he confer so often with an intimate group of friends, as if upon some deep plan, appoint rendezvous with them, and seem to know always which way he must turn next, and when? Why was he so restless, so indomitably eager to make the next move in his mysterious journey? Why did he push on through any weather and look to his mount like a trooper on campaign? Did he mean to upset the country? Men had seen the government of England disturbed before that by fanatics who talked only of religion and of judgment to come. The puritan and the roundhead had been men of this kind, and the Scottish covenanters. Was it not possible that John Wesley was the emissary of a part or of some pretender, or even of the sinister church of Rome?

He lived such calumnies down. No mobs dogged his steps after men had once come to know him and perceived the real quality he was of. Indeed, from the very first men had surrendered their suspicions upon sight of him. It was impossible, it would seem, not to trust him when once you had looked into his calm gray eyes. He was so friendly, so simple, so open, so ready to meet your challenge with temperate and reasonable reply, that it was impossible to deem him subtle, politic, covert, a man to preach one thing and plan another. There was something, too, in his speech and in the way he bore himself which discovered the heart of every man he dealt with. Men would raise their hands to strike him in the mob and, having caught the look in his still eye, bring them down to stroke his hair. Something issued forth from him which penetrated and subdued them,--some suggestion of purity, some intimation of love, some sign of innocence and nobility,--some power at once of rebuke and attraction which he must have caught from his Master. And so there came a day when prejudice stood abashed before him, and men everywhere hailed his coming as the coming of a friend and pastor. He became not only the best known man in the kingdom,--that of course, because he went everywhere,--but also the best loved and the most welcome.

And yet the first judgment of him had not been wholly wrong. A sort of revolution followed him, after all. It was not merely that he came and went so constantly and moved every countryside with his preaching. Something remained after he was gone: the touch of the statesman men had at first taken him to be. He was a minister of the Church of England. He lover her practices and had not willingly broken with them. It had been with the keenest reluctance that he consented to preach in the fields, outside the sacred precincts of a church, "having been all my life," as he said, "so tenacious of every point relating to decency and order that I should have thought the saving of souls almost a sin if it had not been done in a church." He never broke with the communion he loved.

11

But his work in the wide parish of a whole kingdom could not be done alone, and not many men bred to the orders of the church could be found to assist him; he was forced by sheer drift of circumstances to establish a sort of lay society, a sort of salvation army, to till the fields he had plowed. He was a born leader of men. The conferences he held with the friends he loved and trusted were councils of campaign, and did hold longplans in view, as his enemies suspected. They have a high and honorable place in the history of the statesmanship of salvation. It was a chief part of Wesley's singular power that everything he touched took shape as if with a sort of institutional life. He was not so great a preacher as Whitefield or so moving a poet as his brother Charles; men counseled him who were more expert and profound theologians than he and more subtle reasoners upon the processes of salvation. But in him all things seemed combined; no one power seemed more excellent than another, and every power expressed itself in action under the certain operation of his planning will. He almost unwittingly left a church behind him.

It is this statesmanship in the man that gives him precedence in the annals of his day. Men's spirits were not dead; they are never dead; but they sometimes stand confused, daunted, or amazed as they did amidst the shifting scenes of the eighteenth century, and wait to be commanded. This man commanded them, and kept his command over them, not only by the way he held the eye of the whole nation in his incessant tireless journeys, his presence everywhere, his winning power of address, but also by setting up deputies, classes, societies, where he himself could not be, with their places of meeting, their organizations and efficient way of action. He was as practical and attentive to details as a master of industry, and as keen to keep hold of the business he had set afoot. It was a happy gibe that dubbed the men of his way *Methodists*. It was the method of his evangelization that gave it permanance and historical significance. He would in any case have been a notable figure, a moving force in the history of his age. His mere preaching, his striking personality, his mere presence everywhere in the story of the time, his mere vagrancy and indomitable charm, would have drawn every historian to speak of him and make much of his picturesque part in the motley drama of the century; but as it is they have been constrained to put him among statesmen as well as in their catalogues of saints and missionaries.

History is inexorable with men who isolate themselves. They are suffered oftentimes to find a place in literature, but never in the story of events or in any serious reckoning of cause and effect. They may be interesting, but they are not important. The mere revolutionist looks small enough when his day is passed; the mere agitator struts but a little while and without applause amidst the

12

scenes and events which men remember. It is the men who make as
well as destroy who really serve their race, and it is noteworthy
how action predominated in Wesley from the first. The little
coterie at Oxford, to which we look back as to the first associates
in the movement which John Wesley dominated, were as fervent in
their prayers, in their musings upon the Scripture, in their visits
to the poor and outcast, before John Wesley joined them as afterward. Their zeal had its roots in the divine pity which must lie
at the heart of every evangelistic movement,--pity for those to
whom the gospel is not preached, whom no light of Christian guidance had reached, the men in the jails and in the purlieus of the
towns whom the church does not seek or touch; but he gave them
leadership and the spirit of achievement. His genius for action
touched everything he was associated with; every enterprise took
from him an impulse of efficiency.

Unquestionably this man altered and in his day governed the
spiritual history of England and the English-speaking race on both
sides of the sea; and we ask what was ready at his hand, what did
he bring into being of the things he seemed to create? The origina-
tive power of the individual in affairs must always remain a mystery, a theme more full of questions than of answers. What would
the eighteenth century in England have produced of spiritual better-
ment without John Wesley? What did he give it which it could not
have got without him? These are questions which no man can answer.
But one thing is plain: Wesley did not create life, he only summoned it to consciousness. The eighteenth century was not dead;
it was not even asleep; it was only confused, unorganized, without
authoritative leadership in matters of faith and doctrine, uncertain
of its direction.

Wesley's own Journal affords us an authentic picture of the
time, mixed, as always, of good and bad. He fared well or ill upon
his journeys as England was itself made up. The self-government of
England in that day was a thing uncentered and unsystematic in a degree it is nowadays difficult for us to imagine. The country gentlemen, who were magistrates, ruled as they pleased in the countrysides, whether in matters of justice or administration, without dictation or suggestion from London; and yet ruled rather as representatives than as masters. They were neighbors the year around to
the people they ruled; their interests were not divorced from the
interests of the rest. Local pride and a public spirit traditional
amongst them held them generally to a just and upright course. But
the process of justice with them was a process of opinion as much
as of law. It was an inquest of the neighborhood, and each neighborhood dealt with visitors and vagrants as it would. There was
everywhere the free touch of individuality. The roads were not po-
liced; the towns were not patrolled,--good men and bad had almost
equal leave to live as they pleased. If things went wrong the

13

nearest magistrate must be looked up at his home or stopped in his carriage as he passed along the highway and asked to pass judgment as chief neighbor and arbiter of the place. And so Mr. Wesley dealt with individuals,--it was the English way. His safety lay in the love and admiration he won or in the sense of fair play to which his frank and open methods appealed; his peril, in the passions of the crowds or of the individuals who pressed about him full of hatred and evil thoughts.

The noteworthy thing was how many good men he found along these highways where Tom Jones had travelled, how many were glad to listen to him and rejoiced at the message he brought, how many were just and thoughtful and compassionate, and waited for the gospel with an open heart. This man, as I have said, was no engaging orator, whom it would have been a pleasure to hear upon any theme. He spoke very searching words, sharper than any two-edged sword, cutting the conscience to the quick. It was no pastime to hear him. It was the more singular, therefore, the more significant, the more pitiful, how eagerly he was sought out, as if by men who knew their sore need and would fain hear some word of help, though it were a word also of stern rebuke and of fearful portent to those who went astray. The spiritual hunger of men was manifest, their need of the church, their instinct to be saved. The time was ready and cried out for a spiritual revival.

The church was dead and Wesley awakened it; the poor were neglected and Wesley sought them out; the gospel was shrunken into formulas and Wesley flung it fresh upon the air once more in the speech of common men; the air was stagnant and fetid; he cleared and purified it by speaking always and everywhere the word of God; and men's spirits responded, leaped at the message, and were made wholesome as they comprehended it. It was a voice for which they had waited, though they knew it not. It would not have been heard had it come untimely. It was the voice of the century's longing heard in the mouth of this one man more perfectly, more potently, than in the mouth of any other,--and this man a master of other men, a leader who left his hearers wiser than he found them in the practical means of salvation.

And so everything that made for the regeneration of the times seemed to link itself with Methodism. The great impulse of humane feeling which marked the closing years of the century seemed in no small measure to spring from it: the reform of prisons, the agitation for the abolition of slavery, the establishment of missionary societies and Bible societies, the introduction into life, and even into law, of pity for the poor, compassion for those who must suffer. The noble philanthropies and reforms which brighten the annals of the nineteenth century had their spiritual birth in the eighteenth. Wesley had carried Christianity to the masses of the people, had

14

renewed the mission of Christ himself, and all things began to take color from what he had done. Men to whom Methodism meant nothing, yet, in fact, followed this man to whom Methodism owed its establishment.

No doubt he played no small part in saving England from the madness which fell upon France ere the century ended. The English poor bore no such intolerable burdens as the poor of France had to endure. There was no such insensate preservation of old abuses in England as maddened the unhappy country across the Channel. But society was in sharp transition in England; one industrial age was giving place to another, and the poor particularly were sadly at a loss to find their places in the new. Work was hard to get, and the new work of pent-up towns was harder to understand and to do than the old familiar work in the field or in the village shops. There were sharper contrasts now than before between rich and poor, and the rich were no longer always settled neighbors in some countryside, but often upstart merchants in the towns, innovating manufacturers who seemed bent upon making society over to suit their own interests. It might have gone hard with order and government in a nation so upset, transformed, distracted, had not the hopeful lessons of religion been taught broadcast and the people made to feel that once more pity and salvation had sought them out.

There is a deep fascination in this mystery of what one man may do to change the face of his age. John Wesley, we have had reason to say, planned no reform, premeditated no revivification of society; his was simply the work of an efficient conviction. How far he was himself a product of the century which he revived it were a futile piece of metaphysic to inquire. That even his convictions were born of his age may go without saying: they are born in us also by a study of his age, and no century listens to a voice out of another,-- least of all out of a century yet to come. What is important for us is the method and cause of John Wesley's success. His method was as simple as the object he had in view. He wanted to get at men, and he went directly to them, not so much like a priest as like a fellow man standing in a like need with themselves. And the cause of his success? Genius, no doubt, and the gifts of a leader of men, but also something less singular, though perhaps not less individual,--a clear conviction of revealed truth and of its power to save. Neither men nor society can be saved by opinions; nothing has power to prevail but the conviction which commands, not the mind merely, but the will and the whole spirit as well. It is this and this only that makes one spirit the master of others, and no man need fear to use his conviction in any age. It will not fail of its power. Its magic has no sorcery of words, no trick of personal magnetism. It concentrates personality as if into a single element of sheer force, and transforms conduct into a life.

15

John Wesley's place in history is the place of the evangelist who is also a master of affairs. The evangelization of the world will always be the road to fame and power, but only to those who take it seeking, not these things, but the kingdom of God; and if the evangelist be what John Wesley was, a man poised in spirit, deeply conversant with the natures of his fellow-men, studious of the truth, sober to think, prompt and yet not rash to act, apt to speak without excitement and yet with a keen power of conviction, he can do for another age what John Wesley did for the eighteenth century. His age was singular in its need, as he was singular in his gifts and power. The eighteenth century cried out for deliverance and light, and God had prepared this man to show again the might and the blessing of his salvation.

¶ Letter to Georgia Trustee John Burton.

(Taken from *The Letters of the Rev. John Wesley* (Epworth Press, 1931), I, 188, 191.)

October 10, 1735.

DEAR SIR,—I have been hitherto unwilling to mention the grounds of my design of embarking for Georgia, for two reasons,—one, because they were such as I know few men would judge to be of any weight: the other, because I was afraid of making favourable judges think of me above what they ought to think; and what a snare this must be to my own soul I know by dear-bought experience.

But, on farther reflection, I am convinced that I ought to speak the truth with all boldness, even though it should appear foolishness to the world, as it has done from the beginning; and that, whatever danger there is in doing the will of God, He will support me under it. In His name, therefore, and trusting in His defence, I shall plainly declare the thing as it is.

My chief motive, to which all the rest are subordinate, is the hope of saving my own soul. I hope to learn the true sense of the gospel of Christ by preaching it to the heathen. They have no comments to construe away the text; no vain philosophy to corrupt it; no luxurious, sensual, covetous, ambitious expounders to soften its unpleasing truths, to reconcile earthly-mindedness and faith, the Spirit of Christ and the spirit of the world. They have no party, no interest to serve, and are therefore fit to receive the gospel in its simplicity. They are as little children, humble, willing to learn, and eager to do the will of God; and consequently they shall know of every doctrine I preach whether it be of God. By these,

16

therefore, I hope to learn the purity of that faith which was once delivered to the saints; the genuine sense and full extent of those laws which none can understand who mind earthly things.

*   *   *

To the other motive--the hope of doing more good in America--it is commonly objected that 'there are heathens enough in practice, if not theory, at home; why, then, should you go to those in America?' Why? For a very plain reason: because these heathens at home have Moses and the Prophets, and those have not; because these who *have* the gospel trample upon it, and those who have it not earnestly call for it; 'therefore, seeing these judge themselves unworthy of eternal life, lo, I turn to the Gentiles.'

If you object, farther, the losses I must sustain in leaving my native country, I ask,--Loss of what? of anything I desire to keep? No; I shall still have food to eat and raiment to put on--enough of such food as I choose to eat and such raiment as I desire to put on; and if any man have a desire of other things, or of more food than he can eat, or more raiment than he need put on, let him know that the greatest blessing which can possibly befall him is to be cut off from all occasions of gratifying those desires, which, unless speedily rooted out, will drown his soul in everlasting perdition.

¶   Second Savannah Journal.

(Taken from *The Journal of the Rev. John Wesley* (Epworth Press, 1909, 1938), I, 197-214).

Not finding, as yet, any door open for the pursuing our main design, we considered in what manner we might be most useful to the flock at Savannah. And we agreed (1) to advise the more serious among them to form themselves into a sort of little society, and to meet once or twice a week, in order to reprove, instruct, and exhort one another. (2) To select out of these a smaller number for a more intimate union with each other, which might be forwarded, partly by our conversing singly with each, and partly by inviting them all together to our house; and this, accordingly, we determined to do every Sunday in the afternoon.

MAY 5, *Wed.*--I was asked to baptize a child of Mr. Parker's, second Baliff of Savannah; but Mrs. Parker told me, 'Neither Mr. Parker nor I will consent to its being dipped.' I answered, 'If

you "certify that" your "child is weak, it will suffice" (the rubric
says) "to pour water upon it."' She replied, 'Nay, the child is not
weak; but I am resolved it shall not be dipped.' This argument I
could not confute. So I went home, and the child was baptized by
another person.

Sun. 9.--I began dividing the public prayers, according to the
original appointment of the Church (still observed in a few places
in England). The morning service began at five; the Communion Office
(with the sermon), at eleven; the evening service, about three; and
this day I began reading prayers in the court-house--a large and convenient place.

Mon. 10.--I began visiting my parishioners in order, from house
to house; for which I set apart the time when they can not work, because of the heat, viz. from twelve till three in the afternoon.

¶   Miss Sophy.

        (Taken from *The Journal of the Rev. John Wesley*,
        (Epworth Press, 1909, 1938), I, 355-356).

        I was in doubt whether I could admit Miss Sophy to the Com-
munion till she had, in some manner or other, owned her fault and declared her repentance. I doubted the more, because I was informed
she had left off fasting, and because she neglected all the morning
prayers, though still acknowledging her obligation to both, which
made a wide difference between her neglect and that of others. But
after much consideration, I resolved to take Mr. Delamotte's advice
and to bear with her till I had spoken with her once more.

¶   Afterthoughts.

        (Taken from *The Journal of the Rev. John Wesley*, (Ep-
        worth Press, 1909, 1938), I, 421-424).

        Toward evening was a calm; but in the night a strong north wind
brought us safe into the Downs. The day before, Mr. Whitefield had
sailed out, neither of us then knowing anything of the other. At
four in the morning we took boat, and in half an hour landed at Deal;
it being *Wednesday*, FEBRUARY I, the anniversary festival in Georgia
for Mr. Oglethorpe's landing there.

It is now two years and almost four months since I left my
native country, in order to teach the Georgian Indians the nature
of Christianity. But what have I learned myself in the meantime?
Why, what I the least of all suspected, that I, who went to America
to convert others, was never myself converted to God. 'I am not
mad,' though I thus speak; but 'I speak the words of truth and sober-
ness'; if haply some of those who still dream may awake, and see,
that I am, so are they.

Are they read in philosophy? So was I. In ancient or modern
tongues? So was I also. Are they versed in the science of divinity?
I too have studied it many years. Can they talk fluently upon spiritual things? The very same could I do. Are they plenteous in alms?
Behold, I gave all my goods to feed the poor. Do they give of their
labor as of their substance? I have laboured more abundantly than
they all. Are they willing to suffer for their brethren? I have
thrown up my friends, reputation, ease, country; I have put my life
in my hand, wandering into strange lands; I have given my body to be
devoured by the deep, parched up with heat, consumed by toil and
weariness, or whatsoever God should please to bring upon me. But
does all this--be it more or less, it matters not--make me acceptable
to God? Does all I ever did or can know, say, give, do, or suffer,
justify me in His sight? Yea, or the constant use of all the means
of grace? (which nevertheless, is meet, right, and our bounden duty).
Or that I know nothing of myself; that I am, as touching outward,
moral righteousness, blameless? Or (to come closer yet) the having
a rational conviction of all the truths of Christianity? Does all
this give me a claim to the holy, heavenly, divine character of a
Christian? By no means. If the oracles of God are true, if we are
still to abide by 'the law and the testimony,' all these things,
though, when ennobled by faith in Christ, they are holy and just and
good, yet without it are 'dung and dross,' meet only to be purged
away by 'the fire that never shall be quenched.'

This, then, have I learned in the ends of the earth,--that I
'am fallen short of the glory of God': that my whole heart is
'altogether corrupt and abominable'; and consequently my whole life
(seeing it cannot be that an 'evil tree' should 'bring forth good
fruit'): that, 'alienated' as I am from the life of God, I am 'a
child of wrath,' an heir of hell: that my own works, my own sufferings, my own righteousness, are so far from reconciling me to an
offended God, so far from making any atonement for the least of those
sins, which 'are more in number than the hairs of my head,' that the
most specious of them need an atonement themselves, or they cannot
abide His righteous judgement: that 'having the sentence of death'
in my heart, and having nothing in or of myself to plead, I have no
hope, but that of being justified freely, 'through the redemption
that is in Jesus'; I have no hope, but that if I seek I shall find
Christ, and 'be found in Him, not having my own righteousness, but

19

that which is through the faith of Christ, the righteousness
which is of God by faith.'

If it be said that I have faith (for many such things have I
heard, from many miserable comforters), I answer, So have the
devils--a sort of faith; but still they are strangers to the covenant of promise. So the apostles had even at Cana in Galilee, when
Jesus first 'manifested forth His glory'; even then they, in a sort,
'believed on Him'; but they had not then 'the faith that overcometh
the world.' The faith I want is 'a sure trust and confidence in
God, that, through the merits of Christ, my sins are forgiven, and
I reconciled to the favour of God.' I want that faith which St.
Paul recommends to all the world, especially in his Epistle to the
Romans: that faith which enables every one that hath it to cry out,
'I live not; but Christ liveth in my; and the life which I now live,
I live by faith in the Son of God, who loved me, and gave Himself
for me.' I want that faith which none can have without knowing that
he hath it (though many imagine they have it, who have it not); for
whosoever hath it, is 'freed from sin, the' whole 'body of sin is
destroyed' in him: he is freed from fear, 'having peace with God
through Christ, and rejoicing in hope of the glory of God.' And
he is freed from doubt, 'having the love of God shed abroad in his
heart, through the Holy Ghost which is given unto him'; which
'Spirit itself beareth witness with his spirit, that he is a child
of God.'

2. PLANTING BY LAY PEOPLE AND CULTIVATION
BY WESLEY'S PREACHERS

With copious sentiment and nostalgia J.B. Wakeley recalled the early days of Methodism in New York. As a historically minded pastor in New York Annual Conferences, he delved into the "lost chapters" of John Street church, one of the earliest sites of Methodist work in America. Because the architectural monuments still stood in his time, he could summon to familiar settings those determined lay spirits, Barbara and Paul Heck, Philip and Margaret Embury, and Captain Thomas Webb, lay preacher extraordinary resplendent in his bright military uniform. Webb especially was a mover and doer in the growth of the movement in its infancy.

Thomas Rankin, to whom praise of other men than John Wesley did not come easily, paid a handsome tribute to this unlearned but sincere preacher, American prototype of the Methodist lay man, as Heck was of the Methodist lay woman. The brief passage is taken from the manuscript of Rankin's "Journal" preserved in Garrett-Evangelical Theological Seminary.

One of the key documents is the letter from Thomas Taylor of New York to John Wesley, 11 April 1768. It opened the way for an organized missionary effort under Wesley's direct authority, as a result of which regularly appointed preachers (unordained all) were sent two-by-two in the years before the American Revolution, beginning in 1769 with Richard Boardman and Joseph Pilmore. The letter is given here in the more complete and accurate form provided by Frank Baker in Methodist History, *III[2] (Jan. 1965), 3-9.*

Among the missionaries sent by Wesley, Francis Asbury stood preeminent. John Wesley Bond, a minister who served as his traveling companion during his later years, has left a charming, candid, and perceptive literary portrait. It is based on day-to-day personal observation, and hence offers a more human and more profound picture than the ordinary adulations.

Two of his contemporaries, also journal writers, were Joseph Pilmore and Thomas Rankin. The first of these has been worthily edited and published; the other lies fallow in manuscript. The first was a Methodist by persuasion, but capable of thought and action independent of his English leader. The second was more "Wesleyan" than Asbury himself.

One of many evangelically inclined clergymen, who nevertheless remained firmly in the Anglican fold, was Devereux Jarratt of Virginia, whose involvement in the spiritual awakening of the 1770s brought him into fruitful contact with the Methodists.

Please compare the complete record of the General Minutes for the year 1773, the date of the first Annual Conference, with the most recent volume of the General Minutes--or even with any accessible Annual Conference Journal. This is one way to measure change.

¶ Early lay founders.

> (Taken from J.B. Wakeley, *Lost Chapters Recovered from the Early History of American Methodism* (1858), 34-36, 42-49).

Mr. Embury emigrated to America in the early part of 1765. He settled in the city of New-York, and for some time resided in John-street, where his son Samuel was born on the 24th of September, 1765. Mr. Embury was a carpenter and joiner by trade, and, like Paul, labored with his own hands and lived in his own hired house. Mr. Embury was a local preacher in Ireland before he came to this country.

About the same time a number of emigrants from the "Emerald Isle" came to New-York, who had been Methodists in their own land. They were not only "strangers and foreigners," but were like "sheep without a shepherd." They were away from the means of grace, from a preached gospel, from class-meetings, and love-feasts; and their

> "Faith forsook its hold,
> Their hope declined and love grew cold."

. . . Among the emigrants who arrived the next year was a pious family by the name of Hick [Heck], from Balligarane, Ireland.

Mrs. Barbara Hick was a "mother in Israel;" she felt for the honor of God, for the cause of bleeding Zion, and for the souls of those who were about making "shipwreck of faith."

One evening she went into a company of the backslidden Methodists, and found them engaged in playing cards. She seized the pack of cards, and with a holy indignation threw them into the fire, determined to burn up their idols. Mrs. Hick then warned them of the danger to which they were exposed, and expostulated with them in the most pathetic and earnest manner. Then going to Mr. Embury, she exclaimed, "Brother Embury, you must preach to us, or we shall all go to hell, and God will require our blood at your hands!"

Poor Embury! to him it was like a thunder-peal in a clear sky; it was like an earthquake shock; it was like the alarm of the sound of the last trump! Her manner, her countenance, the tone of her

voice, as well as what she said, aroused, astonished, and alarmed
him. He felt as David did when Nathan said to him, "Thou art the
man!" And yet Mr. Embury wished to quiet his conscience and hush
his fears, so he inquired, "How can I preach, for I have neither a
house nor a congregation?" Plausible as this excuse appeared, she
had an answer ready, and said with peculiar emphasis, which Mr. Embury never forgot: "Preach in your own house and to your own company first." She seemed to him like a messenger from the invisible
world, addressing him with the impressive eloquence of eternity. No
wonder the warning was astounding and her appeal irresistible, and
his excuse, when "weighed in the balance, found wanting." His re-
sponsiblity was so pressed upon him that he could not shake it off,
and he agreed to comply with her request, to hold a meeting in his
own house, while she was to collect as many hearers as were willing
to attend. Only six attended the first meeting. They sung and
prayed, and Mr. Embury instructed them in the doctrines of salvation.
Influenced by a desire to "flee the wrath to come, and to be saved
from their sins," and to be kept from falling, they enrolled their
names into a class, and resolved to attend regularly at the house of
Mr. Embury for further instruction. Thus their numbers gradually
increased till the place became too strait for them. They then obtained a more commodious room in the neighborhood, where they could
worship the God of their fathers. Here they assembled for mutual
edification. The rent of the room was defrayed by voluntary collections. Mr. Embury continued to lead their devotions, and to expound
to them the word of life. Very useful was he to the "little flock"
to whom it was their Father's good pleasure to give the kingdom. The
first class was organized in 1766.

*   *   *

A most singular event soon brought the little band of Methodists
into notice. It was the appearance of a military officer in their
meeting, in full uniform, with his sword hanging at his side. No
wonder there was some nerve shaking to receive a visit so unexpect-
edly from an officer of the royal American troops. What could be
the object of his visit? All eyes were upon him. Had he come to
persecute them, to interrupt their religious services, or prohibit
them from worshiping?

They were astonished, and their hearts overflowed with gratitude,
as they discovered that, instead of appearing among them from sinister
motives, he had come to join in their devotions. When they prayed
he kneeled down in the attitude of an humble worshiper, and his
countenance sent forth a correct report of the religion that dwelt
in his bosom, that breathed, "Glory to God in the highest, on earth
peace, and good will to men." They dismissed their fears and threw
away their needless anxieties, when they saw his devotional appear-

ance; and though he was clad in the habiliments of war, they recognized in him a worshiper of "the Prince of Peace."

When the service was over, he introduced himself to the Methodists as Captain Thomas Webb, of Albany, also as a soldier of the cross, and a spiritual son of John Wesley; and they were overjoyed, and hailed him as a "brother beloved." They invited him to preach for them. He accepted the invitation, and from that time became one of the principal agents in establishing Methodism in America.

At that period it was customary for military men on all occasions to wear their regimentals. Mr. Webb was a local preacher, and appeared in public with his coat of scarlet with its splendid facings, with his sword lying before him, and the "sword of the Spirit" alongside of it, and can we wonder that he attracted attention? It was so novel, so unlike what they had ever seen before, that curiosity drew many to hear the "old soldier," and to see a military man in the pulpit. Then his style of preaching arrested their attention. He wielded the sword of the Spirit naked. He wrapped no silk around it lest it should be too sharp, and was careful that the point was not too dull. The old members used to speak of his manly eloquence, his holy boldness, his honest appeals, his faithful warnings, his tremendous home thrusts at the human heart.

In a very blunt and emphatic manner, he would bring out in a thunder tone, *"You must repent or be forever damned;"* at the same time he would bring his uplifted hand down upon the desk, and thus thunder terror into the "hearts of the king's enemies." Many yielded to the Conqueror, and said,

"I yield, I yield;
I can hold out no more;
I sink, by dying love compell'd,
And own him conqueror."

In 1766, Captain Webb preached in a hired room, near the barracks.

. . . We now introduce to our readers the far-famed "Rigging Loft," so celebrated in the early history of American Methodism.

. . . This Rigging Loft was occupied by the Methodists in 1767. It was to the early Methodists what the "upper room" in Jerusalem was to the disciples on the day of pentecost. The hired room had become too small to accommodate the congregation, and they rented a Rigging Loft in what was called *Horse-and-Cart-street,* now William-street. It was called so from the fact that there were many horses and carts accommodated therein; there was also an inn there that had

a horse and cart painted on the sign.

The Rigging Loft was not distinguished for its magnificence or architectural beauty. It was sixty feet long and eighteen wide. Humble as it was, it had attractions for the early Methodists in this city that few places had, however splendid. It was their *Bethel*. . . .

In this humble place, twice on Sunday, and on Thursday evening, Philip Embury or Captain Webb preached a *full, free,* and *present* salvation; and here the worshiping assemblies were "fed with the sincere milk of the word," and they grew thereby. Here they wept and prayed, rejoiced and praised.

This building, thus identified with the early history of Methodism in this country, stood until about three years since, an honored memorial of the trials and victories of earlier days. Oft I have visited that Rigging Loft, (120 William-street,) but never entered it without devotional feelings. Many hallowed associations cluster around it. Thought was busy calling up the past. Here Embury preached, and Captain Webb wielded the "sword of the Spirit;" here sinners were awakened and converted to God; here the "sons of God" presented themselves before the Lord, and "devout women" wrestled with God in prayer, and the fires of pentecost were re-kindled in many hearts. These walls have echoed with voices long since silent in death. Mighty plans have been formed here, and no doubt, among others, that of erecting a house of worship for God.

It is somewhat singular, that while all the buildings that were erected about the time of the Rigging Loft had passed away, this edifice remained so long, alone in its glory, a time-honored relic of the past. It is singular that it remained thirty-four years after Wesley Chapel was numbered among the things that were.

It was a little, plain, modest building, that stood with its gable-end toward the street. . . It had been for several years used as a store, and was last occupied by a card engraver. It was taken down in 1854 to make way for a more commodious building.

. . . Great numbers attended divine service at the Rigging Loft, and it could not contain half the people who desired to hear the word of the Lord; therefore the necessity of erecting a house of worship. We bid adieu to the Rigging Loft, and introduce to the reader the cradle of American Methodism, or the first Methodist Church erected in John-street.

¶ Captain Webb.

(Taken from John Pritchard, *Sermon Occasioned by the Death of the Late Capt. Webb* . . . (Bristol, 1797), 12-17, 22-23).

Captain Webb was in his younger days a very useful servant of the crown; in which situation he received a wound in his arm, and lost his right eye in the same campaign that General Wolfe lost his life. He was always a man of moral character, and much respected in the army as an officer and a friend. From the earliest dawn of reason upon his mind, he had frequent convictions from that light which enlighteneth every man that cometh into the world; his conscience accusing or excusing, according to his general conduct.

In the year 1764, being about forty years of age, it pleased that God who knoweth the heart of man, which in its natural state is deceitful above all things and desperately wicked, to convince him by the power of his Spirit alone, of this important truth, deeply inpressing his mind with his awful situation as a fallen creature. Not having any spiritual friend at this time to advise with, it pleased God, who had begun this blessed work, to lead him in a very remarkable way to the knowledge of salvation by the remission of sins. He was frequently very much distressed, almost to despair; suffering grievously from the temptations of Satan, who often suggested to his mind, that there was no mercy for him, and tempted him to put an end to his existence. While under this temptation, in extreme agony of soul, he besought the Lord to seal his doom, or direct him to some comfortable passage of scripture; when, with a trembling hand, he opened the Bible, and cast his eye upon Isaiah liv. 7, 8. For a small moment have I forsaken thee, but with great mercies will I gather thee: In a little wrath I hid my face from thee for a moment, but with everlasting kindness will I have mercy on thee, saith the Lord they Redeemer. He took great comfort from these words, and was singularly directed in a dream to a Moravian Minister, (a Mr. Cary) whom he met with on his way from London to Bristol, and whose person he knew as soon as he saw him, in consequence of his dream ; wherein also it had been suggested to him, that that man would lead him to Christ. As soon as they arrived in this city, he took an opportunity of opening his mind to Mr. Cary, who told him, he must lie at the feet of the Lamb, and be washed in his blood: giving him at the time an invitation, which he accepted, to hear him preach the next day. This was on March 23, 1765. While the Minister was speaking on the sufferings of Christ, and his love to mankind, it pleased the Lord to set before him the cross, and the Saviour of the world bearing his sins in his own body on it; when, in a moment, his burden was removed, peace and joy through believing

26

filled his mind; having, according to the language of the Homily of the Church of England, "a divine persuasion, or confidence, that all his sins were blotted out, and he reconciled to God by the merits of Christ;" And, according to the language of scripture, Rom. v. 1. Being justified by faith, he had peace with God through our Lord Jesus Christ. Soon after this, it pleased the Lord to strengthen him with repeated tokens of his favour; giving him a full assurance of hope, that he should one day be with him in glory, which assurance he enjoyed to the day of his death, being more than thirty years.

He became acquainted with the Methodists through the late Rev. Mr. Roquet a few days after his conversion, who introduced him to the acquaintance of several pious people, among whom he found that spirit and experience which answered to his own, and which together with a divine impression on his mind, whereof he often spoke, determined him to live and die with those people.

The first time of his bearing a testimony of the truth was in Bath; when the preacher not coming as was expected, he was desired to speak to the people, which he did, and gave an account of his own experience. This was all he knew about preaching at that time, and the people were much blessed.

Soon after this he had occasion to go to America in his military capacity, where he was appointed Barrack-Master of Albany. As soon as he arrived there he made a point of holding family prayer in his house, at which his neighbours frequently attended; after a little while he ventured to give them a word of exhortation, and from the good effects that appeared in their conversion, he was encouraged to go farther still, even into the highways and hedges.

. . . This man (of whom the world is not worthy) from the love he bore to the souls of men, issued forth like lightning from one end of the land to the other, to bind up the broken hearted, and proclaim liberty to the captives. In one place we see him breaking forth like a mighty tempest, and thundering from mount Sinai upon the impenitent: In another place we behold him, like a benificent[sic] cloud, pouring the spirit of grace and consolation in copious steams upon the mourners in Zion.

. . . He came not out among us, like the philosophical Divines of the day, to teach us to number the stars, to know their rounds, and to discover the secrets of nature; but to convince his fellow sinners of sin, and righteousness, and of judgment; to teach us that the world passeth away and the fashion thereof; and that there is nothing more dangerous than forming an undue alliance with its customs and fading pleasures. He came not among us to instruct us in

27

state affairs, and rules of civil policy, which is frequently nothing but the art of deceiving; but to discipline us for heaven. Though a soldier by profession, he came not to inspire us with the love of conquest and triumph, which animated the Alexanders and Caesars of former times, and the heroes of the present age; but to conquer self, and to inflame our minds with the love of Jesus and eternal happiness.

The doctrines he taught, and for which he met the fiercest opposition, were the same that awakened the scorn and rage of the world ever since the beginning; and which many, who call themselves christians, oppose with all their zeal: such as, The Divinity of Christ, and the Holy Spirit; proving from the scriptures and other records, that they were one with the Father, whose glory is equal, whose majesty is co-eternal, and that the Church has always believed and maintained it. The Holy Spirit is not from himself as the Father is, for that being supposed, there would be more principles than one, consequently, more Gods than one, which is contrary to the whole tenor of the scriptures. The Father must be the first principle of all essence, the Son in the Father, and the Holy Spirit deriving his essence from both, and reproducing them in the world, and in the heart of man.

The doctrine of Free and Universal Grace. He believed and taught us that the grace of God was free for every man. That Jesus Christ tasted death for every man, and that in virtue of it, a measure of grace was given to every man to profit withal, and consequently that man is free to choose or refuse. For if a man cannot do that which is lawful and right, he cannot do that which is unlawful and wrong: for what he seems to do is done in him and for him, either by irresistible depravity, or irresistible grace: a doctrine in opposition to sense and reason, and constant experience, which convinceth us that we have a power of acting and choosing. It can be no objection to this truth that according to the scripture we cannot please God without his assistance; for this is so far from being an objection, that it is a proof of our freedom to accept of such assistance and to concur with it. For as a Divine of the established church said, "It must be a barbarism of language, to talk of assistance to a creature that hath no activity or power of its own; it is like a man talking of assisting a mere machine or a burthen that he takes up by main force."

The doctrine of the Sinner's Justification by Faith in Christ, without any respect to works, but such as proceed from that faith, and manifest it. This is the one only condition of our justification the gospel recommends, and from which we cannot be excused. Thy faith hath saved thee: faith hath made thee whole; and again, O woman, great is thy faith. Yet be it remembered, that she had first proved her faith by an act or work springing from it. In prayer the

same condition is required;--whatsoever ye shall ask in prayer believing, ye shall receive; again, what things ye desire when ye
pray, believe that ye receive them, and ye shall have them. God
requires faith because he hath given us abundant reason to credit
his word. . . .

To convince you how much he deserves our love and regard,
it is sufficient to explain, in a few words, the effects which his
labours have produced since he began his ministry. He was, under
God, the first instrument of planting Methodism in America; and not
satisfying himself with the success of his own labours in Philadelphia, New York, and other places, he stretched out his hands to the
British Conference, and prayed them, "Come over and help us." Ministers were accordingly sent from this country to America; and many
were raised up among themselves, who are now mutually labouring to
bring down Antichrist, to reduce sin, and to erect the Saviour's
kingdom upon its ruins. By him many, but a degree from the brute,
enemies to church and state, have learned to render unto Caesar
the things that are Caesar's, and unto God the things that are God's.
Let us bring to mind what God has wrought for us, and for his Church
among us, by this his servant, whose memory we now embalm with our
tears. Has not the Angel of the Covenant, by him, brought many
through the wilderness into friendship with us, and caused them to
favour the things of the Spirit? He was the man that planted them
in a well-ordered church, where they are quickened by God's grace
through a lively and faithful ministry, where the gifts of Christ
are watered by the powerful prayers of his saints, the preaching of
his word, and the holy Sacraments; where many run to and fro that
knowledge may be increased; and where discipline is for a wall and
bulwark, and our hearts warmed by the communion of his saints. By
his influence Preaching-houses were erected in New York, Philadelphia, and many other places in the wide continent of America; and
even this house (Portland-Chapel) he was the first and principal
Agent in erecting.

¶   (Taken from Thomas Rankin, *Journal*, typed MS p. 206,
     in Library, Garrett-Evangelical Theological Seminary).

Now I am speaking of Captain Webb (as he is now gone to his
eternal reward;) suffer me to pay a small tribute to his memory. In
the beginning of that glorious work (which the Lord in mercy had
carried on; and hath done since that period to the present time); he
was made a lively instrument for the good of many souls, and in a
great measure laid the foundation both in New York and elsewhere of
that revival of the power of heart felt religion; which has now
spread itself over a vast part of North America. He was a man of much

private prayer, and loved to retire and convene with God alone.
This I well knew, by being at different times, weeks together with
him. His gifts were calculated to be of great use in new places;
and having the name of an officer of the army, many came to hear
him, who would not attend the ministry of others. Let my soul be
where his is happily landed!

¶   Thomas Taylor writes to Wesley.

        (Taken from *Methodist History*, III[2] (Jan. 1965),
        9-15).

                                    New York, 11th April, 1768

Rev. and very Dear Sir,

    I intended writing to you for several weeks past, but a few of
us had a very material transaction in view. I therefore postponed
writing until I could give you a particular account thereof. This
was the purchasing of ground for building a preaching-house upon,
which by the blessing of God we have now concluded. But before I
proceed I shall give you a short account of the state of religion
in this city. By the best intelligence I can collect there was
little either of the form or power of it till Mr. Whitefield came
over thirty years ago; and even after his first and second visit
there appeared but little fruit of his labours. But during his
visit fourteen or fifteen years ago there was a considerable shaking
among the dry bones. Divers were savingly converted and this work
was much increased in his last journey, about four years since,
when his words were really as a hammer and as a fire. Most part of
the adults were stirred up, great numbers pricked to the heart, and
by a judgment of charity several found peace and joy in believing.
The consequence of this work was, the churches were crowded and subscriptions raised for building new ones. Mr. Whitefield's example
provoked most of the ministers to a much greater degree of earnestness. And by the multitudes of people young and old, rich and poor,
flocking to the churches, religion became an honourable profession--
there was no outward cross to be taken up therein. Nay, a person
who could not speak about the grace of God and the new birth was
esteemed unfit for genteel company. But in a while, instead of
pressing forward and growing in grace (as he exhorted them) the
generality were pleading for the remains of sin, and the necessity
of being in darkness. They esteemed their opinions as the very essentials of Christianity, and regarded not holiness either of heart
or life.

The above appears to me to be a genuine account of the state of religion in New York eighteen months ago, when it pleased God to rouse up Mr. Embury to employ his talent (which for several years had been as it were hid in a napkin) by calling sinners to repentance and exhorting believers to let their light shine before men. He spoke at first only in his own house. A few were soon collected together and joined in a little society—chiefly his own countrymen, Irish. In about three months after brother White and brother Sause from Dublin joined them. They then rented an empty room in their neighbourhood, which was in the most infamous street of the city, adjoining the barracks. For some time few thought it worth their while to hear. But God so ordered it by His providence that about fourteen months ago Captain Webb, barrack master at Albany (who was converted about three years since at Bristol) found them out and preached in his regimentals. The novelty of a man preaching in a scarlet coat soon brought greater numbers to hear than the room could contain. But his doctrines were quite new to the hearers, for he told them point blank "that all their knowledge and profession of religion was not worth a rush unless their sins were forgiven and they had the 'witness of God's spirit with theirs, that they were the children of God.'" This strange doctrine, with some peculiarities in his person, made him soon be taken notice of, and obliged the little society to look out for a larger house to preach in. They soon found a place that had been built for a rigging-house, sixty feet in length and eighteen in breadth.

About this period Mr. Webb, whose wife's relations lived at Jamaica on Long Island, took a house in that neighborhood, and began to preach in his own house and several other places on Long Island. Within six months about twenty-four persons received justifying grace, near half of them whites, the rest Negroes. While Mr. Webb (to borrow his own phrase) was "felling the trees on Long Island," brother Embury was exhorting all who attended on Thursday evenings and Sunday mornings and evenings at the rigging-house to flee from the wrath to come. His hearers began to increase, and some gave heed to his report, about the time the gracious providence of God brought me safe to New York after a very favourable passage of six weeks from Plymouth. It was the 26th day of October last when I arrived, recommended to a person for lodging. I inquired of my host (who was a very religious man) if any Methodists were in New York. He informed me there was one Captain Webb, a strange sort of man, who lived on Long Island and sometimes preached at one Embury's at the rigging-house. In a few days I found out Embury. I soon found what spirit he was of, and that he was personally acquainted with you and your doctrines, and had been a Helper in Ireland. He had formed two classes, one of the men and another of the women, but had never met the society apart from the congregation, although there were six or seven men and about the same number of women who had a clear sense of their acceptance in the Beloved.

31

You will not wonder at my being agreeably surprised in meeting with a few here who have been and desire again to be in connection with you. God only knows the weight of the affliction I felt in leaving my native country. But I have reason now to conclude God intended all for my good. Ever since I left London my load has been removed and I have found a cheerfulness in being banished from all near and dear to me, and I made a new covenant with my God that I would go to the utmost parts of the earth provided He would raise up a people with whom I might join in His praise. On the great deep I found a more earnest desire to be united with the people of God than ever before. I made a resolution that God's people should be my people, and their God my God, and (bless His holy name!) I have since experienced more heartfelt happiness than ever I thought it possible to have on this side eternity. All anxious care even about my dear wife and children is taken away. I cannot assist them, but I daily and hourly commend them to God in prayer, and I know He hears my prayers, by an answer of love in my heart. I find power daily to devote myself unto Him, and I find power also to overcome sin. If any uneasiness at all affects me, it is because I can speak so little of so good a God.

Mr. Embury has lately been more zealous than formerly, the consequence of which is that he is more lively in preaching, and his gifts as well as graces are much increased. Great numbers of serious people came to hear God's word as for their lives. And their numbers increased so fast that our house for this six weeks past would not contain the half of the people.

We had some consultations how to remedy this inconvenience, and Embury proposed renting a lot of ground for twenty-one years, and to exert our utmost endeavours to collect as much money as to build a wooden tabernacle. A piece of ground was proposed, the ground rent was agreed for, and the lease was to be executed in a few days. We, however, in the mean time, had two several days for fasting and prayer for the direction of God and His blessing on our proceedings— and Providence opened such a door as we had no expectation of. A young man, a sincere Christian and constant hearer, though not joined in society, would not give anything towards this house, but offered ten pounds to buy a lot of ground, (and) went of his own accord to a lady who had two lots to sell, on one of which there is a house that rents for eighteen pounds per annum. He found the purchase money of the two lots was six hundred pounds, which she was willing should remain in the purchaser's hands on good security. We called once more upon God for His direction, and resolved to purchase the whole. There are eight of us, who are joint purchasers, among whom Mr. Webb and Mr. Lupton are men of property. I was determined the house should be on the same footing as the Orphan House at Newcastle and others in England, but as we were ignorant how to draw the deeds we purchased for us and our heirs until a copy

of the writings from England was sent us, which we desire may be sent by the first opportunity.

Before we began to talk of building the devil and his children were very peaceable, but since this affair took place many ministers have cursed us in the name of the Lord, and laboured with all their might to shut up their congregations from assisting us. But He that sitteth in Heaven laughed them to scorn. Many have broke through and given their friendly assistance. We have collected above one hundred pounds more than our own contributions, and have reason to hope in the whole we shall have two hundred pounds: but the house will cost us four hundred pounds more, so that unless God is pleased to raise up friends we shall yet be at a loss. I believe Mr. Webb and Lupton will borrow or advance two hundred pounds rather than the building should not go forward, but the interest of money here is a great burden, which is seven per cent. Some of our brethren proposed writing to you for a collection in England, but I was averse to this, as I well knew our friends there are overburdened already. Yet so far I would earnestly beg: if you would intimate our circumstances to particular persons of ability perhaps God would open their hearts to assist this infant society and contribute to the first preaching-house on the original Methodist plan in all America—excepting Mr. Whitefield's Orphan House in Georgia. But I shall write no more on this head.

There is another point far more material, and in which I must importune your assistance not only in my own name but in the name of the whole society. We want an able, experienced preacher—one who has both gifts and graces necessary for the work. God has not despised the day of small things. There is a real work in many hearts by the preaching of Mr. Webb and Mr. Embury, but although they are both useful, and their hearts in the work, they want many qualifications necessary for such an undertaking, where they have none to direct them. And the progress of the gospel here depends much on the qualifications of the preachers.

I have thought of Mr. Helton, for if possible we must have a man of wisdom, of sound faith, and a good disciplinarian, one whose heart and soul are in the work; and I doubt not but by the goodness of God such a flame would be soon kindled as would never stop until it reached the great South Sea. We may make many shifts to evade temporal inconveniences, but we cannot *purchase* such a preacher as I have described. Dear sir, I entreat you for the good of thousands to use your utmost endeavours to send one over. I would advise him to take shipping at Bristol, Liverpool, or Dublin, in the month of July or early in August; by embarking at this season he will have fine weather in his passage and probably arrive here in the month of September. He will see with his own eyes before winter what progress the gospel has made. With respect to the money for

payment of a preacher's passage over, if they could not procure it, we would sell our coats and shirts and pay it.

I most earnestly beg an interest in your prayers, and trust you and many of our brethren will not forget the church in this wilderness.

I remain with sincere esteem, Rev. and Dear Sir,
                    Your very affectionate brother and servant,

                              T. T.

¶   Anecdotes of Bishop Asbury.

   (Taken from "John Wesley Bond's Reminiscences of
   Francis Asbury," *Methodist History*, IV[1] (Oct. 1965)
   10-26).

It has been said by some, that persons designed by Providence to fill important stations or as extraordinary characters are frequently distinguished in infancy by some remarkable event. Whether this be true in the general I know not; but certainly our venerable friend was in eminent danger of violent death when very young; and was providentially preserved. The circumstance I had from his own mouth. A room attached to the house in which his father resided, had been occupied for the use of some machinery that caused a large hole to be left in the floor of the second story, over the hearth below. The Bishop's Father being a gardener by trade, used to put up his gardening tools, consisting of long shears, pruning saws, hoes, rakes, etc. in this place. One day Francis, (the only son) was left in this upper room; nor was his danger thought of until his Father, calling to his Mother said, "Where is the Lad; I hear him cry." His mother than ran into the room and found he had crawled to the hole in the floor and fallen through. But by the kind   providence of God, the gardening tools had been recently removed, and a larger boiler nearly filled with ashes put in their place, into which he fell; this broke his fall, or the world would most probably have been forever deprived of the labours of Bishop Asbury.

I received my appointment to travel with Bishop Asbury, at the Baltimore Conference, March 1814. Previous to the appointment being fixed, he took me by the hand and let me know that if I went with him it must be a voluntary thing; that he would feel delicate in receiving the attentions of any man who might accept the station merely in conference appointment.

The Bishop was at this time in a very infirm state of health. He had taken cold in the fall of 1813, which was several times renewed through the winter, and he was moreover in a very bilious habit. He tarried a few days at Perry-Hall and took medicine when finding himself a little better we set out for the Philadelphia Conference on the first of April 1814. By the importunity of his friends at Philadelphia he was prevailed on to have a top put to his Sulky, having travelled through the winter without any.

Friday, 15th April. Though the Bishop was still unwell, and the weather unfavorable, yet we set off for the New-York Conference; the Bishop having a string of appointments through New-Jersey. We crossed the Delaware in the steam-boat. It came on to rain very hard, and as there was no shelter to the boat, and the Bishop was taken very sick, and had a severe spell of vomiting on board; we had a very disagreeable passage: yet he seemed cheerful, as though these were scenes with which he had been familiar. We however landed safe through mercy, and the weather clearing off we continued our way; but the Bishop was taken sick again on the way and vomited much. He wished to obtain a little wine or porter; hoping it would stop his vomiting; but though we stopped at several places none could be had. I was pleasingly surprised to see with what cheerfulness he bare his affliction, and how composedly he met every disappointment. After travelling eleven miles we came to Woodsberry, and the Bishop being still very unwell consented to tarry at the house of one of our friends, and let Brother Michael Coate go on and fill his appointments. This night he took medicine which kept him up great part of the night; he however appeared a little better in the morning and set out for his appointment twenty miles distant and got there while Brother Coate was preaching. When he had concluded the Bishop went into the house, and first apologized for his not being in time: stating his ill health, which indeed his looks but too fully confirmed. He mentioned his sacred regard of character, and determination to be found in the punctual discharge of those lessons of industry which he in conjunction with the conferences constantly inculcated on the younger preachers. After which he gave a lengthy and pathetic exhortation. While almost the whole congregation was in tears. We then went 3 miles for dinner and 7 more for lodgings; in all thirty miles.

In conversation with Bishop Asbury, on the subject of his extraordinary exertion to reach his appointments; I endeavoured to dissuade him from it, stating that such was the state of his health, that it must be greatly *impaired* if not *destroyed* by such exertions. But he remarked that, "Sometimes circumstances were such as would justify a preacher's disappointing a congregation, were the people acquainted with the reasons that detained him. But when the people collected and there was no preacher, every one would form his own conjecture on the subject, and might think the preacher negligent and lose confidence in him and so be discouraged. It has never

35

been my practice to say to the younger preachers 'Go Boys. - but - Come.' I have ever set an example of industry, and punctuality; and if ever the young men should neglect their appointments, it must not be by our example."

After tarrying about a week in Philadelphia to recruit, at the house of his faithful friend, our dear Brother Thomas Haskins, since gone to his reward; we set out for the Ohio Conference, to be held in Cincinnati. To get to which the Bishop manifested more than ordinary concern; frequently expressing his fears that Bishop McKendree would not be able to reach there. We took in the carriage with us a number of Bibles, and Testaments from the "Philadelphia Bible Society." And it was truly gratifying to see what pleasure he manifested in giving them away, especially when he met with a poor person who he thought would be likely to make good use of them. And many such we found; especially when we had gotten beyond the market towns; where the women had not an opportunity of obtaining a little money by means of small marketing. One I particularly recollect in the state of Kentucky, who tho' her husband possessed property, yet when we gave her a Bible, she endeavored for a time to conceal her feelings but when she found her tears flowed too fast to be concealed, gave vent to them and said, she "Believed God had sent us there to bring her the Bible; that she had been trying for years to get one but could not succeed." Surely the love of money is the root of all evil. Influenced by this principle, this man would withold from his wife and children several of which were nearly grown, the holy scriptures, whose precepts alone could preserve their morals and instruct them in the way to Heaven.

I could but mark what an agreeable effect the rural scenes of the country had upon the Bishop. His mind seemed fatigued with the noise and bustle of the City; but he had not proceeded more than ten or twelve miles into the country when he appeared all life, -all pleasantry,-all affection. And on one occasion he remarked to me that, "No one knew what effect it had upon him to get into a retired situation, in a quiet, plain and pious family." And he appeared to enjoy much solemn delight when he reached the mansion of his late, venerable friend, the Rev. Martin Boehm, of Lancaster county Pennsylvania. While he viewed the old mansion, the Chapel and Burying-grounds which contained the earthly remains of his old Friend, with several others who once lay near his heart; his mind seemed to rise above all earthly things; and sweetly anticipate the moment when he should join them in the paradise of God.

July the third we reached Little-York, and put up with our worthy friend Mr. Francis Hollingsworth, in whose hands the Bishop placed his Manuscript Journal to be prepared for publication. Bishop Asbury called on Mr. Hollingsworth again the ensuing year, and tarried near a week, reviewing his Journal as revised by Mr.

Hollingsworth and left with him such part as he had kept through the year. Afterwards in conversation with me on the subject of his Journals the Bishop appeared much pleased; and spake in high terms of what Mr. H⌈ollingsworth⌉ had done.

It was about this time, he received a letter from the Rev. Daniel Hitt giving an account of the great deficiency in the preacher's quarterage in the New-England Conference. The Bishop thought it most likely that the same deficiency would prevail in the Ohio and Tennessee Conference, and that many of the preachers, especially those with families, would suffer, or have to locate; in order to seek support by their own industry in some secular employment. To prevent which he now first drew up what he termed his "Mite-Subscription:" with the intent of relieving such Conferences as might be in distress. The object of this subscription he afterwards so enlarged as to embrace a Missionary Plan: hoping to obtain German, French, and possibly in time Spanish Missionaries. He was led to this by seeing there were numbers of these people in our country who do not understand the English language: and the French especially tho' there are so many of them in our sea ports, yet they have no place of religious worship in the U⌈nited⌉ S⌈tates⌉ except possibly in Orleans, and an old Church in Charleston, S.C. which I believe is not occupied. On this work his heart was much set. He in Chilicothe, Ohio, met with an intelligent french Gentleman from Gernsey, or Jersey, who was acquainted with the Methodist Society there. And through this Gentleman he wrote a letter in the french language to one of those islands inviting missionaries to the United States.

Through much weakness he reached Chambersburg, Pa. on the fifth of July, where he met the society in Br. Thos. Johns' house, for the first time he had attempted any thing in public since his illness in New-Jersey. And thinking it probably would be the last time he should see them, he gave them some account of himself: stating his early awakenings and conversion to God; his call to the ministry, and volunteering to come to America, with a summary of his labours and sufferings here. He stated moreover that, in the forty years he had laboured here he had never found time to "purchase land, to build himself a house, or even to marry a wife. That his labours in the ministry had called for all his time, and all his thoughts." On one subject eluded ⌈sic⌉ to above, the Bishop afterwards in conversation stated to me that he did not believe that any person entertained more honourable views of marriage than himself. And that this was one reason why any man, however highly he might have conceived of him, sunk in his estimation the moment he discovered him to be influenced by any unworthy motive in forming so close a union. That as to himself, had he entered into such a state, it would have been his duty to have paid to his family a suitable attention. But that such was the nature of his calling, and such the demands upon him that, he never could think of dividing his time.

We observed above that every part of the work shared in his concern and his prayers. But it was not that alone which was under his own superintendency, that lay near his heart: our brethren abroad had constantly a place therein. Once at the Leesburg Conference, when rising from prayer, he cried out, "Pardon us Mighty God! we forget our Brother Coke." He then in a most impressive manner, implored the blessing of the great Head of the church on the Doctor and the weighty missions in which he was engaged; together with the rest of our European brethren, and the work of God at large. (Of Doctor Coke, Bishop Asbury always spake with much affection, and in the highest terms of applause. When the account of the Doctors death reached America, the New-York Conference, then sitting in Albany, requested Bishop Asbury to preach his funeral. On which occasion, after stating the Doctor's parentage, birth and education; his good standing as a citizen, and prospects in life; his conversion and call to the ministry; his disinterestedness, liberality, zeal, travels and sufferings; with his usefullness as a minister, and missionary superintendent etc. observed, on his character, "He was in his temper, quick.-It was like a spark; touch it and it would fly; and was soon off.-Indeed it is natural in a Welch-Man to be quick.-But jealousy, malice, or envy; dwelt not in a soul so able as that of Coke.") His mind was not of that narrow cast which sought the good of his own particular party. He rejoiced to hear of the spiritual prosperity of Zion every where. And when he received an account of a revival of true religion in any particular church; he rejoiced to report it in his travels, that he might stimulate others of the same community to spirituality and zeal by the example of their brethren. So when passing through New-Jersey in 1815 he heard of the revival in some of the congregations of our Presbyterian brethren. I have heard him relate it with much apparent satisfaction in Carolina and elsewhere. In like manner he was distressed at any account which was calculated to wound the cause of religion, whether the subject of it was a member of his own particular church or not. In December 1815 while in South Carolina, he received the account of the accusation brought against the Rev. Mr._____of Baltimore. His very soul seemed grieved: he often mentioned it to me with expressions of sorrow. He said he knew it would cause a number of his members to join the Methodist Church. But said he "What of that? We never wish to build on the ruin of others." He then adverted to the opposition there had been in that church between what was called the "Formal," and the "Evangelical" or "Spiritual" ministers. And said that this minister having stood high in the party who contended for spiritual reform, the opportunity would be seized; and spirituality spoken of with reproach: besides the occasion it would furnish for the infidel to scoff at all religion.

Though he well knew that God had given us in the holy scriptures, one consistent, and closely connected chain of doctrine; and that there alone must be looked for the most approved form of church

38

government; and that the adopting and maintaining this, was no small part of the duty of an individual, or community; yet he was well convinced that all the essential parts of christian doctrine and discipline, were held by most of our neighbouring churches. Hence he ever sought to cultivate a friendship with them; saying it was better that christians should try to find out in what they *did* agree, than in what they *did not*; and make *that* the subject of conversation; and from the good principles which they held in common with each other, to try to excite each other, to serve God.

It cannot be reasonably supposed that a mind so philanthropic as his, could look with an eye of indifference on the cruel slaver of the poor Blacks in the southern and some of the middle states. He frequently spake of it with deep concern; and said he had examined it every way of which his mind was capable: that in parts of the country there were difficulties in the way of freeing them: the poor things have no protection. And evil disposed people would abuse them. That under such circumstances he did not see what we as a ministry could do better than to try to get both masters and servants to get all the religion they could, and get ready to leave a troublesome world. That this would make the owners humane and the servants trusty: and would therefore make the situation of both, much better, even in this world, and infinitely so in the next. But he said their condition after they were free was too often made a pretext for holding them, when the true cause was avarice. That where this was the case, he considered the person to be a slave-holder in *soul;* and that he could not see how a person who had a slave-holding soul in them could ever get to the Kingdom of Heaven. He thought, he said, that in the places where the strongest prejudice prevailed against an immediate and indiscriminate emancipation, from the uncultivated state of their minds; yet no objection could in reason lay against allowing the slave to purchase his freedom, and allowing him certain privileges or perquisites with that intent. And that he thought every Legislator ought to favor this. That it would give a spur to industry and economy and would excite a laudable ambition to maintain a fair character; and would tend to a gradual improvement of the mind and manners. That it would cut off the objection, "That the emancipation of some makes the rest discont[ent]ed." For all would know that if they conducted themselves as others had done, they might enjoy the same advantages.

The Bishop appeared to derive much satisfaction from the reflection, that the condition of the slaves was ameliorated where ever Methodist influence prevailed. Once in S[outh] Carolina seeing a number of negro children out at play, I remarked to the Bishop that, I was gratified at seeing them comfortably clothed, but mentioned that I expected he could remember when things were different. He answered, "Yes, formerly they generally ran naked."

Bishop Asbury was thought by many, to be a stern man and rather austere in his manner. Perhaps by nature he was; and it was his own opinion that by nature he was suspicious. These tempers when indulged, and suffered to follow the corrupt leading of fallen nature are certainly much to be dreaded. But as it is not the office of grace to destroy human nature, but to sanctify it: I am fully convinced that every natural feature of the human mind has its use; and when brought properly under the influence of grace, fits the individual for that particular station for which an ever ruling providence designed him. Thus altho these features of the mind mentioned above; though when found in a governor, or even in an irreligious *head of a family,* tend to destroy the peace and safety of themselves and others: yet when corrected by the love of God and our neighbour, they will produce much good; especially in an executive officer. When a person is continually exposed to the flatteries and persuasions of men, endeavoring either from design or a blind fondness to draw him from his duty; and has frequently to deal with men tho' in the general mean well, yet are human beings, and have many of the weaknesses of humanity about them: and are ever seeing difficulties in the way; he must not possess too much flexibility of disposi[ti] on. And in gathering up his mind, (so to speak) and fixing himself not to be swerved from duty; the countenance and voice may assume an appearance, which a person not acquainted with human natures, especially if they themselves be a little displeased, will be very likely to mistake for anger, or other improper tempers. And this from two years opportunity of observing, I am convinced was frequently the case with Bishop Asbury. And suspicion itself may also be rendered subservient to the most useful purposes. For when a person is almost continually engaged in intricate business, coming on in rapid succession, and finds himself straitened for time; he will be under frequent temptations to take things on trust, or presum[p]tion. And it was no doubt this natural temper of mind brought properly under the government of grace, which induced him to thrust himself into every part of his charge, lest something might be wrong-lest some part of the cause of God might suffer. These natural turns of mind certainly require great watchfulness and much grace to keep them in a right direction; and so does every other disposition of the human heart. And in Bishop Asbury, they had a right direction-He had feeling:-few men perhaps had more: though he had firmness and decision. He had confidence;-few men perhaps had more unshaken confidence in his friends: though he seemed determined to be blind to the faults of none.

¶   Joseph Pilmore.

(Taken from *The Journal of Joseph Pilmore*
(1969), 112-13, 202-03, 210).

New York, [1770 or 1771]

My Dear Dear Br.

You much esteemed favour came safe to hand, & was made a
Blessing to my Soul. Nothing gives me so much pleasure as to
hear that you are well, & that the pleasure of the Lord prospers
in your Hands. When we preach and live the Gospel, this must
necessarily be the Case. It was the pure Doctrine & upright
lives of the primitive Xtians & preachers that prevailed over
all the opposition of Jews and Gentiles, & stood as a barrier
against all the projects which a Subtile Devil could Invent &
this in all ages of the World will stand as a sure Basis, that
will support every Minister of the Gospel under all his Trials
and Tribulations.

From what you write of Yorkshire I am led to believe "wherein
sin abounded Grace hath much more abounded" O! Grace, Grace!
Unbounded Grace! "Ho! ye despairing Sinners, come & trust upon
the Lord"

I have been waiting with eager expectation for some of the
Brethren to come over to our Macedonia & help us, but Ah me!
There are so many things to give up, before one can cross the
Atlantic, that it seems to be too much even for a Methodist
preacher! I find by Mr. Wesley's letter that none were willing
to come, so it is very uncertain whether ever we shall have an
opportunity of returning to Old England or no. But blessed be
God, we know what was our Intention in leaving all that was dear
to us, in order to visit those dear, dear Americans: & as we came
in singleness in heart, the Lord has greatly blessed us both, in
N. York & Philadelphia. Our Congregations are very large, &
very serious; triffling [sic] seems to have no place at present
for Sinners are engaged about the vast important affairs of the
Invisible World, even the poor Negroes are turning to God, &
seeking to wash their robes and make them white in the Blood of
the Lamb.

A few days ago the Lord was pleased to manifest his Love to
a poor Black, her Mistress has persecuted her very much because
she came to the Methodist Church, but she thought it was better
to be "beaten for hearing the word of God here; than to burn in
Hell to all eternity." We have about twenty Black women that
meet in one Class, & I think upon the whole they are as happy
as any Class we have got.

41

Many people of Superior rank come to hear the word and are very friendly. The chief difficulty we labour under is want of Ordination & I believe we shall be Obliged to procure it by some means or other. It is not in America as it is in England, for there is no Church that is one Establish'd more than another. All Sects have equal authority with the Church of England; I do believe if we should form a Church we should soon have the largest congregations in these two Cities. The fields are white already, but the labourers are very few, there are hundreds of Sinners in this Country who dont hear a Sermon above once a quarter & some for not half a Year, & many of them would gladly hear, if they had anybody to preach to them; but in many places they have not a Minister of any Denomination for forty or fifty miles.

What a field for Methodist preachers! Whils't I was in Pensylvania [sic] I had the favour of opening the New Methodist Church about twenty miles from Philadelphia; and what was most remarkable, the poor plain Country people have called it Bethel, i.e. *the House of God*.

I have preach'd several times in an English Church, and the people flock'd to gather from all Quarters in such multitudes that I was oblig'd at last to stand upon a Table in the Churchyard, & to preach the Word to a crowded Multitude who stood all around under the Shady Trees.

Perhaps you will say I speak too much in favour of the Americans, but I do assure you one half is not yet tould [sic] you. And I freely wish, that you would come and prove the truth of what I say, if you will but come, I assure you that you will want nothing that is good. The people here are very kind & take pleasure in provoiding [sic] for the Methodist preachers.

Robt Williams is in Maryland preaching to the poor Convicts & I trust the Lord makes him useful. Mr. Webb is now in New York. He is a genuine Wesley & labours hard to promote the Cause. His Gifts are small, but he is very zealous and honest, & that you know is very precious in a preacher.

I could still add more but you see my paper is just done, & therefore must take my leave of you for the present wishing you an increase of every Gift and Grace necessary for that office to which the Lord has called you unto

I am Dear Brother whilst yours for ever

Joseph Pilmore

On Itinerating

Wed: 18. This day I had many persons from the country *entreating* me to visit them. The longer I stay here, the more work is laid out for me. God is opening a great and effectual door for his gospel, and the dear people in all parts where I go, are eagerly desirous of hearing the word of life.

Fri: 20. After Intercession I set off with a Friend for German Town where I intended to preach in the School house but the Presbyterians opened their Church for me, so I gladly accepted of it, and was comforted in preaching on the twelvth of Isaiah, "O Lord I will praise Thee &c."

Sat: 21. I had some Young Quakers to visit me, and was glad of an opportunity of conversing Freely with them of the things of God. Just before preaching, Mr. Boardman arrived from New York, and we concluded the day togither in peace.

Sun: 22. Set off early in the morning for Whitemarsh Church: as the roads were very bad, and the weather disagreable I thought we should have but few to hear, but I found the Church as full as it could hold, and God did not disappoint his people. My heart rejoiced in the Lord, and my tongue was fully at liberty to publish free salvation through the blood of the Lamb. I was so engaged for God, and so united to the dear people, that I could not tell how to give over. Parhaps the Seed sown this day, may hereafter produce a plentiful harvest, and be a mean [s] of bringing some souls to glory. In our way home we dined with my kind Friend Mr. Mather, who always behaves to me with the utmost tenderness and civility. Though of a different Society, our hearts are truely united, and I feel such affection for the family that it is difficult to part--but we shall meet again hereafter to part no more forever. At six I preached my farewell sermon in Philadelphia, and it was indeed a time of love. These people in general receive my message as from God, and my way is perfectly open and free. At present I have a most delightful prospect of doing good, not only in the City, but also in all the Country round about, as the Churches of Episcopalians, Lutherans, Sweeds, and Presbyterians, are open to me, and vast multitudes attend the word and seem to embrace it. Yet I am obliged to submit. This is rather trying, not to leave this Place, but to leave the Work at this time when God is so manifestly Working by me; however as it is not *my* doings, I hope it will not be laid to my charge. May God give his blessing to my dear fellow-labourer, and crown him with more abundant success.

Mon: 23. As Mr. Boardman was so *urgent*, I went to two or three places to take leave of my friends, and about two oClock left Philadelphia. Several of my select friends were a good deal dissatisfied at the manner in which I was hurried away, and resolved to accompany me as far as Burlington. They hired a Coach, and Messrs. Wallace, Dowers, Salter, & Coates, set of [off] with me for Bristol where we arrived just in the dusk of the evening; they put us over the River immediately and we just go to Burlington in time to preach. The congregation was large and deeply serious, so that I thought myself well rewarded for the pains I had taken to visit them.

Tues: 24. Took leave of my dear Friends; they returned to Philadelphia in the Coach, and I set forward on a hired Horse for N. [New] York. The frost was the most sharp I ever knew, I was in the utmost danger of being frozen, and was obliged to run on foot to prevent it. And even then, my fingers would frequently freze [freeze] so as to lose all their sencibility. The only method in my power was, to rub them upon my cloaths with all the force I had to bring them to life, and prevent losing the use of my hands. As I wanted, if possible, to be [in] N. [New] York on Xmas Day, I pushed forward as fast as I could, and rode a good while within night. But, as the road was very intricate, and having no guid [guide], I lost my way. After I had travelled some time in uncertainty, it was strongly impressed upon my mind to return to the place where the roads divided, and take the other road, which I did, and pursued it till it brought me to a House, which, to my great comfort, was an Inn. So I took up my aboad [abode] for the night, and was heartily glad that I had found a place of rest. After a little refreshment, I proposed family prayer, to which they readily consented, and God gave me uncommon freedom to wrestle with him for their salvation and eternal happiness. As the night was bitter cold, I was glad to have a very large fire in my room, took the cloaths off another bed, and likewise my own wearing apparel, and spread them all over me, yet it was with some difficulty I weathered out the night.

Pilmore Appraises the Southern Journey

It is now above a year since I left this City: I set out with a consciousness of *duty*, and was determined to *obey* what to me was a Call from above. I was totally unacquainted with the people, the road, and every thing else, only I knew there were multitudes of souls scattered through a vast extent of country and was willing to encounter any difficulty, and undergo the greatest hard ships so I might win them to Christ. My plan was to following the leadings of Providence, and go wherever the "tutelary cloud" should direct. With this view I turned my face to the South and went forward above

a thousand miles through the Provinces, visited most of the Towns
between Philadelphia and Savannah in Georgia, where I have preached
the Gospel of Christ.

At Savannah I had several Invitations to go forward towards
Florida, but my mind was so strongly drawn towards the people
where I had already been, who entreated me to turn my face towards
the North and visit them again [I] judged it to be the will of God,
and was so affected that I resolved to comply with their request,
and ventured through the country again where I revisited all the
places where I had gone preaching the Gospel, where I found to my
great satisfaction, that I had not labored in vain. I have been
in many dangers by land and by water--my difficulties in passing
through so many Provinces without a guide, and without so much as
a single acquaintance, except one in Maryland, whom I met with in
Philadelphia, have been very considerable, and often discouraging--
the Slanderous reports that were raised of me, together with the
opposition I some times met with, made my way sufficiently rough,
and tried me to the uttermost, yet the Lord has brought me safe
through all and made me more than conqueror through faith in the
Lamb. My Constitution has suffered very much, and is never likely
to be restored, but all is well, since I have spent my strength
for him who bought me with the price of his blood--And I rejoice
that I have preached the Gos people [Gospel] to so many thousands
of sinners, not indeed as I would have done, but in the best manner
I could; and I can say with the utmost confidence, I have done it
in great sincerity and uprightness of heart, and blessed by God,
I have not laboured in vain. His presence was with me, his Word
ran and was glorified, and sinners were gathered to the Shepherd of
Israel, and savingly converted to God. This affords me the most
pleasing satisfaction, and is a good reward for all my fatigue.
In a little time the scene will be closed, and all the storms of
life eternally over. O happy--happy day when I shall be an exile
no more, but enter into the heaven of love, where there is fulness
of joy, and pleasures that never decay.

First Methodist Conference in America (July 1773)

Tues: 13. We had appointed to meet in Conference in Philadelphia, and several of us met in our Church at six in the morning,
but as two of the Preachers were not arrived, we agreed to adjourn
till the next day. At seven in the evening, Mr. Boardman preached
a most excellent sermon on the important work of the Gospel Ministry. *Wednesday* morning we met, and entered upon our business
in the Fear of the most high God. As Mr. Boardman and I had been
shamefully misrepresented to Mr. Wesley, and Mr. Rankin sent over
to take the whole management upon himself, it was expected we should

have pretty close work. Had we given place to *nature,* and followed our own *temporal interests,* it would probably have been so; but
we considered & preferred the interests of religion and the honour
of God, above all the riches and honours the whole world can bestow,
and were determined to submit to any thing consistent with a good
conscience, rather than injure the work of the Lord. In this Spirit
we were kept during the Conference; we consulted togither under the
tender visitations of the Almighty, and were favoured with the
presence and blessing of God. So the enemy of souls was disappointed, and all our matters were settled in peace.

It is now near four years since Mr. Boardman and I arrived
in America, we have constantly laboured in the great work of the
Lord, and have preached the Gospel through the Continent for more
than a thousand miles, and formed many Societies, and have aboute
a thousand Members, most of whom are well grounded in the doctrins
of the Gospel, and savingly converted unto God. This hath God
wrought, and we will exalt and glorify His adoreable name.

Sun: 18. I preached at seven in the Morning with much freedom, and happiness of mind. The power of the Highest was present
with us, and his Word was made Spirit and life to the hearers.
Afterwards had the happiness of hearing Mr. Duche, and in the
afternoon, when [went] to the Presbyterian Church, where I was
greatly entertained and edified with the discourse. At night Mr.
Rankin preached, and then we had a Love-feast for the Society. A
few people spoke of the goodness of God, and we were favoured with
a visit from our Heavenly Lord, but nothing like what we have
known in months that are past.

¶   (Taken from Thomas Rankin, *Journal,* typed MS, in
    Library, Garrett-Evangelical Theological Seminary)

The chapel would scarce hold the number that attended. As for
the poor black people, they were glad to hear at the doors and
windows. After preaching, I met the society. The Divine Presence,
was in the midst of the morning, under the sermon more so in the
afternoon; but in meeting the society some trembled, many wept,
while others rejoiced in hope of the glory of God. After the
service was over, Brother Williams and I rode to the house of a
friendly man, Mr. Richard Dellam (Brother to Joseph Dellam of
Swan Creek) who is one of the members of the assembly. He
received us with kindness and much affection. Here we spent an
agreeable evening after the labour of the day. Blessed be the
name of the Lord, for his love and consolation to my soul.

Monday, 7th November, 1774: We rode to Henery Waters, near Deer Creek, where we intended holding our quarterly meeting for Baltimore and Kent circuit on the eastern shore. In the afternoon the preachers and many of the people came together, and some from a great distance. In the evening, I preached for the first time in the new preaching house, and the presence of the Lord was with us.

Tuesday, 8th: When I arose this morning, my mind was much oppressed by the powers of darkness, but I was enabled to struggle through the painful opposition and look to Jesus. After an early breakfast we spent about 2 hours in the affairs of the circuits. At 10, our general love feast began. There were such a number of white and blacks as never had attended on such an occasion before. After we had sung and prayed, the cloud burst from my mind, and the power of the Lord descended in such an extraordinary manner as I had never seen since my landing at Philadelphia. All the preachers were so overcome with the Divine presence, that they could scarce address the people; but only in broken accents saying; "This is none other than the house of God and the gate of heaven"! When any of the people stood up to declare the loving kindness of God, they were so overwhelmed with the Divine presence that they were obliged to sit down and let silence speak his praise. Near the close of our meeting, I stood up and called upon all the people to look towards that part of the chapel where the poor blacks were. I then said, "See the number of the black Africans, who have stretched out their hands and hearts to God." While I was addressing the people thus, it seemed as if the very house shook with the mighty power and glory of Sinai's God. Many of the people were so overcome, that they were ready to faint, and die under His almighty hand. For about 3 hours the gale of the spirit thus continued to break upon the dry bones, and they did live, the life of glorious love. As for my self, I scarce knew whether I was in the body or not: and so it was with all my brethren. We did not know how to break up the meeting or part asunder. Surely the fruits of this season will remain to all eternity. After a little refreshment, we finished our business of the circuit, and then concluded the day with a watch night. The same spirit and power of our God was displayed among the people; all the time our meeting continued. This has indeed been a mighty day of the Son of Man, to many, very many souls. All glory be to God on high, and to the Lamb that sits on the throne, forever and forever!

*   *   *

Thursday, 20th July, 1775: I rode to the chapel at the forks of Gunpowder Falls and preached to a numerous congregation. This being the day set apart for a general fast by the Congress, throughout all the British Provinces, all the serious part of the inhabitants paid a particular attention to the same. I endeavoured

47.

to open up and enforce the cause of all our misery. I told them that the sins of Great Britain and her colonies had long called aloud for vengence and in a peculiar manner the dreadful sin of buying and selling the souls and bodies of the poor Africans, the sons and daughters of Ham. I felt myself, but poorly when I began to preach, but the Lord was my strength and enabled me to speak with power and divine pungency; and to meet the society afterwards. After the service was over, I rode to Mr. Gough's at Perry Hall. He and his wife had by the mercy of God lately found a sense of the Divine favour; and now cheerfully opened their house and hearts to receive the ministers and children of God. I spent a most agreeable evening with Mr. and Mrs. Gough and the rest of the family. A numerous family of servants were called in to prayer and exhortation, so that with them and the rest of the house, we had a little congregation. The Lord was in the midst and we praised Him with joyful lips. The simplicity of spirit discovered by Mr. and Mrs. Gough was truly pleasing. At every opportunity, he was declaring what the Lord had done for his soul: still wondering at the matchless love of Jesus, who had plucked him as a brand from the burning. A gentleman in Bristol, who had died some years ago, left Mr. Gough an estate of money, houses and land, to the value of upwards of 60 or 70 thousand pounds. In the midst of all this, he was miserable and unhappy, nor never found true felicity, till he found it in the love of God his saviour. O, that he may live to be an ornament to the religion of Jesus Christ, both by example and precept.

Friday: I left Mr. Goughs and rode to Captain Ridgely's where I preached in the afternoon. Some were deeply cut to the heart, under the word so that they roared out from the disquietness of their souls: some of these I hope will not easily forget this hour.

Tuesday, 22nd August, 1775: We had our quarterly meeting for the lower circuit. The Lord was present at our love feast, and the preaching that followed. I find a want of liberality among the people of this circuit in order to carry on the work among them.

Wednesday: I returned to Philadelphia. On Tuesday, I was seized with a flux and fever, which has given me a good deal of pain, and attended with much weakness. I continued poorly all the week, but at the same time, enabled to read and write a good many letters. I remained in this city and supplied the chapel here till the beginning of October. By my being but poorly, the most of the time, I had quite work enough for my strength. I had a good deal of writing to attend to, by the number of letters, I was called to answer. As the work increased, this part of my labour increased also. The hurry and confusion that now reigned throughout this city made it rather uncomfortable to me at this period. My present station exposes me to trials of different

48

kinds more than ever. I cannot I dare not, countenance the measures taken to oppose Great Britain; and yet at the same time, I would do nothing to hurt, the inhabitants of America. How difficult to stand in such a situation; and not to be blamed by violent men on both sides? I had frequent opportunities from the first general congress that was held in Philadelphia, till now; to converse with several of its members; and also with many members of the Provincial Congress, where I travelled. I found liberty to speak my mind with freedom and so far as I could see they were not offended. I could not help telling many of them, what a farce it was for them to contend for liberty, when they themselves, kept some hundreds of thousands of poor blacks in most cruel bondage? Many confessed it was true, but it was not now the time to set them at liberty. While I was in the city we had rumor upon rumor of what was going forward. I endeavoured according to my little abilities to lead all those who heard me, (among whom were some-times some of the members of the Congress) to a proper improvement by turning with our whole hearts to the living God. A little while, and this dream of life will soon be over and trying as well as pleasing scenes will flee away!

"Then come bright day, which nee'n shall have a cloud,
   Come cheering smiles, from the bright face of God."

Keep me O Lord, holy and humble, and let me do and suffer all thy blessed will and so endure to the end, that I may be eternally saved. In the midst of all the public distractions, I found much pleasure in receiving different letters from my Christian friends in England and on this continent. But there were none that gave the joy to me, compared to what I felt, in the receiving one from Mr. Wesley. He had been near unto death, this summer in Ireland; but now I was assured of his recovery, by a letter with the August Packet. I hope to live, to see him, and my Brethren in England once more.

*   *   *

Tuesday, 27th August, 1776: Our quarterly meeting began as usual with our love feast, and ended with our watch afternoon. Surely this was a day of the Son of Man; and great was our glorying in God our Saviour. From morning to evening, prayer and praise, engaged all our ransomed powers. In the love feast, the flame of Divine love, run from heart to heart; and many were enabled to de-clare the great things which the Lord had done for their souls. Early in the morning, some of our kind friends came, and told me, that they were informed a company of the militia (with their officers) intended to come and take me and the other preachers up. Some of our good women came and with tears would have persuaded me to leave the place, and go to some other friends' house for safety. I thanked them for their love and was obliged to them for their

49

kind attention to my personal safety, but I added, "I am come here by the providence of God, and I am sent on an errand of love to the souls that shall attend, and thus engaged in my Lord's work. I fear nothing, and will abide the consequences be what they will." Our love feast passed off in quietness, and attended with much of the Divine presence as observed before. After some refreshment, we began to prepare for the rest of the service. I had retired a little by myself, when one and another came to my room door and begged I would not venture out to preach for the officers and their men were come. I felt no perturbation of mind, but was perfectly calm and recollected. I told our friends, their business was to pray and mine to deliver the message of God. Soon after I went to the arbour (which was fitted up for preaching) and then I beheld the officers and soldiers, in the skirts of the congregation. After singing, I called on all the people to lift up their hearts to God as the heart of one man. They did so indeed and in truth. When we arose from our knees, most of the congregation were bathed in tears; and I beheld several of the officers and their men wiping their eyes also. I had not spoke 10 minutes in preaching when a cry went through all the people; and I observed some of the officers as well as many of the soldiers trembling as they stood. I concluded my sermon in peace, and the other preachers prayed and exhorted after me, till the conclusion of the service. I was informed afterwards, by some of our friends who heard what some of the officers said, when they asked their commanding officer, "shall we execute the commands, we came for"? "God forbid (he replied) that we should hurt one hair of the head of such a gentlemen and minister of the Lord, Jesus Christ, who has this day so clearly and powerfully shown us the way of salvation." They departed to their own homes, and we spent the evening in peace and love. This afternoon and in particular in the evening, I had a strong impulse upon and pre-sentiment in my mind, that there had been an engagement between the British and the American troops. I mentioned it to one of the preachers and added, "we shall soon hear, whether this be of God or not".

Wednesday: We set off early on our way for Philadelphia, and reached Newcastle, on the Delaware River on Thursday afternoon. About 10 o'clock that evening an express arrived that there had been a general engagement on Long Island (near New York) and that some thousands of the American troops were cut to pieces. After preaching by the way, I came in safety to Philadelphia on Saturday forenoon.

¶   Devereux Jarratt meets Robert Williams and the Methodists

(Taken from letter in *Arminian Magazine*, (1786),
397, quoted in W. W. Sweet, *Virginia Methodism*
(1955) 65-66; and letter to Edward Dromgoole,
31 May 1785, 110).

Virginia (the land of my nativity) has long groaned through
a want of faithful ministers of the gospel. Many souls are perishing for lack of knowledge, many crying for the bread of life, and
no man is found to break it to them. We have ninety-five parishes
in the colony, and all except one, I believe are supplied with
clergymen. But, alas! You will understand the rest. I know of
but one clergyman of the Church of England who appears to have the
power and spirit of vital religion; for all seek their own, and not
the things that are Christ's. Is not our situation then truly
deplorable? And does it not call loudly upon the friends of Zion
on your side of the Atlantic to assist us? Many people here
heartily join with me in returning our most grateful acknowledgements for the concern you have shown for us in sending so many
preachers to the American colonies. Two have preached for some
time in Virginia: Mr. Pilmoor and Mr. Williams. I have never had
the pleasure of seeing Mr. Pilmoor, but by all I can learn, he is
a gracious soul and a good preacher. With Mr. Williams I have
had many delightful interviews. He has just now returned to my
house from a long excursion through the back counties. I hope he
will be able to write you joyful tidings of his success. But, after
all, what can two or three preachers do in such an extended country
as this? Cannot you do something more for us? Cannot you send us
a minister of the Church of England, to be stationed in that one
vacant parish, I mentioned? In all probability he would be of
great service. The parish I am speaking of is about forty miles
from me. The people are anxious to hear the truth. The parishes
around it afford a wide field for itineration; for I would have no
minister of Jesus, as matters stand, confined to one parish. Mr.
McRoberts, the gentleman referred to above, is an Israelite indeed.
He is a warm. zealous, striking preacher. He is constantly making
excursions toward Maryland and Pennsylvania in the North and North-
west, while I make a tour of the parishes to the South and Southwest.
Now, if we had one to take this station forty miles to the west, we
should be able to go through the country. I flatter myself it will
be so. I shall wait with expectation till I am favored with an
answer from you. I trust it will be such an answer as will rejoice
my heart and the hearts of thousands.

[From 1773, the date of Williams' first contact with Jarratt,
to 1784, Jarratt and the Methodists were in full cooperation in
Virginia, and out of this cooperation came the first great Methodist
awakening in America, which reached its peak during the years 1775
to 1776.]

. . . My not being at conference was not owing to want of inclination, but not being invited by either of the superintendents, I imagined my company was not desired; and since I have been more convinced of it for I wrote to Dr. Coke intreating him and Mr. Asbury to pay me a visit before they left the state, to which the Doctor did not vouchsafe a verbal answer and Mr. Asbury a very slight one. If ever I was worthy of the love and esteem of Mr. Asbury or any preacher in connection with him, I am so still. For I am the same both in principle and practice as I was the first day he ever saw me. I have suffered no change at all. I love and honor those who fear the Lord, let their station in life be what it will; but my peculiar attachment has been to the Methodists; and considering the persecution I have suffered on their account, the many hundred miles I have rode through all weathers and at all seasons to serve them in every respect, I cannot conceive how I have deserved to be treated so coldly, to say the least. Surely it proceeds from no good spirit. However, I am no stranger to such treatment. . . .

¶   Minutes
                                of

              Some Conversations Between the Preachers
                      in connection with

                    The Rev. Mr. John Wesley
                  Philadelphia, June (July), 1773

The following queries were proposed to every preacher:--
   1. Ought not the authority of Mr. Wesley, and that Conference, to extend to the preachers and people in America as well as in Great Britain and Ireland?
   Ans. Yes.
   2. Ought not the doctrine and discipline of the Methodists, as contained in the Minutes, to be the sole rule of our conduct, who labour in the connection with Mr. Wesley in America?
   Ans. Yes.
   3. If so, does it not follow that if any preachers deviate from the Minutes we can have no fellowship with them till they change their conduct?
   Ans. Yes.
The following rules were agreed to by all the preachers present:
   1. Every preacher who acts in connection with Mr. Wesley and the brethren who labour in America is strictly to avoid administering the ordinances of baptism and the Lord's supper.
   2. All the people among whom we labour to be earnestly exhorted to attend the Church, and receive the ordinances there; but in a particular manner to press the people in Maryland and Virginia to the observance of this minute.

3. No person or persons to be admitted into our love-feasts oftener than twice or thrice unless they become members; and none to be admitted to the society meetings more than thrice.

4. None of the preachers in America to reprint any of Mr. Wesley's books without his authority (when it can be gotten) and the consent of their brethren.

5. Robert Williams to sell the books he has already printed, but to print no more, unless under the above restrictions.

6. Every preacher who acts as an assistant to send an account of the work once in six months to the general assistant.

Quest. 1 *How are the preachers stationed?*

New York, Thomas Rankin, to change in four months.

Philadelphia, George Shadford, to change in four months.

New-Jersey, John King, William Waters.

Baltimore, Francis Asbury, Robert Strawbridge, Abraham Whitworth, Joseph Yearbry.

Norfolk, Richard Wright
Petersburg, Robert Williams.

Quest. 2 *What numbers are there in the Society?*

New-York	180
Philadelphia	180
New-Jersey	200
Maryland	500
Virginia	100
	1160

Preachers 10

3. THE AMERICAN REVOLUTION

The early Methodists were relaxed about record-keeping--
in striking contrast to some of their successors. The Minutes
of the first Annual Conferences are notoriously incomplete and
inaccurate. This is especially true of the meetings held during
the Revolution, when at one time northern and southern segments
were effectively out of communication. Through the agency of
Edward Schell and Elizabeth Hughey we have at hand the unofficial
but far more complete Minutes kept by Philip Gatch and published
in the Western Christian Advocate, *19 and 26 May 1837. Offered*
here are those for 1777, which deal with organizational matters
occasioned by the Revolution, and 1779, which cover the issues
surrounding the Fluvanna meeting on ordination. Neither of these
meetings was adequately reported in the printed Minutes.

Two contrasting views of military service by Methodist
ministers are given by Jesse Lee and Thomas Ware. Conflated
in the material are the two related but disparate issues of
Christian pacifism and ministerial exemption. The experience of
Freeborn Garrettson was more immediate and exemplifies the violence
done by both American superpatriots and Anglophiles.

Wakeley preserves an eye-witness account of what happened
to John Street church during the Revolution. Thomas Jackson
preserves the record of a historic conversation between George
Shadford and Francis Asbury. It helps to explain why the latter,
of all of Wesley's missionaries except a couple who located, was
the only one to remain in America during the Revolution.

William Watters' early and rare autobiography has one
valuable account of what happened as a result of the ordinations
at the Fluvanna Conference. The later, somewhat jaundiced
interpretation of the Methodist Protestant historian Edward J.
Drinkhouse, provides interesting contrast as well as an exercise
in the use of historical sources.

¶ Minutes of a Conference held in Baltimore, May, 1777.

(Taken from the *Western Christian Advocate*,
May 19 & 26, 1837 Vol. 4 #4, 5, duplicated
by Edwin Schell).

Q. 1. What preachers are admitted this year, and who remain
on trial?
A. Caleb Pedicord, Hollis Hanson, Joseph Cromwell, Thomas
Chew, Michael Debruler (1), Robert Wooster, John Tunnel,
Philip Adams (1), Samuel Strong, William Gill, John
Littlejohn, Edward Pride, Leroy Cole, Joseph Reece (1),
John Dickins, Reuben Ellis, Edward Baily, Samuel Roe (1).

Q. 2. What numbers are in society?
A.

New York,	96	Leesburg	330
Philadelphia,	96	Hanover,	262
Jersies,	160	Amelia,	620
Kent,	720	Brunswick,	1360
Chester,	136	Sussex,	727
Baltimore,	900	Pitsylvania,	150
Anapolis,	120	Carolina,	930
Frederick,	361	In all,	6968

Q. 3. What is the yearly collection (3)?
A. In all,L 23 6s. 11d.

Q. 4. What shall be done with respect to the administration of
the ordinances?
A. Let the preachers and people pursue the old plan, as from
the beginning.

Q. 5. What alteration may we make in our original plan?
A. Our next conference will, if God permits, show us more
clearly.

Q. 6. What shall the preachers' quarterage be?
A. If there be 3, 4, or 5 pound remaining, let it be divided
among those who want it.

Q. 7. Who act as assistants this year?
A. Thomas Rankin, Francis Asbury, George Shadford, Martin
Rodda, Edward Drumgoole, Samuel Spragg, Daniel Ruff,
William Waters, Philip Gatch, James Foster, John King,
William Duke.

Q. 8. What preachers are admitted this year?
A. Nicholas Waters, John Sigman, Joseph Hartly, Isham Tatum,
James Foster, Freeborn Garretson, Thomas M'Clure, William
Wren.

Q. 9. Are there any objections against the preachers?
A. Examine them one by one. (This was done.)

Q. 10. Where are the preachers stationed this year?
A. Philadelphia, William Duke.
Jersies, Henry Kennedy, Thomas M'Clure
Chester, Robert Lindsay.
Kent, Martin Rodda, William Glendening, Isaac Cromwell, Robert Wooster.
York, Thomas Webb.
Baltimore, George Shadford, John Littlejohn, Joseph Hartly, William Gill.
Anapolis, William Wren, Francis Asbury.
Fredericktown, Samuel Spragg, Caleb Pedicord.
Leesburg, Daniel Ruff, Thomas Chew, John Cooper.
Hanover, James Foster, Nicholas Waters, Samuel Strong.
Amelia, Edward Drumgoole, Joseph Reece, Reuben Ellis.
Brunswick, William Waters, John Tunnell, Freeborn Garretson.
Sussex, Philip Gatch, Hollis Hanson.
Pitsylvania, Isham Tatum, John Sigman.
Carolina, John King, John Dickins, Edward Pride, Leroy Cole.
Norfolk, Edward Bailey.

Q. 11. Can any thing be done in order to lay a foundation for a future union, supposing the old preachers should be, by the times, constrained to return to Great Britain? Would it not be well for all who are willing, to sign some articles of agreement, and strictly adhere to the same, till other preachers are sent by Mr. Wesley, and the brethren in conference?
A. We will do it.

Accordingly, the following paper was wrote and signed "We, whose names are underwritten, being thoroughly convinced of the necessity of a close union between those whom God hath need as instruments in his glorious work, in order to preserve this union, are resolved, God being our helper,
1. To devote ourselves to God, taking up our cross daily, steadily aiming at this one thing, to save our souls and them that hear us. 2. To preach the old Methodist doctrine, and no other, as contained in the Minutes. 3. To observe and enforce the whole Methodist Discipline, as laid down in the said Minutes. 4. To choose a committee of assistants to transact the business that is now done by the general assistants, and the old preachers who came from Britain (2),

William Waters,	James Foster,	Daniel Ruff,
Robert Wooster,	William Glendening,	Caleb Pedicord,
Philip Gatch,	Hollis Hanson,	Freeborn Garretson,
Thomas Chew,	Henry Kennedy,	William Wren,
Robert Lindsay,	Thomas Rankin,	William Duke,

Francis Asbury,	Thomas M'Clure	Martin Rodda,
John Cooper,	George Shadford,	Richard Owens,
Samuel Spragg,	Richard Webster,	Edward Drumgoole,
		Joseph Hartly."

Q. 12. Who shall act as a committee of assistants agreeably to
the preceding plan?

A. Daniel Ruff, William Waters, Philip Gatch, Edward Drumgoole,
William Glendening.

Q. 13. Have not preaching funeral sermons been carried so far as
to render that venerable custom as some sort contemptible?

A. Yes; therefore let all the preachers inform every society,
that we will preach none but for those we have reason to
believe have died in the fear and favor of God.

Q. 14. To whose care shall we leave Mr. Wesley's books (4)?

A. To William Waters, Daniel Ruff, Philip Gatch,
Edward Drumgoole.

Q. 15. When and where shall our next conference be?

A. At Baltimore town, or brother Waters', on the 3d Tuesday
in May, 1778.

NOTES FOR 1777, BY THE EDITORS. (1) These four persons' names,
viz, Michael Debruler, Philip Adams, Joseph Reece, and Samuel Roe,
are not in the printed Minutes of this year, and the name of Joseph
Reece only is on the list of stationed preachers. (2) This plan of
union is precisely the same with that recommended by Mr. Wesley
himself, in the year 1776, and which was carried finally into effect
both in Europe and America, under different modifications. Twenty-
five preachers signed these terms. (3) This, down to the 6th
question inclusive, is not in the printed Minutes. (4) From this
to the end is wanting in the printed Minutes.

*   *   *

Minutes of a Conference held at Roger Thomson's, in Fluvanna
County, VA., May 18, 1779 (1).

Q. 1. What preachers are admitted this year?
A. Caleb Pedicord (2).

Q. 2. Are there any objections to any of the preachers?
A. Examine them one by one (which was done).

Q. 3. What numbers are in society (3)?
A. As follows:

| Hanover, | 281 | Charlotte, | 186 |
| Frederick, | 480 | Brunswick, | 656 |

Fairfax,	309	Pitsylvania,	500
Barkley, (sic)	191	Roanoke,	470
Fluvanna,	300	Tarr River,	455
Amelia,	470	Newhope,	542
Sussex,	655	Charles city,	77
Lunenburg,	489	Buckingham,	25
		Total,	6086

Q. 4. Shall any of the preachers receive quarterage money, who are able to travel and do not travel?
A. No.

Q. 5. Shall preachers reduced, or broke down by preaching, or sickness, receive any support from the society?
A. 1st. If they are able to support themselves, they are to receive no support from the society. 2. If they are in real want, they are to be assisted.

Q. 6. In what light are we to look on those preachers who receive money for preaching by subscription?
A. As excluded from Methodist connection.

Q. 7. What is the conference collection?
A. As follows:

	Ł.	s.	d.		Ł.	s.	d.
Frederick,	6	0	0	Lunenburg,	10	0	0
Fairfax,	6	0	0	Pitsylvania,	12	12	3
Fluvanna,	34	0	0	Roanoke,	24	0	0
Hanover,	15	0	0	Tarr River,	12	8	6
Amelia,	15	0	0	In the steward's			
Sussex,	30	0	0	hands,	26	6	11
Brunswick,	15	0	0		Ł205	7	8

Q. 8. How was it expended?
A.

Preacher's expenses to and from conference,	83	19	6
Expenses at conference,	50	0	0
Thomas Morris,	20	0	0
Nelson Reed,	46	12	2
Servants,	0	4	16
	Ł205	7	8

Q. 9. What shall the preachers be allowed per quarter?
A. Something equivalent to five pounds, Virginia currency four years ago.

Q. 10. How are the preachers stationed this year?
A. As follows

Frederick,	Sussex,
Fairfax,	Brunswick,
Barkley,	Mechlenburg,
Buckingham,	Charlotte,

58

Fluvanna,	Pitsylvania,
Hanover,	Roanoke,
Charles city,	Tarr River,
Amelia, Samuel Roe, Isham Tatum.	New Hope.

Q. 11. How are the local preachers and exhorters to be ruled, in order to make matters regular?

A. Every local preacher and exhorter to go according to the direction of the assistant, where, and only where he shall direct him.

Q. 12. Is any helper to make any alteration, or appoint preaching in the circuit, or in any new place, without consulting the assistant?

A. No.

Q. 13. What directions shall this conference give the several assistants, for the promoting Discipline and order in the several rounds?

A. That the assistants require every local preacher, exhorter, or temporary traveler, to take a note from quarter to quarter; and the assistants and stewards of the societies, and the trustees of preaching-houses, are to suffer none to preach or exhort without having such a note as aforesaid.

Q. 14. What are our reasons for taking up the administration of the ordinances among us?

A. Because the Episcopal Establishment is now dissolved, and therefore in almost all our circuits the members are without the ordinances, We believe it to be our duty.

Q. 16.(sic) What preachers do approve of this step?

A. Isham Tatum, Henry Willis, Charles Hopkins, Frank Poythress, Nelson Reed, John Sigman, Reuben Ellis, Leroy Cole, Philip Gatch, Carter Cole, Thomas Morris, James Kelly, James Morris, William Moore, James Foster, John Majors, Andrew Yeargin, Samuel Roe.

Q. 16. Is it proper to have a committee?

A. Yes, and by the vote of the preachers.

Q. 17. Who are the committee?

A. Philip Gatch, James Foster, Leroy Cole, and Reuben Ellis.

Q. 18. What powers do the preachers rest in the committee?

A. They do all agree to observe all the resolutions of the said committee, so far as the said committee shall adhere to the Scripture.

Q. 19. What form of ordination shall be observed, to authorize any preacher to administer?
A. By that of a presbytery.

Q. 20. How shall the presbytery be appointed?
A. By a majority of the preachers.

Q. 21. Who are the presbytery?
A. Philip Gatch, Reuben Ellis, James Foster, and in case of necessity, Leroy Cole.

Q. 22. What power is vested in the presbytery by this choice?
A. 1st. To administer the ordinance themselves. 2d. To authorize any other preacher or preachers, approved of by them, by the form of laying on of hands and of prayer.

Q. 23. What is to be observed as touching the aministration of the ordinance, and to whom shall they be administered?
A. To those who are under our care and Discipline.

Q. 24. Shall we re-baptize any under our Discipline?
A. No.

Q. 25. What mode shall be adopted for the administration of baptism?
A. Either sprinkling or plunging, as the parent or adult shall choose.

Q. 26. What ceremony shall be used in the administration?
A. Let it be according to our Lord's command, Mat.,xxviii, 19, short and extempore.

Q. 27. Shall the sign of the cross be used?
A. No.

Q. 28. Who shall receive the charge of the child after baptism, for its future instruction?
A. The parents, or persons who have the care of the child, with advice from the preacher.

Q. 29. What mode shall be adopted for the administration of the Lord's supper?
A. Kneeling is thought the most proper, but in cases of conscience, may be left to the choice of the communicant.

Q. 30. What ceremony shall be observed in this ordinance?
A. After singing, praying, and exhortation, the preacher delivers the bread, saying, "The body," &tc., according to the church order.

Q. 31. When and where shall our next conference be?
    A. At American town, the second Tuesday in May.

NOTES ON GATCH'S MINUTES FOR 1779, BY THE EDITORS.
    On consulting the printed Minutes, it will be seen that a
conference was held in Kent county, Delaware, April 28th, 1779.
There were only six assistants at this conference, and 17 preachers
only were stationed. This conference was not appointed at the
previous one, but must have been called by Mr. Asbury and a few
others. But the conference that met at Fluvanna seems to be the
one that was properly the successor of the conference of 1778, as
the Delaware conference was an extraordinary one, and called on
an especial occasion. In the Fluvanna conference there were 11
assistants, and 32 preachers stationed.

¶   Jesse Lee on Military Service.

               (Taken from Minton Thrift, *Memoir of
               the Rev. Jesse Lee* (1823) 26-34).

    "I weighed the matter over and over again, but my mind was
settled; as a Christian and as a preacher of the gospel I could not
fight. I could not reconcile it to myself to bear arms, or to kill
one of my fellow creatures; however I determined to go, and to
trust in the Lord; and accordingly prepared for my journey.

    "Monday July 17th, 1780, I left home and set out for the army,
and travelled about 25 miles to Mr. Green Hill's, where I was
kindly used -- I tarried there all night.

    "Wednesday 19th, I set off early in the morning and travelled
about 16 miles to Mr. Hines'. In the afternoon we had much conversation on spiritual matters, and in the evening, felt my heart
more engaged with God in prayer than usual. I felt my dependence
upon God, and though I believed that great difficulties lay before
me, yet I resigned myself into the hands of God, and felt assured
that he would protect and take care of me.

    "I did not join the army till the 29th. On the evening of
that day I came in sight of the camp, and was soon called on parade,
and orders were given for all the soldiers to be furnished with
guns. I then lifted up my heart to God and besought him to take
my cause in his hands, and support me in the hour of trial.

    "The sergeant soon came round with the guns, and offered one
to me, but I would not take it. Then the lieutenant brought me
one, but I refused to take it. He said I should go under guard.
He then went to the colonel, and coming back, brought a gun and
set it down against me. I told him he had as well take it away

or it would fall. He then took me with him and delivered me
to the guard.

"After a while the colonel came, and taking me out a little way
from the guard, he began to converse with me, and to assign many
reasons why I should bear arms; but his reasons were not sufficiently
cogent to make any alteration in my mind. He then told the guard to
take care of me, and so left me.

"Many of the people came and talked with me and pitied me, and
would leave me with tears in their eyes. We lay encamped at a
tavern a few miles from the site of what was afterwards the seat of
government for North Carolina. After dark, I told the guard we must
pray before we slept; and, having a Baptist under guard, I asked
him to pray, which he did. I then told the people if they would
come out early in the morning, I would pray with them. I felt
remarkably happy in God under all my trouble, and did not doubt
but that I should be delivered in due time. Some of the soldiers
brought me some straw to lay upon, and offered me their blankets
and great coats for covering. I slept pretty well that night,
which was the first, and the last night I was ever under guard.

"Sunday 30th. -- As soon as it was light, I was up and began
to sing, and some hundreds of people soon assembled and joined
with me, and we made the plantation ring with the songs of Zion.
We then kneeled down and prayed; and while I was praying, my soul
was happy in God, and I wept much and prayed loud, and many of the
poor soldiers also wept. I do not think that I ever felt more
willing to suffer for the sake of religion than what I did at that
time.

"A little after we were done prayer, Mr. Thomas, the tavern
keeper, came out and talked with me, and told me he was in bed
when he heard me praying, that he could not refrain from tears, and
he had called to see me, and know if I would be willing to preach
to them that day, it being sabbath? I told him I would preach
provided he would procure a block, or something for me to stand
upon; which he readily promised to do. I told him, withal, I wished him to go to the colonel, for we had no higher officer amongst
us, and obtain leave for me to preach; which he did, and liberty
was granted. It is but just to state, that Colonal Bru*** was a
man of great humanity, although a profane swearer. When he heard
that I was about to preach, it affected him very much, so he came
and took me out to talk with me on the subject of bearing arms.
I told him I could not kill a man with a good conscience, but I
was a friend to my country, and was willing to do any thing that I
could, while I continued in the army, except that of fighting.
He then asked me if I would be willing to drive their baggage
wagon? I told him I would, though I had never drove a wagon before;
he said their main cook was a Methodist, and could drive the wagon

when we were on a march, and I might lodge and eat with him; to which I agreed. He then released me from guard, and said when I was ready to begin meeting I might stand on a bench by his tent. When the hour arrived, I began under the trees, and took my text in Luke xiii.5. *Except ye repent, ye shall all likewise perish.* After I had been speaking awhile it began to rain, and we were under the necessity of going into the house, where I resumed my discourse. I was enabled to speak plainly, and without fear; and I wept while endeavouring to declare my message. Many of the people, officers as well as men, were bathed in tears before I was done. That meeting afforded me an ample reward for all my trouble. At the close of the meeting, some of the gentlemen went about with their hats to make a collection of money for me, at which I was very uneasy, and ran in among the people and begged them to desist. I could not at that time feel willing to receive any compensation for preaching. I thought if the people could afford to sit and hear me, I could well afford to stand and preach to them. I felt my heart humbled before God, and was truly thankful to him for the grace communicated to my soul at that time. I had no doubt but that all things would work for my good.

"On Monday I took charge of the wagon, and felt much resigned to the will of God."

. . . "Sunday 13th of August, we lay by and did not march; about 3 o'clock in the afternoon, I preached to a large number of soldiers, from Isa. iii. 10, 11. *Say ye to the righteous, &tc.* Many of the hearers were very solemn, and some of them wept freely under the preaching of the word. I was happy in God, and thankful to him for that privilege of warning the wicked once more. It was a great cross for me to go forward in matters of so much importance, where there were few to encourage, and many to oppose; but I knew that I had to give an account to God for my conduct in the world -- I felt the responsibility laid upon me, and was resolved to open my mouth for God. I often thought I had more cause to praise and adore God for his goodness than any other person. For some weeks I hardly ever prayed in public, or preached, or reproved a sinner, without seeing some good effects produced by my labours.

"Thursday 17th, about 10 o'clock in the morning, we received the unexpected news of general Gates' defeat, near Campden, which took place the day before; the news spread through the camp, and all were called out on parade. All appeared solemn; not an oath was heard for several hours. The mouths of the most profane swearers were shut. We then commenced a retreat back to North Carolina.

"Monday 28th, we marched down to Romney's Mills, on Deep River. On the 29th, I was taken very sick. The next day I went to Mr. Crump's about three miles from the camp. I was so sick that I

could not return to camp that night. I was brought to examine my heart closely concerning my hope of heaven; and was comforted to find that I had no doubt of my salvation; for I believed that should the Lord see fit to remove me from this world, I should be called to join the armies of Heaven.

"Tuesday the 5th of September, the army marched from Deep River, and I joined them though quite unwell.

"On the following morning the Colonel told me, inasmuch as I was not willing to bear arms, I must join the pioneers. I was afterward appointed sergeant of the pioneers, which was a safe and easy birth; there were but few in that company, and I had to direct them in their labours, which was not hard. The soldiers suffered much for the want of provision, for the greater part of the week. We crossed Harraway River, and came through Randolph County; we were frequently alarmed at night, so that I was much fatigued by severe marches by day, and sleeping little at night. But the best of all was, my soul was kept in peace, and at times, I felt great fellowship with the Father and with the Son!

"On the 15th of September, at night, some of our men took a noted tory from under guard and carried him a little way off, and hung him up, without judge or jury. Some inquiry was made about it the next day, but no person would confess the fact, and it passed over. This circumstance took place near Salisbury, where we tarried four nights.

"Sunday the 24th, Mr. Green Hill preached in the camp; his text was 1 Thes. v. 19. 'Quench not the Spirit.' The next morning before day we had orders to prepare and leave the ground in ten minutes, for the British were expected to be on us in a short time. We left the ground before day, and the wagons came on towards Salisbury about 16 miles, and then had orders to turn back to the Cross-Roads, which was about 9 miles; we retreated about 7 miles, and halted to get something to eat; we then had orders to march immediately. The enemy came to Charlotte, and had an engagement with our people, and several men were killed. Some who overtook us, who were with the baggage, were wounded and bleeding. We marched about 18 miles that day, and made it quite late in the night before we came to a halt. We stayed two or three hours, and cooked something, and eat a little; and then marched immediately, without taking time to sleep. We marched again sometime before day, and the roads were thronged with people, men, women and children, with their property, flying from the face of the enemy. The colonel rode up and said to me, 'Well, Lee! don't you think you could fight now?' I told him I could fight with switches, but I could not kill a man. We came to Salisbury and encamped in town that night, expecting the enemy would be after

us every hour. The night was very cold.

"On Thursday, 28th of September, we crossed the Yadkin, at Island Ford, on account of the water being very high.

"On Sunday, the 8th of October, I was but poorly employed; we had no religious meeting.

"Tuesday the 10th, general Butler came into camp with a number of men, and took command of the whole army.

"At night the news arrived in camp that on Saturday last the Americans had a skirmish with the British and tories in Kings' Mountain, where our men gained a complete victory, and killed many of the enemy, and took the rest prisoners. We were all glad to hear the news; but some rejoiced with horrid oaths, and others determined to get drunk for joy. For my part, I felt thankful to God, and humbled before him, knowing that the battle is not to the strong.

"October 13th, colonel Morgan joined us with a part of his regiment -- some of our soldiers were very sick -- I went among them where they lay in barns, at the point of death, and talked to them about their souls; and begged them to prepare to meet their God. When convenient, I attended the funeral of those who died, and prayed at the grave.

"Wednesday the 18th, we had a sharp frost, which was a great advantage to those who were sick. In the evening Col. Washington, with his troop of horse joined us. The next day we crossed the Yadkin River to the South, and the day following, marched a small distance above Salisbury, and took up late at night. On Saturday we were up before day, and after some consultation among the officers, we were informed that we were not to march that day. We were in constant expectation of an attack from the enemy. I felt my mind calm and stayed on God; but having my rest so much broken of late, I felt quite dull and heavy.

"In the evening, by general Butler's order, 500 men were de-patched in search of the enemy. In the evening I walked out into the woods alone to pray and meditate; and it was to me a time of comfort and peace. I had such a deep sense of the love of God, that I was humbled in his presence, and my soul was filled with gratitude and love.

"Sunday 22nd October, we continued in camp all day and had no religious meeting. On Tuesday following, Gen. Jones came into our camp with his men. Many of the militia officers and soldiers began to be very uneasy about remaining any longer, as they supposed their time of service had expired, and several had already deserted.

"Saturday 28th. They drummed out of camp two captains and one ensign for deserting.

"Sunday Oct. 29th. -- On this morning I obtained my discharge. The general said as there were two sergeants of the pioneers, and one was sufficient, it would be best for me to resign, and as I was the oldest in office, I might have the privilege if I chose it. I accepted the offer -- took my discharge -- settled some business -- took leave of many of my old acquaintances, and left the army."

¶   Thomas Ware on Military Service.

(Taken from Thomas Ware, *Sketches of the Life and Travels of Rev. Thomas Ware* (1842) 29-30).

Others pleaded conscientious scruples against bearing arms, and were excused on that account, though their property was laid under requisition to support the war. Having now abjured my king, and taken up arms against him, I had time to think and reason with myself on the part I had taken in this great national conflict; and some of my reflections I can never forget while memory lasts. The cause I held to be just. On this point I had no misgivings. But whether we should be able to sustain our ground, appeared to me a much more doubtful question. There must be, I was sure, much hard fighting, and many valuable lives sacrificed, to gain the boon of our independence, if we should succeed at last. And what will they gain, thought I, who fall in the struggle? The thanks of their country? No; they will be forgotten. But then the principles for which we were contending, it appeared to me, were worth risking life for. Our example would be followed by others, and tyranny and oppression would be overthrown throughout the world. Still the question recurred, "Can you meet the martialled hosts of the British nation -- you, who know little or nothing of the arts of war, and whose officers know not much more than yourselves -- with any hope of success?" This was an appalling view of the subject. Yet, with the views I entertained of the justness of our cause in the sight of Heaven, I could not doubt, and resolved for one on liberty or death. "But there is a hereafter," was suggested to my mind. True, thought I, but I will do the best I can, and trust in God. And so it was, that as a soldier in the army I was more devout than when at home; and I prayed until a confidence sprang up within me, that I should return to my home and friends in safety, or not be cut off without time to make my peace with God.

66

¶   Garrettson's Beating.

(Taken from Nathan Bangs, *History of the Methodist Episcopal Church* (1839), I, 125-26).

Mr. Freeborn Garrettson was at that time actively and successfully engaged in preaching the gospel in Queen Anne's county, in the
state of Maryland. After having paid a visit to Mr. Asbury in his
seclusion at Judge White's, where he had an opportunity of preaching to a small company, he returned to Queen Anne's and preached.
The next day, as he was on his way to Kent, he was met by one John
Brown, formerly a judge of that county, who seized his horse's
bridle; and notwithstanding the remonstrances of Mr. Garrettson,
who assured him that he was on the Lord's errand, peaceably engaged in persuading sinners to be reconciled to God, Brown
alighted from his horse, seized a stick, and began beating Mr.
Garrettson over the head and shoulders, in the meantime calling
for help. As some were approaching, as he thought with a rope,
Brown let go the bridle, when Mr. Garrettson gave his horse the
whip, and thus cleared himself from the grasp of his persecutors.
He was, however, soon overtaken by his pursuer, who struck at him
with all his might, when Mr. Garrettson was thrown from his horse
with great violence. Providentially a lady passed along with a
lancet and he was taken to a house and bled, by which means he
was restored to his senses, of which he had been deprived by
the blows he had received, and the fall from his horse. He then
began to exhort his persecutor, who, fearing that death would
ensue, exhibited some sorrow and great trepidation of heart, offering to take Mr. Garrettson in his carriage wherever he wanted to go.
No sooner, however, did he perceive that the patient sufferer was
likely to recover, than he brought a magistrate, more wicked than
himself, both of whom, says Mr. Garrettson, "appeared as if actuated
by the devil." The following is his own account of the termination
of this affair: --

"With a stern look the magistrate demanded my name. I told
him; and he took out his pen and ink, and began to write a mittimus
to commit me to jail. 'Pray, sir,' said I, 'are you a justice of
the peace?' He replied that he was. 'Why, then,' said I, 'do you
suffer men to behave in this manner? If such persons are not taken
notice of, a stranger can with no degree of safety travel the road.'
'You have,' said he, 'broken the law.' 'How do you know that,'
answered I; 'but suppose I have, is this the way to put the law in
force against me? I am an inhabitant of this state, and have
property in it; and , if I mistake not, the law says for the first
offence, the fine is five pounds, and double for every offence
after. The grand crime was preaching the gospel of the Lord
Jesus Christ, in which I greatly rejoice. My enemy,' said I,
'conducted himself more like a highwayman than a person enforcing
the law in a Christian country. Be well assured, this matter will

67

be brought to light,' said I, 'in awful eternity.' He dropped his pen, and made no farther attempt to send me to prison. By this time, the woman who bled me came with a carriage, and I found myself able to rise from my bed and give an exhortation to the magistrate, my persecutor, and others who were present."

From this time Mr. Garrettson went on his way rejoicing in all the mighty things which the Lord did by his instrumentality; for he wrought wonderfully by his means in the states of Maryland and Delaware.

¶   John Street Church During the Revolution.

(Taken from Wakeley, *Lost Chapters*, 458-59).

To my friend, G. P. Disosway, Esq., I am indebted for the following anecdotes illustrative of the times. He received them from Hannah Baldwin, who was present when the events took place. They occurred while Peter (Williams) was sexton.

"Religious meetings at night were then generally forbidden, but allowed in the Methodist Church, as the British imagined, or rather desired, that the followers of Wesley should favor their cause. Still the services were sometimes interrupted and disturbed by the rude conduct of men belonging to the army. They would often stand in the aisle with their caps on during Divine worship, careless and inattentive. On one occasion, before the congregation was dismissed, they sang the national song, *'God save the king.'* At its conclusion the society immediately began, and sang to the same air, those beautiful lines of Charles Wesley:

'Come, thou almighty King,
Help us thy name to sing,
    Help us to praise!
Father all-glorious,
O'er all victorious,
Come,and reign over us,
    Ancient of Days.

'Jesus, our Lord, arise,
Scatter our enemies,
    And make them fall!
Let thine almighty aid
Our sure defense be made;
Our souls on thee be stay'd;
    Lord, hear our call,'" etc.

"Upon a Christmas eve, when the members had assembled to celebrate the advent of the world's Redeemer, a party of British officers, masked, marched into the house of God. One, very properly personifying their master, was dressed with cloven feet, and a long forked tail. The devotions of course soon ceased, and the chief devil, proceeding up the aisle, entered the altar. As he was ascending the stairs of the pulpit, a gentleman present with his cane knocked off his Satanic majesty's mask, when lo, there stood a well-known British colonel! He was immediately seized, and detained until the city guard was sent to take charge of the bold offender. The congregation retired, and the entrances of the church were locked upon the prisoner for additional security. His companions outside then commenced an attack upon the doors and windows, but the arrival of the guard put an end to these disgraceful proceedings, and the prisoner was delivered into their custody."

¶ George Shadford Returns to England.

(Taken from Thomas Jackson, ed., *The Lives of Early Methodist Preachers, Chiefly Written by Themselves*, 6 vols. (London, 1873),VI, 172-73).

At our Quarterly Meeting I said to Brother Asbury, "Let us have a day of fasting and prayer, that the Lord may direct us. ...We did so, and in the evening I asked him how he found his mind. He said he did not see his way clear to go to England. I told him I could not stay, as I believed I had done my work here at present; and that it was as much impressed upon my mind to go home now as it was to come over to America." He replied, "Then one of us must be under a delusion." I said, "Not so; I may have a call to go and you to stay; and I believe we both obeyed the call of Providence." We saw that we must part, though we loved as Jonathan and David. . . .

¶ William Watters Visits Southern Brethren.

(Taken from William Watters, *A Short Account* (1806) 80-81).

We found our brethren as loving and as full of zeal as ever, and as fully determined on persevering in their newly adopted mode; for to all their former arguments, they now added (what with many was infinitely stronger than all the arguments in the world) that the Lord Approbated, and greatly blessed his own ordinances, by them administered the past year. We had a great deal of loving conversation with many tears; but I saw no bitterness, no shyness, no judging each other. We wept, and prayed, and sobbed, but

neither would agree to the other's terms. In the mean time I was requested to preach at twelve o'clock. As I had many preachers and professors to hear me I spoke from the words of Moses to his father-in-law. "We are journeying unto the place of which the Lord said, I will give it you: come thou with us and we will do thee good: for the Lord hath spoken good concerning Israel".

After waiting two days, and all hopes failing of any accommodation taking place, we had fixed on starting back early in the morning but late in the evening it was proposed by one of their own party in conference, (none of the others being present) that there should be a suspension of the ordinances for the present year, and that our circumstances should be laid before Mr. Wesley and his advice solicited in the business, also that Mr. Asbury should be requested to ride through the different circuits and superintend the work at large. The proposal in a few minutes took with all but a few. In the morning instead of coming off in despair of any remedy, we were invited to take our seats again in conference, where with great rejoicings and praises to God, we on both sides heartily agreed to the above accommodation. I could not but say it is of the Lords doing and it is marvellous in our eyes. I knew of nothing upon earth that could have given me more real consolation, and could not but be heartily thankful for the stand I had taken, and the part I had acted during the whole contest. I had by several leading characters, on both sides been suspected of leaning to the opposite; could all have agreed to the administering the ordinances, I should have had no objection; but until that was the case, I could not view ourselves ripe for so great a change. In a letter I received from Mr. _____ in the course of the year -- he observed amongst other things, nothing shakes Bro:_____like your letters -- you will I hope continue to write and spare not. We now had every reason to believe that every thing would end well, that the evils which had actually attended our partial division, would make us more cautious how we should entertain one thought of taking any step that should have the least tendency to so great an evil.

¶   Drinkhouse's Critical Judgment.

        (Taken from Edward J. Drinkhouse, *History
        of Methodist Reform* (1899), I, 219).

From the silence of the annalists of these early days it must not be inferred that the two parties into which the societies and the preachers were now divided did not press their divergent views of Conference polity, the one under the lead of Gatch, unfortunately for the cause now retired, and for this reason not so influential as he would have been, supported by Poythress, Ivy, Willis, Dickins, Yeargan, O'Kelly, Tatum, Gill, Cole, Glendinning, Reed, Major,

Tunnell, Ellis, as well as Watters and others, to the number of
nearly thirty out of the forty-four preachers, paving the way for
a Presbyterian system; while Asbury, with the less hearty support
of some dozen American preachers, Ruff, Garrettson, Cooper, Hartley,
Chew, Cromwell, and Peddicord being the principals, predetermined
that it should be hierarchal, an Episcopacy of three orders, with
property rights and ecclesiastical authority exclusively vested
in the preachers, as in Wesley's day. The former were equally
conscientious, and if they had been equally firm in the maintenance of their convictions, the organic form of American Methodism
would have been conformed to the precedents of the New Testament
churches, which established the priesthood of the people with a
ministry to serve in honor for their works' sake. Had it prevailed, it is patent that the O'Kelly secession of 1792 would have
been forestalled, and the societies saved the most disastrous
destruction of their unity they ever experienced, until the climax
of disunion in 1844. Had it prevailed, a strong probability would
be established, as will be seen, that the organic unity of American
Methodism would have been preserved, with what advantages denominationally, and what honor as a magnificent section of Christ's
earthly fold, the pen of the historian cannot describe. All the
Scripture, all the methods of the primitive Church for two
centuries, all the logic, all the rights of manhood Christianized,
all the political sentiments of the American Methodists and
revolutionary people, were on the side of the Fluvanna's large
majority of the preachers and three-fifths of the people.

4. FORMATION OF THE METHODIST EPISCOPAL CHURCH

The process whereby the Methodist movement grew into the Methodist "connection," and thence to visible form as the Methodist Episcopal Church is a fascinating study in institutional nurture. It is also fraught with a number of troublesome, and in some cases, troubling problems. This process says a great deal about what the Methodist church really is and about Methodists' doctrine of the church.

The organization of the church resulted indirectly from the coincidence of two factors: (1) American victory in the Revolutionary War and subsequent independence, and (2) the problem of administration of the sacraments and Wesley's ordinations. A short series of documents below includes most of the pertinent evidence on what Wesley did, or thought he was doing.

Thomas Ware was one of the participants in the Christmas Conference of 1784. His judgments, in the Sketches, should be taken seriously. In the absence of formal minutes of this crucial meeting, this kind of evidence is very important. Thomas Coke's ordination sermon for Francis Asbury is likewise significant for his understanding of the process. Years later, when at last Asbury was laid to rest, Ezekiel Cooper, best known as second publishing agent of the Methodist Publishing House, reviewed his career and contribution, and offered a seasoned interpretation of the founding of the church.

¶   Background of Wesley's Ordinations.

(Taken from Wesley, *Journal*, III, 232).

Mon. 20 Jan. 1746 - I set out for Bristol. On the road I read over Lord King's *Account of the Primitive Church*. In spite of the vehement prejudice of my education, I was ready to believe that this was a fair and impartial draught; but, if so, it would follow that bishops and presbyters are (essentially) of one order, and that originally every Christian congregation was a church independent on all others!

(Taken from *Letters*, III, 182, to J. Clark, 1756).

. . . As to my own judgement, I still believe 'the Episcopal form of Church government to be both scriptural and apostolical': I mean, well agreeing with the practice and writings of the Apostles. But that it is prescribed in Scripture I do not believe. This opinion (which I once heartily espoused) I have been heartily ashamed of ever since I read Dr. Stillingfleet's *Irenicon*. I think he has unanswerably proved that neither Christ or His Apostles prescribed any particular form of Church government, and that the plea for the divine right of Episcopacy was never heard of in the primitive Church.

But were it otherwise, I would still call these 'smaller matters than the love of God and mankind'. And could any man answer these questions, - 'Dost thou believe in the Lord Jesus Christ, God over all, blessed for evermore?' (which, indeed, no Arian, semi-Arian, or Socinian can do); 'Is God the centre of thy soul? Art thou more afraid of offending God than of death or hell?' (which no wicked man can possibly do, none that is not a real child of God); - if, I say, any man could answer these questions in the affirmative, I would gladly give him my hand.

This is certainly a principle held by those that are in derision called Methodists, and to whom a Popish priest in Dublin gave the still more unmeaning title of Swaddlers. They all desire to be of a catholic spirit; meaning thereby, not an indifference to all opinions, not an indifference as to modes of worship: this they know to be quite another thing. 'Love, they judge, alone gives a title to this character. Catholic love is a catholic spirit.'

As to heresy and schism, I cannot find one text in Scripture where they are taken in the modern sense. I remember no one scripture where heresy signifies error in opinion, whether fundamental or not; nor any where schism signifies separation from the Church, either with or without cause. I wish, sir, you would re-consider this point, and review the scriptures where these terms occur.

(Taken from Wesley, *Letters*, VII, 20, to Charles, 8 June 1780).

DEAR BROTHER, - Read Bishop Stillingfleet's *Irenicon* or any impartial history of the Ancient Church, and I believe you will think as I do. I verily believe I have as good a right to ordain as to administer the Lord's supper. But I see abundance of reasons why I should not use that right, unless I was turned out of the Church. At present we are just in our place.

Mr. Galloway's is an excellent tract. He is a clear writer. Shall I print it in the *Magazine*, or a separate pamphlet? Yet I can by no means agree with him that taxation and representation are inseparable. I think I have fully proved the contrary. But those who are taxed without being represented are under a despotic Government. No; the will of the King is not their law any more than it is ours.

I would not read over Dr. Watt's tract for an hundred pounds. You may read it, and welcome. I will not, dare not move those subtle, metaphysical controversies. Arianism is not in question; it is Eutychianism or Nestorianism. But what are they? What neither I or any one else understands. But they are what tore the Eastern and Western Churches asunder.

I am fully persuaded the Bishop will never meddle with us. He is a wiser man.

But this time you might understand me better. I *use* people whom I do not *trust*. I meant, I will not trust him to correct the next edition of the Hymn-Book.

The *Ecclesiastical History* will be printed first. If I live a little longer, Hook may follow.

It is well I accepted none of Lord George's invitations. If the Government suffers this tamely, I know not what they will not suffer.

Mr. Collins is not under my direction; nor am I at all accountable for any steps he takes. He is not in connexion with the Methodists. He only helps us now and then. I will suffer no disputing at the Conference.

Undoubtedly many of the patriots seriously intend to overturn the Government. But the hook is in their own nose. Peace be with you all!

(Taken from Wesley, *Letters*, VII, 30-31, to
Robert Lowth, Bishop of London, 10 Aug. 1780).

MY LORD, - Some time since, I received your Lordship's favour;
for which I return your Lordship my sincere thanks. Those persons
did not apply to the Society because they had nothing to ask of
them. They wanted no salary for their minister; they were themselves able and willing to maintain him. They therefore applied
by me to your Lordship, as members of the Church of England, and
desirous so to continue, begging the favour of your Lordship, after
your Lordship had examined him, to ordain a pious man who might
officiate as their minister.

But your Lordship observes, 'There are three ministers in that
country already.' True, my Lord; but what are three to watch over
all the souls in that extensive country? Will your Lordship permit
me to speak freely? I dare not do otherwise. I am on the verge of
the grave, and know not the hour when I shall drop into it. Suppose
there were threescore of those missionaries in the country, could I
in conscience recommend these souls to their care? Do they take
any care of their own souls? If they do (I speak it with concern!)
I fear they are almost the only missionaries in America that do.
My Lord, I do not speak rashly: I have been in America; and so
have several with whom I have lately conversed. And both I and they
know what manner of men the far greater part of these are. They
are men who have neither the power of religion nor the form - men
that lay no claim to piety nor even decency.

Give me leave, my Lord, to speak more freely still: perhaps it
is the last time I shall trouble your Lordship. I know your Lordship's abilities and extensive learning; I believe, what is far
more, that your Lordship fears God. I have heard that your Lordship is unfashionably diligent in examining the candidates for Holy
Orders - yea, that your Lordship is generally at the pains of examining them *yourself*. Examining them! In what respects? Why,
whether they understand a little *Latin* and *Greek* and can answer a
few trite questions in the science of divinity! Alas, how little
does this avail! Does your Lordship examine whether they serve
Christ or *Belial*? whether they love God or the world? whether
they ever had any serious thoughts about heaven or hell? whether
they have any real desire to save their own souls or the souls of
others? If not, what have they to do with Holy Orders? and what
will become of the souls committed to their care?

My Lord, I do by no means despise learning; I know the value of
it too well. But what is this, particularly in a Christian minister, compared to piety? What is it in a man that has no religion?
'As a jewel in a swine's snout.'

Some time since, I recommended to your Lordship a plain man,

whom I had known above twenty years as a person of deep, genuine piety and of unblameable conversation. But he neither understood Greek nor Latin; and he affirmed in so many words that he believed it was his duty to preach whether he was ordained or no. I believe so too. What became of him since, I know not; but I suppose he received Presbyterian ordination, and I cannot blame him if he did. He might think any ordination better than none.

I do not know that Mr. Hoskins had any favour to ask of the Society. He asked the favour of your Lordship to ordain him that he might minister to a little flock in America. But your Lordship did not see good to ordain *him*; but your Lordship did see good to ordain and send into America other persons who know something of Greek and Latin, but who knew no more of saving souls than of catching whales.

In this respect also I mourn for poor America, for the sheep scattered up and down therein. Part of them have no shepherds at all, particularly in the northern colonies; and the case of the rest is little better, for their own shepherds pity them not. They cannot; for they have no pity on themselves. They take no thought or care about their own souls.

Wishing your Lordship every blessing from the great Shepherd and Bishop of souls, I remain, my Lord,

Your Lordship's dutiful son and servant.

(Taken from Wesley, Letters, VII, 191 to the
preachers in America, 3 Oct., 1783).

DEAR BROTHER, – 1. Let all of you be determined to abide by the Methodist doctrine and discipline published in the four volumes of *Sermons* and the *Notes upon the New Testament,* together with the *Large Minutes* of the Conference.

2. Beware of preachers coming from Great Britain or Ireland without a full recommendation from me. Three of our travelling preachers have eagerly desired to go to America; but I could not approve of it by any means, because I am not satisfied that they throughly like either our discipline or our doctrine. I think they differ from our judgement in one or both. Therefore, if these or any other come without my recommendation, take care how you receive them.

3. Neither should you receive any preachers, however recommended, who will not be subject to the American Conference and cheerfully conform to the Minutes both of the American and English Conferences.

4. I do not wish our American brethren to receive any who make any difficulty of receiving Francis Asbury as the General Assistant. Undoubtedly the greatest danger to the work of God in America is likely to arise either from preachers coming from Europe, or from such as will arise from among yourselves speaking perverse things, or bringing in among you new doctrines, particularly Calvinism. You should guard against this with all possible care; for it is far easier to keep them out than to thrust them out.

I commend you all to the grace of God; and am

Your affectionate friend and brother.

(Taken from Luke Tyerman, *The Life & Times of the Rev. John Wesley, M.A.* (London, 1870-71), III, 428, Thomas Coke to Wesley, 17 Apr., 1784).

HONOURED AND VERY DEAR SIR, – I intended to trouble you no more about my going to America; but your observations incline me to address you again on the subject.

If some one in whom you could place the fullest confidence, and whom you think likely to have sufficient influence and prudence and delicacy of conduct for the purpose, were to go over and return, you would then have a source of sufficient information to determine on any points or propositions. I may be destitute of the last mentioned essential qualification (to the former I lay claim without reserve); otherwise my taking such a voyage might be expedient.

By this means, you might have fuller information concerning the state of the country and the societies than epistolary correspondence can give you; and there might be a cement of union, remaining after your death, between the societies and preachers of the two countries. If the awful event of your decease should happen before my removal to the world of spirits, it is almost certain, that I should have business enough, of indispensable importance, on my hands in these kingdoms.

I am, dear sir, your most dutiful and most affectionate son,

Thomas Coke.

(Taken from Tyerman, III, 429, Coke to Wesley, 9 Aug., 1784).

HONOURED AND DEAR SIR, – The more maturely I consider the subject, the more expedient it appears to me, that the power or ordaining others should be received by me from you, by the imposition of your hands; and that you should lay hands on brother Whatcoat and

77

brother Vasey, for the following reasons: (1) It seems to me the most scriptural way, and most agreeable to the practice of the primitive churches. (2) I may want all the influence, in America, which you can throw into my scale. Mr. Brackenbury informed me at Leeds, that he saw a letter from Mr. Asbury, in which he observed that he would not receive any person, deputed by you, with any part of the superintendency of the work invested in him; or words which evidently implied so much. I do not find the least degree of prejudice in my mind against Mr. Asbury; on the contrary, I find a very great love and esteem; and am determined not to stir a finger without his consent, unless necessity obliges me; but rather to be at his feet in all things. But, as the journey is long, and you cannot spare me often, it is well to provide against all events; and I am satisfied that an authority, formally received from you, will be fully admitted; and that my exercising the office of ordination, without the formal authority, may be disputed, and perhaps, on other accounts, opposed. I think you have tried me too often to doubt, whether I will, in any degree, use the power you are pleased to invest me with, farther than I believe absolutely necessary for the prosperity of the work.

In respect of my brethren Whatcoat and Vasey, it is very uncertain whether any of the clergy, mentioned by brother Rankin, except Mr. Jarratt, will stir a step with me in the work; and it is by no means certain, that even he will choose to join me in ordaining; and propriety and universal practice make it expedient, that I should have two presbyters with me in this work. In short, it appears to me, that everything should be prepared, and everything proper be done, that can possibly be done, on this side of the water. You can do all this in Mr. C____n's house, in your chamber; and afterwards, (according to Mr. Fletcher's advice,) give us letters testimonial of the different offices with which you have been pleased to invest us. For the purpose of laying hands on brothers Whatcoat and Vasey, I can bring Mr. Creighton down with me, by which you will have two presbyters with you.

In respect to brother Rankin's argument, that you will escape a great deal of odium by omitting this, it is nothing. Either it will be known, or not known. If not known, then no odium will arise; but if known, you will be obliged to acknowledge, that I acted under your direction, or suffer me to sink under the weight of my enemies, with perhaps your brother at the head of them. I shall entreat you to ponder these things.

Your most dutiful, THOMAS COKE.

(Taken from Wesley, *Journal*, VII,
15-16, 31 Aug., 1784).

Tues. 31. - Dr. Coke, Mr. Whatcoat, and Mr. Vasey came down
from London in order to embark for America.

Sept. 1, Wed. - Being now clear in my own mind, I took a step
which I had long weighed in my mind, and appointed Mr. Whatcoat
and Mr. Vasey to go and serve the desolate sheep in America.

Thur. 2. - I added to them three more; which, I verily
believe, will be much to the glory of God.

Sun. 29. - Prayed, letters, tea, on business; 9.30 prayers,
Mark vii, 27! communion; 1 at brother Ewer's dinner, conversed;
2 sleep, on business, prayed, tea, conversed; 5 Acts xxviii 32!
society; 7 the singers; 8 supper, within, prayer; 9.30. [Diary]

Mon. 30. - Prayed, Heb. vi. 1, writ plan; 8 tea, conversed,
prayer, Accounts, Journal; 12 select society; 1 at brother Pine's,
dinner, conversed, prayer; 2.30 letters, within to some prayer;
5 at P. Gad's tea, conversed; 6 prayed, Lu. xii 15 within, supper,
conversed, prayer; 9.30.

Tues. 31. - Prayed, letters; 1 tea, conversed, prayer, letters;
12 on business, Dr. Coke within; 1 at Jo(hn) Ellison's with
Charles, dinner, conversed; 2.30 writ narrative, prayed, prayer; 5
tea, conversed; 6 prayed; 6.30 read the letters, the leaders, at
sister Jo(hnson's), supper, conversed, prayer; 9.45.
Mark vii, 38; Lu xii. 15; 1 Cor. xi. 14.

Sept. 1, Wed. - Prayed, ordained R(ichar)d Whatcoat and
T(homas) Vasey, letters; 8 tea, conversed; 9 letters, writ
narrative; 2 dinner, conversed, prayer, visited some; 5 tea, conversed, prayer, visited; 6.30 prayer, Rom. ii 28! 8 at sister
Jo(hnson's), supper, conversed, prayer; 9.30.

(Taken from Wesley, *Letters*, VII,
238-39, to our brethren in America,
10 Sept., 1784).

1. By a very uncommon train of providences many of the
Provinces of North America are totally disjoined from their Mother
Country and erected into independent States. The English Government has no authority over them, either civil or ecclesiastical,
any more than over the States of Holland. A civil authority is
exercised over them, partly by the Congress, partly by the Provincial Assemblies. But no one either exercises or claims any
ecclesiastical authority at all. In this peculiar situation some
thousands of the inhabitants of these States desire my advice; and

in compliance with their desire I have drawn up a little sketch.

2. Lord King's *Account of the Primitive Church* convinced me many years ago that bishops and presbyters are the same order, and consequently have the same right to ordain. For many years I have been importuned from time to time to exercise this right by ordaining part of our travelling preachers. But I have still refused, not only for peace' sake, but because I was determined as little as possible to violate the established order of the National Church to which I belonged.

3. But the case is widely different between England and North America. Here there are bishops who have a legal jurisdiction: in America there are none, neither any parish ministers. So that for some hundred miles together there is none either to baptize or to administer the Lord's supper. Here, therefore, my scruples are at an end; and I conceive myself at full liberty, as I violate no order and invade no man's right by appointing and sending labourers into the harvest.

4. I have accordingly appointed Dr. Coke and Mr. Francis Asbury to be Joint Superintendents over our brethren in North America; as also Richard Whatcoat and Thomas Vasey to act as elders among them, by baptizing and administering the Lord's Supper. And I have prepared a Liturgy little differing from that of the Church of England (I think, the best constituted National Church in the world), which I advise all the travelling preachers to use on the Lord's Day in all the congregations, reading the Litany only on Wednesdays and Fridays and praying extempore on all other days. I also advise the elders to administer the Supper of the Lord on every Lord's Day.

5. If any one will point out a more rational and scriptural way of feeding and guiding those poor sheep in the wilderness, I will gladly embrace it. At present I cannot see any better method than that I have taken.

6. It has, indeed, been proposed to desire the English bishops to ordain part of our preachers for America. But to this I object; (1) I desired the Bishop of London to ordain only one, but could not prevail. (2) If they consented, we know the slowness of their proceedings; but the matter admits of no delay. (3) If they would ordain them now, they would likewise expect to govern them. And how grievously would this entangle us! (4) As our American brethren are now totally disentangled both from the State and from the English hierarchy, we dare not entangle them again either with the one or the other. They are now at full liberty simply to follow the Scriptures and the Primitive Church. And we judge it best that they should stand fast in that liberty wherewith God has so strangely made them free.

(Taken from E. T. Clark, *et al*, eds.,
The Journal & Letters of Francis Asbury
(1958), I, 471, 473-74).

Sunday, 14 Nov., 1784. - I came to Barratt's chapel: here, to
my great joy, I met these dear men of God, Dr. Coke, and Richard
Whatcoat, we were greatly comforted together. The Doctor preached
on "Christ our wisdom, righteousness, sanctification, and
redemption." Having had no opportunity of conversing with them
before public worship, I was greatly surprised to see brother
Whatcoat assist by taking the cup in the administration of the
sacrament. I was shocked when first informed of the intention of
these my brethren in coming to this country: it may be of God. My
answer then was, if the preachers unanimously choose me, I shall
not act in the capacity I have hitherto done by Mr. Wesley's
appointment. The design of organizing the Methodists into an
Independent Episcopal Church was opened to the preachers present
and it was agreed to call a general conference, to meet at Baltimore
the ensuing Christmas; as also that brother Garrettson go off to
Virginia to give notice thereof to our brethren in the south.

*　　　　*　　　　*

Tuesday, 14 Dec., 1784. - I met Dr. Coke at Abingdon, Mr.
Richard Dallam kindly taking him there in his coach, he preached on,
"He that hath the Son hath life." We talked of our concerns in great
love.

Wednesday, 15 Dec., 1784. - My soul was much blest at the
communion, where I believe all were more or less engaged with God.
I feel it necessary daily to give up my own will. The Dr. preached
a great sermon on, "He that loveth father or mother more than me,"
&tc.

Saturday, 18. - Spent the day at Perry Hall, partly in preparing
for conference. My intervals of time I passed in reading the third
volume of the British Arminian Magazine. Continued at Perry Hall
until Friday, the twenty-fourth. We then rode to Baltimore, where
we met a few preachers: it was agreed to form ourselves into an
Episcopal Church, and to have superintendents, elders, and deacons.
When the conference was seated, Dr. Coke and myself were unanimously
elected to the superintendency of the Church, and my ordination
followed, after being previously ordained deacon and elder, as by
the following certificate may be seen.

Know all men by these presents, That I, Thomas Coke, Doctor of
Civil Law; late of Jesus College, in the University of Oxford,
Presbyter of the Church of England, and Superintendent of the
Methodist Episcopal Church in America; under the protection of
Almighty God, and with a single eye to his glory, by the imposition

of my hands, and prayer, (being assisted by two ordained elders,) did on the twenty-fifth day of this month, December, set apart Francis Asbury for the office of a deacon in the aforesaid Methodist Episcopal Church. And also on the twenty-sixth day of the said month, did by the imposition of my hands, and prayer, (being assisted by the said elders,) set apart the said Francis Asbury for the office of elder in the said Methodist Episcopal Church. And on this twenty-seventh day of the said month, being the day of the date hereof, have, by the imposition of my hands, and prayer, (being assisted by the said elders,) set apart the said Francis Asbury for the office of a superintendent in the said Methodist Episcopal Church, a man whom I judge to be well qualified for that great work. And I do hereby recommend him to all whom it may concern, as a fit person to preside over the flock of Christ. In testimony whereof I have hereunto set my hand and seal this twenty-seventh day of December, in the year of our Lord 1784. THOMAS COKE.

Twelve elders were elected, and solemnly set apart to serve our societies in the United States, one for Antigua, and two for Nova Scotia. We spent the whole week in conference, debating freely, and determining all things by a majority of votes. The Doctor preached every day at noon, and some one of the other preachers morning and evening. We were in great haste, and did much business in a little time.

> (Taken from Wesley, *Letters*, VII, 262, to Barnabas Thomas, 25 Mar., 1785).

DEAR BARNABAS, - I have neither inclination nor leisure to draw the saw of controversy; but I will tell you my mind in a few words.

I am now as firmly attached to the Church of England as I ever was since you knew me. But meantime I know myself to be as real a Christian bishop as the Archbishop of Canterbury. Yet I was always resolved, and am so still, never to act as such except in case of necessity. Such a case does not (perhaps never will) exist in England. In America it did exist. This I made known to the Bishop of London and desired his help. But he peremptorily refused it. All the other bishops were of the same mind; the rather because (they said) they had nothing to do with America. Then I saw my way clear, and was fully convinced what it was my duty to do. As to the persons amongst those who offered themselves I chose those whom I judged most worthy, and I positively refuse to be judged herein by any man's conscience but my own. - I am, dear Barnabas,

> Your affectionate brother.

(Taken from Tyerman, III, 439, Charles
Wesley to Dr. Chandler, 28 Apr., 1785).

I never lost my dread of separation, or ceased to guard our
societies against it. I frequently told them: 'I am your servant
as long as you remain in the Church of England; but no longer.
Should you forsake her, you would renounce me.'

Some of the lay preachers very early discovered an inclination
to separate, which induced my brother to print his 'Reasons against
Separation.' As often as it appeared, we beat down the
schismatical spirit. If any one did leave the Church, at the same
time he left our society. For near fifty years, we kept the sheep
in the fold; and, having filled the number of our days, only waited to depart in peace.

After our having continued friends for about *seventy* years,
and fellow labourers for above *fifty*, can anything but death part
us? I can scarcely yet believe it, that, in his eighty-second
year, my brother, my old, intimate friend and companion, should have
assumed the episcopal character, ordained elders, consecrated a
bishop, and sent him to ordain our lay preachers in America! I was
then in Bristol, at his elbow; yet he never gave me the least hint
of his intention. How was he surprised into so rash an action?
He certainly persuaded himself that it was right.

Lord Mansfield told me last year, that ordination was separation.
This my brother does not and will not see; or that he has renounced
the principles and practice of his whole life; that he has acted
contrary to all his declarations, protestations, and writings; robbed
his friends of their boasting; and left an indelible blot on his name,
as long as it shall be remembered!

Thus our partnership here is dissolved, but not our friendship.
I have taken him for better for worse, till death do us part; or
rather, reunite us in love inseparable. I have lived on earth a
little too long, who have lived to see this evil day. But I shall
very soon be taken from it, in steadfast faith, that the Lord will
maintain His own cause, and carry on His own work, and fulfil His
promise to His church, 'Lo, I am with you always, even to the end!"

What will become of these poor sheep in the wilderness, the
American Methodists? How have they been betrayed into a separation
from the Church of England, which their preachers and they no more
intended than the Methodists here! Had they had patience a little
longer, they would have seen a real bishop in America, consecrated
by three Scotch bishops, who have their consecration from the
English bishops, and are acknowledged by them as the same with
themselves. There is, therefore, not the least difference betwixt
the members of Bishop Seabury's church, and the members of the

Church of England. He told me he looked upon the Methodists in America as sound members of the Church, and was ready to ordain any of their preachers whom he should find duly qualified. His ordination would be indeed genuine, valid and episcopal. But what are your poor Methodists now? Only a new sect of presbyterians: And, after my brother's death, which is now so near, what will be their end? They will lose all their influence and importance; they will turn aside to vain janglings; they will settle again upon their lees; and, like other sects of Dissenters, come to nothing.

(Taken from Tyerman, III, 443-44, Charles Wesley to John Wesley, 14 Aug., 1785).

DEAR BROTHER, - I have been reading over again your 'Reasons against a Separation,' printed in 1758, and your Works; and entreat you, in the name of God, and for Christ's sake, to read them again yourself, with previous prayer, and stop, and proceed no farther, till you receive an answer to your inquiry, 'Lord, what wouldst *Thou* have me to do?'

Every word of your eleven pages deserves the deepest consideration; not to mention my testimony and hymns. Only the seventh I could wish you to read, - a prophecy which I pray God may never come to pass.

Near thirty years, since then, you have stood against the importunate solicitations of your preachers, who have scarcely at last prevailed. I was your natural ally, and faithful friend; and while you continued faithful to yourself, we two could chase a thousand.

But when once you began ordaining in America, I knew, and you knew, that your preachers here would never rest till you ordained them. You told me, they would separate by-and-by. The doctor tells us the same. His Methodist episcopal church in Baltimore was intended to beget a Methodist episcopal church here. You know he comes, armed with your authority, to make us all Dissenters. One of your sons assured me, that not a preacher in London would refuse orders from the doctor.

Alas! what trouble are you preparing for yourself, as well as for me, and for your oldest, truest, and best friends! Before you have quite broken down the bridge, stop, and consider! If your sons have no regard for you, have some regard for yourself. Go to your grave in peace; at least, suffer me to go first, before this ruin is under your hand. So much, think, you owe to my father, to my brother, and to me, as to stay till I am taken from the evil. I am on the brink of the grave. Do not push me in, or embitter my last moments. Let us not leave an indelible blot on our memory; but let us leave behind us the name and character of honest men.

This letter is a debt to our parents, and to our brother, as well as to you, and to

Your faithful friend,

CHARLES WESLEY

(Taken from Wesley, *Letters*, VII, 284, to Charles Wesley, 19 Aug., 1785).

DEAR BROTHER, - I will tell you my thoughts with all simplicity, and wait for better information. If you agree with me, well; if not, we can (as Mr. Whitefield used to say) agree to disagree.

For these forty years I have been in doubt concerning that question, 'What obedience is due to 'heathenish priests and mitred infidels"? I have from time to time proposed my doubts to the most pious and sensible clergymen I knew. But they gave me no satisfaction; rather they seemed to be puzzled as well as me.

Some obedience I always paid to the bishops in obedience to the laws of the land. But I cannot see that I am under any obligation to obey them further than those laws require.

It is in obedience to those laws that I have never exercised in England the power which I believe God has given me. I firmly believe I am a scriptural ἐπίσκοπος as much as any man in England or in Europe; for the *uninterrupted succession* I know to be a fable, which no man ever did or can prove. But this does in no wise interfere with my remaining in the Church of England; from which I have no more desire to separate than I had fifty years ago. I still attend all the ordinances of the Church at all opportunities; and I constantly and earnestly desire all that are connected with me so to do. When Mr. Smyth pressed us to 'separate from the Church,' he meant, 'Go to church no more.' And this was what I meant seven-and-twenty years ago when I persuaded our brethren 'not to separate from the Church.'

But here another question occurs: 'What is the Church of England?' It is not 'all the people of England.' Papists and Dissenters are no part thereof. It is not all the people of England except Papists and Dissenters. Then we should have a glorious Church indeed! No; according to our Twentieth Article, a particular Church is 'a congregation of faithful people' (*coetus credentium*, the words in our Latin edition), 'among whom the word of God is preached and the sacraments duly administered.' Here is a true logical definition, containing both the essence and the properties of a Church. What, then, according to this definition, is the Church of England? Does it mean 'all the believers in England (except the Papists and Dissenters) who have the word of God and the

sacraments duly administered among them'? I fear this does not
come up to your idea of 'the Church of England.' Well, what more
do you include in that phrase? 'Why, all the believers that adhere
to the doctrine and discipline established by the Convocation under
Queen Elizabeth.' Nay, that discipline is wellnigh vanished away,
and the doctrine both you and I adhere to. I do not mean I will
never ordain any while I am in England, but not to use the power
they receive while in England. [sic]

All those reasons against a separation from the Church in this
sense I subscribe to still. What, then, are you frightened at?
I no more separate from it now than I did in the year 1758. I submit still (though sometimes with a doubting conscience) to 'mitred
infidels.' I do, indeed, vary from them in some points of doctrine
and in some points of discipline - by preaching abroad, for instance,
by praying extempore, and by forming societies; but not an hair's
breadth further than I believe to be meet, right, and my bounden
duty. I walk still by the same rule I have done for between forty
and fifty years. I do nothing rashly. It is not likely I should.
The high-day of my blood is over. If you will go hand in hand with
me, do. But do not hinder me if you will not help. Perhaps, if
you had kept close to me, I might have done better. However, with
or without help, I creep on. And as I have been hitherto, so I
trust I shall always be.

Your affectionate friend and Brother.

(Taken from Minutes of Conferences (England),
I, 189-91, 30 Aug., 1785).

OF SEPARATION FROM THE CHURCH

1. Ever since I returned from America, it has been warmly
affirmed, 'You separate from the Church.' I would consider, How
far, and in what sense, this assertion is true.

2. Whether you mean by that term, the building so called, or
the congregation, it is plain I do not separate from either: for
wherever I am, I go to the Church, and join with the congregation.

3. Yet it is true that I have in some respects varied, though
not from the doctrines, yet from the discipline of the Church of
England; although not willingly, but by constraint. For instance:
Above forty years ago, I began *preaching in the field;* and that
for two reasons: First I was not suffered to preach in the Churches.
Secondly, No Parish Church in London or Westminster could contain
the congregation.

4. About the same time several persons who were desirous to
save their souls, prayed me to meet them apart from the great

congregation. These little companies (*societies* they were called) gradually spread through the three kingdoms. And in many
places they built houses in which they met, and wherein I and my
brethren preached. For a few young men, one after another, desired
to serve me, as *sons in the gospel*.

5. Some time after, Mr. Deleznot, a clergyman, desired me to
officiate at his chapel in Wapping. There I read prayers, and
preached, and administered the Lord's Supper to a part of the
Society. The rest communicated either at St. Paul's, or at their
several Parish Churches. Meantime, I endeavoured to watch over all
their souls, as one that *was to give an account;* and to assign to
each of my fellow-labourers the part wherein I judged he might be
most useful.

6. When these were multiplied, I gave them an invitation to
meet me together in my house at London; that we might consider in
what manner we could most effectually *save our own souls,* and *them
that heard us*. This we called a *Conference,* (meaning thereby, *the
persons,* not *the conversation* they had.) At first I desired all the
Preachers to meet me; but afterwards only a select number.

7. Some years after, we were strongly importuned by our
brethren in America, to 'come over and help them.' Several
Preachers willingly offered themselves for the service; and several
went from time to time. God blessed their labours in an uncommon
manner. Many sinners were converted to God; and many Societies
formed, under the same rules as were observed in England: insomuch,
that at present the American Societies contain more than eighteen
thousand members.

8. But since the late revolution in North America, these have
been in great distress. The clergy having no sustenance, either
from England, or from the American States, have been obliged almost
universally to leave the country, and seek their food elsewhere.
Hence those who had been members of the Church, had none either to
administer the Lord's Supper, or to baptize their children. They
applied to England over and over: but it was to no purpose. Judging
this to be a case of real necessity, I took a step which, for peace
and quietness, I had refrained from taking for many years: I
exercised that power, which I am fully persuaded the great Shepherd
and Bishop of the Church has given me. I appointed three of our
labourers to go and help them, by not only preaching the word of
God, but likewise administering the Lord's Supper, and baptizing
their children throughout that vast tract of land, a thousand miles
long, and some hundreds broad.

9. These are the steps, which not of choice, but necessity, I
have slowly and deliberately taken. If any one is pleased to call
this *separating from the Church,* he may. But the law of England

does not call it so; nor can any one properly be said so to do unless out of conscience he refuses to join in the service, and partake of the Sacraments administered therein.

JOHN WESLEY.

Camelford, August 30, 1785.

After Dr. Coke's return from America, many of our friends begged I would consider the case of Scotland, where we had been labouring for many years, and had seen so little fruit of our labours. Multitudes indeed set out well, but they were soon turned out of the way: chiefly by their ministers either disputing against the truth, or refusing to admit them to the Lord's Supper; yea, or to baptize their children, unless they would promise to have no fellowship with the Methodists. Many who did so, soon lost all they had gained, and became more the children of hell than before. To prevent this, I at length consented to take the same step with regard to Scotland, which I had done with regard to America. But this is not a separation from the Church at all. Not from the Church of Scotland, for we were never connected therewith, any further than we are now: not from the Church of England, for this is not concerned in the steps which are taken in Scotland. Whatever then is done either in America or Scotland, is no separation from the Church of England. I have no thought of this: I have many objections against it. It is a totally different case.

But, for all this, is it not possible there may be such a separation after you are dead? Undoubtedly it is. But what I said at our first Conference above forty years ago, I say still, "I dare not omit doing what good I can while I live, for fear of evils that may follow when I am dead."

> (Taken from Thomas Jackson, *The Life of the Rev. Charles Wesley* (London, 1841), II, 396-97, Charles to John Wesley, 8 Sept., 1785).

Dear Brother, - I will tell you my thoughts with the same simplicity. There is no danger of our quarrelling; for the second blow makes the quarrel; and you are the last man upon earth whom I would wish to quarrel with.

That juvenile line of mine,

Heathenish Priests, and mitred infidels,

I disown, renounce, and with same recant. I never knew of more than one 'mitred infidel,' and for him I took Mr. Law's word.

I do not understand what obedience to the Bishops you dread. They have let us alone, and left us to act just as we pleased, for these fifty years. At present some of them are quite friendly toward us, particularly toward you. The churches are all open to you; and never could there be less pretence for a separation.

That you are a scriptural Ἐπίσκοπος , or Overseer, I do not dispute. And so is every Minister who has the cure of souls. Neither need we dispute whether the uninterrupted succession be fabulous, as you believe, or real, as I believe; or whether Lord King be right or wrong.

Your definition of the Church of England is the same in prose with mine in verse. By the way, read over my 'Epistle,' to oblige me, and tell me you have read it, and likewise your own 'Reasons.'

"You write, 'All those reasons against a Separation from the Church, I subscribe to still. What then are you frighted at? I no more separate from it than I did in the year 1758. I submit still to its Bishops. I do indeed vary from them in some points of discipline; (by preaching abroad, for instance, praying extempore, and by forming societies;)' (might you not add, and by ordaining?) 'I still walk by the same rule I have done for between forty and fifty years. I do nothing rashly.'

If I could prove your actual separation I would not; neither wish to see it proved by any other. But do you not allow that the Doctor has separated? Do you not know and approve of his avowed design and resolution to get all the Methodists of the three kingdoms into a distinct, compact body? a new episcopal Church of his own? Have you seen his ordination sermon? Is the high-day of his blood over? Does he do nothing rashly? Have you not made yourself the author of all his actions? I need not remind you, *qui facit per alium facit per se.*

I must not leave unanswered your surprising question, 'What then are you frighted at?' At the Doctor's rashness, and your supporting him in his ambitious pursuits; at an approaching schism, as causeless and unprovoked as the American rebellion; at your own eternal disgrace, and all those frightful evils which your 'Reasons' describe.

'If you will go on hand in hand with me, do.' I do go, or rather creep on, in the old way in which we set out together, and trust to continue in it till I finish my course.

'Perhaps if you had kept close to me, I might have done better.' When you took that fatal step at Bristol, I kept as close to you as close could be; for I was all the time at your elbow. You might

89

certainly have done better, if you had taken me into your council.

I thank you for your intention to remain my friend. Herein my heart is as your heart. Whom God hath joined, let not man put asunder. We have taken each other for better for worse, till death do us - part? no: but unite eternally. Therefore in the love which never faileth, I am

Your affectionate friend and brother.

¶   Coke's Sermon at Asbury's Ordination

(Taken from Thomas Coke, *The Substance of a Sermon...27th of December, 1784* (Baltimore, 1785, reprint 1840) 5-15).

Text: Rev. 3:7-11. The most important part of a minister's duty is to insist on the great fundamental truths of Christianity. But he is called occasionally to consider subjects of a more confined and peculiar nature; and the intention of the present meeting more especially requires such an attempt. I shall therefore, with the assistance and blessing of God,

In the first place, vindicate our conduct in the present instance.

Secondly, open the words of my text.

And thirdly, delineate the character of a Christian bishop.

The Church of England, of which the society of Methodists, in general, have till lately professed themselves a part, did for many years groan in America under grievances of the heaviest kind. Subjected to a hierarchy which weighs every thing in the scales of politics, its most important interests were repeatedly sacrified to the supposed advantages of England. The churches were, in general, filled with the parasites and bottle companions of the rich and the great. The humble and most importunate entreaties of the oppressed flocks, yea, the representations of a general assembly itself were contemned and despised; every thing sacred must lie down at the feet of a party, the holiness and happiness of mankind be sacrificed to their views; and the drunkard, the fornicator, and the extortioner, triumphed over bleeding Zion, because they were faithful abettors of the ruling powers. But these intolerable fetters are now struck off, and the antichristian union which before subsisted between church and state is broken asunder. One happy consequence of which has been the expulsion of most of those hirelings"who ate the fat and clothed themselves with the wool, but strengthened not the diseased, neither healed that which was sick, neither bound up that which was broken, neither brought again that which was driven away, neither sought that which was lost," Ezek. xxxiv, 3,4.

The parochial churches in general being hereby vacant, our

people were deprived of the sacraments, through the greatest part of those States, and continue so still. What method can we take at this critical juncture? God has given us sufficient resources in ourselves, and, after mature deliberation, we believe that we are called to draw them forth.

But what right have you to ordain? The same right as most of the reformed churches in Christendom: our ordination, in its lowest view, being equal to any of the Presbyterian, as originating with three presbyters of the Church of England.

But what right have you to exercise the episcopal office? To me the most manifest and clear. God has been pleased, by Mr. Wesley, to raise up in America and Europe a numerous society, well known by the name of Methodists. The whole body have invariably esteemed this man as their chief pastor, under Christ. He has constantly appointed all their religious officers from the highest to the lowest, by himself or his delegate. And we are fully persuaded there is no church office which he judges expedient for the welfare of the people intrusted to his charge, but, as essential to his station, he has a power to ordain. After long deliberation he saw it his duty to form his society in America into an independent church; but he loved the most excellent liturgy of the Church of England, he loved its rights and ceremonies, and therefore adopted them in most instances for the present case.

Besides, in addition to this, we have every qualification for an episcopal church which that of Alexandria (a church of no small note in the primitive times) possessed for two hundred years. Our bishops, or superintendents, (as we rather call them,) having been elected or received by the suffrages of the whole body of our ministers through the continent, assembled in general conference.

*   *   *

But I proceed to open my text.

"To the angel of the church in Philadelphia, write." It is evident to every discerning reader that the words bishop, elder, overseer, &c., are synonymous terms throughout the writings of St. Paul. Nor do I recollect a single instance in the New Testament where any peculiar title is given to the superior officers of the church, (such as were Timothy and Titus,) except in the epistles of our Lord to the seven churches of Asia, where they are distinguished by the name of angel - the prime messengers of Christ to his churches. St. John wrote the Revelation in the isle of Patmos, near the close of his life, when the gospel had gained considerable ground in the world, and many numerous societies of Christians had been formed. Among the principal of these were the seven churches of Asia, which were evidently

(what we now call) episcopal churches. For it will hardly admit of a doubt, but these capital societies had in each of them a college of presbyters. And had these been all on an equality, our Lord would never have directed these epistles respectively to a *single* angel. And *all of them* being thus addressed, we have reasonable ground to presume that the churches in general, even before the death of St. John, were of the episcopal order. And of how great importance must the office of these angels have been, when the Lord addressed himself only to them, as if the welfare of their respective churches entirely depended on them!

*   *   *

Having just touched on the general character of this amiable bishop of the church of Philadelphia, as displayed in my text, which, had it been the will of God, we could wish to have seen at fuller length, I proceed to consider the grand characteristics of a Christian bishop.

1. His *humility*. This is the *preservatrix virtutum,* the guard of every other grace. As some one beautifully observes, other graces, without humility, are like a fine powder in the wind without a cover. Let a man be ever so zealous, ever so laborious, yet if he wants humility, he will be only like Penelope with her web in the ancient fable, undoing at one time what he does at another. There is something interwoven with human nature which immediately recoils at the very appearance of pride. But this man is clothed with humility. When no other grace shines forth, still we discern this beautiful veil. We give him credit for every thing. And when, in spite of all his caution, some hidden gem peeps out, it sparkles with redoubled lustre. But, above all, he is a vessel fit for his Master's use. His eye is single, he moves directly on; his only desire is to glorify God and benefit mankind, yea, he lives for no other end. He is "in a strait between two, having a desire to depart and be with Christ," and at the same time a fervent desire to be a blessing to his fellow-creatures. "He is crucified to the world, and the world to him." And his soul, disentangled from every selfish view, and emptied of every selfish desire, is a fit receptacle of all the divine gifts which God is willing to bestow. He continually lies at the feet of his Lord, and the language of his heart is, "Not unto me, not unto me, but unto thy name, O Jehovah, be all the praise!"

> "Flow back the river to the sea,
> And let my all be lost in Thee."

There is no impediment in his soul to the divine operations. He is as the clay in the hand of the potter, as the pen in the hand of the ready writer. His humble spirit simply inquires into the will of its God, and when that is discovered, confers no longer with

flesh and blood, but fulfils it with the most entire resignation and great delight.

2. His *meekness*. This is a *passive* grace. It is the sacred ballast of the soul - that evenness, that divine serenity of spirit which "is not provoked," which nothing can move to wrath - that moderation spoken of by St. Paul, which harmonizes all the passions, and holds every power of the heart in sweet subjection - it ties them all to the horns of the altar. In this the Christian bishop eminently shines. Amid all the contradictions of sinners, and the provoking of tongues, he still retains his gracious temper, and discovers no emotion but that of pity and compassion - all is softness, all is love. This is the quiet spirit, whose price is great in the sight of God. 1 Pet. iii, 4. It is the Spirit of the Lamb, whose voice was not heard in the streets; who was oppressed and afflicted, yea, was brought as a lamb to the slaughter; and as a sheep before her shearers is dumb, so he opened not his mouth. O how contrary to the spirit of the meek and lowly Jesus is the turbulence and violence of many who call themselves the ministers of Christ! "But the sheep will flee from such, for they know not their voice."

3. His *gentleness*. This is an *active* grace, which flows out in the converse and the carriage. It is Christian courtesy. This also the Christian bishop possesses in a high degree. "Grace is poured into his lips," for "out of the fulness of his Lord he receiveth grace for grace." Nothing that is grating drops from his mouth. His very reproofs are dipt in oil. How insinuating is all his language, while the hearer hangs upon his tongue! His words "drop like the gentle rain from heaven upon the place beneath." His looks, and every gesture, and every feature, beam forth love. This is a key to open hearts with. What an amazing field of action does this engaging temper, accompanied by the blessing of God, gradually open to his zealous soul! He makes religion appear amiable even in the judgment of the world itself. And excepting when employed in the severer duties of his function, he knows nothing of the pain of giving pain.

4. His *patience*. This is the grace that "endures all things" - that flows out in sufferings and trials, and bears up the soul under every difficulty - *sub pondere crescit*. The more it is exercised , the stronger it grows. Let us view the Christian bishop in this respect. Behold, with what a steady pace he moves! Equally unshaken by the smiles or frowns of men, he gently moves along, like a mighty river, that bears down all before it, and yet waters every fertile meadow on its sides. His great Zerubbabel proceeds before him, and every mountain drops into a plain. His soul "looks to Jesus, who endured the cross, despising the shame," and earnestly endeavors -

"To trace *his* example, the world to disdain,
And constantly trample on pleasure and pain."

He smiles at persecution, and thanks his God for the opportunity of
displaying an example to the world of the religion he proclaims.
Thus does he go on, till he has finished the work which God has
given him to do. And when the organs of his body have been weakened
and enervated by the diseases which sooner or later assault the
mortal frame, he still puts forth his little strength for the
glorious cause in which he has been so long engaged, till having
"fought the good fight, and finished his course," he drops asleep
in the arms of his God.

5. His *fortitude*. His soul is far above the fear of temporal
dangers. He possesses this cardinal virtue in all its strength
and vigor. He "adds to his faith, *courage,* 2 Pet. i, 5. And
though it is so divinely tempered by all the softer passions, as to
be hid to all but the discerning eye, when not drawn out to action;
yet there it ever resides, even in his inmost soul, like an iron
pillar strong. But when the church, which he fosters in his anxious
bosom, is in danger, he always steps out the foremost. He stands
in the front of the battle, and endeavors to receive himself all
the fire of the enemy. Like a faithful shepherd he steps between
the wolf and the sheep, and is perfectly willing to lay down his
life for their sake. If you touch the church of God, you touch the
apple of his eye. And though he is not entirely ignorant of the
value of his life and labors, yet when the cause of Zion calls him
forth, "he mocketh at fear, and is not affrighted, neither turneth
he back from the sword:" he beholds his once suffering, but now
exalted Saviour. He looks up to the noble army of martyrs, "the
cloud of witnesses," and follows their glorious track,

"Pain, want defies; enjoys disgrace;
Glories at dissolution near."

6. His *impartiality*. This is the rarest of all the virtues, and
yet one of the most important for a ruler of the church. There is
nothing more intolerable to mankind than partiality in him that
governs; and it always springs in part from a meanness and baseness
of mind. It meets with such immediate and effectual resistance,
that all the reins of discipline are dropped, and the vineyard of
the Lord thrown open to every beast of prey. But the Christian
bishop is "without partiality and without hypocrisy." He moves by
equal rules. He seeks not the praise of men, but serveth the Lord
Christ. He meets with the constant and effectual support of those
whom only he esteems - the upright and the good. And when the
welfare of the church demands the separation of a rotten member,
however rich, however honorable, however powerful, he clothes himself with the dignity of his office, and executes the will of God.

7. His *zeal*. In this he is eminent indeed. For though it is softened and corrected by the other graces, yet it wraps up his heart in the interests of Zion, and "the zeal of the Lord's house eats him up." He pants for the conversion of the whole world, and cries out with the souls under the altar, "How long, O Lord?" How far does his rapid spirit rise above the honors, the riches, and the pleasures of the world! He leaves them at a distance behind. His whole attention is swallowed up by greater things than these. While the men of the world are variously employed in the pursuit of earthly objects, he endeavors, in the Spirit of his Lord, to extract honey out of every flower, good out of every evil. He watches the opportunity, runs through every open door, and "spends, and is spent," for the good of mankind.

8. His *wisdom*. This reigns over all his soul. He is prepared for it by the God of *nature*, and endued with it by the God of *grace*. He was born to govern. He is "as wise as a serpent." His eye continually pervades the whole circle of his work, and yet who so blind as he? Isa. xlii, 19. He is all ear, and yet none is so deaf. He sets his feet in the centre of his sphere, and feels the smallest motion through every parallel. He knows with clear precision when to speak, and when to be silent; when to move, and when to be still; when to parry, and when to thrust. He has a quick discernment of men and manners; but he "lays hands *suddenly* on no man." His choice of laborers proceeds from the ripest judgment, and from the clearest evidence that can be procured. He feels all the strength of his resources, as if they were wholly centred in himself, and knows how and when to draw them forth. He is acquainted with the various views, the knowledge, the situation, the circumstances and the wishes of the people; and the various gifts, graces, and abilities of the pastors. He makes them all to tally. He brings out all his force against the common enemy, he spreads out all his sails to every favorable wind, he keeps in motion every wheel of the machine, and uses to the uttermost every person and every thing within his power for the glory of God and the prosperity of his church.

9. His *communion with God and confidence in him*. These support him under all his trials. He lives within the veil. His soul cleaves to God; and he waters all his endeavors with fervent prayers. He bears upon the altar of his heart the interests of the church of Christ, and sends them up to the throne of grace with all the sacred fervor of devotion. He spreads out all his hopes and all his fears before his God, and "makes all his requests known unto him;" and then returns to his labors with cheerfulness and vigor. He "walks with God," and moves with a full confidence and divine assurance of success, so far as the means he uses can answer the great end of every thing he does - the glory of God and the good of mankind.

Lastly: his *seriousness*. Though he lies at the feet of all the lovers of Jesus, yet he never debases himself. He knows his station, and "magnifies his office." The enemies of God may fear and hate him, but they cannot despise him. No lightness of spirit is observable in him; all is dignity as well as love. The company of the greatest upon earth affects him not. He lives in the presence of his Master, and says nothing but what is becoming the audience chamber of the King of king.

¶   Thomas Ware's Report of Formation of Methodist
         Episcopal Church.

         (Taken from *Sketches of the Life and Travels
         of Rev. Thomas Ware* (1842), 101-02, 105-08,
         112-14).

The Methodist Episcopal Church in the United States was organized in 1784, soon after the close of the revolution. It was not practicable during the war for Mr. Wesley, the father and founder of the Methodist societies, to furnish an organization suited to our necessities. But after its termination, Mr. Asbury, who lived in the feelings and possessed the entire confidence of both preachers and people, according to their general wish and expectation, made application to Mr. Wesley in behalf of the American societies, and he resolved without delay to send over Dr. Coke, whom he first set apart by the imposition of hands to the office of superintendent, with instructions to carry his plan into effect. He furnished the doctor with forms of ordination for deacons, elders, and superintendents; and appointed him, jointly with Mr. Asbury, to preside over the Methodist family in America.

When Dr. Coke arrived in America he first saw Mr. Asbury at Judge Barrett's, (Barrett's Chapel), in the state of Delaware, and exhibited to him his credentials. Mr. Asbury rejoiced for the consolation of being able to hope that relief would be afforded to the societies, but said, "Doctor, we will call the preachers together, and their voice shall be to me the voice of God." It was accordingly agreed to have a conference, to meet in Baltimore, on the ensuing Christmas.

Nearly fifty years have now elapsed since the Christmas conference; and I have a thousand times looked back to the memorable era with pleasurable emotions. I have often said it was the most solemn convocation I ever saw. I might have said, for many reasons, it was sublime. During the whole time of our being together in the transaction of business of the utmost magnitude, there was not, I verily believe, on the conference floor or in private, an unkind word spoken, or an unbrotherly emotion felt. Christian love predominated; and, under its influence, we "kindly thought and sweetly spoke the same."

At the Christmas conference we met to congratulate each other, and to praise the Lord that he had disposed the mind of our excellent Wesley to renounce the fable of uninterrupted succession, and prepare the way for furnishing us with the long-desired privileges we were thenceforward expecting to enjoy. The announcement of the plan devised by him for our organization as a church filled us with solemn delight. It answered to what we did suppose, during our labours and privations, we had reason to expect our God would do for us; for in the integrity of our hearts we verily believed his design in raising up the preachers called Methodists, in this country, was to reform the continent, and spread scriptural holiness through these lands; and we accordingly looked to be endued, in due time, with all the panoply of God. We, therefore, according to the best of our knowledge, received and followed the advice of Mr. Wesley, as stated in our form of Discipline.

After Mr. Wesley's letter, declaring his appointment of Dr. Coke and Mr. Asbury joint superintendents over the Methodists in America, had been read, analyzed, and cordially approved by the conference, the question arose, "What name or title shall we take?" I thought to myself, I shall be satisfied that we be denominated, The Methodist Church, and so whispered to a brother sitting near me. But one proposed, I think it was John Dickins, that we should adopt the title of METHODIST EPISCOPAL CHURCH. Mr. Dickins was, in the estimation of his brethren, a man of sound sense and sterling piety; and there were few men on the conference floor heard with greater deference than he. Most of the preachers had been brought up in what was called, "The Church of England;" and, all agreeing that the plan of general superintendence, which had been adopted, was a species of episcopacy, the motion on Mr. Dickins' suggestion was carried without, I think, a dissenting voice. There was not, to my recollection, the least agitation on the question. Had the conference indulged a suspicion that the name they adopted would be, in the least degree, offensive to the views or feelings of Mr. Wesley, they would have abandoned it at once; for the name of Mr. Wesley was inexpressibly dear to the Christmas conference, and especially to Mr. Asbury and Dr. Coke.

After our organization, we proceeded to elect a sufficient number of elders to visit the quarterly meetings, and administer the ordinances; and this it was which gave rise to the office of presiding elders among us.

From what I have said, it will be understood that, when the Methodist Episcopal Church was organized, I was present. But, as I was little more than a spectator of the interesting transactions of the Christmas conference, I shall take the liberty to speak of

the character of the preachers who constituted that body, as if not numbered among them.

In practical wisdom they appeared to me to excel; and although few of them affected the scholar, yet they prized learning as a desirable accomplishment. Some of them were acquainted with the learned languages; and most of them were not deficient in general and polite literature. But what eminently distinguished them as a body of Christian ministers was, that they possessed, in a high degree, the happy art of winning souls. In preaching and in debate they were workmen who needed not to be ashamed; and they made wise and useful improvement of the knowledge they possessed, and the talents God had given them. Hence the high estimation in which they held the Bible. Many of them were in the habit of reading it regularly on their knees; and some made it a point to read it once through every year in that attitude. We may, therefore, venture to say, that few men, in any age of the church, knew better how to estimate the sum of good which Heaven kindly wills to man, and few have been so successful in recommending the Bible and Bible religion to their fellow-men.

*　　　*　　　*

I have said the preachers who composed the Christmas conference did hold human learning to be a desirable accomplishment. They know, indeed, that learning and piety had no necessary connection, from the fact that there have been some eminent scholars, whose lives have evinced that they were far from being pious, and there have been many pious souls who have made no pretensions to human learning. Yet, when learning and piety are united, they are mutually beneficial in promoting the best interests of man. Such views prevailed among the preachers at that early period of our history. In proof of this, it may be sufficient to mention that, at the Christmas conference, they passed a resolution forthwith to erect a college, or public school, and to publish a plan of it immediately after the conference should adjourn.

¶ Wesley Scorches Asbury and Coke

(Taken from Wesley, *Letters*, VII, 91,
to Asbury, 20 Sept., 1788).

MY DEAR BROTHER, – There is, indeed, a wide difference between the relation wherein you stand to the Americans and the relation wherein I stand to all the Methodists. You are the elder brother of the American Methodists: I am under God the father of the whole family. Therefore I naturally care for you all in a manner no other persons can do. Therefore I in a measure provide for you all; for

the supplies which Dr. Coke provides for you, he could not provide were it not for me, were it not that I not only permit him to
collect but also support him in so doing.

But in one point, my dear brother, I am a little afraid both
the Doctor and you differ from me. I study to be little: you study
to be great. I creep: you strut along. I found a school: you a
college! nay, and call it after your own names! O beware, do not
seek to be something! Let me be nothing, and 'Christ be all in all!'

One instance of this, of your greatness, has given me great
concern. How can you, how dare you suffer yourself to be called
Bishop? I shudder, I start at the very thought! Men may call me a
knave or a fool, a rascal, a scoundrel, and I am content; but they
shall never by my consent call me Bishop! For my sake, for God's
sake, for Christ's sake put a full end to this! Let the Presbyterians
do what they please, but let the Methodists know their calling
better.

Thus, my dear Frank, I have told you all that is in my
heart. And let this, when I am no more seen, bear witness how
sincerely I am   Your affectionate friend and brother.

*   *   *

¶   A Methodist Protestant View

(Taken from Drinkhouse, I, 275-77).

It is no loss, perhaps, to the religious world that no minutes
were ever made, much less published, of the conversations between
Coke and Asbury in that after-dinner talk at Barratt's home, "a
private conversation on the management of our affairs in America."
What Wesley directed them to do and what they afterward did were so
incongruous, and so questionable, that it is well that no man knows
to this day. Asbury discloses a single feature, and it is pregnant
of consequences, "My answer then was, if the preachers unanimously
choose me, I shall not act in the capacity I have heretofore done
by Mr. Wesley's appointment." It may be safely assumed that in
that Sabbath afternoon private interview Coke showed Asbury the
plan, or the "little sketch," his credentials as a superintendent,
conveying authority to set him apart for the same position, and the
circular letter to be printed and circulated among the societies.
A crisis had arrived and Asbury was quick to perceive it, hence
his demurrer. A joint superintendent with Coke. It did not accord
with his purposes. Did Coke inform him how solemnly Wesley had
charged him that the title of bishop as synonymous with superintendent should not be assumed, as Coke had given him reason to suspect
would be the case? Under Asbury's cross-examination it may be concluded that nothing was kept back. He finds Asbury a pronounced

hierarchist and a believer in apostolical succession, views most in accord with his own. A joint superintendent with Coke. He was to be watched and reported to Wesley by one equal in authority. Had he not been the paternal head of the American Methodists for thirteen years? Was he still to be under "tutors and governors," the chief three thousand miles distant? There were reasonable and honest objections to it, and it will be found that a few years after, when Wesley more fully appreciated what was done at the Christmas Conference and remonstrated with Asbury for his apparent insubordination, he frankly uncovered. Wesley writes, 1789, "I received some letters from Mr. Asbury affirming that no person in Europe knew how to direct those in America." Prior to this he had written to Brackenbury, as Coke relates in his famous letter to Wesley, urging his own ordination, "he saw a letter in London from Mr. Asbury, in which he observed that he would not receive any person deputed by you to take any part of the superintendency of the work invested in him, or words evidently implying so much." In the introductory chapter the position is taken for this stage of the History that a "tripartite contention will be disclosed as the key to the mystery of otherwise unaccountable transactions of these three in dealing with each other." The beginning of it is disclosed. It shall be developed step by step, and the conclusion then reached vindicated.

In the hours of the Sabbath afternoon in a private interview Coke and Asbury arrived at an understanding. What it was will be unfolded at the Christmas Conference. Other details were talked about, for Coke says, "he and I have agreed to use our joint endeavors to establish a school or college." It is the sequel to suggestions which had been made by John Dickins, who had the English Kingswood school in mind, some time before. Just forty days would elapse before Christmas. An immense amount of work had to be done meantime. Garrettson to notify all the eighty-three preachers widely scattered, and mail facilities almost nugatory for such hasty business. Asbury generalled the campaign. Coke says farther of the Barratt meeting: "Mr. Asbury had also drawn up for me a route of about a thousand miles in the meantime. He has also given me his black man (Harry by name) and borrowed an excellent horse for me. I exceedingly reverence Mr. Asbury; he has so much wisdom and consideration, so much meekness and love; and, under all this, though hardly to be perceived, so much command and authority." It is a pen-picture indeed. He was already under the spell of that magnetic presence.

¶ Appraisal by Ezekiel Cooper

(Taken from Cooper, *The Substance of
a Funeral Discourse*...the 23rd of
April, 1816 (1819), 108-11).

It was at that meeting, at Barrett's chapel, of which I have
spoken, that by mutual consent and agreement, of the preachers there,
that the General conference was called, to meet in Baltimore, on the
Christmas following, to take into consideration, the proposals and
advice of Mr. Wesley. Intelligence was sent off, to every part of
the connexion. Brother Garrettson, was appointed to go through
Maryland, into Virginia, and to give the information, to the south
and west, and to call the preachers together.

The conference met, the 27th of December, 1784, and continued
their deliberation and sitting until sometime in Jan. 1785. It was
unanimously agreed, that circumstances made it expedient for the
Methodist societies, in America, to become a separate body, from the
church of England, of which until then, they had been considered as
members. They also resolved to take the title, and to be known in
future, by the name of THE METHODIST EPISCOPAL CHURCH. - They made
the episcopal office elective and the bishops, or superintendants [sic]
to be amenable, for their conduct, to the body of preachers, or to
the General conference. - Mr. Asbury, though appointed by Mr. Wesley,
would not be ordained, unless he was chosen by a vote, or the
voice of the conference. He was unanimously elected, and Dr. Coke,
was also unanimously received, jointly with him, to be the Superintendants, or Bishops, of the Methodist Episcopal Church. From that
time, the methodist societies, in the United States, became an
independent church, under the Episcopal mode and form of government -
Designing, professing, and resolving "to follow the scriptures, and
the primitive church," according to the advice and counsel of Mr.
Wesley, and in perfect unison with the views, the opinion, and wishes
of Mr. Asbury. This step met with general approbation, both among
the preachers and the members. Perhaps we shall seldom find, such
unanimity of sentiment, in a whole community, upon any question, of
such magnitude, proposed to be adopted by them. And do we profess,
in our church government, and order, to be founded on, to be
governed by, and to follow, the Scriptures, and also the usages of
the primitive church? Well brethren, let us be careful, firmly to
adhere to the good old way; and never depart from the Scripture
rule! Let us continue to follow the best lights we can obtain,
from the apostolick and primitive usages and customs, both as to
doctrines, morality, discipline, and church government.

From the time that the church was constituted, and he was clothed
with Episcopal functions, until the day of his death, which was more
than thirty years, Bishop Asbury continued to be, uninterruptedly,
the approved, the diligent, the indefatigable, and useful Superintendant of the Methodist Episcopal church, in the United States and

extensive territories thereof. He made it his constant, regular, and only business. Once a year, he, generally, passed through the widely extended bounds of his vast and important charge. He usually travelled about five thousand miles, annually; and his tour, generally presided in six, seven, or eight conferences; fixed the stations and appointments, of, from two to six hundred preachers; ordained a great number of travelling and local elders and deacons; and likewise, had the general oversight of the whole connexion, and body of the church, amounting, at the close of his labours, to more than two hundred thousand members. - Beside all this, there were other ministerial cares and arduous labours - such as public preaching; an extensive epistolary correspondence, business of divers kinds with the trustees, of different churches, societies, and the various other official members; and in overseeing, less or more, the temporalities, and spiritualities of the whole church. To which may be added, his remarkable attention to, and constant diligence in social and family prayer, and religious conversations, admonitions, and counsels, wherever he went, and into whatsoever place or circle he came; together, with his attention to reading, to study, and to private and secret devotions, in promoting, and establishing, and maintaining, his own communion and fellowship with the Father and the Son, and to keep his own soul alive to God. Wonderful man! Every day, and every hour, almost every minute, appeared to be employed, and devoted, in close application to some excellent work and useful purpose! But he appeared to have nothing to do with the things of this world, only as they promoted the cause of God.

5. ORIGINS OF UNITED BRETHREN AND EVANGELICAL ASSOCIATION

Genuine source materials for the antecedents of the Evangelical United Brethren, who merged with the Methodist Church in 1968 to form the United Methodist Church, are scarce. A few key documents have been brought together by Arthur C. Core, in Philip William Otterbein, *published in 1968. Some of them are reprinted here. He also privately duplicated a "Church Reader" for the EUB in 1963.*

One of several persons whose lives intersected both former denominations is Henry Boehm, whose father was one of the founders of the United Brethren, and who himself became a Methodist preacher and traveling companion of Bishop Asbury. He was at pains in his autobiographical Reminiscences *to correct several alleged misinterpretations of the relations between his father and the Methodist movement. On one of the controverted issues, that of Asbury's attitude toward the Germans and the German language, a letter from the bishop to Jacob Gruber offers evidence.*

One of the most valuable and comprehensive original materials is the autobiography of Christian Newcomer. This Life *and* Journal, *published in 1834, contains many insights into the problems of the early struggling group of United Brethren, who resisted pressure to regard themselves as a "church." The volume also offers impressive evidence that United Brethren were not laggard in following the ideal of the itinerating circuit rider.*

Jacob Albright, who lacked education but made up for it with zeal and determination, left no literary remains. His close friend, George Miller, prepared a short spiritual biography in 1811 in which he presumed to speak as if in the autobiographical words of his friend. The words are Miller's, but the spirit is Albright's. Another very important source, unfortunately not published as was Newcomer's, is the "Day Book" of John Dreisbach. Here are a few selections on the subjects of discipline, organization of General Conference of the Evangelical Association, and union discussions with the United Brethren.

¶ The Constitution and Ordinances of the Evangelical Reformed
Church of Baltimore, Maryland, 1785

(Taken from H. G. Spayth, *History of the Church of the
United Brethren in Christ* (1851), 43-54, reprinted in
Arthur C. Core, *Philip William Otterbein* (1968),
109-14).

By the undersigned preacher and members which now constitute
this church, it is hereby ordained and resolved, that this church,
which has been brought together in Baltimore, by the ministration
of our present preacher, W. Otterbein, in future, consist in a
preacher, three elders, and three deacons, an almoner and church
members, and these together shall pass under and by the name - The
Evangelical Reformed Church.

2d. No one, whoever he may be, can be preacher or member of
this church, whose walk is unchristian and offensive, or who lives
in some open sin. - (1 Tim. iii.: 1-3. 1 Cor. v.: 11-13.)

3d. Each church member must attend faithfully the public
worship on the Sabbath day, and at all other times.

4th. This church shall yearly solemnly keep two days of humilia-
tion, fasting, and prayer, which shall be designated by the preacher;
one in the spring, the other in the autumn of the year.

5th. The members of this church, impressed with the necessity
of a constant religious exercise, suffering the word of God richly
and daily to dwell among them, - (Col. iii.: 16. Heb. iii.: 13: -
x: 24, 25) - resolve that each sex shall hold meetings apart, once
a week, for which the most suitable day, hour, and place, shall
be chosen, for the males as well as the females: for the first, an
hour in the evening, and for the last, an hour in the day time, are
considered the most suitable. In the absence of the preacher, an
elder or deacon shall lead such meetings.

(a) The rules for these special meetings are these: No one
can be received into them who is not resolved to flee the wrath
to come, and, by faith and repentance, to seek his salvation in
Christ, and who is not resolved willingly to obey the disciplinary
rules, which are now observed by this church, for good order, and
advance in godliness, as well as such as in future may be added by
the preacher and church Vestry; yet, always excepted, that such
rules are founded on the WORD OF GOD which is the only unerring
guide of faith and practice.

(b) These meetings are to commence and end with singing and
prayer; and nothing shall be done but what will tend to build up
and advance godliness.

104

(c) Those who attend these special meetings but indifferently, sickness and absence from home excepted, after being twice or thrice admonished, without manifest amendment, shall exclude themselves from the church, (*versamlung.*)

(d) Every member of this church (who is the head of a family) should fervently engage in private worship; morning and evening prayer with his family; and himself and his household attend divine worship at all times.

(e) Every member shall sedulously abstain from all backbiting and evil-speaking, of any person, or persons, without exception, and especially of his brethren in the church. - (Rom. xv:1-3. 2 Cor. xii:20. 1 Peter ii:1. Ja. iv:11.) The transgressor shall, in the first instance, be admonished privately; but, the second time, he shall be openly rebuked in the classmeeting.

(f) Every one must avoid all worldly and sinful company, and, to the utmost, shun all foolish talking and jesting. - (Ps. xv:4. Eph. v:4-11.) This offense will meet with severe church censure.

(g) No one shall be permitted to buy or sell on the Sabbath, nor attend to worldly business; not to travel far or near, but each spend the day in quietness and religious exercises. - (Isa. lviii:13, 14.)

(h) Each member shall willingly attend to any of the private concerns of the church, when required so to do, by the preacher or Vestry; and each one shall strive to lead a quiet and godly life, lest he give offense, and fall into the condemnation of the adversary. -(Math. v:14-16. 1 Pet. 11:12.)

6th. Persons expressing a desire to commune with us at the Lord's table, although they have not been members of our church, shall be admitted by consent of the Vestry, provided that nothing justly can be alleged against their walk in life; and more especially when it is known that they are seeking their salvation. After the preparation sermon, such persons may declare themselves openly before the assembly; also, that they are ready to submit to all wholesome discipline; and thus they are received into the church.

7th. Forasmuch as the difference of people and denominations end in Christ, - Rom. x:12. Col. iii:11) - and availeth nothing in Him but a new creature - (Gal. vi: 13-16) - it becomes our duty, according to the gospel, to commune with, and admit to the Lord's table, professors, to whatever order, or sort, of the Christian church they belong.

8th. All persons who may not attend our class-meetings, nor partake of the holy sacrament with us, but attend our public worship,

shall be visited, by the preacher, in health and in sickness, and on all suitable occasions. He shall admonish them, baptize their children, attend to their funerals, impart instructions to their youth; and, should they have any children, the Church shall interest herself for their religious education.

9th. The preacher shall make it one of his highest duties to watch over the rising youth, diligently instructing them in the principles of religion, according to the word of God. He should catechise them once a week; and the more mature in years, who have obtained a knowledge of the great truths of the gospel, should be impressed with the importance of striving, through divine grace, to become worthy recipients of the holy sacrament. And in view of church membership, such as manifest a desire to this end, should be thoroughly instructed for a time, be examined in the presence of their parents and the Vestry, and, if approved, after the preparation sermon, they should be presented before the church, and admitted.

10th. The church is to establish and maintain a German school, as soon as possible; the Vestry to spare no effort to procure the most competent teachers, and devise such means and rules as will promote the best interests of the school.

11th. That, after the demise or removal of the preacher, the male members of the church shall meet, without delay, in the church edifice, and, after singing and prayer, one or more shall be proposed by the elders and deacons. A majority of votes shall determine the choice, and a call shall be made accordingly; but, should the preacher on whom the choice falls, decline the call, then, as soon as possible, others shall be proposed, and a choice made. But here it is especially reserved, that, should it so happen that before the demise or removal of the preacher, his place should already have been provided for, by a majority of votes, then no new choice shall take place.

12th. No preacher shall stay among us who is not in unison with our adopted rules, and order of things, and class-meetings, and who does not diligently observe them.

13th. No preacher can stay among us who teacheth the doctrine of predestination, (*Gnadenwahl*) or the impossibility of falling from grace, and who holdeth them as doctrinal points.

14th. No preacher can stay among us who will not, to the best of his ability, CARE for the various churches in Pennsylvania, Maryland, and Virginia, which churches, under the superintendence of William Otterbein, stand in fraternal unity with us.

15th. No preacher can stay among us who shall refuse to sustain, with all diligence, such members as have arisen from this or some other churches, or who may yet arise, as helpers in the work of the Lord, as preachers and exhorters, and to afford unto them all possible encouragement, so long as their lives shall be according to the gospel.

16th. All the preceding items (*punckte*) shall be presented to the preacher chosen, and his full consent thereto obtained, before he enters on his ministry.

17th. The preacher shall nominate the elders from among the members who attend the special meetings, and no others shall be proposed: and their duties shall be made known unto them, by him, before the church.

18th. The elders, so long as they live in accordance with the gospel, and shall not attempt to introduce any new act contrary to this constitution and these ordinances, are not to be dismissed from their office, except on account of debility, or other cause: should any one desire it, then, in that case, or by reason of death, the place shall be supplied by the preacher, as already provided.

19th. The three deacons are to be chosen yearly, on New Year's day, as follows:
The Vestry will propose six from among the members who partake with us of the holy sacrament. Each voter shall write the names of the three he desires for deacon, on a piece of paper, and, when the church has met, these papers shall be collected, opened, and read, and such as have a majority of votes shall be announced to the church, and their duties made known unto them, by the preacher, in presence of the church.

20th. The almoner shall be chosen at the same time, and in the same manner, as the deacons, who, at the next election, will present his account.

21st. The preacher, elders, and deacons, shall attend to all the affairs of the church, compose the Church Vestry, and shall be so considered.

22nd. All deeds, leases, and other rights concerning the property of this church, shall be conveyed, in best and safest manner, to this church Vestry, and their successors, as trustees of this church.

23rd. Should a preacher, elder, or deacon, be accused of any known immorality, and, upon the testimony of two or three creditable witnesses, the same should be proven against him, he shall be immediately suspended; and, until he gives sure proof of true

107

repentance, and makes open confession, he shall remain excluded from this church. The same rule shall be observed and carried out in relation to members of the church, who shall be found guilty of immoral conduct. - (1 Cor. v:11-13. 1 Tim. V:20. Tit. iii:10.)

24th. All offenses between members shall be dealt with in strict conformity with the precepts of our Lord. - (Matt. xviii: 15-18.) No one is, therefore, permitted to name the offender, or the offense, except in the order prescribed by our Savior.

25th. No member is allowed to cite his brother before the civil authority, for any cause. All differences shall be laid before the Vestry, or each party may choose a referee from among the members of the church, to whom the adjustment of the matter shall be submitted. The decision of either the Vestry or referees shall be binding on each party; nevertheless, should any one believe himself wronged, he may ask a second hearing, which shall not be refused. This second hearing may be either before the same men, or some others of the church; but whosoever shall refuse to abide by this second verdict, or, on any occasion, speak of the matter of dispute, or accuse his opponent with the same, excludes himself from the church.

26th. The elders and deacons shall meet four times in the year, viz.: the last Sabbath in March, the last Sabbath in June, the last Sabbath in September, and the last Sabbath in December, in the parsonage house, after the afternoon service, to take the affairs of the church into consideration.

27th. This constitution and these ordinances shall be read every New Year's day, before the congregation, in order to keep them in special remembrance, and that they may be carefully observed, and no one plead ignorance of the same.

28th. We, the subscribers, acknowledge the above-written items and particulars, as the ground-work of our church, and we ourselves, as co-members, by our signatures, recognize and solemnly promise religious obedience to the same.

> William Otterbein, *Preacher*.
>
> Lehard Herbach, Henry Weitner,
> Peter Hofman, *Elders*.
>
> Philip Bier, William Baker,
> Abraham Lorsh, *Deacons*.

Baltimore, January 1st, 1785.

¶ Minutes of the United Brotherhood in Christ Jesus

(Taken from *Minutes of the Annual and General Conferences of The Church of The United Brethren in Christ 1800-1818*, trans. and ed. A. W. Drury 9-18, reprinted in Arthur C. Core, *Philip William Otterbein* (1968), 120-27).

Here now follows what the United Brotherhood in Christ Jesus from the year 1800-the *United* till 1800-have done in their annual conference, how the preachers and church members should conduct themselves.

SEPTEMBER 25, 1800, the following preachers assembled at the house of Peter Kemp in Frederick County, Maryland: William Otterbein, Martin Boehm, John Hershey, Abraham Troxel, Christian Krum, Henry Krum, George Pfrimmer, Henry Boehm, Christian Newcomer, Dietrich Aurand, Jacob Geisinger, George Adam Geeting, Adam Lehman.

Each person spoke first of his own experience, and then declared anew his intention with all zeal, through the help of God, to preach untrammeled by sect to the honor of God and [the good] of men.

1. Resolved that two preachers shall go to Smoke's and investigate whether D. Aurand should baptize and administer the Lord's supper.

2. Resolved that yearly a day shall be appointed when the unsectarian [*unpartheiische*] preachers shall assemble and counsel how they may conduct their office more and more according to the will of God, and according to the mind of God, that the church of God may be built up, and sinners converted, so that God in Christ may be honored.

3. The meeting was opened with prayer, then a chapter read, a short discourse delivered by Brother Otterbein, and then again closed with prayer.

SEPTEMBER 23, 1801, we again assembled at Peter Kemp's in order to counsel together and instruct one another how we might be pleasing to God and useful to our fellowmen.

The following preachers were present: William Otterbein, Martin Boehm, Christian Newcomer, Daniel Strickler, George Adam Geeting, Peter Senseny, John Neidig, David Long, Abraham Mayer, Frederick Schaffer, Jacob Geisinger, John Hershey, Thomas Winter, Ludwig Duckwald, David Snyder, Peter Kemp, Matthias Kessler, Christian Krum, Abraham Hershey, Michael Thomas.

1. After prayer, Otterbein gave a discourse. He said that salvation depends on Christ alone and his mercy, and that whoever here becomes free from sin and a party spirit has God to thank. Thus he declared his mind, and then each of the preachers spoke of his experience, and then was the following resolved.

2. A letter was read from Rev. Pfrimmer, and it was resolved to make no answer, because that seemed right to every one.

3. A letter was received from Aurand at Smoke's, and resolved to grant his desire and to notify him through Christian Newcomer.

4. To-day's session closed with a song and a hearty prayer that God would bless us and make us true and faithful laborers in his vineyard. Oh, that the Lord would send upon us all his Holy Spirit, that we might proclaim with power the word of God. Amen.

1. The 24th of September, 1801, we again assembled in God's name in Peter Kemp's house; and first a chapter of the Revelation of John was read, namely, the fourteenth chapter. Then followed singing and hearty prayer that each one might be willing to preach the gospel and that he also be careful, and that he also so walk as he preaches to others. [For 1802 see p. 112]

2. The preachers were examined as to whether they are willing according to their ability to labor in the work of the Lord, through the grace of the Lord.

3. It was asked who are willing to take charge of a circuit and preach at the appointed places. Then the following preachers offered themselves: Christian Newcomer, David Snyder, Michael Thomas, Abraham Hershey, Daniel Strickler, Abraham Mayer, Frederick Schaffer, David Long, John Neidig, Peter Kemp.

4. Resolved that each preacher, after the sermon, shall hold conversation with those who would be converted, be they who they may, if they are determined from the heart to give themselves to God.

5. Resolved that the preachers shall be brief and avoid unnecessary words in preaching and in prayer; but if the Spirit of God impels, it is their duty to follow as God directs. O God, give us wisdom and understanding to do all things according to thy will. Amen.

1. At nine o'clock we again came together. We began the session again with singing and hearty prayer that God would bless us with wisdom and understanding and with hearty love to God and one another. Amen.

2. Resolved that our preachers' meeting [conference] next year shall be October 5, 1803, at David Snyder's, and whoever of the preachers cannot come shall write to the conference.

3. Resolved that the last Sunday in August a great meeting shall be held at Sleepy Creek.

4. Our present meeting was now closed; and indeed with a hearty prayer, which may the Lord out of grace grant for Jesus' sake. Amen.

Martin Boehm, William Otterbein, George Adam Geeting.

1. OCTOBER 5, 1803, we assembled at David Snyder's, in Cumberland County, Pennsylvania. The preachers present were the following: William Otterbein, Martin Boehn, Christian Newcomer, David Snyder, John Hershey, Peter Kemp, Abraham Mayer, Christopher Grosh, Christian Krum, Valentine Flugle, John Winter, Frederick Schaffer, George Adam Geeting, George Benedum.

We began the session with the reading of the second chapter of First Timothy, and then with singing some verses of a hymn, and with prayer. Thou, dear Saviour, bless our coming together to the honor of thy name and to the edification of us all. O Lord, answer us for Jesus' sake. Amen.

2. Each one of the preachers spoke as to his condition, how it stood with him; and of his renewed determination in upright love with all, with earnest determination in uprightness toward one another, and bound together in love, to walk in the ways of God; to preach the gospel through the power of Jesus. Amen.

3. Resolved that Daniel Strickler and Christian Krum shall call the preachers in Virginia together and with one another determine how they should preach and rightly arrange their plan. The Lord give them wisdom and power from above.

4. October 6, at two o'clock, our session again began with the reading of a chapter and with prayer. In the forenoon there was preaching by Otterbein and Boehm.

5. The work in Maryland was considered. It was left to the preachers in Maryland themselves to arrange.

6. Resolved that Martin Boehm and Grosh place the preachers in order in Pennsylvania as may tend most to the honor of God and the benefit of the hearers and the bettering of the church of God.

7. Resolved that David Snyder and Abraham Mayer and Benedum shall make their own arrangement, how they shall serve their

111

preaching places, as may be best for the kingdom of God. May the Lord help them. Amen.

8. It is ordered that Christian Newcomer and Henry Krum go to Christian Berger's and preach the gospel in his part of the country wherever they can find an entrance to the praise of our Lord Jesus Christ.

9. Resolved that the preachers named shall give to Christian Berger authority to baptize, but nothing more at this time.

10. October 7 we began our session again with the reading of the Fourteenth Psalm, and very hearty prayer.

11. Concerning Brother Flugle it was resolved that Brother Hershey visit his place to administer the Lord's supper.

12. There being a complaint against D. Aurand, resolved that Brother Snyder and Brother Neidig should go thither and make an investigation.

13. Resolved that our next conference again be held at David Snyder's, if the Lord will, the first Wednesday in October, 1804, and a great meeting Saturday and Sunday following. The Lord grant it his blessing.

At length it was resolved that concerning the recording of the people's names every one has the freedom to do according to his understanding, and that they love one another as brethren. Further, it was resolved that the preacher after the sermon should converse with awakened souls as in the circumstances it might seem proper.

William Otterbein, Martin Boehm, George Adam Geeting.

Here must be inserted the minutes of the Conference of 1802. These were on a sheet by themselves. I have just now found them. I record them here now as follows (Drury).

At Cronise's, in Frederick County, [Maryland] we, the following preachers, came together to hold counsel: William Otterbein, Martin Boehm, Christian Newcomer, John Hershey, Christopher Grosh, Abraham Troxel, Henry Krum, Michael Thomas, Dietrich Aurand, David Snyder, Peter Kemp, Matthias Kessler, George Adam Geeting.

We began our meeting with singing, then with right hearty prayer to God that the kingdom of God might come and the will of God be done on earth as in heaven. May God will to send us preachers the grace of love to love God and all men.

112

2. Each of the preachers spoke of his condition, how it is with him in his preaching and how his purpose is further to do in his office, to call heartily upon God for his help, and that ever he might through humility give to another higher esteem than to himself. May God give to us preachers grace that we may become very humble to the honor of God and the good of men.

3. Resolved that Valentine Flugle have a certificate from us that he is allowed to exhort and persuade the people that they be converted. The Lord give him his blessing.

4. Resolved that we write to Pfrimmer that for the present we will have nothing to do with him.

5. At the close of the session Ludwig Duckwald and William Ambrose from Sleepy Creek, Virginia, arrived.

6. October 7 the sermon began, which was preached by Otterbein and Boehm, on Hebrews 13:17, with great blessing. To God be all the glory for this. May the sermon never be forgotten by us preachers and all the hearers.

7. The first thing that was taken up was that John Miller with our approval shall exhort the people to incite them to good works as much as he can through God's grace.

8. It appeared that in the matter of the recording of names, twelve votes were in favor and nine against. It is therefore with consent laid over the present.

9. The preachers shall establish prayer-meetings where they preach, if it is possible.

10. It is permitted to Ludwig Duckwald to baptize and to administer the outer signs of the Lord's supper according to God's Word.

11. On the 26th of September there was a sermon preached by our Brother Otterbein, from the fourteenth verse to the end of the Epistle of Jude, and that with great blessing. In the afternoon our consultation was resumed.

12. A proposal was made relating to the collecting of a sum of money for poor preachers. Nothing, however, was done.

13. Resolved that if a preacher does anything wrong or scandalous, the nearest preacher shall go and talk with him alone. If he refuse to hear or heed, said preacher shall take with him one or two more preachers. If he refuse to hear them, he shall be silent till the next conference.

14. Resolved that George Adam Geeting in the spring and fall shall visit the societies on Frederick Circuit.

15. Resolved that Christian Newcomer visit Cumberland Circuit twice yearly.

16. Resolved that Martin Boehm twice yearly visit the circuits in Pennsylvania beyond the Susquehanna, to ascertain the condition of things in their societies.

17. Resolved that Jacob Baulus and Valentine Baulus shall make house-visits in Middletown and Fredericktown and their vicinity.

18. Further, it is laid down as a rule [*vest gesetzt*] that when one of our superintendents [or elders, *eltesten*] dies, namely Otterbein or Martin Boehm, who now are appointed to the place [*gesetzt sind*], then shall another always be chosen in his stead. This is the wish of both, and all of the preachers present unanimously consent and are agreed that it be thus.

Now for this time is the session closed in God's name.

William Otterbein, Martin Boehm.

This yet here to mention: Peter Senseny, Ludwig Duckwald, John Neidig, are authorized to baptize and administer the Lord's supper, with all belonging thereto.

OCTOBER 3, 1804, the conference met at David Snyder's. Few preachers came, however, on account of the prevailing sickness and mortality. Present, Christian Newcomer, Martin Boehm, Frederick Schaffer, David Snyder, Matthias Bortsfield.

They counseled together and resolved, the Lord willing, that the next conference be held near Middletown, Maryland, on Wednesday before Whitsunday, 1805.

1. MAY 29, 1805, we, the following preachers, assembled at the house of Christian Newcomer. Both our [superintendents] were present - Otterbein and Boehm. John Hershey, George Adam Geeting, Daniel Strickler, Frederick Schaffer, Peter Kemp, Lorenz Eberhart, George Benedum, David Snyder, Christian Krum, Frederick Duckwald, William Ambrose, Jacob Baulus, Jacob Geisinger, Christian Berger, Abraham Mayer, Christian Newcomer.

2. We began the session with hearty prayer. Otterbein gave a short address. May the Lord Jesus grant his blessing to the same. Amen.

3. The assembled preachers resolved through the grace of Jesus Christ to urge forward the work of God with more earnestness than ever before. O dear Saviour, help us, poor and unworthy, for the sake of thy suffering and death. Amen.

4. According to the confession of the preachers the grace of God was with them and their work. May the Lord bless them in their office. The Lord make each one very faithful.

5. Pfrimmer received permission to preach among us.

6. The following preachers arrived: Ludwig Duckwald, Daniel Troyer, Jacob Dehof.

7. At eight o'clock, May 30, we again assembled. A portion from God's Word was read, followed by prayer to God in the name of Jesus, and thus the session began.

8. With the advice and consent of the preachers Newcomer determined to preach the whole year in Maryland and a part of Pennsylvania; and Christian Krum in Virginia. Resolved that each receive forty pounds yearly.

9. Resolved that George Adam Geeting shall be present at the usual great meetings in Maryland and on this side of the Susquehanna in Pennsylvania.

10. It was decided by the preachers' meeting that Geeting should not take up his residence at Hagerstown, but that Hagerstown should be served by our preachers.

11. The preachers who preach where they desire, according to their inclination, shall have no compensation. When, however, they receive money, they shall bring the same to the conference, to be given to the regular preachers.

12. It is allowed in our preachers' meeting that Frederick Duckwald of Sleepy Creek, and Christian Berger, of Westmoreland, baptize, administer the Lord's supper, and solemnize marriage.

13. The conference will be held next year at Lorenz Eberhart's, the Tuesday before Whitsunday, 1806, and that there on the Saturday following a great meeting shall begin. May the Lord be with us.

14. With this the session was brought to a close after the reading of a chapter and an exhortation that we should live to the honor of God.

William Otterbein, Martin Boehm.

¶ Henry Boehm's Defense of His Father and His Methodist
Relations
(Taken from H. Boehm, *Reminiscences* (1866), 377-86).

It is a matter of deep regret that I am under the necessity of
noticing a grave attack upon the character of my father and of the
Methodist Episcopal Church, made by the historians of the "United
Brethren in Christ."

The attack was first made thirty-nine years after my father was
in the grave, and was repeated eleven years later. So half a
century after my father's death I, an old man in my ninety-first
year, am obliged to vindicate his character from those who profess
to revere his memory, who eulogize him, who place him next to the
great Otterbein. Beautiful garlands they bring with which to adorn
their victim. These historians say:

In justice to his memory, to the Church in whose origin he was
so intimately concerned, and to the truth of history, we must
pause at the grave of this venerable patriarch to review an account
of William Otterbein and Martin Boehm, which first appeared in the
Methodist Magazine, volume vi, pp. 210-249. The sketch purports to
have been furnished to Bishop Asbury a short time previous to his
death, by his friend, F. Hollingsworth, the transcriber of the
bishop's journal; it has also been embodied in the history of the
Methodist Episcopal Church, by Dr. Bangs, and may be found in
volume ii, pp. 365-376. Here is the matter referred to:

"Martin Boehm, of whom we desire to speak, was born in November,
1725. As a professor of religion and minister of Christ, the labors
and experience of his life may be pretty justly estimated by what
we learn from himself, communicated in answers to certain questions
propounded to him by his son Jacob, which we transcribe.

"*Ques.* Father, when were you put into the ministry?
"*Ans.* My ministerial labors began about the year 1756. Three
years afterward, by nomination to the lot, I received full pastoral
orders.
"*Q.* What was your religious experience during that time?
"*A.* I was sincere and strict in the religious duties of prayer
in my family, in the congregation, and in the closet. I lived and
preached according to the light I had: I was a servant and not a
son; nor did I know any one, at that time, who would claim the
birthright by adoption but Nancy Keaggy, my mother's sister; she was
a woman of great piety and singular devotion to God.
"*Q.* By what means did you discover the nature and necessity
of a real change of heart?

"A. By deep meditation upon the doctrine which I myself preached, of the fall of man, his sinful estate, and utter helplessness; I discovered and felt the want of Christ within, etc., etc.

"Q. Were your labors owned of the Lord in the awakening and conversion of souls?

"A. Yes; many were brought to the knowledge of the truth. But it was a strange work; and some of the Mennonist meeting-houses were closed against me. Nevertheless, I was received in other places. I now preached the Gospel spiritually and powerfully. Some years afterward I was excommunicated from the Mennonist church, on a charge truly enough advanced, of holding fellowship with other societies of a different language. I had invited the Methodists to my house, and they soon formed the society in my neighborhood, which exists to this day. My beloved wife, Eve, my children, and my cousin Keaggy's family, were among the first of its members. For myself, I felt my heart more greatly enlarged toward all religious persons and all denominations of Christians. Upward of thirty years ago I became acquainted with my greatly beloved brother, William Otterbein, and several other ministers, who about this time had been ejected from their churches as I had been from mine, because of their zeal, which was looked upon as an irregularity. We held many large meetings in Pennsylvania, Maryland, and New Virginia, which generally lasted three days. At these meetings hundreds were made the subjects of penitence and pardon. Being convinced of the necessity of order and discipline in the Church of God, and having no wish to be at the head of a separate body, I advised serious persons to join the Methodists, whose doctrine, discipline, and zeal suited, as I thought, an unlearned, sincere, and simple-hearted people. Several of the ministers with whom I labored continued to meet in a conference of the German United Brethren; but we felt difficulties arising from the want of that which the Methodists possessed. Age having overtaken me with some of its accompanying infirmities, I could not travel as I had formerly done. In 1802 I enrolled my name on a Methodist class-book, and I have found great comfort in meeting with my brethren. I can truly say my last days are my best days. My beloved Eve is traveling with me the same road, Zionward; my children, and most of my grandchildren, are made the partakers of the same grace. I am, this 11th of April, 1811, in my eighty-sixth year. Through the boundless goodness of God I am still able to visit the sick, and occasionally to preach in the neighborhood: to His name be all the glory in Christ Jesus."

*   *   *

It is a duty I owe to my venerated father, to the memory of Bishop Asbury, and to the ministers that were in charge of the Church at Boehm's Chapel in 1802, that I should correct the misrepresentations contained in the history of the "United Brethren in Christ."

There was a mistake in the account in the Methodist Magazine, and copied in Bangs's history and the "History of the United Brethren." It says the questions were asked by Martin Boehm's son Jacob. It should have been Henry. I asked the questions, and wrote the answers. This was fifty-three years ago last March. I have the original copy with my father's signature, and the reader can see a fac-simile of his autograph. I asked the questions, and took down the answers at the request of Bishop Asbury, who wished the history of my father. The bishop had taken down from the lips of Otterbein the answers giving his history. It was at my father's house where the questions were asked and the answers given. To the animadversions that have been made to my statement I make the following replies: 1. It is objected that my father did not understand English, and that he wrote neither the questions or answers. He did understand English very well. He conversed very readily in English, and had quite a library of English works, which he read with great pleasure and profit; among others, Wesley's Sermons and Fletcher's Checks. These were great favorites with him.

As my father was aged and infirm I wrote the questions and answers. He fully understood them both, and it was voluntary on his part, and not the least influence was exerted over him. I carefully wrote every word of the answers from his mouth, and then read them over to him, and he pronounced them correct, and then deliberately affixed his signature to them. My father was not one who would sign a document when he was ignorant of its contents, or that he knew to be untrue.

At that time neither Bishop Asbury or myself supposed it would ever be a matter of controversy. It was not obtained for any such object, or to prove my father was a Methodist, but simply to obtain his history correctly.

2. Another error is this: that his son had warped the statement. This is both uncharitable and unjust. It was not enough to hint that I took advantage of my father's ignorance of the English language, but now I am accused of warping what he said. I would as soon have cut off my right hand. If I had been guilty of an act so mean, so unjust to my father, and so false to others, I should have despised myself all the rest of my life. The insinuation has not the semblance of truth. Those answers were not warped; there was no false coloring, but sober truth. I took them down from his lips as he answered in honest simplicity, and in the same spirit I wrote them down.

3. This historian [Spayth] speaks of Boehm's Chapel being built on Martin Boehm's land, principally by him and his German brethren, and then the Methodists denying him the privilege of his own meeting-house, etc. Now all this is a mistake. It was not built upon my father's land, but upon that of my brother Jacob, who

118

gave the site for the church. Nor was it built principally by my
father and "the German Brethren." I suppose he means by this the
United Brethren. As a body they had nothing to do with it. My
father gave something, and so might some of them; but it was built
for the Methodists, and principally by the Methodists. It was not
my father's church any more than it was mine, and it is sheer none-
sense to talk of the cruelty of shutting him out of his own church.
No such thing ever did or could take place, simply from the fact
that he never owned any church, and therefore the thing was impossible. It was built for a Methodist church, the plan was furnished by a Methodist minister, and it was deeded to the Methodist
Episcopal Church. After the lapse of seventy years it is still a
Methodist Episcopal Church, and their ministers still preach in it.

4. Another error is accusing the Methodists at Boehm's Chapel
of double dealing. In the first place "forming a class under a
liberal construction of their rules," so that Father Boehm, not a
member, could attend a class, and then "withdrawing such liberal
construction," and bringing it to bear on Father Boehm, so he was
excluded from the class-meeting and love-feast. Any one acquainted
with the Methodist Discipline knows that no such thing could take
place. No individual Methodist society makes and unmakes terms
of membership. We have a Discipline, and the terms are fixed by the
General Conference. We are not independent bodies to make rules
for ourselves. Furthermore, I was there at the time, and know that
no such thing ever took place. William Hunter then had charge of
the circuit, an honest man as ever came from the land of Erin. He
was an outspoken man, open as the light of day, and incapable of
duplicity.

But to "the gist of the matter." Father Boehm, says this
writer, was entreated, "for form's sake," to have his name go on to
the class-book nominally. So, according to this statement, he never
joined the Methodists, he was only a "nominal member." Here the
Methodists are accused of deception, and my aged father of complicity
with them: they pretending that he was a member, and he allowing his
name to be entered as a member, all the while knowing that he was
not one. My father would never have stooped to such meanness. He
did not consider himself a nominal, but a real member of the
Methodist Church. He was not only a member of the class, and used
to meet in it, but he was a member of the Quarterly Conference; he
used to meet and take a part there, by virtue of his office, as a
local preacher of the Methodist Episcopal Church. He was an ordained minister and used to administer the ordinances, Baptism and
the Lord's Supper.

But it is said "he was entreated to do this for peace' sake."
For whose peace? My father was not so easily persuaded to do a
wrong action for the sake of peace. He always preferred purity
to peace: "First pure, then peaceable."

(Taken from F. Asbury, *Journal and Letters*, III,
504-05, letter to Jacob Gruber, 7 July, 1814, corrected).

Great grace be with us. Brethren my heart's desire and prayer
to God is that Israel might be saved. I am willing to go and to die at
Jerusalem! I could wish myself accursed from the example of Christ,
perhaps he might mean crucified. I suppose we English Americans hold
4000 traveling and local preachers and living exhorters to supply 3
million of souls annually. I say 200,000 Germans, and their descendants, on the east side of the Ohio including Pennsylvania, Maryland
and Virginia, not one gospel minister among them; perhaps 100 settlements
and congregations vacant.

What are the Lutherans, what are the Reformed, the Friends, what
are the Albrights, but deceitful apes and opposers of Methodists, what
are the United Brethren? But you may ride a circuit or let it alone,
you may meet in class --- or let it alone.

Should my life be spared, to return which is very doubtful, one more
attempt for a German missionary, a kind of presbytery preaching at least
half their time in German. Lay out the country, in proper divisions,
meeting quarterly but taking our complete form of discipline and hymn
books in German translation and putting them into every hand and house.
And when there is a good German settlement and a prospect, let one
missionary stay and work till a regular society is formed, and given up
to the circuit preachers. Yet let the missionaries visit them quarterly
to remove difficulties, to explain things the English preachers cannot,
for want of language. Where is the money to support 4 missionaries?
Make collections once a quarter and let them dividend with Baltimore and
Philadelphia conferences. Where are the men, Jacob Gruber, Henry Boehm,
John Swartswelder and William Folks. Now, think on this, for God's sake,
for Christ's sake; and for the sake of the many thousands of souls, that
live in blindness. Mind you preach English half your time. And receive
all the help they can give of entertainment, but see if in 45 years we
have preached in Pennsylvania, we have 6000 members in the old circuits
and need Philadelphia left out as a city. Think it over, consult your
God, and your brethren. As the most active man, I think, you ought to
preside, as ruling elder, and there ought to be a strict discipline, like
a well regulated flying army.

I am your feeble Father; and let it be known, that one of the
grand acts of his life was a capital mission to the American Germans,
but lived not to finish it, or that the conferences did not see eye to
eye with the Bishop in this great undertaking or that the missionaries,
the men of his choice, though well qualified, and of full descent
from father and mother, and educated in the German language and of sound
constitution; yet would not nobly volunteer; but I hope better

things, though I thus write. I hope the Lord will direct us; and make the path of duty plain. My soul has been without a doubt, or a cloud in all my affliction, though the greatest, I have ever experienced, and the most difficult to recover from. My copy was correct made, employ an amanuensis not having written more than three letters 13 weeks. I am if possible more than ever yours,

F. Asbury

¶   Christian Newcomer's Journal

(Taken from *The Life and Journals of The Reverend Christian Newcomer* (1834), 13-14, 69, 74, 201, 217, 232-33).

*   *   *

Already for a considerable time, I had become acquainted with William Otterbein and George Adam Geeting, two preachers of the German Reformed Church, and had frequently heard them preach in the neighborhood of my place of residence. These individuals endowed by God, preached powerfully, and not like the Scribes: their discourses made uncommon impressions on the hearts of the hearers; they insisted on the necessity of genuine repentance and conversion, on the knowledge of a pardon of sin, and in consequence thereof, a change of heart and renovation of spirit. Many secure and unconcerned sinners were, by their instrumentality, awakened from their sleep of sin and death - many converted from darkness to light - from the power of Sin and Satan unto God. They soon collected many adherents to, and followers of the doctrines which they preached, from the multitude that congregated to hear them. Those persons who held to, and embraced these doctrines, were by them, formed into societies, and were called Otterbein's people, and the worldly-minded, gave them the nick-name *Dutch Methodists,* which in those days, is rather considered slanderous.

Whereas these men preached the same doctrine which I had experienced, and which according to my views and discernment so perfectly agreed with the doctrine of Jesus Christ and his Apostles; therefore I associated with them and joined their society: and blessed be God, although I withdrew myself from the Mennonite society, on account of the want of the life and power of religion among them, I never felt in any wise accused within for so doing; - on the contrary, have received many a blessing of God when assembled with my new brethren.

The work of grace now spread very rapidly among the German population in the States of Maryland & Pennsylvania: from every quarter resounded the call, "Come over and help us." The harvest was great, and the laborers few.

*   *   *

Sunday 8th June, 1800 – My prayer is this morning, O! that God of his infinite mercy, may be with us in power, and may signs and wonders be done in the name of the holy child, Jesus. A vast multitude of people were collected to-day; Br. Draksel preached the first sermon. The people were remarkably attentive, and the grace of God wrought powerfully. At night we held meeting at Abr. Hershey's; a young Methodist Brother preached first; I followed him. We had a blessed time. 9th – This morning we held our Love feast, and administered the ordinance of the Lord's Supper; it proved a happy day to many souls. I staid this night at A. Long's. 10th – This day I preached a funeral sermon. The great mass of the people here appear to rest contentedly in their carnal security: may God have mercy on them. I came to Bear's, my brother-in-law, where I staid for the night. 11th – This day I visited my relations in this section of the country, and lodged at Buckwalter's. 12th – This day I came to Br. Martin Boehm's; found Br. Robinson, a Methodist preacher there; we spent several happy hours. How profitable it is to be in company with the godly, and how easy to preach to a congregation of praying people. 13th – This evening I preached at Br. Strickler's, from Luke 24; v. 45, 46, 47. 14th – I came to York, and tarried for the night with a Mr. Baer.

*   *   *

Sunday, 22d Mar., 1812 – This forenoon I preached at Henry Frey's from Matth. 21, v. 14, 15, 16, to an attentive congregation; in the afternoon I heard Br. James Smith, in Leesburg, where I met Bishops Asbury and McKendree; I lodged with Mr. Busy. The Methodist Conference was here in session, and I tarried until the 27th, when the Conference was closed; rode with Asbury and Henry Boehm to Noland's Ferry, where we crossed the Potomac river. Before we parted, Asbury gave me an invitation to attend the Philadelphia Conference, in order to assist in effecting a union and brotherly fellowship within the bounds of the Philadelphia Conference, between the Methodist church and the United Brethren in Christ. I lodged this night at the widow Kemp's. 28th, and

Sunday 29th – We had a Quarterly meeting in Shauman's church; Bishop McKendree was present. At night he preached at Schnebly's, I exhorted after him; we both lodged at Jacob Hess's. 30th – Our meeting still continued; Br. Fechtig preached first, McKendree followed; several persons were happily converted to God, others had their spiritual strength renewed, and some were enabled to jump and shout for joy: unto God be all the glory.

April 2d – To-day I was at Peter Stadtler's, where I received the information through Br. Henry Spayth, that old Father Martin Boehm had departed this life, aged 86 years, 3 months and 11 days; he died March 23d, and was buried March 25th, 1812.

122

Sunday 29th Aug., 1813 - This forenoon I preached in Lyday's schoolhouse, in the German and English language; in the afternoon I spoke in Middle-town. 30th - To-day I stopped for refreshment with Henry Huber; rode to Zanesville and lodged at a public house. 31st - This evening I stopped with a Quaker family and lodged with them for the night.

September 1st - This evening I reached Steubenville; having no acquaintances in the place, I stopped at a public house. 2d - The Ohio Conference is here in session. I went this morning to pay a visit to Bishop Asbury, who is present; he lodges with Mr. Wells, where we took breakfast together; I went with him to Conference, and delivered a communication from our Conference. Here I found several brethren to whom I was known; was cordially invited to lodge at Br. Noland's, during my stay, which invitation I cheerfully accepted.

Sunday 5th - Bishops Asbury and McKendree both preached to-day to a congregation estimated at more than 2000 persons. 6th - This forenoon I received a communication from the Conference to the Brethren in our next Conference which is to assemble in Montgomery county, Ohio. After taking an affectionate farewell of the two Bishops and the other Brethren, I dined once more with my kind host Br. Wm. Noland; commended him and his amiable family to God in prayer, and set out at three o'clock in the afternoon; crossed the Ohio river, and staid for the night in a little village.

22d Mar., 1815 - I set out for Baltimore, to the Methodist Conference, came to Mr. Barsh's and staid for the night. 23rd - I reached the city and lodged with John Hildt. 24th - This morning I paid a visit to Bishops Asbury and McKendree, went with them to the Conference room. At 11 o'clock Enoch George preached an ordination sermon, Bishop McKendree gave an exhortation; seven Brethren were then solemnly ordained. At night James Smidt preached a powerful sermon; I lodged again with Hildt. 25th - I attended Conference again; in the evening I was at Eutaw meeting house, and returned to my lodgings at Hildt's. I have a room to myself at his house: (like the Prophet Elisha with the woman of Shannon,) where I can go in and out as I please.

Sunday 26th - This forenoon Br. George Geeting preached in Otterbein's church, I exhorted after him; Br. John Swartzwelder preached in the afternoon. At night I heard Asa Shinn preach in Eutaw meeting house; he is a wonderful orator and reasoner. 27th - I was again at the Conference; Br. Hoffman preached in Light street meeting house at 11 o'clock; I exhorted after him; in the afternoon

the session of the Conference was brought to a close. 28th - This day I bid Bishops Asbury and McKendree farewell; rode a short distance out of the city to Kalbfus's and staid for the night. 29th - This morning I feel my spiritual strength renewed, and fresh courage to be more engaged than ever. O Lord! strengthen this resolution, and grant that my old days may be appropriated to thy name's glory. Came to Mr. Sumwalt's and staid for the night. 30th - I rode to Jacob Kleinfelter's. 31st - I visited W. Bentz, and lodged with old Mr. Naylor; had a bad night's rest, and wrestled for a clean heart.

April 1st - I attended a meeting of the Albright Brethren, near Conewago, and returned to Naylor's.

Sunday 2d - This day I was in York; Bishop McKendree and Henry Smidt preached in the meeting house; I spoke after them in German, lodged with W. Bentz. 3d - This morning my poor soul is drawn out in prayer to God for sanctifying power: O! Lord, impart into my soul thy nature and thy perfect love. I rode with Br. Henry Smidt to Jacob Kleinfelter's; the Albright Brethren had their Conference here; about 14 or 15 preachers were assembled. I made another attempt to effect a union between the two societies, but in vain. 5th - I left them, rode to Bishops in Little's-town, and staid for the night. 6th - I felt the love of God powerfully in my soul; rode all day long joyfully and serene. Towards evening I reached Benedict Sauder's, where I tarried for the night. 7th - This day my soul was also enabled to rejoice on account of the presence of the Lord; came to Middle-town and lodged with Valentine Bowlus. 8th - Returned home.

Sunday 9th - I preached at Schnebly's. 12th - I left home, called at Henry Kumler's, and lodged at night with Abr. Huber, at the Rocky Springs. 13th - This morning I set out early; stopped at John Meyer's and took refreshment; rode to Peter Brown's, in Sherman's Valley, where I tarried for the night. 14th - I rode all day over hills and vallies, and staid for the night with David Long. 15th - Rode to Michael Mase's, in Union county.

Sunday 16th - This morning I rode to Martin Dreisbach's where I preached with great liberty. 17th - I preached at George Miller's, from 2d.Peter 1, v.5 to 8. 18th - I remained here and had a long conversation with Miller and Niebel respecting the union of our respective societies, but all in vain; we could not bring matters to bear.

Jacob Albright's Experience as Told
by George Miller in 1811

(Taken from Miller's biography in German, translated and published by the Historical Society of
the E.U.B. Church (1959)).

Jacob Albright was born May first, in the year of our Lord 1759,
in Douglas Township, Montgomery County, Pennsylvania. His parents
presented the infant for holy baptism and saw to it that he was
taught to read and write in the German language, and to learn the
fundamental teachings of Christianity, according to the Evangelical
Lutheran doctrine, and in due time he became a member of said congregation in Douglas Township. He was married in 1785 and soon thereafter settled in Earl Township, Lancaster County, Pennsylvania.

Jacob Albright's soul-condition prior to reaching the age of
thirty-two, seems not to have been the best, at least he always
thought of it with regret, repentance and deep humility, and often
in speaking to his friends expressed deep sorrow concerning the
same. But we shall let him tell his own story, in a manner in which
he often told it to his friends, at sundry times and places, somewhat after this fashion:

"I traveled with frivolous and trifling disregard, the path of
life; was happy with the pleasure-bent, and thought little of the
purpose and goal of human existence; was regardless of human responsibility and thoughtless of living a Christian life. I lived
as though the span of my sinful life was unending and committed
many a sin for which God had promised severe punishment.

*   *   *

"Undoubtedly it would have continued in this manner for long,
perhaps forever, had not the grace of God brought to my attention
so many circumstances, I had hitherto completely neglected. I had
come at times into grave danger to life and limb and my deliverance
was often so sudden and wonderful, that I marvelled. Unwillingly
then I was drawn often to gratitude for the gracious providence. I
felt my breast tighten and my heart beat high and I would break out
in prayers of thanksgiving. But as often as I lifted my eyes to
heaven, I heard the voice of conscience say: 'You are unworthy of
the grace of God; the offerings pleasing to God are only pure
hearts.' O that humiliated me deeply.

"God stretched his hand toward me in still another way. I had
in my early youth received catechetical instruction in the Christian
religion. At that time I could not yet fully comprehend the great
truths thereof nor vividly experience the same; nevertheless from
that day forward there remained with me a feeling of reverence toward

God, which now to be sure, was very dim, but it went so far as to reverence every place where God was worshiped, regardless of manner and place. And never did a thought of mockery or ridicule of such persons, who engaged in the worship of God enter my mind and heart, regardless of what Confession or sect they belonged.

*   *   *

"This reverence caused me repeatedly to visit such places of worship and religious services and I listened with rapt attention to the exhortations of the ministers. Through the working together of the inner feelings of my soul and the voice of the Gospel, I came at last to the full recognition of what is required of God to fulfill one's responsibility and obligations as a person, as a Christian to stand justified before Him who knows the innermost thoughts of the human heart, from whom no secrets are hidden.

. . ."I was terrified concerning my state of soul life. The judgment of God stood out in my imagination. My spirit experienced deep depression which no urge of perceptive faculty could enliven. The feeling of my unworthiness grew daily, until in my 32nd year, on a specific day in the month of July, it had grown to such proportion that it bordered on despair. I felt myself so small and my sins so great, that I could no longer comprehend how the righteousness of the just judge who would judge according to dessert and merit could save me from being cast into the bottomless pit of damnation. The fear of my heart increased every minute, so that I wanted to cry out: 'Ye mountains fall over me, and ye hills cover me.'. . .

"So as my heart experienced this lively repentance and this firm resolve for improvement came before my soul, I felt at the same time the need of prayer to pour out my heart before God. I felt a power within, heartily, and with dedication to pray to God. I fell upon my knees, tears of bitter repentance rolled down my cheeks and a long fervent prayer for grace and forgiveness of my sins ascended to the throne of the Most High.

"This continuous and earnest petitioning brought me at last nearer and nearer to my illumination. I felt power to dedicate myself to the good; to surrender my will to the will of God. I heard the voice of the Comforter in my inner being, for I learned to recognize and became convinced, that God does not desire the destruction of the sinner, but rather that he be converted and live, and that God looked with gracious and forgiving eyes upon my sincere repentance, sorrow, and broken heartedness and that the merit of my Savior, his bitter suffering and death completed the work of my salvation.

*   *   *

Was it only accidental that your heart and just your heart, should be so overflowing with sympathy and concern for the well-being of your brethren? Is not here just in this, the hand of God visible, whose wisdom guides the destiny of individuals and nations? What if his eternal love which desires to lead every soul into Abraham's bosom, should have chosen *you* to show your brethren the way into the knowledge of God and to prepare them for the acceptance of the mercy of God?'

*   *   *

"However, the fulfillment of all this I postponed from time to time. Always I believed to some hinderance in the way of immediate obedience, and when such had been removed, I convinced myself of the existence of other obstacles.

"For such indecision and procrastination God punished me with severe illness, a constant increasing pain of body went through all my nervous system. I lost weight constantly, until I was reduced to a shadow of my former self. An indescribable weakness paralyzed every muscle in my body so that I could not engage in any work of whatsoever kind. And what was still more terrible to me than all bodily affliction was that at times the terrific feeling overwhelmed my soul, as though I had been completely forsaken of God. What I endured in body, soul, and spirit during this illness is difficult to describe. In time of such sensation of being completely forsaken, I cried out so bitterly, that all who were near me, and saw and heard me, turned away from me in horror and frightfulness.

"In this visitation from God I saw now more clearly than ever God's finger and learned with the utmost conviction that a man can do nothing better than to submit himself fully to the will of his creator and be obedient to His will without a backward or forward look. So wretched my condition was, nevertheless the Lord granted me his unmerited favor and mercy to keep me in the state of grace. I therefore continued in prayer, humbled myself before his throne and promised solemnly and made the firm resolve, that should I become well again I would immediately follow his call and go preaching his gospel throughout the land, wherever he would send me, if only he would go with me.

"As soon as this firm resolve became rooted in my heart it seemed as though a heavy load had been rolled from my soul. I felt a complete alleviation and the peace within returned to my heart. So as soon as restfulness of soul was re-established just so quickly I lost all pain in my body. My strength returned and my life coursed through my body and in short time I was fully restored to health.

"Soon thereafter I made ready to travel and prepared myself in such manner as I felt was expedient. The strength and equipment to

preach the gospel I sought alone of the Lord, in continuing prayer and in the study of his reward.

....."In the possession of such grace, the gift of the Lord God equipped me with the power of his righteousness and holiness, sealed by his Spirit in love, faith and hope. I began my travels in the year 1796, in the month of October, in order to be obedient to the call of God, according to the revelation of his holy will through the Gospel.

"I traveled through a large part of Pennsylvania and Virginia, and the Lord granted me his blessing so that I found entrance to preach in churches, school houses, and private homes. I also received some temporal support, here and there, so that I could continue my itinerating in the service of the Gospel. For this ministry was fruitful so that many sinners were converted to God as his spirit awakened them to their need.

"When I had preached about four years and had specifically determined to preach the Gospel at such places where the life and Christian order and decorum were yet unknown, so I also sought to minister to such awakened and converted souls and determined to provide them with proper religious instruction as to how they might best in fellowship with others, in the unity of the faith, work out their souls' salvation and develop the spiritual life."

¶   John Dreisbach's "Day Book "

(Taken from typed manuscript copy in Garrett-Evangelical Theological Seminary, III, 5-6, 41-42, 60).

After the meeting I asked the friends to gather about in front, for brother R. McKreh [exhorter on trial] had promised to humble himself, and I began an investigation of him. First, I told the friends of our rules, and then I told brother McKreh of his wrong doing viz.: 1. Careless and arrogantly he deported himself among the people of the circuit. 2. Disobedience toward his older brethren in office as they admonished him. 3. Slandering the brother preachers. 4. The breaking of the marriage rule. Then I told him of his ill-temper at the conference, his slanderous untruth about us after the conference. Then I said, now decide if we have done you right or wrong? I am convinced of the truth by the omnicient God before whom we all must appear and McKreh's conscience will convince him that it is the truth. Now, because he promised me to humble himself, it shall be made known to you if he, in truth, has done so. Now brother McKreh, I ask you the following questions, which you must answer by a yes or no as to your mind in this matter. First question: Do you recognize and confess your transgression and wrongdoing? He arose and answered, Yes, I am guilty. Second

question: Brother McKreh, I ask you before the omnicient God, are
you sorry of heart and do you sincerely regret it? He arose and
answered, Yes, I regret it from my heart. Third question: Brother
McKreh, do you confess before God and this society that the conference did right? He arose and answered, Yes, I believe it did right.
Fourth question: Brother McKreh, I ask you in God's name, will you
in the future give heed to the good advice and exhortation of your
older brethren in office, being submissive and obedient, humbling
yourself and seeking the grace of God for the service they may
assign you. According to our rules in the Lord, will you then arise
and testify before God and the congregation by saying, Yes? He
stood up and said, "Yes, by the grace of God and with His help I
am determined so to do." Now brother McKreh you have not only
given this witness to me and the present congregation, but also to
the omnipresent omniscient God. O, brother, prove it now with the
deed that you are sincere and honest. And so I am permitting
brother McKreh to exhort in this class and work with brother
Deuberman for God's honor, and he shall be on trial until the next
big meeting and quarterly conference, which then will decide his
case by majority vote. I also admonished his wife publicly to
humility and earnest prayer. In closing we had prayer, a wonderful
victory, and a blessed time. Now my dream of April 25 has come
true. Praise God for it. Amen.

*   *   *

Monday, October 14, 1816
The delegates gathered, and the first General conference
opened. It was the First General Conference we ever held. We
examined the records, and had an interview with Newcomer and Roth
who came to us to learn of the possibility of a merger with the
United Brethren in Christ. The name of the Society was changed from
"The So-Called Albrights", to "The Evangelical Association".

The Joint Committee appointed to effect the proposed union met
in the house of Henry Kumler in Autrim township, Franklin county,
Pa., Feb. 14, 1817. The difficulties in the way seemed greater
than had been anticipated. Also at this our General Conference a
general Book Agent and an assistant was elected as follows: Solomon
Miller, agent and Henry Niebel, assistant. We had a profitable
blessed time, for which we thank God and that peace and brotherly
love prevailed.

Friday, October 18, 1816
Our First General Conference adjourned after a reverent
devotional prayer service, when every one went his way while I with
several other brethren rode to Longstown and helped publishing press
for today and tomorrow.

Sunday, October 20, 1816
    I preached in Buffalo at Peter Schmitt's, and in the
afternoon at my father's. The text of the forenoon service was
Heb. 12:15, and for the afternoon was Psalm 73:28. I was blest in
preaching and the congregation appeared likewise blest. Thank God!

Monday, October 21, 1816
    This entire week, I shall again be kept busy at the
Publishing press. I also was priviledged to attend several meetings, and I can say that the Lord has blest me with his grace.

*   *   *

Friday, February 14, 1817
    We met at brother Cumler's to discuss the union of the two
denominations, but it could not be accomplished because we of our
side insisted that only itinerant ministers, and such who travelled
and did much preaching and those now retired should have a seat with
a full vote in their annual conference. But the United Brethren
delegation did not have the authority to agree to such arrangements
because of their aged retired preachers. We also discussed matters
relating to discipline, doctrine and knowledge, which then led to
sharp critical accusations; from our delegation because some did not
consider them as good and pure as we ourselves, and so there were
accusations also against us as proud, and not sincere loving people.
At last and finally it appeared we could agree in doctrine and
discipline, but on other points we could not agree. We held days
of fasting and prayer before and after the discussion of various
subjects when grace and the blessings of God was bestowed upon us.
We closed the conference with the suggestion, exhortation and
promise to love one another, despite our differences and to pray
for one another and to honor and treat one another at all times as
Christians.

II.

PIONEER DEVELOPMENT, 1784-1860

6. THE SHAPE OF THE CHURCH AND MINISTRY

For all their insistence on separation of church and state American denominations have been inordinately impressed with historic contacts. Much rivalry has circulated around the question of who was first to send greetings to the first President of the United States. Methodists have claimed first place. Nathan Bangs prefaced his printing of this greeting with an extended explanation of the date and authenticity of these documents.

The uncertain direction of the infant Methodist Episcopal Church, and also the ambiguous relation with the "mother church" is indicated by the curious approach (in letters and personal conversations) which Thomas Coke on his own made to William White in 1791, when the latter was bishop of the new Protestant Episcopal Church. For context see "Coke-White Correspondence" in Encyclopedia of World Methodism. *Although nothing came of this episode except pique in Asbury, it is symbolic of a continuing unique relationship of the two denominations both rooted so strongly in the Anglican tradition.*

The writings of James O'Kelly, which arose from his controversy with Asbury and hence with the M. E. Church, form an early corpus in the democratic side of Methodism. His fervor, which was balanced by his ineptitude, glitters in his several publications, all of which are extremely rare. One visible effect was the inclusion of explanatory notes in the Discipline of 1798, designed to prove the scriptural and traditional foundations of Methodist polity, which O'Kelly had attacked.

Book editors rarely have time to write books themselves. This was the fate of Ezekiel Cooper, second Agent of the Methodist Publishing House, who left (in voluminous manuscripts held in Garrett-Evangelical Theological Seminary) several projects in various states of incompletion. Here is a first plan for an archives and a history of the new church.

Both Wesley's and Asbury's authority were matters of debate in the early years. Ware's judgments on the notorious "removing Mr. Wesley's name from the Minutes" are fair and moderate. Watters' defense of Asbury's authority includes a strong support for the itinerant ministry and the appointive power of the bishop.

Both Watters and Snethen emphasized the key role of the local preacher, who backed up, and sometimes outdistanced, the better known circuit rider itinerant preacher, member of an Annual Conference. It may be argued that both forms of ministry are essential, neither being feasible without the other. Abel Stevens provides a typical defense of itinerant ministry, based on scriptural precedents such as Timothy and Titus as "traveling bishops."

The last three selections deal with the institution of the class meeting, which, along with bands and select societies, put into visible form the Reformation and Wesleyan doctrines of the priesthood of all believers and going on to perfection. Obviously by the middle of the nineteenth century the class meeting was in trouble. The appearance of books in its defense and official reaffirmations only reveal the extent of the trouble.

¶ Address of the Bishops of the Methodist Episcopal Church.

(Taken from *Gazette of the United States*, 6 June 1789,
reprinted in Nathan Bangs, *A History of the Methodist
Episcopal Church* (1839), I, 284-85).

To the President of the United States: –

Sir, –We, the bishops of the Methodist Episcopal Church, humbly
beg leave, in the name of our society, collectively, in these United
States, to express to you the warm feelings of our hearts, and our
sincere congratulations on your appointment to the presidentship of
these States. We are conscious, from the signal proofs you have
already given, that you are a friend of mankind; and under this
established idea, place as full confidence in your wisdom and
integrity for the preservation of those civil and religious liberties
which have been transmitted to us by the providence of God and the
glorious revolution, as we believe ought to be reposed in man.

We have received the most grateful satisfaction from the humble
and entire dependence on the great Governor of the universe which
you have repeatedly expressed, acknowledging him the source of every
blessing, and particularly of the most excellent constitution of these
States, which is at present the admiration of the world, and may in
future become its great exemplar for imitation; and hence we enjoy
a holy expectation, that you will always prove a faithful and
impartial patron of genuine, vital religion, the grand end of our
creation and present probationary existence. And we promise you our
fervent prayers to the throne of grace, that God Almighty may endue
you with all the graces and gifts of his Holy Spirit, that he may
enable you to fill up your important station to his glory, the good
of his Church, the happiness and prosperity of the United States,
and the welfare of mankind.

Signed in behalf of the Methodist Episcopal Church.

Thomas Coke,
Francis Asbury.

New-York, May 29, 1789.

To the Bishops of the Methodist Episcopal Church in
the United States of America.

Gentlemen,- I return to you individually, and through you to
your society collectively in the United States, my thanks for the
demonstrations of affection, and the expressions of joy offered in
their behalf, on my late appointment. It shall be my endeavor to
manifest the purity of my inclinations for promoting the happiness
of mankind, as well as the sincerity of my desires to contribute
whatever may be in my power toward the civil and religious liberties
of the American people. In pursuing this line of conduct, I hope,
by the assistance of divine Providence, not altogether to disappoint
the confidence which you have been pleased to repose in me.

It always affords me satisfaction when I find a concurrence of
sentiment and practice between all conscientious men, in acknowledgments of homage to the great Governor of the universe, and in
professions of support to a just civil government. After mentioning
that I trust the people of every denomination, who demean themselves
as good citizens, will have occasion to be convinced that I shall
always strive to prove a faithful and impartial patron of genuine
vital religion - I must assure you in particular, that I take in the
kindest part the promise you make of presenting your prayers at the
throne of grace for me, and that I likewise implore the divine
benediction on yourselves and your religious community.

George Washington

¶ Bishop Coke's Approach to Bishop William White on Merger.

(Taken from Drinkhouse, I, 398-400).

Right Reverend Sir, - Permit me to intrude a little upon your
time, upon a subject of great importance.

You, I believe, are conscious that I was brought up in the
Church of England, and have been ordained a presbyter of that church.
For many years I was prejudiced, even I think to bigotry, in favor
of it; but through a variety of causes and incidents, to mention
which would be tedious and useless, my mind was exceedingly biassed
on the other side of the question. In consequence of this, I am
not sure but I went further in the separation of our church in
America than Mr. Wesley, from whom I had received my commission,
did intend. He did indeed solemnly invest me, as far as he had a
right so to do, with episcopal authority, but did not intend, I
think, that our entire separation should take place. He being
pressed by our friends on this side the water for ministers to
administer the sacraments to them, (there being very few clergy
of the Church of England in the states,) went farther, I am sure
than he would have gone, if he had foreseen some events which

followed. And this I am certain of - that he is now sorry for the separation.

But what can be done for a reunion, which I wish for, and to accomplish which, Mr. Wesley, I have no doubt, would use his influence to the utmost? The affection of a very considerable number of the preachers and most of the people, is very strong toward him, notwithstanding the excessive ill usage he received from a few. My interest also is not small; and both his and mine would readily, and to the utmost, be used to accomplish that (to us) very desirable object; if a readiness were shown by the bishops of the Protestant Episcopal Church to reunite.

It is even to your church an object of great importance. We have now above 60,000 adults in our society in these states; and about 250 travelling ministers and preachers; besides a great number of local preachers, far exceeding the number of travelling preachers, and some of these local preachers are men of very considerable abilities; but if we number the Methodists as most people number the members of their church, viz., by the families which constantly attend the divine ordinances in their places of worship, they will make a larger body than you possibly conceive. The society, I believe, may be safely multiplied by five on an average, to give us our stated congregations, which will then amount to 300,000. And if the calculation, which I think some eminent writers have made, be just, that three-fifths of mankind are unadult (if I may use the expression), at any given period, it will follow that all the families, the adults, which form our congregations in these states amount to 750,000. About one-fifth of these are blacks.

The work now extends in length from Boston to the south of Georgia; and in breadth, from the Atlantic to Lake Champlain, Vermont, Albany, Redstone, Holstein, Kentucky, Cumberland, etc.

But there are many hinderances in the way. Can they be removed?

1. Our ordained ministers will not, ought not to give up their right of administering the sacraments. I do not think that the generality of them, perhaps none of them, would refuse to submit to a reordination, if other hinderances were removed out of the way. I must here observe that between 60 and 70 only, out of the 250, have been ordained presbyters, and about 60 deacons (only). The presbyters are the choicest of the whole.

2. The preachers would hardly submit to reunion if the possibility of their rising up to ordination depended upon the present bishops in America. Because, though they are all, I think I may say, zealous, pious, and very useful men, yet they are not acquainted with the learned languages. Besides they would argue,

if the present bishops would waive the article of the learned languages, yet their successors might not.

My desire of a reunion is so sincere and earnest, that these difficulties make me tremble; and yet something must be done before the death of Mr. Wesley, otherwise I shall despair of success; for though my influence among the Methodists in these States, as well as in Europe, is I doubt not increasing, yet Mr. Asbury whose influence is very capital, will not easily comply, nay, I know he will be exceedingly averse to it.

In Europe, where some steps had been taken tending to a separation, all is at an end. Mr.Wesley is a determined enemy of it, and I have lately borne an open and successful testimony against it.

Shall I be favored with a private interview with you in Philadelphia? I shall be there, God willing, on Tuesday, the 17th of May. If this be agreeable, I'll beg of you just to signify it in a note directed to me at Mr. Jacob Baker's, merchant, Market Street, Philadelphia; or if you please, by a few lines sent me by the return of the post, at Philip Rogers', Esq., in Baltimore, from yourself or Dr. Magaw; and I will wait upon you with my friend Dr. Magaw. We can then enlarge upon the subjects.

I am conscious of it that secrecy is of great importance in the present state of the business, till the minds of you, your brother bishops, and Mr. Wesley, be circumstantially known. I must, therefore, beg that these things be confined to yourself and Dr. Magaw, till I have the honor of seeing you.

Thus you see that I have made a bold venture on your honor and candor, and have opened my whole heart to you on the subject as far as the extent of a small letter will allow me. If you put equal confidence in me, you will find me candid and faithful.

I have notwithstanding been guilty of inadvertences. Very lately I found myself obliged (for the pacifying of my conscience) to write a penitential letter to the Rev. Mr. Jarrett, which gave him great satisfaction; and for the same reason I must write another to the Rev. Mr. Pettigrew.

When I was last in America I prepared and corrected a great variety of things for our magazine, indeed almost everything that was printed, except some loose hints which I had taken of one of my journeys, and which I left in my hurry with Mr. Asbury, without any correction, entreating him that no part of them might be printed which could be improper or offensive. But through great inadvertency (I suppose) he suffered some reflections on the characters of the two above mentioned gentlemen to be inserted in

the magazine, for which I am very sorry; and probably shall not rest till I have made my acknowledgements more public - though Mr. Jarrett does not desire it.

I am not sure whether I have not also offended you, sir, by accepting one of the offers made me by you and Dr. Magaw of the use of one of your churches, about six years ago, on my first visit to Philadelphia, without informing you of our plan of separation from the Church of England. If I did offend, (as I doubt I did, especially from what you said to Mr. Richard Dallam of Abingdon,) I sincerely beg yours and Dr. Magaw's pardon. I'll endeavor to amend. But, alas! I am a frail, weak creature.

I will intrude no longer at present. One thing only I will claim from your candor: that if you have no thought of improving this proposal, you will burn this letter and take no more notice of it, (for it would be a pity to have us entirely alienated from each other if we cannot unite in the manner my ardent wishes desire,) but if you will further negotiate business, I will explain my mind still more fully to you on the probabilities of success.

In the meantime permit me, with great respect, to subscribe myself, right reverend sir,   Your very humble servant in Christ,
                                                      Thomas Coke.

The Rt. Rev. Father in God, Bishop White.
     Richmond, April 24, 1791

¶   The O'Kelly Schism

(Taken from James O'Kelly, *The Author's Apology* (1798), 32-39).

                    CHAP. XIII.

The proceedings of the Committee that night; and of the Conference the day following.
I met the select number that evening, according to appointment, and found them engaged in revising our old book of discipline.
    2. My thoughts were many, but my words were few. They looked at one another, and one turned toward me, and addressed me in the following manner;
    3. Will you pass your word to abide by what this conference may do?
    4. My answer was, "You alarm me! Tell me (continued I) what you intend to do?" They answered and said, We cannot tell; but we will pass our word to abide by the decision of this conference.
    5. I utterly refused to pass my word. I then saw why they wanted me in that meeting.

6. And it came to pass on the morrow, that conference met persuant to adjournment.

7. Then arose Thomas, the president, and reported to conference the resolves of the committee, &c.

8. Moreover, Thomas continued his speech and said, "The members of this conference are the representatives of the people;

9. "And we are to all intents the legislature of the Methodist Episcopal Church: and the government is Aristocratical. You may call me a weather-cock."

10. This speech effected many minds, because they justly expected the affairs of the council to have come before them; that being the business for which they were called together.

11. Some of the members at sundry times would interrogate the president, after this manner;

12. But where is the council affairs, &c. ? That being the cause of this meeting.

13. Thomas would arise and warmly oppose, and demand silence on the subject: and silence it was.

14. In our debates if at any time we were led to speak of the conduct of Francis, he would leave the house.

15. The debates of the synod turned chiefly on episcopal dignity.

16. The Virginians, for a while did distinguish themselves in defending their ecclesiastical liberties, but they fainted in the struggle.

17. Richard Ivey, exceeded himself, he spake with tears, and in the fear of God, and much to the purpose; crying popery, etc.

18. If at any time a minister would move to abridge (in any degree) the bishop's power,

19. The defenders of that faith, would not only oppose the motion, but would charge the member with something like treason, as it were.

20. We still complained heavily of such illegal and radical alterations. Their cry was, "Every general conference is possessed of a right to form their own preliminaries."

21. Thus we see, the government is subject to perpetual innovations.

*   *   *

5. I then arose, and stood before the assembly, with the New Testament of our Lord Jesus, in my hand,

6. And spake after this manner; Brethren, hearken unto me, put away all other books, and forms, and let this be the only criterion, and "that will satisfy me."

7. I thought the ministers of Christ, would unanimously agree to such a proposal. But alas, they opposed the motion!

8. A certain member whose name was John, withstood me, and spake after this manner: The scripture is by no means a sufficient form of government.

9. "The Lord has left that business for his ministers to do, Suitable to times and places," &c. I withstood him for a season, but in vain: the motion was lost.

10. I now saw, that moderate Episcopacy was rising to its wanted and intended dignity. I discovered also, that districts had lost their suffrage.

11. I considered that the stations of the Lord's ministers rested entirely with Francis, so, that unless that absolute power could be abridged, the best of men might ever be injured, and run out of the connection.

12. I now moved again, after this manner; Let a preacher who thinks himself injured in his appointment, have an appeal to the district conference.

13. The motion was seconded, and warmly debated. William McKendre, with several more, did, with holy zeal strive with me for liberty.

14. Conference adjourned till the second day of the next week: at which time they reassumed the debate with double vigour.

15. Some professed fears, that if an appeal was allowed, it would reflect on the wisdom, and goodness of the bishop, etc.

16. Others saw, or thought they saw, that such liberty would be injurious to the church, because preachers would ever be appealing;

17. And they would take each others part; so that easy and wealthy circuits, would be crowded with preachers, while poor circuits would be left desolate.

18. Heavy reflections on the conference; had any other people said as much, it would have been thought hard persecution. Was this ignorance, or policy?

19. It was urged by several, that the bishop always appointed well, as far as they knew. I prayed them not to arrogate infalibility to the bishop:

20. For in my judgment, he made many very injudicious appointments.

*   *   *

14. A little after the going down of the sun, conference adjourned to the Dutch church, where the long dispute was finished by candle-light.

15. The debates were more powerful than ever, yet with a deal of Christian moderation. I was entirely silent.

16. Hope Hull, a worthy Elder, sounded a proper alarm! He exceeded himself by far: I could wish his words were written in a book.

17. He spake after this manner; O Heavens! Are we not Americans! Did not our fathers bleed to free their sons from the British yoke? and shall we be slaves to ecclesiastical oppression?

18. He lift up his voice, and cried, "What, no appeal for an injured brother? Are these things so? Am I in my senses?"

19. Henry arose, and displayed his political abilities, exclaiming against a balance of power; with an essay on church-history.

20. Stephen Davis, in whom was the spirit of wisdom, withstood the celebrated Henry, assuring of us, that the last arguments were badly founded. "We are far gone into POPERY!"

21. Quickly after this, the votes were taken; ah fatal hour, the motion was lost; and out of an hundred, and more, we had a small minority.

22. Some withdrew from that hour, resolving to enjoy their liberties at the expence of society: and hold fast faith, and a good conscience.

23. Will not these words cause the ears of an American to tingle. "Shall an injured man have an appeal? No!" . . . . . .

It was surely a very fatal hour of papal darkness, in which a law passed, that an injured brother and minister in the Church of Christ, should have no redress!

2. Men may make a thousand turns, yet the declaration remains a solemn truth; which gave birth to a seperation!

3. After conference adjourned, I discovered my worthy friend and loving brother Woods, standing at my side, waiting to conduct me, and my few true brethren, through the dark to his house.

4. There were we tenderly received, and refreshed. The Lord remember him in mercy; and his worthy Christian Lady, whose name is Mary: whom I dearly love in the Lord.

5. Should they, hereafter reject and dispise me, I hope forever to love and esteem them both.

6. I spent great part of that night in groans and tears! On the morrow I implored the God of heaven to give me understanding. I consulted my friends, and in the fear of God, resolved not to return to conference. "O Dort, Dort."

> (Taken from *An Address to the Christian Church*
> (179-?), 19-23).

A plan of union proposed, &c.

Should I, who talk of union, attempt to set the example, or lay down a plan; where should I begin?

2. I am acquainted with those of the Baptist order, that my soul has fellowship with; but the door into that church is water – and I cannot enter because of unbelief.

3. I am acquainted with some of the Presbyterian order, whom I love in the Lord. But before I can be a minister in that society, I must accede to, or acknowledge a book called "The Confession of Faith."

4. This I cannot do, until I can believe that God eternally decreed some angels and men to eternal life, and the rest to eternal death – and this unalterably fixed.

5. Should I propose to unite with my old family, the Methodists, to whom my attachment is greater than to any people in the world; notwithstanding their treatment to me;

6. I could not be received, unless I could subject myself to a human head, and subscribe to an oppressive, and unscriptural form of government!

7. I would propose to promote Christian union by the following method, viz: Let the Presbyterians lay aside the book called the confession of faith,

8. Which faith, is proposed to ministers before they are received; and instead thereof, present the Holy Bible to the minister who offers himself as a fellow-labourer.

9. Let him be asked if he believes that all things requisite and necessary for the church to believe and obey, are already recorded by inspired men.

10. Let the Baptists open a more charitable door, and receive to their communion those of a christian life and experience; and they themselves eat bread with their father's children.

11. Let my offended brethren, the Mothodists [sic] lay aside their book of discipline, and abide by the government laid down by the apostles - seeing those rules of faith and practice were given from above,

12. And, answer for doctrine, reproof, correction, instruction in righteousness; that the man of God may be perfect, thoroughly furnished unto all good works. II Tim. 3.16.17

13. What more does the church need, than is above inserted! Let their Episcopal dignity submit to Christ, who is the head, and only head of his church; and then we as brethren will walk together, and follow God as dear children.

14. O, how this would convince the world that we were true men, and not speculators. This would give satan an incurable wound; and make deism ashamed.

15. Again, as each church is called by a different name, suppose we dissolve those unscriptural names, and for peace sake, and for Christ's sake, call ourselves Christians? This would be - "The Christian church."

¶   Annotations in the Discipline of 1798.

(Taken from *The Doctrines and Discipline of the Methodist Episcopal Church* (1798), 5-8).

The preachers and members of our society in general, being convinced that there was a great deficiency of vital religion in the church of England in America, and being in many places destitute of the christian sacraments, as several of the clergy had forsaken their churches, requested the late Rev. John Wesley to take such measures, in his wisdom and prudence, as would afford them suitable relief in their distress.

In consequence of this, our venerable friend, who, under God, had been the father of the great revival of religion now extending

143

over the earth, by the means of the Methodists, determined to ordain ministers for America; and for this purpose, in the year 1784, sent over three regularly ordained clergy; but preferring the episcopal mode of church-government to any other, he solemnly set apart, by the imposition of his hands, and prayer, one of them, viz. Thomas Coke, Doctor of Civil Law, late of Jesus-college in the university of Oxford, and a presbyter of the church of England, for the episcopal office; and having delivered to him letters of episcopal orders, commissioned and directed him to set apart Francis Asbury, then general assistant of the Methodist society in America, for the same episcopal office, he the said Francis Asbury being first ordained deacon and elder. In consequence of which, the said Francis Asbury was solemnly set apart for the said episcopal office, by prayer and the imposition of the hands of the said Thomas Coke, other regularly ordained ministers assisting in the sacred ceremony. At which time the general conference held at Baltimore, did unanimously receive the said Thomas Coke and Francis Asbury as their bishops, being fully satisfied of the validity of their episcopal ordination.

N O T E S

It cannot be needful in this country, to vindicate the right of every christian society, to possess, within itself, all the privileges necessary or expedient for the comfort, instruction, or good government of the members thereof. The two sacraments of baptism and the Lord's supper have been allowed to be essential to the formation of a christian church, by every party and denomination in every age and country of christendom, with the exception only of a single modern society: and ordination by the imposition of hands has been allowed to be highly expedient, and has been practised as universally as the former. And these two points as above described, might, if need were, be confirmed by the Scriptures, and by the unanimous testimony of all the primitive fathers of the church for the three first centuries; and indeed, by all the able divines who have written on the subject in the different languages of the world down to the present times.

The only point which can be disputed by any sensible person, is the episcopal form which we have adopted; and this can be contested by candid men, only from their want of acquaintance with the history of the church. The most bigotted devotees to religious establishments (the clergy of the church of Rome excepted) are now ashamed to support the doctrine of the apostolic, uninterrupted succession of bishops. Dr. Hoadley, bishop of Winchester, who was, we believe, the greatest advocate for episcopacy, whom the protestant churches ever produced, has been so completely overcome by Dr. Calamy, in respect to the uninterrupted succession, that the point has been entirely given up. Nor do we recollect that any writer of the protestant churches has since attempted to defend what all the

learned world at present know to be utterly indefensible.

And yet nothing but an apostolic, uninterrupted succession can possibly confine the right of episcopacy to any particular church. The idea, that the supreme magistrate or legislature of a country, ought to be the head of the church in that nation, is a position which, we think, no one here will presume to assert. It follows, therefore, indubitably, that every church has a right to choose if it please, the episcopal plan.

The late reverend John Wesley recommended the episcopal form to his societies in America; and the general conference, which is the chief synod of our church, unanimously accepted of it. Mr. Wesley did more. He first consecrated one for the office of a bishop, that our episcopacy might descend from himself. The general conference unanimously accepted of the person so consecrated, as well as of Francis Asbury, who had for many years before exercised every branch of the episcopal office, excepting that of ordination. Now, the idea of an apostolic succession being exploded, it follows, that the Methodist church has every thing which is scriptural and essential to justify its episcopacy. Is the unanimous approbation of the chief synod of a church necessary? This it has had. Is the ready compliance of the members of the church with its decision, in this respect, necessary? This it has had, and continues to have. Is it highly expedient, that the fountain of the episcopacy should be respectable? This has been the case. The most respectable divine since the primitive ages, if not since the time of the apostles, was Mr. Wesley. His knowledge of the sciences was very extensive. He was a general scholar: and for any to call his learning in question, would be to call their own. On his death the literati of England bore testimony to his great character. And where has been the individual so useful in the spread of religion? But in this we can appeal only to the lovers of vital godliness. By his long and incessant labours he raised a multitude of societies, who looked up to him for direction: and certainly his directions in things lawful, with the full approbation of the people, were sufficient to give authenticity to what was accordingly done. He was peculiarly attached to the laws and customs of the church in the primitive times of christianity. He knew, that the primitive churches universally followed the episcopal plan: and indeed bishop Hoadley has demonstrated that the episcopal plan was universal till the time of the reformation. Mr. Wesley therefore preferred the episcopal form of church government; and God has (glory be to his name!) wonderfully blessed it amongst us.

To the observations above made, we would add, that it must be evident to every discerning reader of the epistles of St. Paul to Timothy and Titus, that Timothy, who was appointed by St. Paul, bishop of the Ephesians, and Titus, who was appointed by the same apostle, bishop of the Cretians, were bishops in the proper episcopal

145

sense, and that they were traveling bishops. The episcopal office in all its parts was invested in them. Timothy is charged (1) to be attentive to the teachers, respecting the purity of their doctrine, and to regulate every thing with due authority: "I besought thee to abide still at Ephesus, - that thou mightest charge some, that they teach no other doctrine, &c." I Tim.i.3, &c. "these things command and teach," iv.II. (2) To superintend the elders of the church: "Rebuke not an elder, but intreat him as a father," v.I. "let the elders that rule well, be counted worthy of double honour, especially they who labour in the word and doctrine," ver. 17. "against an elder receive not an accusation, but before two or three witnesses. Them that sin, rebuke before all, that others may fear," &c. ver. 19.21. (3) To lay on hands for the ministry: "Lay hands suddenly on no man," ver. 22. (4) To choose men for the preaching of the gospel: "The things that thou has heard of me among many witnesses, the same commit thou to faithful men, who shall be able to teach others also." 2 Tim. ii.2. And throughout these two epistles, St. Paul addresses himself to Timothy as one who had the chief superintendance over the private members of his church, and in all the affairs thereof. He also authorizes Titus to ordain elders (a peculiar part of the episcopal office) and to regulate every thing: "For this cause left I thee in Crete, that thou shouldest set in order the things that are wanting, and ordain elders in every city, as I had appointed thee." Titus i. 5.

Nor is it less evident, that the seven angels of the seven churches of Asia Minor (the seven stars held in the right hand of Christ) mentioned in the 2d and 3d chapters of the Revelation, possessed all the parts and requisites of the episcopal office. For our Lord would never have addressed those epistles, which so deeply concerned the interests of those churches, to single individuals, if those single individuals had not been, by the superior offices with which they were invested, proper representatives of those churches respectively. We must also observe, that each of those churches belonged to a great metropolitan city, to which many other cities, towns and villages, were considered as adjoined: so that as Titus, bishop of Crete, was required to "ordain elders and to set in order the things that were wanting, in every city" in the Isle of Crete, so the other bishops (as soon as possible) had each an extensive diocese, through which they travelled, and over which they superintended.

Nor must we omit to observe, that each diocese had a college of elders or presbyters, in which the bishop presided. So that the bishop by no means superintended his diocese in a despotic manner, but was rather the chief executor of those regulations, which were made in the college of presbyters, which answered to the convocations, synods, or conferences of all the well-organized churches in modern times.

146

But in all we have observed on this subject, we by no means intend to speak disrespectfully of the presbyterian church, or of any other: we only desire to defend our own from the unjust calumnies of its opponents.

¶ William Colbert on General Conference, 1796.

(Taken from William Colbert, "Journal," 15 Oct. 1796, manuscript in Garrett-Evangelical Theological Seminary).

Saturday 15 My colleague is changed I have Joseph Whitby instead of Thomas Sergeant. Left Philadelphia in company with five preachers-- Seelee Bunn, William Hardesty, Joseph Rowen, Joseph Whitby, and John Lackey. A Chester we fell in with Bishop Asbury and Elder Whatcoat, who invited us to dine with our good old friend, the widow Withy, after which we rode on to Wilmington. Brother Bunn and I was kindly entertained at the old widow Toppins.

Sunday 16 Bishop Asbury preached this fornoon in Wilmington from Rev. 2 ch. 1-7 verses. Elder Whatcoat exhorted: in the afternoon Seelee Bunn preached from Heb. 11 ch. 24-26 vs. At night Elisha Pelham preached from Gal. 3 ch. 1st v. and when he had done I spoke I Cor. 13 ch. 13 v. The congregation was large.

Monday 17 We picked up Jacob Colvert another preacher, and he with Seelee Bunn and my rode to the widow Stephens in Harford County Maryland.

Tuesday 18 We rode to Micheal Mather's near Abingdon where we fell in Valentine Cook, and Joseph Rowen Calver staid behind with Cook, and we rode on to Geo. Garrettsons.

Wednesday 19 We rode to Baltimore, where Joseph Rowen left us, and Seelee Bunn and I rode to Hookstown.

Thursday 20 Began the General Conference. At night Francis Poythress preached from Heb. 3d ch. 7 & 8 vs. and George Roberts (who is an excellent speaker) gave an exhortation.

Friday 21 At 1 oc Thornton Fleming preached from Rev. 20 ch. 11-15 vs. At 2 oc. the General conference met, and the Committee brought before them several thing's. That which was debated most-- was, whether the probation of the preachers should be lengthened to 4 years, or stand as it does--it was put to vote, and lost as it ought to be. So it stands as it was.

At night Freeborn Garrettson preached on Perfection from Heb. 6 ch. 1 v. Valentine Cook exhorted after him. For two nights, the exhorters have, by far been the best preachers.

147

Saturday 23 Shadrach Bostwick preached from Eph. 3 ch. 8 v. Solomon Sharp prayed after him with power. I gave a quarter of a dollar for the sight of an Elephant, which I expect I had better given to the poor. This principle business this afternoon in the General Conference was the subject of the Chartered Fund.

Sunday 25 This morning a Love feast was held, after which Doctor Coke preached, and John Dickins gave an exhortation. In the afternoon George Roberts preached a powerful sermon in the Meetinghouse in old Town from 1 Peter 4 ch. 2 and a preacher by name of Ray gave an exhortation after him. At night Doctor Coke preached in the Old Town meetinghouse from John 16 ch. 8-11 verses which was followed by a lively exhortation.

Monday 24 spent the forenoon in writing, and at 2 oc. went into the General Conference, and heard them debate on the Chartered Fund, preachs Fund, and Book Fund, which was thrown all into one. I did not attend preaching to night, but went to the Meetinghouse, and there was a great stir. I have felt better in my mind today than I have for some time past.

Tuesday 25 Spent in Conference.

Wednesday 26 Debated--how long a preacher should travel before he was to be considered ellegible to the Office of an Elder.--Some wanted it 4 years--some 3 years--some 2 years, and some 1 year--but it terminated in favour of his ellegibillity to the office of an Elder after traveling two years after he is Deacon, as a preacher travels 2 years before he is a Deacon.

Thursday 27 Doctor Cooke preached a delight sermon from Philipians 4 ch. 4 v. and John Dickins gave us a beautiful exhortation. After the service one of the preachers broke out in an extacy of joy, which affected many. I was a time of a gracious Shower for my own part I was tendered.

Friday 28 Yesterday there was much talk about another Bishop, and in the afternoon Doctor Coke made an offer of himself,--it was not determined whether they would receive him, But to day I suppose there was not a dozen out of an handred that rejected him by their votes. This gave me satisfaction. The afternoon was spent, debating whether the Local Deacons should be made elligible to the office of Elders and it went against them.

At night George Roberts preached an excellent sermon from Luke 16 ch. 31 v. and James Tollos gave an exhortation.

Saturday 29 The subject of Negro Slavery was brought forward, and more said in favour of it than I liked to hear.

<u>Sunday 30</u> This morning heard Doctor Coke preach in Light Street, from Isaiah 66 ch. 10th v. It was a time of refreshing at the Point.

<u>Monday 31</u> The debate on the subject of Slavery resumed and when put to vote, it went in favour of its standing as it had.--They who hold Slaves are to be continued in Society.

<u>Tuesday Nov. 1</u> Debated, whether we should continue in society such as distilled spiriting, and whether continue such an order of men in the Church as Presiding Elders, and when it was ended by a vote, we stand as we were. At night Richard Whatcoat preached from Col. 1 ch. 21, 22, 23 vs. his sermon was followed by an exhortation.

<u>Wednesday 2</u> Much said on the manner of trying members--whether the Members should by the church, guilty or not guilty, or that the preacher should retain or expel them according to his own judgment of the nature of their offence. When it was put to vote it stands as it was. Much was also said on the subject of marriage-The Rule stands with an adition of some explanations.

<u>Thursday 3</u> An address in the Minutes of 1795 & 6 disaproved, and the General Conference rose. I rode to my father's.

¶   Ezekiel Cooper's Plan for a History of Methodism.

(Taken from duplicated typescript published by the Baltimore Conference Methodist Historical Society (1958)).

At your [Baltimore Conference] request I submit to you a copy of my brief remarks upon a proposed plan to collect materials and documents, and to compile and publish a complete history of the Methodist Episcopal Church in America. With sentiments of great respect I am yours
          Balt. March 26 1811   Ezekiel Cooper

I. <u>Plan for collecting materials & documents.</u>
1. Let every circuit preacher collect all the information in his power from the members and other friends within his circuit, and acquaintance; particularly from the old members, local preachers, stewards, etc.
2. Let the presiding elders collect all they can within the bounds of their respective districts, from the preachers, and others; and use their influence to excite every one to contribute the knowledge they have to the stock of information.
3. Let every preacher commit to writing all the information within their knowledge of any and every part of the connection, where they have travelled, whether districts, circuits, station or otherwise.

4. Let the Bishops take a general oversight of this work, and
   press it upon the preachers and others, in every part of the
   connection, to attend to it, as a matter of importance to the
   present and future generations; and also, let the superintendants give all the information within their knowledge, and
   which they can collect, from the various sourses within their
   power.

   II. Items, on which information ought to be collected.

1. A short geographical account of the several or particular parts
   of the country, where the circuits, districts, etc. are formed.
   Vis. the latitude, longitude, and bearings of the plans, as
   nigh as can be assertained; the face of the country; level or
   mountanous; furtile or barren; bays, rivers, lakes, creeks etc.
   of note, and where and what waters they fall into untill they
   enter the ocean; the names of mountains, valleys, and other
   noted parts, and circumstances relative to places etc. and the
   connection of different mountains & waters, their courses and
   bearings etc. Through what countries, states, counties etc. they
   pass, with the discription of the bounds of states, counties etc.
   and their size, connection etc. and where and how our districts,
   circuits etc. are formed within the states, & counties etc.
   and also to what conference united, together with the bounds
   or extant of the conference, as to the states & country through
   which extended.

2. General historical sketches, of the first settlement of the
   different places, by whom, from where, in what manner etc. the
   present population, the general state of civil and social
   society, literary and religious education, their mode and manner
   of education, schools and seminaries, regulations, advantages
   etc. the manners, customs, information and occupation and
   pursuits of the people - agriculture, manufactories, progressive
   improvements from the first settlement to the time being; natural
   productions, mineral, vigitable or animal etc. Whether the
   place or places be healthy or sickly,prevalent diseases, causes
   etc. Whether the people generally are long or short lived,
   industrous habits or not, wealthy or poor, and the causes of
   prosperity or adversity as the case may be. The form of civil
   goverment, in the legislative, executive, and judiciary departments of state. Constitutional privileges and suffrages in
   elections and appointment of officers etc. whether of the
   United States or of particular states etc. Charters and orgina-
   tions of cities, boroughs etc. Account of literary, benevolent,
   humane, scientifical or religious associations - different
   denominations of christians, their doctrines, forms and modes
   of worship, discipline, ceremonies etc. honestly and plainly
   stated in candid and mild terms - together with any remarks
   whatever of a historical nature calculated to give entertainment
   or information, whether material, artificial, civil, moral, or
   religious.

3. Religious information relative to the Methodist Episcopal church – when the Methodist preachers first came to any place, such preachers names, the causes or circumstances, of an opening for them, and of their going to such places, whether by invitation, missionary enterprize, or what particular providential circumstance, the success they had, the difficulties to encounter, whether persecution, opposition, or otherwise – the religious and moral state and prejudices of the people, their views and ideas of the Methodists, the ground and causes of their prejudices, views etc. how overcome and changed in their sentiments whether from the truth and force of doctrine, the upright deportment of preachers & members, the visible good done and changes in the manners of the people, or by any other additional circumstances – when the first Methodist society was formed in any place or places among the rich, poor, or mediocrity, the progress of the work and societies, the probable benefit we have been to others, either particularly or generally, to ministers, churches or people who never joined us – the general changes of manners, sentiments etc. among the people from the time we entered among them to the time being – our number of members, and probable number of regular hearers, and of irregular hearers on particular occasions – account of special revivals, particular outpourings and manifestations of divine grace & power – how revivals were carried on, time of continuance – of quarterly, camp, and other meetings which were very remarkable – of general, and annual conferences, any circumstances of a public or private nature, among the preachers or people, of note worthy of record or history – number of local preachers, societies, preaching houses, preaching places, etc.
4. Biographical sketches of the lives, usefulness and deaths of eminently pious persons, preachers, or other members, men or women – together with all and every kind of information about religion, and other circumstances connected with the rise, progress, and affairs of the Methodist Episcopal Church in America.
5. Let every person giving information be careful to give as correct account as possible, not only of the facts, but of the dates and places of occurance; and also let them sign the statements with their names, and places of their residence.
   III. The disposition of the materials.
1. Let the whole of the documents from every part be collected and deposited with some confidential person appointed to take charge of them.
2. Let a committee of revission of three be appointed to examine, collate and arrange them, and to compare them with our discipline, minutes, and other authorities of history, geography, doctrines, etc. – to assertain as nigh as possible the correctness thereof, as the case may be.
3. Then let the whole be put into the hands of a person appointed to be the compiler and writer of the history, the said person to be

151

authorised to call the aid of the committee, appointed to collate etc. to counsell or assist him in revising and arranging; and also let him be authorised to employ at his discretion, a good amanuensis, or assistant writer, capable of a pure and correct historical style.

4. Let the superintendants and also the committee of revission, read and examine the manuscript when compiled and fully written, and compare with the documents and authorities, to see if fairly and correctly written. Let them alter nothing in the manuscript, but make their remarks, objections, and proposed alterations or additions, on paper, pointing to the pages and passages to be amended - after which, the compiler to re-examine and correct, and prepare the manuscript for the press, and superintend the printing of the same.

5. Let all the original documents be preserved in a place of safe deposit, as evidence of the authority and sourses from whence the materials were obtained, in case any dispute shall arise with respect to the truth or correctness of the history.

6. Let an account of the West Indies, upper & lower Canada, New Brunswick, and Nova Scotia, and any other part in America where Methodism is extended, be included in the work, or added, as a suppliment, and let measures be adopted to obtain information from those places.

7. I would advise, that, in a full introduction to the history, there be a concise and full relation, of Methodism in Europe, an account of the existant amity between them and all other of the Methodists every where, in doctrine and christian fellowship - of our first preachers coming from there etc. etc. etc. Also, the ground and reasons of our history being published; the plan of collecting materials, the credibility of the sourses etc. etc. etc. etc.

Yours respectfully

Ezekiel Cooper

¶ Rescinding the Rule on Wesley's Authority, 1787.

(Taken from Ware, *Sketches*, 130-31)

Mr. Wesley had been in the habit of calling his preachers together, not to legislate, but to confer. Many of them he found to be excellent counsellors, and he heard them respectfully on the weighty matters which were brought before them; but the right to decide all questions he reserved to himself. This he deemed the more excellent way; and as we had volunteered and pledged ourselves to obey, he instructed the doctor, conformably to his own usage, to put as few questions to vote as possible, saying, "If you, brother Asbury, and brother Whatcoat are agreed, it is enough." To place

the power of deciding all questions discussed, or nearly all, in the hands of the superintendents, was what could never be intro- duced among us - a fact which we thought Mr. Wesley could not but have known, had he known us as well as we ought to have been known by Dr. Coke. After all, we had none to blame so much as ourselves. In the first effusion of our zeal we had adopted a rule binding ourselves to obey Mr. Wesley; and this rule must be rescinded, or we must be content, not only to receive Mr. Whatcoat as one of our superintendents, but also, as our brethren of the British conference, with barely discussing subjects, and leaving the decision of them to two or three individuals. This was the chief cause of our rescinding the rule. All, however, did not vote to rescind it. Some thought it would be time enough to do so when our superinten- dents should claim to decide questions independently of the confer- ence, which, it was confidently believed, they never would do.

We were under many and great obligations to Mr. Wesley, and also to Dr. Coke, who had done much to serve us, and all at their own expense. As to Mr. Wesley, there were none of us disposed to accuse him of a desire to tyrannize over us, and, in consequence, to withdraw our love and confidence from him. But there was, perhaps, with some, a lack of cautiousness not to cause grief to such a father. There were also suspicions entertained by some of the preachers, and, perhaps, by Mr. Asbury himself, that, if Mr. Whatcoat were received as a superintendent, Mr.Asbury would be recalled. For this none of us were prepared.

¶   Asbury's Authority; Local Preachers

(Taken from Watters, *Short Account* (1806), 103-07, 116-19).

My dear Brother,
                    That there should be those who through prejudice, think the Methodists, since they have had Bishops amongst them, are quite a different people, is not strange. But is it not strange, that any who have known them from the beginning, should admit such a thought, 'till they have investigated the matter thoroughly? All must know that names do not alter the nature of things. We have from the beginning had one amongst us who has superintended the whole work. At first this person was solely appointed by Mr. Wesley, and called the General Assistant; at a time when there was none but European preachers on the continent. But why was the name of General Assistant, ever changed? All that will open their eyes may know why. The Methodists in England and in America, formerly did not call themselves a particular church; but a religious society in connextion with different churches, but mostly with the Episcopal church. After the revolutionary war, the Episcopal Clergy became very scarce, and in far the greatest number of our societies, we had no way of receiving the ordinances of baptism and

153

the Lords supper. It was this that led many of our preachers, as
you well know, to take upon them the administration of the
ordinances. Mr. Rankin, who was our first General Assistant, after
staying the time in this country he came for, returned home. This
was at a time when we had no intercourse with England, and Mr.
Asbury, the only old preacher that determined (in those perilous
times) to give up his parents, country, and all his natural
connections, was finally and unanimously chosen by the preachers
(assembled in conference,) our General Assistant. He continued
such, until the year 1784, when the Doctor came over, and not only
the name of General Assistant was changed to that of Superintendant,
but we formed ourselves into a separate church. This change was
proposed to us by Mr. Wesley, after we had craved his advice on
the subject; but could not take effect till adopted by us: which
was done in a deliberate, formal manner, at a conference called
for that purpose: in which there was not one dissenting voice.
Every one of any discernment, must see from Mr. Wesley's circular
letter on this occasion, as well, as from every part of our mode of
church government, that we openly and avowedly declared ourselves
Episcopalians; though the Doctor and Mr. Asbury, were called
superintendants. After a few years, the name from Superintendant
was changed to Bishop. But from first to last, the business of
General Assistant, Superintendant, or Bishop, has been the same;
only since we have become a distinct church, he has, with the
assistance of two or three elders ordained our ministers; whose
business is to preside in our conferences, and in case of an
equal division on a question, he has the casting vote; but in no
instance whatever, has he a negative, as you are told. He has
also the stationing of all the travelling preachers, under certain
limitations. Which power as it is given him by the general conference
so it can be lessened, or taken from him at any time conference sees
fit. But while he superintends the whole work he cannot interfere
with the particular charge of any of the preachers in their stations.
To see that the preachers fill their places with propriety, and to
understand the state of every station, or circuit, that he may the
better make the appointments of the preachers, is no doubt, no
small part of his duty; but he has nothing to do with receiving,
censuring, or excluding members: this belongs wholly to the
stationed preacher and members. His power I confess is great, but
let it be well observed, that it intirely respects the travelling
preachers, and none else. It never can from the nature of things,
be put into the hands of any man, but one in whom the whole have
the highest confidence, and that no longer than he faithfully
executes his trust. I know of no way the preachers can be as well
stationed, as by one that goes through the whole work, and is
without his local prejudices in favor of, or against any place: as
he seldom stays longer in one place than another. The whole body
of preachers in conference cannot station themselves, I am well
assured; and a committee chosen by them for that purpose, would
find many insurmountable difficulties: as they could have but a

very superficial knowledge of the particular gifts of many of the
preachers, or state of many of the circuits. The sacrifice that a
preacher makes in giving up his choice, and going wherever he is
appointed, is not small. But no one is worthy of the name of a
travelling preacher, that does not cheerfully go any where he can,
for the general good. If he is so circumstanced, that he cannot go
any where, and every where that is thought best, he should say so,
when he first offers himself to conference. If it so happens, after
he has been travelling, he ought to let it be known as soon as
possible; and whenever he cannot be accommodated, with a circuit
that he can fill, he ought to be contented to stop, till he can.
You will say, this is the hardships I complain of. Every station
in life has its difficulties. But this cannot be remedied in the
present state of things. It is then our duty to do the best we can,
under unavoidable difficulties. Better many individuals suffer, than
the work at large should. I would rather be in the more general
work; yet if circumstances prevent, let me be content, to act in some
humble way. As for my own part, I am so fearful of seeing the
travelling connection clogged, with the local preachers, that I
never wish a seat in conference, as a member, unless I can fill
some proper station. They can do well enough without my weak
counsel, while I withhold my labors, whether I do it willingly or
through necessity.

But a greater charge than the love of power has been brought
against Mr. Asbury; (though I believe only by a few) even that of
the love of money. I think a devil ought to blush (if it were
possible) at such a charge. Where is all that he has been heaping
up for near these forty years? I confess if this was his object,
he has stood so high in the estimation of many that he might have
accumulated considerably by this time. But is it so? Where is it?
I have been as long, and as intimately acquainted with him as most
men in America, and I must give this testimony. Of all men that I
have known he is in my estimation, the clearest of the love of
money, and the most free to give away his all, in every sense of
the word. I ask Mr. Asbury's pardon for taking this liberty in
defending a character, that speaks louder for itself than many such
witnesses can for it; but the time and place I live in, shall be my
apology for so doing.

I am as ever yours, &c.
Wm. WATTERS

To Mr. B____
  March 1806.

*   *   *

I have learned from experience that though a travelling preacher has, in most particulars, far the advantage of obtaining useful
knowledge, and of being useful, yet, not so in all things.- The

travelling preacher that comes into, and passes through a neighbourhood, and especially in a time of a revival, generally sees the best side of professors, but the local preacher who resides amongst them has an opportunity of taking into view the whole of their conduct, and from his more intimate knowledge (if a man of attention and observation), he can suit their particular cases beyond what any one can who wants such information. The same observation I have often made with regard to the irreligious. I never found myself better furnished with arguments for attacking and convincing sinners, than while in a located situation, and such as I lived in the midst of. I have heard it observed by some that their particular calling in life, so exposed them to the company of the wicked, that they could not preach to them with the same freedom as before. Hence I have made it a point never to go amongst such, without real business, and then not to stay longer than was actually necessary. I have my doubts whether this is necessarily the case in pursuing any lawful calling, and that when ever it so happens, it is owing to unfaithfulness or imprudence, or both. But should it be necessarily the case with any calling, then I would immediately quit it, though the most profitable in the world, rather than not be able to meet my bitterest enemy in the pulpit, before God and the congregation.

Although a travelling ministry is in my estimation one of the greatest blessings, with which a people can be blessed, and to be commissioned to go to the ends of the earth, to deliver the glad tidings of the gospel, salvation to saints and sinners, is the greatest honor ever conferred on mortal man; yet a local ministry has undoubtedly its use. And in the purest ages of the Church was by the Lord, joined to a travelling ministry, and though they have often been divided, yet it ought never to be the case. Hence there ought to be the greatest attention in the government of every Church, so to unite and settle these two particular spheres of action in such a manner as for neither to clog, much less destroy the other. I know of no plan adopted by any of the Reformed Churches, or any that could be adopted to equal ours. Hence we see the success that has attended it from the beginning, and need not wonder that restless, designing spirits should be so uneasy under it, for no part of our discipline as it respects our ministry, has any respect to individuals, but the general good is the object throughout. The man that commences a travelling preacher humanly speaking, makes a great sacrifice to leave all, and to have not the least hope of any greater worldly compensation, than barely food and raiment, and that only while he is able to fill his appointment. The man that acts as a local preacher, however, pressing his wants of a worldly nature may be, has no dependence on one shilling for any services amongst us; while perhaps his gifts are such that he could command his hundreds elsewhere.

These are trying circumstances, and if the preacher has any object in view but the glory of God in the salvation of souls, he hardly can stand his ground long. Hence one and another have turned their backs on us, after making the most public declarations of their attachments; and though many have rejoiced to draw off such from us, and many mourned their loss, yet I am well satisfied that this is one means of purging our ministry, both local and travelling, and as such, has had a blessed tendency to keep us of the same spirit of which we were in the beginning of the work.

I have found that a local preacher's sphere of action is much more extensive than I thought it was before I tried it. And though I much prefer that of a travelling preacher; yet I think the great thing is in either state to be instant in season, and out of season endeavouring to do all we possibly can in so good a cause, taking care not to pull down with one hand any part of what we build up with the other. This is a sore evil whenever it happens, from which good Lord deliver us all.

¶   Nicholas Snethen on Lay Preachers

(Taken from *Snethen on Lay Representation* (1835), 88-91, and *Western Repository*, I (1822), 332).

Letters to a Young Preacher, No. IV.

My Dear Young Friend,

The intervention of a wide ocean betwixt this and the then mother country, is well known to have been one of the causes which led to our independence. A similar cause led to a similar effect in respect to the Methodist society. We were too far removed from the parent stock even while the national relation existed, to reciprocate the feelings and affections of one body or family, unless some other means had been resorted to than that of occasional visits from missionaries. But though we obtained Mr. Wesley's consent to become an episcopal church, it does not appear on the face of the communications and transactions, that he anticipated all the events which actually took place. The election of Mr. Asbury by the American preachers before he would be ordained, placed him beyond the power of recall by Mr. Wesley; and the omission of the name of the latter in our minutes, gave rise to feelings of a very unpleasant nature. Dr. Coke, whose sensibilities were constitutionally too quick and powerful for his prudence, actually commenced the complaint in the pulpit, and was only restrained by the timely and resolute interference of some of the more judicious of the preachers. The circumstantial evidence is sufficiently strong to induce a belief that Mr. Asbury had an eye to his own security in making his election a previous condition of his ordination. The leaving of Mr.

157

Wesley's name out of the American minutes, resulted almost exclusively from political considerations; and we are safe in conclud-
ing that the reason why Mr. Asbury did not make a more strenuous
opposition to the measure, arose from a thorough knowledge of the
danger of the case. He had witnessed all the difficulties which the
American preachers had encountered in consequence of the public
notoriety of Mr. Wesley's early opposition to our national cause.
To revive an inveterate national prejudice so soon after the war,
would certainly have been hazardous. The prayer book and the gown
were not so quietly given up, particularly the latter, in behalf of
which a considerable struggle was maintained, and some ungracious
tempers provoked. A certain preacher being introduced to a friendly
gentleman in New Jersey, as a great advocate for the gown, his
reply was, "If I could have my will they should be all tied tail to
tail, like Sampson's foxes, and fire brands placed between them."
No habit could be more inconvenient for a horseman, and the want of
a vestry or dressing-room to the country chapels, exposed the
gown-men not only to much difficulty, but also to some ridicule.
These trappings of episcopacy were finally given up, and all the
heart-burnings that they occasioned have long since subsided. The
advocates for the prerogative, unlike their European predecessors,
had discernment sufficient to foresee that they were nowise essential
to the existence or the exercise of power, especially in this country,
and therefore judiciously yielded to the popular prejudice.

As nothing contributes so much to the development of human
character and conduct as a knowledge of the principles under which
men act, it is desirable that you should make yourself intimately
acquainted with the principles of your ministerial ancestors. I
shall not hesitate, therefore, as often as convenient, to bring
principles into review. You may recollect that lay-preachers were
considered in the English conferences, as a sort of extraordinary
missionaries, raised up and sent forth in a providential, as well
as gracious way, to provoke the regular clergy of the national
establishment to jealousy. The recorded peculiarities and varieties
of the belief of our ancestors, is to us a kind of inheritance, or
property, and not a mere deposit committed to us for safe keeping.
If we can use this property so as to make ourselves wiser than they
were, we have a right so to do. The most fastidious advocate for
primitive Methodism is found to have varied his faith in God's
designs in raising up lay-preachers and the people called Methodists,
&c.&c. We do not believe now-a-days, if a young man professes to be
called to preach, that there is any thing so very extraordinary in
the case, as was once supposed. He is sent forth without any
reference to the clergy of the church of England, or any other church,
to preach the gospel to every person who is disposed to hear him at
any hour of the day, though others may be preaching at the same time.
The primitive preachers believed that a preacher ought to have the
judicial power over all the members of the society; and this power,
they conceived, they ought to exercise over the members of an inde-

pendent church, as well as while they were members of a national church; and of the society at the same time; and their excommunications from the latter, did not affect their standing in the former. No Methodist preacher, before ordination was introduced among us, could deprive any person of the sacrament, and yet the members of the conference of 1784, all preachers as they were, did not scruple to entrust this awful power exclusively to their own hands and the hands of their successors. The cautious policy of Mr. Wesley, and his prudential movements in regard to the national church, I am not disposed to criticise; but it appears to me, that it led both him and his followers into a species of empyricism in cases where only abstract principles should have guided them. If it could have been possible for Mr. Wesley, on the supposition that he was properly addressed by the Methodists in this country, after the acknowledgment of our independence by the British government, to have replied to their request to be acknowledged by him as an independent church, that, Whereas the United States had become independent, and application had been made to him, &c.&c. he did consent that they should meet together personally or by delegates chosen by and from among themselves, and make and adopt such form and plan of church government as they in their judgment might judge both scriptural and best adapted to their local and national situation, &c.&c. And had it been possible for the American Methodists and preachers to have proceeded in this way, and have formed a system by which the legislative, executive and judicial powers of the church should so mutually balance each other, as to prevent any man or order of men in the ministry or membership, from infringing upon the rights of others, &c.&c. our condition at this time, I am inclined to think, would have been rendered much more prosperous. Now, the impossibility in this case did not arise from a want of goodness or wisdom, but from the prejudices of education, local partialities, and the habits of mind which they were calculated to engender. With a heart full of good wishes, I remain, &c.

Senex.

¶   Abel Stevens Defends Itineracy.

(Taken from *An Essay on Church Polity* (1847), 140-44).

   2. It comports with the design of the Christian ministry. Christianity was not designed to be, like Judaism, a local system, but aggressive, until it should be universal. The missionary idea should not be incidental, as it is in the systems of most modern churches - dependent on casual impulses and occasional liberality, but should be incorporated into the very constitution of the ministry - its ostensible characteristic. Such was the meaning of the divine commission, "Go ye into all the world." Such was the character of the primitive ministry during its itinerant operations. The truth broke forth on the right and on the left, till it over-

spread and outspread the Roman empire. When it pleased God to raise up Wesley, only about two or three of even incidental forms of aggressive action were to be found in the Protestant churches. He was providentially led to introduce an arrangement which should put Protestant lands themselves under a great system of missionary operations – itinerant circles of ministerial labor, which, while they conveyed the gospel to the millions of domestic heathen who had scarcely been affected by the existing localized system, should also send forth tangents of evangelic light to the millions abroad.

3. It has an inestimable influence on the ministry itself. It is an heroic training which the greatest military captains might applaud. We need not enlarge here. Any reflecting mind must perceive that such a system as the Methodist itinerancy is remarkably adapted, as a vehicle, for the enthusiastic energy which characterizes fervid and highly devotional minds, and is equally fitted to keep alive that energy. It is also well suited to preclude men of false character, for it is almost entirely a system of sacrifice. By its access to all classes, it affords an invaluable knowledge of human nature; by its constant exercise, it produces athletic frames and energetic devotedness to one work; by its frequent changes, a pilgrim spirit. . . . .

Do we assert too much when we say, that for one hundred years the Methodist ministry, though mostly uneducated, have transcended in labors, in results, and in conservative adherence to their great principles, any other body of men engaged in moral labor on the earth?

4. It distributes in turn, to most of the societies, the various talents of the ministry. This is an important consideration to those who have witnessed its operation, but it can only be alluded to here. Many men of fervid spirit and deep piety have little talent for disciplining the church. Their discourses are chiefly hortative; they are instrumental in great revivals and additions to the membership. It is obvious that such talents need a rapid distribution. The soul must not only be converted, but trained in piety. By an itinerant system such men are changed from position to position, arousing dull churches, breaking up new ground, invading and reclaiming ungodly neighborhoods. By the same system prudent men, with talents for instructing and edifying the converted masses, follow the former, gathering up and securing the fruits of their labors. Some pastors are addicted chiefly to experimental and practical preaching, others to the illustration and defense of doctrinal truth. Some are most effectual in the social services and in pastoral labors, others in the ministrations of the pulpit. Some have ability only for spiritual labors, others are skillful in managing and invigorating the fiscal resources of the church, in erecting new chapels, and promoting the benevolent enterprises of the times. Now it is clear that the frequent distribution of these various gifts, wisely adapted

160

to the local wants of the various churches, must be an extra-ordinary cause of energy and success, and such we shall by and by see has actually been its effect.

5. It produces a sentiment of unity throughout the church. In no sect is there more co-operation - more of the esprit du corps. Scarcely is a church erected, or any important measure attempted, that does not enlist the common sympathy of the body; and this results, to a great extent, from our having pastors who, by frequent changes, become individually common to us all.

6. By it one preacher can supply a plurality of societies. This is one of its capital advantages. In a sparse population, a single circuit sometimes takes in ten or twenty appointments. Methodism has thus supplied our frontier for fifty years with the gospel. The usual stationary ministries wait for the call of the people, except in their collateral missionary labors: the Methodist ministry goes forth to call the people. This is one of its strong-est points of contrast. It is the missionary church. Its adapta-tion in this respect to our own country is worthy of remark.

＊　　　＊　　　＊

7. It provides for poor churches. At least one-third of our societies do not afford a competent support; yet we supply them with preachers, and by annual or biennial changes these preachers are replaced, and the disadvantages of such places relieved, by being shared among them. By any other plan, such societies must be abandoned. Do away the itinerancy, and Methodism would at once contract, by at least one-third, its sphere of labor, and lose nine-tenths of its moral power. This, under God, is the great secret of its triumphs. Pages could be written on the subject.

8. This system has been found by experiment not only practicable, and, in connection with our classes and other means, perfectly adapted to the pastoral and other wants of our densest communities as well as the wilderness, but also the most success-ful one yet adopted by Protestant Christendom. We would not speak of it with sectarian gratulation, but in proof of our position, and in humble gratitude to the great Head of the church, who, in his mercy, has made us "a peculiar people," "which in time past were not a people, but are now the people of God."

¶ Class Meetings.

(Taken from Charles C. Keys, *The Class-Leaders Manual* (1851), 137-51).

THE DIFFICULTIES AND TRIALS CONNECTED
WITH THE OFFICE OF A LEADER.

In a world cursed by sin, and peopled with sinners, it cannot be expected that the instrumentalities employed for the diffusion of truth and godliness will meet with no resistance, or that those who are personally engaged in this work will encounter no difficulties. "The carnal mind is enmity against God," and so far as it may be permitted to have sway, will oppose itself to the progress of his cause. And a thousand other hindrances - where no fixed and determined opposition to the principles of true religion exists, but connected in the manner of cause and effect, with a world in ruins - will be found to arise in the prosecution of any benevolent or evangelical enterprise.

Occupying, as he does, an elevated and prominent position in the Church of God, the class-leader will not be able to discharge his responsibilities without his share of trial and difficulty. It will be well, therefore, for him to prepare his mind for these things, to be ready for the storm when it may arise, and thus be strengthened to resist the influences which may be made to bear against him.

1. In the first place, you will, without doubt, feel the importance of your position, and perhaps be oppressed with the weight of your responsibilities. Much is expected from you, and many eyes are gazing upon you. "A city set upon a hill cannot be hid." Many wait for your halting, and are ready to detect the smallest deviation from duty or consistency, and to rejoice in the occasion you may give for their reproach and mockery. You are a mark to be shot against. And the honour of Christ is more concerned in your fidelity, than in that of the ordinary professor. Everything depends upon the uniformity with which you maintain your Christian character, and perform the duties of your office. It is not to be wondered at, therefore, if you sometimes tremble in view of your situation, and are tempted to think that you want the qualifications which are necessary to your office. Your feelings may vary at different times; you may not always be equally fervid and happy, or you may not at all times meet with the same amount of success in your ministrations and labours, and, discouraged by any positive failure, or unfavourable change, you may be inclined to relinquish your charge. But I advise you not to indulge in these feelings. You have been providentially called to take part in the pastoral work; you stand approved of your minister, as well as of your brethren; and, until there is an intimation from the proper

source that your services are no longer required, it should generally be considered as your duty to maintain your post, and to acquit yourself in that post, as well as you may be able. Always bear in mind your dependence, and forget not your privilege at the throne of grace. "If any man lack wisdom, let him ask of God, who giveth to all men liberally, and upbraideth not; and it shall be given him," (James i,5.) If you would serve the cause of Christ, and if you would not deteriorate in personal piety, and endanger your personal salvation, neglect not "the gift that is in thee," and the work to which you have been called by the Church.

2. Like the minister of Christ, you will often be tempted to sadness and discouragement, previous to those ministrations in which, from time to time, you are engaged.

*   *   *

3. It may also be suggested, that you are disappointing the expectations of those by whom you have been appointed; that you are not fulfilling the designs of your office; and that you should, therefore, make way for a more competent person, by vacating your position.

But surely these thoughts are gratuitous. You must suppose the preacher in charge, from whom you received your appointment, to have acted in good conscience, when he invited you to share in his labours and responsibilities as a pastor of the flock, and it is hardly becoming in you to question his good judgment in continuing you in office. The presumption is, that the opinion of others concerning you is more favourable than that which you have formed concerning yourself, and that your exercises in this respect constitute only a very common form in which temptation is presented to the minds of those who are engaged in any good work. And as to making room for others, there is no lack of opportunity to those who are seeking it to do good. The labourers in the vineyard of the Lord are not so numerous as that we can well spare any well-intentioned, though comparatively weak and inefficient, person, who is willing to do what he can in cultivating Emmanuel's grounds. "When he saw the multitudes, he was moved with compassion on them, because they fainted, and were scattered abroad, as sheep having no shepherd. Then saith he unto his disciples, The harvest truly is plenteous, but the labourers are few." (Matt. ix, 36,37.)

*   *   *

4. You may be tempted on the ground of worldly interest. Properly to discharge your duties will take considerable time, and that time must, in part, though not ordinarily, be subtracted from the hours of business. You may not have so good an opportunity to make money, as those

163

"who spend the day, and share the night"

in the worship of mammon, and the accumulation of gold. But what
are the great purposes of life, and what is the nature of the warfare upon which you have entered? "Is not the life more than meat,
and the body than raiment?" "Man shall not live by bread alone."
"What shall I eat, and what shall I drink, and wherewithal shall I
be clothed?" are not the inquiries that should be permitted to
engross the mind, and to corrode the heart. "Having food and
raiment," therefore, "let us be therewith content." Ours is a
holier and more honourable vocation. You are justly expected, in
some measure, to participate in the self-denial of those who "leave
all to follow Christ," and to preach the gospel.

*   *   *

5. You will find your difficulties, too, in the character of
those who are under your care.

Some, on account of their inexperience, will be easily led
away, and disappoint the sanguine hopes you have cherished concerning them. Some, on account of their ignorance and want of culture,
will be exceedingly slow to receive your instructions, and others
again, of a higher grade of intellect, will be inflated with views
of their self-sufficiency, and will fail to manifest that spirit of
docility which you have a right to expect from them. Perhaps, instead
of being "swift to hear, slow to speak, slow to wrath," they are
directly the opposite; - "contentious," and indisposed to "obey the
truth." They may have permitted prejudice to sour their minds
against you, they may be unreasonable and obstinate in their
opinions, and at the same time inconsistent in their moral conduct.
They receive, perhaps, the reproofs you administer, in a manner that
does not correspond with your charitable intentions, and take
offence at the close scrutiny you find it necessary to institute into
their experience and general character. You will sometimes find
uncharitableness and disagreement among themselves. Instead of going
on to perfection, they may show their "need" of learning "which be
the first principles of the oracles of God," and be "such as have
need of milk, and not of strong meat." Or, you may be tried with
their irregular attendance. Sometimes they are at class, and sometimes not. Sometimes there in good season, and then again not
coming until you are half way through. Perhaps they are exceedingly
inconstant. At one time very zealous, and seeming to give promise of
great piety and eminent usefulness, and soon after reflecting dishonour upon the Church, and wounding its friends by the folly and
impropriety of their conduct, and making you to feel that your labour
has been in vain in the Lord. Or you may be tried by their penurious-
ness. You are expected to see that the various class collections
are attended to, and in your efforts to obtain subscriptions, find
some of your members falling far behind the mark, which their

circumstances would justify you in expecting them to approach. Perhaps the more affluent members, as it too often happens, give no more (if as much) than the poor ones. As a consequence, the amount you raise is smaller than what is expected from you, and you may be called to bear the opprobrium which justly belongs to others. Now as you "have no greater joy" than when your members "walk in the truth," and give evidence of spiritual prosperity, so all these things, evincing their spiritual delinquency, are a source of pious grief and pain. Here is, perhaps, your severest trial. But remember, all God's servants have their trials. And those who are most diligent and faithful, are sometimes tried with greater severity than those who are exercised by no anxiety as to the final result of their labours. The most fervent, the most prayerful, the most laborious, and the most useful ministers of Christ, are sometimes called to pass through deep waters, and like their divine Master, are made to groan in spirit over the multiplied ills which crush a world that they aim to save, and render the work in which they are engaged more difficult and stupendous. Cheer yourself, then, by the company you keep, while a source of higher consolation is found in that grace, which is "sufficient for thee," and which will never fail thee. Expect these trials, and prepare to meet them in that spirit which is authorized by the unfailing promises of God, "Be strong in the Lord, and in the power of his might."

6. But after doing your best, you are sometimes found fault with, and this occasions you sorrow.

"But," says the apostle, "he that judgeth me is the Lord." To your own master you stand or fall. There always will be captious and complaining persons in the Church. And frequently those who do the least, complain the most. Now, I know not that you have anything to do with the careless and casual observations which may be made concerning the manner in which you discharge the duties of your office. One thing is certain; you are not accountable to such persons. They have no authority over you. It will be time enough for you to be troubled on this account, when a suggestion is made by your minister that you have committed an error, or when, through other friendly counsel, you have intimated that there is room for improvement. But even in this case, if you have a proper view of the matter, you will perceive that nothing more is required than that you should avail yourself of such suggestions, so as to make yourself more useful and available to the Church. Farther than this, you are not required to heed the rumours and suggestions which float upon the wings of the wind, and which, in many cases, pass away with the breath which gave them currency. Stand then to your post. Pursue the even tenor of your way, through evil report and through good report; and so discharge your duty as ever to have impressed upon your mind, that you are to give account to God, and not to man. With an eye single to his glory, and the good of his cause, do your utmost in the station which you occupy, without respect to "the

honour" or good opinion "which cometh from man." Thus in the day of
his coming you may say, -

> "I have fought my way through;
> I have finish'd the work thou didst give me to do!"

And then from your Lord you'll receive the glad word, -

> "Well and faithfully done!
> Enter into my joy, and sit down on my throne."

¶   John Miley on Class Meetings.

(Taken from *A Treatise on Class Meetings* (1851), 31-43).

Class meetings form an important part of Methodist economy;
especially of what is peculiar to that economy. In their requirements and provisions, in their duties and privileges, they pertain
alike to every member, and address themselves directly to the
Christian experience and character of all. The custom of weekly
meetings, for purposes of personal, Christian intercourse, where
the subject of communion is religious experience and deportment,
and where all the exercises of communion, of exhortation, and
encouragement are characterized by that plainness and candor which
earnest religious interest and mutual confidence inspire, must
produce a strong and benign influence upon all properly engaged in
these exercises.

The principle of Christian association being common, more or
less, to the various branches of the Church, can not be claimed as
a peculiarity of Methodism. The degree to which Methodism adopts
it, and the mode through which she avails herself of it, form its
peculiarity to her. She avails herself of the principle specially
through her class meetings; and here it is done to an extraordinary
degree; and there is hereby supplied to our societies that of which
there is a great lack in many others.

It seems to us plain that the social principle in religion, as
it obtains in various branches of the Church, is far below what it
should be - that it fails, in a great measure, to secure that
intimacy of Christian communion which accords with our relation to
each other as the children of God, and which has often been exemplified in the history of the Church. As Christians, we sustain
an intimate and endeared relation to each other. It is more than
that existing between members of the same community or commonwealth;
it is that sustained to each other by members of the same family.
"Fellow-citizens with the saints" we are; but we are more; we are
members, in common, "of the household of God." We are alike the
children of God and brethren in Christ; and we are,therefore, exhort-

166

ed to cultivate that unity and communion and to cherish toward each other those brotherly affections which are proper to this intimacy of relationship.

This intimacy of fellowship in Christ, this ardor and kindness of brotherly affection, have often been exemplified in the history of the Church. "Then they that feared the Lord spake often one to another." Here is an instance among the godly of the Jewish Church. The details are not given; yet, from the general statement, and from the circumstances of the times, we are warranted in the belief of an intimate, brotherly association among these people of God. Witness the meetings of the disciples, where Christ came and stood in their midst. Here are evidences of the same brotherly communion and love. Thus, too, when the day of Pentecost was fully come, the disciples were all together, with one accord, in one place; and, after the addition of three thousand upon the day of Pentecost, the same heavenly fellowship was kept up.   .   .   .

The early history of the Christian Church furnishes many other instances of like fellowship.   They are also furnished at different times through the whole progress of the Church. They were particularly revived under Mr. Wesley. Intimate association was highly characteristic of his earlier religious meetings. It was a great leading measure in that wonderful reformation so gloriously wrought out through his instrumentality. He found that, by an intimate association of those who were awakened and turned to the Lord, the work of reformation was far more permanent, efficient, and successful. Such is the account Mr. Wesley has furnished us himself. Those who were awakened to the importance of religion, particularly sought his instruction and direction; and he says, "I asked, 'Which of you desire this? Let me know your names, and places of abode.' They did so; but I soon found they were too many for me to talk with severally so often as they wanted it. So I told them, 'If you will all of you come together every Thursday, in the evening, I will gladly spend some time with you in prayer, and give you the best advice I can.'

"Thus arose, without any previous design on either side, what was afterward called a society."   .   .   .   .

Here was the measure, and here were the benefits of an intimate Christian association.

There surely is great danger of falling far below this measure of Christian association. Often the tone of piety and the external circumstances of the Church are both unfavorable to it. It is only an earnest tone of religion, and an ardent state of Christian affections, that will lead us to seek such association. As experimental religion declines, and the intensity of the religious affections abates, the children of God will find themselves drawn away

from each other; they will so far lose even their relish for "the communion of saints." This is a truth that accords with much personal experience, and is supported by the most extended observation upon Christian denominations. Then, whenever Christian experience, earnestness, and enjoyment decline, and the religious affections lose their fervency, the true social principle, in religion, is in danger; it must so far be weakened, and fail of its preserving and sustaining efficiency, and of its abundant good fruits. Here, then, upon these grounds, there is great danger to the principle of true Christian association. It is sadly in accordance with Christian experience, and with the history of the various Churches, that there is ever a tendency to fall below - far below - the true standard of Christian experience and enjoyment, brotherly kindness and love. And the liability to this is only the greater, in the absence of some efficient measure of Christian communion , which may serve to cultivate and develop our religious experience, and our brotherly love and care for each other. And in this the Churches generally are greatly deficient.

But we apprehend the greater danger now, to the true principle of Christian association, from the state of the Church in relation to society or the world. There have been many periods in the history of the Church, when the pressure of circumstances from without brought Christians close together in intimate communion, and earnest concern and sympathy for each other.   .   .   .

Such has been, almost constantly, the condition of the Church. But is not that condition now much changed? The numbers of the Church are greatly increased. Her social position and influence are elevated and enlarged. The Church has greatly influenced the society without her pale; and that society, in its turn, tends greatly to influence her. Thus there is a mutual approximation. The consequences are these: Christians are drawn away to mingle more freely in the society of the world; and, by so much, they are drawn away from an intimate association with each other. All this is very plain, and needs no further illustration. Here, then, is the great danger, at present, to the true principle of Christian association. It arises from the present position of the Church in relation to society or the world.   .   .   .

As stated above, the measure provided in our branch of the Church, in order to secure these great objects, is specially the institution of class meetings. This measure has great advantages; it has the elements of peculiar adaptation and efficiency. The meetings of our classes are stated and regular. The duty of attendance extends alike to all. The subjects of communion are religious experience and deportment. Here plainly is true Christian association. And thus the principles of religious experience, and the strength of Christian affections, are promoted, which, in turn, strengthen and sustain it. And some such measure - some provision

of similar adaptation and results, seems to us indispensable to the
higher spirituality and piety, the higher prosperity and welfare of
every branch of the Church.   .   .   .

We have dwelt thus long upon this subject, because we wished
to develop somewhat this great fundamental, living principle of
Christian association upon which class meetings are instituted.
We wished, also, to indicate, with some clearness, how fully and
how efficiently this principle was embraced in our class meetings.
The fuller consideration of this point will, however, remain as the
subject of a future section of this treatise. We know of no measure,
in any branch of the Church, that so fully and efficiently embraces
and employs this indispensable principle as our class meetings.
The principle of intimate Christian association is necessary to
every well-ordered Church government. Without it there can not be
a high development of spirituality and moral force; there can not
be great permanence, progress, or prosperity. And it is to the
adoption of this principle, to so great an extent, and in so
appropriate and efficient a mode, as in her class meetings, that
Methodism owes much of her vigor and growth, much of her
spirituality and power, and, consequently, much of her efficiency
in doing good. Class meetings should, therefore, be dear to all
the friends of Methodism, and should receive the hearty approval
and support of all in her communion.

¶   A Southern View of Class Meetings at General Conference.

(Taken from *The Methodist Quarterly Review* ‾_South_‾ , XII (1858),
510-15, 526-29).

In regard to the subject referred to your committee, no one of
the memorialists to General Conference seems for a moment to
question the practical utility and superior excellence of the
institution of Class-Meetings. On the contrary, all admit this
most readily, and express great desire that the meetings should be
continued 'as a prudential means of grace;' but ask that they be
put in the same category with prayer-meetings and love-feasts;
and that it be left entirely optional with the membership whether
they attend them or not. In other words, they ask that Answers
1st and 2d to Question 1st, of chapter iv., section iii., in the
Discipline, p. 122, be either entirely stricken out, or so modified
as to remove all penalty whatever for non-attendance, and let the
Church action be altogether advisory, and not mandatory in its
character, as at present. For this the memorialists urge various
reasons, some of which it may be proper briefly to notice. First,
they contend the Church has no express Scripture warrant for the
institution of Class-Meetings, and in the absence of such warrant
has no right to make attendance upon them a condition of membership. .   .   .

But what are the facts in the case? Why, first, it can easily be proved from the Scriptures that it devolves on the Church to adopt such regulations as will secure communion and fellowship among the members one with another. This some branches of the Church have done in one way, and some in another. We have chosen to do so by means of Class-Meetings; and who will pretend to say this is not as efficient and every way as successful a means for the accomplishment of the proposed end as any ever used? The Scriptures having enjoined the end, and left it for the Church to adopt means for the attainment of that end, and these means, after a trial of many years, proving highly efficient and successful, we very properly, we think, infer their scriptural authority.   .   .   .

Again, the Scriptures enjoin whatever tends directly to the improvement of personal piety; the cultivation and perpetuation of unity in the Church; the strengthening of Christian fellowship; and the increase of Christian sympathy and affection; all of which is done by Class-Meetings, as the experience of thousands can testify; hence again we argue their scriptural authority.   .   .   .

The assertion of the memorialists, that thousands are kept out of our Church because of the rule on this subject, is simply a question of fact, and can be settled by facts only. Until the facts shall be produced, your committee must be allowed to entertain a different opinion, especially as the memorialists elsewhere assert the rule is obsolete, and we are unable to understand how an obsolete rule could work such sad results.   .   .   .

To the minds of your committee, in view of the fact that Class-Meetings, together with the rule now complained of, have been part and parcel of Methodistic policy from the organization of the Methodist Episcopal Church to the present hour, and when properly attended to and judiciously managed, have always worked well; and of the further fact, that their decline has oftener been the fault of the preachers rather than of the people, it is plain that we now need a mild, prudent, and faithful observance, rather than an abrogation of the rule. We, therefore, recommend that this Conference take such measures as will secure a more faithful and uniform observance of our rules as they are, particularly in regard to the proper division of societies into classes, and the change of leaders, as contemplated by the Discipline, and that the attention of the Annual Conferences severally may be called to this subject, and the course of their members strictly inquired into; and may induce local preachers also to give greater attention to the matter of meeting the classes at their several appointments; and make it the business of all the preachers, travelling and local, to meet the classes at all the regular preaching-places where societies have been or may be formed. We are satisfied the united and well-directed efforts and example of all the preachers on this subject, would not fail in the end to recover whatever we may have lost in regard to

the acceptableness and usefulness of the Class-Meeting institution.

Finally, although your committee do not say, or intend to intimate, that the ends proposed by Class-Meetings may not be attained by some other means, they do say that, in their judgment, no other means they have known to be used, have reached those ends so readily or so efficiently. And they further give it as their opinion, that at this particular time there are many and strong reasons why the Church should hold to her distinctive peculiarities, both as to doctrines and discipline, with zealous and watchful care.

Entertaining these views, the committee cannot, therefore, agree with the memorialists, nor recommend that their prayer be granted; but submit the following:

"Resolved, That the prayer of the memorialists, asking the rule making it the duty of the members of our Church to attend Class-Meetings be stricken from the Discipline, be not granted.

"Resolved, That the Annual Conferences severally be and hereby are instructed to inquire dilligently into the conduct of their members on this subject, and hold them to a strict accountability to the existing rules and regulations of the Church.

"Resolved, That inasmuch as Class-Meetings are frequently neglected under the plea of attending preaching in the bounds of the different societies, the local preachers be and hereby are urged either to hold Class-Meetings, or make arrangements for them to be held by the leaders, at all their appointments, wherever such may be at all practicable."

*   *   *

The following substitute for the resolutions of Drs. Smith and Rosser was offered by A. M. Shipp and N. Talley, and adopted by the Conference:

"Whereas, no official information has been laid before this General Conference of any general dissatisfaction with the institution of Class-Meetings as now established in our Church; and whereas, nevertheless, statements have been made by several delegates to the effect that said meetings have been neglected in many portions of the Church; therefore,

"Resolved, That the College of Bishops be requested to give the institution of Class-Meetings a prominent place in the proposed Pastoral Address to the Methodist Episcopal Church, South, and to give such advice and counsel on this general subject as in their godly judgment the circumstances of the case may demand; and also, to keep the institution prominently before the Annual Conferences, by inquiring carefully how far it is fostered, and attendance upon it enforced."

171

In accordance with this request, the Bishops, in their Pastoral Address, use the following strong and unambiguous language:

"If Class-Meeting be, as we believe, a good institution, important to the spirituality of the Church, we cannot, we ought not to revoke our laws upon the subject, and, by making a stand once upon it, voluntarily commit ourselves to the absurdity of saying or admitting that, with all its advantages as a means of grace, those who neglect are as acceptable and praiseworthy as those who observe it. While, therefore, we have been memorialized by a few, (and we are glad to say a very few of our people,) for some modification of this and other peculiarities of our economy, for the reasons just given, and others that might be added, we have inaugurated no important changes in our book of Discipline."

On the whole, we are not sorry that the subject was brought before the General Conference. Its discussion in that body developed a strong regard to this institution of the Church. Even those who wished to cancel the test-law spoke in as high terms of the Class-Meeting itself as those who contended for its perpetuation. If the test-law were not in the Discipline, there would, perhaps, be no great necessity to put it there; as we do not want any to enforce attendance on the Lord's Supper, family prayer, fasting, and other duties recognized in the Bible and the General Rules. But as it is there, were we now to expunge it, it might be thought that we have seen cause to modify our opinion concerning the importance and scriptural character of the institution itself. We are satisfied that a candid and thorough examination of the Class-Meeting system would result in a confirmation of the views set forth by the Conference, and endorsed by the Bishops, in regard to the value of this feature of our economy.

*   *   *

The following course seems to be agreeable to the spirit and principles of the gospel. 1. Let the delinquent be tenderly but faithfully admonished by his leader. 2. Let the pastor visit him to ascertain his reasons for non-attendance, to remove his objections, to bring him to a sense of his duty, and to stir him up to its discharge. 3. Let these visits be repeated, if possible, and at sufficient intervals to allow of thought, reflection, and determination, as some minds are slow in their operation, and this is a case in which considerable latitude may be allowed. 4. After several weeks or months have elapsed, according to circumstances, let the delinquent be summoned before the church of which he is a member, or a select number of its members, to show why he does not attend his class. In nine cases out of ten, after the steps we have specified have been taken, the delinquent will not appear before the society or the committee. In that event the act of excommication on the part of the Church is but little more than a ratification of the delinquent's own act. But if he should appear, he may be able

to show, to the satisfaction of the society or committee, that some cause other than contumacy, or a want of proper regard to the institutions of the Church, occasions his neglect, and then, of course, his standing in the Church is not affected thereby. If, however, he can show no such cause, and will make no promise of amendment, the Church would be as derelict as he, were it not to disown an individual so impracticable and insubordinate. But even in that case - so sacredly are the rights of membership guarded by the Church - the delinquent has the right of appeal from this decision to a superior court. If the decision be affirmed by the court of appeals, we cannot see why it ought not to be final. Surely he must have strange notions of personal rights, and ecclesiastical prerogatives, who can suppose that the former have been invaded, and the latter extended beyond the limitation of Scripture and reason, when a delinquent member has been disowned by such a process as this. For our own part, we are not yet prepared to pull down all the fences, and turn the "field which the Lord hath blessed" into a common.

7. WESTWARD MOVEMENT AND CAMP MEETINGS

Digging into the diaries and journals of the circuit riders provides not only data and understanding on the involvement of Methodism in the Westward Movement, but also evidence of the educational level of the participants. Many of them were admirably self-educated, like Asbury; but the paucity of formal training shows up in grammar and style. What these preachers learned, they learned the hard way.

Hence one notes a contrast between the journals of John Smith, rough-hewn circuit rider of the Greenbriar, and Oxford-educated Thomas Coke. Both, however, testify to the challenges and difficulties of frontier ministry. The same may be said of the records of Richard Whatcoat and John Kobler. Somewhat more formal and polished are the autobiographies which benefited from publication, such as those of James B. Finley and Alfred Brunson. These later offer colorful portraits of ministerial life, the one in Ohio and the other in Illinois and Wisconsin. Brunson's especially is comparable to the better known life of Peter Cartwright, which for that reason is not included in this collection. Materials illustrative of the share of Methodism in the Westward Movement are abundant. Only a sampling is undertaken here. A comprehensive collection already in print is William Warren Sweet, Religion on the American Frontier, Vol. IV: The Methodists (1946).

All three groups--Methodists, United Brethren, and Evangelicals-- shared the heady experience of frontier revivalism and camp meetings. Henry Boehm bridges the first two, since he came from a UB background into Methodism. John Dreisbach represents the Evangelical Association. In a broader context the camp meeting phenomenon belongs to the world view of Romanticism. This is amply illustrated in the account by A. P. Mead in Manna in the Wilderness. *Here is camp meeting as romantic primitivism, nostalgia for the good old days when Annual Conferences were occasions for revivals and plenteous conversions and when every church member was supposed to be able to recall the turning point of his life. The comments of Washington Irving indicate that he was vastly intrigued by these camp meeting Methodists, but was able to keep them at a safe distance.*

¶   Early Travels on Appalachian Frontier.

(Taken from Lawrence F. Sherwood, Jr., ed. *The Journal of John Smith,* (Oct. 1966), 12-41. Original is in G-ETS).

A Journal for the year of Our Lord 1787 -

Began the 4th Day of July which I Spent in Baltemore with the two followg. had some comfort in company with Revd. Mr. Watcoat, and Others, Dureing my stay. O My god enable me to Spend the remnant of my days to thy glory. give me thy perfect Love for Christ's sake Amen.

Friday 6th. Rode about 6 Mile out of town Preached & met society at Wm. Perego's found som comfort in waiting before ye Lord

Sat. 7 Rode 16 Miles on my way to my circuit. Lodged at Bror. Jones's in company with Jesse Lee - - - - -and on the Sabbath Rode with him to his Preaching place the stone Chappl. gave an Exortation and assisted in the Love-feast-

In the evening I Preached at Zoar Chap. but was somewhat indisposed-

Mon. 9th. We Rode to Randal's where was a few souls met we both spoke A little and return'd to Brother Jones's

Tuesd. we parted Lord grant that we may meet in thy King-dom Above -

Wed 11th. (July 11, 1787) Set of in company with Mr. Watcoat traveled and preached together For several Days I was weak in body and but little appetite for food, but the Lord was often Very precious in manefesting his presence to my soul.

Sat. 14 Met with Mr. Asbury and heard him Preach 3 times on Sunday once in Hagartown twice about two Miles from town -

Mon 16 Set off and got a Bath and Staid there two or three Day I often Drank out of the Springs and found Some benefit therefrom -

Thury. 19th. Let Bath in company with Mr. Asbury Rode to Wiggin's the people were gather'd for Worship the spirit I trust was in the word

Frid 20 We rode to Old town I was still very weak and feble and low in Spirit -

Sun. 22st Heard Mr. Asbury Preach and receiv'd the supper
of the Lord from his hand I also gave an Exortation the
Lord was present and we fed on Angel's food.

Mon 23 Rode 40 Mile up the South branch of Potomack A fine
levil road hedg'd in on either Side by Mountains Some places
the Rocks towing Aloft Over Our heads near 200 feet high O
how wonderfull is the works of the Lord - Rode thro' A
couple of little Villages Rumney & Morefield Lodg'd at Bror.
Vanmeters in company with Br. Todd and some Others -
Tues 24th. Rode 20 Miles Up the Sout fork of the Branch to
Cobern were A few souls met together to make prayer I gave an
Exortation Our souls Drank at the fountain head and bursting
Joys split and I believe the heavenly Quire took the chorus
and the city rang With loud Hosanahs -

Wed. 25 Rode 20 Miles Fed at Hick's Lodg'd at a little
cabbin in the Mountain where lived a couple of Old
Decipels and a little boy was kindly entertain'd with such
things as the place could afford. Was a happy as if I'd
been in A fine castle feasting on the Richest dainteys -

Thurs 26 Rode 40 Miles left the sout fork and got on the
cow pastures Bated at A Dutchmans one Posley Hovers Din'd
upon the provision I along with me Lodg'd at Matthias
Benson's the Old Man and Woman were very hospitible they
were baptist decipels but of A catholic spirit -

Frid. 27 Rode Forty Miles to day Over Mountains and Rocks.
Killed a Rattle Snake for the first Fed at the warm
Springs and took A Drink of the Water much stronger and
Warmer than the waters at Bath. Called at the Hot Springs
the water so warm that by Bathing in it causes great sweats.
by putting my hand in the water at first it seem'd like
scalding and I believe that water made as worm Over the
fire would Scawld. I had rather Drink it than the Warm
spring water. Lodg'd at Morris's A man that was A
methodist in Ireland but I fear he has Out liv'd the power
of religion but was very kind and hospitible -

Sat 28 Travil'd 40 Miles Fed on the road and eat such things
as I had with me called at the Red Springs and took A drink
of the Water it tasting so much like Tarter I could hardly
bear it. -

In the evening I call'd at the Sweet Spring where I drank
freely it being of a Soft Sweet nature. Seem'd Something
more Agreeable than the Red Springs it being near Night
and no place for A Methodist Preaching to lodge at I set
out into the Wilderness to seek lodging after riding 5 or

176

6 miles I got to an house where an Old Dutchman lived
It being dark I ask'd for lodging, but he had not consider'd
the Apostel's Exortation (viz) be not forgetfull to
entertain Strangers therefore I was Oblieg'd to Seek
farther and After riding A Mile I got to an House where
lived the Man his Wife & nine children Were Siting round
the fire I call'd for Lodging which was readily granted.
I suped on A little Joney cake and Milk Went to prayer with
them found my Soul Very Happy and drawn out after God

I lay down to Rest on Some Straw laid on boards being weary
and Fatieug'd I Slep tolerable well. Arose in the morning
and commended them to God it being Sunday the 29 I rode 7
or 8 Miles to the Sinks of Greenbrier. Where the Rehoboth
Society met together and I trust the Lord was present with
us and gave us to feed on Angels food.

Mun. 30 Met the Children God was present and I believe
reach'd many of their hearts I trust it will be A memorable
day to many that were present. O God raise up the riseing
generation as A seed to Shew forth thy praise Lodg'd at
Edward Kenans Tribulation Flees

Tues 31 Preach'd at Rehobath Church the Lord was present
and many felt the power of his word all I want is to do the
will of God my soul is happy but not full Lord give me an
intire conformety to thy will -

Lodg'd at Alexander Hosicks Tribulation Flees

August Wed 1st. (1787) Rode over the Mountain to Pott's Creek
Call'd at the Sweet Springs. A place of wickedness Drank
freely of the water was Somewhat Poorly -

Lodg'd at Mitchel Porterson Pott's Creek met with Bror.
Doddridge was much indispos'd by reason of A Violent pain
in my head -

Thurs 2 Preach'd at Daniel Prentices found Some liberty to
declare the counsel of God to poor sinners. Lodg'd in a
Cabin at the Red Springs -

Fry 3 Preach'd at the Sweet Springs where was a number of
Souls Assembled in order to git the benefit of the Waters
I invited them to come to Christ and be made Whole I hope
some will be perswaded to come to the Living Waters that
flows So freely for every soul Lodg'd at P. Cinders -

Sat 4 Preach'd there at 11 O'Clock Shew'd them that the
Righteous is more Exelent than his Neighbour...at 3 O'Clock

Preach'd at Scarbrow's and met Society there was A Shaking
amongst the dry bones and while I was talking to the Children
the People were all in A flood of tears I hope they'll never
forgit the advice given

Sun 5 was at Rehobath Church Many were Assembled together
and I reasoned with them on Righteousness Temperance and
Judgment to come felix I believe trembled and I'm in hopes
Some of them will no longer put of there futer concern
Lodg'd at Garret Greens an Old Dutch friends –

Some when I Preach'd hear last were so affected that for
some day they were expected to die and glory to God there
Sickness was Unto death for it termenated in their conversion –

¶   Dr. Coke as Frontiersman.

(Taken from Thomas Coke, *Extracts of the Journals* (1793),
105–06, 147).

A great part of the way we had nothing in the houses of the
Planters but bacon and eggs, and Indian corn bread. Mr. Asbury
brought with him tea and sugar, without which we should have been
badly off indeed. In several places we were obliged to lie on the
floor, which indeed I regarded not, though my bones were a little
sore in the morning. The Preachers in Europe know but little, in the
present state of Methodism, of the trials of two thirds of the
Preachers on this Continent. And yet in what I believe to be a
proper view of things, the people in this country enjoy greater
plenty and abundance of the mere necessaries of life, than those of
any country I ever knew, perhaps any country in the world. For I
have not in my three visits to this Continent, in all of which I
have rode about 5,600 miles, either met with, or heard of, any
white men, women or children, that have not had as much bacon, Indian
corn, and fuel for fire, as they wanted, and an abundance to spare:
nor are they badly off for clothing.

The great revival, however, and the great rapidity of the work
of God, the peculiar consolations of God's Spirit which he has
favoured me with, and the retirement I met with in these vast
Forests, far overbalanced every trial. Many other circumstances
also amply compensated for the disagreeable part of my journey.
Sometimes a most noble Vista of half a mile or a mile in length,
would open between the lofty Pines. Sometimes the tender fawns
and hinds would suddenly appear, and, on seeing or hearing us,
would glance through the woods, and vanish away. Frequently indeed
we were obliged to lodge in houses built with round logs, and open
to every blast of wind, and sometimes were under the necessity of
sleeping three in a bed. Often we rode sixteen or eighteen miles

without seeing a house, or human creature but ourselves, and often were obliged to ford very deep and dangerous rivers, or creeks (as they are here called.) Many times we ate nothing from seven in the morning till six in the evening; tho' sometimes we carried refreshments with us, and partook of our temperate repast on stumps of trees in the woods near some spring or stream of water.

*   *   *

March 9th. I have again entered into my romantic way of life. For there is something exceedingly pleasing in preaching daily to large congregations in immense forests. O what pains the people take to hear the gospel! But it is worthy of all pains. 11th. I am now come among the Peach trees: and they are in full bloom. Truly they assist a little, under the Supreme Source of Happiness, to make the heart gay.

It is one of my most delicate entertainments, to embrace every opportunity of ingulphing myself (if I may so express it) in the Woods. I seem then to be detached from every thing but the quiet vegetable Creation, and MY GOD. The Ticks indeed, which are innumerable, are a little troublesome: they burrow in the flesh, and raise pimples, which sometimes are quite alarming, and look like the effects of a very disagreeable disorder. But they are nothing when opposed to my affection for my Lord. Yea

> I'll carve thy passion on the bark:
>   And every wounded Tree
> Shall drop, and bear some mystic mark
>   That Jesus died for me.
> The Swains shall wonder, when they read
>   Inscrib'd on all the Grove,
> That Heaven itself came down and bled
>   To win a mortal's Love.

¶   Another English Itinerant.

(Taken from *The Original Journal of Richard Whatcoat*, Manuscript bound in three volumes, Garrett-Evangelical Theological Seminary; I, 1 Jan. 1791).

Some remarks on the year 1790, in the former part of it I Traveled with Bishop Asbury, through the Lower parts of Virginia, North and South Carroline, Georgia, and Holston. May the Seventh we Took the Wilderness for Coontuckey, and arived Safe at Wm Magwiens Near Matson Courthouse the tenth; Conference began at Rich. Mastersons near Lexington Courthouse, the fourteenth, we had a

179

Blessed Time, the power of the Lord was present to heal maney Souls
etc. Bishop Asbery and I preachd thirteen Sermons, besids
exhortations etc etc. we Traveled about a 106 miles through
Cantuck Settlement. the 24th we Marcht from the Crab Orchard through
the wilderness, and arived at Capt. Emes at the Head of Grapey
Valley the 27; preachd at General Rupels the 30th and Began
Conference at Georg McHights June the 3; the Lord was powerfuly
present to Wound and heal; we Rode to petersburg Virginia, Began
our Conference the 14th. after which we Rode through Greebryer to
Redstone; Began our Conference at Beesentown the 28th of July.
Crost Loral hill the 2d of Augt. We stopt two Nights at Baltimore,
and arived at philadelphia the 20th of august. I supose we
Traveled about four thousand Miles in 8 Months. Our Travels by
Day and Night, over Mountains and Rivers, and allmost impracticable
Roads, beside the want of proper Refreshment, and the Danger of the
Savage hands, was Niether easy, Nor pleasing to the flesh; But
Seeing the Gospel spred the Travel of the Redeemer Coming home and
the Divine Consolations flowing in to my own Soul Makes the Cross
Seem Light and the Burthen easy.

¶   John Kobler's Journal.

(Taken from Maxwell P. Gaddis (1855) 504-11. Original in
Lovely Lane Museum, Baltimore).

     Lord's day, August 12, 1798. - Preached in Dayton, a little
village by that name on the bank of the Big Miami river, and just
below its junction with Mad river. Here are a few log houses and
eight or ten families residing. Here I saw some tokens for good;
the people seem to receive the word preached with all readiness of
mind; indeed, several in the little company were much affected.
When divine service was over I saw an Indian standing in the yard
reading. I expect he was the fruit of the Moravian missionaries
toward the north, as his book was in the German language, and he of
the Shawnee tribe. As he could speak a little English, I asked him
if he knew for what intent we had met together, and what we had
been doing. He said, 'To worship the Great Spirit and to do good.'
I asked him if he knew that Christ died for sinners. 'O , yes,'
said he, 'I know that Jesus came a little baby into the world, and
that he died upon the cross to save us from our sins, and bring us
to heaven at last.'

     In this neighborhood there are six or eight Methodists settled,
and among them there is a local preacher by the name of Hamer. I
think he came down from the Redstone country; is from forty to
forty-five years of age. Last year he raised a class of the few
scattered Methodists here, and for awhile met them as leader. I
visited each of them severally, as far as possible, examined into
the state of their souls, and found some of them filled with

prejudice. I held a second public meeting among them, and read the rules of the society; laid before them the great necessity of Christian union in Church membership, and invited all those of them who could fellowship each other to come forward and join in class. So we organized a regular class of eight members, of whom brother Hamer was appointed leader.

It is impossible for a person of intelligence to explore this region of country, and not be deeply impressed with a forcible conviction of its future prosperity. Nature appears to have united all her advantages of land and water to pour forth, at a future day, immense treasure into the hands of the rising generation. The lands are a beautiful level, and as fertile soil as heart could wish. The rivers abound with clear, fresh, wholesome running water, affording every convenience for hydraulic power, and sufficiently navigable to carry down all the produce of the country and tradesmen to a good market.

Monday, August 13, - Rode down the Big Miami river twelve miles, and preached in an old fortress to a small company, consisting chiefly of the few families that lived in the fort. On inquiry I found that this fortress was on the frontier, and no settlement around or near them. The inhabitants of this country are poverty-stricken in the extreme. The sustenance for man and horse can scarcely be obtained through the parts of the country which I have passed. However, they set before me the principal dish I have subsisted on since forming this circuit - a dish of boiled corn, in its soft state of which I gladly partook with a joyful heart. Rode on several miles to a little village called Franklin, where I was kindly entertained by a gentleman whom they called Captain Ross. His companion was indeed a fine-disposed lady, who spared no pains to render my situation agreeable. I preached in his house by candle-light to the inhabitants of the place, which consisted of six or eight families. I was much taken with the appearance and seriousness of this company, several of whom appeared to hear for their souls, and felt deeply, as was manifest by their tears.

*   *   *

Tuesday, August 14. - I rode down the Miami thirty-six miles to explore the country. I found the settlement very sparse, only now and then a white family. About four o'clock, P.M., I came to an old garrison called Fort Washington, situated on the bank of the Big river. It bore the appearance of a declining, time-stricken place. Here are a few log buildings beside the fortress, and a few families residing, together with a small printing-office, just put into operation, and a small store, opened by a man of the name of Snodgrass. This, I was told, was the great place of old for the rendezvous of the Federal troops, when going to war with the Indians. Here, alas! General St. Clair made his last encampment with his

181

troops before he met his lamentable defeat. Here I wanted to preach very much, but could find no opening or reception whatever. I left the garrison to pursue my enterprise, with the full intention of visiting it again, and making another effort with them on my next round; but this I was not permitted to do.

August 19. - I preached at a brother M'Cormick's, eleven miles from where Cincinnati now stands, to a considerable company of attentive hearers.

Thursday, August 24, - Visited a new settlement called Sycamore, and preached at the house of a man by the name of Dusky, from these words: 'The Son of man is come to seek and save that which was lost.' The following day I preached at a Mr. Ramsey's on faith and love, and the day following at Mr. Vinyard's. Next morning rode twenty miles to Beaver creek, and preached at Johun's. The next day I pushed on to the Mad river settlement, and reached brother Sink's weary and faint. Here I met with one of Baron Swedenborg's disciples. He appeared to be a man of good natural sense, but his mind, alas! as to religion and spirituality, is as visionary as that of Mohammed himself. He moved from Philadelphia. Here I saw a grist-mill in operation grinding corn. The dam across the creek was constructed and built entirely by the beavers, where lay a tree twelve inches in diameter, the stump of which I measured with my own hands, which they had cut down with their teeth. The limbs of the tree were cut off in the same manner, and all wrought up in the dam in the best possible manner. If this is not reason, it is certainly verging very near to it.

August 26. - Preached in Dayton, on Sabbath, to all the people which town and country could afford, who were but few at best. My diary, before me, states that the word preached, at this time and place, was brought to bear upon the company with a powerful, quickening influence. All present appeared to be struck under conviction, and some made the inquiry, 'What must I do to be saved?' Some followed me to the house where I staid, and expressed an increasing desire to be wholly devoted to God. The success of the Gospel on this missionary field is no longer a problem.

I was at this time a very sick man. Started from Dayton down to my appointment at Hold's station, twelve miles; reached the place; the people were collected; was not able to preach. Under present circumstances I was at a loss to know what course to pursue. To travel and preach was impossible, and to lie sick at any of the houses in these parts would be choosing death, as it is next to impossible for a well man to get food or sustenance, much more for one prostrate on a bed of sickness. Next morning started to brother M'Cormick's, about fifty miles distant, as the only place where I could stay with any degree of comfort. I rode this day twenty-five miles under circumstances trying to feeble nature. I had taken no

sustenance in the morning and could reach no house. When my fever became high I had recourse to the ground for a bed for about two hours. I then rode on to the house of a Mr. Harlan, who received me kindly.

January 1, 1799. - Preached in Dayton to a mixed company of traders from Detroit, some Indians, French, and English. Knowing that they all had immortal souls to be saved, I took for my text, 'In every nation he that feareth God and worketh righteousness is accepted of him.' I lifted up my voice like a trumpet, cried aloud, and spared not; laid before them the corruptions of their wicked hearts, and the fearful consequences of a life of sin, in such pressing terms that many of them looked wild, and stood aghast, as if they would take to their heels. After preaching I met the class, and found them in a prosperous state, walking in the fear of the Lord.

January 2. - On Monday expounded the 126th Psalm at Hold's station, with considerable success.

March 25. - Preached at Ramsey's, and again at night met the society. As there were no candles to be had for night-reading and study, necessity invented the following plan: Take clarified beeswax, and, while in a warm state, roll it out in the shape of a tube, one end of which is rolled into a coil, which answers for the candlestick. In daytime we had recourse to the woods to study and read the Bible.

April 2. - Preached in Dayton, for the last time, to all that town and country round about could afford, which were not many. Subject of discourse was Esau selling his birthright. I improved the subject by showing that every soul living has a spiritual birthright by virtue of the death and merits of our Lord Jesus Christ; that by improving it as the Gospel directs, we become heirs of God and joint-heirs with Christ to an eternal inheritance; yet this bequest may be sold, and is often sold, for a mere sinful trifle, which never fails to meet the Divine displeasure here and hereafter. I then met the class, read the rules, and pressed on the society the various duties devolving upon them as Church members; to attend class meeting, and follow peace with all men, and walk in love one with another.   .   .   .

Next morning on my way, I called to see a young man that was reported to be dying. I found him lying on some scraps of rags, apparently breathing his last. He cried to God, with uplifted hands, to save his body from death, and his soul from ruin! Preached at Hold's station and at Franklin at night. In time of the first prayer a company of fifteen Indians came to the door. When we rose up from prayer the old chief fixed his eye on me, and pushed through the company to give me his hand. He was strung out with jewels in

his ears, nose and breast. When the service was over the chief gave me his hand, and they all retired in good order."

¶   James B. Finley in Ohio, 1810 ff.

(Taken from *Autobiography* (1855), 193, 194, 223, 285-86, 295).

It seemed to me that I was about to leave the world and part from all my relatives, and wife, and little daughter forever. After prayer I rose, embraced them all, mounted my horse, and started. After riding some distance, I came to a point where the road diverged, and desiring to take a last look at the loved ones behind, I turned and saw them weeping. It was a severe struggle with nature, but grace proved triumphant, and I journeyed on.

Several days' travel brought me to Zanesville, [Ohio] the principal appointment on my circuit. When I arrived in town it was raining hard. In lieu of an overcoat, to protect me from the storm, I had procured a blanket, and cutting a hole in the middle of it, I thrust my head through it and found it a good protection. Riding up to the door of one of the principal Methodists of the place, I asked for lodgings, informing the brother that the conference had sent me there as the preacher. Eyeing me closely from head to foot, he replied, "You look like any thing else than a preacher." I told him he should not judge too rashly, as he might, perhaps, think better of me on a closer examination, and I suggested the propriety, at least, of his giving me a fair trial. To this he assented, and I tarried with him. The next day being Sabbath, I preached, in the morning, in the log court-house, and, after leading the class, rode six miles to brother Joseph's, where I preached again in the afternoon and met class.   .   .   .

I entered upon this work with great fear and trembling. No where, in all the round, could I find a place for my family to live, and hence I was driven to the necessity of building a cabin, which I located on the Leatherwood fork of Wills creek, fourteen miles west of Barnesville. After getting it ready for occupancy, I wrote to my father, requesting him to bring my family, and after a separation of four months we had the pleasure of meeting again. We took possession of our humble cabin, twelve by fourteen feet, which proved sufficiently capacious, as we had nothing but a bed and some wearing apparel. My funds being all exhausted, I sold the boots off my feet to purchase provisions with; and after making all the preparation that I could to render my family comfortable, started out again upon my circuit, to be absent four weeks.   .   .   .

At the conference which was held November 1, 1810, I was appointed to Knox circuit. This circuit was taken from Fairfield circuit at the conference held in Cincinnati on the thirtieth of September,

184

1809, and, of course, this was the second year of its existence.
Though a large circuit, still it was not so large as Wills Creek.
It commenced at the mouth of Licking opposite Zanesville, and
embraced all the settlements on that stream up to Newark; thence
up the south fork of Licking to Holmes's, and on to Granville,
extending as far as Raccoontown, now Johnstown; thence on the north
fork to Robinson's mill and Lee's, on to Mount Vernon and Mitchell
Young's; thence down Owl creek to Sapp's and John's, and down to the
mouth of Whitewoman; thence down the Muskingum, including the
Wapatomica country, to the place of beginning. It took four full
weeks to travel around this circuit. It was well supplied with
local help, there being eight local preachers living within its
bounds, as follows: James Smith, John Green, _____Rapp, Joseph
Pigman, James Fleming, Joseph Tharp, _____Parks, and _____Pumphrey.
Six of these were from Virginia, and the other two from Monongahela.
At that time they were all pious men, and devoted zealously to their
Master's cause.

                    *   *   *

At the conference all the Bishops were present - M'Kendree,
Roberts and George. Bishop Asbury had ceased his labors, and followed his beloved Coke to heaven. It was an interesting session to
both preachers and people. One day a messenger came to me and informed me that Bishop M'Kendree wished to see me at his room. I
went accordingly, and when I arrived he said, "I am going to put
you in charge of the Ohio district." I told him candidly I
thought he might make a much better selection; and, besides, I was
entirely too young in the ministry for such a post. "Well," said
he, "you must go and learn. You are not too young to learn."
Accordingly, when the appointments were read out, my name stood in
connection with the Ohio district. I felt exceedingly depressed, and
groaned under the load; but I resolved, God being my helper, to enter
the field and do the best I possibly could under the circumstances.
My district embraced eight circuits, extending from the mouth of
Captina, on the Ohio river, to the lake at the mouth of Huron, including the state of Ohio, all the Western Reserve, all western
Pennsylvania, from the Ohio, and Alleghanies, and western New York,
as far down as Silver creek, below Fredonia. On this field of labor
were ten traveling preachers and a membership of four thousand and
fifty. My first round of quarterly meetings commenced October 19th
and 20th, at Leesburg, on Tuscarawas circuit. The next was on
Beaver circuit, at the Falls of Big Beaver, on the 26th and 27th;
Grand River and Mahoning, at Hartford, Western Reserve, on November
2d and 3d; Erie circuit, at Oil creek, on the Alleghany river, in
western Pennsylvania, November 9th and 10th; Chatauque circuit at
Broken Straw, November 16th and 17th; Shenango circuit, at Jackman's
meeting-house, four miles below Pittsburg, November 23d and 24th;
Steubenville circuit, at Long's meeting-house, November 30th and
December 1st; West Wheeling, December 7th and 8th, at Andrew Scott's,

near Wheeling. The most of these quarterly meetings were seasons
of great interest, and attended with Divine manifestations. It was
customary, in consequence of the newness of the country and the
sparseness of the population, to hold prayer meetings at different
places, on Saturday night of the quarterly meeting. These meetings
were attended with great good, and when they would all meet in love-
feast in the morning, and speak of the blessings received at
different places where the meetings were held, it would kindle the
spirit of piety; and I have no doubt if this practice had been
continued it would have resulted in vastly more good to the Church
than the preaching of Saturday night. A custom prevailed at these
meetings which was strange to me. No one was called on to pray.
The leader would say, "If any of you feel like taking up the cross
and delivering your mind, do so." Sometimes three or four would
commence at once. This was altogether upon the voluntary principle.
The practice was carried into the public meetings, and if any one
male or female felt inspired, no matter who was preaching, they
would rise and deliver their impressions.

*   *   *

At this meeting we were assisted by that veteran pioneer preacher, Dr. Shadrach Bostwick, who had for fourteen years labored in the
itinerant field. He entered the traveling connection in 1791, and
traveled successively the following circuits: Milford, Talbott,
Bethel, Flanders, Elizabethtown, Cambridge, Saratoga, and New
London. He then traveled as presiding elder four years on Pittsfield
district. In 1803 he was sent as a missionary to the Western
Reserve, and formed a circuit called Deerfield. During his second
year on this circuit, he married and located. He studied medicine,
and after he had mastered the science entered upon the practice.
During all the time he continued to preach, as circumstances would
admit. He was a most amiable man, and had a lovely family, beloved
and respected by all. Such was his piety, and uniform consistency
of character, that he won the affection and esteem of all. His
letters breathe an ardent spirit of piety. I have several, which I
shall keep as precious mementoes of affection. As David and
Jonathan, we were one in life, and I trust in death we shall not be
divided.

¶   Brunson on Michigan Circuit.

(Taken from Alfred Brunson, *A Western Pioneer* (1872), I, 267-68).

The circuit, at that time, extended to all the white settlements
in the Territory, except the one at St. Mary's outlet of Lake
Superior, which was, perhaps, hardly white. From Detroit we went
north to Pontiac, then but a small village. From thence we went
down the Upper Huron, now the Clinton River, to Mount Clemens, and

thence down Lake St. Clair and river to Detroit; from thence again to the River Rouse, and up that stream some seven miles to the upper settlement; thence back to the river and lake road leading to Monroe, on the River Raisin; up that nine miles, mostly on an Indian trail, to the upper settlement, and back by the same path to the lake road, and on to the Maumee at the foot of the rapids; and thence right back on the lake road fifty-eight miles, to Detroit. It required four weeks to get round, though we had but twelve appointments.

We arranged a plan so as to preach every Sabbath in the old council-house in the city, and once in two weeks at the other places. To aid in our support a subscription paper was circulated in Detroit, on which some $200 were pledged, but only $100 was actually paid.

¶   Camp Meeting at Annual Conference.

(Taken from Henry Boehm, *Reminiscences* (1865), 206-07).

The conference met on October 1 at Liberty Hill, Tenn., at Rev. Green Hill's. He was a local preacher, had emigrated from North Carolina, where Bishop Asbury had been well acquainted with him.

A conference was held at his house in North Carolina as early as 1785, and Dr. Coke and Asbury were both there. Another conference was held there in 1792, at which Bishop Asbury presided. He and his family emigrated to Tennessee when all was a wilderness, and they had to make their way through a cane-brake to the place where their house was located. Liberty Hill was twelve miles west of Nashville, and Nashville was then but a very small village. This was the first conference I attended with Bishop Asbury as his aid, and all I saw and heard were full of interest.

It was the first conference William M'Kendree attended as bishop. I saw him when he filled the episcopal chair for the first time, and so I did Bishop Whatcoat. M'Kendree had left Baltimore at the close of the General Conference and gone West by the most direct route. He was one of the fathers of the Western Conference, where his influence was unbounded. The preachers gave the new bishop as well as the old one a hearty welcome.

There was a camp-meeting connected with the conference, and the preachers ate and slept in their tents. There were eighty ministers present, and there had been an increase of twenty-five hundred members during the year. It was a most pleasant conference, and the discussions were interesting.

There were noble men belonging to the conference: Learner

Blackman, William Burke, John Sale, Jacob Young, and James Ward.
These were the presiding elders, and they were on districts that
were large enough for conferences. There were present also Jesse
Walker, the pioneer of Missouri. He was a young man then, only six
years in the ministry. Samuel Parker, the Cicero of the West. He
was a deacon. Peter Cartwright, young, strong, courageous; but he
had not graduated to elders' orders. Twelve were admitted on trial,
six ordained deacons, and ten elders, among whom was the eccentric
James Axley.

The names of the districts now appear strange: Ohio District,
John Sale, Presiding Elder; Kentucky District, William Burke;
Mississippi District, Jacob Young.

¶   Another at Rushville, Ohio, 1812.

(Taken from James B. Finley, *Autobiography* (1855), 252-53).

This year a camp meeting was held at the Rushville camp-ground.
At this meeting we were blessed with the presence of both of our
beloved Superintendents - Asbury and M'Kendree. A row was raised,
on Saturday, by about twenty lewd fellows of the baser sort, who came
upon the ground intoxicated, and had vowed they would break up the
meeting. One of the preachers went to the leader for the purpose
of getting him to leave, but this only enraged him, and he struck
the preacher a violent blow on the face and knocked him down. Here
the conflict began. The members saw that they must either defend
themselves or allow the ruffians to beat them and insult their wives
and daughters. It did not take them long to decide. They very soon
placed themselves in an attitude of defense. Brother Birkhammer, an
exceedingly stout man, seized their bully leader, who had struck the
preacher, and with one thrust of his brawny arm crushed him down
between two benches. The aiddecamp of the bully ran to his relief,
but it was to meet the same fate; for no sooner did he come in reach
of the Methodist than, with crushing force, he felt himself ground
on the back of his comrade, in distress. Here they were held in
durance vile till the sheriff and his posse came and took possession,
and binding them, with ten others, they were carried before a justice,
who fined them heavily for the misdemeanor.

As soon as quiet was restored, Bishop Asbury occupied the pulpit.
After singing and prayer, he rose and said he would give the rowdies
some advice. "You must remember that all our brothers in the Church
are not yet sanctified, and I advise you to let them alone; for if
you get them angry and the devil should get in them, they are the
strongest and hardest men to fight and conquer in the world. I
advise you, if you do not like them, to go home and let them alone."

The work of the Lord commenced at this point, and meetings were

kept up without intermission till Tuesday morning. Upward of one hundred were converted to God and joined the Church. Many more gave in their names, and they were handed over to the leaders, to be presented to the next preacher who should come upon the circuit. At the close of the camp meeting we left for conference, which was held in Chilicothe, October 17, 1812.

¶   Evangelical Association Camp Meeting, 1816.

(Taken from John Dreisbach, "Day Book," typescript of manuscript, 18-20).

Mon., May 27, 1816. We travelled to David Beier's, where the announced tent meeting is to be held.

Tue., May 28, 1816. I helped the friends yesterday and today in making preparation for the meeting.

Wed., May 29, 1816. By light I preached on the last petition in the Lord's prayer, Matt. 6:13 for the opening of the services. I had no special victory in speaking, yet the audience and especially the believers were attentive and interested when I laid emphasis on prayer. There were two conversions and shoutings among the believers. The weather was very cold for this time of year and almost too fresh to be living in tents, which I believe was also a hindrance to the meetings.

Thur., May 30, 1816. At 9 o'clock brother Erb preached from Eph. 4:15 and J. Schilling exhorted with power. I, too, exhorted and invited the penitent sinners forward and several of them were heavy burdened with their sins. I had faith, and a number were saved and this morning before the meeting two souls were saved. Praise God for his work. This forenoon, many people were touched and almost overcome by the power of God. I feel wholly comforted in God and encouraged in his work. O praise the Lord for his favor. At 2 p.m. J. Frueh preached from Psalm 50:14, which was quite weak, when Thomas followed exhorting in blessing with good results. By light, A. Ettinger preached from Isa. 55:7 and several brethren exhorted. A goodly number of souls were converted during this day.

Fri., May 31, 1816. At 9 o'clock D. Thomas preached from John 8:36 with conviction and power and brother Schmitt of Kestenburg exhorted. At 2 p.m. I preached with grace and power. And I think it was not in vain as I spoke from Heb. 12:14, 15. I pointed out: 1. To make peace with God for himself, and with others also, which must not be neglected. 2. Holiness of life and service. 3. The fruitage of holiness. We then held our quarterly conference with blessing with 33 members present. Four or five souls were saved after the service, and I believe many have found holiness

189

power. The ungodly wicked crowd pulled one seeking soul away, but it returned and was converted. At night, J. Kleinfelter preached from Eph. 5:1. J. Dehoff exhorted and Erb also in closing. There were no results during the public service, but after it closed there were a number of conversions for which we thank God.

Sat., June 1, 1816. Early in the morning, we observed the Lord's Supper in blessing, following which 10 persons were baptised. We also had a profitable hour in a testimony meeting. Praise God. In the afternoon, brother J. Dehoff preached from Heb. 2:3. He preached with unction, plain, and with good effect. By candle light, it was for A. Hersch to preach, but there arose a rain storm, so that we held a prayer meeting instead, having a successful meeting. Praise God.

Sun., June 2, 1816. At 9 o'clock I preached with favor from Mark 16:15. I had much freedom and grace in preaching, and the audience was very attentive and interested, though there was no movement. At 2 o'clock brother Abraham Hersch preached from Eph. 1:13, 14. He was followed by the aged John Walter preaching from Rom. 8:18. He spoke well and with inspiration yet with bodily weakness. During the sermon, the ungodly pulled a newly converted woman out of the service and kept her in a shut up room until she escaped and ran back again into the meeting. Brother Shilling in German in the evening, from ISa. 3:10, 11 and brother Frueh spoke in the English language from Acts 17:30. After midnight the wicked and ungodly endeavored to storm in upon us as a mob with clubs and stones and asked the leaders to come out, or they would storm the camp. With God's power, loud shoutings, prayer and song we drove them back several times. And as they came again, we caught the foreman, a large black negro. I tripped him and he fell to the floor when we tied him with cords. And the other three we put under guard. The believers were strengthened and took courage. Praise God, for the others of the mob took their flight. We watched until day and early sent for the Justice of Peace, Ensmonger.

Mon., June 3, 1816. At 10 o'clock brother Erb preached from I John 3:8. I only heard him in closing for I had to appear in the court in Manheim against the rioters who disturbed our meeting last night, who were put under the power of the law to keep the peace. It was threatening to rain, and I gave a brief exhortation in closing and we said farewell of the camp ground with blessings and victory. As near as we could determine, there were 24 souls saved who confessed the forgiveness of their sins. Praise God! At eventide we came to Henry Eby's. In the group were A. Ettinger, D. Thomas, J. Kleinfelter and I.

¶ A Romanticized Camp Meeting.

(Taken from A. P. Mead, *Manna in the Wilderness* (1860), 402-03, 407-13).

The bell has rung, and the few who slept are called to greet the rising sun. It is a happy morning! A happy morning to many who had no hope in Christ as the sun went down last night, but the day star has arisen in their hearts, and the Sun of Righteousness shines on their rejoicing souls. May the light they have never go out! What a victory was achieved last night! Victory belongs to the saints of the Most High. Many happy countenances greet you as you pass around the ground. The soldier rejoices after the enemy is routed or taken.

"What a glorious night was that!" says a brother in allusion to the many conversions of last evening.

"Yes, and I trust its fruits will last with you and me."

"God grant it; but if we could only have another day!"

"Perhaps it is better to retire from the field with banners flying! We will want to come again. This is but a commencement. We should carry our zeal home; it is needed there."

"You have it; we should go home with the spirit of labor. The work is yet to be done."

As the above conversation concludes, we hear the voice of singing and prayer. Many are performing their morning devotions. A company at the left of the stand are singing

"There will be no more sorrow there."

Men in groups are talking, and we will pass around near the tents to greet familiar faces, and catch a word that shall indicate the spiritual pulse. It is strong and regular, depend on it! Some are taking breakfast. O Lord, give them bread from heaven!

*   *   *

Bow down in prayer for the divine blessing! Prayer should sanctify every parting here, for praise will celebrate our greeting in the skies. Dr. Peck prays. How humble and simple his acknowledgements at a throne of grace! The order of the meeting, the conversion of souls, the quickening of believers, the sanctification of the Church, all made themes of thanksgiving. He prays that we may go home to toil for the Lord; to live our religion in sunshine and storm. Hear his

191

FAREWELL ADDRESS!!

"I shall say but little. I am gratified with the order that has been observed upon the ground. Our worship has not been disturbed. The people, generally, have acted with becoming propriety. My heart is encouraged, and I must approve the course of the brethren. You have been prudent in your conduct; but the best of all is, God has been with us. I think just as a brother said when it rained:*"The work began right; it began in the hearts of believers."*

Some came here partially backslidden from God, and they have been brought to experience anew the work of grace in their hearts. They are now in favor with God. May they go away better men, and better women, than when they came. Some have experienced perfect love - *sanctification*. This sanctification is the joy of my heart, and has been for many years. This salvation from sin is the sanctification taught in the Bible. It was the joy, and theme, and power, of Wesley. It has gladdened my heart, that you have experienced this blessing, and that you have borne testimony to it. I hope you will continue in this grace. Let your light shine. Take the blessing to your homes, and retain its power, and exhibit its fruit there.

A word to young converts! You are young in experience, and you may expect trials in professing what the Saviour has done for you. The report has gone before you, that you have been converted at this camp meeting. Don't be alarmed. Put yourselves under the watch-care of the Church as soon as possible. Choose the people of God for your associates. Settle it in your mind that you will never backslide. Calculate on living religion at all times and at all hazards. Let it be said, when God shall open the books and read the account of this meeting, "This one and that one was born there." Turn neither to the right nor the left; go straight from this camp ground to heaven.

Brethren, take care of these lambs of the flock. They need nursing; they are in a wicked world. Watch over them, and help them in the way to heaven. Young converts and all, especially you who have experienced the blessing of sanctification, go home to scatter the hallowed fire; go to labor for God and souls, and to die happy!

Awakened sinner! A word to you. You feel your need of salvation; go home to seek it (if you do not obtain it before reaching home). Go call on your pious neighbors, and ask them to pray for you. Go to the house of God, and hear the word of life preached, and may God bring you into his everlasting kingdom. O, that great results may follow this meeting! Carry the fire with you, my brethren; and may we see through the whole year, yea,

and in all time to come, a flaming revival of religion.

We are about to part! (Here the speaker's voice grew
tremulous with emotion, and tears started from many eyes.) These
separations are painful: we may never meet again! We must part, -
we cannot remain here! This is only the means of grace; it is a
help that we use, and pass on. We must leave this hallowed place
to go into active service, to live and labor and die for God. We
will march around the ground; and the ministers, on arriving in
front of the stand, will pause, and we will take the parting hand:
I like this old-fashioned mode of saying farewell."

The procession forms, headed by Dr. Peck, Presiding Elder of
the District, and Rev. Wm. Wyatt, Presiding Elder of Honesdale
District; Brothers Gorham, Van Valkenberg, and Schoonmaker follow
next, to lead the singing. Nearly a score of ministers fall into
line immediately, and the procession begins to move on, singing,

"We are homeward bound."

The procession starts from the right of the stand, and passes
on within the inner circle of tents. We call it circle, though, as
the Revelator said of heaven, "it lieth four square, and the length an
and the breadth thereof are equal." At such a time, how the mind
links the past, the present, and the future! We are marching to
the music of Zion! We are in the grove! The winds are still; and
on each tree and leaf the sun shines a silent "God bless you!"
We are as soldiers marching around the field of conquest; but we
think of our release from the army, and the day when we shall
receive our reward. Our feelings are lively indeed; and keeping
up the figure of our song, we seem to be gliding into the harbor.
Space and time seem to be annihilated, so vivid are our anticipations while we sing, -

Into the harbor of heaven now we glide,
We're home at last,
Softly we drift on its bright silver tide,
We're home at last.
Glory to God, all our dangers are o'er,
We stand secure on the glorified shore,
Glory to God, we will shout evermore,
We're home at last.

Now the ministers pause, and the farewell begins. How touching
is the scene! Here is manhood with its strength and hope; but who
can resist the current of sympathy that flows from heart to heart?
Who can be indifferent to the impressions made by such a farewell?
Look at that strong man; he seems almost overcome with emotion.
Whence his feelings? He is grasping again the hand of the minister
that led him to Christ. Years have passed, and now they meet again.

193

It may be the last. A fervent, "God bless you," falls from each lip, and they part. Do you not read in the countenance of the minister, evidence of an humble, grateful satisfaction that he has not labored in vain? And more: he covenants anew to meet his spiritual children in heaven. "He that goeth forth and weepeth, bearing precious seed, shall doubtless come again, bringing his sheaves with him."

Here are the aged, with whitened locks and faltering steps. They look like the heroes of other days. They have come down to us from days of peril. A half a century ago they welcomed the wayworn itinerant to their homes. They gave the ministers of Jesus comfort and shelter in the wilderness. They pronounce a benediction upon us as they pass in the procession. They have been to many a camp meeting. They hardly expect to see another. Some of them have sons in the ministry, and like all other men, they think much of that in which they have much invested.

"Preach Jesus!"

"We will! Good-bye, fathers! We have knelt at your altars, and we have seen your children converted. We have seen some of them pass over Jordan, and they sang as they went. Your treasures are in heaven! We will meet you there."

Here are the mothers. God bless the mothers - aged mothers. Some prayed for strength to attend one more "Feast of Tabernacles," and God answered their prayers. Here comes one who is almost home. She has been a mother in Israel for more than two-score years. What though her once beautiful tresses have whitened upon her brow, and the wrinkles of age and care furrow her face? still there is a sweet happy look on the countenance. With tears, we say: -

"Good-bye, mother; thou shalt soon have a crown."

.   .   .   . The singing continues, and the procession moves on. Here is "Elisha;" but he says not a word. Is he musing and praying over a scene of such touching, such awful interest? Now he has shaken hands with all the preachers, and has taken his place by the side of the procession to witness proceedings. He catches the words that are sung,

"We'll be gathered home."

He can hold still no longer. "Glory to God! Glory to Jesus! We will be gathered home. So we will, HALLELUJAH!" Amen! So let it be.

Here are the children. We shake their little hands, and think of the words of Christ, "Suffer little children to come unto me, and

194

forbid them not, for of such is the kingdom of heaven." They will never forget that parting scene. When they hear us preach the Gospel, they will remember that we kindly pressed their hands, and bid them "good-bye," and we shall have more ready access to their hearts. The impression now made will eventuate in salvation. Good-bye, children!!

Here are some clad in mourning, and they weep, and we weep with them. They are reminded of other and sadder separations. Thank God, there is joy for the lonely widow, and the fatherless. The hour is approaching when the garments of mourning will be exchanged for the robes of heaven. Young converts, good-bye. How happy you look!

> Tongue can never express,
> The sweet comfort and peace
> Of a soul in its earliest love.

¶ Washington Irving on Camp Meetings, 1823.

(Taken from Pierre M. Irving, *Life and Letters of Washington Irving* (1864), IV, 344-45; reprinted in *Methodist History*, VI[2] (Jan. 1968), 48-49).

February 13th, 1823. - Mr. Irving came home with us after the opera, which is always over early, and stayed a long while talking as usual, before he wished "good night." He was exceedingly entertaining, and gave us a vivid description of the gatherings of the Methodists in America, which occur from time to time, and at one of which he was present. "These gatherings were generally on a spot particularly well suited to the occasion. Mr. Irving described it as a promontory or peninsula which spread itself out in an expansion of the Hudson, carpeted with verdure, and shaded by groves of splendid trees, while the whole is backed by mountain scenery of great beauty. Here thousands of persons are assembled from different parts of America, and remain encamped for three or four days."

As Mr. Irving approached the place, he said he saw, "innumerable rows of carriages, wagons, &c., standing round; and the sound of female voices, singing in chorus, struck most pleasantly on his ear. Persons of this sect pay particular attention to their vocal music; and the psalms thus chanted in the open air, by voices of great power and sweetness, had a solemn and a thrilling effect. Some favorite preachers were surrounded by immense congregations, while others drew a smaller number of hearers round them; but many of them would suddenly stop, and launch into severe anathemas against any unfortunate strangers whose more elegant dress would show them to be mere spectators of the scene. In other parts of

the grove, processions would be seen moving slowly and solemnly along - elders of the tribes leading their flocks to this holy place of meeting, and occasionally halting to offer up a short but fervent prayer. But the whole has such a striking effect, that many persons are converted at the moment - or fancy themselves so. The black population throng to these places as much as the white; and young girls would fall down senseless, and lay to for some time; "for, says Mr. Irving, "it requires a great struggle to send the devil out of a negro; but when they are once turned Methodists, they are the most sturdy in their doctrine."

Irving said, "that he passed a group of negroes, an old white-headed man, and several old black women standing by him, who looked upon him with great contempt. The old man, casting a look over his shoulder, ejaculated: 'Ay' (here mentioning the name of our holy Savior), 'ay, He will carry the day!' as if he were speaking of an election; and then added: "If God Almighty were not too strong for the devil' (here another fierce and sidelong look at Mr. Irving), 'there would be no living in the 'arth!' We hope his faith was greater than his charity, and wished him an increase of the latter article."

8. BEGINNINGS OF BLACK METHODISM

Frequent references to the presence of Negroes in the early days of Methodism in America occur in the journals of Asbury, Whatcoat, Pilmore, and others. Some examples are given from Pilmore's Journal. Segregation was already present, but relations were quite informal and unstructured. William Colbert in his manuscript journal described an active class meeting composed of black members.

One of the most valuable documents on the early times is the brief autobiography by **William Allen,** *first bishop of the African Methodist Episcopal Church. It was written between 1816 and 1831, but published only in 1880, recently reprinted by Abingdon Press in 1966. Here is the classic account of the walkout of black members from St. George's church in Philadelphia in 1787. Here also an account of the formation of the denomination.*

One of the steps on the way to separation from the M. E. Church and formation of a new denomination was the organization of autonomous local churches. The Charter of the Zion Church in New York illustrates the process as the African Methodist Episcopal Zion Church came into being. The process was not completed, however, until 1820, as related in the early history of A.M.E. Zion Methodism by Christopher Rush in 1843. Note that, in spite of the title, this book deals with Zion Methodism. In all cases, whether of A.M.E., A.M.E.Z., or the smaller but very early African Union Methodist Protestant Church, the same forces of racial discrimination and struggle for black self-expression played a central role.

Other issues concerned ordination of ministers and control of church property. The white church did what it could to provide ordained ministerial leadership, but it seems somewhat grudgingly. Lack of education was part of the problem. The difficulty over church property is rooted in the principle, derived from Wesley himself and established in the General and Annual Conferences in the United States, that title is vested not in trustees of a local church but in Annual Conference Boards of Trustees. This raised difficulties when black Methodists sought to buy or build their own churches, and to free themselves from continued control by white church leaders.

¶ Earliest Origins of Black Methodism.

(Taken from duplicated manuscript by Lewis Baldwin, selections
from the Journal of Joseph Pilmore).

⌈September 3, 1770 - Philadelphia.⌉ Wednesday, we met togither to
break bread. Our meeting was rather heavy and dull in the beginning;
but we cried unto God, and he presently gaves (gave) us his blessing
of peace. Then the people spoke freely of what he had done for their
souls, and even the poor Negroes came forth and bore a noble testimony
for God our Saviour.

⌈August 1, 1771 - New York.⌉ Was a busy day indeed. Many people
attended for direction in matters of the highest importance, and want
to know how they may obtain salvation. In the evening we had our
Quarterly Love-feast, which was a special season of love to the
believers in general. They spoke freely of the goodness of God,
while a profound awe and divine reverence seemed to sit upon every
countenance. One of the poor Negroes declared, her heart was so full
of divine love that she could not express it, and many more of them
were exceedingly happy in their minds. If the people who keep them
in a state of *slavery* would but take pains to have them instructed in
the Religion of Jesus, it would be some compensation for the loss of
their *liberty*; but this, alas! is too much neglected. Yet there are
a goodly number of Masters in America, who are glad to do all in their
power for them.

⌈November 10, 1771 - Philadelphia.⌉ After morning preaching, a
person put a Letter into my hands from a poor Negro Slave, part of
which ran thus-
    "Dear Sir, These are to acquaint you, that my *bondage* is
"such I cannot possibly attend with the rest of the Class to
"receive my Ticket therefore beg you will send it. I wanted much
"to come to the Church at the Watch-night, but could not get
"leave; but, I bless God that night, I was greatly favoured with
"the spirit of prayer, and enjoyed much of his divine presence.
"I find the enemy of my soul continually striving to throw me
"off the foundation, but I have that within me which bids
"defiance to his delusive snares. I beg an interest in your
"prayers that I may be inabled to bear up under all my difficulties
"with patient resignation to the will of God."

⌈June 4, 1772 - On the road to Maryland.⌉ . . .after crossing the
Ferry I went forward about five miles to Mrs. Dallams where I found
honest Robert Williams preaching. We spent the evening togither with
the family in great comfort, and rested in peace. The next day, as
it had been published, we had a fine congregation, and the Lord inabled
me to preach glad tidings to the poor and meek. After preaching we
spent the evening with Mr. Husband, a man of pretty extensive reading

and tolerable good understanding: if he had but a sense of the favour of God he would be happy: but without that all other knowledge will vanish away. After supper many poor Negroes came in; we joined in an Hymn of praise, I gave them an Exhortation, & concluded the day with prayer. While we were on our knees wrestling with God, I observed one of the Negroes go out, and thought he was affected in his mind, and so it happened, for we heard him calling loudly upon God to bless him and save his soul from sin. How many of these poor Slaves will rise up in judgment against their Masters, and, porhaps, enter into life, while they are shut out.

[August 5, 1772 - Portsmouth, Virginia] Wednesday . . . I returned to Portmouth and preached to a pretty congregation with enlargeness of heart on the nature of free justification through the Righteousness of Christ; After preaching two poor slaves came to me and beged I would instruct them in the way of salvation so I gave them a short and plain account of the Plan of the Gospel, and shewed them how sinners may come to God and be saved. We then joined in singing and prayer, and they expressed great thankfulness for what they had heard, and seemed determined to be Christians. . . .

[August 9, 1772 - Norfolk] Sunday. . . . I preached . . . in the evening at Norfolk. As the ground was wet, they persuaded me to try to preach within and appointed men to stand at the doors to keep all the Negroes out till the white people were got in, but the house would not hold them; however I went into the pulpit; (and) began, but present a plank gave way, and the stage, on which the pulpit was fixed, began to sink down at one side, which so terrified the people that they cried out amain. As I perceived it would be impossible to quiet the people, I slipped out - ordered a Table and began sin(g) ing in the large plain adjoining the house; this happened to be the very thing, the people drew out of the house, and I had a noble congregation of white and black, to whom I freely declared the whole counsel of God, and pressed them to obey the word of the Lord.

[August 16, 1772 - Norfolk] . . . I was in time to preach at Norfolk in the evening. Just before preaching, we had a thunder shower that kept some of the delicate ones from the preaching. Yet we had the house perfectly (full) of white people, and a vast multitude of black people stood around about the outside. As I was much fatigued before I began, I was afraid I should not be able to preach to the great congregation so as to be heard, but God was better to me than all my fears, and made his word like a sharp two-edged sword, piercing into the hearts of sinners.

[April 25-26, 1773 (near Portsmouth)]. Monday. . . . went
down to Capt'n Connors, where I preached at three oClock with
more happiness of mind than I usually feel in the country . . . In
the morning all the Negroes were called in, and I expounded a
Chapter and prayed; then set off for Norfolk again . . .

¶   A Black Class Meeting, 1794.

(Taken from William Colbert, "Journal," manuscript in Garrett-
Evangelical Theological Seminary).

Thursday 23 I preached to a congregation of Black people at
Oxenhill on the Banks of Pottomac partly oposite Alexandria from
Matt. 5 ch. 5th v. Some years past a few of these Black people
obtained their freedom and embraced religion, loved our society and
built us a Meeting House, began to exhort the people of their
Coulour to flee from the wrath to come and God has blessed the
labour in an extraordinary manner, their society is very numberous,
and very orderly, and to their great credit with pleasure I assert,
that I never found a white class so regular in giving in their
Quarterage, as these poor people are, and the greater part of them
are slaves, of whom never request anything. But they will enquire
when the Quarterly Meetings are from time to time, and by the last
time the preacher comes round before the Quarterly Meeting they
will have five Dollars in silver tied up for him: as they are so
numberous the circuit preacher cannot meet them all, there are 2
leading characters among them, that fill their station with dignity.
They not only have their Class meetings, but their days of examination in order to find out anything that may be amiss among them and
if they can settle it among themselves they will, if not, as the
Elders of Israel brought of matters which they concieved were of too
great importance for them to decide on before Moses, so would these
people bring matters of the greatest moment before the preacher. I
lodged at Mr. Baynes a very kind family, tho' not members of our
society two brothers and two sisters are living to gether, their
parents are dead and they are single.

¶   Walkout from St. George's.

(Taken from Richard Allen, *The Life Experience and Gospel
Labors*. . . (1880, rep. 1966), 25-29).

A number of us usually attended St. George's church in Fourth
street; and when the colored people began to get numerous in attending the church, they moved us from the seats we usually sat on, and
placed us around the wall, and on Sabbath morning we went to church
and the sexton stood at the door, and told us to go in the gallery.
He told us to go, and we would see where to sit. We expected to

take the seats over the ones we formerly occupied below, not knowing any better. We took those seats. Meeting had begun, and they
were nearly done singing, and just as we got to the seats, the
elder said, "Let us pray." We had not been long upon our knees
before I heard considerable scuffling and low talking, I raised
my head up and saw one of the trustees, H_____M_____, having
hold of the Rev. Absalom Jones, pulling him up off of his knees,
and saying, "You must get up—you must not kneel here." Mr. Jones
replied, "Wait until prayer is over." Mr. H_____M_____ said
"No, you must get up now, or I will call for aid and force you
away." Mr. Jones said, "Wait until prayer is over, and I will
get up and trouble you no more." With that he beckoned to one of
the other trustees, Mr. L_____S_____ to come to his assistance.
He came, and went to William White to pull him up. By this time
prayer was over, and we all went out of the church in a body, and
they were no more plagued with us in the church. This raised a
great excitement and inquiry among the citizens, in so much that I
believe they were ashamed of their conduct. But my dear Lord was
with us, and we were filled with fresh vigor to get a house erected
to worship God in. Seeing our forlorn and distressed situation, many
of the hearts of our citizens were moved to urge us forward; notwithstanding we had subscribed largely towards finishing St.
George's church, in building the gallery and laying new floors, and
just as the house was made comfortable, we were turned out from enjoying the comforts of worshipping therein. We then hired a store-
room, and held worship by ourselves. Here we were pursued with
threats of being disowned, and read publicly out of meeting if we
did continue worship in the place we had hired; but we believed the
Lord would be our friend. We got subscription papers out to raise
money to build the house of the Lord. By this time we had waited on
Dr. Rush and Mr. Robert Ralston, and told them of our distressing
situation. We considered it a blessing that the Lord had put it
into our hearts to wait upon those gentlemen. They pitied our
situation, and subscribed largely towards the church, and were very
friendly towards us, and advised us how to go on. We appointed Mr.
Ralston our treasurer. Dr. Rush did much for us in public by his
influence. I hope the name of Dr. Benjamin Rush and Robert Ralston
will never be forgotten among us. They were the first two gentlemen who espoused the cause of the oppressed, and aided us in building the house of the Lord for the poor Africans to worship in. Here
was the beginning and rise of the first African church in America.
But the elder of the Methodist Church still pursued us. Mr. John
McClaskey called upon us and told us if we did not erase our names
from the subscription paper, and give up the paper, we would be
publicly turned out of meeting. We asked him if we had violated any
rules of discipline by so doing. He replied, "I have the charge
given to me by the Conference, and unless you submit I will read
you publicly out of meeting." We told him we were willing to abide
by the discipline of the Methodist Church, "And if you will show us
where we have violated any law of discipline of the Methodist Church,

we will submit; and if there is no rule violated in the discipline
we will proceed on." He replied, "We will read you all out." We
told him if he turned us out contrary to the rule of discipline, we
should seek further redress. We told him we were dragged off of our
knees in St. George's church, and treated worse than heathens; and
we were determined to seek out for ourselves, the Lord being our
helper. He told us we were not Methodists, and left us. Finding
we would go on in raising money to build the church, he called upon
us again, and wished to see us all together. We met him. He told
us that he wished us well, that he was a friend to us, and used
many arguments to convince us that we were wrong in building a
church. We told him we had no place of worship; and we did not
mean to go to St. George's church any more, as we were so
scandalously treated in the presence of all the congregation present;
"and if you deny us your name, you cannot seal up the scriptures
from us, and deny us a name in heaven. We believe heaven is free
for all who worship in spirit and truth." And he said, "So you are
determined to go on." We told him, "Yes, God being our helper." He
then replied, "We will disown you all from the Methodist connection."
We believed if we put our trust in the Lord, he would stand by us.
This was a trial that I never had to pass through before. I was
confident that the great head of the church would support us. My
dear Lord was with us. We went out with our subscription paper, and
met with great success. We had no reason to complain of the liberality of the citizens. The first day the Rev. Absalom Jones and myself
went out we collected three hundred and sixty dollars. This was the
greatest day's collection that we met with. We appointed a committee
to look out for a lot - the Rev. Absalom Jones, William Gray, William
Wilcher and myself. We pitched upon a lot at the corner of Lombard
and Sixth streets. They authorized me to go and agree for it. I did,
accordingly. The lot belonged to Mr. Mark Wilcox. We entered into
articles of agreement for the lot. Afterwards the committee found a
lot in Fifth street, in a more commodious part of the city, which we
bought; and the first lot they threw upon my hands, and wished me to
give it up. I told them they had authorized me to agree for the lot,
and they were all well satisfied with the agreement I had made, and
I thought it was hard that they would throw it upon my hands. I
told them I would sooner keep it myself than to forfeit the agreement
I had made. And so I did.

We bore much persecution from many of the Methodist connection;
but we have reason to be thankful to Almighty God, who was our
deliverer. The day was appointed to go and dig the cellar. I arose
early in the morning and addressed the throne of grace, praying that
the Lord would bless our endeavors. Having by this time two or
three teams of my own - as I was the first proposer of the African
church, I put the first spade in the ground to dig a cellar for the
same. This was the first African Church or meetinghouse that was
erected in the United States of America. We intended it for the
African preaching-house or church; but finding that the elder

stationed in this city was such an opposer to our proceedings of erecting a place of worship, though the principal part of the directors of this church belonged to the Methodist connection, the elder stationed here would neither preach for us, nor have anything to do with us. We then held an election, to know what religious denomination we should unite with. At the election it was determined--there were two in favor of the Methodist, the Rev. Absalom Jones and myself, and a large majority in favor of the Church of England. The majority carried. Notwithstanding we had been so violently persecuted by the elder, we were in favor of being attached to the Methodist connection; for I was confident that there was no religious sect or denomination would suit the capacity of the colored people as well as the Methodist; for the plain and simple gospel suits best for any people; for the unlearned can understand, and the learned are sure to understand; and the reason that the Methodist is so successful in the awakening and conversion of the colored people, the plain doctrine and having a good discipline.

¶ Allen's Letter in Walker's *Appeal*.

(Taken from David Walker's *Appeal, in Four Articles; Together with A Preamble, to the Coloured Citizens of the World* (1829), Charles M. Wiltse, ed., Hill and Wang, New York, 1965, 56-59).

Before I proceed further with this scheme, I shall give an extract from the letter of that truly Reverend Divine, (Bishop Allen,) of Philadelphia, respecting this trick. At the instance of the editor of the Freedom's Journal, he says, "Dear Sir, I have been for several years trying to reconcile my mind to the Colonizing of Africans in Liberia, but there have always been, and there still remain great insurmountable objections against the scheme. We are an unlettered people, brought up in ignorance, not one in a hundred can read or write, not one in a thousand has a liberal education; is there any fitness for such to be sent into a far country, among heathens, to convert or civilize them, when they themselves are neither civilized or Christianized? See the great bulk of the poor, ignorant Africans in this country, exposed to every temptation before them: all for the want of their morals being refined by education and proper attendance paid unto them by their owners, or those who had the charge of them. It is said by the Southern slave-holders, that the more ignorant they can bring up the Africans, the better slaves they make, ('go and come.') Is there any fitness for such people to be colonized in a far country to be their own rulers? Can we not discern the project of sending the free people of colour away from their country? Is it not for the interest of the slave-holders to select the free people of colour out of the different states, and send them to Liberia? Will it not make their slaves uneasy to see free men of colour enjoying liberty? It is against the law in some of the Southern States, that a person of colour should receive an

203

education, under a severe penalty. Colonizationists speak of America being first colonized; but is there any comparison between the two? America was colonized by as wise, judicious and educated men as the world afforded. William Penn did not want for learning, wisdom, or intelligence. If all the people in Europe and America were as ignorant and in the same situation as our brethren, what would become of the world? Where would be the principle or piety that would govern the people? We were stolen from our mother country, and brought here. We have tilled the ground and made fortunes for thousands, and still they are not weary of our services. But they who stay to till the ground must be slaves. Is there not land enough in America, or 'corn enough in Egypt?' Why should they send us into a far country to die? See the thousands of foreigners emigrating to America every year: and if there be ground sufficient for them to cultivate, and bread for them to eat, why would they wish to send the first tillers of the land away? Africans have made fortunes for thousands, who are yet unwilling to part with their services; but the free must be sent away, and those who remain, must be slaves. I have no doubt that there are many good men who do not see as I do, and who are for sending us to Liberia; but they have not duly considered the subject - they are not men of colour. - This land which we have watered with our tears and our blood, is now our mother country, and we are well satisfied to stay where wisdom abounds and the gospel is free."

> "RICHARD ALLEN,
> "Bishop of the African Methodist Episcopal
> "Church in the United States."

I have given you, my brethren, an extract verbatim, from the letter of that godly man, as you may find it on the aforementioned page of Freedom's Journal. I know that thousands, and perhaps millions of my brethren in these States, have never heard of such a man as Bishop Allen - a man whom God many years ago raised up among his ignorant and degraded brethren, to preach Jesus Christ and him crucified to them - who notwithstanding, had to wrestle against principalities and the powers of darkness to diffuse that gospel with which he was endowed among his brethren - but who having over-come the combined powers of devils and wicked men, has under God planted a Church among us which will be as durable as the founda-tion of the earth on which it stands. Richard Allen! O my God! The bare recollection of the labours of this man, and his ministers among his deplorably wretched brethren, (rendered so by the whites) to bring them to a knowledge of the God of Heaven, fills my soul with all those very high emotions which would take the pen of an Addison to portray. It is impossible my brethren for me to say much in this work respecting that man of God. When the Lord shall raise up coloured historians in succeeding generations, to present the crimes of this nation, to the then gazing world, the Holy Ghost will make them do justice to the name of Bishop Allen, of

Philadelphia. Suffice it for me to say, that the name of this very
man (Richard Allen) though now in obscurity and degradation, will
notwithstanding, stand on the pages of history among the greatest
divines who have lived since the apostolic age, and among the
Africans, Bishop Allen's will be entirely pre-eminent.

¶   Organization of A.M.E. Church.

(Taken from Richard Allen, *The Life Experience and Gospel
Labors*, 30-35).

In 1793 a committee was appointed from the African Church to
solicit me to be their minister, for there was no colored preacher
in Philadelphia but myself. I told them I could not accept of their
offer, as I was a Methodist. I was indebted to the Methodists,
under God, for what little religion I had; being convinced that they
were the people of God, I informed them that I could not be anything
else but a Methodist, as I was born and awakened under them, and I
could go no further with them, for I was a Methodist, and would
leave you in peace and love. I would do nothing to retard them in
building a church as it was an extensive building, neither would I go
out with a subscription paper until they were done going out with
their subscription. I bought an old frame that had been formerly
occupied as a blacksmith shop, from Mr. Sims, and hauled it on the
lot in Sixth near Lombard street, that had formely been taken for
the Church of England. I employed carpenters to repair the old
frame, and fit it for a place of worship. In July 1794, Bishop
Asbury being in town I solicited him to open the church for us which
he accepted. The Rev. John Dickins sung and prayed, and Bishop
Asbury preached. The house was called Bethel, agreeable to the prayer that was made. Mr. Dickins prayed that it might be a bethel to the
gathering in of thousands of souls. My dear Lord was with us, so
that there were many hearty "amen's" echoed through the house. This
house of worship has been favored with the awakening of many souls,
and I trust they are in the Kingdom, both white and colored. Our
warfare and troubles now began afresh. Mr. C. proposed that we
should make over the church to the Conference. This we objected
to; he asserted that we could not be Methodists unless we did; we
told him he might deny us their name, but they could not deny us a
seat in Heaven. Finding that he could not prevail with us so to do,
he observed that we had better be incorporated, then we could get any
legacies that were left for us, if not, we could not. We agreed to
be incorporated. He offered to draw the incorporation himself,
that it would save us the trouble of paying for to get it drawn.
We cheerfully submitted to his proposed plan. He drew the incorporation, but incorporated our church under the Conference, our property
was then all consigned to the Conference for the present bishops,
elders, ministers, etc., that belonged to the white Conference, and
our property was gone. Being ignorant of incorporations we cheer-

fully agreed thereto. We labored about ten years under this incorporation, until James Smith was appointed to take the charge in Philadelphia; he soon waked us up by demanding the keys and books of the church, and forbid us holding any meetings except by orders from him; these propositions we told him we could not agree to. He observed he was elder, appointed to the charge, and unless we submitted to him, he would read us all out of meeting. We told him the house was ours, we had bought it, and paid for it. He said he would let us know it was not ours, it belonged to the Conference; we took counsel on it; counsel informed us we had been taken in; according to the incorporation it belonged to the white connection. We asked him if it couldn't be altered; he told us if two-thirds of the society agreed to have it altered, it could be altered. He gave me a transcript to lay before them; I called the society together and laid it before them. My dear Lord was with us. It was unanimously agreed to, by both male and female. We had another incorporation drawn that took the church from Conference, and got it passed, before the elder knew anything about it. This raised a considerable rumpus, for the elder contended that it would not be good unless he had signed it. The elder, with the trustees of St. George's, called us together, and said we must pay six hundred dollars a year for their services, or they could not serve us. We told them we were not able so to do. The trustees of St. George's insisted that we should or should not be supplied by their preachers. At last they made a move that they would take four hundred; we told them that our house was considerably in debt, and we were poor people, and we could not agree to pay four hundred, but we agreed to give them two hundred. It was moved by one of the trustees of St. George's that the money should be paid into their treasury; we refused paying it into their treasury, but we would pay it to the preacher that served; they made a move that the preacher should not receive the money from us. The Bethel trustees made a move that their funds should be shut and they would pay none; this caused a considerable contention. At length they withdrew their motion. The elder supplied us preaching five times in a year for two hundred dollars. Finding that they supplied us so seldom, the trustees of Bethel church passed a resolution that they would pay but one hundred dollars a year, as the elder only preached five times in a year for us; they called for the money, we paid him twenty-five dollars a quarter, but he being dissatisfied, returned the money back again, and would not have it unless we paid him fifty dollars. The trustees concluded it was enough for five sermons, and said they would pay no more; the elder of St. George's was determined to preach for us no more, unless we gave him two hundred dollars, and we were left alone for upwards of one year.

Mr. Samuel Royal being appointed to the charge of Philadelphia, declared unless we should repeal the Supplement, neither he nor any white preacher, travelling or local, should preach any more for us; so we were left to ourselves. At length the preachers and stewards

206

belonging to the Academy, proposed serving us on the same terms that
we had offered to the St. George's preachers, and they preached for
us better than twelve months, and then demanded $150 per year; this
not being complied with, they declined preaching for us, and we were
once more left to ourselves, as an edict was passed by the elder,
that if any local preacher should serve us, he should be expelled
from the connection. John Emory, then elder of the Academy, published a circular letter, in which we were disowned by the Methodists.
A house was also hired and fitted up for worship, not far from
Bethel, and an invitation given to all who desired to be Methodists
to resort thither. But being disappointed in this plan, Robert R.
Roberts, the resident elder, came to Bethel, insisted on preaching
to us and taking the spiritual charge of the congregation, for we
were Methodists he was told he should come on some terms with the
trustees; his answer was, that "He did not come to consult with
Richard Allen or other trustees, but to inform the congregation, that
on next Sunday afternoon, he would come and take the spiritual
charge." We told him he could not preach for us under existing
circumstances. However, at the appointed time he came, but having
taken previous advice we had our preacher in the pulpit when he
came, and the house was so fixed that he could not get but more than
half way to the pulpit. Finding himself disappointed he appealed
to those who came with him as witnesses, that "That man (meaning the
preacher), had taken his appointment." Several respectable white
citizens who knew the colored people had been ill-used, were
present, and told us not to fear, for they would see us righted, and
not suffer Roberts to preach in a forcible manner, after which Roberts
went away.

The next elder stationed in Philadelphia was Robert Birch, who,
following the example of his predecessor, came and published a
meeting for himself. But the method just mentioned was adopted and
he had to go away disappointed. In consequence of this, he applied
to the Supreme Court for a writ of mandamus, to know why the pulpit
was denied him. Being elder, this brought on a lawsuit, which
ended in our favor. Thus by the Providence of God we were delivered
from a long, distressing and expensive suit, which could not be
resumed, being determined by the Supreme Court. For this mercy we
desire to be unfeignedly thankful.

About this time, our colored friends in Baltimore were treated
in a similar manner by the white preachers and trustees, and many of
them driven away who were disposed to seek a place of worship, rather
than go to law.

Many of the colored people in other places were in a situation
nearly like those of Philadelphia and Baltimore, which induced us,
in April 1816, to call a general meeting, by way of Conference.
Delegates from Baltimore and other places which met those of
Philadelphia, and taking into consideration their grievances, and

in order to secure the privileges, promote union and harmony among themselves, it was resolved: "That the people of Philadelphia, Baltimore, etc., etc., should become one body, under the name of the African Methodist Episcopal Church."

¶   Articles of Association of the Trustees and Members of the
     African Methodist Episcopal Church called "Bethell Church,"
                              1796

(Taken from Afro-American History Series, No. 201 (Rhistoric Publications, h.d., 3-11, 17-19).

ARTICLE 1. It is provided and declared that the style and title of this corporation shall be "The African Methodist Episcopal Church of the City of Philadelphia in the Commonwealth of Pennsylvania"- and shall consist of John Morris, William Hagan, Robert Green, Jupiter Gibson, William Jones, Jonathan Trustey, Peter Lux, Prince Pruine and Richard Allen, Trustees and Members of "Bethell Church" aforesaid, and their successors, duly qualified, elected and appointed in such manner as hereinafter is provided and directed, who shall be Trustees (for the purposes, and with the powers and privileges hereinafter granted and specified) of the church called "Bethell Church," and of all and every such other church and churches as do now or hereafter shall become the property of the corporation.

ART. 2. The corporation aforesaid, and their successors forever do, and shall have and hold the said building, called "Bethell Church," and all other churches which are now, or shall become, the property of the corporation, in trust for the religious use of the ministers and preachers of the Methodist Episcopal Church, who are in connection with the General Conference of the said Church, and likewise for our African brethren, and the descendants of the African race, as hereafter specified; and also for ministers and teachers of our African brethren duly licensed or ordained according to the form of discipline.

ART. 3. It is provided and declared, That the rents, issues, profits and interests of the real and personal estate of and belonging to the said Church, and trustees and their successors, shall from time to time be applied and laid out for repairing and maintaining their said Bethell Church, and all and any other place or places of public worship, lot or lots of ground, burial grounds or buildings which now do, or at any time hereafter may or shall belong to the said Church or trustees, as shall from time to time be thought proper and expedient, by two thirds of the trustees for the time being; and after the year one thousand eight hundred, if the funds and revenues be sufficient, the trustees may and shall be permitted, in their own discretion, to allow a reasonable and proportionable part for the support of the ministers. And if it

shall so happen, that the trustees shall be divided with respect to a proposed application or appreperiation of money, and two thirds do not coincide in opinion; then and in such case, the elder of the Methodist Episcopal Church for the time being, in the city of Philadelphia, who shall be appointed by the Conference of the said Church to the charge of the Methodist Society in the said city, shall have a voice in the decision of the question; and his vote whether it be with the majority or minority of the trustees shall be final and definitive against the proposed appropriation; but shall never have effect to confirm the proposed appropriation or application of money with a minority.

ART. 4. It is provided and declared, That the said trustees, and their successors shall not by deed or any otherwise, grant, alien, convey, or otherwise dispose of any part or parcel of the estate real or personal in the said corporation, vested or to be vested, or in any way to mortgage or pledge the said real estate for the payment of any debts by them contracted, to any person or persons whatever; unless such grant, alienation and conveyance, be made by and with the consent of the elder for the time being, regularly appointed by Conference; and two thirds of the regular male members of the said church, of at least twenty-one years of age, and one year's standing.

ART. 5. It is provided and declared, That the trustees shall consist of nine persons, duly qualified, Chosen and appointed as is hereafter mentioned; who shall be and continue trustees of the said church, until they be removed in manner and form following, that is to say: one third part in number of the said trustees, being the third part herein first named, shall cease and be discontinued on the second Monday after Easter, which shall be in the year of our Lord, one thousand eight hundred; - upon which day a new election shall be had and held of so many others in their place and stead by a majority of the male members of the said congregation, duly qualified to vote as is hereinafter mentioned, and that such election shall and may be held in such manner and at such places, as the corporation shall from time to time appoint and direct. . .

ART. 6. It is provided and declared, That none but coloured persons shall be chosen as trustees of the said African Episcopal Bethell Church, and such other Church or Churchs as may or shall hereafter become the property of this corporation, and none shall be eligible to the office of a trustee but such as are received and acknowledged to be members of the said church, by the elder of the Methodist Episcopal Church, in the City of Philadelphia, appointed as aforesaid; and in case of the death, expulsion or resignation from the said corporation, of any of the said trustees or their successors, then the members of the said Church shall convene together within one month from the time of such death, expulsion or resignation, and shall chuse from among themselves, by a majority of

legal votes, a person or persons to fill up such vacancy; and the person or persons so elected shall be and continue in office so long as the person or persons in whose place or stead he or they shall have been so elected would or might have continued, in order to preserve and keep up the number of nine trustees sorever. But before any of the aforesaid elections are held, public notice shall be given to the congregation, on the preceding Sunday, after divine service, before the said congregation be dismissed.

ART. 7. All elections for trustees shall be held by ballot of the male coloured members, in close communion with them, or as many of them as attend after being duly warned thereto; and no male member shall have a right to vote for trustees, until he has been a member standing in full connection, one year at least. And no coloured person shall be chosen a trustee of the said corporation, until the said person shall have been a member in full connection and standing, at least two years. And no person shall be admitted into close connection with their classes, or be enrolled on their books, but Africans and descendants of the African race.

ART. 8. It is provided and declared, that the trustees aforesaid, and their successors forever, are and shall be empowered to have, and shall have the entire direction and disposal of the temporal revenues of the aforesaid African Bethell Church; and, after paying the ground rent for the said Church, are to apply the remainder for the benefit of the said Church, as a majority of the aforesaid trustees and their successors shall, from time to time, direct. And the aforesaid trustees and their successors forever, shall have the disposal and management of the temporal concerns of the aforesaid "African Methodist Episcopal Church," - subject nevertheless, to the provisions, and under the regulations made and provided in the third and fourth articles of this instrument.

ART. 9. It is declared, that the trustees and members of the African Methodist Episcopal Church do acquiesce in, and accord with the rules of the Methodist Episcopal Church, for their church government and discipline, and with their creeds and articles of faith; and that they and their successors will continue forever in union with the "Methodist Episcopal Church of Philadelphia," subject to the government of the present Bishops and their successors in all their ecclesiastical affairs and transactions (except in the temporal right and property of their aforesaid Bethell Church, which is to be governed as therein directed) as long as the said articles and creeds of the said Church remain unchanged."

ART. 10. It is declared, that the Elder of the Methodist Episcopal Church, for the time being, in the city of Philadelphia, appointed as aforementioned, shall have the direction and management of the spiritual concerns of the said Bethell Church, and any other

church or churches which may or shall be built hereafter by the Corporation aforesaid, or by any other means become their property, agreeably to the form of discipline of the said Methodist Episcopal Church. Provided always, That the said Elder shall receive no person into the African Bethell Society, but such as are previously recommended by a trustee or trustees of the said African Bethell Church. . . .

ART. 11. It is agreed and declared that the Elder of the Methodist Episcopal Church in the city of Philadelphia, appointed as aforesaid, shall from time to time forever hereafter nominate the preacher who shall officiate in said African Methodist Episcopal Bethell Church, and any and all other church or churches which shall hereafter become the property of the corporation, and shall attend to the said church and churches himself, to administer the ordinances of Baptism and the Lord's Supper, as often as he the said elder can make inconvenient. And the said elder for the time being, shall license to exhort and preach, anyone or more of the coloured brethren, who are or shall be members of the said church, and shall appear, to the satisfaction of the said elder, to be adequate to the task, and to have grace and gifts proper to appear in public. And if either of the said coloured brethren shall graduate into holy orders, it shall be done in such manner and way as the General Conference shall direct. And it is provided and agreed, that the said elder may claim, and shall have and possess a right to preach once on every Sunday, and once during the course of the week (and no more) in any or all the houses set apart and built, or to be set apart and built by the aforesaid trustees or their successors, of the said African Bethell Church, in the city and suburbs of Philadelphia, in the commonwealth of Pennsylvania.

*   *   *

We cannot forget to acknowledge the tender care and kindness of a number of our friends, among the white people, in striving to break from off our necks the cruel bands of slavery, which a great part of our race now labour under, and a few years ago nearly all; but the Lord hath raised up many spiritual Moseses, and hath sent them to our cruel oppressors, to persuade them to let the oppressed go free. We are thankful some have obeyed, and have submitted to the word of truth and to their own conscience, and have freed their poor slaves; while others keep them in abject slavery, and put grievous burdens on them - too grievous to be borne. We pray God to hear the groans of the oppressed, and work out a glorious deliverance for them. We are thankful for as many friends as we have among the white people, and some of the most worthy characters. We cannot but regret the loss of that great and good man WARNER MIFFLIN, whose memory will not be forgotten for ages to come; whose labours and anxiety were great for the freedom of our race; who for many years devoted his time to that service, and who has been instrumental in

the hands of God, in liberating hundreds, if not thousands of the African race. Though he was rejected and despised by many who held our fellow creatures in bondage, like a good soldier he stood to his integrity, took up his cross daily, and despised the shame of befriending those despised people. He died in that work he had been engaged in for many years – and departed this life on the 16th of October, 1798. We hope that every slave he has been instrumental in freeing, is a star in his garment, and that he will shine unto the perfect day. He was an useful member of civil as well as religious society, and fought not the honours of this world. . . .

We can but be thankful for the many friends that the Lord has given us, in the state of Pennsylvania, as well as in Massachusetts and other neighbouring states. We find many worthy characters who espouse the cause of the poor oppressed Africans; who devote their time and services freely to work out a deliverance for the poor African race; we acknowledge their kindness and friendly assistance, and hold ourselves indebted to them, for the religious concern that rests upon many of their minds for us, when the yoke of bondage is broke from off the necks of the people of colour, for their care to cultivate them, in order to make them fit members for religious and civil society. We are thankful that their labours have not been in vain – for there is three houses erected for divine worship: two of them are under the care of the Bishop and conference of the Methodist churches, and one under the care of the bishops of the church of England; our houses of worship are generally filled with hearers, particularly on the Sabbath day, for then it is most convenient for them to attend. We hold ourselves most indebted to the inhabitants of this city, who have kindly assisted us with their friendly advice, as well as their money. We have reason to pray for the long life of that most worthy and benevolent character Dr. Benjamin Rush, who was the first gentleman that assisted us with advice; and he has manifested his friendship by contributing largely towards building our houses of divine worship – as well as numbers of other citizens. We now join those who are our friends in exhorting and persuading our African brethren to flee from the wrath to come, and to keep a conscience void of offence towards God and man. Unto you, our friends and brethren, seeing that the Lord hath raised up so many friends to espouse our cause, let us strive to adorn the gospel, and walk worthy of our profession where-in we are called, that the gospel be not blamed. – We desire to be truly thankful to the great giver of every good and gracious gift bestowed upon us; and may he give us grace and understanding, so that we may do his will here upon earth, at last be received up to glory, where pain and parting is no more.

Signed by order, and in behalf of the trus-)
   tees incorporation of Bethell Church.   )

                        RICHARD ALLEN

(Taken from Christopher Rush, A Short Account of the Rise and Progress of the African Methodist Episcopal Church in America (1843), 37-43).

On Sunday night the 16th of July, 1820, the Elder, William M. Stilwell, who had the charge of Zion and Asbury Churches, came to the Rose Street Academy, a little before the conclusion of Divine Worship, and when the service was ended he informed the official brethren, as many as were present, that he and several hundred of his (white) brethren had that day withdrawn from the Methodist Episcopal Church, in consequence of some resolutions of their preachers in Conference, which they thought were improper measures for preachers of the Gospel to resort to, and which would be injurious to the temporal concerns of the church - the chief resolution was to petition the Legislature of the State of New York for a special Act of Incorporation, in order to give the preachers more power over the Trustees, in regard particularly to the temporalities of the churches under their government in this State. This information was somewhat alarming; for the Trustees and the other official members of our church had been several times threatened and spoken to unkindly by Elders having charge of the circuit and of our church, which had already caused considerable dissatisfaction in the minds of the official brethren, and now to hear of this special Act of Incorporation, as aforesaid, they were roused to a consideration of what would be for the best interest of our Zion Church, and some of them imbibed a belief that the time had arrived when we might loosen Zion Church from under the government of the white Bishops and Conference. The following Tuesday, the 18th instant, the Trustees were notified to meet the Presiding Elder, at the residence of Peter Williams, in Liberty Street - they went accordingly, and Abraham Thompson, the oldest preacher and Deacon in our church, accompanied them to the place appointed, where they found the presiding Elder, Peter P. Sandford, Aaron Hunt, Joshua Soule and Thomas Mason. There were several questions and answers interchanged; the presiding Elder informed the Trustees that William M. Stilwell had withdrawn from the Methodist Episcopal Church, and therefore had no further charge of our church, and that he wished to know what our church intended to do. The Trustees told him that they would consult on the case, and give him an answer as soon as possible. The Preachers of Zion Church being unpleasantly exercised in mind about a resolution of the white Methodist Preachers in one of their Conferences, relative to a Local Preachers' Conference, they had previously appointed a meeting, and had requested our Trustees to meet them and council each party in regard to what they had heard, and the appointed time happened to be on the night of the same day that the Trustees met the aforesaid Preachers at Peter Williams', in Liberty Street; they accordingly met together at the residence of James Varick, in Orange Street, in order to see what

was best to be done. After considerable consultation, they resolved to appoint Abraham Thompson, James Varick, John Dungy and George Collins a committee, to call on Doctor Phoebus, an old Elder of the Methodist Episcopal Church, (who was said to be neutral in the case of the division) and William M. Stilwell, to gain some further information on the subject, and to obtain from William M. Stilwell a copy of the resolution of the last General Conference, which had caused the schism in the white Methodist Church. They also agreed to request a meeting of all the official members of Zion Church, at the Rose Street Academy, the following Friday night, at which time they hoped to come to a final decision among the official brethren.

On Friday night, July 21st, 1820, the official members met together in the Rose Street Academy, according to request, and after due deliberation they agreed upon the following: –

WHEREAS, a very grievous schism has taken place in the Methodist Episcopal Church in this city, in consequence of a resolution of the last General Conference, and that resolution acted upon by the annual Conference of the New York District, the substance of which is (as we are informed) that a memorial shall be drawn up, subscribers obtained by the Preachers, and the same to be presented to the Legislature of the State of New York, at their next sitting, praying for a special Act of Incorporation, to suit the peculiarities of the Methodist Discipline, so that the Preachers may have more authority to exercise their functions in the church than they now have; and whereas, it is reported that, should the Legislature deem it expedient to grant the request of the memorialists and enact the said special Act of Incorporation, it will very materially change the present manner of conducting the temporal concerns of the said church; (as the Trustees or Stewards to be appointed according to the contemplated mode, will hold the property of the Society in trust for the Preachers in Conference instead of, or more than for the members of the Society) and whereas, in consequence of the aforementioned schism, a very different explanation is given relative to the contents of the said memorial, and fearing that the said report is true, and that our church property will be involved in the same difficulties should the contemplated Act of Incorporation be obtained, having no desire to transfer our church property to the Methodist Preachers in Conference; therefore, we have Resolved –

1. That we cannot fairly understand the intention of the said Preachers, in praying the Legislature for a special Act of Incorporation, and having some reason to fear that the above mentioned report is correct, we are much dissatisfied and do highly disapprove of the said memorial.

2. That in consequence of the dissatisfaction and doubt existing on our minds, relative to the intended special Act of Incorporation, and to the conduct of the Preachers in Conference requiring such an

Act, we decline receiving any further services from them as respects our church government.

3. That George Collins, Tobias Hawkins and William Brown be a committee appointed to inform the presiding Elder of the District, or the ruling elder in the city of New York, of the above resolutions.

4. That we request William M. Stilwell to continue his services with us for the remainder of the year.

5. That we recommend the above to the members of our Society.

They also agreed to call a meeting of the whole Society, male and female, which they did on the next Wednesday night, the 26th inst.; whereupon, a large number of the members crowded the Rose Street Academy and unanimously sanctioned the foregoing resolutions.

The Trustees being informed that they could not hold meetings in the Circus any longer, were now obliged to turn their attention towards going home and holding meetings within the walls of the new building, which were at this time a little more than half up and the floor beams laid, so that by laying down planks on the beams and making temporary seats, some hundreds might be accommodated. Thither we repaired on Sunday morning, July 30th, and William M. Stilwell preached within the new walls of Zion Church for the first time. It began to rain soon after the text was taken and continued during Divine service; nevertheless there were but few went away; those who had umbrellas stood it out with apparent composure. The weather cleared up time enough to hold meeting in the afternoon, when Abraham Thompson preached and James Varick closed the meeting. We had a comfortable time; and John Dungy preached in the evening, commencing at half past 6 o'clock; so that the third meeting concluded before candle-light. . . .

The official members, therefore, came together in the Rose Street Academy, on Friday night, August 11th, 1820, and the Preachers informed them that they had held a meeting for the purpose of considering the present state of our Church, and that there were two grand questions put and answered at that meeting, viz. - Shall we join Bishop Allen? Answer, No. Shall we return to the white people? Answer, No - and that they therefore determined to consult with the rest of their official brethren, upon the subject of establishing a firm church government of our own, by ordinations, &c. After several of the brethren had given their opinions, it being late, the meeting was adjourned to the following Tuesday night.

(Taken from Rush, 49-51).

The case of our Church being at this time in a very precarious state, in regard particularly to the want of Elders in the Church, it became essentially necessary that something must be done to relieve her from that religious pressure; whereupon, a meeting of all the official members of the Church was held in the Rose Street Academy, on Wednesday night, September 13th, at which time the Elder, William M. Stilwell, informed the brethren that he called them together to consult about the propriety and necessity of electing an Elder, and read to them several extracts from books, written by Methodist Preachers, to prove the validity of such proceedings in cases of necessity. He also advised them to pursue or adopt the plan, as it would be a case of real necessity with them, being an African Methodist Church without an Elder, and he not having a sufficient number of Elders connected with him at present to perform ordination. A vote was then taken, in order to know whether the official brethren approved of the measure and were ready to act upon it; which was carried in favour of being ready. They then proceeded to nominate Abraham Thompson and James Varick, to be recommended to the Society as persons to be elected to the office of Elders in the Church.

Bishop William McKendree having arrived in the city, and being desirous to see some of the official members of our Church, nine of them, viz., Abraham Thompson, Leven Smith, John Dungy, Christopher Rush, Timothy Eatto, Samuel Bird, Tobias Hawkins, William Brown, and George Collins called on him, on Sunday, September 24th, 1820, immediately after Divine service in the afternoon, at his lodgings (he being unwell) at the residence of Joshua Soule, where they had a mutual conversation on the subject of our withdrawing from our white brethren. The Bishop said that he desired to see them, in order to know what they wanted him to do for them. They told him what they wanted, what they had done, and how far they were willing to go, in order to be in union with or governed by the white Bishops and Conference, and asked him whether he could ordain Elders for them. He said that he was limited in his office and could not at the present, but advised them to wait until the sitting of the ensuing annual Conference, and have the case brought regularly before that body, so that, if they should agree on the subject, our Preachers might be ordained by him. Our brethren then informed him that such was the state of their spiritual affairs they could not wait until that time, but would be obliged to proceed and elect Elders as was contemplated, and gave him to understand that they probably would wait the result of the said Conference relative to ordination.

216

On Sunday afternoon, October 1st, 1820, being the time appointed to elect the two brethren who were nominated on the 13th of September last for that purpose, the members of the Society, both male and female, were requested to tarry after the dismission of the congregation, for special business; and after the Elder, William M. Stilwell, had given a satisfactory explanation of the purpose for which the members of the Society were detained, Abraham Thompson was offered, and all who were in favour of his being elected were requested to hold up their right hand, which was done in a very solemn manner by a large majority (if not by the whole body); then James Varick was offered, and was in the same manner solemnly elected. These two brethren, being thus elected, were considered as having full power to exercise the peculiar functions of Elders in the Church with us, or any society of coloured people in connexion with us, until an opportunity offered to ordain them by the hands of proper authority. The whole process was conducted with much apparent solemnity and satisfaction. *elder by election*

¶   African Methodist Episcopal Zion Relations with
        Methodist Episcopal Church, 1821

(Taken from Bradley, I, 84-86, and Rush, 65-69).

To the Bishops and Preachers of the Philadelphia and
New York Conferences, Assembled:

Respected Brethren:

We, the official members of the African Methodist Zion and Asbury Churches, in the city of New York, and of the Wesleyan Church, in the City of Philadelphia, on behalf of our brethren, members of the aforesaid Churches; likewise of a small society at New Haven, and some of our colored brethren on Long Island, beg the favor of addressing you on a subject, to us, of great importance, and, we presume, not a matter of indifference to you.

In the first place, suffer us to beg you will accept of our humble and sincere thanks for your kind services to us when in our infant state, trusting that the Great Head of the Church, the all-wise and gracious God, has, and will continue to reward you for your labors among us, having made you the instruments of bringing us from darkness to light. And from the power of sin and Satan, to Him, the true and living God.

In the next place we proceed to say: - When the Methodist Society in the United States was small, the Africans enjoyed privileges among their white brethren in the same meeting-house, but as the whites increased very fast the Africans were pressed back; therefore, it was thought essentially necessary for them to have

meeting-houses of their own, in those places where they could obtain them, in order to have more room to invite their colored brethren yet out of the ark of safety to come in; and it is well known that the Lord has greatly enlarged their number since that memorable time, by owning their endeavors in the conversion of many hundreds. Many preachers have been raised up among them, who have been very useful in a located state; but they have hitherto been confined; they have no opportunities to travel, being generally poor men, and having no provisions made for them to go forth and dispense the Word of Life to their brethren, their usefulness has been greatly hindered, and their colored brethren have been deprived of those blessings which Almighty God might have designed to grant through their instrumentality. And now, it seems, the time has come when something must be done for the prosperity of the ministry amongst our brethren; and how shall this be accomplished? for we have not the least expectation that African or colored preachers will be admitted to a seat and vote in the Conference of their white brethren, let them be how much soever qualified for the work of the ministry; nor do we desire to unite with our brother Richard Allen's connexion (for our brethren, the members of the Wesleyan Church in Philadelphia, withdrew from them to build their present house of worship, named as above); therefore, our brethren in the City of New York, after due consideration, have been led to conclude that, to form an itinerant plan, and establish a Conference for African Methodist preachers, under the patronage of the white Methodist Bishops and Conference, would be the means of accomplishing the desired end. Believing that such an establishment would tend greatly to the prosperity of the spiritual concerns of our colored brethren in general, and would be the means of great encouragement to our preachers, who are now in regular standing in connexion with the white Methodist Episcopal Church in the United States, and also to such as may be hereafter raised among us, who may be disposed to join the said Conference and enter on the traveling plan. And, in order to commence this great work, the two societies in the City of New York united and agreed that the title of the connexion shall be "The African Methodist Episcopal Church in America," and have selected a form of discipline from that of the mother (white) church, which, with a little alteration, we have adopted for the government of the said connexion, and to which we beg to offer you.

After the perusal of our selection and the consideration of our case, should our proceedings meet your approbation, and you should be disposed to patronize the same, we will stand ready, and shall be glad to receive such advice and instruction as you may think proper to give us, through our father in the Lord, Bishop McKendree, or any other person the Conference may be pleased to appoint.

On the subject of ordination to Eldership (a privilege which our preachers have been long deprived of) permit us to say that we

might have obtained it from other sources, but we preferred and determined to follow the advice of Bishop McKendree, given to our brethren in New York the last time he was with them, and wait until the meeting of your Annual Conference in this and the district of New York, in order to understand what encouragement we may look for from the mother church. But, in consequence of some uneasiness in the minds of some of our members in New York, occasioned by our brother Richard Allen's determination to establish a society of his connexion in that city, our brethren there have been under the necessity of solemnly electing three of their deacons to the office of Elders, and some of their preachers to the office of deacons, to act only in cases of necessity, and to show to our people that our preachers can be authorized to administer the sacrament of the Lord's Supper as well as those of brother Allen's connexion - that thereby they might keep the body together, and we believe it has had the desired effect, for very few have left the Societies there, notwithstanding the efforts made to induce them to leave us.

We expect that our first yearly Conference will be held in the City of New York, on the 14th day of June next, at which we hope to have the happiness of hearing that our Father in the Lord, Bishop McKendree , presided, and commenced his fatherly instructions in an African Methodist Conference, formed under the patronage of the Methodist Episcopal Church in the United States of America. With this hope we shall rest, waiting your answer; meanwhile praying that the great Shepherd and Bishop of souls and our most merciful Father will be pleased to bless and guide you in your deliberations on our case, so that your conclusions may be of such as shall be pleasing in his sight, and tend most to the prosperity of his kingdom amongst the Africans, and consequently prove an everlasting blessing to many precious souls.

N.B. Should the above address be sanctioned by your respected body, and you should be pleased to act upon it, we will thank you to transmit the same to the New-York Annual Conference, for their consideration, and should the time appointed for the sitting of the African Conference be inconvenient for the person who may be appointed to organize the same, we are willing that it should be altered to a few days sooner or later, provided you would be pleased to give us timely notice of said alteration. But should you be disposed not to favor the said address in any respect, you will please have the goodness to return it to the bearer.

Signed, in behalf of the official members of both Societies, at a meeting called especially for that purpose, March 23rd, 1821, in the City of New York.

James Varick, President
George Collins, Secretary

Reply from Philadelphia Conference:

The committee, to whom was referred the memorial of the official members of the African Methodist Zion and Asbury Churches, in the city of New York, and the Wesley Church, in the city of Philadelphia, in behalf of themselves and others of their coloured brethren, proposing and requesting the organization of a Conference for the African Methodist Preachers, under the patronage of the Bishops and Conferences of the white Methodist Episcopal Church, having had the subject under serious and close consideration, in its various bearings and relations, ask leave now to report:

1. We view it as a subject of great importance to the coloured people, demanding from us our friendly patronage and pastoral attention, so far as circumstances will admit of it. We have always acted upon the principle toward the people of colour, of doing them all the good that was in our power, in promoting and improving their moral and religious instruction and character, and in protecting and defending them in all their just rights and privileges, and more particularly we have, as instruments under God, laboured much for the conversion and salvation of their souls. They know, and it is generally known and acknowledged, that our labours of good will and christian love toward them for many years past, have been crowned with gracious success and much good effect among them, as it respects both their moral and religious character, and also to the improvement to some considerable degree, of their condition and circumstances in life.

2. There are at this time various societies and congregations of coloured people, in different places, who have been collected and raised under our ministerial labours, and who have erected and built themselves houses for the public worship of God, wherein they assemble separate from the white people for their religious devotions; and also, there are a considerable number of pious coloured men, whom we have reason to believe are qualified to preach the word of life and salvation, and to be useful in their labours among the people of their own colour; but upon our present plan, under existing circumstances and regulations, their privileges as ministers are very much circumscribed, and their opportunities for improvement and usefulness are very limited. There exists no expectation or prospect, that the coloured Preachers will be admitted to a vote or seat in our Conferences, or participate in sundry other privileges among the white Preachers, in their labours and pastoral care of the churches and societies generally; neither is it understood that they wish or desire it. They request a Conference themselves in unity and friendship with, and under the patronage of the Bishops and Conferences of the white Preachers, and that our Bishops should preside among them and ordain their Preachers, and extend to them their superintending

220

protection, counsel and direction in their itinerant regulations and ministerial operations. It appears that they could obtain orders from another quarter, and become a connexion distinct from, and independent of the white Bishops and Conferences, but they prefer and desire patronage from, and a certain degree of union with us. They have refused to unite with Richard Allen and his African connexion, being dissatisfied with their general manner of proceedings.

3. From every view of the subject we have been able to take, we are of opinion the time is come when something must be done, more than yet has been done, for our coloured people, especially for such as are situated and circumstanced as the memorialists are, in order to enlarge their sphere of labours, and to extend their privileges and opportunities of usefulness among themselves, under our protection and direction, otherwise we shall lose their confidence in us and our influence over them, and they will become separate from, and independent of us, and then our usefulness among them will in a great measure be lost. And it appears in the present case under consideration, that they are fixed and resolved to have a Conference among themselves, whether patronized by us or not, and they have appointed the time for holding it, but that they wish us to take them under our patronage: Therefore, your committee proposes the following resolutions to the Conference for adoption, viz.

First, Resolved, that the Philadelphia Conference do advise and recommend that one of our Bishops do attend and preside in the African Conference, appointed to sit in New-York, and to superintend their organization as an African Methodist Conference, under the patronage of our Bishops and Conferences, agreeably to the proper plan, viz. (if the New-York Conference concur with us.)

1. One of the Bishops always to preside in the said Conference, or in case no Bishop be present, then, such white Elder as the Bishop shall appoint is to preside.

2. Our Bishops to ordain all their Deacons and Elders, such as shall be elected by their own Conference and approved of by the Bishop as qualified for the office.

3. The Bishop, or the Elder appointed by him, to preside in the Conference, with an advisory committee of three, chosen by the Conference, to make out the stations and appointments of the Preachers.

4. All the other proceedings of the Conference to be as comformable to the rules and regulations generally followed in our Conferences, as circumstances will admit of.

5. Their Discipline, doctrines, government, and rules of order in all things, to be as comformable to ours as possible, so as to secure to themselves their own peculiar rights and privileges.

6. The Bishop, or such Elder as shall be appointed by him, with his proper instructions, together with the said African Conference, to agree upon the several points, terms and considerations of unity and amity mutually to exist, as reciprocal duties and obligations between them and us. This agreement to take place and be entered into at the time or organizing the said Conference.

Secondly, Resolved, that a copy of this report be forwarded with the African Memorial to the New-York Conference, and that the said New-York Conference be recommended and requested to concur with us in the proposed plan of organizing the said African Conference under our patronage, with such additons to, or alterations of the above items, as to them may appear best.

EZEKIEL COOPER,)
THOMAS WARE,   )   Committee
ALWARD WHITE,)

The above report was adopted by the Philadelphia Conference, and the Secretary was instructed to communicate a copy of it to the New-York Conference.

SAMUEL COX, Secretary.

Milford, April 19, 1821.

9. THE REFORM MOVEMENT

The close association of political and ecclesiastical issues in the 1820's is uncanny. Here if anywhere the Methodist movement and the American way of life ran parallel. The same outlook pervaded both the halls of Congress and the General Conferences of the church. There was a "Jacksonian era" in the history of the Methodist Episcopal Church. Although the nation was not yet rent, passions in both state and church ran deep, whether over a national bank and the forced removal of the Eastern Indians on the one hand or over the election of presiding elders and the rights of lay people on the other. For Methodist history this decade of agitation over reform is a classic prototype of that pervading theme, which runs like a guiding thread throughout the story, of democracy versus authority.

The arguments over appointment or election of presiding elders, which would determine whether these officers would be known as the bishops' lieutenants or representatives of the body of ministers, were ably summarized by Nathan Bangs. Although he was deeply involved, he managed to present a fair case for both sides in his History. Later on, at the point of schism, he was impelled to make a strong defense of the connectional system, which he thought was threatened by the extremes to which the reformers were going. Thus he quoted the entire report to General Conference prepared by John Emory as an answer to the reformers' memorial (III, 413-29). It is not included in this collection of readings because it rehashed arguments made more effectively by others.

Among the many protagonists who sought to present the case for one side or the other Nicholas Snethen stands out. His essays, printed in the Reform magazine Wesleyan Repository, later Mutual Rights, were brought together in one volume entitled Snethen on Lay Representation. Even after the passage of a hundred and fifty years his pieces are thought-provoking. Although he was caught up in the passionate struggle in which personalities were involved as well as issues, he maintained a high degree of integrity and good sense. Snethen, who once rushed to Asbury's defense against O'Kelly and then later joined the dissident Reformers, is one of the major neglected figures in the American Methodist tradition.

Although he can scarcely be credited with objectivity, Edward Drinkhouse performed a valuable service by bringing into an appendix of his two volume History key documents related to the Methodist Protestant Church. Among these are the Constitution of the church and Henry B. Bascom's "Declaration of Rights," the

latter identifying the ecclesiastical issues of church government with the heady ideas which were current in the political realm during the terms of Andrew Jackson.

(Taken from Nathan Bangs, *A History of the Methodist Episcopal Church* (1838), II, 338-43).

Those in favor of the change, alleged,

1. That it is more in conformity to the genius of the American people to have a voice in the election of those who are to rule over them; and as the presiding elders were, by the usages of the Church, entrusted with a controlling influence over the preachers, they ought to have a choice in their selection.

2. It was contended that so long as they were appointed by the bishop, it necessarily augmented the power of the episcopacy, as, by virtue of this appointment, the presiding elders were amenable to the bishop alone for their official conduct, and not to their brethren in the conference.

3. Hence, the preacher, let him be oppressed ever so much in his appointment, has no medium of redress within his reach, as his case is represented to the appointing power through an ecclesiastical officer over whom he has no control, and who is completely in the bishop's confidence and at his disposal.

4. These things, it was contended, were incompatible with the natural and civil rights of freemen, and with that equality among brethren of the same ministerial order, as is the case in respect to presiding elders and all the other elders in the Methodist Episcopal Church.

5. As to a council to advise with the bishops in stationing the preachers, it was pleaded that however wise and good the bishop might be, it was impossible for him to have that knowledge of the local state of the people and peculiar circumstances of the preachers, which is essential to enable him to make the most judicious appointments; and hence he assumed a responsibility for which he could not rationally account.

6. And then to give one man the complete control over five hundred others, many of whom may be equal to him in age and experience, and perhaps also in wisdom, learning, and goodness, and as likely to be as disinterested in their views and feelings, was an anomaly in legislation and an absurdity in practice for which no arguments could be adduced, derived from either Scripture or the fitness of things.

7. That however safely this prerogative might be exercised by Bishop Asbury, especially in the infancy of the Church, when the number of preachers was few, it had now become impossible, on the

increase of preachers and people, for a bishop to exercise such a tremendous power intelligibly and safely to all concerned. Bishop Asbury, it was argued, was the *father* of the connection, and felt for the entire family in a way that no one else could, and therefore no one else ought to be entrusted with the same power which he had exercised.

8. The example of our British brethren was cited, who, after the death of Mr. Wesley, had given the power of stationing the preachers to a committee, and then they were allowed an appeal to the conference.

To these arguments, it was answered,

1. That the Church of Christ was founded, in some respects, upon very different principles from those on which civil governments rested, and therefore, though analogous in some particulars, yet in others the contrast was so obvious as to neutralize all analogical arguments. That though the people elected their legislators, president, and governors, yet most of the executive officers were appointed by the president; and as presiding elders were executive officers, their appointment by the bishop might be justified even from analogy.

2. Though it was admitted that they strengthened the hands of the episcopacy, yet being appointed by him saved the Church from an evil more to be dreaded than mere episcopal power, and that was an electioneering spirit, which must keep the conferences in perpetual agitations – engendering a strife incompatible with the spirit of harmony and brotherly love.

3. Hence, though a preacher might, either from inadvertence or design, be injured in his appointment, yet to make the presiding elder dependant on the choice of an annual conference might make him fear to do his duty, in respect to enforcing discipline, and in exacting vigilance from those under him in the discharge of duty; moreover his redress was always with the bishop and the annual conference, to whom con-jointly the presiding elder is responsible for his official conduct.

4. As to natural and civil rights, it was retorted, that though a Methodist preacher retained them as a citizen, yet the moment he entered the itinerancy, he became subject to ecclesiastical restraints which, though not incompatible with his rights as a freeman, were nevertheless essential to the preservation and efficient operation of the itinerancy.

5. In respect to the necessity, arising from the limited information and want of local knowledge of a bishop, of associating others with him in stationing the preachers, this was remedied in practice by his receiving all the information he could from presiding elders and others, and then acting according to the dictates of an unbiased

judgment, which was less likely to be influenced by local prejudices than those who, from their more limited sphere of information, were liable to be biased by partial interests and local feelings.

6. As to an unlimited control over five hundred men, more or less, while it was admitted that many of them might be equal to the bishop in general wisdom and experience, yet they could not, from their position, have that comprehensive knowledge of the whole work, and that experience arising from extensive travel and information which belonged to an itinerating episcopacy; and, moreover, this control had a check in annual conferences, who might ultimately determine whether a preacher was justified or not in refusing to go to his appointment, and also by the General Conference, under the inspection of which the bishop's conduct passed every fourth year.

7. Though it be admitted that Bishop Asbury sustained a fatherly relation to the Church which none of his successors could, and had a more intimate knowledge of preachers and people, both from his having grown up with them, and the comparative smallness of their number, yet from having an increased number of bishops, and from those restraints constantly thrown around them by a watchful diligence among their brethren, it was contended, would prevent any wanton exercise of power, and render it still safe in their hands.

8. As to our British brethren they had no other visible head than their conference. But we have, and therefore can act more efficiently through this medium, than we could do by a stationing committee. It was still further contended, and with great force of argument, that if this power were taken from the bishops, it would be extremely difficult to keep up an interchange of preachers from one annual conference to another, a difficulty not felt in England, where they were all united in one conference, in which all their business was transacted.

In the course of this discussion two opposite views were taken of the doctrine of responsibility. Some of those who contended for reserving this power in the hands of the bishop, insisted that the episcopacy was responsible for the entire executive administration, in all its ramifications, and therefore, in order that it might exercise it safely, it must have the control of the appointments, not indeed to office, but to the several stations, so that if those acting under its appointment did not discharge their trusts with fidelity, they might be removed or changed at pleasure; and as a strong and commanding motive for a wise and faithful execution of this high trust, the episcopacy was held responsible to the General Conference, which had entrusted to the bishops the preservation of our itinerancy in all its parts; and this they could not do if the power of appointment were taken from them.

To this it was replied, that though this seemed very plausible in theory, it was not possible to exemplify it in practice - that it was loading the episcopacy with a weight of responsibility too heavy for any mortal and fallible man to bear, and therefore must ultimately crush the episcopacy beneath its pressure. To prevent this it would be most judicious to divide the responsibility among the several annual conferences, and hold the presiding elders especially strictly responsible to them for their official as well as their moral and Christian conduct - as it was admitted on all hands that the preachers were held accountable to their respective conferences for their ministerial and Christian conduct, it was in vain to contend that the episcopacy should be more liable to censure for their malversation. The former traced responsibility from the General Conference, who made the regulations and judged of episcopal acts, to the episcopacy, and thence down through the several grades of Church officers: the latter traced it up through the societies, to quarterly and annual conferences, to the General Conference; while others contended, with more truth than either, it is believed, that each body and officer was accountable for its and his own conduct, and the latter to the tribunal from which he received his authority, and held the right to call him to an account for his acts and deeds.

¶   Nicholas Snethen's Essays on Democracy

(Taken from *Snethen on Lay Representation* (1835), 67-69, 75-78, 119-129, 342-46, articles in *Wesleyan Repository* and *Mutual Rights*).

The Present State of Things

It was a singular and perhaps a providential circumstance, that the General Conference [1820] was equally divided on the motion to suspend "the reconciliation" for four years. An event so unlikly [sic] on so momentous a question, was certainly well calculated to teach moderation to both parties; but so it seemed not to the managing spirits. The alarm was sounded, the constitution is violated - and forty-five votes were pledged beyond the doors of the conference and redeemed within them - thus was the conciliatory propositions of the second bishop; the solemn agreement of a committee of equal numbers from both sides; the votes of more than two-thirds of the General Conference; the expression of satisfaction and tears of joy, &c. all thrown to the winds: and the peace and harmony of the preachers, if not their final union, put in jeopardy for the sake of gaining four years to electioneer through the annual conferences. Scarcely had the preachers returned to their circuits, before it began to be rumored that the motives and the moral integrity of one-half the travelling preachers, or at least of their representatives was questionable. The friends of the sole power of the bishops to

choose presiding elders, whispered about (as we hear) that the preachers in the north and east, and a certain number in the Baltimore Conference, aimed to destroy the itinerancy and introduce congregationalism, &c. We may just remark in passing that our plan, and the congregational plan, are the two extremes in church government. In ours, all the power is in the hands of the bishops and preachers - in theirs, in the people. If we must believe those preachers to be sincere who can propagate such suspicions against their brethren, we cannot believe that their understandings are equal to their sincerity. How terrible must the imaginations of men be alarmed by fears, who in despite of every evidence which the nature of the case can furnish, conjure up images of the most extreme ideal danger. If they really believed that those preachers aim at more than they profess, why not believe that they aim at some modification of our episcopacy. Men who were contending for their rights, when they gave up principles, dear to every lover of religious liberty, should have been promptly met by those who were required to give up almost nothing; but all terms are not only refused them; their honesty and veracity is held up in their absence in more than doubtful character. Those who think they do God service by propagating their own suspicions against their brethren, may remain blind to the consequences, but to us who take no part in this election campaign of four years long, and have no immediate interests in the issue, it is plain that they are making a schism among traveling preachers, and are using the very means to render it incurable. Who can have any confidence in any proposed plans of reconciliation, who remembers what was the fate of that of 1820? It was an awful and portentous hour that fixed the character of "truce breakers" upon forty-five members of the General Conference. But though the present mode of proceeding is calculated to destroy all our hopes of a restoration of mutual confidence among travelling preachers, yet, in our opinion, the spell which had suspended free inquiry is dissolved forever, and every year will give rise to new doubts respecting the wisdom of the organization of our hierarchy. But whoever may have the majority in the next General Conference, we think it can easily be forseen, that the people will not be suffered to remain neutral, for, though they will not be permitted to touch the hem of the garments of *the powers that be,* they will add too much to the pomp and grace of the triumph to be left out of the train.

The probability is, that there will be no reconciliation among the preachers at the next General Conference. We may calculate therefore, that the defeated party will come among us, not like the conquered bull in the fable among the frogs in the marsh, to tread us to death, but to seek our sympathy. In such an event, the members of the church will no longer have to tell the story of their complaints to a deaf man. On some future occasion we may essay something in the form of a memorial by way of anticipation. In the meanwhile we think it very advisable that brethren should be wary

of taking sides with those of any party who are contending for themselves, and for themselves only.

*   *   *

We do not remember to have seen a discourse on this explicit
declaration of the origin, and positive nature of relegious freedom,[sic]
in which its social, as well as individual bearing is brought fairly
into view. The commentators and the preachers mostly treat of it in
reference to experimental religion, as a freedom from the guilt, the
power, and the principles of sin; and it is certain, that he who is
under the power of either of these, is not morally or religiously
free indeed. Upon this plan the nature of church freedom is seldom
brought under consideration; but the difference between private and
social freedom is of importance, and involves consequences of the
most interesting nature. If, as is generally believed, Jesus Christ
intended that his disciples and followers should exist together in
a social state as fellow subjects of his kingdom, or members of his
church, we cannot forbear the inquiry, whether he meant that they
should be socially free indeed, or whether they should pass under
the yoke to ecclesiastical masters. As such masters are not fond to
be called by their right names, it is probable that no one will be
forward to assert, that this latter condition of the church, is
agreeable to the will of its founder. Should any one, however, be
found bold enough to attempt to father either the principles, or
the practices of religious bondage in the church, upon the authority
of Jesus Christ, we hold that he may be effectually refuted by these
words, "If the son shall make you free, ye shall be free indeed," for
they imply no doubt of his readiness and willingness to make us free;
but of our acceptance of his glorious and substantial freedom. Let
us enquire into the nature of church freedom, as distinct from personal
and civil freedom, for it is evident that neither of the latter
necessarily involve the former. The very essence of church freedom,
consists in having a voice personally, or by our representatives, in
and over the laws by which we are to be governed, and in being judged
by our peers. If one man or any set of men, who have no dependence
upon the church or legislative responsibility to it, may or can make
its laws, it has not the shadow of freedom any more than the substance;
all church powers and privileges are thus cut off at their fountainhead. Nor would the church be at all benefited, if the by-laws and
written forms were dispensed with, and all church proceedings referred
to the letter of the New Testament, if men of the same irresponsibility
were to be interpreters and executors of the sacred authority; the
danger on the contrary would be increased, as without precedents they
might add caprice to injustice. It is certain, that the letter of
no institution can execute itself, and it would be an idle waste of
time to attempt to prove that implicit confidence in men with
absolute power, is utterly fallacious. There is not a man living, who
can foresee how power will effect him before he make the trial, and
it is well known how often the most sagacious judges of human nature,

230

are disappointed in their anticipation of religious as well as civil officers. Judges of courts of justice, who are made as independent as possible of other branches of civil government, are only appointed during good behaviour, but such a latitude is found to be by no means safe in the office of lawmakers; those who are invested with the legislative authority in free communities, are held under the perpetual responsibility of periodical elections. The priestcraft of which we have heard reiterated complaints, is nothing more than a modification of human ambition, or a vice of nature converted into a vice of office. It is seldom if ever, that we find on the pages of ecclesiastical history, a fair and correct development of the principles of social freedom. The struggle between the great contending parties, when the priesthood was concerned, was, who should be the greatest, not how powers should be equalized and balanced. When violence and force was resorted to, it was natural, and indeed unavoidable, for the weaker party to have recourse to artifice. The boasted advantages of separating the church from the state, are neutralized to the members of the latter; if there is no balance of power between them and their officers; and it may also happen, that their condition may be thus changed for the worse; as the political power may have an interest in protecting the church from the unlimited influence of the priesthood, though it must be confessed that they have most frequently combined their force, and made the people a common prey. We do not profess to be competent judges of the actual state of religious freedom among other denominations in our country, but if we may trust to appearances we should be led to conjecture, that in some instances, where the greatest zeal for liberty is expressed, the check giving principles are either not well understood or steadily carried into practical operation. The reformers themselves seem not to have understood the principles of church freedom as well as the founders of our republic did those of civil freedom. Though nothing can be more hostile to our views and feelings than a union of church and state, yet as human nature is the same, and, like gravity, acts by uniform laws, we are fully persuaded that any means which are found, on experiment, sufficient to check and control the natural ambition of the human heart in one case, has strong claims to our attention in the other. As the American doctrine, that tyranny consists in undivided power being in the same hands, is as fully demonstrated by the priestcraft of ecclesiastical history, as the kingcraft and aristocratical policy of civil history, why may not the converse of the case hold true. Men who have the same interests will be prone to act alike; and as long as they perceive that their interests are mutual, they will act together. It would be a miracle, that is, an event contrary to the course of nature, if either priests or preachers, with the legislative and executive power of the church in their own hands, should not manage the interests of others, so as to promote their own. The security of a church against the tyranny of its own officers is out of the question, so long as its members remain ignorant of, or inattentive to those constitutional principles, on

231

whose reaction the health of social, as well as natural bodies depend. The cause and effects of a fever in the human body are in many points analogous to tyranny in the body social. Both proceed from some derangement in the parts and powers of the system, and both by an excess of circulation to the head, if not corrected, eventuate in death. Ambition, as we have said, is like gravity, and can only be overcome by opposing force to force, and resistance to resistance. If the interests of the church could be placed upon one end of a beam or lever, and the interests of priests or preachers at the other, though the former might be much the more weighty, yet the balancing of the two would not depend upon that circumstance, but upon the position of the rest or fulcrum. There is not, nor can there be, a form of religious government devised, that may not become tyrannical by deranging the balance of power; and this we conceive to be the reason why the scriptures are so silent upon the forms and modes of church government, and also why so little has been gained by changing its modes and names, in order to bring it more near to the scripture plan. The eagerness with which some men search for precedents of religious governments, seems to us to be of no more importance than that of a mechanic, who ransacks every country, in order to find models for steelyards, or should prefer the ancient Roman one to any other. No model would be of any use, if he should not know how to construct this kind of balance scientifically, or by experiment. The tenacity with which the different denominations cleave to their different modes of government on account of their supposed conformity to the primitive church government, betrays a want of science and a neglect of experiment. Among the churches which have adopted the episcopal form, there are no two who have given the same division of power to their episcopal officers; and an indefinite number more might differ among themselves, and from all the rest. The same thing might happen to a presbyterian, or congregational, or any form of government, and probably has happened. If any one will prove to us that the primitive church was not free indeed, we can prove that it is no precedent for us, and that in this respect we ought not to follow its example. Any government which is founded on principles, which secure to the preachers and the members of the church their mutual rights and privileges, is scriptural enough for our faith and practice. Is it not remarkable that the American people who have a government *sui generis* of their own originating and making, should be so tenacious of the religious polity of the European churches from which their ancestors sprung? Could this difference in the influence of the prejudice of education have existed, if the principles of religious government were as well understood as those of civil liberty? We are inclined to think that much of the asperity which exists among different sects, is to be traced to the want of some guiding and directing principle, which though it might direct men through different roads, could hardly fail, if steadily followed, to conduct them to the same end. Our church which has neither legislative voice nor will, with the millstone of the absolute power of the preachers about her neck, can

never see the pleasant light, or breathe the vital air of freedom. The waves and billows of despotic government must roll eternally over her head, unless by some means she can extricate herself from this dead weight.

*   *   *

A View of the Primitive Church and its Government.

As our fathers and brethren gave us, in their wisdom, a form of church government without furnishing us with any scriptural rules, principles, or doctrines, by which to illustrate and defend it, does it not behoove us to go to the source and fountain head of all information and authority, instead of taking the scriptural character of our discipline for granted, and continuing to build upon a foundation which we have not proved? What would be our condition, were our religion as destitute of scripture support as is our discipline? Nothing can be more plain than our plan of salvation; nothing more perplexed than our plan of government. In the one case, rules and precedents are furnished to us at all points; in the other, all is dogmatical. Our church government may be compressed into the following maxim: "All power must be in the hands of the preachers; none in those of the members of the church." .   .   .   .

In the New Testament the acts of ministers were not confounded with those of the church; nor those of the church with the acts of the ministry, any more than their names. It may surprise those who have been accustomed to hear of the primitive church, to find, that in Paul's writings no such phrase exists; but that he uniformly writes to, and speaks of churches.

With the opinions of Romanists or Reformed, we have nothing to do, when we are seeking principles. These, I repeat, must be expressed in the New Testament, or they must originate from it, by plain and obvious consequence or inference. If any change take place, even one month after the canon of scripture was closed, or without the authority of the apostles, it is of no more importance in deciding a question of scripture principle, than as though it had happened in the eighteenth century.

From the New Testament, we find, then, the following principles: first, that in the very beginning, churches were local assemblies. Secondly, that each and every church possessed an identity of existence. Thirdly, that each church was distinguished from its office bearers. These three principles of church existence, are three natural, simple, and obvious means of preserving the rights and liberties of churches. By giving to each church identity of existence, every individual one must be destroyed before the genus can become extinct. The church of any name or country may be destroyed, and yet, if any single christian church remains, in any part

233

of the world, the gates of hell have not prevailed against it. Nothing is more notorious, from the whole tenor of ecclesiastical history, than the process by which churches have been enslaved. Individual churches must be swallowed up, to make dioceses, provinces, &c. This is not only a well known, but a necessary process of a hierarchy. One ministerial head, or sovereignty over many churches, is out of the question. Hierarchists have always aimed to make the church one and indivisible. Be the name, or the form of the head what it may, every part of the body is made equally dependent upon it, and must die if it be cut off.

But the indivisibility of the church has neither scripture, example nor precept for its support. The union of the primitive churches was maintained among themselves upon federative principles. Believers are, indeed, considered as composing one church, as it respects God, and Christ; as, "the church of the living God - head over all things to the church," &c. - but when we attend to the addresses of the apostolic epistles, a distinction of the churches among themselves most evidently appears. . . .

"And he gave some apostles, and some prophets, and some evangelists, and some pastors and teachers; for the perfecting of the saints, for the work of the ministry, for the edifying of the body of Christ" - "God hath set some in the church, first, apostles; secondly, prophets; thirdly, teachers; after that miracles, then gifts of healing, helps, governments." In these two passages, and they are the most detailed account of the primitive office of any in the New Testament, bishops and elders are not mentioned by name. The pastors and teachers in the first, may be supposed to answer to the teachers and governments in the second. The apostles, prophets, evangelists, miracles, gifts of healing, &c. are confessedly extraordinary, for they are equally wanting in all other ages and countries. The idea that bishops are successors of the apostles, in the only sense it can possibly be admitted, is precluded by their co-existence. Nothing is more plain, than that pastors, governments, bishops or elders, were contemporary with the apostles. "And Paul sent for the elders, and said take heed to the flock of God over the which the Holy Ghost hath made you overseers" - "And we beseech you, brethren, to know them who labor among you, and are over you, in the Lord, and admonish you, and to esteem them very highly in love for their work's sake" - "Remember them who have the rule over you, who have spoken unto you the word of God, whose faith follow." It may be remarked in passing, how little this style savours of the dictatorial. But these passages prove, most unequivocally, that in Ephesus, in Thessalonica, and among the Hebrews, St. Paul recognised overseers, rulers, pastors or governments, as well as teachers. A succession to oversight or government, in the churches, must, therefore, be to those, and not to the apostles; for by the shewing of Paul himself, the apostles and evangelists had not the oversight or rule, in the churches enumerated above; and no one overlooked them all; their

bishops were among them. Now does it not follow, by analogy, where no evidence is found to the contrary, that the case was similar to other churches? That is, that there were elders in every city and church, whom the Holy Ghost made overseers.

Apostles, evangelists, prophets, gifts, miracles, &c. &c. might have been necessary in the planting of churches, and the completion of written revelation; but this extraordinary work once accomplished, the extraordinary succession would destroy the identity of the original. . . .

We will now proceed to search for the principle of the primitive government, as found in the examples recorded in the New Testament.

In the Acts of the Apostles there is a circumstantial account of the manner in which the controversy between the judaizing teachers and Paul and Barnabas was decided. "When, therefore, Paul and Barnabas had no small dissention and disputation with them (the certain men who came from Jerusalem) they (the brethren) determined that Paul and Barnabas, and certain others of them (their own body) should go up to Jerusalem, unto the apostles and elders, about this question. How were the certain others of them selected? Did Paul and Barnabas choose them, or did they offer their own services, or were they chosen by the brethren who were vexed? Nothing but the most positive evidence to the contrary ought to influence any man to imagine that the latter mode was not adopted in preference to the two former. But if it was, then, there were delegates, or representatives in this case: "And when they were come to Jerusalem they were received of the church, and of the apostles and elders. And the apostles and elders came together to consider this matter. And when there was much disputing, Peter rose and said, men and brethren, - then all the multitude kept silence, and gave audience to Barnabas and Paul. James said, men and brethren hearken unto me. Then it pleased the apostles and elders, with the whole church." The vote was unanimous without a dissenting voice. The address of the letter is, "The apostles, elders, and brethren, greeting, unto the brethren which are of the Gentiles, in Antioch and Syria and Cilicia." These newly planted churches of Gentile converts refer an important dispute, which was occasioned by certain men who came from Jerusalem, to that mother church. The church and its office-bearers, as well as the apostles, all meet, and all vote; and they write back, "that it seemed good unto the Holy Ghost, and unto us." It would seem that there were no upper house in those days, nor closed doors.

This was not a general council, nor a general conference, it is true; and it is equally true, that they did not write their letter to the universal church, but to the brethren of the Gentiles in Antioch, and Syria, and Cilicia, who had written to them. The whole of this transaction deserves to be studied with great care and attention. Neither the judaizing teachers, nor the brethren, seem to have enter-

tained very awful notions of apostolic supremacy in this instance.
And whatever may have been the actual power of apostles in such
matters, it is certain that the great apostle to the Gentiles, and
his colleague, the son of consolation, interposed no legislative
prerogatives to the exclusion of the elders and brethren. The
multitude kept silence only while Peter and Paul and Barnabas and
James were speaking, neither of whom, it would seem, took the
floor, until an advanced stage of the debate, for there had been
much disputing before Peter arose. The church, in the whole
business, is contradistinguished from the apostles and elders, so
that it is impossible for the art of man to confound them. The
parent church at Jerusalem did not volunteer in this affair, but
acted by particular request. Rome seems to have had no more to do
with it than Geneva, or Canterbury, or Baltimore.

*   *   *

Another principle of great importance, which we are to search
for in the New Testament, if it be not given or revealed, is,
respecting the manner in which the officers of the churches were
originally selected. But concerning the apostles, properly so
called, there can be no question, their very name imports their
immediate commission from the head of the church; and all the particulars of their being chosen by the Lord Jesus Christ, as well as
their very names, are circumstantially recorded by the evangelists.
When one was to be ordained to be a witness, with the eleven, of
the resurrection, in the place of Judas, they appointed two, and
they prayed, and said, thou Lord, who knowest the hearts of all
men, shew whether of these two thou hast chosen.   .   .   .

Evangelists seem to have been qualified for their extraordinary
office of helpers to the apostles, by supernatural gifts, and to have
done all the duties common to apostles, except the identical, and
essential ones, of bearing witness to the resurrection of the Lord
Jesus Christ, and of writing scripture. That they bore an important
part in planting, and establishing churches, is evident; but how
many of them there were, or whether they all continued in their
office for life or not, the scripture is silent. It can only be
logically inferred, that the secondary office ceased with its
principle.   .   .   .

Modern ministers of the gospel are successors to the powers and
prerogatives of the ancient pastors and teachers; and if any among
them pretend to anything more, sooner or later, they will be convicted of ignorance or error. The earliest case on record in the
penticostal dispensation, of a regular election, is in the iv. of
the Acts: "Then the twelve called the multitude of the disciples,
and said, it is not reason that we should leave the word of God,
and serve tables; wherefore, brethren, look ye out among you seven

men of honest report, full of the Holy Ghost and wisdom, whom we
may appoint over this business; but we will give ourselves continually to prayer and to the ministry of the word. And the saying
pleased the whole multitude: and they chose Stephen, &c. &c. whom
they set before the apostles, and when they had prayed, they laid
their hands upon them." Here, it is worthy of remark, that the
apostles did not even nominate. Of the manner in which the elders
were chosen we have no account; but as it is clear from the above
passage, that the laying on of hands, and of course ordaining, does
not imply, or include the choosing of the men, is it not to be
inferred that the multitude chose or elected, in the one case, as
well as in the other? May it not be reasonably presumed, that one
cause why the New Testament is so silent upon the subject of the
election of elders or bishops, is that it is a mere common sense
process? The qualifications for the office being stated, as they
are, in a very full and detailed manner, nothing but a positive
prohibition, from divine authority, should prevent churches from
choosing or electing their own officers.

*   *   *

An Address to the Friends of Reform [1827]

You have heard of what was done in the bounds of the Virginia
conference; and will hear of the proceedings of the Baltimore annual
conference, in the case of Dennis B. Dorsey. I notice this last case
as proof of the fact, that the itinerant preachers have taken a stand
against reform, or representation, which must change our relation to
them. We are no longer to consider ourselves as standing upon the
open and equal ground of argument with those brethren in behalf of a
principle; but as the supporters of what we conceive to be truth and
right, opposed by power. From the beginning, I have considered the
avoiding of written discussion by almost all the itinerant preachers
on the old side, as ominous of this issue, and have not ceased to
anticipate the time when a display of the plenary powers in their
hands would in effect place us as lambs among wolves, and call upon
us to be "wise as serpents and harmless as doves."

I understand the text in its original application, "I send you
forth as lambs among wolves," that is, with truth and right, among
those who have both the power and disposition to resist your
principles and to destroy you, but I give you no means of self
defence, but the wisdom of the serpent, tempered with the harmlessness of the dove. We have all along asserted, that there is power
enough in the rulers of the Methodist Episcopal Church, to excommuni-
cate us all, and we are still of the same opinion; but if any one
should doubt it, let him remember, that the body of men of whom we
mean to ask for a fish, may give us a scorpion; that the very
General Conference of 1828, may make rules, if they conceive they are
not already made, to reach every reformer.

Our relation I say was changed in point of fact, from the day the power of the itinerant preachers waked into action. The most distinguished preacher who should advocate the principle of representation would find himself obnoxious to power, as well as the least member in the church. No man among us has power to oppose to power; and truth or right in the mouth of a minister would not lose its lamb-like helplessness, when assailed by the power of a majority of itinerant preachers. This majority have all the claws and all the teeth, and therefore, every man may be made to fear.   .   .   .

Heretofore it is doubtful if a single travelling preacher has written for the Wesleyan Repository or the Mutual Rights, who was not known to his superiors. The writers themselves often confided their proper names to their brethren, and so they felt not like lambs among wolves; but a few examples in the annual conferences will put an end to this kind of generous rivalship. Travelling preachers themselves will be thus painfully taught the wisdom of the serpent - taught to elude power by policy. What a temptation will this prove to trespass upon the innocence of the dove? Brother Dorsey, it seems, was advised by his friends (in this advice I did not participate) not to answer any question which might criminate himself. This refusal to answer questions, this putting the conference upon the proof of his guilt, made a part of his offence. Who then did he thus offend? No one but the members of the annual conference. Now mark brethren, the importance of this whole transaction: not to brother Dorsey merely, but to us all. Let this procedure be established as a precedent, and of what avail will the maxim of our Master be to us? How can we maintain the harmlessness of the dove? How escape the jaws of power without dissimulation? Surely if we have no right to keep our own secrets among those who make a man an offender for a word, we have no means of self preservation, but in the unqualified wisdom of the serpent. Brother Dorsey by a vote of the annual conference, is deprived of a station for one year. Will either of these voters feel any twitches or qualms of conscience in treating either of us relatively in the same way, if we refuse to answer and to promise as they may please, and punish us for contumacy, or contempt of court? And that too, while in our courts of law no man is required to answer any question which goes to criminate himself. If brother Dorsey were imprisoned or banished for one year, by an annual conference for contumacy, all of the state of Maryland would be up in arms. The sound of the outcry of the deed would reach the ends of the earth. Persecution! would be re-echoed in all directions; and yet, in case either of imprisonment or banishment, he might preach quite as much in the capacity of a travelling preacher as these brethren intend he shall in this case. The truth is, brethren, that there is the very essence of persecution in this act of the Baltimore annual conference. As a precedent, it deprives us of our last, our only resort to defend ourselves against power, which we can imploy consistently with our christian character. Is not punishment for telling the truth and a reward for dissimulation, in effect, the same? I know brethren, that we shall be accused of

238

party spirit and party purposes, in espousing the cause of this brother, but it is not so; by this dispensation we are sent forth as lambs among wolves, power has usurped authority over truth; we are not to be reasoned with, but punished. In this new condition, what are we to do? We must go to the New Testament for direction and instruction; and there we learn, that we must be wise as serpents and harmless as doves. Must we not then espouse the principle, and can we do this without espousing the cause of the first martyr of it in the Baltimore annual conference? Your turn, my turn, may come next. It is an awful thing to be driven by the power of a majority from the last asylum of harmlessness - to be reduced to the dreadful alternative of dissimulation or bearing witness against one's self. . . .

I deem it proper, brethren, that in this portentous change, in this state of your affairs, that you should hear my voice, should see my name. It will, I know it will, it must be asked, now the time is come to try men's souls, where is Philo Pisticus? Where is Adynasius? Where is Senex [his pseudonyms] Where is the man who was among the foremost to challenge us to the cause of representation? Where is Snethen? I trust that while he is among the living, but one answer will be given to this question - he is at his post, he is in the front of the contest, he is shouting on, brethren on! and if he fall, it will be with a wound in his breast, and with his head direct towards the opponent. . . .

Of the labor of seven years, I make no account. I was not a lamb among wolves. My courage, my resolution was not put to the test. I have never been questioned, never called to account, not even threatened. The fiery trial has come upon one who is as the shadow of a man, a walking skeleton, and I yet go free! Mysterious providence! Thank God, the afflicted man's soul is in health, his fortitude is unimpaired by disease, he has the courage and the constancy of a martyr: Lord, let the young man live and not die! Let not the wife of his youth be a premature widow. I cannot now desert the cause and be innocent before God or man. I cannot now be silent and be harmless. I therefore advertise you of the change, and earnestly entreat you to conform to it by conforming to the directions of the Master, "Be ye, therefore, wise as serpents, and harmless as doves." Your affectionate fellow laborer in the great cause of church representation.

N. SNETHEN.

¶   Henry Bascom's "Declaration of Rights," 1830.

(Taken from Drinkhouse, II, 600-07).

Article 1st. God, as the common Father of mankind, has created all men free and equal, and the proper equality and social freedom of

the great brotherhood of the human race, in view of the gifts and grants of the Creator, are to be inferred from all his dispensations to men. Every man by the charter of his creation, is the equal of his contemporaries; - the essential rights of every generation are the same. Man as the child of God's creation, continues man immutably, under all circumstances; - and the rights of ancestry are those of posterity. Man has claims which it becomes his duty to assert, in right of his existence, such as the indefeasable right of thinking and acting for himself, when thought and action do not infringe the right of another, as they never will, when truth and justice are made the basis of human intercourse. These rights, common to the great family of man, cannot be abolished by concession, statute, precedent, or positive institution; and when wrested or withheld from the multitude of mankind, by their rulers, may be reclaimed by the people, whenever they see proper to do it.

Art. 2d. Man was created for society, his natural rights are adapted to the social state, and under every form of society, constitute properly, the foundation of his civil rights. When man becomes a member of civil society, he submits to a modification of some of his natural rights, but he never does, he never can, relinquish them. He concedes the exercise of these rights, for his own and the general good, but does not, cannot, cast them off. His rights receive a new direction, but do not terminate; and that government which deprives man of rights, justly claimed in virtue of his creation, and interwoven with the constitution of his nature, and the interests of society, denies to him the gifts of his Creator, and must be unjust. God can be the author of no government, contravening the wisdom of his arrangements in the creation of men.

Art. 3d. In every community there is a power, which receives the denomination of sovereignty, a power not subject to control, and that controls all subordinate powers in the government. Now whether this power be in the hands of the many, or a few, it is indubitably certain, that those members only of the community are free, in whom the sovereign power resides. The power of a community, is essential to its freedom, and if this power be confined to a few, freedom is necessarily confined to the same number. All just government must be founded upon the nature of man, and should consult alike the natural rights, civil wants, and moral interests of his being. All rightful authority is founded in power and law; all just power is founded in right, and as one man's natural right to the character of lawgiver, is to all intents, as good as another's, it follows, that all legitimate law must have its origin in the expressed will of the many.

Art. 4th. As all men are essentially equal, in their rights, wants, and interests, it follows from these, that representative government, is the only legitimate human rule, to which any people can submit. It is the only kind of government that can possibly reconcile, in any consistent way, the claims of authority, with the

advantages of liberty. A prescriptive legislative body, making laws without the knowledge or consent of the people to be governed by them is a despotism. Legislators without constituents, or peers and fellows, deputing them, as their representatives and actors - thus constituting themselves a legislature beyond the control of the people, is an exhibition of tyranny in one of its most dangerous forms. In the momentous affairs of government, nothing should be made the exclusive property of a few, which by right, belongs to all, and may be safely and advantageously used by the rightful proprietors. The justice of every government, depends essentially upon the original consent of the people; - this privilege belongs to every community, in right of the law of nature; and no man or multitude of men, can alter, limit, or diminish it. Constitutional law is an expression of the will of the people, and their concurrence in its formation, either personally, or by representation, is essential to its legitimate authority.

Art. 5th. No community can be said, without mockery, to have a constitution, where there is a consolidation of the different powers of government in the hands of the same men, and the remaining portion are left of course, without any security for their rights. Such a case, presents an absolute government; a government of men not principles. A constitution is not the creature of government; the nature of things renders it impossible that it should be an act of government. In strict propriety, it exists anterior to government; - government is based upon, proceeds from, and is the creature of the constitution. A constitution contains the elements and principles of government, and fixes the nature and limits of its form and operations; but is an instrument distinct from government, and by which government is controlled. It is a preliminary act of the people, in the creation of government. It sustains to government the same relation that laws do to the judiciary; the latter is not the source of law, cannot make laws, or annul them, but is subject to, and governed by law. A constitution recognizes the rights of the people, and provides for their assertion and maintenance. It settles the principles and maxims of government. It fixes the landmarks of legislation. It is the sovereign voice of the people, giving law and limit, to themselves and their representatives.

*   *   *

Art. 9th. The right to be represented, where law is made to govern, is not only essential to civil freedom, but is equally the basis of religious liberty. Civil and religious liberty are intimately connected, they usually live and die together; and he who is the friend of the one, cannot consistently be the enemy of the other. If liberty, as is admitted on all hands, is the perfection of civil society, by what right can religious society become despoiled of this crowning excellence of the social state? The New

241

Testament furnishes the principles, but not the forms of church government; and in the adaptation of forms to these principles, Christian bodies should be governed mainly by the few facts and precedents, furnished in the apostolic writings. The will and mind of the Great Head of the church, on this subject, so far as clearly revealed, whether by express statute, or fair implication, cannot be contravened without impiety; but in relation to a variety of topics, connected with the internal police, and external relations of the church, on which the Scriptures are silent, it is left to every Christian community, to adopt its own regulations, and the same is true of nations. Ministers and private Christians, according to the New Testament, are entitled to equal rights and privileges - an identity of interests implies an equality of rights. A monopoly of power, therefore, by the ministry, is a usurpation of the rights of the people. No power on the part of the ministry, can deprive the people legitimately of their elective and representative rights; as the ministry cannot think and act for the people, in matters of principle and conviction, so neither can they legislate for them, except as their authorized representatives.

Art. 10th. The government of every Christian church, should be strictly a government of principle, in relation to the governed; and every private Christian, is as deeply and reasonably interested as the ministry. Dominion over conscience, is the most absurd of all human pretensions. The assumption, that absolute power in the affairs of church government, is a sacred deposit in the hands of the ministry, libels the genius and charities of the New Testament. Whenever a Christian people place themselves under a ministry, who claim the right of thinking and deciding for them, in matters of faith and morality, they are guilty of impiety, however unintentional, to the Great Head of the church, inasmuch, as it is required of every Christian, to reflect and determine for himself, in all such cases, and the duty cannot be performed by another. And those ministers who aim at a principality of this kind, in the personal concerns of faith and practice, are plainly guilty of usurped dominion over the rights and consciences of the people.

Art. 11th. Expedience and right are different things. Nothing is expedient that is unjust. Necessity and convenience, may render a form of government useful and effective for a time, which afterward, under a change of circumstances, and an accumulation of responsibility, may become oppressive and intolerable. That system of things, which cannot be justified by the word of God, and the common sense of mankind, can never be expedient. Submission to power, gradually and insidiously usurped, should seldom or never be received as proof of the legitimate consent of the people, to the peculiar form of government, by which they are oppressed; as such submission may be the result of principles, attachments and energies, which owe their existence to causes foreign from the government,

which is supposed to produce them. Peaceable submission by the people, to a system of government, can never be construed into a proper approval of it, as one of their own choice; for, as men by birth and education, may become the subjects of a form of civil government they do not approve, so thousands may be born into the kingdom of God, and nurtured in his family, under forms of ecclesiastical polity, materially inconsistent with the lights and notices of revelation on this subject. The continued sufferance and submission of the people, so far from proving the divine right of those who govern, does not even furnish proof of any right at all, except the claim which arises from mere forbearance.

Art. 12th. Without insisting upon those portions of the New Testament, which go directly against the right of the ministry, to exclusive rule, the well known indefiniteness of its language, on the subject of church government, should admonish the claimants of such power, that their pretensions cannot be sustained. Nevertheless, in all ages since the apostolic, and in all parts of the world, with but few exceptions, a large majority of those calling themselves Christian ministers, have shown a disposition, both in ecclesiastical and civil affairs, to maintain an influence in matters of government, independent of the people, and to suppress the right of inquiry, and freedom of discussion. And this is readily accounted for, by adverting to the fact, that the liberty of thinking and acting, and especially the free expression of opinion, have always lessened the influence of ministerial pretensions, and abridged the claims of an aspiring ministry, to irresponsible domination. It is lamentably true, that in a thousand instances, in the various divisions of papal and protestant Christendom, oppression has been exercised under pretence of duty, and professed veneration for the dead; and their doings; and an earnest contention for preëxisting customs have been urged, as sufficient reasons, for withholding the rights of the people, and lording it over God's heritage.

Art. 13th. It is true, to a great extent, that throughout all the divisions of the Christian world, intellect has taken but comparatively little hold of the subject of religion, and still less of the subject of church government; and this affords the ministry an opportunity of misleading the people, on the subject of their rights, and in but too many instances, they resign themselves the passive subjects of their religious teachers, without once inquiring, whether in doing so, they do not dishonour the Great Head of the church, in his members. Christian ministers are men of like passions with other men, they are equally liable to err, and become depraved; they should not be watched with an eye of malignant jealousy, but their errors, oppressions, and usurpations, should be met and resisted by the people, with confidence and firmness. The people should teach their rulers, that they will find them alike free from the spirit of faction, and the tameness of servility. They should let them know, that with every disposition to render

243

proper obedience, they are determined not to be oppressed.

Art. 14th. Whenever the members of a church resign the right
of suffrage, and of discussing freely and fearlessly the conduct of
their rulers, whether it be done by direct concession, or indirectly
by attaching themselves to, and continuing within the pale of a
church, where such a system of polity obtains, they renounce to a
fearful extent, one of the first principles of the protestant
religion, and bring dishonour upon its name. Whenever spiritual
rulers, attempt to check a perfectly free communication of thoughts
and feelings among the people, - when the lips and the pens of the
laity are interdicted, without their oversight and license; - when
they attempt to repress honest convictions and free inquiry; - when
their disapprobation is shown to all, who do not support them, and
their displeasure incurred by the diffusion of intelligence among
the people, not calculated to increase their power and reputation;
then it becomes the duty of the people, to decline their oversight,
as men unworthy to rule the church of God. The rock on which the
church has split for ages, is that the sovereign power, to regulate
all ecclesiastical matters, (not decided by the Scriptures, and
which of right belongs to a Christian community, as such,) has by
a most mischievous and unnatural policy, misnamed expediency, been
transferred to the hands of a few ministers, who have been in part,
the patricians of the ministry, and the aristocracy of the church.

*   *   *

Art. 17th. No power possesses so fatal a principle of increase
and accumulation in itself, as ecclesiastical power. Its facilities
for reproduction and multiplication are many and fearful, and should
be vigilantly guarded against by all, who consider the image of God,
as closely connected with the rights of man. And whenever the
growth and manifestation of this power, in any of its innumerable
forms and modes of operation, shall clearly amount to an invasion
of Christian rights, the injured and oppressed, should resist the
encroachment with manly decision and unyielding remonstrance. In
every church, where the principle of representation is excluded,
in the affairs of its government, the right of private judgment
becomes a nullity, and faith and practice, are necessarily, to a
great extent, the offspring of prescription. The right of deciding
what are the will and mind of God, in matters of faith and discipline,
by prescriptive interpretation, is conceded in the scriptures, to
no man, or body of men exclusively: of course, the right of judgment
belongs to all, equally and inalienably; and when the ministry
avail themselves of the indifference, inattention, or ignorance of
the people, brought under their charge from time to time, to constitute themselves their legislative masters and executive guardians,
they usurp the dominion of conscience, and although never complained of, are *de facto* religious tyrants, because they assume and
exercise rights, that do not, and cannot in the nature of things,

belong to them. It should not be overlooked, moreover, that when
the ministry are considered by the laity, as the sole judges and
depositories of faith and discipline, the people lose the only
powerful motive, the only direct incentive, they can possibly have,
to inquire and decide for themselves, in the infinitely momentous
concerns of truth and duty. Such a monopoly of power by the
ministry, tends directly to mental debasement, consequent indecision
of character, insincerity, and misguided zeal.

*   *   *

Art. 22d. Any movement by the oppressed, to recover their
rights, will be resisted by those who have oppressed them; but
suffering and persecution, in a cause, which the love of God and
man requires, should be fearlessly met and resolutely borne.

¶   Constitution of the Methodist Protestant Church, 1830.

(Taken from Drinkhouse, II, 257-58, 261-65).

PREAMBLE

We, the Representatives of the Associated Methodist Churches,
in General Convention assembled, acknowledging the Lord Jesus
Christ, as the only head of the Church, and the word of God, as
the sufficient rule of faith and practice, in all things pertaining to godliness; and being fully persuaded that the representative
form of church government is the most scriptural, best suited to our
condition, and most congenial with our views and feelings as
fellow-citizens with the saints, and of the household of God; and,
Whereas, a written Constitution, establishing the form of Government, and securing to the Ministers and Members of the Church
their rights and privileges, is the best safeguard of Christian
liberty; We, therefore, trusting in the protection of Almighty God,
and acting in the name and by the authority of our constituents,
do ordain and establish, and agree to be governed by the following
elementary principles and Constitution: -

ELEMENTARY PRINCIPLES

1. A Christian Church is a society of believers in Jesus Christ,
and is of divine institution.
2. Christ is the only Head of the Church; and the word of God the
only rule of faith and conduct.
3. No person who loves the Lord Jesus Christ, and obeys the gospel
of God our Saviour, ought to be deprived of church membership.
4. Every man has an inalienable right to private judgment, in
matters of religion; and an equal right to express his opinion, in
any way which will not violate the laws of God, or the rights of

245

his fellow-men.

5. Church trials should be conducted on gospel principles only, and no minister or member should be excommunicated except for immorality; the propagation of unchristian doctrines; or for the neglect of duties enjoined by the word of God.

6. The pastoral or ministerial office and duties are of divine appointment and all elders in the church of God are equal; but ministers are forbidden to be lords over God's heritage, or to have dominion over the faith of saints.

7. The Church has a right to form and enforce such rules and regulations only, as are in accordance with the holy scriptures, and may be necessary or have a tendency to carry into effect the great system of practical Christianity.

8. Whatever power may be necessary to the formation of rules and regulations, is inherent in the ministers and members of the Church; but so much of that power may be delegated,from time to time, upon a plan of representation,as they may judge necessary and proper.

9. It is the duty of all ministers and members of the Church to maintain godliness, and to oppose all moral evil.

10. It is obligatory on ministers of the gospel to be faithful in the discharge of their pastoral and ministerial duties; and it is also obligatory on the members, to esteem ministers highly for their works' sake, and to render them a righteous compensation for their labours.

11. The Church ought to secure to all her official bodies the necessary authority for the purposes of good government; but she has no right to create any distinct or independent sovereignties.

*   *   *

Article VII
Composition and Powers of the Annual Conference

I. There shall be held annually, within the limits of each district, a Conference, to be denominated the Annual Conference, composed of all the ordained itinerant ministers belonging to the district; that is, all ministers properly under the stationing power of the Conference, and of one delegate from such circuit and station for each of its itinerant ministers, provided, however, that every circuit and station shall have at least one delegate. Each Annual Conference shall regulate the manner of elections, in its own district, provided, however, that the election of delegates to the first Annual Conference, under this Constitution, shall be according to such regulations as may be adopted for that purpose by the Quarterly Conferences of the respective circuits and stations.

II. The Annual Conferences, respectively, shall be vested with power to elect a president, annually; to examine into the official conduct of all its members, to receive by vote, such ministers and

246

preachers into the Conference as come properly recommended, and
who can be efficiently employed as itinerant preachers, or
missionaries; to elect to orders those who are eligible and competent to the pastoral office; to hear and decide on appeals; to define
and regulate the boundaries of circuits and stations; to station the
ministers, preachers and missionaries; and to perform such other
duties as may be prescribed by this Convention or the General
Conference.

III.   To make such rules and regulations as may be necessary to
defray the expenses of the itinerant ministers, preachers, and
their families; to raise their salaries as fixed by this Convention;
and for all other purposes connected with the organization and
continuance of said Conferences.

IV.   The Annual Conferences, respectively, shall also have
authority to perform the following additional duties: -
        1st. To make such special rules and regulations as the
peculiarities of the district may require; provided, however, that
no rule or regulation be made, inconsistent with this Constitution.
And provided, furthermore, that the General Conference shall have
power to annul any rule or regulation which that body may deem
unconstitutional.
        2nd.   To prescribe and regulate the mode of stationing the
ministers and preachers within the district; provided always, that
they grant to each minister or preacher stationed, an appeal, during
the sitting of the Conference.   *Reformed*
        3rd.   Each Annual Conference shall have exclusive power to
make its own rules and regulations for the admission and government
of its colored members and to make for them such terms of suffrage
as the Conferences respectively may deem proper.
        But neither the General Conference nor any Annual Conference
shall assume powers to interfere with the constitutional powers of
the civil government or with the operations of the civil laws; yet
nothing herein contained shall be so construed as to authorize or
sanction anything inconsistent with the morality of the holy
scriptures.

*   *   *

Article   X
Restrictions on the Legislative Assembles

I.   No rule shall be passed which shall contravene any law
of God.
        II.   No rule shall be passed which shall infringe the right
of suffrage, eligibility to office, or the rights and privileges
of our ministers, preachers, and members, to an impartial trial by
committee, and of an appeal, as provided by this Constitution.
        III.   No rule shall be passed infringing on the liberty of

speech, or of the press; but for every abuse of liberty, the offender shall be dealt with as in other cases of indulging in sinful words and tempers.

IV. No rule, except it be founded on the holy scriptures, shall be passed authorizing the expulsion of any minister, preacher or member.

V. No rule shall be passed appropriating the funds of the Church to any purpose except the support of the ministry, their wives, widows and children; the promotion of education, and Missions; the diffusion of useful knowledge; the necessary expenses consequent on assembling the Conferences, and the relief of the poor.

VI. No higher order of Ministers shall be authorized than that of Elder.

VII. No rule shall be passed to abolish an efficient itinerant ministry, or to authorize the Annual Conferences to station their ministers and preachers longer than three years, successively, in the same circuit, and two years successively in the same station.

VIII. No change shall be made in the relative proportions, or component parts of the General or Annual conferences.

* * *

Article XIII

Suffrage and Eligibility to Office

I. Every Minister and Preacher, and every white, lay, male Member, in full communion and fellowship, having attained to the age of twenty-one years, shall be entitled to vote in all cases.

II. Every Minister and Preacher, and every white, lay, male Member, in full communion and fellowship, having attained to the age of twenty-five years, and having been in full membership two years, shall be eligible as a representative to the General Conference.

III. No person shall be eligible as a delegate to the Annual Conference, or as a steward, until he shall have attained to the age of twenty-one years, and who is not a regular communicant of this Church.

IV. No Minister shall be eligible to the office of President of an Annual Conference, until he shall have faithfully exercised the office of elder two years.

10. INVOLVEMENT IN SLAVERY AND DIVISION

*The Episcopal Address to General Conference, 1836, set the
tone for the official position over the next decade.. Don't rock
the boat. Avoid destructive controversy.*

*That all could not be solved by such a policy is shown by the
violence done on Luther Lee, as reported in Lucius Matlack's
intense account of Methodism and slavery, published in 1849 when
the fires were very hot. Contrast this volume with the measured
objectivity (mostly) of Donald Mathews' book of similar title
(*Methodism and Slavery*), published over a hundred years later in
1965. Matlack offers many insights, although of course his interpretations are part of the source material, not modern historical
judgments. When Orange Scott and his followers withdrew in 1843,
the church was shocked by this "backdoor" departure. Everyone
concerned for the unity of the church had been feverishly guarding
the front door to keep the South in.*

*Alfred Brunson's account of the underground railroad may stand
contrasted to the highly convoluted arguments of William A. Smith,
who did his best to justify slavery in the 1850s, and at least
convinced many Southerners. Methodists were not the only ones to
become enmeshed in slavery, as the book reviews in the* Methodist
Quarterly Review *indicate. These outdated arguments carried
considerable weight in the pre-war years. They exacerbated the
bitterness which followed the division of the church in 1844.*

*The debates in the long General Conference of 1844 have been
largely preserved in a massive volume. A sample of the arguments
includes an emotional but sincere defense by Bishop James Andrew,
the "man in the middle," and James B. Finley's rejoinder. Many
books appeared on both sides after the separation, all of them designed to prove the validity of what each side did. George Peck
wrote extensively on the issue of episcopal authority in relation
to the action of General Conference; but his detailed and legal
points are too cumbersome and irreducible to give here. But he
did include in an appendix an able speech by Leonidas Hamline, one
of the central figures in the debates. He was the editor of the
new* Ladies Repository, *and was elected bishop at the General
Conference of 1844.*

*A massive literary gun was shot off by Charles Elliott in a
book whose theme is announced in the title,* History of the Great
Secession, *published in 1855. It did not contribute to healing
the wounds of division. For that matter, very little that was
either said or written before the Civil War had therapeutic value.
A lot of steam was released, however.*

¶ Episcopal Address, General Conference, 1836.

(Taken from *Journal of General Conference*, 8-10).

6. We now approach a subject of no little delicacy and difficulty, and which we cannot but think has contributed its full proportion to that religious declension over which we mourn. It is not unknown to you, dear brethren and friends, that, in common with other denominations, in our land, as well as our citizens generally, we have been much agitated in some portions of our work, with the very excitable subject of what is called abolitionism. This subject has been brought before us at our present session - fully, and we humbly trust, impartially discussed, and by almost a unanimous vote highly disapproved of; and while we would tenderly sympathize with those of our brethren who have, as we believe, been led astray by this agitating topic, we feel it our imperative duty to express our decided disapprobation of the measures they have pursued to accomplish their object. It cannot be unknown to you, that the question of slavery in these United States, by the constitutional compact which binds us together as a nation, is left to be regulated by the several state legislatures themselves; and thereby is put beyond the control of the general government, as well as that of all ecclesiastical bodies; it being manifest that in the slaveholding states themselves, the entire responsibility of its existence or non-existence rests with those state legislatures. And such is the aspect of affairs in reference to this question, that whatever else might tend to meliorate the condition of the slave, it is evident to us, from what we have witnessed of abolition movements, that these are the least likely to do him good. On the contrary, we have it in evidence before us, that the inflammatory speeches, and writings, and movements, have tended, in many instances, injuriously to affect his temporal and spiritual condition, by hedging up the way of the missionary who is sent to preach to him Jesus and the resurrection, and by making a more rigid supervision necessary on the part of his overseer, thereby abridging his civil and religious privileges.

These facts, which are only mentioned here as a reason for the friendly admonition which we wish to give you, constrain us as your pastors, who are called to watch over your souls as they who must give an account, to exhort you to abstain from all abolition movements and associations, and to refrain from patronizing any of their publications; and especially from those of that inflammatory character which denounce in unmeasured terms those of their brethren who take the liberty to dissent from them. . . .

From every view of the subject which we have been able to take, and from the most calm and dispassionate survey of the whole ground, we have come to the solemn conviction, that the only safe, Scriptural, and prudent way for us, both as ministers and people,

to take, is wholly to refrain from this agitating subject, which is now convulsing the country, and consequently the Church, from end to end, by calling forth inflammatory speeches, papers, and pamphlets. While we cheerfully accord to such, all the sincerity they ask for their belief and motives, we cannot but disprove of their measures, as alike destructive to the peace of the Church, and to the happiness of the slave himself.

¶   Luther Lee mobbed in Herkimer Co., 1838.

(Taken from Lucius Matlack, *History of American Slavery and Methodism* (1849), 201-02).

At the session of the Black River Conference for 1838, Luther Lee located; and from that time forward, devoted himself wholly to the advocacy of anti-slavery sentiments, being an agent for the New-York State Society. At the close of one of his lectures in Utica, N.Y., 130 names were added to the Wesleyan Anti-slavery Society. As a specimen of the opposition he had to contend with, in advocating abolitionism at that period, the following letter is inserted: -

"Dear Brother: - A few weeks since, I gave you a little account of a mob, since which, it has occurred to me, that it might be interesting to your readers, to furnish, from time to time, an account of the most important occurrences, which may attend my labors, as a lecturing agent of the New-York State Anti-slavery Society - for you are already apprized that such is my calling for the present year.

"On Friday, after the mob already described, I was blest with another, as I was delivering a lecture in the Methodist meeting-house, at Crane's Corners, in Litchfield, Herkimer County, N.Y. This, like the former, was got up by the lovers of whiskey. I discovered, as I entered the Church, that a rude company were collecting about the door, and concluded that we should have some disturbance, but the leading brethren were not expecting any such thing, as we had no Christians in this place, who did not care if the abolitionists were mobbed. Soon after meeting commenced, it was manifest to me, that Satan was on the spot, attended by his faithful ally, king alcohol, for the noise and shout of a king was heard in Satan's camp. I proceeded, however, without much interruption, until I had nearly finished my discourse, when the enemy charged. The first shot did not take effect, for some cause, but they soon reloaded, and one was heard to say, 'now shoot him in his eyes;' and the next instant, the charge came, which did execution, though the eyes escaped. The reader must not be alarmed for my safety, for had I been killed, I could not have given an account of it: 'He that fights and runs away, may live to

fight another day, - but he that is in battle slain, can never live to fight again.'

"However, I neither run nor fell on this occasion. If the reader wishes to know what kind of a gun the enemy used on the occasion, he is informed it was a squirt gun, charged with whiskey and lamp black. I finished my discourse, for I found that I could talk with a black face just as well as with a white one, and remarked, in conclusion, that no doubt that was the best argument they had, with which to oppose abolition, and that though the congregation could all see that it was a very striking argument, one which a man could not get rid of so easy as some others, yet it was not a convincing argument, and could never prove abolitionists to be wrong. It reminded me of the cowardly sailor, who hid himself at the commencement of a battle among some casks; but soon a cannon ball struck a tub of butter near him, and covered him with its contents, whereupon he rushed into the scene of action, crying, 'there is no danger, they shoot nothing but butter' - and so, they have got to shoot something at me worse than whiskey and lamp black, before I shall be conquered or discouraged, in pleading the cause of the oppressed. I do not know but some would contend that this mob was got up under the 'golden rule,' for the mob, no doubt, would, all of them, like to have whiskey put into their faces, and most of them, rather than not to have the whiskey, would be willing to take a little lamp black with it!

"Yours, for God and the oppressed,
"Luther Lee.

Peru, N.Y. Oct. 16, 1838."

¶ Petition on Black Testimony, 1840.

(Taken from Matlack, 218-20).

PETITION,

"From the official members of the Sharp-street and Ashbury colored
    M.E. Churches, Baltimore,
To the General Conference of the M.E. Church, convened in this
    city.

Dear Brethren, - We have learned with profound regret, with unutterable emotion, that your venerable body adopted on the 18th instant, a resolution which substantially declares that is is inexpedient and unjustifiable to admit the testimony of colored persons against the white members of the Church, in those States where colored testimony against white persons in civil and criminal cases, is illegal.

The adoption of such a resolution, by our highest ecclesiastical judicatory, a judicatory composed of the most experienced
and the wisest brethren in the Church, the choice selection of
twenty-eight Annual Conferences, has inflicted, we fear, an
irreparable injury upon eighty thousand souls for whom Christ died -
souls, which, by this act of your body, have been stripd of the
dignity of Christians, degraded in the scale of humanity, and
treated as criminals, for no other reason than the color of their
skin! Your resolution has, in our humble opinion, virtually declared that a mere physical peculiarity, the handy work of our
all-wise and benevolent Creator, is prima facie evidence of
incompetency to tell the truth, or is an unerring indication of
unworthiness to bear testimony against a fellow being whose skin
is denominated white.

We feel called upon most solemnly to protest against this act
of the General Conference, whereby every colored member of the
Church is unjustifiably and unnecessarily disfranchised and degraded.
We protest against this act of the Conference, because it justifies
the wicked and 'condemns the just,' and is, consequently, an
'abomination to the Lord;' because its tendency is to make one
portion of the community proud, haughty, vain-glorious and over-
bearing; and produces in the other a state of imbittered feeling,
which effectually impedes the free course of the gospel among
them, when proclaimed by those to whom they have been accustomed
to look as their spiritual guides.

Brethren, out of the abundance of the heart we have spoken.
Our grievance is before you! If you have any regard for the
salvation of the eighty thousand immortal souls committed to your
care; if you would not thrust beyond the pale of the church,
twenty-five hundred souls in this city, [a few words lost] - if
you would not incur the fearful, the tremendous responsibility, of
offending not only one, but many thousands of his 'little ones;'
we conjure you to wipe from your journal, the odious resolution
which is ruining our people.

¶   Poem on Bishop Soule as "Mr. Facing - both - ways."

(Taken from Matlack, 252-53).

                    TO BISHOP SOULE.

            "When day with all its wiles is fled,
              And thou in deep and searching thought,
            Survey at each act and word thou'st said,
              And each with good or evil fraught -

Mark! Can'st thou then to God appeal,
  And say, thou know'st my hands are clear,
No slave have I! I've set my seal –
  Nor can oppression 'gainst me bear!

But oh, the heart, by sin deceived,
  Can only see its crimson fade;
It dims the soul which it received,
  'Till guilt seems pure whate'er its shade.

And thus, mistaken man, art thou,
  In calling thine, clean, holy hands:
Go, go, repent thou even now,
  For thou has tightened slav'ry's bands!

Where was thy Bible – where thy mind?
  When truth had fir'd an honest heart,
To break the yoke, the chain unbind,
  And bid the oppress'd in peace depart?

Yes, they'd have left dark slav'ry's home,
  Tho' he was mild who swayed their lives,
Nor outcast would he've bid them roam,
  But bought them lands for babes and wives;

Had'st thou not said to him, thou'rt kind,
  They're happier here than in that State,
Where equal laws they cannot find,
  And slav'ry here's a better fate.

But I would ask, couldn'st thou secure
  This Christian master length of days?
Or couldn'st thou then, their peace insure,
  'Gainst change, should age hedge up his ways!

I'd ask thee more in candor, too,
  Would'st thou, tho' treated tender, kind,
Consent to be a slave, in view
  Of freedom sweet tho' unrefin'd?

What, tho' they had not all their rights,
  Yet might they taste of purest joy;
For nature's ties would yield delights,
  When slavery could no more annoy.

¶ Withdrawal of Orange Scott and Jothan Horton, 1842.

(Taken from Matlack, 308-09, 311-13, 315-17).

With the date of this communication, closes our connection
with the Methodist Episcopal Church. We take this step after years
of consideration, and with a solemn sense of our responsibility to
God - we take it with a view to his glory and the salvation of
souls.

Twenty years, and upwards, of the best part of our lives, has
been spent in the service of this Church - during which time, we
have formed acquaintances which have endeared to our hearts multitudes of Christian friends. Many of these are true kindred spirits,
and we leave them with reluctance. But the view we take of our
responsibility is not local in its bearings, nor limited in its
duration. While we live, and when we die, we wish to bear a
testimony which shall run parallel with coming ages; nay, with the
annals of eternity. Many considerations of friendship, as well as
our temporal interests, bind us to the Church of our early choice.
But for the sake of a high and holy cause, we can forego all these.
We wish to live not for ourselves, nor for the present age alone,
but for all coming time; nay, for God and eternity. We have borne
our testimony, a long time, against what we considered wrong in the
M. E. Church. We have waited, prayed, and hoped, until there is no
longer any ground for hope. Hence we have come to the deliberate
conclusion, that we must submit to things as they are, or peaceably retire. We have unhesitatingly chosen the latter.

It is, however, proper, in leaving the Church, that we assign
our reasons. These are, mainly, the following:

1. The M. E. Church, is not only a slaveholding, but a
slavery defending, Church.
2. The Government of the M. E. Church contains principles not
laid down in the Scriptures, nor recognized in the usages of the
primitive Church - principles which are subversive of the rights,
both of ministers and laymen.

That the M. E. Church is a slaveholding Church, none will deny.
It is not, of course, meant that slaves are a part of our church
funds, though it is believed the fruits of slaveholding or of slave-
buying and selling, make a large portion of these funds. But what
we mean, is, that the M. E. Church allows her members and ministers
unrebuked, to hold innocent human beings in a state of hopeless
bondage - nay, more, that she upholds and defends her communicants
in this abominable business! All her disciplinary regulations,
which present a show of opposition to Slavery, are known and
acknowledged to be a dead letter in the South. And they are as
dead in the North as in the South. Even the general rule has been

altered, either through carelessness or design, so as to favor the
internal slave trade; and yet the last General Conference refused
to correct the error, knowing it to be such!

*   *   *

And finally, she has adopted a resolution on colored testimony,
which disfranchises eighty thousand of her members – thus giving the
weight of her influence to that slaveholding legislation which, in a
civil point of view, disfranchises millions of our fellow countrymen.

Add to this, the fact, that all her official papers, are so much
under the influence of slaveholding, that no Abolitionist can be
heard on the subject of Slavery and abolition, however he may be
abused, traduced and misrepresented.

In view of these facts, we ask, is not the M. E. Church, one
of the main supporters of Slavery in this country? Has she not
defended it in almost every conceivable way? And is there any
prospect that this Church will ever be reformed, so long as Slavery
exists in the country? If not, can we obey the commands of God, and
continue in fellowship with a Church which receives, shields and
defends, thousands and tens of thousands, who, according to Mr.
Wesley, are 'exactly on a level with men-stealers?" If a large
portion of our ministers and members were sheep-stealers or horse-
stealers, there would be more propriety in covering them; – but
when we consider that they make merchandise of the souls and bodies
of men, or do that which is tantamount to such a traffic, without
rebuke, how can we co-operate with them in the great work of reforming the world? Others must judge for themselves, but we feel
it our duty to 'come out of her' – to 'have no fellowship,' or
connection, 'with the unfruitful works of darkness' but to 'come
out from among them and be separate!' By this course, we solemnly
believe, we can do more for the cause of the bleeding slave, than
by continuing in a Slavery-defending Church, when there can be no
hope of reforming her till the country is reformed. But,

2d. The government of the M. E. Church contains principles
not laid down in the Scriptures, nor recognized in the usages of
the primitive Church – principles which are subversive of the
rights both of ministers and laymen.

While we admit that no form of Church government is laid down
in the Scriptures, we contend that, principles are laid down which
are in direct contravention with some existing forms.   .   .   .

The power which our bishops claim and exercise, in the Annual
Conferences, is contrary to the plainest principles of Christian
responsibility. All religious associations must, in the nature of
things, have the right to express, without restraint, their opinions

on any moral question. But this, no annual or quarterly conference, in the M. E. Church, can do, without the consent of the bishop or presiding elder. But no body of Christian men has any more right to submit to such restraints, than they have to commit the entire keeping of their consciences to other hands. That holy men of God should consent, in this enlightened age, to exercise such power over the consciences of their brethren, is truly astonishing! but not more so, than that ministers can be found who will peaceably submit to such innovations upon their responsibilities to God!!

Scarcely less objectionable, is the power conferred upon the bishops of the M. E. Church, in the appointment of the preachers. That the entire destinies of three or four thousand men should be in the hands of some five or six bishops, so far as their fields of labor are concerned, seems to be forbidden by the fact that, these bishops are fallible men – that they are often ignorant both of the preachers and people; and that they cannot control the openings of Providence, and the calls of God. We know the presiding elders are usually called upon for advice in this matter; but there is no obligation on the part of the Episcopacy to advise with any one. And when all must admit that it would be dangerous for the bishops to exercise the power they possess, what advantage can there be in their possessing such power?

*   *   *

Another serious objection to Methodist Episcopacy, is the election of bishops for life. Both Bishop Hedding and Dr. Luckey, have expressed the opinion, that the office of bishop may be periodically elective, and that the ceremony of ordination may be dispensed with; and, that too, without invalidating any of the essentials of Episcopacy. But now once a bishop always bishop, however incapacitated to the performance of the duties of the office from bodily or mental infirmities. But we have not time to enlarge on any of these topics.

We will mention but one thing more. And that is, that feature in the economy of the Methodist E. Church, which gives the power to the preacher, of excluding almost any member he may wish to get rid of. True, the discipline requires the forms of trial, in case of expulsion; but as the preacher has the sole power to appoint the Committee, and that without giving the accused any right of challenge, it is not, in general, difficult, for a preacher to punish whom he pleases, and that for trifling causes, as many can testify. And, as he has the sole right to appoint all the leaders, and nominate all the stewards, it is of but little consequence for an expelled member to appeal to the Quarterly-meeting Conference, if the preacher is known to be strongly prejudiced against him – however unfounded that prejudice may be.

Such, in brief, are some of our reasons for leaving the M. E. Church. We shall have more to say, on these matters, hereafter.

*   *   *

And now, dear brethren of the M. E. Church, we bid you farewell. Many of you we know and love. And while we do not impeach your motives or honesty, we hope, in turn, you will not treat us as barbarians. There is room enough for us all. Let us have no unchristian contention.

Jotham Horton, Orange Scott, La Roy Sunderland.

Providence, R.I., Nov. 8, 1842.

¶   Pastoral Address to the Utica Convention, 1843.

(Taken from Matlack, 338-44).

Beloved Brethren and Friends, - The Convention having accomplished the object for which it assembled, we deem it proper, before we retire to our respective fields of labor, to address you on the subject of its happy issue, and the duties and prospects that lie before us.   .   .   .

We would congratulate you in view of the new relation in which the action of the Convention places you to each other, and to the Christian world. We are now an organized Christian community, and have an existence and a name among the sister Churches of our country; and though we are the youngest of them all, and small in comparison with many of them, yet we trust in God that we shall so adhere to the spirit and truth of primitive Christianity, and so subsist upon the 'sincere milk of the word,' that we shall soon be equal in proportions, strength and usefulness, to the oldest, and never be surpassed by those who may hereafter be added to the common family. Most of those who at present compose the New Connection, have been members of the M. E. Church, and have for years been looked upon and treated as refractory children, rebelling against the lawful authority of our Mother's family government, but this charge can no longer be preferred against us. We are now of lawful age, and have entered upon the responsibilities of a distinct community, to be governed upon principles more in accordance with our views of primitive Christianity, and we believe better adapted to the security of individual rights, and to the general development of Christian zeal and enterprise throughout the ministry and membership. We may still respect our Mother for the good she has done in the world, and for the blessings wherewith she has blessed many of us; but we can no longer acknowledge her authority, and with her oppression of the poor, with her corrupting herself with Slavery,

and with the arbitrary features of her government, we can have no fellowship.

We can do no less than congratulate you, brethren, on the organization of a Christian community, free from the above-named objectionable features, while it retains all that is valuable in Methodism, all that most of us ever loved, in view of which we joined the M. E. Church, and for the sake of which many of us spent the ardor of our youth and the strength of our manhood to build her up. Did we leave behind the valuable features of Wesleyan Methodism, we should think we were making a sacrifice indeed, but such is not the case; we retain all that is essential to it, all that is peculiar to the whole family of Wesleyan Methodists in Europe and America, while we have thrown off those peculiarities which distinguish the M. E. Church from the other portions of the Wesleyan family.

The most important changes which we have made consist in our repudiation of all connection with Slavery and slaveholders, and our rejection of the prerogative system of Episcopacy, and in these it cannot be pretended that we have sacrificed any essential part of Wesleyan Methodism. That our divorce from Slavery and slaveholders cannot be considered a sacrifice of Wesleyanism is plain, since its founder said, that 'Slavery is the sum of all villainies,' and that 'all men-buyers' (slaveholders) 'are exactly on a level with men-stealers.' Nor can it be contended that Episcopacy is any part of Wesleyan Methodism, for it forms no part of the economy of the Wesleyan Connection in Europe and Canada, but is peculiar to the Methodist E. Church in this country.

We may then congratulate ourselves, on the ground of having retained all that is essential to the identity, life, body and soul of Wesleyan Methodism, while we have separated ourselves from some of its objectionable features, which have been engrafted upon it in this country, and which have, from time to time, disturbed and agitated the M. E. Church from its organization to the present day.
. . . .

Brethren, we are now but small in number, in comparison with many other denominations, but remember that we have just entered upon existence, and have commenced our career with fuller developments of life, and stronger pulsations, than did most or all of our older sisters, when they, like ourselves, first assumed the responsibilities of organized and distinct members of the Christian family. Instead of feeling disheartened in view of our present numbers, we ought to thank God and take courage, on the ground that we are so strong, and that so many have been found to consecrate themselves to the cause of God and humanity. When we consider the circumstances of the case, the powerful influences that have been brought to bear against us, and the force of early imbibed prejudices, and the strength of long-cherished connections, we look upon our

present numbers as the clearest evidence of the power of our principles, and as a strong assurance of our future success. 'Let the weak say, I am strong.' 'A little one shall become a thousand, and a small one a strong nation.' Our principles are of God, and will prevail.

We must expect to meet with opposition, endure reproach, and make sacrifices, but these we can cheerfully bear, in the cause of God, justice, mercy and humanity. Let the strength of our principles support us; let the magnitude of the cause in which we are engaged, stimulate our exertions; let the true spirit of Christianity give direction to all our efforts; and let the glowing prospect of success, which brightens upon the not very distant future, inflame our zeal. What have we, brethren, to fear, so long as we are conscious of doing the will of God? 'If God be for us, who shall be against us?' There are no prisons, no chains, no fiery faggots in reservation for us in this land. What if our characters are assailed, if we feel that our names are written in heaven, beyond the reach of poisoned words? What if our motives are impugned, so long as God reads the heart? What if the reputations of some of us should be blighted, so long as we know that the glory remains, yet to be revealed, with which the loss of all on earth cannot compare?

But, brethren, we deem it proper to caution you against indulging in an improper spirit towards those from whom you may receive wrong treatment. Though we would have you fearlessly, at all times, speak the truth in the love of it, yet we trust you will never render evil for evil, or oppose a bitter spirit with the same ill temper of mind. You must expect to be misrepresented, and have your motives impugned; those who remain in the M. E. Church cannot be expected to appreciate your reasons for secession; did they, they would follow your example, - hence they will be led to invent reasons for your course other than the dictates of an enlightened judgment and honest conscience; and this they will do as an excuse for their own course.　　.　　.　　.

The cause of the bleeding slave, you will never forget; nor will you overlook the cause of Temperance, which has already done so much for the restoration of the degraded, and to make the wretched happy. In a word, we desire that every member of the Wesleyan Connection should not only be a zealous advocate of every branch of moral reform, but co-workers, even in the front rank, battling side by side with those who contend with the Lord's enemies.

But above all, brethren, we exhort you to make holiness your motto. It is holiness of heart and life that will arm you against every assault, that will give you moral power to oppose the evils and corruption in the world, against which we have lifted up a standard. It is holiness that will insure success in our enterprise that will crown us with a useful life, a triumphant death,

and with the fullness, power and glory of eternal life in the world of redeemed spirits. We will then close with the apostolic prayer, "And the very God of peace, sanctify you wholly; and we pray God your whole spirit, and soul, and body, be preserved blameless unto the coming of our Lord Jesus Christ. Faithful is he that called you, who also will do it.'

Luther Lee, Chairman.

G. Pegler, J. Watson, M. Swift, R. Bennett.

Utica, N.Y., June 8, 1843.

¶ The Underground Railroad, 1822-3.

(Taken from Alfred Brunson, *A Western Pioneer* (1872), I, 269-72).

In the course of this year I saw the operation of the "Under-ground Railroad." At Judge Lee's, at Monroe, I saw an old negro and his wife, older, indeed, from hard and cruel usage than from years. They were wending their way to the land of freedom below Malden, or Amherstburg, in Canada. He said he "was forty-five years old last corn-planting time," but his wrinkled face and gray hairs indicated over sixty.

I inquired, "Why did you leave your master?"

"O, my master he be dead, and all we poor slaves were sold to pay his debts, and were on the way down to Orleans to be sold again."

"Have you any children?"

"Yes, massa, we have eight."

"Why did you leave them?"

"Why, when we get down the river to Orleans, and be sold, one goes one way and another another way, and we should be separated anyhow, and me and the old woman thought if we could get our liberty, though we be separated from our children, which must take place anyhow, it would be better for us, and no worse for them."

"Where did you leave them?"

"On the Ohio River. We came down from Wheeling in a flat-boat, and tied up on the Ohio side one night, and we made our escape and traveled all night to the north. We lay by days in the woods, and traveled nights til we got into the woods; then we traveled days

261

and rested nights."

"Were you not afraid of being pursued and taken back?"

"Not much. 'Cause there was eighty others in the boat, and
they be afraid to leave them to follow us old folks, lest the young
ones escape too. But still, for fear, we lay by of days a few
times, till we reach the woods, then we travel in the daytime."

"Did you not hate to part with your children?"

"Yes; but it make no difference, for in Virginia they were no
use to us. We was not allowed to have any help from them. If I
asked my son to bring me a drink, when I was tired, in the field,
the overseer wouldn't let him, but curse me to get my own drink,
and if we had gone on with them and been sold to different masters,
it would have been no better. We should not likely go all to the
same plantation, and if we did it would be no better than it was in
Virginia."

"How did you know who were your friends, and whom to call on to
get food and lodging?"

"O, these good men's names are all known among the slaves
South."

"How did you obtain this information?"

"Why, some slaves who have escaped, after a while came back
privately to get their friends away, and they tell us; and when we
get started, and find one good friend he tells us of others on the
road, and so on."

The Judge told me that one morning, as he was walking down
by the bridge to see if any negroes were about, as he was wont to
do, and frequently found them stopped there by the tollgate, or
waiting till morning to find him - for his name was known all the
way into slavedom - he saw a young negro, about eighteen years old,
crawl out from under the bridge, who showed fear of detection. As
he called to him not to fear, as he was his friend, the negro
approached and asked for Judge Lee. "I am Judge Lee," was the reply,
when the negro's eye danced for joy, and he asked, "Please, massa,
give me something to eat?"

"Yes, you follow that path under the bank up to that brick
house, and go into the cellar kitchen door, and I'll be there soon."

The negro was hardly out of sight before two men rode up; one,
who was hired at the Maumee, had a musket, the other had pistols.
They inquired if he had seen a young negro there that morning; they

knew he could not have got further than that place, for they had heard of him on the road.

"Yes," the Judge told them, "I saw one here not long since, and the last I saw of him he was going up the river, as fast as he could well travel," and off they went at full speed. The Judge then went into the house and told the negro that his pursuers had come, and he had sent them up the river; and directing some food for him, told him, after eating, to go into the cellar and remain hid till he came back. In about an hour they came back cursing the Abolitionists, as some of them must have hid the fellow.

The Judge assured them that he saw the negro going up the river, and was sure he had not returned, as he had been there all the time, and he was also sure that he had not crossed the river, as that was impossible, except at the bridge.

The pursuers rode round for a while, but getting no further information of the runaway, gave up the pursuit and went back, cursing the whole fraternity of Abolitionists. In a few hours the negro was over the river and on his way to Brownstown, from whence he could cross into Malden, where he probably arrived that night.

I was also told of one of the meanest of the mean tricks ever played off, and that by a negro himself. He came with his master from Kentucky, to decoy a fugitive into his master's hands, and succeeded too well. He went over into Canada and found the fugitive, and told him that he also had made his escape and wanted the fugitive to go over and help him get over his goods, as he had lots of them, and he would pay him well.

The fugitive did not like to cross the river lest some trick should be played upon him; but after a long parley the decoy succeeded in inducing the fugitive to cross with him. As they approached the house, the master stepped out, with pistols in hand, and demanded of the decoy, "What, Jim, are you here to?" Jim pretended to be alarmed, but soon turned in and helped iron the prisoner, and conveyed him back to bondage and suffering.

¶   Is Slavery Sinful?

(Taken from William A. Smith, *Lectures on the Philosophy and Practice of Slavery* (1856), 11-12, 208-09, 278-79).

The great question which arises in discussing the slavery of the African population of this country - correctly known as "Domestic Slavery" - is this: Is the institution of domestic slavery sinful?

263

The position I propose to maintain in these lectures is, that slavery, per se, is right; or that the great abstract principle of slavery is right, because it is a fundamental principle of the social state; and that domestic slavery, as an institution, is fully justified by the condition and circumstances (essential and relative) of the African race in this country, and therefore equally right.

*　　　*　　　*

On the general question, Is the system of domestic government existing amongst us, and involving the abstract principle of slavery, justified by the circumstances of the case, and therefore right? we reach an affirmative conclusion, for the reasons:

I.   That the Africans are a distinct race of people, who cannot amalgamate to any material extent with the whites, and who, therefore, must continue to exist as a separate class.

II. That they are, as a class, decidedly inferior to the whites in point of intellectual and moral development, so much so as to be incompetent to self-government. Although they have shared largely in the progress of civilization, they have not reached this point. The proof is:

1. Such is the almost universal opinion of the most intelligent and pious communities throughout the whole Southern country, who certainly are well acquainted with their character and capabilities, and therefore fully competent to judge in their case.

2. The experiments at domestic colonization which have been made in this country prove it.

3. The experiments in the case of the free colored population spread through the country are equally in proof.

4. The colonization experiment on the coast of Africa is still more conclusive.

III. That domestic slavery is the appropriate form of government for a people in such circumstances, is fully exemplified by the Divine procedure in the case of the heathen subdued by the ancient Israelites.

We infer:

1. That they have no right to social equality or to political sovereignty - that to accord them either, in their present moral condition, would be a curse instead of a blessing. It would in all probability lead to the extermination of the race, and inflict a deep injury both upon the moral and physical condition of the

whole country.

2. That every consideration of humanity and prudence requires that, until a better form of subordinate government shall be devised, they must be continued under the system of domestic slavery now in operation.

*   *   *

It has been shown in previous lectures that the principle of slavery accords fully with the doctrine of abstract rights, civil and social; and that a system of domestic slavery in the United States is demanded by the circumstances of the African population in the country. But it by no means follows that the conduct of all masters, in the exercise of their functions as masters, is proper, any more than that the conduct of all parents, or the owners of apprentices, is such as it should be. The opinion is entertained that the domestic government of children does not more than approximate propriety as a general thing; and that the government of apprentices and of African slaves falls far short of what is proper. In this lecture it is proposed to deal with the relations of masters to slaves, that is, the duties they owe them. The doctrine that the system of domestic slavery assumes that the slave is a "mere machine - a chattel," has been fully exploded. The Bible particularly regards the slave an accountable being. It requires him to yield a willing obedience to his master, and teaches him that such service is accepted of the Lord as service done unto himself, Ephesians vi. 5-8; and in the 9th verse, the master is required to "do the same things unto them, forbearing threatening: knowing that your Master also is in heaven." And again, (Colossians iv. 1,) "Masters, give unto your servants that which is just and equal." Hence, in the strictest sense, religion holds the scales of justice between masters and slaves. Each one is held to a strict accountability for the faithful performance of his duty, the one to the other - "for there is no respect of persons with God."

It behooves us, then, who are masters, or who expect to become masters, to inquire into the duties of this relation. The master who does not inform himself on this subject, and endeavor conscientiously to do his duty, is strangely wanting in important elements of Christian character, and, indeed, even in some of those attributes which enter materially into the character of a good citizen.

A most fanatical spirit is abroad in the land on the subject of domestic slavery. The inhumanity of masters at the South is greatly exaggerated. (Instances in which the institution of slavery is abused no doubt contribute to this excitement.) Even those who are deficient in the duties they owe their domestics and apprentices - quite as much so as is common at the South with the

masters of African slaves – lend a willing ear to political
demagogues and fanatical party-leaders in their denunciations of
the South. Want of sympathy for hired servants, and instances in
which they are overreached and oppressed beyond the means of legal
redress, are as common in certain quarters as are the cases of
inhumanity to the slaves at the South. But this does not help the
matter. Evils of this kind are to be deplored whether they occur
at the North or the South. The injunction of the apostle reaches
every case of the kind – "Masters, give unto your servants that
which is just and equal: knowing that ye also have a Master in
heaven."

¶   Review of Pro-Slavery Books.

(Taken from the *Methodist Quarterly Review* (South), XI
(Jan. 1857), 40-43).

In view of such overwhelming testimony afforded by these
scriptures of the Divine approbation of slavery, can it be credited
that they are appealed to as condemning it? Yet it is even so.
Many of the bitterest opponents of slavery declare their opposition
to it because it is inconsistent with the will of God as set forth
in the Bible. They read there a law which says, "Thou shalt love
thy neighbor as thyself;" and again, "All things whatsoever ye
would that men should do unto you, do ye even so to them." They
discover in these two precepts a principle diametrically opposed to
slavery. One of these has said – a man not given to drawing hasty
or incorrect conclusions – "Were this precept (the one last cited)
obeyed, it is manifest that slavery could not in fact exist for a
single instant. The principle of the precept is absolutely subversive of the principle of slavery." This is the stronghold of the
anti-slavery advocate; and if we compel him to surrender it, we
shall have gone far to convert him to the truth. The answer we
think is complete. Jesus Christ declared of the "law" that its
essence was contained in two items – supreme love to God, and love
to one's neighbor: "Thou shalt love the Lord thy God with all thy
heart, and soul, and strength, and thy neighbor as thyself. On
these two commandments hang all the law and the prophets." This
"law" of which the Saviour spake embraced the law of the Decalogue,
from which we have before cited, and in which, as we have seen,
slavery is protected, and the injunction is given, "Thou shalt not
covet thy neighbor's wife, nor his man-servant, nor his maid-
servant, nor his ox, nor his ass, nor anything that is thy neighbor's."
Can it be possible that the Lawgiver of Sinai and Christ are at
issue?   .   .   .   .

If it be true, as he says it is true, that the principle of
slavery and the Bible principle of love to one's neighbor are
antagonistic, then there is no escape from the conclusion that the

266

God of Sinai and the Christ who expounded his law are at issue. But
we will take a lower position, and endeavor to "justify the ways of
Jehovah," and to remove this contrariety by showing that the interpretation put upon the command to love your neighbor as yourself, by
modern anti-slavery writers, is not the true one. We say it with all
the emphasis of which we are capable, that the principle of slavery
does not conflict with the proper lines of the law of human love;
that,on the contrary, in many cases, and in the particular case of
American slavery, the proper exercise of the principle, "Love your
neighbor as yourself," demands the continuance of the institution.

By the precept, "Love your neighbor as yourself," and by that
other precept, (being the same in another form,) "Do unto others as
you would that others should do unto you," we are not to understand
as taught that whatever one man may lawfully desire in one condition
of life, another may lawfully desire in another condition of life;
and that the master is, therefore, in applying the rule of love, to
measure the proper desires of his servant by his own. If it be
right for the servant, taking into consideration justice to the master,
the safety and welfare of society, and the welfare of the servant
himself; if it be right for the servant, in view of all these considerations, to desire freedom, then it is certainly true that the
master, in the proper exercise of this Christian principle of love,
should set him free. But if, on the other hand, it be not right for
the servant to desire freedom, because of any of the considerations
named, or for any other sufficient reason, then it is equally clear
that, in the exercise of the same principle, the master should not
manumit him, but should hold him in bondage. Let us illustrate the
practical operation of this principle in a hypothecated case, the
parallel to which any Southern city can furnish. A. is a servant
of rare mechanical genius. B. has purchased him at a very high
price. With his powers as a mechanic, A. is nevertheless naturally
unthrifty, negligent, and lazy. He needs an overseer - some one to
compel him to work; otherwise, he would become a drunken and
dissipated wretch, scarcely able to earn bread enough to live upon,
much less to rear up a family. A. is now in B.'s service, and works
well. The master gives him food and raiment, and supplies him with
all the necessaries of life. He has a wife and family, all of whom
are under the control of his master, and A. is as happy and contented as is the master who owns him. In such a case, the question of
manumission is presented to B. One at his elbow suggests, "You have
no right to hold A. in bondage. The God that made you declares that
'you must love your neighbor as yourself;' that you 'must do to others
as you would have them do to you.' If you were in A.'s place, you
would desire freedom. Christian love to A. must prompt you to set
him free." "But," responds B., "I cannot set him free. As he is,
he is filling the station God designed him to fill. He is a faithful, steady servant. He works well as a servant. His labors are of
great pecuniary advantage to me, and of utility to the town in which
I live. He has all the necessary comforts of life; a wife and family

267

well taken care of, and provided for as he is himself. If I manumit
him, I will do him an injury. I will not deny that he may desire
freedom, but he is (as all of his race are) naturally unthrifty and
negligent, and he lacks forethought. If I set him free, together
with his family, as my neighbor N. did in the case of his servants,
like them, in a few months - years at farthest - A. and his family
will become vicious and filthy in their habits, an eyesore to all
passers-by, and some of them, perhaps, tenants of the jail or
penitentiary. I believe my duty to A. and to A.'s family, and the
love you speak of, alike require that I should keep him in his
present state of servitude. He is a happier and better man, as a
servant, than he would be if he were free." In the case put, is not
B.'s reasoning sound? Yet if B. had measured A.'s desires by his own,
he would have given him and his family their freedom; and in so doing,
would have violated rather than obeyed the law of Christian love, by
inflicting upon his servants the evils he enumerates. The servants
were not prepared for struggling as freemen in the battle of life:
they were not fitted for the position into which they would be
thrust by manumission; hence their ruin by securing freedom. Dr.
Bledsoe has happily expressed the thought we are here enforcing:
*"A foolish desire, we repeat, in one relation of life, is not a good
reason for a foolish or injurious act in another relation thereof."*

*   *   *

If this reasoning be sound, it follows that, in some cases, it
is an act of disservice and positive injustice to the slave to manumit
him. In such cases, it is clear that slavery does not conflict with
the proper exercise of the principle, "Love your neighbor as yourself."
Slavery, as it exists at the present day in the Southern States of
this Union, constitutes, we think, one of the cases in which justice
and love to the slave require that the institution should continue
to exist. Our opponents will admit that slavery, as known among us,
is of the most mitigated form.

*   *   *

We say more: Our slavery has exalted the race who are its
subjects from a state of gross barbarism to a state of comparative
civilization. We say more: The race subjected to slavery among us is
yet incompetent to govern or provide for itself; and if such a thing
as universal emancipation were practicable, and could the race at
once be separated from the whites, it would again speedily lapse into
barbarism. Even amid the restraining influences of the highest
civilization, the individual instances of emancipation attest what
we have said, that, as a people, they are incompetent and improvident, and utterly unable to maintain decently themselves or their
families. In the character of slaves, they have been useful, and
have advanced rather than retarded the prosperity of our people.
Such being the advantages, on the one hand, of keeping them in

servitude, and such being the disadvantages, on the other, of setting them free, the argument for the extinction of slavery must be overwhelming, indeed, before we can be brought to believe that it is either just or right or expedient to manumit our slaves.

¶ Debate in General Conference, 1844.

(Taken from *Debates in the General Conference of the Methodist Episcopal Church* (1844), 148-52).

Bishop Andrew then rose, evidently labouring under powerful emotion, and spoke as follows:

Mr. President, - I have been on trial now for a week, and feel desirous that it should come to a close. For a week I have been compelled to listen to discussions of which I have been the subject, and I must have been more than man, or less than man, not to have felt. Sir, I have felt and felt deeply. I am not offended with any man. The most of those who have spoken against me, have treated me respectfully, and have been as mild as I had any right to expect. I cherish no unkind feelings toward any. I do not quarrel with my abolition brethren, though I believe their opinions to be erroneous and mischievous. Yet so long as they conduct themselves courteously toward me, I have no quarrel with them. It is due that some remarks should be made by me, before the conference come to a conclusion upon the question, which I hope will be speedily done, for I think a week is long enough for a man to be shot at, and it is time the discussion should terminate.

As there has been frequent reference to the circumstances of my election to the episcopal office, it is perhaps proper that I give a brief history of that matter. A friend of mine (brother Hodges) now with God, asked me to permit myself to be put in nomination for that office. I objected - the office had no charms for me. Finally I consented, with the hope of failure; but I was nominated and elected. I was never asked if I was a slaveholder - no man asked me what were my principles on the subject - no one dared to ask of me a pledge in this matter, or it would have been met as it deserved. Only one man, brother Winans, spoke to me on the subject; he said he could not vote for me because he believed I was nominated under the impression that I was not a slaveholder. . . .

A friend who has taken ground in favour of the resolution before you suggested: "Why," said he, "did you not let your wife make over these negroes to her children, securing to herself an annuity from them?" Sir, my conscience would not allow me to do this thing. If I had done so, and those negroes had passed into the hands of those who would have treated them unkindly, I should have been unhappy. Strange as it may seem to brethren, I am a slaveholder for conscience'

sake.   .   .   .

What can I do? I have no confession to make - I intend to
make none. I stand upon the broad ground of the Discipline on which
I took office, and if I have done wrong, put me out. The editor of
the Christian Advocate has prejudged this case. He makes me the
scape-goat of all the difficulties which abolition excitement has
gotten up at the north. I am the only one to blame, in his opinion,
should mischief grow out of this case. But I repeat, if I have
sinned against the Discipline, I refuse not to die. I have spent
my life for the benefit of the slaves. When I was but a boy, I
taught a Sunday-school for slaves, in which I taught a number of
them to read; and from that period till this day I have devoted my
energies to the promotion of their happiness and salvation; with all
my influence in private, in public, with my tongue, with my pen, I
have assiduously endeavoured to promote their present and eternal
happiness. And am I to be sacrificed by those who have done little
or nothing for them? It is said, I have rendered myself unacceptable
to our people. I doubt this: I have just returned from Philadelphia,
where they knew me to be a slaveholder; yet they flocked to hear me,
and the presence of God was with us; we had a good, warm, old-fashioned meeting. I may be unacceptable in New-York, yet from the
experience I have had, I doubt even that. To whom am I unacceptable?
Not to the people of the south - neither masters nor slaves. Has my
connection with slaves rendered me less acceptable to the coloured
people of the south - the very people for whom all this professed
sympathy is felt? Does the fact that I am a slaveholder make me
less acceptable among them? Let those who have laboured long among
them answer the question. Sir, I venture to say, that in Carolina
or Georgia I could to-day get more votes for the office of bishop
from the coloured people, than any supporter of this resolution, let
him avow himself an emancipator as openly as he pleases. To the
coloured people of the south there, and to their owners, - to the
entire membership of the slaveholding conferences, I would not be
unacceptable - but, perhaps, they are no part of "our people;" in
short, sir, I believe that I should not be unacceptable to one half
of the connection - but on this question I have nothing to say.
Should the conference think proper to pass me, there is plenty of
ground where I can labour acceptably and usefully.   .   .   .

The country is becoming agitated upon the subject, and I hope
the conference will act forthwith on the resolution.

Mr. Finley said, - Mr. President, I arise with some trepidation,
and think I should not speak at all if I were not placed in the
situation I am, as the mover of the substitute on your table. When
I proposed it, it was with the purest motives, I am sure, and
believing it would be more acceptable than the original resolution.
In framing that substitute, I thought I took ground on the
constitution of our Church; and I am sure I have expressed nothing

in the preamble but what are the acknowledged facts in the case.
The resolution is only to express the sense of the General Conference
in reference to the facts as they exist, in connection with the
situation in which these circumstances have placed the superintendent.

Now, sir, in regard to the ground taken, this General Conference
is restricted against doing anything which will destroy our itinerant
general superintendency. This principle must be conceded. That
Bishop Andrew has become connected with the great evil of slavery, he
himself has declared on this floor, and says he is a slaveholder.
This fact will not be denied; and that this connection with slavery
has drawn after it circumstances that will embarrass his exercising
the office of an itinerant general superintendent, if not in some
places entirely prevent it. I ask any man on this floor to deny these
things. Now, sir, are not all the facts true, and true to the life?
Hence, the question follows, Will this General Conference permit one
of its vital and constitutional principles to be broken down and
trampled under foot, because one of her general officers has seen fit
to involve himself in circumstances which will trammel that office in
more than half of all the field of his labour? Now, sir, I take my
stand here this day to oppose, to my utmost, the violation of so
sacred a principle. Was Bishop Andrew involved in these circumstances when he was elected to that office? No, sir: no man here
will say he was. And could he have been elected to that office if
he had been? No, sir: no man here will assert that he could. He
was chosen with the declaration of southern men that he was not then,
and never had been, connected with the evil of slavery; and we had
reason to believe he never would be, or he could not have been chosen
to that office. Well now, sir, what is the state of the case? He
has become a slaveholder. I ask you, sir, whose fault is this? It
is his own voluntary act, in view of all the circumstances. This
voluntary act has thrown this great body of ministers, and the whole
Church, into this tremendous state of agitation, of which he could now
relieve us, if he would, by his resignation.

But, sir, what does this resolution request of him? The mildest
and most moderate thing the case is capable of, without giving up the
whole principle, viz., "that it is the sense of this General
Conference that he desist from the exercise of his office until these
impediments be removed." This resolution was modified to the most
easy requirement it could be to meet the feeling of southern brethren,
and to cover the principle, and from this ground I will not be moved.
So, sir; on this ground will I stand until I die. There are two
great principles to be determined in this resolution which have not
been decided in the Methodist Episcopal Church. One is this: Has
the General Conference a right, or has it the power, to remove from
office one, or all of the bishops, if they, under any circumstances,
become disqualified to carry out the great principles of our
itinerant general superintendency? The second is: Will the Methodist
Church admit the great evil of slavery into the itinerant general

271

superintendency? Now, sir, they never have done it; and if there should be one elected at this conference, he will not be a slaveholder. But I cannot, for my life, perceive the difference between continuing one of them in that office who has seen proper to connect himself with it, and voting directly to put one into it who holds slaves. It is the same principle. . . .

But, sir, it is plead here, in the case of Bishop Andrew, that the conservativeness of the Discipline fully covers his case. Now I wish to meet this argument. It has been reiterated again and again that the Discipline of the Methodist Episcopal Church is conservative toward slavery. This assumption I most positively and emphatically deny. Methodism and the Methodist Discipline have always been, and are now, and I hope will be while the world stand, belligerent toward slavery, and have branded it in the forehead, so that all the world may see it as a great evil. Now, sir, how a grave body of ministers of the Methodist Episcopal Church can hold that this great moral evil can be justified and sanctified by the Methodist Discipline, is a strange paradox to me. Any man who can say it is right for him to hold his fellow-being in bondage, and buy and sell him at pleasure, put him under an overseer, and drive, whip, and half starve him, and that this is connived at by the Methodist Church, I think must have a queer view of the Church and her Discipline. I now say, in my place, before God, that whenever the Methodist Episcopal Church shall sanction this doctrine, as much as I love her, I will leave it and seek another community. Now I say again, there is not one item in the Discipline of the Methodist Episcopal Church that has any conservative principle toward slavery as a great moral evil; yet I will say, sir, it has some conservativeness toward her ministers and members, who, through necessity, are connected with it, and cannot help themselves, and this conservativeness is clearly defined. Yes, sir, I repeat, clearly defined, so that none may be mistaken on this subject. And what is this conservativeness? It is this: when the master cannot set his slave free and that slave enjoy his freedom; when it is beyond the power of the master to free his slave, or that slave to enjoy his freedom, slavery is fixed on the absolute necessity of the case; and if there be any such case, it could not and should not be called a sin. But I hold that this conservativeness goes not one step further to extenuate any man from crime; as a slaveholder, it is the necessity of the case that saves him from crime. . . .

Before I close this speech, I must answer some things which have been stated on this floor. The first is this: that, in the infant state of Methodism, the slaves could be set free in every state of the Union; but whenever the Methodist Church began to take action against slaveholding, the states began to make laws to contravene their freedom. Now, sir, I ask, what was it that first moved the Church to this course? The Church always considered it a great evil, and had some hope that the preaching of the Gospel would eventually

effect much toward its destruction. Then the preachers were free from slavery themselves; then they could, and did, preach against it, and the cause of the poor slave was taking deep root in the public mind. Then preachers began to connect themselves with this great evil, and the other preachers thought it was time to do something to prevent it, believing that the connecting of slavery with the ministry would rivet the chains of slavery the tighter. .   .   .

Now, sir, to answer a few more things that have been urged, and I am done. It has been argued that they hold slaves out of charity to them. Sir, I am at a great loss to know what sort of charity this is, to hold a fellow-creature in bondage, and make him work hard all his life, and appropriate all his labour to the master's use, for charity to the poor slave; to buy and sell him as we do animals, is a queer charity to me, just such as I pray to God may never be exercised toward me. Again, it is said we treat them as we do our children. Now, sir, I ask, do those brethren teach their children that it is better to be slaves than freemen? Do they put their children into the field and set overseers over them? Do they clothe and feed these slaves as they do their own children? Do they teach them to read the Bible, and qualify them to be useful citizens? I leave all these answers for others.

I never will agree that slavery shall be connected in any way with episcopacy, nor anywhere else only by necessity. I must state again, that from this principle I never will be removed. .   .   .

Having thus expressed my position fearlessly, but I trust with no bad feeling toward any brother, on the ground which I believe the Church has always occupied, I take my seat, and shall wait the issue with as much composure and prayer as I am capable of.

¶   Hamline's Speech.

(Taken from George Peck, *Slavery and the Episcopacy* (1845), 128-30, 136-37).

I do not rise, Mr. President, with the hope that I shall "communicate light" on the topics before us; but rather for the purpose of imploring light from others. It cannot be unkind in me to suggest that this discussion has taken an unprofitably wide range; for many whispers within the bar, and the complaints of several speakers on the floor, show that this is the case. We have drawn into the debate many questions which have but a very slight connec-tion with the propositions contained in the resolution. I would, if possible, call the attention of the conference from matters so remote to the real issue in the case. It is complained that we seem to have forsaken all argument, and a call is made for our "strong reasons." We ought, indeed, to argue on both sides. And if I should not do it,

273

I will, at least, refrain from addressing a word to the galleries, or to the spectators.

There ought to be two questions before us. First. Has the General Conference constitutional authority to pass this resolution? Second. Is it proper or fitting it should do it? The first question should be first argued; but so far it has scarcely been touched. If we have not authority to pass the resolution, to discuss its expediency is surely out of place; for it can never be expedient to violate law, unless law violates justice. I shall leave the question of expediency to others, or only glance at it; but I ask your attention to the topic of conference authority.

The resolution proposes to suspend the exercise of a bishop's functions on a certain condition to be performed by him. If I mistake not, the resolution is a mandamus measure. Its passage will absolutely suspend the exercise of the superintendent's functions, until he complies with the prescribed condition. The measure of power required to do this is the same which would be requisite to suspend or depose a bishop for such reasons as the resolution mentions, or, in other words, for "improper conduct." Have we, then, such authority? I shall assume that we have; hoping, if I prove nothing, to provoke proof, pro or con, from the brethren who surround me.

I argue this authority in the General Conference, first, from the genius of our polity on points which the most nearly resemble this. Strict amenability in church officers, subordinate and superior, is provided for in our Discipline. From the class-leader upward, this amenability regards not only major but minor morals - not only the vices, but also the improprieties of behavior.   .   .   .

In all these instances the matter of removing from office is peculiar. First. It is summary, without accusation, trial, or formal sentence. It is a ministerial, rather than a judicial act. Second. It is for no crime, and generally for no misdemeanor, but for being "unacceptable." Third. Most of these removals from office are by a sole agent, namely, by a bishop or preacher, whose will is omnipotent in the premises. Fourth. The removing officer is not legally obliged to assign any cause for deposing. If he do so, it is through courtesy, and not as of right. Fifth. The deposed officer has no appeal. If indiscreetly or unnecessarily removed, he must submit; for there is no tribunal authorized to cure the error, or to rectify the wrong. But we believe that there are good and sufficient reasons for granting this high power of removal to those who exercise it. It promotes religion. It binds the church in a strong and almost indissoluble unity. It quickens the communication of healing influences to the infected and the enfeebled parts of the body ecclesiastical. In a word, it is a system of surpassing energy. By it executive power is sent in its most efficient form,

274

and without loss of time, from its highest sources or remotest fountains, through the preachers and class-leaders, to the humblest member of the church. The system is worthy of all eulogy.

We will now inquire as to the bishop. In his case is this strong feature of Methodism lost sight of? Is he, who can at discretion, by himself or by his agents, remove from office so many, among whom are thousands of his co-ordinates or peers, subject in turn to no such summary control? We have seen that to lodge this power of removal in superior, and impose submission to it on inferior, officers is the fashion of Methodism. She loves the system. She carries it up through many grades of office until we reach the bishop. Does it suddenly stop there? If so, on what ground? I can conceive none. If any can, let the reasons be arrayed before us. I can perceive none, Mr. President, in being; but I can conceive them possible under given circumstances. In church and in state there must always be an ultimate or supreme authority, and the exercise of it must be independent, so far as systematic responsibility is concerned. But is the episcopacy in regard to this question supreme? Certainly not. The General Conference, adjunct in certain exigencies with the Annual Conferences, is the ultimate depository of power in our church. And I beg to dwell here. For, in the second place, I shall argue our authority to depose a bishop summarily for improprieties morally innocent, which embarrass the exercise of his functions, from the relations of the General Conference to the church, and to the episcopacy.

* * *

I have argued that the conference has power, from the grant of the constitution, (which is a catholic grant, embracing all, beyond a few enumerated restrictions,) to try a bishop for crime, and to depose him summarily for "improper conduct." Is this hard on the bishop? Does he not summarily remove, at discretion, all the four years round, two hundred presiding elders, and two thousand of his peers; and shall he complain that a General Conference, which is a delegated body - in a word, that all these two thousand peers of his, whose authority converges through the channels of representation, and concentrates here, should do to him what he so uniformly does to them? Shall one elder, holding a high office at our hands, be so puissant, that, like the sun in the heavens, (though he be a planet still, and in his office reflects no light which we have not shed upon him,) he must bind and control all, but is in turn to be controlled by none? No, sir. This conference is the sun in our orderly and beautiful system. . . .

I said, Mr. President, that if I noticed the question of expediency, it would be only by a glance. I will remark, generally, that in determining what is proper, after having ascertained what is lawful, we should look two ways. As first in importance we should

consider the interests of the church.   Second, we should consult
the feelings of the officer. And we should inquire as to the church,
how is she likely to be affected by the improper conduct of her
officer?   .   .   .   .

In regard to the officer, it should be inquired if the unfitness
he has brought on himself for his sphere of action was by some
imperative necessity, and if not, whether it was in presumable
ignorance of the grief and misfortunes he was about to inflict on
our Zion? Or must he have known what would follow, so that his act
proceeded from, or at least was associated with, some degree of
indifference, if not of wantonness, in regard to results? These
things, sir, should be well weighed in settling the question of
expediency.

A bishop's influence is not like a preacher's or class-leaders's.
It is diffused like the atmosphere, everywhere. So high a church
officer, (I will not say, sir conference officer, though just now
I take you to be such, at least, for the time being,) I say, so
high a church officer should be willing to endure not slight
sacrifices for this vast connection. What could tempt you, sir, to
trouble and wound the church all through, from centre to circum-
ference? The preacher and the class-leader, whose influence is
guarded against so strongly, can do little harm - a bishop infinite.
Their improper acts are motes in the air - yours are a pestilence
abroad in the earth. Is it more important to guard against those
than against these? Heaven forbid! Like the concealed attractions
of the heavens, we expect a bishop's influence to be all-binding
everywhere - in the heights and in the depths - in the centre and
on the verge of this great system ecclesiastical. If instead of
concentric and harmonizing movements, such as are wholesome, and
conservative, and beautifying, we observe in him irregularities,
which, however harmless in others, will be disastrous or fatal in
him, the energy of this body, constitutionally supreme, must
instantly reduce him to order, or if that may not be, plant him in
another and a distant sphere. When the church is about to suffer a
detriment, which we by constitutional power can avert, it is as much
treason in us not to exercise the power we have, as to usurp, in
other circumstances, that which we have not.

¶   Charles Elliott, *History of the Great Secession* (1855).

(Taken from *ibid*, 341-44, 483).

15. We will now present a few observations on the plan and its
provisions.

It was a fixed point, decided in 1828, that the General
Conference could not divide the Church. Hence the failure of Dr.

Caper's plan, and the non-entertainment of that part of Mr. M'Ferrin's resolution, which called for a division of the Church.

The plan was not made because separation was better than union, but because it was an alternative, seeing separation was inevitable.

The plan, indeed, was, however, in advance of supposed secession. It was asked by the minority; and it was supposed to be the most likely method to prevent secession, though it was made in prospect of one.

It was, too, to meet an emergency, to provide for which, as we have said, the ordinary rules of Church polity will not apply. It was a revolution, and a violent one, to meet which the conference had to prepare as best it can. It is true, it might have made no provision to meet it, except denial, resistance, and disownment; but then all thought that this was not the better way, though none were satisfied with the measures adopted.

The General conference did not authorize the secession by its acts; for this must be the sole act of the south themselves.

It was, however, intended as a peace measure, and certainly there is much to be said in favor of such a measure, compared to one founded in a different spirit.

The principal provisions of the plan could not apply till a secession should have taken place.

Hence the south separated themselves. They were neither expelled, nor disowned, till they should disown the Church, and renounce its jurisdiction.

16. As several objections have been made to the report on the declaration, we may now pay attention to some of them.

It is objected that this plan deprives ministers and members in the interior, and ministers on the borders, of their membership, and is therefore unconstitutional or wrong. On this we remark: 1. That there is no act of the conference that deprives them either of trial or appeal, or of their membership. 2. The condition of such is something like that of the state in time of war, when statutory laws, providing for individual rights, must yield to the demands of public good. 3. There were ministers of societies in this country who joined under Mr. Wesley, that were opposed to the organization of the Methodist Episcopal Church, and regarded it as cutting them off contrary to rule. 4. In some places where untoward circumstances break up a Church, there may be minorities of excellent character, who may suffer greatly, whose cases the provisions of the Church can not meet. 5. But there was an emergency. There was a revolution in

the Church, and the ordinary rules of policy could not be made to apply, let the Church do the best she could.

It has also been objected, that the plan contravenes the ministerial call, in shutting it out of the south. The Methodist Episcopal Church does not send its ministers to occupy fields that are cultivated by ministers of the Canadian, Wesleyan, or Irish conferences; yet the cases are very similar to this one. Beside, the commission of our Lord is not confined to the Methodist Episcopal Church, nor to any other Church; yet where there are already faithful ministers in any field, it is not in consistency with our Lord's commission for others to interfere with their labors.

It is said, too, that the plan furnishes a bad precedent, and provides for schism. That our Church went far for peace, and to preserve fraternal relations, is admitted; perhaps, indeed, too far. It is difficult, in an emergency, to keep within proper bounds. But the Church acted on the side of peace, fraternity, and good will; and if a proper use is not made of this by those concerned, it may be going too far to censure her for her moderation.

After all, perhaps, the wisdom of man could not well provide better or more Christian measures than the General conference of 1844 did, in adopting the report on the declaration. Nothing that has since been projected, we think, will compare with it, unless it may be to have done nothing at all. That may have been best; yet we doubt it. To preserve so large a Church in one great confederacy is not the better way, as the history, both of Popery and of great national Churches, fully shows. And even now it may be questioned whether two Methodist Episcopal Churches in the United States are not better than one, provided the new Church were such as the General conference expected it to be. . . .

The Committee on Organization foresaw that something more was necessary to sustain their charge than the cases of Harding and the Bishop. They therefore advert to the abolition excitement in some portions of the Church, as rendering it necessary for the south to dissolve their existing relations. It is unfortunate for this argument that the two preceding General conferences contained each more ultra-abolition delegates than that of 1844, and yet no abolition measure was carried, nor even proposed by any of the committees. The violent agitators had seceded from the Church, and the abolition storm had spent itself before 1844. The only real cause of complaint was, that the General conference refused to sanction slavery in its decisions. This was the real cause, and nothing else.

Indeed, whatever of real or plausible necessity for secession existed when the convention met, seems to have been created by the course of the south, and which did not grow out of the nature of the case. The southern delegates met next day after the adjournment of

the General conference, resolved on the Louisville convention,
fixed the ratio of representation, and sent out an inflammatory
circular to the people. The southern papers hoisted at once the
secession flag, and every effort was employed to get up, not to
allay excitement; to make, but not to prevent the necessity. The
necessity contemplated by the General conference, was one spontaneously arising from the state of things; not one got up or made for the
occasion. The convention can find no reason whatever for its
decision from the provisional plan of the General conference. They
were to find, not to create or make the necessity.

6. What then is the Methodist Episcopal Church, South, but a
secession from the Methodist Episcopal Church? The Report on Organization makes it a secession, by its decision, though it denies it in
its argumentation. The convention renounced the jurisdiction of the
Methodist Episcopal Church; for they renounced the jurisdiction of the
General Conference; but the jurisdiction of the General Conference is
the jurisdiction of the Methodist Episcopal Church; therefore they
renounced the jurisdiction of the Methodist Episcopal Church; and
with it the Church itself.

Beside, they constituted a new Church. And how could they
constitute a new one, and form it from themselves, and therefore
belong to the new Church, without withdrawing, or seceding, or
separating themselves from the Methodist Episcopal Church?

11. PUBLISHING AND CHRISTIAN EDUCATION

The first successful effort at publishing a magazine for Methodists in America was the Methodist Magazine, which began in 1818, eight years before the Christian Advocate. Under various titles (which for convenience are referred to under the generic Methodist Quarterly Review) it continued, with the exception of one year (1829) until 1932; and then went on as an "ecumenical quarterly" entitled Religion in Life. The original "Address" to the readers, and two previews as new editors started a new series, are given here. Joshua Soule and Thomas Mason were followed in 1841 by George Peck. It came to a high point under the editorship of D. D. Whedon, who dominated the journal for a quarter of a century.

The early struggles to establish a publishing house for the Evangelical Association are painfully recorded in the "Day Book" of John Dreisbach, which is quoted via the carefully done history by John H. Ness, Jr. On the other hand, the United Brethren began in 1834 a church magazine, The Religious Telescope, which had a long and honored history in that denomination. The hopes and aspirations of the early editors are expressed in a preview editorial in the first number.

When it came to colleges, the Methodists, though late on the scene, were quick to catch up - lest their sons (only later daughters) might face the spiritual perils of attending schools of other denominations. The first of a long series of "Wesleyan" colleges was located in Middletown, Connecticut, under the leadership of Wilbur Fisk and Laban Clark. The letters indicate some of the many problems that attended establishment of such institutions. The peculiarly Methodist relationship of church-related colleges is illustrated by the report of a committee to Indiana Annual Conference investigating the feasibility of setting up a college in that state. Indiana-Asbury, as it was called, became DePauw University.

Until at least after the Civil War most ministerial leaders thought of theological education in terms of field experience - "brush college" as some fondly called it. Both Ware and Brunson were of this view. But both were led to accept the values of more formal training. Church-related liberal arts colleges were one thing; but theological seminaries were regarded with considerable suspicion. The fine light of the Holy Spirit might all too easily be blurred or shut out. Hence the earliest seminaries, Boston and Garrett, had to prove themselves worthy of cherishing the flame. Brunson, like Peter Cartwright, was an old curmudgeon who viewed any kind of change from the old ways with distaste. But they were both intelligent men who had to learn new ways whether they liked them or not.

280

¶   Editorials in the *Methodist Quarterly Review* (under various
      titles), 1818, 1841, 1884.

(Taken from *Methodist Quarterly Review*, Jan. 1818, 3-7).

    In publishing this periodical Miscellany the Editors feel all
those sensibilities which arise from a conviction that its merits
are to be tested under the inspection of an enlightened community.

    The care and labour inseparable from the agency of the Book
Concern, forbid our devoting as much time and application to the
selection and arrangement of materials for publication in the
magazine, as its nature and importance demand.

    But, notwithstanding these embarrassments exist, we trust the
work will be found both useful and entertaining to the real friends
of Zion.

    The great design of this publication is to circulate religious
knowledge, - a design which embraces the highest interests of
rational existence, as the sum of individual and social happiness
increases on a scale of proportion with the increase of spiritual
light and information.

    In the execution of this design, the strictest care will be
taken to guard the purity and simplicity of the doctrines of the
gospel against the innovations of superstition on the one hand, and
of false philosophy on the other.

    In admitting controversial subjects into this work, the heat
of party zeal, and personal crimmation, will be cautiously avoided.

    Such contentions have already done great evil in the Christian
world, and especially in arming infidels against a religion, the
nature and principles of which are calculated to harmonize, improve,
and sanctify the human species. Every benevolent mind - every friend
of unity and peace - every heart influenced by the social affections -
in short, every lover of God and man, will rejoice to see the spirit
of party zeal retiring, and giving place to candour, moderation, and
charity.

    The few years of the present century which have already passed
away, have opened the most important and auspicious events, relative
to the establishment of the kingdom of Jesus Christ upon earth. The
united exertions of thousands of all denominations of Christians to
spread the holy scriptures - the unadulterated word of God, savours
much of that catholic spirit by which the friends of christianity
should always be governed, and furnishes a pleasing prospect of the
extensive triumph of evangelical truth. To the accomplishment of
such an object we earnestly desire this miscellany may prove an

efficient auxiliary.

We are aware, that, by many readers, no periodical work will be approved, unless it is replenished with curious tales, wonderful narratives, or miraculous phenomena. With such readers we apprehend this work will meet a cool reception. - Curiosity should be indulged only within the limits of reason, and in such a way as to strengthen moral and religious principles. If the Governor of the universe recognises man as a subject of reason, it follows that faith must be grounded in evidence; and therefore we should consider it as an intrusion upon the rights of an intelligent being, to publish a narrative of any wonderful occurrence without the support of competent testimony.

It should never be forgotten that the age of miracles is past; the ends for which they were wrought by Jesus Christ and his apostles being accomplished; and that any pretended addition to them rather weakens than strengthens the evidence they afford of the truth and excellency of the christian revelation.

These observations are far from being intended to eclipse the lustre of the divine administration as displayed in the dispensations of providence and grace.   .   .   .

In forming the general heads under which the various materials are arranged, we have found it necessary to be as concise as possible, both in number and expression. The number and order are as follows. 1. Divinity. 2. Biography. 3. Scripture Illustrated. 4. The Attributes of God displayed in the works of Creation and Providence. 5. The grace of God manifested. 6. Miscellaneous. 7. Religious and Missionary Intelligence. 8. Obituary. 9. Poetry.

It cannot be expected, where the general divisions are so limited, that there should be a critical connection between each head, and every particular which may be placed under it: such connection, however, will be preserved as far as the nature of the subject will admit. A treatise will not always be destined to the Miscellaneous department because it is compounded, or mixed; but its proper place will be determined by its leading character.

Before we close this address, we think it proper to caution our readers in general, and the members of the Methodist Episcopal Church in particular, to guard against two evils. 1. Many persons, after they have read a pamphlet, lay it aside as a useless thing - It soon falls into the hands of children, or servants, where it is defaced or destroyed: or thrown promiscuously with the common news or waste papers, it is forgotten and lost in the lapse of time. Let it not be so with this Magazine. Recollect that it contains many valuable subjects, the completion of which, may require several numbers, and which may sometimes form a chain to connect volumes.

Let parents consider the Methodist Magazine as a legacy for their posterity, and as soon as the last number for the year is received, have the whole bound together and carefully preserved.

2. Without offering any violence to the rights of men, we think ourselves authorized to caution our friends against purchasing, or encouraging the publication, sale, or purchase of any book, or books, directly or indirectly, under the name or title of "Methodist," unless they are published and sold in conformity to the rules of the Discipline in such cases made and provided.   .   .   .

If any man , after having read the sentimental, sublime and spiritual Hymns of Mr. Wesley, and other authors from whose works our Hymn-Book is composed, can sit down and derive either edification or entertainment from the common-place poetry of the day, we are far from wishing to lessen his enjoyment; but the honour of the Church, whose interests we are sacredly bound to promote, calls upon us, as far as our influence extends, to prevent the circulation of such publications under the sanction of her name.

That all persons into whose hands this work shall come may receive instruction, edification and comfort through its instrumentality, is the sincere desire, and earnest prayer of the Editors.

                                        J. Soule & T. Mason.

                    *   *   *

(Taken from *Methodist Quarterly Review*, Jan. 1841, 5-8).

The present is an eventful and an interesting age. Improvements are exceeding, in number and importance, those of all former periods. The various plans for the melioration of human condition are assuming new modifications, and acting with accumulated power. The useful arts, and the institutions of benevolence, are so enlarging their compass, that the defects and embarrassments of the social state are in a way soon to be covered by remedies as near sovereign as the present condition of things will admit.

Among the great instruments of human improvement the press occupies a conspicuous position. It seems especially designed by Providence to exercise a restoring influence upon the understanding and conscience; but it is a lamentable fact that it has not unfrequently been pressed into the service of folly and corruption. To wrest this grand engine from the hand of error, and to employ it in its legitimate work, no effort should be deemed too great a sacrifice. The press should be fully employed in the great object of enlightening and reforming the world: it should furnish every variety of instructive and useful reading; and especially should it correct its own errors, and counteract the evil tendencies it has

occasioned, and of which it is the only effective remedy. . . .

At the late General Conference it was resolved to commence after the close of the volume for 1840, a new series of the work, in an improved form, under the title of the *Methodist Quarterly Review*. The design now is to give the work more fully the character of a Review than it has heretofore sustained, but not in the least to depart from the general purposes contemplated in the former series. Its pages will be devoted to theology, ecclesiastical polity, education, science, and general literature. These subjects will be discussed mostly, but not altogether, in the form of reviews. In extended and elaborate reviews we shall present our readers with the substance of many of the leading publications which from time to time issue from the American and European presses, accompanied with such criticisms and remarks as their character shall demand; and in critical notices shall give our views of the general character of many others. By these means we hope to render much assistance to our readers in ordering books which they may wish to procure, as well as to afford them the means of obtaining the information contained in many others, which they may not have the means or desire to purchase.

For further particulars as to the plan of the work, and our editorial course, we would refer the reader to the prospectus published by the Agents, to our editorial in the July number, and to the present number, which is offered as a specimen.

Such a publication is deemed especially important at the present time. Theology is liable to suffer from the extremes which characterize the age. Adventurous speculation, reckless skepticism, and tame credulity enter largely into the spirit of the times. The grossest errors of the dark ages, together with every species of novelty, find a ready reception even among minds claiming the advantages of a high state of cultivation. And is this any time for the Methodist press to sleep, or to be partial and tame in its instruments of attack and defense? Surely not. If there were ever a time when the true Wesleyan theology, in its clearness, simplicity, and power, required all the means of diffusiveness and extension which can be commanded, the present is that time. A medium for a thorough and full discussion of such topics in theology as have been buried in the mists of false philosophy or unbridled dogmatism is now with us absolutely necessary. And shall the Methodist Episcopal Church prove recreant in such an emergency? Indeed, she cannot. She will fortify every point, and fully equip herself for the important part she is destined to act in the great conflict now in progress between the simple, unsophisticated doctrines of the gospel, and a theology merely speculative on the one hand, or purely dogmatical on the other.

The institutions and government of the church must have due attention. Various questions which many may have supposed long since settled, relating to ecclesiastical polity, are still mooted,

and the principles which they involve are to be contested over and over again. Hence the necessity of being always prepared to defend and explain our own peculiar institutions at length when need requires.

The missionary, sabbath school, and temperance cause, as also our schools and colleges, will come in for a share of our sympathies and co-operation.

Experiments in science are daily bringing to light the secrets of nature, and so enlarging the sphere of human contemplation and enjoyment. It is of immense importance that all branches of the community should keep pace with the progress of scientific discovery, at least so far as the useful arts are affected by this means. It shall be our object to keep our readers sufficiently advised upon this subject.

We hope to pluck now and then a flower from ancient and modern literature, for the gratification of our readers. But those whose morbid appetites can only be satisfied with the creations of a disordered imagination can have little to hope from our labors, or those of our correspondents. The Review will deal in sober realities. And though all due pains will be taken to gratify a well-disciplined taste, its great object will be to make its readers wiser and better.

*   *   *

(Taken from *Index to Methodist Quarterly Review* (1884), 5-9, by Elijah H. Pilcher).

HISTORICAL INTRODUCTION

The use of the press as a means of diffusing religious truth and intelligence was a grand, though natural, conception. The first use to which Gutenberg put his invention of movable type was, in association with the goldsmith, Faust, to issue a large folio edition of the Latin Bible. The high value of the press as a means of multiplying and cheapening copies of the sacred Book was thus early recognized, and, as the art of printing progressed, it was devoted with increasing assiduity to the extension of religious knowledge. It was but natural that the comprehensive intellect of John Wesley should, almost at the beginning of his labors as a religious teacher, have grasped this agency in furtherance of the work of God by printing religious books and tracts, and that he should have followed up this beginning by the establishment of a monthly periodical, the "Arminian Magazine," in 1788.

The following year, 1789, was marked by the commencement of the publishing work of the Methodist Episcopal Church in the appointment of John Dickins, at Philadelphia, as Book Steward, combining in his

own person the multifarious functions of editor, publisher, and book-
seller, in addition to regular work in the pastorate, he being the
only Methodist preacher stationed in that city. He issued, in the
same year, the first volume of the "American Magazine," which was
composed largely of matter reprinted from its English prototype, with,
however, some account of religious affairs in America. A second
volume was given to the public in 1790.

This, the first attempt of the Church at periodical literature,
was then suspended until the General Conference of 1812 instructed
the Book Agents to resume the publication of the magazine in monthly
numbers; but, owing to lack of good management, it was not until
January, 1818, after the General Conference of 1816 had reiterated the
instructions of his predecessor, that the first number of the
"Methodist Magazine" was published, under the editorial supervision
of Joshua Soule - afterward bishop - and Thomas Mason. There being no
weekly paper to furnish religious intelligence to the people, this
monthly served as a medium for the dissemination of religious news of
various kinds, as well as for the presentation of literary matter.
Said the first editors in the "Introductory Address" opening the thin
forty-page pamphlet then issued:

"In forming the general heads under which the various materials
are arranged, we have found it necessary to be as concise as possible
both in number and expression. The number and order are as follows:
1. Divinity. 2. Scripture Illustrated. 4. The
Attributes of God Displayed in the Works of Creation and Providence.
5. The Grace of God Manifested. 6. Miscellaneous. 7. Religious
and Missionary Intelligence. 8. Obituary. 9. Poetry."

These gentlemen, by a liberal use of selections, together with
a few original contributions, consisting in great measure of
obituaries, maintained the journal for four years, when, in 1820, the
election of Mr. Soule to the episcopacy - although he would not consent to be ordained until 1824 - caused a vacancy in the office of
senior Book Agent.

Dr. Nathan Bangs was then appointed senior agent, together with
Thomas Mason who was re-elected assistant. During the ensuing eight
years Dr. Bangs carried upon his shoulders the "entire responsibility
of this establishment, both of editing and publishing the magazine
and books, and overseeing its pecuniary and mercantile department."
In 1828, Dr. Bangs having been transferred to the editorial chair of
"The Christian Advocate and Journal," which he had established as a
weekly paper in 1826, and which in many of its functions had superseded the monthly magazine, the latter was discontinued. The work
that it had done, however, had made its impress upon the Church, and
it was not permitted to die. There was still a vacancy in our
denominational literature, a fact which made a strong impression upon
the mind of Dr. Bangs, to whose earnest intercession was due the

resumption of the magazine, in a somewhat different form, and covering the field of higher religious and moral thought. In the latter part of 1829 appeared the first number of the "Methodist Magazine and Quarterly Review," dated January, 1830, and under the nominal editorship of the Book Agents, John Emory and Beverly Waugh, both of whom were afterward elevated to the episcopacy, although it was generally understood that a large part of the editorial work continued to be done by Dr. Bangs. At the General Conference of 1832 the office of editor of the "Methodist Magazine and Quarterly Review" and general books was established, and Dr. Bangs was removed from the editorship of "The Christian Advocate" to become its first incumbent. This division was of great benefit to the magazine, since it enabled the editor to devote himself exclusively to advancing the character of the literary work presented under his supervision. Hitherto the contents had consisted largely of sermons, or extracts from sermons, and articles reprinted from other publications, together with editorial work, generally of the crudest description. Dr. Bangs, in his "History of the Methodist Episcopal Church," speaks most feelingly of the embarrassment and mortification to which he was subject in his editorial labors, at first both from lack of time and funds, and later from his inability to offer any remuneration to contributors. It is but just to say, however, that notwithstanding this latter defect, the character of the magazine arose greatly upon his installment as its editor, and maintained a position of progressive excellence until his transfer to the secretaryship of the Missionary Society in 1836.

Probably no one man, during the life of the Church in America, has made a deeper or more lasting impression upon her history than Nathan Bangs. A young school-teacher in Canada, converted under the ministry of Joseph Sawyer in 1800, he entered upon a career unparalleled in the amount of work accomplished and the success attending his labors. While not the founder, to his sagacious foresight and business tact must be attributed the wonderful strength of the vast publishing interests of the Church; one of the founders of the Missionary Society and its first secretary, a position which he held for twenty consecutive years, four fifths of the time without salary; the first general editor of the Church, his hand laid the broad foundation upon which is being erected a denominational literature unsurpassed in amount and influence; the father and first editor of "The Christian Advocate;" for eight years editor of the "Methodist Magazine;" the originator of the "Quarterly Review," as a medium for bringing before the Church literature of a higher grade and more permanent character than could be presented in the lighter and more ephemeral weeklies; but few of the successful institutions of the Church were not conceived by his fertile brain or molded by his skillful hand.

The General Conference of 1836 abolished the distinct office of editor of the "Quarterly Review," and elected Dr. Samuel Luckey

general editor, with John A. Collins as his assistant. At this time
the plan of remunerating contributors was adopted. which resulted in
still further elevating the literary merit of the periodical. Dr.
Luckey, although a self-educated man, was for four years principal
of the Genesee Wesleyan Seminary, at Lima, N.Y.; for the same period
general editor at the Book Concern; and for many years a regent of
the University of the State of New York. Under his administration
the periodical pursued the even tenor of its way until 1841, when by
order of the General Conference of 1840, it was detached from its
editorial connection with other periodical literature, greatly enlarged, its title abbreviated to "Methodist Quarterly Review," and
assigned to the editorial direction of Dr. George Peck.

The inauguration of Dr. Peck marked a new era in the history
of the magazine, the more liberal policy adopted by the Church
enabling the editor to devote his time and ability chiefly to its
advancement, and to call to his aid an able corps of paid contributors.
The result was that the literary excellence of the journal increased
with marked rapidity, while, owing to the greater liberality in publication, the mechanical execution and elegance of appearance formed
a decided contrast with preceding volumes. Through a mistaken policy,
however, the names of the authors of contributions, appearing in its
pages, were carefully screened from the profane eyes of the public.
Dr. Peck continued in the editorial chair for eight years, when he
was transferred to the editorship of "The Christian Advocate and
Journal."

By appointment of the General Conference in May, 1848, Dr. John
M'Clintock came from the Chair of Ancient Languages in Dickinson
College to occupy the editorial tripod vacated by Dr. Peck. He was
a man of brilliant and scholarly attainments, and "brought the Review
to the front rank of such publications, giving it a high reputation,
abroad as well as at home, for depth and range of scholarship,
catholicity of temper, and soundness of orthodox theology, coupled
with philosophic and Christian fairness to adversaries." He
introduced the departments of Religious and Literary Intelligence,
and extended that of Critical Notices. Contributions upon topics in
moral and intellectual science were a noticeable feature of the
magazine under his care. Dr. M'Clintock continued as editor during
the eight years immediately following his election.

In 1856, however, Dr. D. D. Whedon was elected to the editorship
of the Quarterly, a position which he has ably filled during the
quarter of a century intervening between that time and the present.
The very satisfactory manner in which he has performed the duties of
his office has given him a hold upon the thought of the Church. Dr.
Whedon's mind is of a metaphysical type, although the practical
element is so fully developed that the periodical has never, under
his charge, leaned toward a theoretical extreme. While he has drawn
to his aid many of the ablest writers of the day, it is his own

contributions to which the regular reader first opens. The Synopsis of the Quarterlies, introduced by him, has grown to be a very important feature, while the Quarterly Book-Table, an outgrowth of the former department of Book Notices, is invaluable. In fact, the wise discrimination and shrewd judgment manifested in the reviews of contemporary literature has constituted the pages occupied by it the most valuable portion of the Review. Under his judicious supervision, the "Quarterly Review" has attained a high degree of prosperity - easily leading the periodical literature of the Church.

Sixty-four years have now passed with their freightage of responsibility since this enterprise was committed to the Church. During this period great changes have appeared, but invariably in the steady line of improvement. It has increased in favor until it has come to be regarded as an indispensable requisite of a minister's library. It has taken rank in the first class of religious Quarterlies. Although Drs. Soule, Bangs, Peck, and M'Clintock have gone to their reward, the noble work which they did in elevating the literature of the Church continues to bear fruit long years after their entrances upon immortality. To the prophetic wisdom of its founders, a fulfillment; to its brilliant succession of conductors, a credit; and to the Church which it so ably represents, an honor - it promises to continue its beneficial career while spiritual life shall animate the denomination which it represents, and a love for learning exist in the minds of her servants.

¶   Early Publishing in the Evangelical Association.

(Taken from John Dreisbach's "Day Book," in John H. Ness, Jr., *One Hundred Fifty Years* (1966), 25-30).

⌈20 Nov. 1815⌉. I began my journey to Philadelphia, Pennsylvania, for the purpose of buying a printing press for the *Gemeinschaft* (Fellowship), and reached Peter Wagner's, near Germantown, four miles from Philadelphia.

Thursday, November 30 - I arrived at Philadelphia, and bought a press, which came to_____. I want to put it all together, including the attachments.

Friday, December 1 - I bought the necessary type. And the total sum was $366.00. I can say that the Lord was with me in these days, in doing business, and had much joy.

Saturday, December 2 - I packed all the material in a box, which I had made to order, costing me $3.64, also 14¢ for steel strappings. Thus making a grand total of $369.78 for the press. (On Sunday he preached in the city.)

Monday, December 4 - After having my breakfast I left Philadelphia, Pennsylvania. The four days with the nights' lodgings, cost me $5.30. God be praised for the grace which I do enjoy. I was in Germantown overnight.

Tuesday, December 5 - I came as far as Goschalopa, at Leonard Miller's, and remained for the night. It was very cold, and I had to face the wind in riding the 30 miles today. My travel expenses to Philadelphia cost me $3.12. I am not feeling very well. (For the next several days he preached in the Reading area.)

Monday, December 11 - I rode to Reading, Pennsylvania, where I had business, relative to the publishing and binding work.   .   .   .

[3 Jan. 1816]. I arrived in Harrisburg, and purchased from the book-printer, Christian Gleim, the Guilder mechanism needed by our denomination for bookbinding, which cost me $21.50. . . (the following six days were spent in filling preaching assignments between Harrisburg and Reading.)

Wednesday, January 10 - In Myerstown (near Lebanon) I bought me a sleigh to ease my travels. . . .

Thursday, January 11 - I began the journey to Philadelphia in order to buy a bookbinding machine. . . .

Friday, January 12 - I arrived at Daniel Bertolet's, in Oley, where I remained for Sunday.

Monday, January 15 - I bade adieu and left for Philadelphia, and intended, with God's assistance, to reach the city. For several days now I have felt discouraged and downcast. . . It was very cold this morning, and in Philadelphia it was said that in fifteen years, the thermometer had not indicated such sharp cold weather. In the evening I reached the city, but during the day was severely tempted, and yet, thank God, also blest . . . .

Tuesday, January 16 - I was busily engaged in purchasing and paying. I paid another, some $30.00, to Ronaldson for printers' type and for two cartons of printers' ink I paid $14.00, which included some other items necessary and belonging to a book bindery. And I grew pale at such an amount, especially that I had to borrow $3.00 for traveling expenses in going home. I loaned them from Samuel Schwertly, on Second Street, at New Marck North, who is a hotel keeper. During the night it rained, and it thawed, even though 18 inches of snow had fallen during the day, and lay on the ground, which, by morning, had about melted away.

Wednesday, January 17 - I hurried away and left Philadelphia at 11 o'clock, after having loaded on my sleigh two boxes of

290

printers' type, weighing approximately 250 lbs., and 2 cartons of
ink, weighing about 30 lbs. and a large baba cover shears (pasteboard
scissors) hoping it would remain in place, and go along safely. But
after 4 miles, arriving at Norristown, I was obliged to unload it and
leave it at Peter Wagner's, instructing him to send it to Reading by
the stage coach. So, now I endeavored to continue on my way, and by
night came near Perkoming.

Thursday, January 18 - In my haste, I arrived as far as Reading
with my sleigh, much of the time slipping on stony ground instead of
snow, which so quickly had melted away. Here a man asked to buy my
sled and harness, offering me his watch and a five dollar note. So
I sold it to him, for I had my saddle and bridle here, leaving it
here when and where I bought the sled. . . .

Saturday, February 3 - We traveled to H. Walter's for a watch-
night meeting and had a helpful service . . . About midnight
we lifted an offering to build a shop for the printing press and
bookbinding machine.

Sunday, February 4 - . . . I arrived at New Berlin, was at
Mr. Wagner's overnight. . . .

Monday, February 5 - I, and brother Niebel, bargained with a man
to build the shop for the printing press and bookbinding machinery,
including all frames and carpenter work, for the sum of $96.00. We
also called on brother Miller, who is sick, and both of us prayed
with, and for him, and the blessing came to him. I asked him if he
had anything he would like to say to us. "Yes," he said, "I have.
I desired to give something to the printing press, but it would
disturb the peace in my home." He said, "I know it is God's work
among us." I comforted him by saying it was all right, and all is
coming along all right in getting the press going . . . Niebel
was present and said, "If any of mine would say of this as not being
right, yet I know it is of God, for His coming Kingdom. . .

Monday, February 12 - I traveled to Longstown (New Berlin),
where I stored my printing press.

Friday, May 3 - I rode to Henry Aurand's near Beavers' Dam and
held a brief meeting preaching to a few people in addition to the
family. I went on my way to Keller's paper mill where I ordered 20
reams of paper of No. 2 quality and continued on to J. Felmry's two
miles from Schweinfort's town.

*   *   *

Monday, June 17 - I arrived at home. Henry Niebel came and we
worked together during this whole week to provide a Discipline and
prepare to have it published. God gave us great grace and blest us
as we performed this service. [No further notes appeared in the

Journal until Saturday, June 22, when they laid aside their work and
held services in the immediate area over the weekend.]

Monday, June 24 - This entire week brother H. Niebel and I are
writing again in preparation of the Discipline and a large song book
to be published for the church - The Geistliche Saitenspiel was
completed on June 29, 1816.

¶   *Religious Telescope* of United Brethren.

(Taken from Vol. I, No. 1, 31 Dec. 1834, p. 2).

We have thought it expedient to send the first No. of the
"RELIGIOUS TELESCOPE," to such of our friends and fellow-citizens,
as we supposed would be likely to patronize a publication of the
kind, without an intention of detracting the intrinsic merits of any
other like publication. But mere thought, or opinion, does not
necessarily constitute a fact! And believing that a mere difference
in opinion, should never create a difference in affection. We shall
therefore consider it no small favor conferred on us by those who
may patronize the establishment; and all such as are otherwise disposed, will please to read, and return the paper to this office, and
no offence will be taken. And their memorialist, as in duty bound,
will pray, &c. &c.

Every person of sober reflection must be persuaded, that information, properly conducted, must be of immense importance to the rising generation of our country; as intelligence and piety, under God,
must be the *palladium* of our civil liberties, and the hope of the
christian church. The lover of his country cannot but tremble for
its rights, its civil and religious privileges, when he witnesses
the thousands of foreigners who are continually pouring into our
country through all her open gates. -- But what will another generation present, when these swelled by natural increase, and augmented
by constant emigration from the old continents, shall amount to
milliens? And feel more than aide by the blessings of heaven, to
wield the destinies of our great world; how important then, that
they should be an intelligent and a virtuous people. Settlements
of strangers are rapidly multiplying through all the west, and the
next generation will doubtless witness millions covering their rich
and fertile plains, and surrounding their mighty rivers and grand
prairies. And shall they not be cared for?

We know that the christian philanthropist stretches his views
to distant climes, and takes thought for the children of heathen
far away. But shall we overlook the swelling thousands of children
in our own kindred states, and leave them destitute of wholesom[sic]

knowledge, and that only which can benefit their couls?[sic]
Every proper consideration and sanctified motive would forbid it.

We are all agreed in the belief that the religion of the Bible
is destined to pervade the earth, and that the time shall come when
every tribe of the human family shall bow at the sacred name of Him
whom we worship as Lord and Saviour. To believe less than this,
seems scarcely compatible with a profession of faith in the truth of
the Scriptures; for however dark the language of prophecy may be in
relation to the times and the causes of the event, the ultimate fact
is declared in terms too absolute to admit of any interpretation but
one.

But uniformity of opinion ends with the belief of this glorious
fact; for as there is room for many suppositions in regard to the
manner in which the convertion[sic] of the heathen world shall be
effected, we suggest that all the newspapers devoted to religion,
and conducted by the spirit of religious enterprise (as well as
the preaching of the Gospel,) will aid in the accomplishment of this
mighty work. For they are calculated to awaken the tyrant from his
dreams of power, and rouse the slumbering genius of an oppressive
people? And like a fore-runner of the sacred Bible, penetrate into
pathless deserts, and have the thrones and diadems of nations--and
speak in thunder on the summit of infidelity! It was with this
instrument, guided by the light of reason and revelation, that
Luther made the Papel power, which had subjugated all Europe to its
domain, tremble to its centre; and gave priestly domination a defeat
from which it can never fully recover.

What person, whose heart grows with zeal for the diffusion of
religious knowledge, should take up his post on the side of opposition,
and adopt a style of animadversion which might render him liable even
to an unfounded accusation of hostile feelings towards one of the
most noble enterprises that the world has ever witnessed.

With how perilous a presumption are we then chargable: if, in
contempt of the well-knonw[sic]principle of labor, we cast this
mighty enterprise upon the billows of confusion, and leave it to the
winds and waves of accident, to supply the place of the wisdom we
will not exercise? Or set all such methods at defiance, and, content
ourselves with the conscientiousness[sic]of the purest intention, and
of the utmost possible dilligence, should cast our efforts upon the
winds, hoping that heaven, in its wisdom, will direct them for good.

We are called upon by a voice from the higher throne to take
the field in the fair conflict of truth, and seeing the evil sword
coming upon the land, to make the alarm and give such evil the
shortest possible date in our power, and thereby provide for the
people of our respective charges, a way of escape from all such
considerations.

How common is it, when some sudden demand is made to administer relief to physical wretchedness, that all rush forward in benevolent wrecklessness, trampling down party distinctions, though rigid as the wintry stream; but when called upon to direct a portion of their aims towards the propagation of truth and religious fruitfulness they either feel no responsibility, or, plead their poverty, and that in view of hundreds and thousands. Religion, it is said, in the days of the apostles, made men generous to the highest pitch, of selling all they had, and pouring the price at the apostle's feet; but men have changed, and not without a cause. To say the best: --the soul of the miser and bigot belongs to the class of the reptiles; and this assertion holds good of the entire genius; for whether the creature be as venomous as the adder, or harmless as the mole, still he can do nothing better than crawl.

I desire nothing, my dear friends, but that those whose hearts are open to considerations of this kind should, with the seriousness which becomes the subject, hear the voice that speake in all that is happening around them, and read, in the language of passing events, the special message sent from the Head of the Church to the citizens of America? And such, who have no feeling for the happiness of man-kind; -- and if feeling, -- have no willingness to aid the torrent of liberality towards this scene of hopeful enterprise--I ask them but once to look abroad into the world, and then turn to the styes of their selfish indulgence and if they cannot be ashamed, I hope at least, they will have the grace to be silent.

The "RELIGIOUS TELESCOPE" shall continue to be devoted to the interests of religion, literature and morality, and every other useful information associated with christianity. The editor will endeavor to apply himself faithfully to this work and exercise the utmost prudence in the management thereof; and trusts that while its financial matters are satisfactorily carried on, the friends and the public will sustain it. It is not the object of the editor to spread language and brilliant literature, and with a high and commanding spirit, conspire to fix upon him the gaze of mankind, but faithfully to rebuke evil and exhibit truth, without seeking to displease, or_____to offend.

¶   Founding and Religious Orientation of
                      Wesleyan University.

(Taken from *Methodist History*, XI (Oct. 1972), 31-32, 40-41).

                                        Wilbraham Sep 12, 1829

Dear Brother, ⌐Clark⌐

I have no other objection to the meeting of the committee in

294

New York than that there seems to be a propriety of our meeting
where we can have personal communication with the Middletown
gentlemen. I am satisfied on reflection that some of the conditions
in their proposition should be altered. I have feared from the beginning that the prescribed sum could not be raised. I have no objection that the trial should be made but I have a strong objection
to set up a school next fall and proceed to raise a confidence in the
publick that we shall have a College and put ourselves to the trouble
and cost of getting it up and of soliciting funds and then in case of
failure in the subscription be liable to be driven from the premises.
And how can we consult on this subject so well as by a personal
interview? Whether the other members of the committee will object
to going to New York I cannot say. As it will probably be too late
for steam boat navigation I should think it would add much to their
journey and expense. Besides some of the committee have never seen
the premises, and this would be desirable in order to their coming
to a decision. B Merritt proposed having the meeting at Middletown.
However, after making this statement and giving these reasons if you
still think it best to have the meeting at New York let me know & I
will notify the other members of our committee. That there should
be a general meeting of the committee somewhere & at some time I am
fully convinced of. The time proposed suits me the best of any as it
is in our vacation. It is the opinion of most of our brethren with
whom I have conversed on this subject, that considering the great
& repeated exertions we have made in our Conference in behalf of the
Academy very little could at present be raised in our Conference for
a College at Middletown. Some of our trustees however seemed willing
to unite in the object provided some permanent arrangement could be
fixed upon by which this seminary could have its existence and
immunities secured to it. But none of us seem willing to put our
hands to an institution which shall in process of time swallow up our
Academy as the "Advocate" swallowed up our "Herald." All this
however can be discussed at the meeting. Be pleased to write again
soon. Yours in Christian Bonds. W. Fisk

*   *   *

New Haven 22d July 1853

Dear Brother

I address this note to you as president of the Board of Trustees
of the Wes. University - At the last meeting of the Board, I handed
in my resignation as Trustee & supposed it was acted upon and accepted, but I received a notice from Prof. Lane, to meet the Board on
Tuesday, Aug. 2d I infer, therefore, that the Board took no action
on my resignation. My desire is that you would lay this before the
Board & that they would now act & accept my resignation, for, after
haveing done all that I have done for the wellbeing of that
Institution & be treated as I have been & have my feelings lacerated

& insulted as they have been - I cannot consent to act any longer as
a member of the Board. One of your Board (a layman of great influence in the Board,) told me that the clergimen were the great hinderance to the prosperity of the Institution & they wished to be rid of
them & they could do better without them & the Joint Board, by
electing a layman, as President, fully indorsed this sentiment - Now
I most sincerely love a religious education & as it is supposed that
I am in the way - I make all speed to take myself out of the way - I
also fear that the object of certain men, in the Board, is to drive
a religious predominance from the University - I can have no fellowship with the movement. If we cannot have a religious education
I desire no education at all. An infidel education I consider as
worse than no education. I may be mistaken, as to the intention of
men and really should be thankful that the future may prove my
fears unfounded - but time will reveal all things.

For you, personally, I have the strongest affection & should
wish, were it consistant with my views of duty, as I have heretofore
done, stand by you, side by side & fight for right & truth - but in
this particular I must break from you & wish you all joy and comfort -
and hope that the University may hereafter persue such a course as
to secure the confidence of our people and its own prosperity &
usfulness.

But aside from all the above considerations such are my prior
engagement that I could not, if I would, be at Middletown on the
2d of Aug. at 8 O'clock A.M. - for I have meeting in New-York on
Monday evening Aug. the 1st

> Our kind regards to sister Clark
> Yours in Bonds of undying love Heman Bangs

¶   A College for Midwestern Methodists.

(Taken from Minutes of the Indiana Conference, 1832, printed
in W. W. Sweet, *Circuit-Rider Days in Indiana* (1916), 101-03).

Next to the religion of the Son of God your committee consider
the light of science calculated to lessen the sum of human woe and
to increase the sum of human happiness. Therefore we are of the
opinion that the means of education ought to be placed within the
reach of every community in general, so that all may have an
opportunity of obtaining an ordinary and necessary education. From
observation and information, your committee are well convinced that
where superior schools and colleges are neglected ordinary schools are
almost universally in a languished state. And many persons are reared, and live and die without any education. We therefore think that
Seminaries and Colleges under good literary and moral regulations
are of incalculable benefit to our country, and that a good Conference

Seminary would be of great and growing utility to our people. We are aware that when a Conference Seminary is named, some of our preachers and many of our people suppose we are about to establish a manufactory in which preachers are to be made. But nothing is farther from our views, for we are fully of Mr. Bernge's opinion who, when comparing ministers to pens, observes, "that although the Seminaries have been trying to make pens for some hundreds of years, they will not write well till God nibs them."

When we examine the state of the literary institutions of our country, we find a majority of them are in the hands of other denominations (whether rightfully or otherwise, we do not take it upon ourselves to determine) whose doctrine in many respects we consider incompatible with the doctrines of revelation, so that our people are unwilling (and we think properly so) to send their sons to those institutions. Therefore we think it very desirable to have an institution under our own control from which we can exclude all doctrines which we deem dangerous; though at the same time we do not wish to make it so sectarian as to exclude or in the smallest degree repel the sons of our fellow citizens from the same.

To accomplish the foregoing desirable objects we most earnestly recommend to the Conference the use of the means that will lead to the end. We would advise that the Presiding Elders of the several districts be required to collect all the information in their power in reference to an eligible site, and the means to build, and present the same to the next Conference. All of which is respectfully submitted.

C. W. RUTER, A. WILEY, JAMES ARMSTRONG.

¶   Training of Ministers.

(Taken from Alfred Brunson, *The Gospel Ministry* (1856), 28-35).

It may be said that in our Biblical Institutes, the student is required to preach, meet class, visit the sick, &c. But preaching before the professors and students is not like preaching to souls to be rescued from hell. The congregation in the institute is small, they are all professors of religion, and all sit as critics on the matter and manner of the performance. This may produce nice, well-arranged discourses; the periods may be well turned, the gesticulation may be as precise as the plates in the old "art of speaking," but there will be "no Holy Ghost in it." The sinner may sleep comfortably under such preaching; the applause of the audience may be gained, which is too often the highest aim, and gaining that, the preacher "has his reward," not in heaven, but on earth.

297

The definition we have given of the acquirements necessary for a useful minister, must save us from the imputation of being opposed to learning in a minister. The whole history of Methodism throws back this charge, by proving the ignorance of those who make it. The course of study required by Wesley and his followers, together with the results of their labors, proves them to be able and among the ablest ministers of Jesus Christ in the present age of the world. If a tree is to be known by its fruits, then this point is established beyond a cavil or a reasonable doubt.

If men have before their conversion, or if they obtain after it, and before they are called of God to the work of the ministry, a liberal or other good education, we are glad of it. The learned Saul of Tarsus had this. But he, like every other truly converted and called man will do, "counted it all loss for the excellence of the knowledge of Christ."

That we, as a Church, are not, and never were, opposed to learning, is amply proven from the facts that our founder, under God, was a man of the most profound science; he put his lay-preachers upon the most extensive course of study; the Church has been, and is now behind none of her age, in getting up and establishing institutions of learning, and at this day has more schools of the higher order than any other Church in the nation. What, then, is the necessity of "the hue and cry" we hear all over the country of the great "want of a more learned ministry?"

We have admitted the necessity of acquirements in the ministry, but we deny the necessity of three or four years' neglect of the necessary and more appropriate labors of men, when called of God to the work, for the sake of tinseling them over with the polish of a school; injuring their health, diminishing their usefulness in the conversion of sinners, marring the itinerancy, the great balance wheel of the moral machinery now revolutionizing the world, and pampering the vanity of the proud and aristocratic of the day. We favor deep, thorough knowledge in theology, but we contend that this can be, as it has been, attained in the ministry by pursuing appropriate studies, while otherwise laboring for the salvation of our fellow-men.

We admit that men can, with teachers, progress in study faster than without, or to be entirely self-taught. But we deny that our young men in the ministry have no teachers. Our Lord instructed his apostles; they instructed those who followed them. Wesley instructed his helpers, and they, in turn, instructed those who followed them. In Theological or Biblical Institutes, lectures and model sermons are delivered; but they are, as in the nature of things they must be, cold, stiff, studied, and for the critic's ear, but without zeal, mental fire, or the power of the Holy Ghost. We all know the difference between preaching to a small congregation, most or all of

298

whom are professors, and a large one, the most of whom are in their sins, and are in danger of perishing in them. It is impossible, in the nature of things, for a preacher in the former case to feel the same degree of interest and anxiety, or to have his soul drawn out, or thrown into his discourse, as it would be in the latter case. The model sermons, then, in these modern cloisters, are but cold, still, and lifeless. They may be logical, but they must be dull; they may be critical and grammatical, but frigid, such as never did and never will, unless human nature is changed, awaken and convert the sinner.

But those who are educated in the ministry have examples of preaching also, but of a very different character, and of an infinitely better quality. In the nature of the itinerant economy, the preachers, traveling and local, are frequently brought together at camp, quarterly, and protracted meetings, when usually the ablest, most aged and experienced among them preach and exhort, not merely for the critic's ear, but to please God and save the people. These model sermons are delivered with a spirit, manner, and a power calculated to make deep and lasting impressions, not only upon the congregations, but especially so upon the young preacher, as a model for him to follow. The impressions thus made on a young mind, seeking to glorify God in the salvation of his fellow-men, will be deeper, more lasting, and of vastly more importance in the formation of his character as a minister of Christ, than thousands of dull, critical, and fine-spun theoretical discourses. And, what is of great additional importance, the doctrines taught by such masters in our Israel, and under such impressive circumstances, take deeper hold upon the affections, because they are usually accompanied by the Divine presence, than cold discourses delivered in the lecture-room of a seminary possibly can do. To this may be attributed, in a great degree, the uniformity of views in doctrine and discipline in our Church, in which, notwithstanding a few differences of opinion among us, we excel other Churches, who boast over us of their superior advantages.

We have admitted the advantages of tuition. But still, the self-taught are admitted to be the greatest and the best scholars, and the most useful men. The best instructors in our schools and colleges have learned that to make good scholars, the student must not depend entirely upon his instructor, but must resort to his own genius and the resources of his own mind. He must have books, or a text to start upon, but then, he must go beyond the duty of the stupid beast who knows just what has been beat into him by repeated bidding; he must think for himself, and penetrate the labyrinths of knowledge, until he finds his way to the light of truth through them. Education *in* the ministry, where we study and preach, preach and study, carrying theory and practice together, with occasional model discourses from older and more experienced men, is calculated to make vastly better ministers than education *for* the ministry, where they cannot have the

same advantages.

The best and safest pattern for the ministry is that set us by the great Head of the Church himself. We assume that he knew better than man does, what kind of preachers he wanted to fill this high commission in saving a lost world. If he had preferred the learned in the modern sense of the word, he would have called such in the first place. He could have converted and called a learned Saul as easily as an unlearned Peter, and if being so deeply learned before-hand was essential to the ministry, then St. Paul mistook his calling, and has published falsehoods to the world under the garb of inspiration. For he says to the Corinthians, "that not many wise men after the flesh, not many mighty, not many noble are called; but God has chosen the foolish things of the world to confound the wise; (and it has done so,) and God hath chosen the weak things of the world to confound the things that are mighty; and base things of the world, and things which are despised, hath God chosen; yea, and things which are not, to bring to naught the things that are." And the great and good reason given for this extraordinary course of the all-wise Jehovah is, "that no flesh should glory in his presence."

12. EARLY THEOLOGICAL EXPRESSION

As Methodism sought a place among the already existing religious groups in the British colonies, it found itself theologically beset on at least two fronts: rationalism and its theological forms of Deism and Unitarianism, and the various expressions of Calvinism among Congregationalists in New England and more widely among Presbyterians and Baptists. The rationalistic threat was the subject of a friendly letter of warning from Nathan Bangs to Laban Clark in 1808.

By far the hottest controversy involved Methodists with the divines of New England, who were busy among themselves restating and revising original Calvinism. One of the few Methodist ministers who really understood the finer points of the theology of John Calvin and its successive redactions in the New England theology was Wilbur Fisk, who held the responsible position of president of new Wesleyan University in Connecticut. His writings had considerable influence not only on Methodist doctrinal preaching, but also on Protestant theology generally.

At the popular level abstruse doctrinal disputes were settled in a more direct fashion, as described in circuit rider John Smith's journal.

Shortly before the M.E. Church was broken apart by the national conflict over slavery, Nathan Bangs brought the first volume of his history of the church to conclusion with an essay on the reasons for the success of Methodism, which came late but rapidly outstripped competition. He has a nice mix, typically Methodistic, of theology and pragmatism.

¶ The Threat of Rationalism.

(Taken from *Methodist History*, III[4] (July 1965), 4-8, letter Nathan Bangs to Laban Clark, 18 Jan. 1808).

Montreal, Jany,18th,1808

My dear brother,

By this I acknowledge the receipt of yours dated Dec. 26th 1807, which contains an account of your health and prosperity in the divine life. I hope to profit by some of the observations which you have sent, as well as to take the exhortation to go on courageously; but I am sorry that I cannot assede[*sic*] to all you say concerning reason. 1st you say, "When reason dictates our will we are virtuous, consistant, uniform, wise." If this were so, what need is there of revelation? Moreover, if that were true, why was not the old heathens virtuous and consistant? How came Socrates to believe and to teach that one supreme inteligence ruled the universe, and at the same time worship the titular Deities in compliance with the prevailing custom of his countrymen? You see that reason taught him to believe in one supreme God, but it did not make him consistant. What he principally lacked, I conclude, was revelation, which would have led him to that Grace which would have influenced his will to have acted consistant. I acknowledge that, as reason teaches us the existance of a God, so it also teaches us that we ought to obey him. If so, the same principal[*sic*-principle] (call it reason if you please) teaches that he ought to give us a knowledge of those laws which we ought to obey. This he has abundantly done in his revealed will. Thus reason, step by step, dictates to us the necessity of revelation; and therefore it says, that when we have it, we ought implicitly to obey it. Now if our will is influenced by this revelation, we shall be, (I do not say virtuous but) religious, consistant, uniform, wise.

2nd You say, "Even that reason which is the eternal fitness of things, and infinitely above the comprehension of mortals." I frankly acknowledge this sentence to be infinitely above my comprehension, for I can see no sense in it. That reason should be the eternal fitness of things is such a paradox, as I am utterly incapable of solving. I can indeed easily perceive that the religion of Jesus Christ is consistant with the nature and fitness of things. To instance, in the nature of God, and the nature of man. But here scripture, not reason, must be our guide, and reason become its handmaid. In scripture God is represented as being holy. Man is therein represented as being unholy. The Christian religion is, by the same, represented as consisting in a union of the soul with God, through faith in the Lord Jesus Christ. If this be so, reason says, God or man must alter, their natures being heterogenious one to the other. Scripture and reason conjointly saith that God is immutable. Of consequence man must be changed. Here is shewn the reasonable-

ness of being born again. But will "reason abiding our will" effect this change of heart? If so, we need no more thank God for the gift of his word and spirit. By the fitness of things I understand that admirable order and harmony which is visible in the natural and the moral world; so that every part thereof is fitted to the place which it occupies, and of course, it ought, in reason, to act conformable to the design of its author. For instance, it is fit and right that there should be civil and ecclesiastical governors; and if so, it is but fit and right that others should submit to be ruled. It is but reasonable then for subjects to obey their lawful Governors – And as God is the great head and governor of the universe, it is but reasonable that all should obey him. Again, every part of the human body is so contrived by infinite Wisdom as to fit its own place, (one part does not interfere with another) and to perform its proper function. In all God's works we behold order, beauty and harmony. But to speak of the eternal fitness of things, which only exist in time, appears to me, not to be consonant to reason. And to say that reason is the fitness of thinks $\lceil sic \rceil$ appears to me absurd. That reason aided by the unering word and spirit of God will lead a man to act consistant with the nature and fitness of things, is, I believe, an incontrovertible truth. And the religion of Jesus Christ becomes reasonable, because it does not contradict, but coincides with that establishment.

3rd "You ask me, Was not Moses dictated by reason, when he choose to suffer affliction with the people of God, having respect unto the recompense of reward?" I answer in the negative. That it was reasonable he should do so, I readily acknowledge. But what made it reasonable? Because God commanded him to go in his Name, to show his wonders unto Pharaoh, and tell him from God to let his people go. Now I ask, did reason or revelation dictate and influence his will? Undoubtedly it was most reasonable, fit and right that Moses should obey because God, who was his rightful Sovereign, had, by his spirit, communicated his will unto him, and thereby made it his indispensable duty so to do. He had respect unto the recompense of reward. I suppose you to understand by this, a reward beyond the grave; and then I would with all submission to your superior judgement, and more extensive information, ask, in what age, or in what nation, reason has made known a future state of rewards and of punishments? Perhaps you will say that many of the ancient heathens believed and taught it. It is true that some of them had some crude, uncertain notions about it. But none of them ever arrived to any certainty. And suppose they had – I think it more reasonable to ascribe it to the light of God's spirit than to reason. We know not how far God might have manifested himself unto them, as he did to Job, Melchisedec, etc.

Yet it remained for Jesus Christ to bring life and immortality (more fully) to light by the Gospel. And this point being firmly and undeniably established by the word and actions of him who could neither lie nor err, I agree with you in saying that it is better

to labour for the meat that perisheth not than for that which
perisheth. Uppon the whole, I cannot but observe the contrast between
your scheme of religion and that laid down in the new Testament. By
Grace are ye saved through faith saith St. Paul. You say, by
reason aiding the will we are made virtuous, consistant, uniform,
wise. I suppose, you mean by such a person, a christian. I do not
wish to speak contemptibly of reason. I think it to be an excellent
gift of God, and that by it we are enabled to perceive many truths,
but not to practise them. It is then, a matter of importance to
be able rightly to appreciate its worth, neither overrating it nor
under-valuing it. And it is verry danderous[sic] to exalt human
reason so as to abuse revelation. Has it not a tendency to engender
pride? For my part I wish not to be wise above what is written, lest
I become a fool. And the moment we depart from the written will of
God we get our minds bewildered in a labarinth of useless speculations,
which endanger our peace and salvation.

I have thus wrote down what occured to my mind in reading your
friendly letter; and I hope you will not be offended at the liberty
which I have taken. I wish ever to posess and to manifest a spirit of
love to all men, and more especially to my brethren in the Ministry,
whom I love and reverence as the servants of God. I hope therefore
that, if I have said anything amiss, you will do as I have done, try
to correct and forgive me. I could not have answered your letter,
without doing as I have; and I think I have done as I would be done
by. I love you, and esteem you as a brother in Christ, and as a
companion in the Kingdom and patience of Jesus. - Br. Madden is in
Quebec, but I expect him up in about a week to take my place here,
as I expect to leave this in about a week. God willing, I expect to
be at Conference, where I hope to have the pleasure of seeing you,
and of taking sweet council with you. My congregation in this place
is large and attentive, especially in the evenings. The society are
going on in love and union, and some others appear under serious
impressions. My self & my other self are well, and we feel determined
to make our way to heaven. God bless you, my brother, and believe
me to be your friend, bro. in Christ, N. Bangs.

¶   Frontier Theology.

(Taken from John Smith, "Journal," edited by L. Sherwood in
Journal of the Greenbrier Historical Society, I[4] (Oct.1968),
26-27).

Mon. 24 Sep,1787 Rode to Jame McClungs the people Assembled
together to hear preaching I took my text and while I was in my
introduction Mr. McCu Stood up & opposed me he said for preaching
false Doctrine the Words I made mention of were in the preceding
part of the Chapter whis was the 4 of Johns firs Epistle I read Over
again to the people and asked them if the Saw any false Doctrin in it

he cryed out it was popery and flew to the table and Snached up my
hymn book and inquired for the Hymn I Sung Which I readily Shew'd him
which he Said was Also rank popery. After blustering A while he
ordered me to resume my discourse I told him I was not obliege'd to
obey him And he said if I did not he would enter into A controversy
with me I told him to come on at which he threw his Stick on the
table and took his Bible out of his pocket and Said that the other
Day I deny'd the final perseverance of the Saints (or to that effect)
I said that I was Still of that Oppinon. Then Said he Explain to me
the 8 Chap. of the Romans. first Said I tell me whether the Scriptures
are conditional or Unconditional At which he flew in a rage and took
up his Stick and made a motion to Strice me. then threw it down
Again And began to read where the Apostle Said I am perswaided. & to
which I said the Apostel did not speak in the possitive And for A
proof to Strengthen me I read our Lords Words in the former part of
the 15 Chap of Johns Gospel. At which time he fell to Abuscing and
blackgarding of me And Said if his office did not prohibit and forbid
him to be A Striker that he would Lace me well I told him I believ'd
that was not all that hinder'd him. and it was as much as he could do
to keep his hands off of me I saw it was to no purpose to Argue with
A mad man And so let him run on. At Last I told the people they might
expect preaching there that day two weeks at which he forbid the man
to let me Preach there, at which he Said he Shou'd Stop no man from
preaching the Gospel in his House. So I kept the feild, and he went
off without Shedding blood Which I every moment look'd for. bless the
Lord O my soul, that I am counted worthy to Suffer for my Master.

¶   Wilbur Fisk on Calvinism.

(Taken from *The Calvinistic Controvery* (1837), 38-54, 92-101).

     But that our doctrine of election is of grace, will appear
evident, I think, from the following considerations. 1. It was pure,
unmerited love that moved God to provide salvation for our world.
2. The gospel plan, therefore, with all its provisions and conditions,
is of grace. Not a step in that whole system but rests in grace, is
presented by grace, and is executed through grace. 3. Even the power
of the will to choose life, and the conditions of life, is a
gracious power. A fallen man, without grace, could no more choose
to submit to God than a fallen angel. Herein we differ widely from
the Calvinists. They tell us man has a natural power to choose life.
Ifso, he has power to get to heaven without grace! We say, on the
contrary, that man is utterly unable to choose the way to heaven, or
to pursue it when chosen, without the grace of God. It is grace that
enlightens and convinces the sinner, and strengthens him to seek after
and obtain salvation, for "without Christ we can do nothing." Let the
candid judge between us, then, and decide which system most robs our
gracious Redeemer of his glory, that which gives man a native and
inherent power to get to heaven of himself, or that which attributes

all to grace. 4. Finally, when the sinner repents and believes, there is no merit in these acts to procure forgiveness and regeneration, and therefore, though he is now, and on these conditions, elected and made an heir of salvation, yet it is for Christ's sake, and "not for works of righteousness which he has done." Thus we "bring forth the top-stone with shouting, crying Grace, grace, unto it." Having gone over and examined the arguments in favour of unconditional election, we come to the last part of our subject; which was, to urge some objections against this doctrine.

1. The doctrine of the unconditional election of a part, necessarily implies the unconditional reprobation of the rest. I know some who hold to the former, seem to deny the latter; for they represent God as reprobating sinners in view of their sins. When all were sinners, they say God passed by some, and elected others. Hence, they say the decree of damnation against the reprobates is just, because it is against sinners. But this explanation is virtually giving up the system, inasmuch as it gives up all the principal arguments by which it is supported. In the first place, it makes predestination dependent on foreknowledge; for God first foresees that they will be sinners, and then predestinates them to punishment. Here is one case, then, in which the argument for Calvinian predestination is destroyed by its own supporters. But again: if God must fix by his decree all parts of his plan, in order to prevent disappointment, then he must fix the destiny of the reprobates and the means that lead to it. But if he did not do this, then the Calvinistic argument in favour of predestination, drawn from the divine plan, falls to the ground.   .   .   .

2. This doctrine of election, while it professes to vindicate free grace and the mercy of God, destroys them altogether. To the reprobates there is certainly no grace or mercy extended. Their very existence, connected as it necessarily is with eternal damnation, is an infinite curse. The temporal blessings which they enjoy, the insincere offers that are held out to them, and the gospel privileges with which they are mocked, if they can be termed grace at all, must be called damning grace. For all this is only fattening them for the slaughter, and fitting them to suffer, to a more aggravated extent, the unavoidable pains and torments that await them. Hence Calvin's sentiment, that "God calls to the reprobates, that they may be more deaf - kindles a light, that they may be more blind - brings his doctrine to them, that they may be more ignorant - and applies the remedy to them, that they may not be healed," is an honest avowal of the legitimate principles of this system. Surely, then, no one will pretend that, according to this doctrine, there is any grace for the reprobate. And perhaps a moment's attention will show that there is little or none for the elect. It is said that God, out of his mere sovereignty, without any thing in the creature to move him thereto, elects sinners to everlasting life. But if there is nothing in the creature to move him thereto, how can it be called mercy or compassion?

he did not determine to elect them because they were miserable, but because he pleased to elect them. If misery had been the exciting cause, then, as all were equally miserable, he would have elected them all. Is such a decree of election founded in love to the suffering object? No: it is the result of the most absolute and omnipotent selfishness conceivable. It is the exhibition of a character that sports most sovereignly and arbitrarily, with his almighty power, to create, to damn, and to save. . . .

3. The doctrine we oppose makes God partial and a respecter of persons; contrary to express and repeated declarations of Scripture. For it represents God as Determining to save some and damn others, without reference to their character, all being precisely in the same state. To deny this, is to acknowledge that the decree of election and reprobation had respect to character, which is to give up the doctrine. Some indeed pretend, that the decree of election was unconditional, but not the decree of reprobation. But this is impossible; for there could be no decree of election, only in view of the whole number from which the choice was to be made; and the very determination to select such a number, and those only, implied the exclusion of all the rest. If it be said, as the Sublapsarians contend, that the decree of election did not come in until all were fallen, or viewed in the mind of God as fallen; and therefore since all might have been justly damned, there was no injustice to those who were left, though some of the guilty were taken and saved; we reply that even this would not wholly remove the objection of partiality. But we need not dwell here, because we have a shorter and more decisive way to dispose of this argument. The truth is, it does not cover the whole ground of our objection. Had God nothing to do with man until his prescient eye beheld the whole race in a ruined state? How came man in this state? He was plunged there by the sin of his federal head. But how came he to sin? "Adam sinned," says Calvin, "because God so ordained." And so every one must say, that believes God foreordained whatsoever comes to pass. Taking all the links together, they stand thus: – God decreed to create intelligent beings – he decreed that they should all become sinners and children of wrath – and it was so. He then decreed that part of those whom he had constituted heirs of wrath, should be taken, and washed, and saved, and the others left to perish; and then we are told there is no unjust partiality in God, since they all deserve to be damned! . . .

4. This doctrine is objectionable, because, contrary to express and repeated passages of Scripture, it necessarily limits the atonement. It will surely not be expected that we should attempt to prove that Christ "tasted death for every man" – that he "gave himself a ransom for all" – that he "died for all" – that he became "a propitiation for the sins of the whole world" – because, these are so many express Scripture propositions, and rest directly on the authority of God. And while these stand, the doctrine of particular

and partial redemption must stand or fall together, has been acknowledged, and is still maintained by most Calvinists; and therefore
they have endeavoured to explain away those passages, which so clearly
declare that "Christ died for all." But in this work they have found
so many difficulties, that others, and among them most of the Calvinistic clergy in New England, have acknowledged a general redemption, and
have undertaken to reconcile with it the doctrine of particular election and reprobation. But this reconciliation is as difficult as the
other. . . .

6. We are suspicious of this doctrine, because its advocates
themselves seem studious to cover up and keep out of sight many of
its features, and are constantly changing their manner of stating and
defending their system. A little attention to the history of the
controversy between predestinarians and their opposers will show the
truth and force of this objection. The charge that Calvinism covers
up and keeps out of sight some of its most offensive features, does not
lie so much against its advocates of the old school; as those of the
modern. With the exception of some logical consequences, which we
think chargeable upon the system, and which they were unwilling to
allow, these early defenders of unconditional election came out boldly
and fearlessly with their doctrine. If modern Calvinists would do
the same, we should need no other refutation of the system. But even
the early supporters of Calvinism, when pressed by their opponents,
resorted to various forms of explanation and modes of proof, and also
to various modifications of the system itself. . . .

How would honest John Calvin, if he could be introduced among
us, with the same sentiments he had when on earth, frown upon the
churches that bear his name! He would not only call them "silly
and childish," but he would, doubtless, in his bold, blunt manner,
charge them with disingenuousness and cowardice, if not with downright duplicity, for thus shunning and smoothing over and covering up
the more repulsive features of their system. How would he chide them
for shifting their ground, and changing their system, while they
nevertheless pretend to build on the same foundation of predestination!
He would, we believe, sternly inquire of them what they meant by
saying, all sinners, not excepting reprobates, may come to Christ
and be saved? - why they pretended to hold to election, and not to
reprobation? - how they could reconcile general redemption with
particular election? - and especially would he frown indignantly upon
that new doctrine, lately preached and defended in what has been
supposed to be the head quarters of orthodoxy in New England, by
which we are taught that derived depravity is not any taint or sinful
corruption of our moral constitution, but consists, exclusively and
entirely, in moral exercise! But probably he would get little
satisfaction from those who profess his creed and bear his name.
They would tell him that the old forms of this system were so
repulsive, the people would not receive them; and that, being hard
pressed by their antagonists, they had thrown up these new redoubts,

and assumed these new positions, not only to conceal their doctrine, but, if possible, to defend it. And as he could get little satisfaction of them, he would get less from us. Could we meet the venerable reformer, we would thank him for his successful zeal and labour in the Protestant cause; but we would expostulate with him for giving sanction and currency to his "horrible decree." We would tell him he had committed to his followers a system so abhorrent to reason, and so difficult to be supported by Scripture, that they had been driven into all these changes in hope of finding some new and safe ground of defence; and that, while we considered this as a striking and convincing argument against the doctrine itself, we viewed it as auspicious of its final overthrow; that these changes, refinements, and concealments were symptoms that the doctrine was waxing old, and was ready to vanish away.

*   *   *

One modification of Calvinism remains to be mentioned. It is known by the name of the "New Divinity." The theological doctors connected with Yale College are the reputed authors of this system. It is evident, however, that the tendency of the Calvinistic theory has been in this direction for a number of years. The "New Divinity," so alarming to some of the Calvinists, is only the ripe fruits of the very plants which they have long cultivated with assiduous care. And why should they start back at results which they have long laboured to produce? This theory, in the first place, is an attempt to make the doctrine, and the technical terms alluded to, coincide. In the second place, it is designed, by a new philosophy of predestination, to get rid of the "logical consequences" that have always pressed heavily upon the old system. Finally, it is a device to reconcile the doctrine of depravity with the former current sentiment, that man has natural ability to convert himself and get to heaven without grace. The two pillars of the new system are, 1. "Sin is not a propagated property of the human soul, but consists wholly in moral exercise." 2. "Sin is not the necessary means of the greatest good;" or, in other words, "Sin is not preferable to holiness in its stead." The Calvinistic opposers of this theory tell us that these sentiments have been held and taught to some extent for the last ten years. They were more fully and more openly announced, however, by Dr. Taylor, of the theological school belonging to Yale College, in a *concio ad clerum* preached September 10th, 1828. From the time of the publication of this sermon the alarm has been sounded, and the controversy has been carried on. The opposers of the new doctrine call it heresy; and in a late publication they seem to intimate that Dr. Taylor and his associates are nearly if not quite as heretical as the author of the sermon on predestination and election [Cf. the foregoing selection]. The doctor and his friends, on the other hand, strenuously maintain that they are orthodox; and to prove it, they repeat, again and again, "We believe that God did, for his own glory, foreordain whatsoever comes to pass." . .

The present advocates of predestination and particular election may be divided into four classes: - 1. The old-school Calvinists. 2. Hopkinsians. 3. Reformed Hopkinsians. 4. Advocates of the New Divinity. By the Reformed Hopkinsians I mean those who have left out of their creed Dr. Hopkins' doctrine of disinterested benevolence, divine efficiency in producing sin, &c., and yet hold to a general atonement, natural ability, &c. These constitute, doubtless, the largest division in the "class" in New-England. Next, as to numbers, probably, are the new school, then Hopkinsians, and last, the old school. These subdivisions doubtless run into each other in various combinations; but the outlines of these four sub-classes are, I think, distinctly marked. . . .

Thus have I endeavoured to glance over the various modifications and present characteristics of that mode of Christian doctrines called Calvinism. Here a few suggestions present themselves, which, from their relation to the present controversy, I will now set down.

It seems singular that, differing as they profess to, so materially, on many points, each individual of each subclass should feel himself injured whenever Calvinism, under this common name, is opposed in any of its features. The sermon on predestination was against Calvinism, and lo! all parties rise up against the sermon. And yet, whether it object to Calvinistic policy or to Calvinistic doctrine, the different parties accuse their opponents of being guilty of the charge, but they themselves are clear. I cannot think of a single important position assumed by the sermon against predestination and election, which is not sustained by Calvinists themselves in opposition to some of their brethren; nor yet of a single charge against their policy, for their changes and ambiguous methods of stating and defending their doctrines, which has not been reiterated by professed Calvinists themselves against their brethren. Thus the sermon is sustained by the Calvinists themselves, and yet they all condemn it!

*   *   *

Will it be said, All this is not argument? I answer, The sermon, it is supposed, contains arguments - arguments which professed predestinarians themselves tell us are unanswerable against the pre-vailing modes of stating and explaining the doctrine. Now let them be answered, if they can be. Let them be answered, not by giving up predestination, in the Calvinistic sense, and still professing to hold it - not by attempting to avoid the logical consequences, by giving the system the thousandth explanation, when the nine hundred and ninety-nine already given have made it no plainer, nor evaded at all the just consequences, so often charged upon it; and when these are answered, it will then be time enough to call for new arguments.

Having prepared the way, as I hope, by the preceding numbers,

310

for the proper understanding of the controversy; and having, by the remarks just made, attempted (with what success the reader must judge) to repel the charges of misrepresentation and bearing false witness, made against me, as the author of the sermon which gave rise to the controversy, I am now prepared, in my next number, to commence an examination of some of the questions of doctrine connected with this discussion.

¶   Fisk on Spirituality and Worship.

(Taken from "A Sermon on John iv. 24, by the Rev. W. Fisk," *Methodist Quarterly Review*, VII (1824), 88-90, 134-25).

When we speak, however, of the necessity of believing the truth, in order to be true worshippers, we include only such truths as effect a spiritual experience, and produce a godly life. Many questions are violently agitated in the Christian world, on which some lay much stress, which do not materially affect man's salvation. These abstract metaphysical propositions, already hinted at, make no essential part of this system of truth, for which we contend. We do not hold it necessary to constitute a man a true worshipper, that he should know whether God's foreknowledge and predetermination are both one, or wherein they differ. Neither do we think it essential whether a man in baptism believe in little or much water. Men may take opposite sides in these and similar questions, and yet be true worshippers.

The essential principles of godliness, are few and plain. They are clearly revealed in the word of God; which is the only and sufficient standard for faith and practice. It is these essential truths, which we expect you will often hear insisted upon, illustrated, confirmed and enforced, from this pulpit.

They are principally as follow:

1. There is one God, eternal, unlimited, and indivisible; and yet, in the mystery of his incomprehensible existence, subsists in a distinction of three, called in scripture, the Father, the Word (or Son) and the Holy Ghost. This distinction is not merely nominal, ideal or official, but positive and substantial; and yet such as not to destroy the divine unity.

This God is the Creator and preserver of all things.

2. Man, the workmanship of God, was made pure and holy. But by his voluntary and unnecessitated act, fell from his state of holiness; and by this apostacy, the whole human race were involved in natural and moral depravity - so that man, unassisted by divine grace, has neither natural or moral ability to serve God, or fit

311

himself for heaven. Not only is "the whole heart faint," but also "the whole head is sick."

3. The Word, the second in the Godhead, took human nature, "became flesh, and dwelt amongst us." And as "God manifest in the flesh," became by his sufferings and death, "a propitiation for the sins of the whole world." So that the provisions of the gospel are universal, and suited to the fallen and debilitated state of the whole human family.

4. Man is convicted, regenerated and sanctified, by the efficient agency of the Holy Ghost, through the merits and righteousness of Jesus Christ; and thus prepared and made meet for the enjoyment of God and Heaven. But repentance towards God, and faith in our Lord Jesus Christ, are conditions, without which, this work will never be accomplished in the soul. This faith and repentance are really the acts of the creature; but they are performed by strength and assistance given, through the mercy of Jesus Christ; for we have already seen, that man's moral weakness is provided for in the gospel; so that all the glory of man's salvation from the foundation to the topstone, is secured to God in Christ; and yet man's agency is intimately and necessarily connected therewith. Hence his condemnation, if he neglect to repent and believe, will rest solely upon himself – Being the known consequence of his own voluntary and unnecessitated choice.

5. Man is kept in a state of acceptance with God by the exercise of faith. But it is abundantly evident from scripture, from experience, and from the very nature of faith and man's agency, that this faith may be lost; or, by neglect, become dead and good for nothing. Therefore the believer is in danger of apostacy: and hence the necessity, if we would preach the gospel in truth, of warning him to take heed; of pointing out his danger, and stirring him up to diligence and perseverance.

6. Without holiness no man can see the Lord. The law of God is exceeding broad, and requires truth in the inward parts. The doctrine, therefore, of entire sanctification, is a necessary article in the faith of a true worshipper. And since this work is not ordinarily completed at conversion, it must be done after – and as it is a preparatory work, it must be done in our preparatory state of existence, that is, in this life – and since it is effected through the cleansing merits of Christ's blood, by the operations of the Holy Spirit, it must be received by faith – Consequently to worship God in truth, we must preach and believe in a present and full salvation, not only from the condemning power and reigning influence of sin, but also from its indwelling and soul-polluting nature. And the same living faith in Christ, which gives this salvation at the first, will, if continually exercised, enable the soul "to serve God without fear in holiness and righteousness before him, all the days of his life."

7. There will be "a resurrection of the dead, both of the just and of the unjust."

8. There will be a general judgment; wherein all shall be judged and condemned or acquitted, "According to the deeds done in the body."

9. The misery of the wicked, and the happiness of the righteous, will be alike eternal. This appears from the very constitution of the gospel. For while it secures immortality and eternal life to the believer, its remedial influences and operations, are no where represented as extending to those who are found sinners in eternity. But on the contrary, many scriptural considerations go to limit them to this world. Besides, the express sanctions of God's law, and the plain declarations of scripture, clearly demonstrate, that after death, "he that is filthy shall be filthy still, and he that is holy shall be holy still." The wicked, at the judgment, shall be sentenced into eternal punishment, and the righteous shall be received into life eternal.

*   *   *

Worship divides itself into private, social and public. I can dwell upon the two former but a moment.

By private devotion is understood those seasons, consecrated from all other employments, in which the soul in secret, engages in meditation, prayer and praise. The necessity for this is found in that command of our Saviour, "Enter into thy closet, and pray to thy Father which seeth in secret." For this there should be set times; for what is left for any time, will probably be performed at no time. "Stated seasons," says one,"for indispensable employments, are absolutely necessary, for so desultory, so versatile a creature as man." On this part of worship, I can only add, that in secret devotion, the heart should be honest before God; should seek to get near him, and hold communion with him; should be fervent, persevering, believing.

The propriety and necessity of social worship, is founded on that Old Testament scripture - "They that feared the Lord, spake often one to another;" and on that encouraging declaration of our Lord, "Where two or three are gathered together in my name, there am I in the midst of them;" and on many other scriptures. This worship is performed in families, in private circles, and in social meetings for religious conversation, prayer and thanksgiving; and affords the advantage of mutual edification, by the united devotion of a number of individuals. The principal thing to be observed peculiar to social worship, is a union of design, of feeling, of faith and of exertion. Unless this union can be secured, social worship cannot be performed in truth; for indeed, without this it is not social - it is disunited, it is discordant. Such devotion gains nothing, but

313

rather loses, for being performed in the presence of a number. But when this union is effected, the time, the place, the mode, are of but little consequence.

But we hasten to speak more largely upon public worship. We have already seen that the worship of God consists in the right dispositions of the heart, and proper exercise of mind, rather than in any outward peculiarity of time, form, or place. But we have also noticed, that, though the acceptableness of worship was to be determined by the frame of the heart, yet this did not render any outward form or place useless. And that form must be a concerted form, that place must be a concerted place, that time must be an appointed time.

So far as the form of worship is not clearly pointed out in the scriptures, so far every church has a right to fix its own forms, and establish its own regulations. And it is worse than vain - it is wicked, in Christians, to have uncharitable contentions and variances with each other, about forms which they only infer, are fixed in the scriptures. It is very evident that the Holy Spirit left many things of this nature undefined, that the church, among all nations, and in all ages of the world, might, in some measure, accommodate its forms of discipline, and modes of worship, to the peculiar circumstances in which it might be placed. But it may be observed, that, since the form is serviceable only as it tends to keep up the spirit of devotion in the heart of the worshipper and extend it to others, that form which will best secure these objects is the best. The leadings of God's providence, corroborated by the test of experience, ought to direct in this matter. These have been the guide in establishing the forms of worship in our church. And since we have found our course a profitable one, we are not disposed to alter it, though it may be thought objectionable by some. Our lively exercises in devotion on the one hand - our fervour and zeal - our hearty accordance of soul, and sometimes of voice, may be thought by some to savour of enthusiasm; but this is to preserve us from dead formality. Our regularity, on the other hand - our strict attention to order and method, may be thought by others, to savour of bondage; but this is to preserve us from disorder and confusion.

It is for the reasons given above, viz. the guidance of God's providence, and the test of experience, that we still continue our warm and zealous method of preaching - our frequent appeals to the passions, and direct assaults upon the heart of the hearer. This was the method so successfully practised by WESLEY and WHITEFIELD, and which has been crowned with so much good, in the hands of the successors. Not that we exclude from our theory or practice, the necessity of enlightening the mind, and informing the judgment. Our ideas on this point have been sufficiently explained, in our first proposition. But experience proves, that the passions, like a strong man armed, keep the palace of the soul, even when the mind is well informed. So that the plainest and most experimental

doctrines, proved by a course of cold reasoning, are not apt to affect
the heart. You may convince men's understandings a thousand times,
and if you do not make them feel you have gained little or nothing.
The heart is bound up in the world - it is settled down in its own
corruptions - it is bound to earth by numerous sensual ties, and
carnal attachments; and can light in the understanding move it? No:
the citadel itself must be attached. The sharp two edged sword must
be piercing - it must not only divide asunder the soul and spirit,
but also the joints and marrow - it must cut its way to the thoughts
of the heart.

¶   Nathan Bangs Explains the Church's Success.

(Taken from *A History of the Methodist Episcopal Church* (1839),
I, 356-65).

Methodism had now existed in this country about thirty-six
years, and numbered in its communion, including preachers and people,
white and colored, sixty six thousand, two hundred and forty-six
souls. The entire population of the United States at that time was
about four millions; if we allow three minors and others, who attended upon public worship among them, to each communicant, the population
of the Methodist Episcopal Church would amount to about one hundred
and ninety-eight thousand. According to this estimation, about one-
twentieth part of the entire population were brought under Methodist
influence in the short space of thirty-six years. This, it should
be remembered, had been effected from nothing, that is, we had no
church members with whom to begin, except the few solitary emigrants
from Ireland, as noted in the second chapter of this work.

*   *   *

We have not, therefore, enumerated the communicants of the
Methodist Episcopal Church as an evidence, of itself, that its
ministry were moving in obedience to God's will, and in the order of
his providence. Though they had been as "numerous as the sands upon
the seashore," had they been destitute of righteousness, they would
be no proof that the instruments of their conversion were sent of
God.

But what we insist upon is, that these men preached the pure
doctrine of Jesus Christ, and that those who were converted by their
instrumentality were really "brought from darkness to light, and
from the power of Satan to God" - that such a reformation of heart
and life was effected as resulted in a uniform obedience to the
commands of God; and that those who were brought under the doctrine
and disciplinary regulations of this Church, brought forth the "fruit
of the Spirit, love, joy, peace, long-suffering, gentleness, goodness,
faith, meekness, temperance" - thus giving evidence that they were

indeed "born of the Spirit," and enjoyed its witness of their adoption into the family of God.

We speak of them as a body. Though it is not probable that there were many hypocrites who came among them – there being no temptation to such to identify themselves with them – yet there were doubtless some such, and others who imposed upon themselves and others; and some who apostatized from the faith – these could not do otherwise than reproach the cause they had espoused. But whenever such were discovered, if they could not be reclaimed from their wanderings, the strict discipline which was enforced cut them off from the communion of the faithful; and thus was the Church freed from the responsibility of their conduct, and kept pure from their corrupting example. By this faithful preaching of the word, and enforcement of discipline, the main body was kept in a healthy state, and presented a living example of the purity and excellence of their religion. This was a resistless argument in their favor.

Another thing which made them more extensively useful was, their itinerating mode of preaching the gospel. Had these ministers confined their labors to insulated congregations, as most of the ministers of other denominations did, they never could have realized that diffusive spread of evangelical religion which actually accompanied their efforts. Had John Wesley, instead of going forth into the "highways and hedges" to call sinners to repentance, settled himself over a parish, Methodism had been either "hid in a corner," or never have had an existence. It was his itinerating so largely, and preaching wherever he could find access to the people, which gave such efficiency to his efforts, and such a wide spread to the gospel by his instrumentality.

But in this country especially, many parts of which were newly settled, and therefore but sparsely populated, had not those preachers carried the gospel to the people by traversing the country, they had remained destitute of the means of salvation. We may, therefore, attribute the success which attended their labors to the blessing of God on an itinerant ministry – on a ministry which went everywhere preaching, "not with enticing words of man's wisdom, but in the demonstration of the Spirit, and with power." This it was which enabled them to "reach even beyond themselves," in preaching the gospel of Christ, and of gathering thousands of souls into his fold.

These men devoted themselves entirely and exclusively to this work, remembering, as their Discipline admonished them, that it was "not their business to preach so many times, and to take care of this or that society, but to save as many souls as possible; to bring as many sinners as they can to repentance, and with all their power to build them up in holiness, without which they cannot see the Lord." It was this diligence in their calling, of being in soul and body devoted to it, which enabled them to accomplish so much in so short

a time, and that, too, in the midst of reproach and opposition.

It was, indeed, this very devotion, this diligence, these zealous efforts in the cause of their divine Master, which provoked much of the opposition which they had to encounter. The lukewarm clergy were aroused to indignation at seeing themselves rivaled by those whom they affected to despise on account of their erratic habits and inferiority in point of literature and science. And as these zealous itinerants made their pointed appeals to the consciences of sinners, denounced the just judgments of God upon hardened offenders, their ire was often kindled against those who thus "reproved them in the gate." Wherever these flaming messengers of Jesus Christ came, they disturbed the false peace of the lukewarm, awakened the conscience of the sleeping sinner, and gave him no rest until he surrendered his heart to Christ. They not only "preached in the great congregation""in the city full," but "into whatever house they entered," they addressed themselves personally to its inmates, urging them to be "reconciled to God;" and they accompanied all their efforts by earnest prayer, both public and private, that God would sanction their labors by sending upon them the energies of the Holy Spirit.

The doctrines, too, which they principally insisted upon, had a direct tendency to produce the desired effect upon the heart and life. While they held, in common with other orthodox Christians, to the hereditary depravity of the human heart, the deity and atonement of Jesus Christ, the necessity of repentance and faith; that which they pressed upon their hearers with the greatest earnestness was, the necessity of the new birth, and the privilege of their having a knowledge by the internal witness of the Holy Spirit, of the forgiveness of sins, through faith in the blood of Christ; and as a necessary consequence of this, and as naturally flowing from it, provided they persevered, holiness of heart and life. On this topic they dwelt with an emphasis and an earnestness peculiar to themselves. The doctrine itself, though held by most orthodox churches, as is manifest from their articles of faith and formularies of religion, was allowed to sleep in their books, or was not brought before the people with that prominence which its importance demands, and with that particularity and definiteness which its vitality in the Christian system renders essential to the success of the gospel ministry.

But on this vital point the Methodist ministers bent their whole force. If they pressed upon the sinner a sense of his depravity and actual guilt, it was to make him feel the necessity of repentance and forgiveness. If they presented to him the death of Christ, as the meritorious cause of the sinner's salvation, it was to encourage him to look to that source for pardon in his blood. If the Holy Spirit was spoken of as the helper of our infirmities, and as a leader into all truth, it was that he might be claimed by the penitent sinner as the sealer of his pardon, and as a witnesser of his "acceptance in the Beloved." Thus all the doctrines of the gospel were brought to

317

have a bearing on this point, that all who were induced to "seek after God" might have no rest until they found "redemption in his blood, even the forgiveness of sins."

By preaching this doctrine everywhere, to all classes of people, making it prominent in every sermon, and exhibiting it as the common privilege of all penitent sinners to experience, they were blessed of God in their labors, and rejoiced over returning prodigals to their Father's house.

III.

SETTLED INSTITUTION, 1860–1914

13. CIVIL WAR AND RECONSTRUCTION

The painful experience of schism in 1844 was irrepressibly followed by the more physically painful trials of civil war. Of course, all of the denominations were embroiled. Much of the involvement followed the ideal of the church as servant, in regimental chaplaincies and services of relief. Much of it, however, carried ecclesiastical conflicts into the public arena.

The infamous War Department Order by Secretary Stanton issued in behalf of Bishop Ames illustrates the degree to which church leaders were willing to seek advantage from the conflict. So also the discussions and resolutions of the Methodist preachers in Boston show how easily Christians fall into secular temptations. The relatively strong position of Northern Methodism is reflected in the Episcopal Address of 1864, and in Abel Stevens' centennial book of 1865.

The friendship of Bishop Matthew Simpson with President Abraham Lincoln is well known. Upon the occasion of his death the bishop delivered a number of memorial addresses, including the funeral sermon in Springfield, Illinois. He made a significant contribution to the martyrology of Lincoln.

On the other hand the Southern branch of the church faced imminent destruction. Some persons actually raised the question whether the struggle for survival was worthwhile. The Palmyra Manifesto of 1865 was a gasp of breath rising from a moribund body. This call for reconstruction of the Southern church as a separate ecclesiastical institution was a prelude to the crucial General Conference of 1866. The bishops in their Address provided an assessment of the condition of the church and a direction for a basic reconstruction of Southern Methodism, which in many ways placed it in advance of the Northern branch.

By the 1880's the South, whether it wished or not, was facing a new era. Atticus Haygood, who was elected bishop in the M. E. Church, South, only two years after the publication of his influential book, The New South (1880), was a leader in rescuing his church—and the South—from its nostalgia for the past, in drawing attention to the challenges of a new era, and in encouraging new opportunities. It began to respond, but excruciatingly slowly.

¶ War Department, Adjutant General's Office, Washington ,
                      November 30, 1862.

(Taken from W. W. Sweet, *The Methodist Episcopal Church in the
Civil War* (1912), 98-99).

To the Generals commanding the Departments of Missouri, the
Tennessee, and the Gulf, and all Generals and Officers
commanding armies, detachments, and posts, and all officers
in the service of the United States in the above mentioned
Departments:

You are hereby directed to place at the disposal of Rev. Bishop
Ames all houses of worship belonging to the Methodist Episcopal Church,
South, in which a loyal minister, who has been appointed by a loyal
Bishop of said Church does not officiate.

It is a matter of great importance to the Government in its
efforts to restore tranquillity to the community and peace to the
Nation, that Christian Ministers, should by example and precept,
support and foster the loyal sentiment of the people.

Bishop Ames enjoys the entire confidence of this Department,
and no doubt is entertained that all ministers who may be appointed
by him will be entirely loyal. You are expected to give him all the
aid, countenance, and support practicable in the execution of his
important mission. You are also authorized and directed to furnish
Bishop Ames and his clerk with transportation and subsistence when
it can be done without prejudice to the service and will afford them
courtesy, assistance, and protection.

¶ Minutes of the Methodist Ministers' Association, Boston, 13 Oct.,
                      1862 and 24 Apr., 1865.

(Taken from Sweet, *Civil War*, 97, 68, the second paraphrased).

Resolved, That, inasmuch as one of the consequences of the war
to suppress the great rebellion in the Southern part of this country
is to open large tracts of country inhabited by many thousands of our
fellow countrymen who are now to a greater or less extent deprived
of Church privileges, we deem it the duty of the Missionary Board of
the Churches to examine the demands of such places for aid from time
to time, and whenever in their judgment the employment of missionaries
in those places would probably promote the cause of Christ and the
salvation of souls, they should establish and sustain such missions.

Resolved, That we believe that it is the imperative duty of the
Missionary Board at once to enter upon this work, and that the
Churches generally would, if properly appealed to, contribute

liberally to sustain them.

*   *   *

The Constitution defines treason and affixes its penalty.
No rank or station, civil or military, should shield from justice
the authors and leaders of the rebellion. . . Any leniency of the
government toward such is worse than wasted, is indeed an undeserved
and grievous cruelty to the insulted sense of justice in the minds
of the brave defenders of the Union and in the heart of the whole
loyal population. Never will the Nation feel its sense of honor
and justice vindicated until the leaders of this unprovoked and
wicked rebellion shall have suffered condign punishment, the
penalty of death; therefore,

Resolved, That no terms should be made with traitors,
no compromise with rebels; that the surrender of rebels should be
unconditional, they should be forced to surrender and should be
held to the strict justice their crimes have merited.

That we hold the National authority bound by the most solemn
obligation to God and man to bring all the civil and military
leaders of the rebellion to trial by due course of law, and when
they are clearly convicted, to execute them.

That in the reconstruction of Southern States no man should
hold office who held a commission in the rebel army or in the
Confederate government, nor shall he be allowed to vote.

It is the duty of the National Government to provide for the
entire extinction of slavery.

The supreme sovereignty of the United States Government must
be maintained in the reconstruction of the Rebel States.

The last resolve pledges most earnest and cordial support to
Johnson if he carries out the policies above set forth.

¶   Episcopal Address, 1864.

(Taken from "Address of the Bishops," pamphlet, 2, 6-7).

The times in which you are assembled are unprecedented. A
"mystery of iniquity," which was working at the date of your last
session, and which had been working for many years, broke forth in
April, 1861, in a gigantic, thoroughly organized, and most defiant
rebellion against the authority of the General Government, and the
integrity and life of the Federal Union. The collisions resulting
inevitably from this unnatural and wicked rebellion have laid waste

large portions of our once fair and beautiful heritage, have sent tens of thousands to a patriot's or a traitor's grave, and have filled the land with lamentation and mourning. The rebellion still rages, but, we are happy to say, with lessening hopes and diminishing resources.

In this great crisis of our national affairs, it gives us pleasure to announce that the Methodist Episcopal Church has proved herself to be eminently loyal. Taking her stand on the sure teachings of the New Testament, and on our Twenty-third Article of Religion, with its appended note, as the true platform of Christian loyalty, and utterly ignoring all partisan political platforms, she has given to the Federal Government her most decided support. Nor has this support been confined to resolutions of approval and sympathy, adopted by all the Annual Conferences, nor to large contributions in money, or its equivalent, for various purposes connected with the war; but her members in large numbers, and many of her ministers, have flocked to the national standard, and have fought side by side with brother patriots on every battle-field of this dreadful war.

It was naturally to be apprehended that, in a crisis of public affairs so dreadful, and during the pendency of a civil war the most gigantic and the most fearful known to history, the Churches in the loyal states, and especially the Methodist Episcopal Church, among the most loyal of those Churches, would be greatly embarrassed in their action and limited in the results of their labor. But we are happy to say that, however it may have been with other Churches, this natural foreboding has not been, to any considerable extent, realized in relation to the Methodist Episcopal Church. On the contrary, she has gone forward in her legitimate work with little interruption and with surprising prosperity. The Annual Conferences have held all their sessions at the times and, with two exceptions - the Missouri and the Kentucky - at the places designated; the organization of the districts and the pastoral charges, with a few exceptions on the extreme war-border, has remained intact, while in nearly all our leading interests there has been a most cheering and even wonderful progress.

*   *   *

The progress of the Federal arms has thrown open to the loyal Churches of the Union large and inviting fields of Christian enterprise and labor. In the cultivation of these fields it is natural and reasonable to expect that the Methodist Episcopal Church should occupy a prominent position. She occupied these fields once. Her net-work of conferences, districts, and pastoral charges, spread over them all: all, indeed, both within and beyond the Federal lines. For nineteen years they have been in the occupancy of the Methodist Episcopal Church South, to the wrongful exclusion of the Methodist Episcopal Church. But her days of exclusive

324

occupancy are ended. The wall of partition is broken down by that very power whose dreadful ministry was invoked to strengthen it. And now, the way being open for the return of the Methodist Episcopal Church, it is but natural that she should re-enter those fields and once more realize her unchanged title as "the Methodist Episcopal Church in the United States of America." She ought never to have been excluded from any portion of the territory of the United States; she ought never to have consented, on any ground, to such exclusion. And now that the providence of God has opened her way, she should not be disobedient to her heavenly calling, but should return at the earliest practicable period.

But how? This is the great question. And while we defer for the full answer to the wisdom of the General Conference, we feel that we ought to say that she should enter those fields as she enters all fields: she should enter preaching Christ and him crucified to all classes of people, laboring with all her might to bring sinners to repentance and to build up believers in that holiness without which no man can see the Lord, and welcoming back such ministers and members as were cut off from her communion without their voluntary act. Yet it is our solemn judgment that none should be admitted to her fellowship who are either slaveholders or are tainted with treason.

We suggest such a change in the Discipline as will permit the recognition of such members and ministers as it may be proper to receive into the Church.

We may add to what is here said, that the bishops, at their meeting in November last, arranged among themselves to have the southern territory then within the Federal lines explored, with a view to making such temporary arrangements as might be found to be practicable for the supply of the spiritual needs of the forsaken people. The bishops have made the exploration more or less thoroughly, either by personal visitation or correspondence, and have temporarily appointed a few preachers.

We deem it proper to call attention to the section in the Discipline in relation to our colored membership. The provision adopted by the General Conference in 1856, though an advance on former legislation, is not, we believe, sufficient to meet the necessities of the colored people. The time has now come, in our judgment, when the General Conference should carefully consider what measures can be adopted to give increased efficiency to our Church among them.

¶ Bishop Matthew Simpson on Lincoln.

(Taken from Simpson, *Our Martyr President, Abraham Lincoln* (1915, originally pub. 1865), 261-64).

Let us pause a moment in the lesson of the hour before we part. This man, though he fell by an assassin, still fell under the permissive hand of God. He had some wise purpose in allowing him so to fall. What more could he have desired of life for himself? Were not his honors full? There was no office to which he could aspire. The popular heart clung around him as around no other man. The nations of the world had learned to honor our chief magistrate. If rumors of a desired alliance with England be true, Napoleon trembled when he heard of the fall of Richmond, and asked what nation would join him to protect him against our Government under the guidance of such a man. His fame was full, his work was done, and he sealed his glory by becoming the nation's great martyr for liberty.

He appears to have had a strange presentment, early in political life, that some day he would be President. You see it indicated in 1839. Of the slave power he said, "Broken by it I too may be; bow to it I never will. The probability that we may fail in the struggle ought not to deter us from the support of a cause which we deem to be just. It shall not deter me. If ever I feel the soul within me elevate and expand to those dimensions not wholly unworthy of its Almighty architect, it is when I contemplate the cause of my country, deserted by all the world besides, and I standing up boldly and alone and hurling defiance at her victorious oppressors. Here without contemplating consequences, before high Heaven and in the face of the world, I swear eternal fidelity to the just cause, as I deem it, of the land of my life, my liberty, and my love. . . .

Standing, as we do to-day, by his coffin and his sepulcher, let us resolve to carry forward the policy which he so nobly began. Let us do right to all men. To the ambitious there is this fearful lesson: Of the four candidates for Presidential honors in 1860, two of them — Douglas and Lincoln — once competitors, but now sleeping patriots, rest from their labors; Bell perished in poverty and misery, as a traitor might perish; and Breckinridge is a frightened fugitive, with the brand of traitor on his brow. Let us vow, in the sight of Heaven, to eradicate every vestige of human slavery; to give every human being his true position before God and man; to crush every form of rebellion, and to stand by the flag which God has given us. How joyful that it floated over parts of every State before Mr. Lincoln's career was ended! How singular that, to the fact of the assassin's heels being caught in the folds of the flag, we are probably indebted for his capture! The flag and the traitor must ever be enemies.

Chieftain! farewell! The nation mourns thee. Mothers shall
teach thy name to their lisping children. The youth of our land
shall emulate thy virtues. Statesman shall study thy record and
learn lessons of wisdom. Mute though thy lips be, yet they still
speak. Hushed is thy voice, but its echoes of liberty are ring-
ing through the world, and the sons of bondage listen with joy.
Prisoned thou art in death, and yet thou art marching abroad, and
chains and manacles are bursting at thy touch. Thou didst fall
not for thyself. The assassin had no hate for thee. Our hearts
were aimed at, our national life was sought. We crown thee as
our martyr – and humanity enthrones thee as her triumphant son.
Hero, Martyr, Friend, FAREWELL!

¶   Methodist Centenary, 1866.

(Taken from Abel Stevens, *The Centenary of Methodism* (1865),
147-53).

WHAT HAS METHODISM ACHIEVED, ENTITLING IT TO THE
PROPOSED COMMEMORATION?

CHAPTER I

ITS SPECIAL ADAPTATION TO THE COUNTRY.

METHODISM, it has been affirmed, was a special provision for
the early religious wants of this nation. The Revolution opened
the continent for rapid settlement by immigration. A movement of
the peoples of the old world toward the new was to set in on a
scale surpassing that of the northern hordes which overwhelmed the
Roman Empire. Much of this incoming population was to be Roman
Catholic, most of it low, if not semi-barbarous. Some extraordinary
religious provision was requisite to meet and counteract its de-
moralizing influence on the country.

The growth of population was to transcend the most credulous
anticipations. The one million and a quarter (including blacks) of
1750, the less than three millions of 1780, were to be nearly four
millions in 1790; nearly five and a third millions in 1800; more
than nine and a half millions in 1820; nearly thirteen millions in
1830. Thus far they were to increase nearly thirty-three and a
half per cent in each decade. Pensioners of the war of the
Revolution were to live to see the "Far West" transferred from the
valleys of Virginia, the eastern base of the Pennsylvania Alleghanies,
and the center of New York, to the great deserts beyond the
Mississippi; to see mighty states, enriching the world, flourish on
the Pacific coast; and to read, in New York, news sent the same day

from San Francisco. Men, a few at least, who lived when the
population of the country was less than three millions, were to
live when it should be thirty millions.

Methodism, with its "lay ministry" and its "itinerancy," could
alone afford the ministrations of religion to this overflowing population; it was to lay the moral foundations of many of the great
states of the West. The older Churches of the colonies could never
have supplied them with "regular" or educated pastors in any
proportion to their rapid settlement. Methodism met this necessity
in a manner that should command the national gratitude. It was to
become at last the dominant popular faith of the country, with its
standard planted in every city, town, and almost every village of
the land. Moving in the van of emigration, it was to supply,
with the means of religion, the frontiers from the Canadas to the
Gulf of Mexico, from Puget's Sound to the Gulf of California. It
was to do this indispensable work by means peculiar to itself; by
districting the land into circuits which, from one hundred to five
hundred miles in extent, could each be stately supplied with
religious instruction by one or two traveling evangelists who,
preaching daily, could thus have charge of parishes comprising
hundreds of miles and tens of thousands of souls. It was to raise
up, without delay for preparatory training, and thrust out upon
these circuits, thousands of such itinerants, tens of thousands of
local or lay preachers and exhorters, as auxiliary and unpaid
laborers, with many thousands of class-leaders who could maintain
pastoral supervision over the infant societies in the absence of
the itinerant preachers, the latter not having time to delay in
any locality for much more than the public services of the pulpit.
Over all these circuits it was to maintain the watchful jurisdiction
of traveling presiding elders, and over the whole system the
superintendence of traveling bishops, to whom the entire nation was
to be a common diocese. It was to govern the whole field by
Quarterly Conferences for each circuit, Annual Conferences for groups
of circuits, Quadrennial Conferences for all the Annual Conferences.
It was to preach night and day in churches, where it could command
them, in private houses, school-houses, court-houses, barns, in the
fields, on the highways. It was to stud the continent with chapels,
building them, in our times at least, at the rate of nearly two a
day. It was to provide academies and colleges exceeding in number,
if not in efficiency, those of any other religious body of the
country, however older or richer. It was to scatter over the land
cheap publications, all its itinerants being authorized agents for
their sale, until its "Book Concern" should become the largest
religious publishing house in the world. The best authority for
the moral statistics of the country, himself of another denomination,
(Dr. Baird,) was at last to "recognize in the Methodist economy, as
well as in the zeal, the devoted piety and the efficiency of its
ministry, one of the most powerful elements in the religious
prosperity of the United States, as well as one of the firmest

pillars of their civil and political institutions." The historian
of the Republic (Bancroft) records that it was "welcomed the
members of Wesley's Society as the pioneers of religion; that the
breath of liberty has wafted their messages to the masses of the
people; encouraged them to collect the white and negro, slave and
master, in the green wood, for counsel on divine love and the full
assurance of grace; and carried their consolation and songs and
prayers to the furthest cabins in the wilderness."

It would indeed appear that the Methodist movement was thus a
providential intervention for the new nation. As we have seen, it
began its operation here at the dawn of the Revolutionary controversy;
its infancy was cotemporaneous [*sic*] with the infancy of the Republic;
it was the only form of religion that possessed much vitality or
made any progress during the Revolutionary struggle; its denominational organization at the Christmas Conference anticipated the national
organization under the Federal Constitution; it fairly started with
the Republic, and has kept pace with it, establishing the ordinances
of religion coextensively with the spread of the population and the
laws of the Government. It not only, by its peculiar system, met
the emergent moral necessities of the opening continent, but exerted
also a most important influence on the other and older religious
provisions of the land. Whitefield's repeated passages through the
colonies had aroused the Churches for the coming wants of the country.
The "Great Awakening" under Edwards, in New England, had subsided,
and even reacted; Whitefield restored the evangelical vitality of
New England, and it has never since been lost. The Presbyterian
and Baptist Churches of the middle states were quickened into their
subsequent and abiding energy by his flaming ministrations. The
earliest religious impulses of the South were given by him.
Methodism, organized, took up the work when he fell in the field,
and it has never ceased to advance, in all evangelical denominations,
beyond any foreign example. Methodism was not designed to supplant
its elder sister Churches in the land, but to provoke them to new
life and labors, while it accomplished its own given work. It
nevertheless quickly surpassed them. We have authentic statistics
of the leading Christian denominations of the United States for the
first half of our century. They attest conclusively the peculiar
adaptation of the ecclesiastical system of Methodism to the moral
wants of the country. During the period from 1800 to 1850 the
ratio of the increase of the ministry of the Protestant Episcopal
Church has been as 6 to 1, of its communicants as 6 to 1; of the
ministry of the Congregationalists as 4 to 1, of their communicants
as 2 2/3 to 1; of the ministry of the regular Baptists as 4 to 1, of
their communicants as 5 2/3 to 1; of the ministry of the Presbyterians
("old and new schools") as 14 to 1, of their communicants as 8½ to 1;
of the ministry of the Methodist Episcopal Church (North and South)
as 19 2/3 to 1, of its communicants as 17 3/4 to 1. It must be borne
in mind, however, that most if not all these religious bodies have,
during the whole of this period, been more or less pervaded by the

Methodistic impulse given by Whitefield and his successors, and much
of their success is unquestionably attributable to that fact.
Methodism has given them thousands of its converts and received but
comparatively few from them.

¶   The Palmyra Manifesto, June, 1865.

   (Taken from W. H. Lewis, *The History of Methodism in Missouri*
   (1890), 175-78).

   Your committee, in considering "the importance of maintaining
our separate and distinct ecclesiastical organization," beg leave
to present the following resolution and accompanying paper:

   Resolved, That we consider the maintenance of our separate
and distinct ecclesiastical organization as of paramount importance
and our imperative duty.

   The reasons are many and obvious. While we have maintained a
separate and distinct ecclesiastical organization for twenty years,
yet we claim original paternity and co-existence as a Methodist
Church with the other branches of the great Methodist family in
the country. Facts will not permit us to yield to any other Church
of that name priority of age; nor in any other light than as an
attempt to deceive the unsuspecting among our people can we regard
the specious claims urged to the confidence and patronage of the
Methodist public under the name of "Old Church."

   In contravention to the Plan of Separation agreed upon by the
General Conference of 1844 - the legitimacy and binding force of
which were recognized by the Supreme Court of the United States -
the Northern wing of the Church has acted in bad faith toward us in
many ways.

   And since that Church was forced by law to give to our Church
her *pro rata* division of property - which she was too mercenary to
do without an appeal to the highest judiciary of the country - she
has persisted in an unprovoked and undesired war upon us - a war
which has aggravated the questions of difference, widened the breach,
and produced an estrangement of feeling and a destruction of fellowship for which she alone is responsible, and which we cannot even
seek to remedy without compromising principles and yielding all self-
respect.

   Those who publish to the world that all differences between
us as swept away with the institution of slavery are either ignorant
of the facts or are trying to mislead the public. The question
upon which the Church divided was not whether the institution of
slavery was right or wrong, per se, but whether it was a legitimate

subject for ecclesiastical legislation. The right or wrong of the institution, its existence or non-existence, could not affect this vital question. It is now abolished by Federal and State legislation, which event we accept as a political measure with which we have nothing to do as a Church. And it remains for us to demonstrate our ability to exist without the institution of slavery, as we have existed with it, which we have already done in California and other places.

Now, if we go into the Methodist Episcopal Church, we will by that act yield the position we have so often taken, admit the charges we have so often refuted, and by accepting political tests of Church-fellowship, stultify ourselves and compromise the essential principles of the gospel. If we seek an alliance with or permit our Church to be swallowed up by any other ecclesiastical body so as to destroy our separate existence as a distinct organization, we admit the charge that with the institution of slavery we stand or fall.

The subject of Church reconstruction or consolidation has been widely discussed by the press and the ministry of the Methodist Episcopal Church (North), and reasons, both political and ecclesiastical, are urged with an ill-disguised pertinacity why we should consent to an absorption of our entire ecclesiastical body by that Church.

It cannot be disguised that what they failed to accomplish during the war by military order and authority they now seek to effect by ecclesiastical strategy and diplomacy - that is, to get possession of our Church property, and rather than recognize us now as a Christian Church entitled to their ecclesiastical fellowship and Christian fraternity (which they by formal vote of their General Conference refused to do in 1848) and in that way, and with a Christian spirit, seek to offer negotiations upon the subject, they prefer to ignore our existence, or, which would suit their purpose better, pronounce us disloyal to the government, and per consequence not entitled to an existence at all; then invade us and by misrepresentations seek to disaffect our people, disintegrate our Church, and inaugurate an ecclesiastical strife that will involve the third and fourth generations.

The only consolidation or reconstruction they would accept would be that we turn over to them our Church property and interests and influence; yield the whole field; confess that we have been in the wrong; indorse the politics of their Church as a condition of membership; and become political hucksters instead of gospel ministers; then even our motives would be suspected, and we looked upon with contempt for our cowardly truckling to party and power.

Again we affirm that our itinerant system has become a great moral agency in elevating the masses of the people, preaching the gospel to the poor and "spreading scriptural holiness over these lands." Under its wide-spread operations we have gathered the people together, planted Churches, organized Sabbath-schools, acquired Church property, built up and endowed institutions of learning, and become a moral and religious element of the country at least equal to any other Protestant Church.

The people have learned to look to our ministry for the gospel, to our Churches and Sunday-schools for religious instruction, and to our influence in restraining vice, encouraging virtue, maintaining law and order, and promoting the well-being of society. We cannot, therefore, abandon our Church and people, or betray the interests and trusts committed to us as a Church, without a plain and culpable disregard of duty that would subject us to the contempt and derision of the Christian public.

We are not at liberty to dissolve our ecclesiastical organization or permit our Church to be absorbed by any other, even should we desire to do so, for our people have been consulted as far as practicable, and they are unwilling to seek any other Church connection, but with great unanimity demand at our hands the maintenance of our Church organization intact.

It is, therefore, due the great mass of the people who oppose the prostitution of the pulpit to political purposes, it is due to our large membership who have been converted and gathered into the fold of Christ under our ministry, and who love our Church doctrines and discipline too fondly to seek any other fold now - it is due every principle of self-respect and ecclesiastical propriety that we maintain, with firm reliance upon the help of the Great Head of the Church, our organization without embarrassment or compromise.

While these are some of the many reasons why we should adopt the above resolution, we desire most ardently to cultivate fraternal relations with all the evangelical Churches, and "as much as in us lies live peaceably with all men."

Wm. M. Leftwich, Chairman; John D. Vincil, Wm. M. Newland.

¶　　　　　　Episcopal Address, M. E. South, 1866.

(Taken from Journal of General Conference, M. E. Church, South, 15-21).

DEAR BRETHREN: - We hail with feelings of devout gratitude the opening of another session of the General Conference of the Methodist Episcopal Church, South. Circumstances connected with the late

unhappy war have prevented us from an earlier meeting; and now that
we are permitted by Divine Providence to assemble, the important
interests that will engage our attention demand that, with all
sobriety and prayerfulness, we address ourselves to their consideration.

We have to review the operations of the Church for eight years -
embracing a period during which important and startling events have
crowded on each other in rapid succession. When the last General
Conference closed, we anticipated an earlier reunion, in this city;
but the well-known condition of things, at the time appointed in
regular order for our meeting, precluded our convening here. And
ever since, until within the last few months, it has been deemed
impracticable to call the Conference together. When it was definitely
decided that the Conference could not meet at the proper time and
place, there being no law in the Discipline authorizing the Bishops
to convene the General Conference, and the state of the country also
being such as to render it doubtful whether any considerable number
of the preachers could be collected together for the purpose of holding such a session if called, the Bishops, feeling the importance of
wise counsel in the emergency, published a card inviting a meeting
of the Bishops, Book Committee, and others, to consult together on
divers important subjects connected with the immediate interests of
the Church. Such a meeting was held, first at Atlanta, Ga.; afterward at Macon, Ga.; and then at Montgomery, Ala. In August last the
Bishops alone met for consultation at Columbus, Ga. These various
meetings were seasons of interest and profit to those who attended
them, and the results of our deliberations, as exhibited in the
resolutions which we published, tended greatly, as we have reason
to believe, to promote the peace and prosperity of the Church.

In order that the character of those meetings may be clearly
appreciated, we would remind you that when they were called it
was distinctly stated that all the acts of such meetings would be
simply advisory. We disclaimed all authority to take any action that
should be binding on the Church, only as it might be approved as
wise and godly. We gave such advice as we judged best for the
Church in her straitened circumstances. If the Annual Conferences
approved it, then they acted in accordance with their own convictions;
if not, then they simply took their own course in all matters that
came before them, without reference to our advice. It is for the
General Conference to decide whether we transcended our authority
in convening such advisory councils.

Early during the war the Bishops had to confine their Episcopal
visitations to the territory east of the Mississippi River. This we
deeply regretted, but in our circumstances it was unavoidable. The
consequence was that the Conferences west of the Mississippi were
deprived of Episcopal supervision during nearly the whole period of
the war. We would not, however, fail to mention in this connection,

that Bishop Kavanaugh, residing as he did within the Federal lines, was able to visit the Missouri, the St. Louis, and the two Kentucky Conferences, and was also able to extend his visitations to the California work. The rest of the Bishops were able to extend their labors to various parts of the work within the Confederate lines. Notwithstanding the fact that our episcopal supervision of the work has been necessarily partial, we are gratified to believe that the preachers have been faithful generally to the interest of the Church of God. With but very few exceptions, the Annual Conferences have been regularly held. The Presiding Elders and Preachers have filled their appointments as of old; and, with humble gratitude to God. We mention the fact that, during the trying years through which we have passed, gracious revivals of religion among our people have attested how the Divine presence has been with us.

We do not attempt in this brief address to enter into a detailed account of the general state of the work. Thank God that we have so safely passed through a most painful and fiery ordeal; that the Church has preserved under His blessing her integrity; that she has in nowise become complicated with political affairs; but keeping in view her own high mission, has been satisfied to perform her legitimate duties.

It is proper to state to you that we found it, in our judgment, needful to the interest of the work to depart in some respects from the strict letter of the law of the Church in our episcopal adminis- tration. Extraordinary exigencies required us to take this respon- sibility. In the journals of the Annual Conferences which will come before you the particular instances in which we have judged it best to assume this grave responsibility will appear. In all such instances we wish it understood that we do not regard such departure from the law as establishing precedents for future guidance, but only as illustrating how extraordinary exigencies may make it necessary to transcend the provisions of even the most wholesome human regula- tions. From this experience, however, the General Conference may find suggestions that are valuable to guide it in providing as far as practicable for contingencies in the future.

It would have been gratifying to us if we had been able to bear the expense of more extensive travel through the work; but in the impoverished state of the Church, and especially in the absence of any provision for more than a bare support of the Bishops, this was impossible. This fact, we hope, will be suggestive to your body. . . .

The publishing interests of the Church suffered greatly in consequence of the war. The Book Concern will require your careful consideration, and some important changes in your plan of operations may be needful for its future efficiency: of this, however, you will be better prepared to judge when you have heard the report of the Agent. With pleasure we have welcomed the revival of our Church papers, and while we regard them as in a high degree creditable to

the Church, we would respectfully submit whether it would not be best to unite Conferences in the publication of a fewer number, in order that they may be better supported and still further improved.

Our missionary work, once the glory of our Church, has been well-nigh ruined. The China mission still lives, and needs your fostering care. Although the financial condition of the country at present forbids the expectation of large collections, yet we may make prospective arrangements for doing a great work in that extensive field.

The interest of the colored population should engage your serious attention. Heretofore the colored people within our bounds have deserved and received a large share of our labors. We have expended our means and strength liberally and patiently for many years for their salvation and improvement, and if in anywise our conduct has not been appreciated by some on earth, nevertheless, our witness is with God, and our record on high. It is grateful to our own feelings to know that if the colored people do not remain under our pastoral care, their departure reflects no discredit upon our labors in their behalf, and is necessitated by no indifference on our part to their welfare. Many of them will probaly unite with the African M. E. Church, some of them with the Northern Methodist Church, while others, notwithstanding extraneous influences and unkind misrepresentations of our Church, will remain with us.

Let us be content to leave to Providence to vindicate in due time our scriptural relation to the interest of the colored people. For those who remain with us the Church should provide generously every thing important to their religious culture. Convinced that your body takes the deepest interest in this subject, and will give it your special attention, we deem it only needful to speak of it in this general and suggestive form; and especially as the Bishops in their Pastoral Address last August brought the subject prominently to the notice of our people.

In respect to the separate and distinct organization of our Church, no reasons have appeared to altar [sic] our views, as expressed in August last. No proposal of fraternal relations has come to us from others, neither do we regard ourselves as in anywise responsible for hostility evinced towards us. While the attempt to take forcible possession of our property and to disintegrate our Church, declare the mind that would destroy us, let it be ours to show the mind that was in Christ. In our conscious integrity we should calmly await the inevitable hour when, in the providence of God, an enlightened public opinion will vindicate our claims as a Church of God and a true type of Methodism. Let us not be impatient for our vindication before the world. The great future is before us, and the great Head of the Church smiles upon us. Our fidelity to God will most perfectly reply to the voice of defamation.

335

If we are to judge from the tone of the religious press, and the action of many of our Conferences, great concern is felt in respect to certain changes in our economy. It is obviously unbecoming in us as Bishops to occupy any other than an impartial relation to those matters. But we take this occasion to urge upon you the importance of giving these subjects your sober and prayerful consideration. From our extensive observation of the state and wants of the Church, we hesitate not to say that some improvement of our economy may be wisely undertaken at this time. Well for us if we can happily avoid extremes and do neither too little nor too much. Let us remember that while innovations are not necessarily improvements, wisdom may demand in the department of ecclesiastical expediency new applications and developments of fundamental principles. The efficiency of Methodism finds its first condition in the prevalence of deep spiritual life; and alterations in our economy are valuable as they coincide with this condition, calamitous when they ignore it. On only one of the points suggested do we regard it becoming in our position to speak directly, and that is in respect to the increase of the number of the Bishops. For such an increase as will give the Church a more efficient episcopacy, we think there is an urgent necessity. The infirmities of age press heavily upon some of us, and diminish our ability to answer to the demands of the work for general episcopal visitation. The great and increasing extent of our territory should be considered. We should by all means have a Bishop, for obvious reasons, residing on the Pacific coast. And while we do not recommend a Bishop for every State or Conference, we are fully persuaded that the number of Bishops should be so increased as to enable them to be pastors of the people as well as chairmen of Conferences and pastors of the preachers. If we would carry out the invaluable plan of our itinerant general superintendency, we must have an addition of a number of vigorous, active, and pious men to your present college of Bishops. . . .

James O. Andrew, Robert Paine, John Early, Hubbard H. Kavanaugh.

¶ Atticus Haygood on "The New South," in "A Thanksgiving Sermon,"
1880.

(Taken from Haygood, *The New South* (1880), 8-12).

Fourthly, there is one great historic fact which should, in my sober judgment, above all things, excite everywhere in the South profound gratitude to Almighty God: I *mean the abolition of African slavery*.

336

If I speak only for myself, (and I am persuaded that I do not,) then be it so. But I, for one, thank God that there is no longer slavery in these United States! I am persuaded that I only say what the vast majority of our people feel and believe. I do not forget the better characteristics of African slavery as it existed among us for so long a time under the sanction of national law and under the protection of the Constitution of the United States; I do not forget that its worst features were often cruelly exaggerated, and that its best were unfairly minified; more than all, I do not forget that, in the providence of God, a work that is without a parallel in history was done on the Southern plantations - a work that was begun by such men as Bishop Capers, of South Carolina, Lovick Pierce and Bishop Andrew, of Georgia, and by men like-minded with them - a work whose expenses were met by the slaveholders themselves - a work that resulted in the Christianizing of a full half-million of the African people, who became communicants of our Churches, and of nearly the whole four or five millions who were brought largely under the all-pervasive and redeeming influence of our holy religion.

I have nothing to say at this time of the particular "war measure" that brought about their immediate and unconditioned enfranchisement, only that it is history, and that it is done for once and for all. I am not called on, in order to justify my position, to approve the political unwisdom of suddenly placing the ballot in the hands of nearly a million of unqualified men - only that, since it is done, this also is history that we of the South should accept, and that our fellow-citizens of the North should never disturb. But all these things, bad as they may have been and unfortunate as they may yet be, are only incidental to the one great historic fact, that *slavery exists no more*. For this fact I devoutly thank God this day! And on many accounts:

1. For the negroes themselves. While they have suffered and will suffer many things in their struggle for existence, I do nevertheless believe that in the long run it is best for them. How soon they shall realize the possibilities of their new relations depends largely, perhaps most, on themselves. Much depends on those who, under God, set them free. By every token this whole nation should undertake the problem of their education. That problem will have to be worked out on the basis of co-operation; that is, they must be helped to help themselves. To make their education an absolute gratuity will perpetuate many of the misconceptions and weaknesses of character which now embarrass and hinder their progress. Much also depends upon the Southern white people, their sympathy, their justice, their wise and helpful co-operation. This we should give them, not reluctantly, but gladly, for their good and for the safety of all, for their elevation and for the glory of God. How we may do this may be matter for discussion hereafter.

2. I am grateful that slavery no longer exists, because it is better for the white people of the South. It is better for our industries and our business, as proved by the crops that free labor makes. But by eminence it is better for our social and ethical development. We will now begin to take our right place among both the conservative and aggressive forces of the civilized and Christian world.

3. I am grateful because it is unspeakably better for our children and children's children. It is better for them in a thousand ways. I have not time for discussion in detail now. But this, if nothing else, proves the truth of my position: there are more white children at work in the South today than ever before. And this goes far to account for the six million bales of cotton. Our children are growing up to believe that idleness is vagabondage. One other thing I wish to say before leaving this point. We hear much about the disadvantages to our children of leaving them among several millions of freed-men. I recognize them, and feel them; but I would rather leave my children among several millions of free negroes than among several millions of negroes in slavery.

But leaving out of view at this time all discussion of the various benefits that may come through the enfranchisement of the negroes, I am thankful on the broad and unqualified ground, that there *is now no slavery in all our land.*

Does anyone say to me this day: "You have got new light; you have changed 'the opinions you entertained twenty years ago.'" I answer humbly, but gratefully, and without qualification: I have got new light. I do now believe many things that I did not believe twenty years ago. Moreover, if it please God to spare me in this world twenty years longer, I hope to have, on many difficult problems, more new light. I expect, if I see the dawn of the year 1900, to believe some things that I now reject and to reject some things that I now believe. And I will not be alone.

In conclusion, I ask you to indulge me in a few reflections that are, I believe, appropriate to this occasion.

And first of all, as a people, let us of the South frankly recognize some of our faults and lacks, and try to reform and improve. I know this is a hard task. And it is all the harder because we are the subjects of so much denunciation and misrepresentation by our critics of the Northern States, and of other countries. Much of this comes through sincere ignorance; much of it through the necessities of party politics; some of it, I fear, through sinful hatred; and much of it through habit. Many have so long thrown stones at us that it has become a habit to do so. The rather Pharisaic attitude that many public men at the North have assumed toward us has greatly embarrassed and arrested our efforts

to discover our faults and to amend them. But all this only furnishes a reason for beginning the sooner and trying the harder. What is really good - and there is much that is good - let us stand by, and make it better if we can.

There are some unpleasant things that ought to be said. They are on my conscience. Will you bear with me while I point out some of the weaker points in our social make-up - some of the more serious lacks in our development?

First, then, let us endeavor to overcome our intense provincialism. We are too well satisfied with ourselves. We think better of ourselves than the facts of our history and our present state of progress justify. Some of us are nearly of the opinion that the words "the South" is a synonym for universe. As a people we have not enough felt the heartbeat of the world outside of us. We have been largely shut off from that world. Slavery did this, and this suggests another reason for gratitude that it exists no more. On this point I will add only one word more. Had we been less provincial, less shut in by and with our own ideas, had we known the world better, we would have known ourselves better, and there would have been no war in 1861.

Secondly, there is a vast mass of illiteracy among us. There is white as well as black illiteracy. There are multiplied thousands who can neither read nor write. They must be taught.

Thirdly, let us recognize our want of a literature. We have not done much in this line of things. It is too obvious to dispute about, it is too painful to dwell upon.

Fourthly, let us wake up to our want of educational facilities. Our public school system is painfully inadequate. Our colleges and universities are unendowed, and they struggle against fearful odds in their effort to do their work. We are one hundred years behind the Eastern and Middle States. We are also behind many of the new States of the West.

Fifthly, consider how behindhand we are with our manufacturing interests. And remember that nature never did more to furnish a people with the conditions necessary to successful manufactures. Does any one say, we lack capital? I answer, No, my friend, it was always so. It was so when we had capital. I have thought of these things a great deal. I have been placed where I was obliged to think of them, and I have reached this conclusion with perfect confidence of its correctness: Our provincialism, our want of literature, our lack of educational facilities, and our manufactures, like our lack of population, is all explained by one fact and one word - slavery. But for slavery, Georgia would be as densely peopled as Rhode Island. Wherefore, among many other reasons, I say again, I thank God that

339

it is no more among us!

I mention, lastly, some traits of character we should cultivate.

First, the humble but all-prevailing virtues of industry and economy in business. There should be no non-producing classes among us - no wasting classes. The Northern people have more money than the Southern people, chiefly for the reason that they work more and save more.

Secondly, let us cultivate the sentiments and habits of political and social toleration. This is sorely needed among us. We need to feel that a man may vote against us and be our friend; we need to feel that we can be his friend although we vote against him.

Thirdly, let us cultivate respect for all law and authority as God's appointment. This is not a characteristic quality of our people. The educating influences of many generations have been unfavorable to the development of this sentiment as a mental habit, or, rather, as a mental characteristic. We must plant ourselves and bring up our children on the platform of St. Paul and St. Peter, as read and considered in the beginning of this discourse. Law, authority, we must reverence and obey as the ordinance of God.

Finally, let us cease from politics as a trust and a trade. Our duty of citizenship we must perform, but we should look no longer to political struggles as the means of deliverance from all our difficulties. If we succeed we would be disappointed. Political success may enrich a few place-hunters, who ride into office upon the tide of popular enthusiasm; but it will bring little reward to the masses of the people. There is no help for it; if we prosper, we must work for it. Our deliverance will come through millions of hard licks, and millions of acts of self-denial, through industry, economy, civil order, and the blessing of God upon obedience.

Secondly, let us look forward. Hitherto I have spoken before some of you of the South of the future. Again I say, Look forward! I do the heroic dead no injustice. But the only rational way in which we can emulate their virtues is to live for the country they died for. We are not called on to die for it, but to live for it; believe me, good friends, a much harder thing to do.

We should not forget what General Lee said to our General Gordon when it was all over: "We must go home and cultivate our virtues." Lee did that. He forthwith set himself to doing good. It is a good example. We are to do the work of today, looking forward and not backward. We have no divine call to stand eternal guard by the grave of dead issues. Here certainly we may say, "Let the dead bury their dead."

My friends, my neighbors, and my pupils, I declare to you today my hope is, that in twenty years from now, the words "the South" shall have only a geographical significance.

If any ask, "Why do you say such things here today?" I answer, Because I remember who are here, and I consider what they are to do and to be when we are gone hence.

I have spoken what I solemnly believe to be the truth. Moreover, the time has fully come when these truths should be spoken by somebody; and I try to do my part, persuaded that before many years there will happily be no longer any occasion or need for them to be spoken.

There is no reason why the South should be despondent. Let us cultivate industry and economy, observe law and order, practice virtue and justice, walk in truth and righteousness, and press on with strong hearts and good hopes. The true golden day of the South is yet to dawn. But the light is breaking, and presently the shadows will flee away. Its fullness of splendor I may never see; but my children will see it, and I wish them to get ready for it while they may.

There is nothing weaker or more foolish than repining over an irrevocable past, except it be despairing of a future to which God invites us. Good friends, this is not 1860, it is 1880. Let us press forward, following the pillar of cloud and of fire always. With health and peace, with friends and homes, with civil liberty and social order, with national prosperity and domestic comfort, with bountiful harvests - with all these blessings, and good hope of heaven through Jesus Christ our Lord, let us all lift up our voices in the glad psalm of praise and thanksgiving: "Oh praise the Lord, all ye nations: praise him, all ye people. For his merciful kindness is great toward as: and the truth of the Lord endureth forever. Praise ye the Lord."

14. WESTWARD WEST

No story of Methodism would be complete without reference to the famous letter by Wyandot William Walker which was printed in the Christian Advocate *of 1 March 1833. In fact no story of the Westward Movement of the nation would be complete without it. It was widely reprinted and raised a hurricane of excitement about either missions to the Indians or settlement in Oregon country, or both, depending on the interests of the reader. In 1831 three Nez Perce and one Flathead traveled to St. Louis to learn more of the white man's way of life, including his religion, about which they already had tantalizing hints. Walker met them, and many months later wrote the letter to his friend Gabriel P. Disoway, who sent it to the* Advocate. *The pious writer undoubtedly improved the story in the telling, romanticizing the Indians' yearning for the new religion.*

About the same time, Alfred Brunson was riding the Methodist circuits in the Middle West, which was then being settled. He gives an uncommonly detailed account of the squatter process as it encountered and organized systematic survey which had no hope of keeping up with the frontier. Methodist circuits and Annual Conferences were carved out in just such an informal first-come first-served basis. Brunson's two-volume autobiography compares favorably with Peter Cartwright's more famous work.

William H. Goode was probably the most widely influential pioneer Methodist preacher in the development of the church in the Great Plains. His work ranged from Kansas and Nebraska to Denver and back. His administrative ability (and durable constitution) repeatedly resulted in his appointment to the opening and organization of new circuits and districts.

Bishop O. C. Baker, his contemporary, was distressed to observe the disastrous effects of white expansion on the Indians, especially those who had already been uprooted from their Eastern homelands and resettled beyond the Mississippi River.

One of the most colorful characters in American history is William Wesley Van Orsdel, the famous "Brother Van" of Montana lore. During the 1870's and 1880's he was in the forefront of the tumultuous settlement of the Big Sky Country by successive waves of exploring, fur-trading, mining, and ranching pioneers. He became to Montana what Johnny Appleseed was for Ohio. One of his many friends was the noted cowboy artist, Charles M. Russell, who recorded the excitement of the quickly passing frontier in magnificent oil paintings and drawings. Through it all Brother Van saw to the planting of Methodism wherever people might be found.

¶ The Oregon Letter, 1833.

(Taken from *The Christian Advocate*, 1 Mar. 1833).

Upper Sandusky, Jan. 19, 1833.

Dear Friend: - Your last letter, dated Nov. 12, came duly to hand. The business part is answered in another communication which is inclosed.

I deeply regret that I have had no opportunity of answering your very friendly letter in a manner that would be satisfactory to myself; neither can I now, owing to a want of time and a retired place, where I can write undisturbed.

I will here relate an anecdote, if I may so call it. Immediately after we landed in St. Louis, on our way to the west, I proceeded to Gen. Clarke's, superintendent of Indian affairs, to present our letters of introduction from the secretary of war, and to receive the same from him to the different Indian agents in the upper country. While in his office and transacting business with him, he informed me that three chiefs from the Flat-Head nation were in his house, and were quite sick, and that one (the fourth) had died a few days ago. They were from the west of the Rocky Mountains. Curiosity prompted me to step into the adjoining room to see them, having never seen any, but often heard of them. I was struck with their appearance. They differ in appearance from any tribe of Indians I have ever seen: small in size, delicately formed, small limbs, and the most exact symmetry throughout, except the head. I had always supposed from their being called "Flat-Heads," that the head was actually flat on the top; but this is not the case. The head is flattened thus:

From the point of the nose to the apex of the head, there is a perfect straight line, the protuberance of the forehead is flattened or levelled. You may form some idea of the shape of their heads from the rough sketch I have made with the pen, though I confess I have drawn most too long a proboscis for a flat-head. This is produced by a pressure upon the cranium while in infancy. The distance they had travelled on foot was nearly three thousand miles to see Gen. Clarke, their great father, as they called him, he being the first American officer they ever became acquainted with, and having much confidence in him, they had come to consult him as they said, upon very important matters. Gen. C. related to me the object of their mission, and, my dear friend, it is impossible for me to describe to you my feelings while listening to his narrative. I will here relate it as briefly as I well can. It appeared that some white man had penetrated into their country, and happened to be a spectator at one of their religious ceremonies, which they scrupulously perform at stated periods. He informed them that their mode of worshipping the supreme Being was radically wrong, and instead

343

of being acceptable and pleasing, it was displeasing to him; he also informed them that the white people away toward the rising of the sun had been put in possession of the true mode of worshipping the great Spirit. They had a book containing directions how to conduct themselves in order to enjoy his favor and hold converse with him; and with this guide, no one need go astray, but every one that would follow the directions laid down there, could enjoy, in this life, his favor, and after death would be received into the country where the great Spirit resides, and live for ever with him.

Upon receiving this information, they called a national council to take this subject into consideration. Some said, if this be true, it is certainly high time we were put in possession of this mode, and if our mode of worshipping be wrong and displeasing to the great Spirit, it is time we had laid it aside, we must know something more about this, it is a matter that cannot be put off, the sooner we know it the better. They accordingly deputed four of their chiefs to proceed to St. Louis to see their great father, Gen. Clarke, to inquire of him, having no doubt but he would tell them the whole truth about it.

They arrived at St. Louis and presented themselves to Gen. C. The latter was somewhat puzzled being sensible of the responsibility [*sic*] that rested on him; he however proceded by informing them that what they had been told by the white man in their own country, was true. Then went into a succinct history of man, from his creation down to the advent of the Saviour; explained to them all the moral precepts contained in the Bible, expounded to them the decalogue. Informed them of the advent of the Saviour, his life, precepts, his death, resurrection, ascension, and the relation he now stands to man as a mediator – that he will judge the world &c.

Poor fellows, they were not all permitted to return home to their people with the intelligence. Two died in St. Louis, and the remaining two, though somewhat indisposed, set out for their native land. Whether they reached home or not, is not known. The change of climate and diet operated very severely upon their health. Their diet when at home is chiefly vegetables and fish.

If they died on their way home, peace be to their manes! They died inquirers after the truth. I was informed that the Flat-Heads, as a nation, have the fewest vices of any tribe of Indians on the continent of America.

I had just concluded I would lay this rough and uncouth scroll aside and revise it before I would send it, but if I lay aside you will never receive it; so I will send it to you just as it is, "with all its imperfections," hoping that you may be able to decipher it. You are at liberty to make what use you please of it.
Yours in haste, Wm. Walker.

¶ Alfred Brunson in Pioneer Country, 1835.

(Taken from Brunson, *A Western Pioneer* (1872), II, 33-34).

At Elkhorn Grove we stopped for breakfast, before taking a twelve-mile prairie, at what we afterwards found to be a back-slidden deacon's. We did not think it necessary to announce our profession for so short a stay and from not seeing any thing like religion about the premises. Being curious to know how the settlers managed to secure their lands when they came into market, all being now "squatters," we asked many questions.

The country had been surveyed into townships, but not into sections. The settlers in this grove had sectionized the township to ascertain the location of the school lands, and also the metes and bounds of their respective claims. The school land, or 16th section, lay entirely within the grove. The settlers had enacted by-laws to govern the settlement. No one was allowed to cut even an ox-gad off the school land, and no one settler was allowed to claim over forty acres of the timber in the grove, but might claim as much prairie outside as he pleased, so that he did not encroach upon older claims already marked out.

"But suppose a man moves into the settlement who will not be governed by your laws?"

"Why, first, we'll not help him to raise a house; secondly, if he comes into our houses at meal time we'll not ask him to eat; and third, if he don't take the hint and leave, we'll tell him to go, and help him to do so."

"But suppose when the land comes into market a man should bid upon one of your claims; how are you going to prevent him?"

"Why, it is agreed by all the settlers in the whole country to have a man present at the sale from each settlement, with our names and the number of our claims, and when the tract is announced for sale he will declare it to be a claim and the claimant will bid the government price - $1.25 - and if any man bids against him he is to be knocked down and dragged out of the house."

"But if he still persists and buys your claim, what will you do?"

"Why, I'll kill him; and, by agreement of the settlers, I am to be protected, and if tried, no settler dare, if on the jury, find a verdict against me."

We found that this was the state of feeling generally in the country among what were called "squatters" on government land, and

345

that a man's life was in danger if he attempted to rob a settler of his hard-earned improvements. The reason for this state of feeling and these measures for self-defense was, that Government had issued what were called "floats," or floating land warrants; that is, a right to enter or bid off at a sale, such lands as the holder of one might select, to the amount called for; and land speculators - called "land sharks" or "land pirates" - had, in many instances, entered the improved farms of the squatter before he was able to do so himself; or would bid off the land, when on sale, at a price above the capacity of the squatter, though below the real value of the improvements. But the pre-emption laws subsequently passed by Congress saved the country from this dangerous state of things, and secured to the settler his rights of property in the lands he improved.

¶   Bishop Baker on Indian Removal.

(Taken from Don W. Holter, *Fire on the Prairie* (1969), 14,16).

[29 Jan. 1857]

My Dear M.:

A strange providence has attended the red man. The Indians residing in the older states were assured by our government, that if they would remove to certain reservations, beyond the Mississippi, they should find permanent homes, and the faith of the Government was solemnly pledged, in their several treaties, to secure to them quiet and peaceable possession, and undisturbed enjoyment of the same, against the claims and assaults of all others. On such pledges, many tribes removed to the West some twenty-five years ago. Such removals greatly interrupted the missionary operations of the different churches, who had established missions among them, and were attended with many unhappy results to the Indians. They had not to be sure, many valuable improvements to leave behind, but there were the graves of their fathers, and cherished memories connected with their former homes. The chiefs generally used their influence to carry out the treaty stipulations with the government, yet many of the people revolted, and were forcibly removed to their assigned reservations. These removals were attended with many unhappy results to the Indians. They were not far removed from the snares of the white man. Their heavy annuities enticed many un-principled men to follow them, and by gaudy, worthless wares, and poisonous liquors, to secure to themselves the government appropria-tions. Some devoted missionaries followed their people, and carried out the plan they had previously adopted for the moral culture of the Indians, and were the means of rendering them much aid. But many of the tribes went alone to their new homes and the moral influences which were thrown around them in their former

346

residences, were soon destroyed. The white man is still building his cabin around him, and where can the red man go? There are no open, unappropriated fields suited to his wants and his habits. There is only one alternative for him, either to adopt the habits of civilized life, or to lie down in the grave.

¶   Opening the Great Plains.

(Taken from William H. Goode, *Outposts of Zion* (1863), 240-41, 312-13).

Soon after the passage of the organizing act [Kansas-Nebraska, October, 1854] three of our Bishops - two of whom are still living, and one departed - met in the city of Baltimore. Attention was turned to the new field providentially presented. The unanimous sentiment was that an early occupancy was important. Little being known, however, as to the actual state and wants of the country, it was thought best, in the first place, to send one who should make a tour of exploration, ascertain its condition, make temporary arrangements, if necessary, for immediate supply to the settlers already there, return and report in time to send out a sufficient body of regularly-appointed preachers from the ensuing session of the several Annual Conferences. At the same interview a selection was made of the man who should conduct the exploration.

Under date of the 15th of May, 1854, I was notified by letter from one of the Bishops, then at Brooklyn, New York, of their action and of my contemplated appointment, with directions to adjust my affairs accordingly. The formal appointment bears date June 3d, and is as follows:

Rev. W. H. Goode:

Dear Brother, - It is understood that emigration is tending largely to Nebraska (a name then embracing both Territories.) It seems probable that the Church ought soon to send some devoted missionaries to that country. But there is not such a knowledge of details respecting the topography and population of these regions as to enable the Church authorities to act understandingly in the premises. You are therefore appointed to visit and explore the country as thoroughly as practicable, for the purpose of collecting information on these points. In performing this work you will be governed by your own judgment, and make full reports in writing of your labor and its results, so that it may be known how many ministers - if any - should be sent, and at what particular points they should be located.

Yours truly,   E. R. Ames,
                Bishop Methodist Episcopal Church.

A letter of instructions also was received, written after consultation with three others of the Episcopal Board, in which the duties required were stated at greater length.

The announcement of my appointment to this new field found me in the position of pastor to the good people of our Church in the quiet city of Richmond, Indiana.

*   *   *

Entered upon our new home, the first thoughts were necessarily directed to arrangements for "a living" through the Winter. High as prices were, it was deemed prudent to lay in, at once, full supplies for the season, that, while absent from home, I might be free from apprehensions of domestic want. This was done at costly rates; and, before I had gone out upon my work, a sufficiency was provided and mainly stored upon the premises. Indian claimants in several departments had to be "bought out" to insure quiet possession, besides the rent to our Wyandott landlord. Other domestic and personal matters were adjusted; dilapidations repaired, unseemly accumulations removed, Indian arrangements overhauled and remodeled more in accordance with Anglo-Saxon ideas of propriety, and a general change effected in the face of things. Our site was pleasant, and the prospect for a temporary home at least *endurable*. In these labors I necessarily bore a large part, and by exposure on a cold day, in a particular department of unaccustomed labor, my fingers were frozen on both hands, thereby laying the foundation of much future suffering up to this time, and probably to the close of life, should my life of exposure continue.

In the course of about three weeks all was arranged, and I set out upon my regular work. No plan for regular quarterly meetings had been arranged, the condition of things not admitting of such plan. Instead of this, the country was to be traveled over at large, new points sought out and occupied, and the different charges visited and labored with as necessity might require and ability allow. My plan was, as Bishop Roberts once said of his habits, "regularly irregular."

All my Winter traveling was performed on horseback. On my first trip I had a young friend as a companion. My first meeting was held upon the Wakarusa, Sabbath, November 26th. Here I found brother Griffing, who had preceded me, and was actively engaged in his work.

Leaving this place, I sought out the residence of the preacher appointed to the Maries Des Cygnes mission. He had not yet visited his charge. I proposed to accompany him on the succeeding day, which he acceded to. Early in the morning we set off for his field of labor, and by noon we found ourselves within its bounds. The next

thing was to find a temporary foothold as a starting-point for our work. Providence directed our way. Stopping at a cabin on the Santa Fe road, we found a kind and hospitable family, consisting of the man, his wife, and several small children, lately moved in. We were made welcome. After the customary inquiries as to former residence, history, etc., we approached the subject of their religious state. Their hearts seemed moved; they told their tale, and wept as they told it. Once they had been members of the Methodist Episcopal Church, and trying to serve the Lord; changes had come over them, followed by repeated removals; Church membership had been forfeited by neglect, and now for years they had been out upon the wide world destitute of religious restraints, supports, and comforts. This, I may add, was in substance the experience that I subsequently heard from the lips of many. We stated to them our character and objects, and it was immediately arranged that the few neighbors should be collected and we should have religious service that evening. The cabin was small, and a considerable space was occupied by a store of groceries and provisions, laid in for the trade, but it was supposed to be sufficient to hold the few settlers by making close quarters.

¶   A Letter from Charlie Russell to Brother Van.

(Taken from Edward L. Mills, *Plains, Peaks and Pioneers* (1947), following p. 128).

[20 Mar. 1918]

Dear Brother Van,

I received an invitation to your birthday party from Reverend Bunch, and am more than sorry that I cant be their but Im on the jury. I think it was about this time of year thirty sevon years ago that we first met at Babcocks ranch in Pig eye bason on the upper Judith. I was living at that time with a hunter and trapper Jake Hoover who you will remember. He and I had come down from the south fork with three pack horses loaded with deer and elk meet which he sold to the ranchers, and we had stopped for the night with old Bab, a man as rough as the mountains he loved but who was all hart from his belt up, and friends an strangers were welcom to shove their feet under his table. This all welcom way of his made the camp a hangout for many homeless mountain and prairie men and his log walls and dirt roof semed like a palice to those who lived mostly under the sky.
The eavning you came there was a mixture of bull whackers, hunters and prospectors who welcomed you with[?] hand shaks and rough but friendly greetings.
I was the only stranger to you, so after Bab interduced Kid Russell

349

he took me to one side and whispered,
Boy, says he, I dont savy maney sam singers,
but Brother Van deels square.
And when we all sat down to our elk meet, beens, coffee and dryed
apples under the rays of a bacon grease light, these men who knew
little of law and one among them I knew wore notches on his gun,
men who had not prayed since they nelt at their mothers knee, bowed
there heads while you, Brother Van, gave thanks; and when you
finished some one said Amen. I am not shure, but I think it was a
man who I heard later was or had been a rode agent.
I was sixteen years old then, Brother Van, but have never
forgotten your stay at Old Babs with men whos talk was generly
emphasized with fancy profanity. But while you were with us, altho
they had to talk slow and carful, there was never a slip. The out
law at Babs was a sinner, an non of us thair were Saints; but our
harts were clean, at least while you gave thanks when the hold up'
said Amen.
You brought to the minds of these hardend homeles men the faces of
there Mothers and few can be bad while she is near.
I have met you many times sinc that, Brother Van, sometimes in
lonely places, but you never were lonsun or alone, for a man with
seared hands and feet stood beside you and near him there is no hate,
so all you met loved you.
Be good and youl be happy is an old saying which many conterdict
and say that goodness is a rough trail over dangerous passes with
wind falls and swift deep rivers to cross. I have never ridden it
verry far myself, but judging from the looks of you its a sinch bet
that with a hoss called faith under you its a smooth flower grone
trail with easy fords where birds sing and cold clear streams dance
in the sun light all the way to the pass that crosses the big devide.
Brother Van, you have ridden that trail a long time and I hope you
still ride to maney birth days on this side of the big range.

             with best wishes from my best half of me your Friend C M Russell

¶   The Trail Blazer.

   (Taken from eulogy quote by Roberta B. West, *Methodist History*,
   V (Apr. 1967), 32-33).

     How few of us today that pay tribute to the fallen leader really
know or comprehend what this pioneer met and overcame. If we could
just see Fort Benton as he saw it that July of 47 years ago, with its
medley of freighters, prospectors, fur traders, Indians, breeds,
gamblers, and outcasts, without law or order except as sustained by
the six-shooter and the Winchester. Not a promising population to
build into the kingdom of God.

There were no trails there to follow. He must make them.
No official board to greet and welcome the boy from Gettysburg. Yet
out of these mule skinners, bullwhackers, prospectors, traders,
gamblers, and outcasts, and the widely scattered homes of this great
state, with a faith that overlooked obstacles higher than the Rocky
Mountains, he sang, prayed, and shouted his way to victory and built
the kingdom of heaven in this land of the Shining Mountains. There
were no trails that led to the hearts of this mass, no order of
service that could ever fit this medley of humanity, but he made a
way into the lives and affections of this people, and left trails
for others to follow.

Sometimes we hear a preacher tell of hardships, how he had gone
to a schoolhouse and built his own fire, swept out the room after the
last dance, furnished the lights, and had a half dozen to service.
But this man had no schoolhouses. The freighters' or cowboys' camp,
the cabin or the ranch home, the Indian tepee, the barroom, or the
street, made him a pulpit. And whatever might be the congregations
he always gave them his best in words and song.

He saw the watering places of the buffalo and the antelope
become the campground of the cowboy and the sheepherder. These
oftentimes gave way to the ranches and towns. He saw wide places
in the trails become cities. He saw the buffalo and the antelope
give way to the cattle and sheep; these in turn gave way to the
farmer. He saw the great prairies turned into golden wheat fields.
And to meet these changes there were no trails, but he made them
and showed us how to follow them.

A two-days' drive in a buggy over unmarked prairies, with half
a dozen out to hear, was victory if some backslider came home to
God. What a joy it was for him to tell of his Lord.

He found no trails when he came, but he left Montana covered
with them, not only literally, but also spiritual ones into the
lives and hearts of men, women and children all over this great
state. How he loved the children! I think that when those children
from the school sang at the grave he asked those about him in heaven
to be quiet so he could hear their voices.

15. BLACK METHODISM

*After the establishment of the three African Methodist groups in
the early nineteenth century the development of the church among
black people went slowly in two directions: continuation within the
Methodist Episcopal Church, north and south, and separation in
racially defined denominations. Division in 1844 did not significantly change this situation, but the Civil War did. Both the rapid
expansion of the older groups and the establishment of a new denomination for Southern Negro Methodists quickly followed cessation of
hostilities. New ways of dealing with race relations involved the
churches.*

*The last theme is illustrated by the letters of James Lynch and
Hiram Revels, as well as by the career of Gilbert Haven. Lynch was
a missionary of the A.M.E. Church to the recently freed black people
of the South. He worked with Bishop Daniel Payne to reestablish the
church and organize the South Carolina Conference. In 1867 he moved
from the African church to the M. E. Church in the belief he could
thereby work more effectively for his race, especially in Mississippi.
He became active in Republican politics and the Freedmen's Bureau.
Revels was another A.M.E. minister who entered the political arena
and also changed to the M. E. Church. He served a year as U.S.
senator from Mississippi, but retained his ministerial relation throughout. Revels' document rose in protest against the move in the
General Conference of 1876 to establish racially separate conferences.
Gilbert Haven was editor of Zion's Herald when he submitted his
resolutions to the General Conference of 1868, was elected bishop four
years later. His animosity against President Johnson rose from his
conviction that Lincoln's successor was destroying the rights black
people had won in the Civil War.*

*The Colored Methodist Episcopal Church (later renamed Christian
Methodist Episcopal) had to defend itself against charges that it
was a puppet of the M. E. Church, South. The M. E. Church decried the
racial segregation involved (ignoring its own form of the same thing).
The older African churches disdained this new group. Isaac Lane and
others pointed out that responsible churchmanship and racial equity
could be achieved by negotiation as well as by conflict.*

*One of the most enduring and unique contributions of Negro
Christianity has been its hymnody. William Milburn approached the
subject via his devotion to camp meeting revivalism. John Jenifer
emphasized denominational heritage in the hymns by B. T. Tanner and
L. J. Coppin, both episcopal leaders of the A. M. E. Church.*

*Self-awareness as a denomination and as expressions of black
self-sufficiency are seen in the passages taken from the works of
Henry McNeal Turner and John Jenifer on ecclesiastical polity.
Turner's book is an extensive commentary on the Discipline.*

352

¶   Black Methodism After the Civil War in Mississippi.

(Taken from *Methodist History*, XI (July, 1973), 9-12),ed. William Gravely).

Jackson Miss
Dec. 3 1868

Bishop M. Simpson D. D.
Rev'd Sir:

Learning by the Episcopal plan 1868-1869 that you will preside at Miss⌊issippi⌉ Conf⌈erence⌉ Canton Jan 28th I beg leave to respectfully and confidingly submit the following for your wise consideration.

Extension of Our Work

It is thought by some that to cultivate well what we have should be the primary object; to increase our church territory, secondary. I do not know but what this line of policy might have been justly inferred from the remarks of Bishop⌊Edward R.⌉ Ames at our last Conference. I have inclined to the opposite view. To increase our church territory is at this moment of primary importance and in comparison with this, the thorough cultivation of what we have is secondary. Because (1) The entire colored population of this state are at this time more impressible than ever they will be in the future (2) Influences are at work to secure them against the Methodist Episcopal Church: one of these is the Methodist Episcopal Church South which holds a colored Conference at Hazelhurst about the date of this letter (perhaps later) They elect to orders and ordain almost any colored man who will follow them: this they do at the white Conferences, if more convenient than waiting for the meeting of the colored. Their ministers are as unscrupulous as are the legates of the Pope, they tell the colored people that the M. E. Church has become corrupt, that it seeks them to make them subjects of taxation in the future to support church interests.

I regret to say that they select some of the vilest democrat negroes in the state as their instruments. The African M. E. Church is equally bitter toward us: it is in a singular position; professing to be radical in politics and opposed to the M. E. Church South, it at the same time endorses every slander breathed against the M. E. Church or its functionaries in the Episcopal and editorial chairs, by the M. E. Church South. The latest of which was the forcible vented by the African M. E. Bishop who visited here a few weeks since to the effect that one of the M. E. Bishops did not want the colored people to live in the United States. The M. E. Church South is moved alone by political considerations, never was a church more partisan; professive to ignore politics. I can prove that it has refused to fellowship some of the best white men in the

state - men of spotless Christian characters and also to renew licenses of local preachers because they were Radical in politics. We must possess the ground or give it up to this politico-ecclesiastical absurdity that is the bellows, blowing into life the dying fires of hostility to the Government. For the African M. E. Church I have a high regard. I honor its history in the past, I affectionately cling to many of the good and true men within its bosom; but reiterating what I have often expressed, it is not in a line with events, its arms are too feeble to be thrown around this great Methodist community of the South.

Everywhere in this state the people are ready to come to us - now is the time to plant our Church in every county of the state and thus, secure the people forever against the influence of a Church that has got the consumption but yet possesses a sufficient lease of life to hinder progress and teach sectionalism. The great argument of the A. M. E. Church as against the M. E. Church has been that colored men organized it, my face knocks this argument dead. Beleiving [sic] then in the importance of extension I am exceedingly anxious that new charges with preachers shall be recognized at our next Conference, and that appointments of bretheren [sic] to counties not yet occupied by us be made, provided men of self sacrificing zeal can be found. I would respectfully recommend that appropriations vary in ammount [sic] according to the resources of the charges to which the preachers are sent. The old charges do not need the inspiration of missionary appropriations to keep them in working order, they have learned to love the Old Mother Church because it is the church of Christ, yet each one of them will want a little something to aid in supporting the preachers. It is our policy to impress the people with the idea of making the churches self supporting as rapidly as possible. I beg further to suggest that in cases where appropriations for old charges are reduced that it not appear that it was done on the recommendation of the Presiding Elders; possibly no such recommendations may be made. Our people are quite ignorant and require much tenderness as well as decision in dealing with them.

As the great cry is continually kept up by the rebel papers that "All the Northern preachers or politicians want is money" it would be a great calamity to throw any part of the support of the Presiding Elders on the people; for whenever amid fierce opposition they attempted to establish a church mercenary considerations would be charged; for let it be remembered that the M. E. South preacher and the demmocrat [sic] politician with intelligence and skill contest every inch of ground with us. The Presiding Elder can do much to raise the salary of the preacher in charge at Quarterly meetings.

Improvement

I am satisfied that you will be pleased and astonished at the

354

great improvement of the bretheren [*sic*] since you last met them.

Colored Citizens Monthly

I have started on my own "hook" a paper with the above title, please find a copy inclosed. I have started it for several reasons (1) I desire to educate the people as to the design, and benefits to be derived from the organization of the M. E. Church, their duties thereto and its importance as an instrumentality for the salvation of souls (2) To educate the black man in the duties of citizenship to teach him to regard his manhood and to develop "back-bone," as well as to inculcate temperance and virtue (3) As the native capacity of the colored men is so poorly thought of I desire to make this paper as far as possible a demonstration of its strength. (4) Designing politicians as unscrupulous as Satan, are preying like wolves upon the Freedmen and they should be unmasked when they imperil their interests.

The paper will advocate the claims of the M. E. Church, the elevation of the colored race and Equal political rights. Proposition has been made to me to consolidate it with our Church paper to be published at Atlanta. I fail to see that I would be doing increased service to my race thereby; but yet if advised so to do by my superiors in the church I will yield with good grace. Yet as I take to editing a paper by almost natural inclination must I think that God may bless my effort in this direction.

Schools

The support of public schools by this state will not be reliable for several years, our meeting houses are generally used by Freedmen's Bureau schools under the auspices of teachers and societies who have no sympathy with Methodism, if the Freedmen's Aid Society of our Church will look after us a little we can have much influence in directing the educational work of this State, which in truth is not prospering in accordance with the large appropriations made.

I am, Bishop, Most Respectfully Yours

James Lynch

¶ Attack on President Johnson by Gilbert Haven, General Conference 1868

(Taken from General Conference Journal, 152).

Whereas, The most solemn act to which the government of the United States, in its judicial capacity, has been called in all its history is near its consummation; and

355

Whereas, The failure of the impeachment of the President will subject the greatest of our generals, and all under his authority, to the power of an infuriated Executive, who has opposed every law that has been made to heal the nation on the only true and permanent basis of equal rights to loyal men; and

Whereas, His release will also reanimate the dying embers of rebellion throughout all the South, sacrifice the lives of many of our fellow-citizens, and thus cast all that region into terror, distress, and danger; therefore,

Resolved, That the General Conference . . . solemnly and earnestly invokes upon the Senate of the United States the blessing of Almighty God, that they may be guided in the great responsibility now devolving upon them, that tyrannical usurpations may be rebuked, the authority of the law may be maintained against the most dangerous hostility of an Executive who avows his irresponsibility to its obligation, and that the peace and safety of our fellow-citizens in all the South may be secured.

¶   Hiram Revels on Segregation.

(Taken from *Methodist History*, VIII (Apr. 1970), 16-20, letters in *Southwestern Advocate* (New Orleans), 4 May 1876).

MR. EDITOR - When I wrote the note at Grenada, which has subsequently published in the columns of your valuable paper, I promised a more lengthy communication on the same and kindred subjects. When the Methodist Episcopal Church, - our church - during and after the war, turned her attention to the condition of the unavoidably poor, and ignorant colored people of the South, I greatly rejoiced, and the wisdom of our church in the adoption of that course, may be seen in the fact that she could have done nothing in the line of Christian duty that would have been more productive of great good in the highest sense of the word. As the result of the late war, about four millions of human beings, emerged from slavery in poverty and ignorance, and knowing as our church did, that they never could be enlightened, and intelligent, and valuable, and useful citizens, without pecuniary aid - literary, moral and religious instruction; she chose the Southern States as a part of the field of her future operations, and sent some of her ablest ministers to her new work, by whom that work has been ably and successfully prosecuted. As the result of this, there are in Mississippi and other Southern States hundreds of regularly organized and prosperous churches, in which thousands of colored people and their children statedly meet, worship God, and receive enlightening instruction from preachers, many of whom are advancing in mental culture, and the acquisition of useful knowledge. Through the instrumentality of our church, every year, shows the colored peoples' advancing to some extent, in the way of social, intellectual, moral and religious elevation, and also, in a more intelligent manner of worship. If the good that has been accomplished

by our church, not merely in organizing churches, for others would
have done that, but especially in instructing and enlightening the
poor, ignorant colored people of the South, by sending among them
in the onset, men of learning and talent to preach the Gospel, and
subsequently aiding every year, in instructing in schools of learning, men of their own race and clime to act as preachers and teachers,
could be seen by the members and friends of our church beyond the
limits of the Southern States, they would at once see that they have
not labored and contributed in vain - that but for the efforts of
the Methodist Episcopal Church, in their favor, thousands of colored
people, who in consequence of those efforts, are now being greatly
elevated, would still be asleep in ignorance and darkness. The
colored people of the South are free American citizens, who under the
organic and statutory laws of our country, enjoy all rights, including
the electoral franchise, of free American citizens. And all know
that unless they are instructed, and advanced in intelligence, the
day will come when the ballot will be a dangerous power in their hands,
just as it would be in the hands of ignorant people of any other
race, and in view of this fact, should not the Methodist Episcopal
Church be commended by all for what she has done in the way of
instructing and informing the colored people through her freedman's
aid and missionary societies? The results of her labors in these
respects may be seen in the large number of comparatively intelligent
colored ministers, who were aided by her when receiving instruction,
in the establishment of high schools of learning, in which tuition
is free to all, and from which some of the most competent and
successful school teachers as well as preachers have come. In this
connection I would call special attention to our flourishing Shaw
University of this State. The influence of the Methodist Episcopal
Church with the colored people of Mississippi is greater than is
that of any other branch of the Methodist Church. Since conference
I could have organized a dozen new churches in my district, but I
have not as yet done much in that way, for the reason that I have
not suitable preachers enough to supply such work.

If it be asked why the Mother Church has so large an influence
with the colored people, the answer is, that when she came among
them to do good - she showed no pride and offishness toward them
on account of their color and previous condition of servitude, but
treated them kindly and affectionately, taking them by hand and
conducting them into the same fold or church with themselves. The
fact of our church making my people a part of herself, instead of
organizing so many of them as would unite with her into churches
and conferences, and then leaving them to themselves to organize
and conduct churches and conferences, when they themselves were
ignorant of the true principles of church government, and management, has lead them fully to believe, that she has for them the
most kindly and friendly christian feeling. The wisdom of our
church in establishing mixed churches and conferences in the Southern States is seen in the fact, that it has had the happy effect of

leading the colored people to abandon the belief that because they are of a colored enslaved race, they are so degraded, it would be vain for them to try by any means to become the equals of their more favored white neighbors in intelligence, pure morals and the adorning virtues of life. They have also been benefitted by coming in contact with their more learned and intelligent white brethren in the transaction of church business, and in divine worship. In view of these indisputable facts, the important question is, will the M. E. Church recede one step from the high christian ground which she took in the commencement of her Southern work, and which has given her such a powerful influence with the colored Southern people, and enable her to be a source of so many blessings to them. As our church has been blamed for making her colored members a part of herself, or, for making no distinctions on account of race or color, in organizing churches and conferences on Southern soil, would not an action of the general conference, dividing the conference and churches on the color line be a virtual acknowledgement that our church has greatly erred, that those who have censured her for her course, were in the right and she in the wrong? Since conference I have visited nine or ten counties in this State, and conversed with quite a number of my people relative to the separation in question, and they declare to me that their earnest hope and prayer is, that the dear mother M. E. Church which has done so much for them in ways already named, will not now abandon that recognition of them which has so much endeared her to them, and led them to hurl from their minds the degrading recollections of slavery, and prompted them to labor for their own and their childrens elevation as otherwise they would not have done. The election of a colored Bishop, is a small matter with them compared with the question of division on the color line. Seeing them as I do, that the separation in question will retard the great work which our church is accomplishing among the poor needy colored Southern people, I am among those who will work and pray against the same. Our white brethren who are now laboring in the South, will not be harmed by continuing in the same relation to their colored brethren that now exists between them. But the sundering of that relation would afford the opponents of our church an opportunity of charging them and the M. E. Church generally with having been insincere toward the colored people *abinitio*. I know that it is said by some, that the colored people people's, want of intelligence and refinement in worship, is so clearly seen and felt, that their intelligent white brethren cannot pleasantly and profitably worship with them, and in reply I would say, that this circumstance only affords intelligent christians an opportunity to do good by going among them and so instructing them by example and otherwise, that they shall abandon what is on christian grounds, objectionable in their manner of worship. There are colored churches in Mississippi where you will find as the result of intelligent instruction and leadership, the same order and decorum in worship that you will find in any white church. In this connection I would say that if preachers of learning and intelligence would point out to

their colored hearers their notions and habits which are not essential
to divine worship, but are the results of ignorance, and exhort them
to abandon the same, they would as a general thing heed their advice.
In most of the colored churches the majority of the members are
opposed to what is objectionable in worship, but they can do nothing
to remedy this state of things, while the Presiding Elders and Pastors
are silent on the subject. In conclusion I would say that I
conscientiously believe that the Head of the church lead the M.W.
Church to enter upon her Southern work, and that with his approval
she cannot abandon it. Then my humble opinion is, that the safe
and wise course for our church to pursue, as regards her Southern
work, is to adhere to the plan on which she commenced that work,
and on which she has succeeded in doing great good. "Let will
enough alone."
Holly Springs, Miss., April 17th, 1786.

¶ How and By Whom the Colored Methodist Episcopal Church in
America was Organized, 1873.

(Taken from <u>Autobiography of Isaac Lane</u> (1916), 23-25).

To the Members of the Colored Methodist Episcopal Church
in America:

We esteem it our duty and privilege most earnestly to recommend
to you, as members of our Church, our form of discipline, which has
been founded on the line of a long series of years, as also on the
observations and remarks we have made on ancient and modern Churches.

We wish to see this little publication in the house of every
Methodist, and the more so as it contains the Articles of Religion
maintained more or less, in part or in whole, by every reformed
Church in the world.

Far from wishing you to be ignorant of any of our doctrines
or part of our discipline, we desire you to read, mark, learn, and
inwardly digest the whole. You ought, next to the Word of God, to
procure the articles and canons of the Church to which you belong.

We deem it proper in this place to give you a brief account of
the organization of our Connection:

From the introduction of Methodism on this continent we have ever
constituted a part of the great Methodist family, first as members
of the Methodist Episcopal Church in America and also after the
change took place by which we were known as the Methodist Episcopal
Church in the United States; and when the division took place, in
1844, which we regard as a legal and constitutional division of the
Church, we formed a part of that division called the Methodist

Episcopal Church, South, which relation we have continued to sustain until the organization of our Church took place at the General Conference held at Jackson, Tenn., which began its session December 15, 1870, which day was spent in prayer and supplication to the Almighty, that his blessings might rest upon us; and on the following day the regular business of the session began, Bishop Robert Paine, D.D., of the Methodist Episcopal Church, South, in the chair.

The circumstances which led to our separate and distinct organizations were as follows:

When the General Conference of the Methodist Episcopal Church, South, met in New Orleans in April, 1866, the Conference found that by revolution and the fortunes of war a change had taken place in our political and social relations which made it necessary that a change should also be made in the ecclesiastical relations, and provision was made for our organization into separate congregations, districts, and Annual Conferences, if we desired it, and that two or more Annual Conferences should be formed, if it was our wish and met the approbation of the bishops of the Methodist Episcopal Church, South; we should have a General Conference organization like that of the General Conference of the Methodist Episcopal Church, South, as deacons and elders; and should a General Conference be organized and suitable men be elected to the office of bishop, that the bishops of the Methodist Episcopal Church, South, would ordain and set them apart as chief pastors among us.

At the General Conference of the Methodist Episcopal Church, South, at Memphis, Tenn. in May, 1870, it was found that five Annual Conferences had been f ormed among us and that an almost universal desire had been expressed on our part that we might be organized into a separate and distinct Church, which was acquiesced in by the bishops of the Methodist Episcopal Church, South, and recommended to said Conference in their address. Whereupon, by our request, the bishops of the Methodist Episcopal Church, South, together with Rev. A. L. P. Green, Samuel Watson, D.D., Edmund W. Sehon, Thomas Whitehead, D.D., R. J. Morgan, D.D., and Thomas Taylor, D.D., were appointed by said Conference to aid in organizing our General Conference at the time and place above specified; and at the succeeding sessions of our Annual Conferences delegates were elected to attend our General Conference, in accordance with the Discipline of the Methodist Episcopal Church, South.

It was further determined by the acts of the General Conference of the Methodist Episcopal Church, South, in 1866 that, should the time arrive when we should be formed into a separate and distinct organization, all property which was intended for the use and benefit of people of color held by trustees of the Methodist Episcopal Church should be transferred to trustees appointed by us, to be held forever

for our use and benefit.

It will be seen from the facts in the case that our record is clear and that we have descended regularly from the very fathers of Methodism and that our organization is both legal and constitutional.

We remain your very affectionate brethren and pastors, who labor night and day, both in public and private, for your good.

William H. Miles, Joseph A. Beebe, Lucius H. Holsey, Isaac Lane.

¶   Negro Hymns.

(Taken from William H. Milburn, *Ten Years of Preacher Life* (1859), 341-42).

> "Jesus, my all, to heaven is gone,
>   And we shall gain the victory;
> He whom I fix my hopes upon,
>   And we shall gain the victory;
> His track I see, and I'll pursue
> The narrow way, till him I view;
>   And we shall gain the victory!
> March on, march on, and we shall gain the victory;
>   March on, and we shall gain the day."

> "There's a rest for the weary, there's a rest
>   for the weary,
> There's a rest for the weary, where they rest
>   forevermore;

> In the fair fields of Eden, in the fair fields
>   of Eden,
> In the fair fields of Eden we'll rest forevermore.

> I've a Saviour over yonder, I've a Saviour
>   over yonder,
> In the fair fields of Eden we'll rest forevermore."

> "Oh, brethren, will you meet me, oh, brethren,
>   will you meet me,
>   Where sorrows never come?"
> What ship is this that will take us all home?
>   Glory! hallelujah!
> 'Tis the old ship of Zion, oh, glory! hallelujah!
> But are you sure she will be able to take us
>   all home?
>   Yes, glory! hallelujah!

361

She's landed many a thousand, and she'll
        land as many more;
King Jesus is the captain! oh, glory! hallelujah!"

(Taken from John T. Jenifer, *Centennial Retrospect History of
the African Methodist Episcopal Church* (1916), 210-12).

"Our Fathers Church"

We are the children of the church,
  Our mothers reared by pray'r,
The church our fathers fortified,
  By faith and manly care.

Refrain

Our fathers' church – our mothers' church –
  Is just the church for me;
Our fathers' church – our mothers' church –
  Mine evermore shall be.

Strong are the massive gates and wide,
  Its walls a towering pile;
Alike impregnable to all
  Who would its courts defile.

Numerous its people as the stars,
  As pledged in days of old;
And will be as the countless sand,
  A number yet untold.

And stirred it is by lofty aims,
  Of love toward man and God,
And will be till the world accepts
  Messiah's staff and rod.

How glorious then this heritage,
  Burdened with storied wealth,
Enriching us and all mankind
  With life, and peace, and health.

Already in our youthful days
  We children prize the gift
That comes with gracious promises,
  Our trodden race t'-uplift.

As gathered on this Children's Day
  We at its altars vow

                    to mark its bulwarks, tell its towers,
                       And hold our place as now."

                              -Rev. B. T. Tanner, D.D.

                       "The Church is Moving On."

A song, I'll sing to you, of men both good and true,
    Who labored, battling for the right:
With righteousness and truth, they started in their youth,
    And never fainted in the fight.

                            Chorus

Oh! the church is moving on, the church is moving on,
    From low-land and from valley, from mountain top they rally,
The battle bow is strung, the banner is out-flung,
    And giant wrong no more is strong, for the church is moving on.

'Twas Richard Allen brave, a legacy who gave
    Of freedom and of courage true:
Then Brown and Walters came, with heart and mind the same,
    And laid down work for us to do.

The western work began, by Quinn a noble son,
    Who labored, preaching night and day;
Then Nazrey took the field, and Payne, with mighty zeal,
    Did go forth lighting up the way.

Then Wayman entered in, and Campbell did begin
    To send forth words of truth and might;
And shorter, Ward and Brown, did labor for the crown,
    And ceased not struggling for the right.

Of Turner next we sing, a mighty host did bring
    Of loyal men and women too,
And Dickerson and Cain, who did not long remain,
    Are resting with the tried and true.

Then Disney from afar, with mighty men of war,
    Did cry out, from across the Sea;
Our only daughter came, and we with heart aflame,
    Will help her good and true to be.

With Gaines and Arnett's force, we'll keep our steady course,
    And millions bring into the fold,
With Tanner and with Grant, we never will recant,
    The landmarks set by men of old.

                              363

And next we sing of Lee, and Salter like as he,
  Will labor bringing souls to God:
And Handy, brave and true, a mighty work will do.
  By trusting in his holy word.

Of Derrick now we sing, and Armstrong, too, we bring,
  And number with the royal band;
And Embry, gone before, to meet upon the shore,
  The loved ones in the glroy land."

                                        –L. J. Coppin.

¶   A. M. E. Bishop Henry McNeal Turner on *Methodist Polity*.

(Taken from Turner, *Methodist Polity* (1885), 36-38, 245-51).

CHAPTER III.

ORGANIZATION OF THE AFRICAN METHODIST EPISCOPAL CHURCH.

91 Q. When was the African M.E. Church organized?
A. In the month of April, 1816.

92 Q. By whom was it organized?
A. Rev. Richard Allen and fifteen others.

94 Q. Why did these men organize a new church?
A. Because they were treated unchristianly by their white brethren.

95 Q. To what white brethren do you refer?
A. To those of the Methodist Episcopal Church, of which they were members.

96 Q. Will you tell me in what that unchristian treatment consisted?
A. In pulling them from their knees while at prayer, forcing them to back seats and in the gallery, and using abusive language to them.

97 Q. What was the result of this treatment?
A. It led to them building a church, where they could worship God unmolested.

101 Q. What were they doing from 1787 up to 1816, when they permanently organized?
A. They were contending for their religious rights.

102 Q. Did God raise them up any friends from among the white people?

A. He did, namely, Dr. Benjamin Rush, R. Ralston, Wm. McKean, Richard Mosely, Jupiter Gibson and Bishop White, of the Protestant Episcopal Church.

103 Q. Who was elected and ordained the first Bishop of the A.M.E. Church?

A. Rev. Richard Allen, a good and great man, who had been ordained to the Christian ministry seventeen years before, by Bishop Francis Asbury of the M.E. Church.

104 Q. When was Richard Allen consecrated a Bishop?

A. April 11th, 1816.

105 Q. Did Bishop White ordain Rev. Richard Allen a Bishop?

A. No; I wish it had been possible, but Bishop Allen was ordained to the Episcopacy by five regularly-ordained ministers, among whom was Rev. Absalom Jones.

106 Q. Who was Absalom Jones?

A. A priest of the Protestant Episcopal Church, who had been ordained by Bishop White.

107 Q. What does tradition say about him?

A. Tradition says that Jones bore the greetings of Bishop White, and assisted in this ordination by Bishop White's consent.

108 Q. What does this establish?

A. That our ordination is not bogus, and connects the A.M.E. Church with historic Christianity.

109 Q. Do you mean that the ordination of the A.M.E. Church is Episcopally historic?

A. No. I mean that it is Presbyterially historic, or, in other words, that through the ordination of four Methodist ministers and Absalom Jones, a Priest of the Protestant Episcopal Church, Bishop Allen received a succession of hands, though through Priests, Presbyters, or elders, which gives his ordination the stamp of primitive Christianity, and made him, through the call of the entire church an ECCLESIASTICAL BISHOP, though not prelatically apostolical.

QUESTIONS TO BE ASKED ON ADMISSION TO THE TRAVELING
CONNECTION BY THE ANNUAL CONFERENCE OR ITS
COMMITTEES

On Personal Character

1. What is your age? What family have you? How long
have you been a church member? When licensed to preach?
Do you enjoy religion? Do you claim sanctification? Have
you the witness of the Holy Spirit?

2. Do you drink whisky? Do you advocate temperance in
your sermons? If not, will you? What books have you?
What are your hours of study? Have you read the Bible
through? If not, will you? Will you read it daily?

3. Do you fast? How often? When did you fast and pray last?

4. Have you considered the hardships of traveling work?
Will you conform to it? Will you obey orders? Go where
appointed?

5. Will you keep your wife on your work? Have you considered the danger of leaving your wife at a distance? Will
you see that your family attend church regularly?

6. Can you sing? Will you sing regularly? Hold family
worship? Will you both be decent in your person and polite
to people? Etc., etc.

I. - On Reading.

1. What is orthography, and what does it embrace?
2. What is articulation, and what does it embrace?
3. What are oral elements, and how are they divided?
4. How may letters by classed?
5. Give a definition for each of the following terms, viz.:
Vowel, diphthong, proper diphthong, improper diphthong,
triphthong, consonant, alphabetic equivalents, dental, lingual,
palatal, cognate.
6. What is a word? Define a primitive, a derivative, a
simple, a compound word.
7. Define syllable, monosyllable, dissyllable, trisyllable,
polysyllable.
8. What is accent? What its use?
9. What is expression of speech? Give its general divisions
and define them.
10. What is the difference between prose and poetry?

II. — On Writing.

1. What is writing?
2. From how many and what sources were the ancient systems of writing probably derived?
3. What are the three essentials of good writing?
4. What does uniformity include?
5. How are the small letters divided?
6. What are the rules for sloping and spacing?
7. What is the rule for shading?
8. What systems of penmanship have you studied, if any, and why do you prefer it?
9. Have you studied book-keeping-single or double entry? If so, whose system?
10. Are you conversant with the art of off-hand flourishing and drawing? How much time have you devoted to this branch of penmanship?

III. — On Spelling.

IV. — On Arithmetic.

V. — On Geography.

VI. — On the Discipline.

1. Why was the A.M.E. Church organized? When and by whom?
2. Name all the Bishops; tell when elected and ordained to that office. If any have deceased, tell whom, where and when.
3. How many Articles of Religion do we accept, and what do they severally treat of? Give the substance of each.
4. Repeat the General Rules; directions for the bands; explain the duties of a leader, and the best method of conducting class-meetings.
5. Give an exposition of the composition and powers of a General Annual, District and Quarterly Conference, Board of Trustee, Official Board, Board of Stewards, Stewardesses, and of the Select Number.
6. What are the duties and powers of a Bishop? Presiding Elder? Elder in charge? deacon? traveling licentiate? local preachers and exhorters?
7. What is probation? How are probationers received? How members from other denominations?
8. What is the duty of preachers to God, themselves and one another? Do you ever contract debts without the probability of paying them?
9. What is the best general and most effective way of preaching?
10. Have you read our form of Discipline carefully? Do you both know and love it, and will you conform yourself thereunto in all things as a son in the gospel?

VIII. – On Binney's Theological Compend.

What does the word theology mean? The word scripture? What does Testament signify? Apocrypha means what? State something of the translations of the Bible. What is meant by a Divine revelation? What does oral revelation mean? What was the necessity for a revelation? Explain a miracle. What is meant by prophecy? State the fulfillment of some. How is the existence of God proved? What are the attributes of God? Name them. What is meant by the Trinity? What was the office of Christ? The Holy Ghost? What is repentance? Justification? Sanctification? Faith? Hope? Charity? What is growth in grace? What is an angel? A devil? Prove by the scriptures a future state. A resurrection. A general judgment. What is the moral law? What duties do we owe to God? To our neighbor? Define baptism. What is the church? Etc., etc.

IX. – Sacred History.

1. Give the history of the church from the creation to the deluge, and tell what you know of the principal characters mentioned.

2. Name the principal events and persons, from the deluge to the departure of the Israelites from Egypt.

3. What were the chief incidents connected with the forty years' wandering in the wilderness?

4. Give the origin of the priestly and prophetic offices, and tell what were the peculiar duties of each.

5. At what time were there judges in Israel? Name them severally. Tell how long each judge served and under what circumstances they came into the office.

6. Name the several kings of Judah and of Israel; their character. Tell when and under whom the ten tribes revolted, and what caused the final seventy years captivity and dispersion.

7. Which are the principal events in the history of the church from the captivity to the restoration under Zerubbabel and Nehemiah?

8. Name all the major and minor prophets; their prophecies, and cite any fulfillments thereof.

9. Give the history of the church from the restoration by Cyrus to the ascension of Christ, and name the principal actors and the parts they performed.

10. Tell what was God's method for the redemption of mankind, and means employed before and since the coming of Christ. How may the church now be known?

X. – Anatomy and Physiology.

XI. – Analogy of Religion.

1. What difficulties have been raised concerning our personal

identity implied in the nation of present and future existence, and how may they be obviated?

2. What analogical proof can you produce of the government of God by means of rewards and punishments?

3. How would you prove from analogy that our probationary life implies trials, difficulties and dangers?

4. Is there such a thing as universal necessity? If so, in what way will it influence our practice?

5. Is God's government a scheme or constitution? If so, how much of it may we comprehend?

6. In what does the importance of Christianity consist and are we competent of judging what was to be expected in a revelation?

7. Explain the system of Christianity in relation to the appointment of a Mediator and the redemption of the world by Him.

8. Is revelation universal? If not, does this supposed deficiency invalidate its claims? If not, why?

9. Give the particular evidence in favor of Christianity.

10. What objections can be urged against the analogy of nature to religion, and by what arguments may those objections be silenced?

¶   African Methodism a Graded Training School for Race Leadership.

(Taken from John T. Jenifer, *Centennial Retrospect History* (1916), 118-21).

Noticing the degrees of efficiency found in the Fathers who lead the church, prior to the advent of schools among them, some have been quisitive as to how they received their training since they were not men of letters. The answer is - being possessed with large degrees of common sense and piety, with native abilities, they kept in sympathetic touch with their constituents; learned useful lessons in the schools of experience and found the functions of the Methodist economy an effective graded training school for leadership.

An illustration of this argument was seen in Alexander A. Wayman subsequently Bishop. He was a fair type of his class; he was not a man of the schools, but a product of his times; schooled in the common condition of his people, a self-made man as some would term him. In a joking manner he would take pride in saying "I, like Frederick Douglass, am a graduate of Tuckeyhoe University" referring to the ten by twelve hut in which he was born at Tuckyhoe Neck in Maryland.

METHODISM A SYSTEMATIC TRAINING SCHOOL FOR THE NEGRO MINISTRY - A CASE IN POINT.

The Baltimore Preachers' Meeting, at the death of Bishop A. W. Wayman, held a Memorial Service at the Cemetery Chapel near the

Bishop's grave. Bishop J. A. Handy presided, and the writer was appointed to deliver the oration. The question arose, among others, as to how Bishop Wayman, who generally boasted of being a graduate of Tuckyhoe University, received an education in his day sufficient to develop the man and the preacher that he was known to be and the following was given as an answer:

It is to be accounted for in the genius of Methodism and the administration of the A.M.E. Church's educational policy. Having united with it, and being trained and developed by the influences and conditions through which he passed, he found his chief training in his Church and by means of its peculiar ecclesiastical economy. This was to Alexander Washington Wayman, afterward Bishop, what it has been to so many other; a *graded school* in which many and marvelous developments of character and efficiency have been produced.

Upon entering a Methodist Church and its ministrations one is brought into contact with agencies that draw out and put into action, every faculty of the soul, having the internal qualifications being born again with the conscious certainty that he is a child of God, with his own free and open Bible to read for his guide, at the altar of his own heart, in his closet, or in the bosom of his family. He is his own high priest who offers sacrifices of prayer and praises to God. At church, in weekly social prayer-meetings with his brethren, he lifts his soul to God in petitions and praises for past blessings, and asks deliverance for himself and others against the ills and evils to come.

At class meeting, where he meets his leader once a week to tell how his soul prospers and to receive comfort and encouragement from the experience of others. At Love Feasts, where Christians meet to break bread, sip water and shake hands in token of love, one toward another. At Revival Meetings where the Church pleads for and puts on new strength, and times of refreshment come from the presence of the Lord. At Camp Meetings where the wilderness and solitary places are made glad and the desert is made to blossom as the rose. At Sunday School, the nursery of the coming Church that is to be, when the present one shall be in Heaven. The Christian Endeavor, where gathers the juvenile church, ambitious, sprightly, hopeful and tactful. Missionary Societies, through which he can preach by proxy, to starving millions abroad, as well as to the heathen at the door. Daughters of Conference, Band Societies, Bible Classes, Literary Societies, Church Aides, Kings Daughters and other benevolent agencies with Choirs, the singers in Zion, each and all ofering a field for the full and free exercise of every gift one possesses.

But these are not all! He that enters finds in an African Methodist Episcopal Church also a form of government with peculiar powers to train and develop men in useful ministrations and governing powers. Its legislative or lawmaking departments, its

judicial or law interpreting departments and its executive or law-enforcing departments, each in operation within its bosom, carrying on the sacred work of teaching and reforming the world in efforts to save mankind.

The several parts connected with each other rising in rank by beautiful gradations, as the interest which each controls increases in scope until they reach the General Conference. Having its Board of Trustees who manage the temporal concerns of the local societies, Official Boards of Stewards, who serve the spiritual interests of the society and look out for the welfare of the preacher, the sick and the poor. Class Leaders, those sub-pastors who assist the preacher to guard well the flock of God; Exhorters, who reprove and encourage men in word and doctrine and lead on the hosts of God in prayer; Local Preachers, who assist the pastor in labors of love, Deacons, assistants in the gospel and in the ceremonies of the sacrament. The Elders, the Shepherds of God, who watch over, feed and guard them, as he who is to give an account; Presiding Elders, the presidents and Pastors of the District and Quarterly Conferences, who see that every part of the law is enforced, who review all the spiritual and temporal machinery of the District, and who lay annually before the Bishop and his Annual Conference, a connected and detailed view of the whole. Then the Bishop chief Pastor of all, the president of the Annual Conference, where all the interests of the Church are reviewed and improved upon, and from which the preachers are appointed and re-appointed to fields of labor for which they have special adaptation and the nature of the work demands.

Lastly we reach the General Conference, where chiefs and subjects are equals in legislative privileges, where they make and revise laws, elect Bishops and department secretaries for the government of this vast reformatory; and while sitting thus assembled near the footstool of the Lord of Hosts, looking down this beautiful ascent over the several orders of agencies, we wonder at and admire the wisdom of the Great Head of His Church, Jesus Christ, who gave us some apostles and some prophets, some evangelists, and some pastors and teachers for the perfecting of the saints, for the work of the ministry, for the edifying of the body of Christ, until we all come into the unity of the faith and of the knowledge of the Son of God unto a perfect man, into the measure of the stature of the fulness of Christ.

Up this grade, by the help of God, the Fathers in the Church came. These ecclesiastical functions prepared them to lead the church; it fitted many to lead the race so that when other public duties devolved upon them, as in and during the Civil War, after Emancipation for political and social re-construction.

371

We will not cite here any examples, for to do so would be injustice to the thousands. The writer may in truth be charged with being prolix in this chapter upon the A.M.E. Church being a graded training school, but the beauty, order and training efficiency of the economy of Methodism is his apology. Yet, it would be narrow and selfish were we to fail to accord to other religious bodies similar strength along similar lines of race enlightenment, uplift and leadership.

16. GOING ON TO HOLINESS AND COMING OUT

One of the major theological movements of the later nineteenth century was the emphasis on holiness, or going on to perfection. The Methodist Episcopal Church, both North and South, provided an important forum. Although much of the action was theological and literary, some schismatic effects were manifest. Earlier the Wesleyan Methodist Connection rose from the combined pressures of sanctification and anti-slavery. A similar combination led to the establishment of the Free Methodist Church, in which B. T. Roberts of Genesee Annual Conference was a main leader. His article in 1857 not only drew the lines of combat but had tremendous influence on the growing holiness movement.

The wider significance of the holiness controversy may be seen in the inflammatory book by William Arthur, The Tongue of Fire, first published in 1856. He was a British Methodist minister who twice visited the United States. His book, for long on the Course of Study of the M. E. Church, South, provided fuel for the revivals associated with holiness.

One of the key figures was John S. Inskip, Methodist minister in New York and leader of the New York Methodist Preachers' Meeting. He contributed a chapter on the rise of the camp meeting movement for McLean and Eaton, Penuel. He was elected first president of the National Camp Meeting Association for the Promotion of Holiness.

Methodism continued to provide a nurturing ground. The First General Holiness Assembly, 1885, took place in the Park Avenue Methodist Episcopal Church in Chicago, with heavy Methodist participation. At least ten denominations were represented, and some tendency toward organization of a separate holiness denomination was evident. "Come-outism" led eventually to formation of splinter-groups.

One of the sturdy opponents of what he regarded as holiness extremism was James Mudge, New England Methodist minister and editor of Zion's Herald. He argued that Wesley's teaching meant growth toward rather than attainment of holiness. Both sides, in fact, claimed Wesley as their own. The holiness movement became closely associated with the pentecostal movement, while opponents tended to align with growing theological liberalism. There were wide individual differences, however, as may be seen in the attitudes of such as Mudge and Gilbert Haven.

¶   "New School Methodism," by B. T. Roberts.

(Taken from *Northern Independent*, 1857, reprinted in Leslie R. Marston, *A Living Witness* (1960), 573-78).

The best seed, sown, from year to year, on poor soil, gradually degenerates. The acorn, from the stately oak, planted upon the arid plain, becomes a stunted shrub. Ever since the fall, the human heart has proved a soil unfavorable to the growth of truth.

Noxious weeds flourish everywhere spontaneously, while the useful grains require diligent cultivation.

Correct principles implanted in the mind need constant attention, or monstrous errors will overtop them and root them out. Every old nation tells the tale of her own degeneracy, and points to the golden age when truth and justice reigned among men.

Religious truth is not exempt from this liability to corruption. "God will take care of His own cause," is a maxim often quoted by the cowardly and the compromising, as an apology for their base defection. When His servants are faithful to the trusts reposed in them, it is gloriously true; when they waver, His cause suffers. The Churches planted by the Apostles, and watered by the blood of martyrs, now outvie heathenism itself in their corruptions. No other parts of the world are so inaccessible to Gospel truth as those countries where the Romish and Greek Churches hold dominion.

As a denomination, we are just as liable to fall by corrupting influences as any were that have flourished before us. We enjoy no immunity from danger. Already there is springing up among us a class of preachers whose teaching is very different from that of the fathers of Methodism. They may be found here and there throughout our Zion; but in the Genesee Conference they act as an associate body. They number about thirty. During the last session of this Conference, they held several secret meetings, in which they concerted a plan to carry their measures and spread their doctrines. They have openly made the issue in the Conference. It is divided. Two distinct parties exist. With one or the other every preacher is in sympathy. This difference is fundamental. It does not relate to things indifferent, but to those of the most vital importance. It involves nothing less than the nature itself of Christianity.

In showing the doctrines of the New School Methodists, we shall quote from *The Advocate* of the sect, published at Buffalo. This is the organ of the party. It is sustained by them. They act as its agents. Where their influence prevails, it is circulated to the exclusion of other religious papers. Its former title was *"The Buffalo Christian Advocate."* But since its open avowal of the new doctrines, it has significantly dropped from its caption, the

expressive word, *"Christian."* This omission is full of meaning. It is, however, highly proper, as we shall see when we examine its new theory of religion. We commend the editor for this instance of honesty. It is now simply *"The Advocate"*; that is, the only Advocate of the tenets it defends.

The New School Methodists affect as great a degree of liberalism as do Theodore Parker and Mr. Newman. They profess "charity" for everybody except their brethren of the Old School. In an article on "Creeds," published in *The Advocate* of April 16th, under the signature of W. the Rev. writer, a prominent New School minister, lays it on to "the sects whose watchword is a creed," in a manner not unworthy of Alexander Campbell himself. He says, "No matter how holy and blameless a man's life may be, if he has the temerity to question any tenet of 'orthodoxy,' he is at once, in due ecclesiastical form, consigned to the Devil - as a heretic and infidel. Thus are the fetters of a spiritual despotism thrown around the human reason. . . And so it has come to pass that in the estimation of multitudes - the teachings of Paul are eclipsed by the theories of Calvin, and the writings of John Wesley are held in higher veneration than the inspired words of St. John." Is not this a modest charge?

But their theory of religion is more fully set forth in the leading editorial of *The Advocate* for May 14th, under the title - *"Christianity a Religion of Beneficence Rather than of Devotion."* Though it appears as editorial, we have good reason to believe that it was written by a leading New School member of the Genesee Conference. It has not been disavowed by that party. Though it has been before the public for months, no one has expressed a dissent from its positions. It is fair to suppose that it represents the views of the leaders of this new movement.

It says, "Christianity is not, characteristically, a system of devotion. It has none of those features which must distinguish a religion grounded on the idea that to adore the Divine character is the most imperative obligation resting upon human beings. It enjoins the observance of but very few sacred rites; nor does it prescribe any particular mode for paying homage to the Deity. It eschews all exterior forms, and teaches that they who worship God must worship Him in spirit and in truth."

The Old School Methodists hold, that "to adore the Divine character" is the most imperative obligation resting upon human beings - that Christianity has *all* of those features that must distinguish a religion grounded on this idea. That he who worships God rightly, will as a necessary consequence, possess all social and moral virtues; that the Gospel does not leave its votaries to choose, if they please, the degrading rites of heathenism, or the superstitious abominations of Popery; but prescribes prayer and praise and the observance of the sacraments of baptism and the Lord's Supper, "as particular modes

for paying homage to the Deity"; that there is no necessity for antagonism, as Infidels and Universalists are wont to affirm, between spiritual worship and the forms of worship instituted by Christ.

The following sneer is not unworthy of Thomas Paine himself. It falls below the dignity of Voltaire. "Christianity in nowise gives countenance to the supposition that the Great Jehovah is so affected with the infirmity of vanity, as to receive with peculiarly grateful emotions, the attention and offerings which poor, human creatures may pay directly to Him in worship."

The above may be sufficient to show what Christianity is not, in the opinion of these New School divines. Let us now see what it is. "The characteristic idea of this system is benevolence; and its practical realization is achieved in beneficence. It consecrates the principle of charity, and instructs its votaries to regard good works as the holiest sacrifice, and the most acceptable which they can bring to the Almighty. . . .

"Whatever graces be necessary to constitute the inner Christian life, the chief and principal one of these is love to man. . . . The great condition upon which one becomes a participant of the Gospel salvation, is - some practical exhibition of self-abnegation, of self-sacrifice for the good of others. Go sell all that thou hast, and give to the poor, were the only terms of salvation which Christ proposed to the young man, who, otherwise, was not far from the kingdom of heaven."

The Old School Methodists hold that benevolence is only one of the fruits of true religion, but by no means the thing itself. In their view, "The principal grace of the inner Christian life" is LOVE TO GOD; and the most acceptable sacrifice we can render Him, is a broken and contrite heart. They teach that the great condition upon which one becomes "a participant of the Gospel salvation" is FAITH IN CHRIST - preceded by repentance. They read in the Gospel that the young man referred to was commanded by Christ to *"come, take up the cross and follow me."* The giving of his goods to the poor was only preparatory to this.

The New School Methodists hold that justification and entire sanctification, or holiness, are the same - that when a sinner is pardoned, he is at the same time made holy - that all the spiritual change he may henceforth expect is simply a growth in grace. When they speak of "holiness," they mean by it the same as do evangelical ministers of those denominations which do not receive the doctrines taught by Wesley and Fletcher on this subject.

According to the Old School Methodists, merely justified persons, while they do not outwardly commit sin, are conscious of sin still remaining in the heart, such as pride, self-will, and

unbelief. They continually feel a heart bent to backsliding; a natural tendency to evil; a proneness to depart from God, and cleave to the things of earth. Those that are sanctified wholly are saved from all inward sin - from evil thoughts, and evil tempers. No wrong temper, none contrary to love, remains in the soul. All the thoughts, words and actions are governed by pure love.

The New School ministers have the frankness to acknowledge that their doctrines are not the doctrines of the Church. They have undertaken to correct the teachings of her standard authors. In the same editorial of *The Advocate*, from which we have quoted so largely, we read: "So in the exercises and means of grace instituted by the Church, it is clearly apparent that respect is had, rather to the excitation of the religious sensibilities, and the culture of emotional piety, than the development of genial and humane disposi-tions, and the formation of habits of active, vigorous goodness."

Here the evils complained of are charged upon "the exercises and means of grace, instituted by the Church." They do not result from a perversion of the means of grace, but are the effects intended to be produced in their institution. It is the CHURCH, then, that is wrong - and so far wrong that she does not even aim at the development of proper Christian character. "The means of grace," in the use of which an Asbury, an Olin, a Hedding, and a host of worthies departed and living, were nurtured to spiritual manhood, must be abolished; and others, adapted to the "development of genial and humane disposi-tions," established in their place. The Lodge must supersede the class-meeting and the love-feast; and the old-fashioned prayer-meeting must give way to the social party! Those who founded or adopted "the exercises and means of grace instituted by the Church" - Paul and Peter, the Martyrs and Reformers, Luther and Wesley, Calvin and Edwards - all have failed to comprehend the true idea of Christianity - for these all held that the sinner was justified by faith in Christ, and not by "some practical exhibition of self - abnegation." The honor of distinctly apprehending and clearly stating the true genius of Christianity was reserved for a few divines of the nineteenth century!

Differing thus in their views of religion, the Old and New School Methodists necessarily differ in their measures for its promotion. The latter build stock Churches, and furnish them with pews to accommodate a select congregation; and with organs, melodeons, violins, and professional singers, to execute difficult pieces of music for a fashionable audience. The former favor free Churches, congregational singing, and spirituality, simplicity and fervency in worship. They endeavor to promote revivals, deep and thorough; such as were common under the labors of the Fathers; such as have made Methodism the leading denomination of the land. The leaders of the New Divinity movement are not remarkable for promoting revivals; and those which do, occasionally, occur among them, may

generally be characterized as, the editor of *"The Advocate"* designated, one which fell under his notice, as "splendid revivals." Preachers of the old stamp urge upon all who would gain heaven the necessity of self-denial - non-conformity to the world, purity of heart and holiness of life; while the others ridicule singularity, encourage by their silence, and in some cases by their own example, and that of their wives and daughters, "the putting on of gold and costly apparel," and treat with distrust all professions of deep Christian experience. When these desire to raise money for the benefit of the Church, they have recourse to the selling of pews to the highest bidder; to parties of pleasure, oyster suppers, fairs, grab-bags, festivals and lotteries; the others for this purpose, appeal to the love the people bear to Christ. In short, the Old School Methodists rely for the spread of the Gospel upon the agency of the Holy Ghost, and the purity of the Church. The New School Methodists appear to depend upon the patronage of the worldly, the favor of the proud and aspiring; and the various artifices of worldly policy.

If this diversity of opinion and of practice among the ministers of our denomination was confined to one Conference, it would be comparatively unimportant. But unmistakable indications show that prosperity is producing upon us, as a denomination, the same intoxicating effect that it too often does upon individuals and societies. The change, by the General Conference of 1852, in the rule of Discipline, requiring that all our houses of worship should be built plain, and with free seats; and that of the last General Conference in the section respecting dress, show that there are already too many among us who would take down the barriers that have hitherto separated us from the world. The fact that the removal is gradual, so as not to excite too much attention and commotion, renders it none the less alarming.

We have thus endeavored to give a fair and impartial representation of New School Methodism. Its prevalence in one Conference has already, as we have seen, involved it in division and disaster. Let it generally prevail, and the glory will depart from Methodism. She has a special mission to accomplish. This is, not to gather into her fold the proud and fashionable, the devotees of pleasure and ambition, but "to spread Scriptural holiness over these lands." Her doctrines, and her usages, her hymns, her history and her spirit, her noble achievements in the past, and her bright prospects for the future, all forbid that she should adopt an accommodating, compromising policy, pandering to the vices of the times. Let her go on, as she has done, insisting that the great, cardinal truths of the Gospel, shall receive a living embodiment in the hearts and lives of her members, and Methodism will continue to be favored of Heaven, and the joy of earth. But let her come down from her position, and receive to her communion all those lovers of pleasure, and lovers of the world, who are willing to pay for the privilege, and it needs no prophet's vision to foresee

that Methodism will become a dead and corrupting body, endeavoring in vain to supply, by the erection of splendid Churches, and the imposing performance of powerless ceremonies, the manifested glory of the Divine presence, which once shone so brightly in all her sanctuaries.

"Thus saith the Lord, Stand ye in the ways, and see, and ask for the old paths, where is the good way, and walk therein, and ye shall find rest for your souls." - Jer. 6:16.

¶   *The Tongue of Fire*, by William Arthur, 1859.

(Taken from *ibid.*, 46-48, 59-62, 72-73, 102-04, 156-57).

The Apostles themselves had doubtless received the Spirit in some measure before the day of Pentecost; for our Lord had breathed upon them immediately after His resurrection, and said, "Receive ye the Holy Ghost." Yet in the time which intervened between that and Pentecost, whatever might have been the advancement of their spiritual condition beyond what it was before, it rested far behind that which immediately followed upon the baptism of fire. It was only then that they were "filled with the Holy Ghost." We find, however, that even the expression, "be filled," is applied broadly to ordinary believers; and that, too, not merely as describing the actual enjoyments of some individuals, but as a precept applicable to all: "Be not drunken with wine, wherein is excess, but be filled with the Spirit." Whatever is meant by being "filled with the Holy Ghost" is, by these plain words, laid upon us as our duty. Looking at it in the aspect of a duty, and thinking of the moral height which the expression indicates above our ordinary life, we shrink. Can such an obligation lie upon us? Is it not commanding the purblind to gaze upon the sun? And yet, whatever is the duty of man must be the will of God. In this view, then, the commandment seems to carry even a stronger encouragement than the promise – seems, in fact, to sum up many promises in one conclusive appeal, saying, "ALL things are now ready. The Lord has provided; the fountain is open; the pure river of the water of life, clear as crystal, is proceeding out of the throne of God and of the Lamb; you are called to its banks, and with you it rests to drink and be filled with the Spirit."

He who has not received the Holy Ghost has not yet entered into the real Christian life, does not know the "peace which passeth understanding," has in no sense "Christ in Him the hope of glory." He is still "in the flesh," in his natural and carnal state; for the Spirit of God does not dwell in him. The difference between receiving the Spirit and being filled with the Spirit, is a difference not of kind, but of degree. In the one case, the light of heaven has reached the dark chamber, disturbing night, but leaving some obscurity and some deep shadows. In the other, that light has filled the whole chamber, and made every corner bright. This state of the soul - being

"filled with the Holy Ghost" - is the normal antecedent of true prophetic or miraculous power, but may exist without it: without it, in individuals who are never endowed with the gift either of prophecy or of miracles; without it, in individuals who have such powers, but in whom they are not in action, as in John the Baptist before his ministry commenced.

Eyesight is the necessary basis of what is called a painter's or a poet's eye; the sense of hearing, the necessary basis of what is called a musical ear: yet eyesight may exist where there is no poet's or painter's eye, and hearing where there is no musical ear. So may the human soul be "filled with the Holy Ghost," having every faculty illuminated, and every affection purified, without any miraculous gift. On the other hand, the miraculous power does not necessarily imply the spiritual fullness; for Paul puts the supposition of speaking with tongues, prophesying, removing mountains, and yet lacking charity, that love which must be shed abroad in every heart that is full of the Holy Ghost.

"Filled with the Holy Ghost!" Thrice blessed word! thanks be to God, that ever the tongues of men were taught it! It declares not only that the Lord has returned to His temple in the human soul, but that He has filled the house with His glory; pervaded every chamber, every court, by His manifested presence.

*　　　*　　　*

In this the power of the Holy Ghost is practically manifested by a reversal of the relations of the human spirit and the flesh. To persons yet in the body, the Apostle says, "Ye are not in the flesh, but in the Spirit, if so be the Spirit of God dwell in you." Not in the flesh, yet in the body! The unconverted man has a spirit, but it is carnalized; the play of its powers - the studies of the intellect, the flights of the imagination, the impulses of the heart, are dictated by motives which all range below the sky and halt on this side of the tomb. The spirit is the servant of the flesh; and man differs from perishing animals chiefly in this, that for carnal purposes and delights he commands the service of spiritual agent - his own soul.

The Holy Spirit, as man's regenerator, reverses this state of things. He quickens the spirit, and through it quickens the frame, so that instead of spiritual powers being carnalized, a mortal body is spiritualized; instead of soul and spirit being subjected by the flesh, flesh and blood become instruments of the Spirit. Limbs move on works of heavenly origin and intent. Thus a direct connection is established between the will of the Supreme Spirit and the material organs of man. A purpose originates in the mind of God; by His Spirit it is silently and swiftly transmitted to the spirit of His child; and by this to the "mortal body." Then, as an iron wire,

on the shore of the Crimea, expresses the will of our Queen in London, so do the earthly members of a mortal express, in the outward and physical world, the purpose of the Holy One. This is redemption achieved: this is adoption in its issues: this is the new life: this is human nature restored, man walking in the light; "God dwelling in him, and he in God." Then his life is a light, and a light so pure, that it gives those on whom it shines, not the idea of "good nature," but of something heavenly. They see his good works, and "glorify his Father which is in Heaven:" not extol his character; but feel that he is raised above his own character, and is "God's workmanship, created anew in Christ Jesus unto good works."

A piece of iron is dark and cold; imbued with a certain degree of heat, it becomes almost burning without any change of appearance; imbued with a still greater degree, its very appearance changes to that of solid fire, and it sets fire to whatever it touches. A piece of water without heat is solid and brittle; gently warmed, it flows; further heated, it mounts to the sky. An organ filled with the ordinary degree of air which exists everywhere, is dumb; the touch of the player can elicit but a clicking of the keys. Throw in not another air, but an unsteady current of the same air, and sweet, but imperfect and uncertain, notes immediately respond to the player's touch: increase the current to a full supply, and every pipe swells with music. Such is the soul without the Holy Ghost; and such are the changes which pass upon it when it receives the Holy Ghost, and when it is "filled with the Holy Ghost." In the latter state only is it fully imbued with the Divine nature, bearing in all its manifestations some plain resemblance to its God, conveying to all on whom it acts some impression of Him, mounting heavenward in all its movements, and harmoniously pouring forth, from all its faculties, the praises of the Lord.

*   *   *

It would be impossible to conceive any form of credential so well framed to certify, that a doctrine was the immediate issue of the mind of God. The bare thought of such a miracle as that of tongues, had it only been a thought, would have made in itself an era in the history of man's intellect; and it may be fairly questioned whether such a thought could have originated in any thing else than in the fact. The leading feature of the new religion was to be a Divine teaching upon things invisible and spiritual - on points of which the unaided powers of man could give no conclusive solution. For such a teaching no attestation could be so apposite as one that accredited it as a message from the Spirit which "searcheth all things." The universal call to man was worthily issued into the world by a sign which showed that it came directly from the only wise God, who gives understanding, and holds the keys of thought. The command of all languages, by one consentaneous impulse, proclaimed the new message to be the WORD OF GOD.

If the amazing revival which characterized the last century,
be viewed merely as a natural progress of mental influence, no
analysis can find elements of power greater than have often existed
in a corrupting and falling Church, or than are found at many
periods when no blessed effects are produced. Men equally learned,
eloquent, orthodox, instructive, may be found in many ages of
Christianity. It is utterly impossible to assign a natural reason
why Whitfield should have been the means of converting so many
more sinners than other men. Without one trace of logic, philosophy,
or any thing worthy to be called systematic theology, his sermons,
viewed intellectually, take an humble place among humble efforts.
Turning again to his friend, Wesley, we find calmness, clearness,
logic, theology, discussion, definition, point, appeal, but none of
that prodigious and unaccountable power which the human intellect
would naturally connect with movements so amazing as those which
took place under his word. Neither the logic of the one, nor the
declamation of the other, furnishes us with the secret of his
success. There is enough to account for men being affected, excited,
or convinced; but that does not account for their living holy lives
ever after. Thousands of pulpit orators have swayed their audience,
as a wind sways standing corn; but, in the result, those who were
most affected, differed nothing from their former selves. An
effect of eloquence is sufficient to account for a vast amount of
feeling at the moment; but to trace to this a moral power, by which
a man, for his life long, overcomes his besetting sins, and adorns
his name with Christian virtues, is to make sport of human nature.

Why should these men have done what many equally learned and
able, as divines and orators, never did? There must have been an
element of power in them which criticism can not discover. What was
that power? It must be judged of by its sphere and its effects.
Where did it act? and what did it produce? Every power has its own
sphere. The strongest arm will never convince the understanding, the
most forcible reasoning will never lift a weight, the brightest
sunbeam will never pierce a plate of iron, nor the most powerful
magnet move a pane of glass. The soul of man has separate regions,
and that which merely convinces the intellect may leave the emotions
untouched, that which merely operates on the emotions may leave the
understanding unsatisfied, and that which affects both may yet leave
the moral powers uninspired. The crowning power of the messenger of
God is power over the moral man; power which, whether it approaches
the soul through the avenue of the intellect or of the affections,
does reach into the soul. The sphere of true Christian power is the
heart - the moral man; and the result of its action is not to be surely
distinguished from that of mere eloquence by instantaneous emotion,
but by subsequent moral fruit. Power which cleanses the heart, and
produces holy living, is the power of the Holy Ghost. It may be
through the logic of Wesley, the declamation of Whitfield, or the

simple common-sense of a plain servant-woman or laboring man; but whenever this power is in action, it strikes deeper into human nature than any mere reasoning or pathos. Possibly it does not so soon bring a tear to the eye, or throw the judgment into a posture of acquiescence; but it raises in the breast thoughts of God, eternity, sin, death, heaven, and hell; raises them, not as mere ideas, opinions, or articles of faith, but as the images and echoes of real things.

$$* \qquad * \qquad *$$

But while on the one hand, we do not expect the permanent presence of the Spirit with the Church in the Romish sense, or in the sense maintained by estimable Christians of the Society of Friends, we must, on the other hand, maintain, as we have said, that without His presence and operation in the hearts of believers, and in Christian agents, we can not have the Christian religion. We do not expect visible signs or miraculous gifts: for these were not the substantial blessing and grace imparted at Pentecost; but were to them only as heralds and ushers. The real grace and blessing lay in what we have called the spiritual influence of the Holy Ghost, acting on the believer's heart; His ministerial influence, acting on the Church; His converting influence, acting on the world. These, we contend, are necessary to the identity of the Christian religion, and were bestowed for all ages, and will to the end of the world be shed on those who perseveringly "wait" for the baptism of fire.

¶ John Inskip on National Camp Meeting, Vineland, N.J., 1867.

(Taken from A. McLean and Joel Eaton, *Penuel; or, Face to Face With God* (1869), 5-13).

The persons who finally assumed the responsibility of holding the National Camp-Meeting, of course expected to be misapprehended by many whose good opinion they would very much regret to lose. They were fully aware they would be misunderstood, and perhaps sometimes misrepresented. Their measures and motives they expected would be assailed, and subjected to the most rigid criticism. It was nevertheless understood and agreed among them, that however severe and uncharitable might be the strictures upon their operations, they would make no attempt to respond except in their spirit and manner of life. It was assumed that what they might *say* in their defence would not be of as much weight as they might *be* and *do*. They could richly afford to wait for the matured and more candid judgment that their brethren would render concerning them after time and opportunity should be given for a clearer and more correct view of their real character and designs. True, some of them felt that a life service in the church ought to protect them against intimations of schismatic, fanatical, or disloyal intentions. If, however, a

whole life given to the interests of religion should not shield them from such inuendoes, they concluded nothing they could say would be deemed satisfactory by their opponents.

They had no doctrinal novelties to propose to the world. They rather sought and inquired for the "old paths." They desired no modification of church polity, but earnestly hoped for a spiritual revolution by which the whole body of Christian believers might be induced to inscribe on their temples, altars, and banners, "Holiness to the Lord." They looked not so much for the diffusion of a dogmatic idea as for the prevalence of a profound religious experience. Holiness, to their minds, appeared to be more in what men *are* and *do*, than in what they *believe*. No doctrinal "shibboleth" was insisted upon, but it was concluded, that as the Spirit and Word might teach, men should be urged to seek more and more of the "mind that was in Jesus." These facts and considerations will explain why this movement has excited so little controversy. The blessed Holy Spirit has also doubtless guided his servants, so that they have not been decoyed into an attitude in which they would compromise the blessed truth they so much desire shall prevail everywhere, and among all of God's dear children.

It was further understood that in speaking of this glorious theme they would be definite, and as far as practicable adhere to the scriptural terms in which, by Divine authority, it is couched. In taking this position, however, it was not designed at all to reflect upon those who feel at liberty to adopt another course. The *nomenclature* of this question, as set forth in the words of Holy Writ, they deemed sufficiently clear and comprehensive. It was adjudged these were to be preferred to those of human origin and device. Hence the object of the meeting was announced to be the "promotion of HOLINESS." The term was understood to imply "entire sanctification," "perfect love," &c.; and being so freely used in the scriptures, it was supposed would be readily apprehended. Still the endeavor among us has been to avoid adherence to mere terms. Terminology, indeed, as such, has been ignored. Facts and ideas, rather than mere words or forms of speech, have attracted attention, and have been made prominent. To elevate the tone of experience more than to correct doctrinal error, has been the object in view. In saying this it is by no means designed to intimate that the doctrinal aspects of this question are unimportant. On the contrary, they are to be urged as fundamental. A people, however, who have had the teachings of Wesley, Fletcher, Watson, Clarke &c. &c., and have used a hymn-book so full of the doctrine as is ours, and had access to such a biographical literature as we have published, to illustrate this great theme, surely need no argument to assure them that it is the will of God they should be "sanctified wholly," and preserved blameless unto the day of his coming." It has been truly said, this doctrine has ever been peculiar and prominent in our religious ideas. It may be found in our hymns, our rituals, our history, our

biography, and all our standard authorities. Hence it was assumed to be more needful to urge this as a privilege than as a doctrine - as a phase of religious life to be enjoyed rather than a creed to be defended. . . .

A call for a larger meeting was submitted for their considera-tion, and in due time was issued, inviting those in favor of holding a camp-meeting for the promotion of holiness to meet in the city of Philadelphia, June 13, 1867.

In pursuance of this call a goodly number of brethren from different parts of the country came together at the Methodist Book Rooms. The city of "Brotherly Love" was a fit place for such a gathering. At a glance it could be perceived this company had met "in the name of the Lord." The venerable Dr. Roberts, of Baltimore, was called to the chair, and Rev. J. Thompson, of Philadelphia, was appointed secretary. It was proposed that some time be spent in prayer for the controlling influences of the Holy Comforter. Each one present appeared to be profoundly impressed with the importance and responsibility of the subject in hand. They moved, therefore, with the greatest solemnity and caution. As one after another led in prayer, the presence of God was more and more sensibly felt. For a time the consciousness of the revelations of the Divine glory and power were almost overwhelming. It was a most extraordinary season - one, indeed, that will never, never be forgotten.

There were many questions to be settled by this meeting. Some of them, it was expected, might be considerably perplexing and difficult. But, under the influence of the mighty and unctuous baptism that came upon all, each embarrassment as it was approached vanished away. It was thought the place of meeting might prove an exciting question; so many came with their minds made up that they had the best position. But a singular unanimity was immediately dis-closed when Vineland was named. It was truly wonderful how all preconceived preferences at once were yielded, and the nomination of Vineland was made unanimous. Such, in fact, was the case all through the consultation. It was the most fraternal and religious business meeting any of us ever attended. There was one continued earnest invocation for the light and aid of the Holy Spirit. The considerate and deferential manner of every one who spoke on the occasion was so marked, as to convince all present God had taken the affair into his hands, and would lead us on to victory and success.

In defining the object of the meeting, we found less difficulty than in giving it a name. Upon conferring one with another, we were persuaded the great body of the people and preachers would sympathize with the object of the meeting. We could scarcely believe that any Christian would not be glad to learn that a fresh and earnest endeavor to "spread scriptural holiness over these lands" was about to be inaugurated. Every true disciple of Jesus loves holiness, and aspires

to attain and enjoy it. There may be some variation in the method of expressing such aspirations, but all who love the Saviour feel and cherish them. He who does not love holiness can make no just pretensions to love its great Author. Christ is a high priest, "holy, harmless, and undefiled." Heaven is a holy place. God and angels who dwell there are holy. Hence, the consistent Christian ever and earnestly loves and seeks after holiness. To hold a camp-meeting for the specific purpose of promoting holiness, it was concluded therefore, we ultimately would, and must have, the sympathy and prayer of all the "household of faith." While we were fully aware many good people might misunderstand, and hence would misrepresent us, yet the assurance that when fully comprehending our aims they would smile on our efforts, made us bold to proclaim to the world what we designed and hoped to accomplish. We were certain that when correctly apprehended, good men of every name would bid us "God speed." Therefore, we dismissed all care and anxiety on that point.

The unusual character of the meeting required it should be so designated as to be understood. Our object was to put in motion influences that would reach the whole country – all churches, in every part of the land. The largest catholicity of spirit was cherished, and it was therefore resolved to invite all denominations to join at once in the great undertaking before us. There was nothing in our plan and purpose from which any need dissent. Our views of minor points could for the time be set aside, or kept in abeyance. Holding them would not in the slightest degree hinder the most cordial and fraternal action upon the all-important question before us. We could be Presbyterians, Episcopalians, Lutherans, Baptists, Methodists, &c., &c., and yet most heartily fraternize in the glorious work contemplated. How far these anticipations have been realized will be disclosed in subsequent chapters.

The adoption of the title, "NATIONAL CAMP-MEETING," was a happy thought. It was thus distinguished from all other camp-meetings. It was never for a moment designed to interfere with these, except to increase their spirituality and power. The time of holding this meeting was fixed early in the season, in order that those attending it might go to the others in the "fulness of the blessings of the gospel of peace." Preachers and people would thus be prepared for joyous and effective service, whether at camp-meeting or elsewhere. At the first meeting at Vineland there were persons present from all denominations, and from almost every State in the Union. How soon would there be diffused among all sects and parties a catholic and fraternal spirit, if the doctrine and experience of Christian purity were generally prevalent, and how firmly might all these States be joined in national unity and friendship.

The intensification of feeling incident to so large an assembly of fervent spirits can scarcely be conceived, except by those who have had the opportunity of witnessing it. To know to what a point

of interest and excitement the mind and heart may be drawn in such circumstances, can be understood only from experience. It was therefore feared that some over-zealous persons, of whom many are apt to be found on all popular occasions, would be led into extremes which would damage them and the cause with which they would thus unfortunately become associated. The fanaticism of this class has done inconceivable injury to the doctrine. It was apprehended they would be drawn to this great gathering of the people, and accomplish their usual unhappy work. Opposers are eager to seize upon such indiscretions and improprieties of speech and conduct as may be alleged against parties of this character. It is well known that fanaticism is sometimes uncontrollable. In all our deliberations and movements we sought to protect ourselves from this peril. In the main, it must be admitted, we were remarkably successful. To God be all the glory. In some instances, doubtless, expressions have been uttered and views have been maintained for which we would be unwilling that the "National Camp-Meeting" should be responsible. It is, however, occasion of devout thanksgiving to our Heavenly Father that our meeting has been much less disturbed in the way intimated than ordinary camp-meetings frequently are.

¶   Declaration of Principles, First General Holiness Assembly, 1885.

(Taken from John L. Peters, *Christian Perfection and American Methodism* (1956), 137–38, abridged by author).

1. The State of Justification. . .including these particulars:
    (1) The pardon of sin, so full and free that all the transgressions of the past life are blotted from the Book of Divine remembrance, and by this act of Divine mercy, the individual is accounted righteous before God, notwithstanding his actual past unrighteousness. (2) The new birth, or moral regeneration, quickening him into spiritual life, and renewing him in the spirit of his mind. (3) Adoption into the Divine family and consequent heirship, witnessed distinctly to the personal consciousness by the Holy Ghost. This great act of justification is received alone upon the ground of the infinite merit of Christ's atoning sacrifice, in the exercise of faith in that atonement, preceded by true repentance, which consists of deep sorrow for the sins committed, restitution, and a full renunciation of sinful habits and associations.
2. Entire sanctification. . .that great work wrought subsequent to regeneration, by the Holy Ghost, upon the sole condition of faith, such faith being preceded by an act of solemn and complete consecration; – including three particulars:
    (1) The entire extinction of the carnal mind, the total eradication of the birth principle of sin. (2) The

communication of perfect love to the soul. . .
(3) The abiding indwelling of the Holy Ghost. . .
There is such a close connection between the
gifts of justification and entire sanctification,
and such a readiness on the part of our Heavenly Father
to bestow the second as well as the first, that
young converts should be encouraged to go up at once
to the Canaan of perfect love.

3. Testimony. It is the duty of all who are made
partakers of entire sanctification. . .to testify
thereof to the praise of the Giver. Such testimony
should be very definite, as much as possible in the
use of Bible terms, and in . . .a spirit of humility
. . .If such testimony be withheld the light of the
soul will soon become darkness.

4. Holy Character. The portraiture of . . .The Sermon
on the Mount, and the thirteenth Chapter of first
Corinthians . . .

5. The attractive Graces. The quieter graces of the
Spirit. . .

6. Growth in Grace . . . should be rapid, constant and
palpable.

¶　　　James Mudge's Critique of "Holiness."

(Taken from *idem, Growth in Holiness* (1895), 156-59, 251-52,
256-59, 261-62).

The question whether entire sanctification is possible in this
life can never be answered satisfactorily or intelligently without a
specification of the sense in which the term is to be taken.
Sanctification being to make holy, entire sanctification will be to
make entirely or perfectly holy - in other words, to produce a
condition wherein the perfect love of God completely controls everything. The same two meanings, lower and higher, which we have
explained with reference to perfection exist here with reference to
entire sanctification, a phrase of precisely similar compass. The
sanctification, or cleansing, or empowering, is entire or perfect at
conversion up to the light then given, so that when justified every
person is in the relative or comparative sense entirely sanctified.
And whenever, at any subsequent point, after a season of retrogression
he comes fully up to his light and once more walks in unclouded
communion he becomes again entirely sanctified, in this lower sense.
Entire sanctification, in the higher or absolute sense, where something more than the partial knowledge and inferior, undeveloped
powers of the young convert come in, where, indeed, complete knowledge and the powers of unfallen humanity are implied, must, as
with the higher perfection, tarry till another life.

Many Methodist theologians vent a great deal of uncalled-for scorn and sarcasm on those who hold that we cannot be sanctified in the fullest sense until the body has been dropped off, charging us with believing in a death purgatory, a heathen philosophy, and the inherent evil of matter and with substituting something else for the blood of Christ as the proper purifier of the soul. All this is wholly beside the mark and comes from confounding things that differ. As is seen by the quotation a few pages back, they really attack John Wesley himself, although far from meaning so to do; for he says that our souls are so pressed down by these shattered bodies that they cannot in this life always think, speak, or act aright. Hence, there is a degree of salvation that cannot come to us until we shake off the body. A greater than Wesley has declared the same things, even the mighty apostle to the Gentiles, who, in Rom. viii, 19-25, fully explains that "the earnest expectation of the creation waiteth for the revealing of the sons of God" . . . .

This can mean nothing but that we are not yet any of us fully saved and, in the largest meaning of the term, not yet completely redeemed, not yet made perfectly whole, not yet, in the complete or absolute sense, entirely sanctified. But this great fact by no means reflects upon the power of Christ, minifies the efficacy of his blood, or gives any aid to the peculiar doctrines of Romanism. All such talk shows superficial thinking. Death is not the means of our deliverance, as though power were attributed to it, but it is the occasion. God's alone is the power. But it is not irreverence to say such are the necessities of the case that he cannot do for us in this life what he purposes to do in another.

It will, perhaps, be sufficiently evident from this what we mean when we say that our whole Christian life on earth should be one of progressive sanctification. That is the proper term for characterizing all the path between the sanctification which marks the entrance on the Christian life and the entire sanctification which marks the close of the earthly Christian life and the entrance on the heavenly. It is quite within our power to be always fully sanctified in the lower sense, according to the knowledge of God's will at any time possessed, and to be making continual advance in this knowledge, as also in the knowledge of our own heart, and so to be growing in holiness. We shall thus have the apparent anomaly of something which is completed and progressing at the same time; but, of course, this cannot be in the same sense. For in whatsoever particulars sanctification is complete, in these particulars its progress has ceased. So far as selfishness or depravity to any degree remains and is being steadily diminished by the cooperation of the divine and human agents that are warring against it, so far and so long our sanctification is progressing, not having yet reached its goal.

*   *   *

John Wesley himself is a shining example of the great difficulty
of strictly classifying by our modern terms one whose views of truth
underwent great changes and who really passed out of one dispensation
into another, instead of simply passing from carelessness to faithfulness of life. Was Wesley really converted or not previous to the
strange warming of his heart in that Moravian meeting in Aldersgate
Street? He finds it hard to say himself. He wrote on one occasion,
"I, who went to America to convert others, was never myself converted
to God." But he subsequently added, "I am not sure of this." Again,
he says, "This, then, have I learned in the ends of the earth, . . .
that, alienated as I am from the life of God, I am a 'child of wrath,'
an heir of hell." The greater wisdom of later years caused him to
correct this hasty judgment by appending, "I believe not," and "I had
even then the faith of a servant, though not of a son." In other
words, he was really at that time accepted of God in the dispensation
of the Father or of the Son, up to which point alone his light had
thus far reached. But of the dispensation of the Holy Ghost, so far
as it meant the joys of conscious adoption through an assured faith
and the clear witness of the Spirit, he as yet knew nothing. So that
wonderful night, May 24th, 1738, when he received the assurance that
his sins were taken away cannot strictly be termed his conversion in
our usual sense, nor can it be said that he then attained entire
sanctification. The facts do not sufficiently bear out either
statement. All that can be truly said is that he entered upon a
decidedly advanced stage of Christian experience, which gave him
very different apprehensions of saving truth and a very much greater
power to do good. .   .   .

What then is "receiving the Holy Ghost," or being "baptized
with the Holy Ghost?" We believe, with John Wesley, that it means,
primarily, the receiving a clear witness to our acceptance with God
and our adoption into his family. This common experience, the witness of the Spirit, shared by all genuine, fully instructed,
thoroughly converted believers, received at the time of their justification if they are taught to look for it, has all the marks of
correspondence, more nearly, at least, than anything else, with the
baptism of the Holy Ghost which we find described in the New Testament.
.   .   .

In fact, any reviving or quickening of spiritual life, any marked influx of blessedness, any strong impression made by the Spirit of
God on the soul may be called, if it is thought best, a baptism of the
Holy Ghost. Whenever any of the fruits of the Spirit, such as love,
joy, peace, are, in a special or sudden way, produced or increased in
the believer, whenever a manifest effect of the Spirit is felt or
seen, there he may find and point out a baptism, or bestowment, or
gift, or anointing of the Spirit. But it is a very different matter
to talk about *the* baptism of the Holy Ghost, as if it were a certain,
definite thing, experienced by the disciples at Pentecost, and
equally obligatory upon, and available for, us now if only we wait

before God in prayer with sufficient earnestness a sufficient length of time. It ought to be declared with great positiveness that Pentecost cannot be repeated. The Holy Spirit has *come* once for all to take the place of Jesus; the promised Comforter is here and will not depart. He abides with and in the Church. His dispensation has been set up and is going on.   .   .   .

Our conclusion is that all true Christians, when they are born of the Spirit, are filled with the Spirit up to their capacity at that time, are baptized with the Spirit, and receive the gift of the Holy Ghost, even the spirit of adoption, or the spirit of holiness, whereby they cry to God, "Father!" and are made holy. Then, as they go on, having it for their chief business to perfect this holiness which has been planted in them, to grow out of infancy into manhood, to become of full age, mature, perfect, they will have, from time to time, other special quickenings, or baptisms, or blessings, from the Holy Spirit. The most important of these they may, perhaps, call the "second" blessing, counting it, as indeed it is, a very wonderful and precious and stirring epoch in their experience. But they should not fall into the habit of calling it "the baptism of the Holy Ghost, in any such way as to obscure or minimize the importance of that first baptism which they had when the Spirit told them they were born again, or of those other subsequent baptisms which they undoubtedly will have if they press diligently on. A close walk with God, such as all Christians may and should have, implies not only constant communion with the Spirit, but also special bestowments of favor, special upliftings and enlightenings and empowerings from time to time, as occasion may demand. Let them come - the more the better. But let no one be in haste to conclude, with reference to any one of them, that it is the final touch, absolutely eradicating or removing the very last possible remnant of depravity; and let no one call it, ignoring the uniform usage of Scripture, "the" baptism with the Holy Ghost.

17. PUBLICATION AND EDUCATION

With an increasing sense of historical tradition the editors of the intellectual and theological quarterly of the Methodist Episcopal Church, the Methodist Quarterly Review , invited James Mudge, in 1894 a minister in the New England Conference and subsequently editor of Zion's Herald, John Faulkner, in 1917 professor in Drew Theological Seminary, and James R. Joy, in 1931 editor of the Christian Advocate, to review the Review. Mudge's seventy-five year anniversary tribute provided the fullest detail, with emphasis on the heyday under Daniel D. Whedon. Faulkner marveled that the journal, now named Methodist Review as a bimonthly, has had such "a distinguished history, an unparalleled achievement," and, having outlasted all its religious rivals, was about to enter a second century, "hale, vigorous, hopeful, with ancient wisdom and a young heart." Joy's task was less happy, to witness the demise of a venerable sister Methodist publication, as long declining subscriptions and sudden financial crisis of the Great Depression forced the end. Or was it rather a transfiguration? Rising from the ashes was Religion in Life, an ecumenical quarterly with strong continuing Methodist overtones.

The second half of the nineteenth century was the time of strong growth of church-related higher education, and especially of that new thing, theological education in seminaries. The beginning of the latter came before the Civil War, with establishment of an enterprise in New England that became Boston University School of Theology. John Dempster moved from there to the Midwest, which he called "this future garden of the New World." Writing in 1864, over ten years after the establishment under his leadership of Garrett Biblical Institute, he combined his enthusiasm for theological training of ministers with his enthusiasm for the westward course of the nation. A more cautious, even suspicious, view was taken by the old curmudgeon, Alfred Brunson, who found himself rather unwillingly appointed to the responsibility of judging the examinations of young men ready to be graduated.

Although some were not convinced that seminaries were a necessity, most leaders were agreed that some form of organized training was important. The General Conference Course of Study was now well established and appeared regularly in the Discipline. Twenty-year samplings illustrate the fare provided for ambitious young preachers.

However debatable were educational requirements for ministry, everyone got excited about the growing phenomenon of Sunday schools. At the center of this movement was John H. Vincent, who from the 1860's until his election as bishop in 1888 was a major figure in the Protestant Sunday school movement. Corresponding Secretary of the Sunday School Union, editor of Methodist Sunday school publications, author, founder of the Chautauqua Sunday-School Teachers'

Assembly--for three decades he dominated the movement.

A leader in youth work, Dan Brummitt, gives insights into the origins of the Epworth League.

¶   James Mudge on the *Methodist Review, 1894.*

(Taken from *ibid.*, July 1894, 524-26, 528-33).

VIII. We come now to the man who more than any other has given
the *Review* its standing and character, and who for no less a period
than twenty-eight years presided triumphantly over its destinies.
As the General Conference of 1856 approached several things combined
to bring forward Dr. Daniel D. Whedon as a candidate for the editorship of the *Quarterly*. His power as a writer had become thoroughly
established, and his great abilities in theology, exegesis, and
literature were by this time widely known in the East and the West
through his various contributions to the journals of the day and
many public addresses. His successful professorship of ten years
at Middletown and of seven years at the University of Michigan had
raised him up a host of friends. His increasing deafness, together
with his strong scholastic bent, largely unfitted him for the pastorate. Moreover, his devotion to the slave, through which he had lost
his position at Ann Arbor, emphasized his fitness for high honor in
the eyes of the more radical antislavery delegates in the General
Conference. He was accordingly chosen, even against so able and
popular an incumbent as Dr. McClintock, by a vote of 108 to 99,
though he was not a delegate to the Conference. Nor was he a member
of any of the six following General Conferences that successively re-
elected him. In 1860 and 1864 he was elected by acclamation, there
being no other nominee. In 1868 a ballot was taken, but out of 227
votes he had 155. In 1872 he had 225 votes out of 366. In 1876 he
was elected by acclamation. In 1880 he received 307 votes out of
373. So long as he was physically capable of the strain of the
editorship no other man was seriously thought of for this high post.
He took hold of the work at once with great vigor, making some
excellent changes. He enlarged "Religious and Literary Intelligence,"
first dividing it into "Religious Intelligence" and "Literary Items,"
and finally substituted two departments entitled, respectively,
"Foreign Religious Intelligence" and "Foreign Literary Intelligence."
He introduced a new department called "Synopsis of the Quarterlies,"
which presented a very valuable *résumé'* and criticism of the leading
articles in these periodicals. He also gave some space, for a while,
at the close of each number to brief editorial remarks. New writers
who have since achieved wide fame very speedily appeared. A goodly
number of laymen furnished acceptable articles. Several missionaries
discussed subjects relating to their respective fields. Three ladies
also appeared among the contributors.

To give anything like an adequate survey of the topics treated
during this long period of twenty-eight years would require, of
course, too great a space; but some idea of the treat furnished the
readers may be gathered from the following partial list. Among the
lighter subjects were these: "The Early Camp Meeting Song Writers,"
"A Plea for the Preacher's Wife," "Is the Modern Camp Meeting a

Failure?" "The Hearing Ear," "The Pacific Railroad," "The Modern Novel,"
"Religious Catalepsy," "Ministerial Transfers," "Toinette," "Plagiarism
and the Law of Quotation," "The Wandering Jew and his Congeners,"
"Florida - Its People and its Productions," "The Territory of Alaska,"
"The Republic of Liberia - Its Status and its Field," "Utah and the
Mormon Problem," "The Medical Profession," "The Temperance Reform,"
"Silence of Women in the Churches," "Should Presiding Elders by Elected?" "Remarkable Problems of our Population," "Our Sunday School
Literature." From all which it will be seen that the demand, perpetually springing up in one quarter or another - shown especially in
a resolution favorably reported to the General Conference of 1868
proposing to modify and popularize the *Review* so as to adapt it to a
larger class of readers, which resolution, however, was promptly laid
on the table - that popular themes be treated so that the average
minister might take more interest in the magazine, was heeded to as
large a degree as could well be done without sacrificing the true
character of the *Quarterly* and lowering it from its proper position
at the head of our periodical literature.   .   .   .

The most marked feature of Dr. Whedon's editorship is yet
to be mentioned - we mean the book notices. He classified them
carefully, a thing which had not been before attempted, and which
of itself indicated a purpose to take hold of the work with thoroughness. Besides a section for foreign theological publications, there
were such divisions as the following: "Religion, Theology, and
Biblical Literature;" "Philosophy, Metaphysics, and General Science;"
"History, Biography, and Topography;" "Politics, Law, and General
Morals;" "Educational;" "Belles Lettres;" "Pamphlets;" "Miscellaneous."
It was frequently the case that as many as fifty books were noticed
under these various heads, from twenty-five to forty-five pages being devoted to them. It was the portion of the *Review* first turned
to by most of the readers. They were certain to find there masterly
delineations, suggestive sentences, pungent paragraphs, and keenest
criticisms. Every page gave evidence that the books had been closely
scrutinized. An immense amount of pertinent and instructive observation was thrown in at all points. While McClintock was not surpassed
in purely literary characterizations and judgment, the new editor
promptly showed that in exegesis and theology a king had come to the
throne. He was called by *The Independent*, as well as by other great
judges, "the best review editor in the country;" and this verdict,
we think, will stand.

*   *   *

It has been calculated that Dr. Whedon gave to the Church in
the pages of the *Quarterly* from his own pen thirty duodecimo volumes
of three hundred pages each. The resolutions unanimously passed by
the General Conference of 1884 unquestionably voice the universal
acclaim. They said:

The service he has rendered the Church, by the devotion of his ripe scholarship, his extraordinary mental acumen, and his trenchant thoughts, to the work of enriching our literature and supplying intellectual food for both ministry and laity, is worthy of grateful mention and permanent record.

IX. The General Conference of 1884, noting the age and unmistakable signs of physical weakness which had overtaken the venerable editor of the *Review*, elected Dr. Daniel Curry in his place, by a vote of 193 out of 353. The Conference also voted, on the recommendation of the Committee on the Book Concern, that it would be well to issue the *Review* at lesser intervals and, so far as possible without lowering at all its high standard or jeopardizing its place among scholars of all denominations, to give such additional matter as would commend it to a wider audience among the people. Accordingly a fifth series was begun with January, 1885. It was changed from a quarterly to a bimonthly, six numbers, each of one hundred and sixty pages, being issued during the year, the periodical from this time being known as the *Methodist Review*.   .   .   .

The post was emphatically congenial to the new editor, who had already spent twelve years in the chair of *The Christian Advocate* and four more in that of the *National Repository*. He contributed no less than seven articles over his own name. Some changes were made in the editorial departments, so that this class of matter was now distributed under six heads, namely: "Current Topics;" "Foreign,Religious and Literary;" "Domestic Religious Intelligence" (though this was soon discontinued), "Missionary Intelligence," "The Magazines and Reviews," and "Book Notices." In "Current Topics" he discussed with great vigor such themes as "Unification of Methodism," "The Higher Criticism in Sunday Schools," "Evangelists and Revivals," "About Evolution," "Bishop William Taylor," "The Irish Land Question," "The Second Advent and the Millennium," "Methodistic Views Respecting Infant Baptism," "The Labor Problem in America," "The Mission of Methodism and Methodist Missions," "The Prohibition Movement," and "City Evangelization." Perhaps the most remarkable thing about the book notices - coming as they were supposed to do from the pen of the great debater who rarely had mercy on an opponent - is the very kindly spirit which they uniformly show. Could these reviews have been written by Daniel Curry, the fierce fighter on many floor?   .   .   .

X. In May, 1888, the Rev. J. W. Mendenhall, D.D., already known as a successful author, was chosen editor on the second ballot, having received 291 votes out of a total of 362. In his introductory address he refers to the general demand for some modification of the *Review* whereby it might be more thoroughly adjusted to the age. He says:

It must assert itself as a potent instrument in the
current strifes of the Church with the doctrinal
errors of modern thinkers and teachers. It is not a
relic of departed giants, but a scabbardless scimeter
to be used in everyday encounter with agnosticism, Old
Testament criticism, and all the cognate upheavals in the
path of Christian culture and progress....Its place is not
the quiet hammock in the summer or the cell of the student
in the winter, but always the arena of combat where intellectual charlatanry prevails, where the diplomacy of evil is in
exercise, where the biblicist is threatened with a cannon
ball, where truth is gashed by the archfiend of hell.

With January, 1889, a few changes were made, chief among them
being the creation of the "Arena," a department for brief discussions
and criticisms by contributors. Subsequently was added "The Itinerants' Club," at first under the charge of Bishop Vincent and designed for the special instruction of younger ministers. The *facsimile*
signature of writers was also introduced. Another feature made prominent was the symposium, grouping under one general head short articles by
different authors on closely related aspects of the same topic. The
subjects thus treated during the few following years were "Character,"
"Theology," "The Heathen," "The New Education," "Language Culture,"
"The American Republic," "The Historic Episcopate," "The Temperance
Movement," "The Christian Sabbath," "Life," "Immigration," and "Divorce."

The main feature, however, of Dr. Mendenhall's administration,
and that by which it must chiefly be judged, was a spirited onslaught
on rationalism, which was almost immediately inaugurated and was maintained with immense vigor to the end. The editor gave himself up with
entire abandon and enthusiasm to this crusade against Old Testament
criticism. The editorials in which he denounced those who had strayed
from the safe paths of orthodoxy, and whom he regarded as wicked dis-
turbers of the peace, amaze one by their length and number.   .   .

No one can question the belief of the author of these articles
that he was divinely called to champion the true faith against a most
dangerous foe. Nor will it be questioned that he did magnificent
service in marshaling the conservative forces and putting his readers
on their guard against such assaults upon Scripture as would destroy its
supernatural character. There can be no doubt as to the general approval
which the editor's course elicited from the Church at large. This was
especially indicated by the greatly increased subscription list which
made the *Review* self-supporting for the first time in a long period; but
the most emphatic indorsement of his work is found in the decided vote
by which the General Conference of 1892 reelected him - 399 out of a
total of 453 ballots.

He took an active part in the chief church questions of the day,
advocating the introduction of women into the General Conference but

not into the ministry, favoring a form of diocesan episcopacy but opposing the election of bishops merely for a limited term, and sternly arraigning "the diabolical alliance with the rum traffic on the part of the Christian community." He secured the writing of a valuable series of articles from strictly conservative scholars on various books of the Bible, such as Isaiah, Job, Daniel, Joshua, Amos, Romans, John, and Mark.   .   .   .

In February, 1893, the Book Committee elected as editor the Rev. William V. Kelley, D.D., a graduate of the Wesleyan University, at Middletown, Conn., in the class of 1865.

The list of those who have guided the destinies of the *Review* during these seventy-five years is not a long one, but it is certainly illustrious. A careful examination of the seventy-five volumes thus far issued profoundly impresses us with the wealth of material presented and preserved. A tempting feast is spread which every lover of wholesome intellectual food cannot fail to enjoy. Topics are provided in all their varied subdivisions - biblical, theological, ecclesiastical, biographical, and philosophical. He who sits down to this banquet hungry will rise up full. We may say of the *Review* in the words of Dr. Elijah H. Pilcher, who prepared with immense labor a complete index to the volumes from 1818 to 1881:

To the prophetic wisdom of its founders, a fulfillment; to its brilliant succession of conductors, a credit; and to the Church which it so ably represents, an honor - it promises to continue its beneficial career while spiritual life shall animate the denomination which it represents and a love for learning exist in the minds of her servants.

¶   John Faulkner on the *Methodist Review (MQR)*, 1917.

(Taken from *ibid.*, Nov. 1917, 862-65).

1818-1918. It has been a distinguished history, an unparalleled achievement. To maintain a periodical of its high class is proved to be very difficult by the failure of many most promising attempts. The mortality among such Reviews is appalling. Ours is the only religious body in America that has succeeded through a whole century. That there has been enough intellectual, religious, and theological life and productivity among us to keep up a Review for a hundred years reflects eternal glory upon our church, whatever the future may bring. Churches that despised us for our alleged sciolism and ignorance have been unable to compete with us here. The English Congregationalists had to give up the great British Quarterly Review (begun 1845), at the end of 1886. The old famous Eclectic Review (London), supported by Baptists and other Nonconformists, went under in 1868, though after a long life - sixty-three years. The North British Review - happy he

who has a set! - back of which was the Free Church of Scotland (1844ff.), went out in 1871. The Congregational Magazine, the Congregational Quarterly (1859-79), the Christian Review (Baptist, 1836-63), are found only in large theological libraries. The Baptist Quarterly (Philadelphia) a most admirable work) died in 1877, after its brief span of ten years. The Baptist Review (1879-1893) could not persist, though its last editor, my friend Professor Vedder, was a scholar, a man of letters, and an editorial genius. The (Protestant Episcopal) Church Review stopped,to my regret, in 1891 (for though in those years a humble pastor on modest salary I was a subscriber to that and several other theological journals of distinction). The American Presbyterian Review reigned with scholarly power from 1869 to the end of 1871, when it was combined with the Princeton. The Presbyterian Review, which filled up my ideal of a perfect theological Review, reposes up there on those shelves, only, alas! from 1880 to 1889 inclusive. I remember my grief when I read the slip announcing that I had received my last number. The Presbyterian and Reformed Review lasted from 1890 to 1902. The old Princeton Review began as the Biblical Repertory in 1825, added its well-known name in 1837, ran under its famous editor, Dr. Charles Hodge (died 1878), for forty-six years, and stopped at the end of 1877. Mr. Libbey started an entirely new periodical of the same name, with the most famous scholars - many of them theological - in the world as contributors, whom he paid lavishly, but the brief years 1878-84 marked its brilliant existence. The British and Foreign Evangelical Review disappeared in 1888 (begun 1856). The Theological Review (Unitarian, where you will find Martineau's powerful essays) shed its light but a short time (1864-79). The Modern Review (also Unitarian, as scholarly as interesting and strong) ceased to come to my library at the end of 1884, after its little life of five years. The Westminster Review, much of it religious, the organ of the George Eliot school - did it queer Robert Elsmere? - finally went out in 1914 after a long and distinguished career of ninety years. The Universalist Quarterly (Boston, 1844-91) was an honor to its denomination, but it, too, had to go. The Unitarian Review, of the same city, represented a church of culture and vast wealth, but its clergy had not enough interest in the Queen of the Sciences to keep the Review agoing (1874-91). Its successor, New World (Boston), a very attractive theological quarterly of high scholarly and literary aims, went out at the end of 1900 after a brief lapse of nine years; and the present Harvard Theological Review, which came in 1908 to take its place, is maintained by an endowment left by the late Rev. Professor Charles Everett. The Christian Quarterly (Disciples of Christ, Cincinnati), though in a church of live doctrinal interest, could not survive (1869-76, '82-'89). The New Englander had a long and eminent career (1843ff.), under the auspices mainly of the professors of the Yale Divinity School, but it finally became more or less secularized and died. The Yale Review took its place in 1892. Its young sister of the same Congregational fold, The Andover Review, I read for ten years (1884-93), but no longer, and had also the honor of being a contributor. The Southern Review (1867ff.), of which our able Rev. Dr. Bledsoe (Church, South),

mathematician and theologian, was editor, was discontinued in 1878, after the death of Dr. Bledsoe in December, 1877. The Presbyterian Quarterly, Richmond, Virginia, did fine work for some years (1887-1902). The Critical Review, Edinburgh, was an English Theologische Rundschau, only much sounder in its theology (1891-1904). The Review of Theology and Philosophy took its place in 1905, but it too, alas! went out in 1915, one of the offerings of this hellish war. With all these departed journals (and some I have purposely omitted) floating away into the dim past like shadows, behind many of which were venerable communions and wide and rich constituencies, that our own Review is about to enter its second century, hale, vigorous, hopeful, with ancient wisdom and a young heart, with eyes open wide to all the new wonders in science, art, literature, and life, and to all the new truth in sociology and religion, with a gracious spirit, catholic toward all churches yet faithful to its own, with undiminished substance of the faith of Christ, of Paul, and of Wesley, the faith once for all delivered to the saints - namely, Christ, the same yesterday, to-day, and forever (when it becomes disloyal to that faith may it die the death it deserves and its memory perish) - that is certainly a gift of God, rare and precious; a gift of which there is hardly a fellow in the long history of his church.

¶   James R. Joyce, *Methodist Review*, 1931.

(Taken from *ibid*, May 1931, 424-25).

The Book Committee of the Methodist Episcopal Church, in session at Cincinnati, Ohio, April 30, 1931, took action as follows:

"The publication of the METHODIST REVIEW shall cease as of July 1, 1931."

With this number, accordingly, the METHODIST REVIEW closes its career of distinguished usefulness. The initial number appeared in January, 1818, under the name *The Methodist Magazine*. Its "great design" was "the circulation of religious knowledge." From 1830 to 1840 it was *The Methodist Magazine and Quarterly Review*. From 1841 to 1884 it was *The Methodist Quarterly Review*. Since 1885 it has been published bi-monthly under the style of the METHODIST REVIEW. . . . .   Yet times have changed, and with them the opinions and tastes of the public, and of the periodicals which serve it. Methodist periodical literature was Wesley's weapon for fighting the foes of the Arminian doctrine which he taught. In America the Methodist press at first had the same battle on its hands, together with the task of winning recognition as a church worthy of intellectual respect. The REVIEW fought both these fights and won. After 118 years it is the last to leave the field and it marches off with banners flying. It has been demonstrated in its own experience and in that of its whilom denomination contemporaries that the work has

been accomplished. Why should it linger superfluous on the stage?

Yet a periodical which has enjoyed a long and vigorous life, into which a succession of able editors have poured the best they had of head and heart, cannot be discontinued without a feeling of regret. While we may and sincerely do approve the action of the Book Committee in discontinuing with this number the METHODIST REVIEW, which had its birth more than a century ago, we believe that not only Methodism, but the Protestantism of America has reason for satisfaction and pride in what this magazine has accomplished in diffusing light and truth from generation to generation. And yet -

> "Men are we and must grieve when even the shade
> Of that which once was great is passed away."

¶　　　　　Brunson on Theological Education.

(Taken from *A Western Pioneer* (1872), II, 328-33).

On the 23rd of October, I went by railroad to Evanston, taking a sleeping car to Milwaukee, reaching Dr. Kidder's, of the institute, on the 24th, in time for dinner. The examination was in progress, and at the organization of the visitors and also the joint board of visitors and trustees I was placed in the chair.

I had never been favorable to these "schools of the prophets," as they are called. Seeing the effects of them in other Churches, from which some learned dunces and hosts of second and third rate preachers had come forth, and a failure in two or three instances from our own institutions, had not given me any more favorable opinion of their utility. In this, my first visit to one of the kind, I desired to see and learn all I could of and concerning them. My mind was open to conviction, and especially as these institutions had been recognized and patronized by the General Conference, and had become "the order of the day" among us, and if there was any good, any thing superior to our old mode of training preachers *in* the work, instead of *for* the work.

In New England for half a century an institution for the education of "indigent pious young men for the ministry" has been in operation among the Congregationalists, and as a result, there are said to be near five hundred clergymen who were thus educated; but after missionating for years in pursuit of "a call," have been unable to obtain one, though there are about as many congregations of the same order without pastors. Now it follows that those "indigent pious young men" were not called of God to the work of the ministry, and that their education did not supply the want of that call. However useful their literary and theological advantages were, these could not and did not qualify them for the work in the estimation of their

own people, or some of their vacant pulpits would have been open to them.

But among the thousands of our ministers who have been educated in the work there can not be found that number, or that proportion of numbers, of failures. In our system of educating in the work, if the candidate is to fail he does it at so early a period as to be laid aside before his ordination.

It is true, in our present station system we have not the advantages attendant on the old circuit system to educate young men in the work. Then a young man usually had an older one over him to instruct him, but now the young man has to be alone. Then, being at a new place every day for four weeks upon a circuit, we could repeat the discourse till we had perfected it; but now, preaching to the same congregation every time, we must have a new subject, which requires a stock of knowledge to be laid in beforehand or extraordinary genius.

Again, our own people have been elevated by and through our ministry to a higher state of intelligence than we found them in, and their acquired knowledge, improved tastes, and aspirations require a more advanced stage of intelligence in a young man to begin with than was formerly necessary. But it should be remembered that the young men now called of God, come from this improved state of society; and as the fathers started from the state of society as it then existed, so our young men now start from the improved state of society, and, of course, have the same relative advantages the fathers did. If the old circuit system were still in use, they could grow as fast, relatively, as the fathers did; but the want of this furnishes one of the strongest arguments in favor of a higher degree of education to commence with that can be advanced. . . .

But our institutes require evidence of a divine call certified to by competent laymen, as well as ministers, before the student can be admitted. And if this certificate is based upon Methodist rule, that is, that there must be "gifts, grace, and usefulness, or fruit," in the conversion of souls, there can hardly be a failure in the candidate. There is a possibility of a mistake or of partiality of feeling from family relation or of taking the gifts of utterance, if there is piety, for fruit, or rather expectation of fruit. But these mistakes will not probably be more numerous than the failures under our old system.

Again, allowing the young man to grow as fast, after entering the work under our present station system, as the fathers did under the circuit system, a thing hardly possible in the nature of things, if equally industrious, having a greater stock of knowledge as a capital to begin with, he will derive a benefit from it.

In view of all the circumstances of the case, the change from the

402

circuit to the station system, each young preacher being alone, instead of having an elder brother with him to teach him, the elevated state of society, and the wish of our people to have educated men - and in this they are more clamorous for education than for talent, they would like, and prefer both, if combined, but prefer the learning without the talent, if but one can be had - and in view of the influence mere tinsel of this kind has upon outsiders in attracting them to our places of worship, it is probably best to have such institutions for such as prefer to go through a theological course before commencing the regular work of the ministry, or such as can not pass muster without it.

But it would be suicidal to require all our young men to have this preparatory course. If we should, the work could not be supplied, and souls must perish, for whom Christ died, on account of it. The General Minutes of conferences for 1864 show three hundred and forty-five to have been admitted on trial in all the conferences. Some years these admissions have been as high as five hundred, or more. Our Biblical institutes graduate not more than from ten to fifteen each, per annum. The wastage of our ministry by deaths, locations, or otherwise, is such that though three hundred and forty-five were added to their number, there were but thirty-three increase in the total number. To depend, therefore, upon our three principal institutions, the Drew Seminary, the Garrett Institute, and the Boston University, for men to fill up the ranks of our ministry, would be to diminish our ministry at the rate of from three hundred to five hundred per annum.

That our Church favors education, with more universities, colleges, seminaries, and institutes, than any other Church in the United States, no one can doubt. No Church has a more rigid and extensive course of theological study required of its ministers than ours, and candidates for our ministry can not be too well educated - the more extensively the better - before applying for admission. But the peculiar studies required of our ministry have, from necessity, been pursued in the work, or after beginning it, thus combining theory with practice. This rule we must adhere to for ages, if not centuries, as our theological institutes can not supply the requisite number of new ministers in less time, if it could even then. But in the mean time it is well to encourage Biblical studies, preparatory to entering the itinerancy, and to provide means for studying in it to all such as can do, being first called of God.

The examinations were very satisfactory. They showed the abilities and skill of the professors, and the attention and diligence of the students. The topics taught and learned were of such a nature as to be useful to a minister, if rightly used and improved upon; but however useful, they can not supply the experience necessary, and that can be attained only in the work.

In the exhibitions the young men acquitted themselves well but as such speeches are the result of long arrangements, writing, rewriting, memorizing, one can hardly form an idea from them of what the pulpit efforts would be of the same person, where less time is necessarily had in the preparation. We can form a better idea of a young man's ability to preach from hearing him a few times in more off-hand efforts. . . .

And it must be admitted that the same amount of knowledge, thought obtained on the circuit or in the station, is as good as if it was obtained in the institute or college; and often, if not generally, it is better, for the reason that it is obtained where theory and practice go hand in hand. It may require more time, but having the advantage of practice with it, it will be better tested and more solid. In truth our most learned and useful men obtain their most varied and useful learning after leaving the schools and engaging in practical life. The school disciplines the mind, and expands the faculties, and thus prepares it for study in after life; and it is always desirable, if possible, to have its advantages. But so many depend entirely upon their scholastic advantages, and neglect future study, that of the two classes the self-taught frequently excel the others in substantial and useful learning.

Evanston may be justly styled the Athens of the North-west portion of the United States. It is beautifully situated on the west bank of Lake Michigan, eleven miles north of Chicago. It was built in a grove, some of the trees large, and so many were left for ornament and shade that they hide the buildings from distant view. It is the seat not only of the Biblical Institute, but also of the North-western University, and the North-western Female College, now a department of the University, to which may be added high and common schools, under the school laws of the State. The morals of the place are of the highest grade and the state of society corresponds with its surroundings and advantages.

¶   The Course of Study.

(Taken from Disciplines of 1860, 1880, 1900, 1920).

    1860
I. For Candidates for Admission on Trial in the Traveling Connection.

    English Grammar-Modern Geography-True's Logic-Newman's Rhetoric.
    (Read Porter's Compendium of Methodism-Wesley's Sermons).

II. For Conference Membership and for Orders.

    FIRST YEAR - The Bible - Doctrines

The Existence of God - The Attributes of God, namely: Unity,
Spirituality, Eternity, Omnipotence, Ubiquity, Omniscience,
Immutability, Wisdom, Truth, Justice, Mercy, Love, Goodness,
Holiness - The Trinity in Unity - The Deity of Christ - The
Humanity of Christ - The Union of Deity and Humanity - Per-
sonality and Deity of the Holy Ghost - Depravity - Atonement -
Repentance - Justification by Faith - Regeneration - Adoption -
The Witness of the Spirit - Growth in Grace - Christian
Perfection - Possibility of Final Apostasy - Immortality of
the Soul - Resurrection of the Body - General Judgment -
Rewards and Punishments.

(The examination on the above to be strictly Biblical, requiring the candidate to give the statement of the doctrine
and the Scripture proofs. To prepare for this he should
read the Bible by course, and make a memorandum of the
texts upon each of these topics as he proceeds.)

Watson's Institutes, 1st Part - Wesley's Plain Account of Christian
Perfection - Fletcher's Appeal - Clark's Mental Discipline.

Essay or Sermon.

(Read Wesley's Notes - Steven's History of Methodism - Wilson's
General History).

SECOND YEAR - The Bible - Sacraments

The Sacrament of Baptism: Its Nature, Design, Obligations, Subjects,
and Mode - The Sacrament of the Lord's Supper: Its Nature, Design,
and Obligation.

(Mode of study and examination same as on Bible in the first year).

Watson's Institutes, 2d Part - Peck's Christian Perfection,
12 mo. - Fletcher's Christian Perfection - Strickland's
Manual of Biblical Literature - Methodist Discipline -
Mitchell's Ancient Geography.

Essay or Sermon.

(Read Bishop Emory's Defense of our Fathers - Powell on Apostolical
Succession - Dr. Emory's History of the Discipline - Wesley on Original Sin, and Wesley's Doctrinal Tracts - Johnston's Natural Philosophy).

THIRD YEAR - The Bible - History and Chronology

Watson's Institutes, 3d Part - Butler's Analogy - Peck's Rule of
Faith - Hibbard on Baptism - Ruter's Church History - Blair's Lectures

on Rhetoric, University Edition – Hedge's Logic.

Essay or Sermon.

(Read Bang's History of the Methodist Episcopal Church – Elliott on Romanism – Fletcher's Works – Rollin's Ancient History – Smith's Patriarchal Age – Hallam's Middle Ages – Russell's Modern Europe).

FOURTH YEAR – Review of the Whole Course

Watson's Institutes, 4th Part – Claude's Essay on the Composition and Delivery of a Sermon – Horne's Introduction, abridged – Stewart's Mental Philosophy.

Essay or Sermon.

(Read Smith's Hebrew People – Mosheim's Ecclesiastical History – Townley's Illustrations of Biblical Literature – Watson's Sermons – History of the United States – Stevens's Church Polity – Hibbard's Palestine: Its Geography and Bible History).

1880
I. For Traveling Preachers. For Admission on Trial.

Common English branches, History of the United States – Ridpath, Scripture History – Smith, (Abridged Edition in one vol.), Catechism of the Methodist Episcopal Church (No. 3), History of Methodism, Stevens (Abridged Edition), Discipline of the Methodist Episcopal Church (Edition of 1880), Compendium of Methodism – Porter, To be Read: Wesley's Sermons (Vol. 1.), Books of Reference: 1. Whitney's Handbook of Bible Geography, Freeman's Handbook of Bible Manners and Customs.

FIRST YEAR –

Biblical Theology: Introduction to the Holy Scriptures – Harman. (Old Testament, chapters i-xxx), Systematic Theology: Compendium of Christian Theology – Pope (Vol. 1), Plain Account of Christian Perfection – Wesley, Ancient History – Thalheimer, Rhetoric – Adams S. Hill, Written Sermon, To be Read: Wesley's Sermons (Vol. II), Foster's Christian Purity, Nast's Introduction to the Gospel Records, Henry and Harris's Ecclesiastical Law and Rules of Evidence.

SECOND YEAR –

Biblical Theology: Introduction to the Holy Scriptures – Harman.(Old Testament, chapters xxxi-lii), Systematic Theology: Compendium of Christian Theology – Pope (Vol. II.), The Sacraments: Baptism, The Lord's Supper, Mediaeval and Modern History – Thalheimer, Lessons in Logic – Jevons, Written Sermon, To be Read: Fletcher's Checks to Antinomianism, Stevens's History of Methodism, Emory's Defense of

Our Fathers, Shedd's Homiletics and Pastoral Theology.

THIRD YEAR –

Biblical Theology: Introduction to the Holy Scriptures – Harman (New Testament, chapters i-xviii), Systematic Theology: Compendium of Christian Theology – Pope (Vol. III.), Atonement in Christ – Miley, History of the Christian Church – Blackburn, Elements of Intellectual Science – Porter, Homiletics – Kidder, Written Sermon, To be Read: Whedon on The Will, Simpson's Lectures on Preaching, Hagenbach's History of Doctrines.

FOURTH YEAR –

Biblical Theology: Introduction to the Holy Scriptures – Harman (New Testament, chapters xix-xlix), Systematic Theology: Theological Institutes – Watson (Part II), Analogy of Natural and Revealed Religion – Butler, God's Word Written – Harbett, Written Sermon, To be Read: Conybeare and Howson's Life and Epistles of Saint Paul, Hurst's History of Rationalism, Fisher's History of the Reformation, Stevens's History of the Methodist Episcopal Church.

Method of Conducting Conference Examinations – 1900

1. In each Annual Conference a Board of Examiners shall be appointed by the Presiding Bishop, consisting of not less than eight nor more than twenty, care being taken to select men with special qualifications for the work, to whom shall be referred all preachers, both traveling and local, pursuing the Course of Study with a view to ordination or Conference Membership. This Board shall be continued for a term of four years, subject to reappointment. Vacancies to be filled at each session of the Annual Conference.

2. This Board shall organize by electing one of its members Chairman and another Registrar, the latter to keep a permanent record of the standing of the students, and report to the Conference when required. This record shall include the credits allowed students for work done in Theological Seminaries and Colleges described in ¶57.§1.

3. The Chairman shall assign to each Examiner the books or subjects in which he is to give instruction by correspondence and final examination, for which examination he shall prepare and send to the Chairman printed or written questions, at least ten in number, two weeks before the time of examination. Vacancies occurring in the Board during the year may be filled by the Chairman until the ensuing Annual Conference.

4. One or two examinations may be held during the year in locations convenient to the students. These examinations shall be under the personal supervision of some member of the Board delegated

by the Chairman.

5. The examinations shall be in writing, if practicable, and in the presence of witnesses, and in that case the papers shall be sent to the Examiners to whom they belong respectively. They shall be graded upon the scale of 100, and none below 70 per cent shall pass. The Examiners shall report the marking of each paper to the Registrar.

6. The provision for mid-year examinations shall not deprive any student of the opportunity of being examined at the seat and time of the Annual Conference.

7. The Board of Examiners shall convene at the seat and time of the Annual Conference, the day before the session opens, to review and complete the work of the year; to examine any students who have not been examined during the year, and to arrange for the work of the year to come. - *Journal*, 1896, p. 296; 1900, p. -

Smaller Scripture History - Smith, History of the Methodist Episcopal Church, Vol. I - Stevens, Student's American History - Montgomery, English and American Literature - Beers, Written Sermon and Essay, To be Read: Discipline of the Methodist Episcopal Church (1900), Selections from Writings of John Wesley - Welch, The Tongue of Fire - Arthur, The Revival and the Pastor - Peck, A Short History of the English People - Green.

FIRST YEAR -

Introduction to the Holy Scriptures (Old Testament. P. 1-447) - Harman, Systematic Theology, Vol. I - Miley, Christian Purity, or the Heritage of Faith - Foster, Discipline of the Methodist Episcopal Church, 1900 (Parts I-V), Principles of Rhetoric - Hill, Preparation and Delivery of Sermons (Parts I, II) - Broadus, Written Sermon, To be Read: Sermons, (Vol. I) I-XXXIII - Wesley, History of the Methodist Episcopal Church, Vol. II - Stevens, The Governing Conference in Methodism - Neely, Christian Science and Other Superstitions - Buckley, Ecclesiastical Architecture - Martin, From the Himalayas to the Equator - Foss, Problem of Religious Progress - Dorchester, History of the Ritual of the Methodist Episcopal Church - Cooke, Asbury's Journal, Vol. I, Methodist Review.

SECOND YEAR -

Introduction to the Holy Scriptures (New Testament. Pp. 448-770) - Harman, Systematic Theology, Vol. II - Miley, Discipline of the Methodist Episcopal Church, 1900 (Part VI to end), Preparation and Delivery of Sermons (Parts III-V) - Broadus, Lessons in Logic - Jevons, Outlines of Universal History - Fisher, One Thousand Questions on Methodism - Wheeler, Essay, To be Read: Sermons (Vol. I) XXXIV-LVIII - Wesley, History of the Methodist Episcopal Church Vol. III - Stevens,

History of Methodism Vol. I - Stevens, Introduction to New Testament -
Dods, Future Retribution - King, Digest of Methodist Law (Edition of
1900) - Merrill, The General Conference and Episcopacy - Harris,
Christian Archaeology - Bennett, The Modern Sunday School (Edition of
1900) - Vincent, Asbury's Journal Vol.II, Methodist Review.

THIRD YEAR -

Biblical Hermeneutics - Terry, Exegetical Studies in the Pentateuch
(The Pentateuch and Isaiah) - Warren, Extemporaneous Oratory - Buckley,
Outlines of Descriptive Psychology - Ladd, History of the Christian
Church, Vol. I - Hurst, The Land of Israel - Stewart, Written Sermon,
To be Read: History of the Methodist Episcopal Church Vol. IV -
Stevens, History of Methodism, Vol. II - Stevens, The Supernatural
Book - Foster, Introduction to Political Economy (Revised) - Ely,
The Historic Episcopate - Cooke, Hymn Studies - Nutter, Asbury's
Journal, Vol. III, The Methodist Review.

FOURTH YEAR -

The Foundations of the Christian Faith - Rishell, Exegetical Studies
in Isaiah (The Pentateuch and Isaiah) - Warren, Christian Ethics -
Smyth, Introduction to Sociology - Fairbanks, History of the Christian
Church, Vol. II - Hurst, Essay, To be Read: Supplementary History of
American Methodism - Stevens, History of Methodism, Vol. III - Stevens,
Analogy of Natural and Revealed Religion - Butler, Life and Epistles
of St. Paul - Conybeare and Howson, The Son of Man - Alexander,
Foreign Missions of the Protestant Churches - Baldwin, History of
Rationalism (Revised Edition 1901) - Hurst, Methodist Review.

English Courses. Traveling Preachers - 1920

   1. Directions for Students and Examiners: Special attention is
called to the "Directions and Helps" as listed in the following
courses. These consist of leaflets and pamphlets giving the student
directions for his work and helps for his study. They indicate also
the work to be done in the regular subjects of the year and in the
"Collateral Reading and Study." The special tasks assigned in them
are a part of the required course. They are to be ordered from the
Book Concern.

   A pamphlet containing suggestions and directions for Conference
Boards of Examiners will be furnished free to each examiner, together
with that part of the "Directions and Helps" which pertains to the
subjects assigned to him. These will be furnished through the Conference Registrars, who are asked to report the names and addresses of
examiners, and the subjects assigned to each on the basis of the new
course.

   Wherever it is at all possible, the Annual Conference is urged to

make provision through its Board of Examiners for a midyear institute, at which examinations may be held, instruction given to the men in the course of study, and lectures and addresses offered for all preachers.

Examinations will be upon the courses noted below until such time as the Commission on Courses of Study constituted by action of the General Conference of 1920 shall have been appointed and the courses approved by the Board of Bishops. Due notice as to these new courses and the time when they will become effective will be given through the Church papers and to the Registrars.

Examination for Admission on Trial:

The English Language: (a) The Art of Writing English – Brown and Barnes, (b) All papers submitted by the candidate shall be examined and marked with reference to the use of English; American History – James and Sanford, Doctrines and Discipline of the Methodist Episcopal Church, with special Reference to the Twenty-five Articles. (For a good commentary on these, see Wheeler, Twenty-five Articles of Religion of the Methodist Episcopal Church). (a) Life of John Wesley – Winchester, (b) Selections from the Writings of John Wesley – New Edition – Welch. Plain Account of Christian Perfection – Wesley. The candidate shall be prepared to write a paper of not less than five hundred words giving a summary of the contents.

The candidate shall be prepared to write a paper of not less than one thousand words upon one of the following subjects, using only the materials found in the Bible: The Life of Moses, the Life of David, the Life of Jesus as recorded in Mark, the Life of Paul as given in Acts. The subject to be written upon shall be assigned at the time of the examination; A written sermon, Directions and Helps for the Examination for Admission (see under §1).

Course of Study for First Year –

New Testament History – Rall, Human Behavior – Colvin and Bagley, The Making of the Sermon – Pattison, How to Study and Teaching How to Study – McMurry, Directions and Helps for the First Year (see under §1). Collateral Reading and Study: The Church School – Athearn, Public Worship – Hoyt, Individual Work for Individuals – Trumbull, The Pastor-Preacher – Quayle, Winning the Fight Against Drink – Eaton, The Life of the Spirit in the Modern English Poets – Scudder, Francis Asbury – Tipple, The Methodist Review.

Course of Study for Second Year –
(a) Dictionary of the Bible (1 Vol. Edition) – Hastings (See Directions and Helps for assignment of work), (b) The Bible in the Making – Smyth, (c) How We Got Our Bible – Smyth. A Short History of the Christian Church – Moncrief. (a) The Pupil and the Teacher – Weigle, (b) The Graded Sunday School in Principle and Practice –

Meyer, The Way to Win - Fisher. Directions and Helps for the Second Year (see under §1). Collateral Reading and Study: The Christian View of the Old Testament - Eiselen, Education in Religion and Morals - Coe, The Preacher, His Life and Work - Jowett, Letters on Evangelism - Hughes, Solving the Country Church Problem - Bricker, History of Methodism (Vol. I) - Stevens, Martin Luther, the Man and His Work- McGiffert, The Methodist Review.

Course of Study for Third Year -

Beacon Lights of Prophecy - Knudson, Foundations of Christian Belief - Strickland, The Social Problem - Ellwood, Introduction to the study of Comparative Religion - Jevons, Directions and Helps for the Third Year (see under §1). Collateral Reading and Study: Studies in Christianity - Bowne, The Fact of Christ - Simpson, Christianity and the Social Crisis - Rauschenbusch, Social Evangelism - Ward, The Community Survey in Relation to Church Efficiency - Carroll, History of Methodism (Vol. II) - Stevens, Life of Phillips Brooks (briefer edition) - Allen, The Methodist Review.

Course of Study for Fourth Year -

Paul and His Epistles - Hayes, System of Christian Doctrine - Sheldon (Except Part I and Appendix), Everyday Ethics - Cabot, (a) The New Home Missions - Douglas, (b) Social Aspects of Foreign Missions - Faunce. Directions and Helps for the Fourth Year (see under §1). Collateral Reading and Study: Historical Geography of the Holy Land - Smith, The Book of Isaiah (Vol. I) Expositor's Bible - Smith, Outline of Christian Theology - Clarke, The Call of the World - Doughty, The Church a Community Force - Tippy, The Minister as Shepherd - Jefferson, History of Methodism (Vol. III) - Stevens, The Methodist Review.

¶   Sunday Schools.

(Taken from John H. Vincent, *The Modern Sunday-School* (1887), 83-87).

The Sunday-school teacher needs just what the normal school aims to secure for the secular teacher. His work is as important in its aims. He deals with the same intellectual powers, and addresses himself, in a peculiar manner, to the more delicate, important, and powerful energies of the soul - the conscience, the affections, the will. The text-book which he employs is as full of difficulties, his pupils are as apathetic. He experiences the same obstacles in the way of quickening the intellect. In his work the curiosity is to be aroused, attention concentrated, voluntary, delighted, and persistent effort to be secured. The Sunday-school normal class is, therefore, based upon the same theory as that which establishes the secular normal school, and it aims at the same worthy and much-needed practical results.

The standard of secular education in these days is so high, and the appliances employed so perfect, that the sabbath school must elevate its standard if it would maintain its power. Children measure their teachers in these days. Many of them are able to do it. No sincerity of character or earnestness of effort can compensate for a poorly prepared lesson, or for habitual incompetency on the part of a Sunday-school teacher. It is a lamentable hindrance to one's success in this field to have his scholars contrasting his matter and style of teaching with those of ordinary teachers in the public schools, or detecting the sophisms or superficial evasions of his explanations. It is not only that the teacher suffers in the estimation of his scholars, but the system of truth he represents also suffers loss.

All truth is divine. We may regard the teachers of natural science and mathematics in our public schools and academies as so many ambassadors of God to the soul of the child. In the Sunday school we have charge of another department of divine teaching. Ours is the ethical and spiritual, and we deal with intellect. We seek to exalt and sanctify it - to connect it with a "pure conscience" and a redeemed heart, that it may become the throne of a "faith unfeigned." The secular teachers tell the little ones of God in nature; we, of God in grace. They conduct them through the outer courts of the cosmos; we lead them beyond the veil, into the innermost sanctuary, where God's voice is heard, and where man may commune face to face with Him. We must, therefore, be "apt to teach." We are to show ourselves "approved" -"workmen that need not to be ashamed, rightly dividing the word of truth." Wisely did the apostle suggest to Timothy, "Give attendance to reading...to doctrine."

The labour of the Sunday-school teacher is voluntary, and performed under the pressure of secular occupations. Mothers come to the Sunday school, as teachers, from the nursery, merchants and clerks from the counter and counting-room, mechanics from the shop, farmers from the field, lawyers from the bar, jurists from the bench, physicians from the bedside, students from the recitation-room. They are engaged six-sevenths of their time in callings wholly unconnected with the specific work of the sabbath school. To perform it they turn aside from their habitual paths of thought and effort. Many of them are wholly deficient in mental discipline, and with no time for preparation, must make sad work with the brain of the pupil and the Book of God on the sabbath. . . .

Yet we can have no permanent theological school for the training of Sunday-school teachers. Nor can the want be realized in every case by teachers' meetings. . . .

Whether, therefore, we look at the best or the poorest of our schools, the conclusion is forced upon us: We must have a general system for the training of teachers - a system that will secure the establishment of regular weekly teachers' meetings where they are not

now held, and provide, in some form or other, a complete preparatory course of training in connection with those schools which have all along sustained the teachers' meeting.

Conventions, local and general, may render assistance by the dissemination of Sunday-school ideas, the comparison of plans, the discussion of principles, and the occasional illustration of approved methods. But the best convention we ever attended left an important work undone. Mere conventions, in which whole counties, and even States, are represented, cannot meet the demand we have specified. The introduction of institute exercises, or normal methods, into these conventions, has been a means of improving their character. But in the midst of these occasional and exceptional exercises we have asked, Is there not yet something more practical - some plan better adapted to the necessities of the work?

The answer is to be found in the normal class exercises hereinafter described.

¶ The Epworth League.

(Taken from Dan B. Brummitt, *Epworth League Methods* (1906), 9-12).

Methodism and Her Young People.

The Epworth League is the young people's society of the Methodist Episcopal Church. Under its banners practically all the young people of the Church are enrolled. No other Church has succeeded in organizing its young life so extensively, and, at the same time, so intensively, as has the Methodist Episcopal Church by means of the Epworth League.

But it must not be supposed that this Epworth League movement was the initial effort of Methodism to promote the social, intellectual, and spiritual culture of her young people. During all the years of her eventful history individual Churches have maintained societies for the special benefit of their younger members. In the years immediately preceding the birth of the Epworth League these organizations had multiplied until, in the larger Churches, they had become quite common. Many of the distinguishing features of these local organizations were retained in the more general organizations, and, in turn, have been inherited by the Epworth League.

The first movement to provide a uniform organization dates back to the year 1872. Some time previous to that date there had been organized by the Rev. Dr. T. B. Neely, in the Fifty-first Street Methodist Episcopal Church, Philadelphia, a Church Lyceum, the chief object of which was to encourage the systematic reading of approved

books. Several similar lyceums were formed in neighboring Churches, and soon it was thought best, for purposes of mutual co-operation, to unite these in a city union. At a meeting of the Board of Managers of this central body, held March 3, 1872, it was resolved to memorialize the General Conference, then soon to assemble at Brooklyn, N.Y., asking formal recognition of the Lyceum. The memorial was referred to a committee, which made a favorable report, but, owing to the great pressure of business at the close of the General Conference session, the recommendations of the committee were not acted upon. At the succeeding General Conference, that of 1876, the request for official recognition was renewed. The Conference adopted *verbatim* the paragraph sent up in 1872.

The Lyceum was received with much favor in different parts of the Church. It did good work in stimulating the intellectual life of the young, and in promoting a taste for the pure and upbuilding in literature. The organization was destined, however, to give place to the Oxford League, a society which retained the idea of intellectual culture, but provided also for special activity in the realm of social and spiritual life.

The Five Original Societies.

The Epworth League is the resultant of the amalgamation of five other societies - the Young People's Methodist Alliance, the Oxford League, the Young People's Christian League, the Methodist Young People's Union, and the Young People's Methodist Episcopal Alliance.

Of these the oldest was the Young People's Methodist Alliance. It came into existence August 25, 1883. Its birthplace was a woody grove on the old and historic Desplaines Camp-ground, not far from the city of Chicago. It emphasized the highest spiritual experience, mutual helpfulness, daily Bible study, the avoidance of doubtful pleasures, and ardent loyalty to all that is embodied in the word "Methodism."

The prime mover in the organization and development of the Oxford League was Dr. John H. Vincent. The General Conference of 1876 made provision for the Lyceum, but it was found that the purpose of this organization did not meet the needs of the young people. Dr. Vincent, keenly alive to the real requirements of the multitudes of young Methodists, sought to supply the vital thing which the Lyceum lacked. He proposed to organize a young people's society that should provide symmetrical spiritual and intellectual culture. This society was called "The Oxford League," after the famous English university in which the "Holy Club," to which the Wesley's belonged, was founded. The new organization was received with favor by many pastors and leading laymen, and was given hearty and significant indorsement at the centennial anniversary of the "Christmas Conference," which was held in Baltimore, December 9-17, 1884.

414

The late Rev. Dr. J. H. Twombly was the originator of the
Young People's Christian League. Years before, in his early pastorate, he organized the young people for service. One of his dreams
had been the gathering of a great Methodist international meeting of
young people. The hour of the fulfillment of his dream was not far
off when the Young People's Christian League was born, in 1887. The
Young People's Christian League was started with broader plans than
any society then existing in the Church. The Young People's Methodist
Alliance at that time had only one class of Members, and the Oxford
League required a uniform constitution, and neither of these societies
was able to group together the already existing societies which were
in many of our Churches. The Young People's Christian League aimed
to unify the interests of these older societies, Lyceums, Guilds,
Bands, etc., with their local histories and associations, by making
them auxiliary to a central body without requiring any change of name
or constitution or method of work, wherever these were acceptable to
their local Church.

The Methodist Young People's Union had its headquarters in
Michigan. The organization was the outcome of a meeting of certain
alert Detroit Conference pastors. For some time they had been impressed that the time had come for the formation of a society for the
social and religious culture of their young people - a society better
fitted for this high purpose than any of those already in existence.
The matter was first broached in November, 1887, and a Conference
organization was formed, known as the "Young People's Society of
Detroit Conference." A comprehensive constitution was adopted. Many
of its best features were ultimately wrought into the plan of the
Epworth League.

The fifth of the "original societies" was but an infant when
the consolidation took place. The organizers doubtless hoped that
they had found the solution of the problem that was vexing the leaders
of the younger hosts of Methodism. One who was high in the councils
of this new organization has said that the North Ohio Conference
Methodist Episcopal Alliance was the outgrowth of a desire for the
consolidation of all Methodist Episcopal societies of young people
into one great connectional society.

18. NEW THEOLOGY

Methodists became more consciously theological as the church expanded and put down roots after the Civil War. Seminaries provided a powerful impetus to systematic thought and organized teaching. But not all theology came from seminaries. Some active leaders, like Bishop Matthew Simpson and editor Daniel Whedon, were self-trained theologians who went on from regular liberal education to independent contributions in Christian thought. Not all of it was polemic, like most of the work in the past. Publications began to take on the aspects of objectivity and systematization. Nevertheless, "Calvinists" and "Deists" continued to lurk in the background. "Arminian" walls were strengthened in defense of Wesleyan theological tradition.

Two who spoke out from episcopal or editorial rather than seminary positions were Simpson and Whedon, the latter long time editor of the Methodist Quarterly Review. *The bishop effectively brought the "message" into the context of the art of preaching. He himself was a master of the pulpit. Whedon took to new levels the debate on freedom of the will, which had arisen in the struggles of Methodism to strike roots in the unfavorable intellectual soil of New England in the days of Nathan Bangs and Wilbur Fisk.*

Concord-Boston, Garrett, and Drew seminaries stimulated scholarly study and writing by their professors. The first to produce systematic theology was Miner Raymond, who in the late 1870's brought out an impressive three volume work under that title. In many ways he clung to the old modes, but the very effort to put the whole into a system was a new departure for practical-minded Methodists. English-born Watson had sufficed for a half century. Raymond sought to make the hard doctrines of depravity more patatable to reasonable people. He was professor at Garrett Biblical Institute from 1864 till 1897.

More forthright in his approach to traditional Wesleyan theology, but not departing from it, was John Miley, professor at Drew Theological Seminary from 1873 till 1895. He too produced an important Systematic Theology, *but became well known as author of a trenchant work on the atonement.*

416

¶   Preaching the Message.

(Taken from Matthew Simpson, *Lectures on Preaching* (1879),
   297-300, 330-35).

    It has become fashionable in certain circles to speak of the
failure of the pulpit. It is represented as belonging chiefly to a
past age, and it is declared that its power over men is passing away.
Some of the writers for the daily press and some of the contributors
to the literary reviews claim for themselves the distinguished honor
of controlling the public mind. They speak of the power of the
press, the number of readers whom they reach by their pen, and the
immense influence which they exert in public affairs. In their
glorification of the press they look upon the pulpit as a diminishing
quantity - as an agency once potent, but which is now almost superseded. A few scientists, also - men of intellectual power and extensive learning, but of skeptical views - have wrought themselves into
the belief that their discoveries in science have invalidated the
authority of the holy Scriptures. They assail the pulpit, not so
much on account of the character of its agency, as because they
fancy the matter of preaching is becoming obsolete. They extol the
triumphs of science, and call in question the possibility of a
revelation from God, and occasionally the very existence of a divine
being. I do not desire to underrate the value of the press; it is one
of the most powerful agencies, as it is, also, the offspring, of a
Christian civilization. It has its place - a conspicuous place - in
diffusing intelligence and in guiding the movements of society.

    There should be no rivalry, much less should there be enmity,
between the press and the pulpit. Each has its appropriate sphere,
and the exaltation of the one does not diminish the glory of the
other. Nor should there be any conflict between the pulpit and men
of true science. Their spheres are widely different: the scientist
is engaged in tracing the laws of matter and ascertaining the
properties with which God has invested it; the preacher is engaged
in proclaiming God's mercy and love as revealed to fallen man, and
the precious promises which he has given of pardon for sin, of
purification of heart, and of a glorious immortality. A few of those
who occupy the pulpit very injudiciously assail the scientists, un-
dervaluing their studies, and reproaching them for their attachment
to science. Sometimes, also, a few who are uncultured, or who have
failed to keep pace with scientific inquiries, announce propositions
almost as absurd as those of the colored preacher of Richmond, who
has recently been lecturing on "The sun, he do move." On the other
hand, there are a few scientists who are as ignorant of the Bible as
the colored lecturer was of astronomy, and who make mistakes if not
so palpable yet quite as ridiculous. Between such extremists in the
pulpit and in the schools of science there is a conflict. But between
the true minister and the true scientist there should be none whatever.
They are engaged in studying different phases of truth. They occupy

                                417

different stand-points, and if the pictures they present do not seem fully to harmonize, it arises from the limits of human vision and from the imperfections of human knowledge. The eye above and at the center can alone perceive and comprehend the harmony of the whole. There is another class of thinkers who are opposed to the pulpit because it proclaims the truths of the Bible; and the Bible is opposed to them. It denounces the judgments of God upon their sinful practices, and they hate the Bible and all who believe it. Such men talk of the failure of the pulpit, and with them "the wish is father to the thought." There are still others so absorbed in business and in various pursuits that they seldom attend a Church or hear a sermon. Possibly when they chanced to attend they were not pleased with the discourse, and their dissatisfaction with one sermon is extended to all; fancying because they care nothing for the pulpit that others sympathize with them, they also glibly talk of its failure.

I do not know precisely what these various classes mean when they use this phrase. Nor am I sure that they perfectly understand themselves. A machine is a failure when it cannot perform the work for which it was designed. But the ignorance, or incapacity, or negligence of a workman, though causing failure on his part, is not properly charged as a failure of the mechanism. So the pulpit is a failure if it is not suited to perform the work for which it was instituted; but it is not a failure simply because some of its preachers may be unskillful or unworthy. There is a clear distinction between failures in the pulpit and the failure of the pulpit itself. The superintendent of a railroad may be a failure, while the railroad itself may be a great public benefit. A cook may be a failure, but the kitchen remains an imperative necessity.

Were I, then, to admit, as I readily do, that some preachers are failures - were I to go further, and admit that many are failures - nay, were we to suppose that nine out of every ten were failures - that would not constitute the pulpit a failure, while even one in ten makes it a grand and glorious success.

*   *   *

The pulpit of to-day should be more powerful than that of any previous age. The preacher has more facilities for an accurate and extensive education, more helps to a thorough understanding of God's word. Investigation and research have brought into clearer light the meaning of various illustrations, and as the ages advance there is a brighter and more beautiful harmony between the volume of revelation and the works of God scattered throughout his universe. In despite of the votaries of a philosophy falsely so called, who seek to invalidate the Bible and to overthrow Christianity, each effort recoils upon its authors, and the claims of the Bible to a divine authorship become more and more apparent. There are glimpses of light long concealed which break forth every now and then, showing that He who inspired the

Scriptures, thousands of years ago, was not unacquainted with those secrets of the universe which are being unfolded in these later times. As some inscription discovered on the bricks of Nineveh, or among the monuments of Egypt, throws light upon the customs of buried nations in the distant centuries; so these occasional glimpses connect the record of the past with the discoveries of the present. With all these helps, imparting both light and confidence, the preacher of to-day should be able to handle the word of the Lord more skillfully. As the Holy Spirit loves truth, and accompanies the truth to the hearts of the hearers, so we may expect a larger spiritual influence to attend the ministrations of the coming day.

The pulpit is still greatly needed. It is the great bond of union between the rich and the poor. Few understand the afflictions through which the lower classes pass, or the trials which they endure. Little do the upper classes of society know of their sufferings and their sorrows; their loss of employment and consequent loss of means of support; their narrow lodgings, scanty fare, and almost untold anguish. They instinctively shrink from the presence of those who live more comfortably and are unwilling to come into association with them. This unwillingness to associate strengthens sometimes into aversion, and then to positive hatred. Not until the minister by some act of kindness, by some manifestation of sympathy, by some effort in their behalf gains their confidence, do they open their hearts even to him.

It is the office of the minister to draw them to himself, that he may draw them to Christ. What a lesson do we find in the example of the blessed Saviour! Wise beyond all human wisdom, pure beyond all human holiness, he stooped to touch the most loathsome and vile. The crowds followed him because he did them good. He healed the sick, he fed the hungry, and then the common people heard him gladly. So, also, did the apostles. They were gifted with miraculous power to do the people good, and wherever they went society was stirred to its foundations. They were miraculously endowed because they had no power of themselves. They had neither money, position or influence. They could command no resources, could confer no benefits. Times have changed. The Church has become strong, wealthy, and influential. The riches of the world are in the hands of Christian nations and Christian communities. While the minister may be able to do but little of himself, he has the public ear and public confidence. He is a bond of union, and the only bond of union, between the various classes of society. Educated and refined, he can associate with the wealthiest and the highest; at the same time, with limited means, and visiting among the masses, his heart is drawn toward them. If he be truly a man of God, he becomes a nucleus around which all the elements gather, attracted by his purity, benevolence, and love. . .

I have now finished, young gentlemen, the present course of lectures. I have invited your attention to the various departments of

your great work. I have presented you glimpses of my own experience, and I have set before you the duties of the sacred office in some measure as they rise before my mind. Before I bid you farewell, may I add a word personal to yourselves. Your exit from this institution, and your entrance practically into the ministry, will mark a great era in the period of your lives. You pass from the retreat of the school into the activity of a busy world; from communion with kindred and cultured minds to become servants of a lost and ruined humanity. You go to lift out of the pit of degradation the most depraved and vicious; to draw the drunkard from his cups, and the young man from saloons of revelry and crime. You need moral courage; you need Christian heroism. Above all, you need power from on high. We are told that the Roman youth of noble family approaching years of maturity entered alone into a private apartment, amid the statues of the gods and of eminent men. In that august and solemn presence he divested himself of the raiment of his boyhood, and put on the manly toga. Then and there he made his vow to imitate the virtues of the great, to rival them in deeds of power, and to make for himself a name worthy of his kindred and ancestry. So as you go forth to enter on your life's duties, make a fresh consecration of all your powers to the service of God. Call around you the unseen; summon to your thoughts the great men of the pulpit who have shaken and moved the world; and there, with a cloud of holy angels above you, and in the immediate presence of the Son of God, whose eyes are like a flame of fire, pray to be clothed with divine power, to be encased in Christian armor, to have "your loins girt about with truth, and having on the breast-plate of righteousness; and your feet shod with a preparation of the Gospel of peace; above all, taking the shield of faith, wherewith ye shall be able to quench all the fiery darts of the wicked. And take the helmet of salvation, and the sword of the Spirit, which is the word of God: praying always with all prayer and supplication in the Spirit." Here resolve that all you are and all you have shall be devoted to this one work: that with all your energies and all your power you will strive against the powers of darkness, and to advance the kingdom of heaven, the Church of the living God; resolve, God helping you, that the Gospel spoken from your lips shall never be spoken in vain, and that you will realize the utmost possibilities of divine power and grace in your ministry among men.

¶   More on Freedom of the Will.

(Taken from Daniel Whedon *Freedom of the Will* (1864), 396-99).

The Maxims of Responsibility.

It is sometimes said that our doctrine of Will fundamentally decides our theology, or rather our theodice. But in truth there is an underlying principle by which our doctrine of the Will itself is likely to be shaped and decided, namely, our fundamental Maxim of

Obligation or Responsibility. If power to act must underlie and be commensurate with obligation to act, then there must be exemption from necessity to obey motive, however strongest, counter to obligation. But if our maxim be that no matter how we come by volition, disposition, state, nature, or what its cause, we are in any case responsible for its intrinsic good or evil, then freedom or non-freedom is morally an unimportant question. This maxim we now consider.

"A man is not to blame for what he cannot help," is the universal language of the moral sense and the common sense. If an act be positively done, without the power of not-doing, or not done for want of power of doing, there can be no guilt. For neither performance of what could not be avoided, nor for non-performance of what could not be done, can there be obligation, responsibility, guilt, blame, or just punishment. The wrong would be in the requirement, not in the non-compliance.

A command requiring an act, requires the exertion of an existing power; and if the power does not exist, then there is the requirement for the exertion of a non-existence or nothing. To require the exertion of a nothing, is to require nothing; that is, the requirement is no requirement.

An act without power adequate to perform it is an event without a cause. To require such an act is to require a causeless effect. No matter what may be the agent or object of whom or which the requirement is made, whether he or it be mind or matter, intelligent or unintelligent, living or lifeless, to require of it a result for which there exists in it no adequate causality is to require a causeless effect. But to require a causeless effect is to require a nothing, and is therefore no requirement at all.

For the non-performance of this non-requirement just penalty is impossible. Pain can indeed be inflicted for nothing. A being of infinite power may inflict all the suffering which a finite being is capable of enduring. He may inflict this pain in consequence of the imposition of a form of requirement which is not a requirement, and in consequence of the non-performance of an action which is no action. But such pain would be no just penalty, nor could the omnipotence of the author make it such. Such action or non-action is no basis for responsibility, for judicial sentence, or for a just retributive divine government.

The axiom that *adequate power must underlie obligation* is equally valid whether the required act be external *or corporeal, or whether intellectual or volitional*. It is equally true that an act for which there exists in the agent no adequate power is not morally requirable; whether it be an unconscious effect of a lifeless cause, as the production of lightening from a solid cube of iron; or an external voluntary corporeal act, as to turn a planet out of its

421

course with my hand; or an intellectual act, as to know the nature and number of the inhabitants of Saturn; or *volitional act,* as to put forth the volitions necessary to call all those inhabitants by their true names. And for just this reason, namely, that all these requirements are alike requirement of a causeless effect, and therefore no requirement at all.

We inaugurate, then, this, what we will call the *axiom of freedom and responsibility,* and hold it as valid as any axiom of geometry. Power must underlie obligation. *There can be no full moral obligation to an act, volitional or non-volitional, for which there is not in the required agent full and adequate power.* Or otherwise, *there can be no guilt or responsibility for act or volition, for avoidance of which there is not complete and adequate power;* that is, for which there is not a *power adequate to counter act or volition.* If guilt, or responsibility, or obligation be a reality, then the power of counter choice is a reality. *Responsibility, therefore, demonstrates free-will.*

The axiomatic character of these propositions is verified by the established *tests* of axioms. These tests are *self-evidence, necessity,* and *universality.* These propositions are *self-evident;* asserting their own truth to the mind that truly understands them; needing no proof, but merely sufficient elucidation to render them perfectly understood. They are characterized by *necessity;* not being able to be otherwise than true, not able to be conceived to be untrue, not possible but to be pronounced true. They are *universal;* ever and everywhere true; and everywhere, and by all minds, assumed and acted upon as true.

¶   Daniel Curry Introduces a First Methodist Systematic Theology.

(Taken from Miner Raymond, *Systematic Theology* (3 vols. 1877-79), I, Introduction).

The science of theology, like every other, may be said to be complete in itself from the beginning, and therefore incapable of increase, or, on the other hand, perpetually changing, and capable of constant enlargement, according as in the one case the original elements of the science are spoken of, and in the other the discovery of its laws and their orderly arrangement and illustration are intended. As a body of truths relating to the divine person and his words and works, the whole of our theology is embraced in the Bible, "so that whatsoever is not read therein, nor may be proved thereby, is not to be required of any man that it should be believed as an article of faith." But back of this just and wise determination arise other highly important questions respecting the real purport of what "may be read therein," and what may be rationally and truly "proved thereby." To respond to these secondary questions is the purpose alike of Biblical criticism and interpretation, and of systematic theology.

While, therefore, as to its fundamental elements, Christian theology was perfected, when the volume of revelation had become complete, yet the duty of thoroughly examining the sacred record, and of properly formulating the things contained in the Bible, was devolved upon the Church, to be carried through all its after stages. And since each age must furnish its own guides and instructors, whether by the living voice or the written page, not only must there be a perpetual succession of living ministers in the Church, but also new books on theology will always be called for. The new ones may not always be essentially better than those to whose places they accede; it is enough if they are better adapted to the demands of their own times.

Methodism, though not primarily and distinctively theological (in the narrower sense of that term), has always held fast to a clearly ascertained and distinctly pronounced system of religious opinions. It is theistical, as opposed to atheism, and its theism is that of the Bible, as understood and accepted by the prevalent consent of the general Church through all its ages; embracing the great truth of the divine unity, as revealed to the patriarchs and prophets of the earlier dispensations, and of the tri-personality of the Godhead, as taught more clearly in the later and fuller revelations of the Gospel. Its doctrinal positions and associations are with the great body of those who accept the essential truths of traditional catholic orthodoxy, holding steadily to the teachings of the Bible in their most direct and rational meaning. It is, therefore, Protestant as opposed to Romish, in respect to both what it rejects and what it allows. It accepts and emphasizes the distinctive doctrines of the Reformation, of sin, of redemption by Christ, of spiritual quickening, and sanctification by the Holy Spirit, of the life of faith on earth, and everlasting life after death. These things, with their resultant considerations and practical consequences were the burden of early Methodist preaching; and because they were assailed from different quarters, Methodism at length became apologetical and polemical, and in its various treatises used alike for defense and explanation, a specific system of theology was developed, distinguished for its simple Biblical orthodoxy and its earnest evangelism and spirituality.

Recognizing the design of theology to be to make men real Christians, the relations of religious doctrines to personal and experimental Christian life are kept always in view, and its strifes, whether defensively or offensively, have all been in favor of those things which appeal most forcibly and directly to the individual Christian consciousness, and which tend most certainly to draw men toward practical godliness.

But there arose in Methodism, as that term was at first used, at a comparatively early day, clearly marked theological differences; and of the opposing types we have now to speak only of the Wesleyan. At a comparatively early stage, controversies arose among those who

bore the common name, respecting the doctrine of predestination, as held and taught by Augustine and Calvin, and by the Reformed Churches of the Continent, and which was violently asserted by the Synod of Dort, and so clearly and ably formulated by the Westminster Assembly. Against that particular doctrinal tenet, which at that time was reckoned by many as an essential part of evangelical orthodoxy, Wesley set himself most decidedly and earnestly, so that his doctrinal teaching became distinguished for its opposition to the doctrine of predestination and its logical concomitants, – and accordingly the theology of Wesleyan Methodism has always been recognized as anti-Calvinistic; and yet beyond that single element, and its inseparable concomitants, there is a marked agreement between the more moderate Calvinists, and the evangelical Arminians, – and especially those of the Wesleyan type. Respecting the purely theological doctrines, – the unity of the Godhead, the Trinity, the person and work of Christ, and the character and work of the Holy Spirit, there is really no difference; while in respect to the nature of sin, and of free grace, and of the work of the Spirit in man, they are also agreed, except that some things which Calvinists confine to the elect, and which are considered as unconditionally certain, Methodists contemplate as universal in purposed beneficence, but conditioned on man's free choice of acceptance or refusal.

When by the force of circumstances Methodism was forced to assume the status of an ecclesiastical body, necessitating some recognized standard of religious belief, certain parts of the writings of Mr. Wesley were raised into the position of a theological standard. But a more effective method of indoctrination was found in the earnest and evangelical style of the preaching, which often in a single sermon, would embody, with more or less fullness, the whole body of evangelical divinity. The hymns of the Wesleys, which their people sung everywhere and continually, were surcharged with their theology, and so it happened that through the agency of Christian psalmody, the doctrinal opinions of the Methodist people became strangely harmonized and greatly intensified. While as yet Methodism was without even a written system of theology, there prevailed an almost unequaled uniformity of doctrinal opinions among them.

It was thirty years after the death of Mr. Wesley, and eighty after the origin of Wesleyan Methodism that its first formal and comprehensive system of theology was issued, – the Theological Institutes of Rev. Richard Watson. As the Methodist bodies of both Great Britain and America had long felt the need of such an exposition and embodiment of "those things which were most surely believed among them," but which had not before been "set forth in order," the advent of that great work was hailed with great joy. And yet its real value for Methodism was but partially appreciated, and its service to the denomination has been great beyond possible computation. The time had come in the growth and development of Methodism that a common standard of doctrines, thoroughly elaborated and set forth with such ability as to command the respect of intelligent

and independent thinkers, was a necessity as a condition of continued harmony in the doctrinal views of the body, and of safety against the seductive influence of the then incipient modern rationalistic un-belief. And this important purpose it accomplished most effectually. To no other single agency is the continued doctrinal unity of Method-ism so much indebted as to the extensive use of Watson's Theological Institutes. In the two capacious volumes in which the work has usually appeared is contained a complete system of theological instruc-tion and culture, - Evidences, Doctrines, Institutions, and Morals. In style it is grave, yet animated, and not inelegant. It is learned, yet not at all pedantic, and though treating of subjects that are sus-tained by the most sacred sanctions of authority, yet is there an almost entire absence of dogmatism. And though, from the necessities of the case it is the farthest removed from light reading, yet to the interested student of the highest possible truths, its matter can not fail to afford at once pleasure and profit. This great work has been the standard of Methodist theology for a full half century; and, in respect to the substance of Christian doctrine, it was never more thoroughly acceptable than at the present time.

The second generation of Methodist ministers, reared under its teachings, have now possession of the pulpits of the denomination, who are sound theologians and able ministers of the New Testament, because they have made the thoughts and the arguments of the "Institutes" their own.

But fifty years is a very long time for any single work to retain its hold upon the public mind, and especially to continue to be an interpreter of the thoughts of a large community of Christians. The last half century has also been an exceedingly active period, especially in the study of theology,- and so it has required frequent re-examina-tions of evidences and arguments, and restatements of conclusions. Nor have these been wanting in Methodist literature. A succession of valuable theological treatises, chiefly, in the form of monographs, have been given to the public, - most of them in England, but some also in this country. An original and comprehensive system of theology, by Rev. William B. Pope, of the Wesleyan Methodist Conference of Great Britain, was published a little more than a year ago, which has been very favorably received by the Church on both sides of the sea. It is at once succinct, and comprehensive, exceedingly clear in its statements, and both progressive and conservative in its doctrinal views and statements, and most thoroughly orthodox according to the standards, and the traditional teachings of Methodism. It is reported that the author intends thoroughly to revise his work, so as to express more satisfactorily his own opinions, and embody the doctrinal system of Wesleyan Methodism, and better to adapt it to general use.

The work of Dr. Raymond, herewith given to the public, is the fruit of a long course of studies and teachings in the subjects dis-cussed. It goes forth without official authorization, further than

its authorship, and the medium through which it proceeds gives it a
semi-official character. It professedly sets forth the doctrinal
convictions of its author, - all which, however, are believed to be
in substantial agreement with the generally accepted doctrines of
Methodism. Because of its comprehensiveness, covering the whole
field of theological discussion, brevity and conciseness in the
several parts became a necessity. Its first aim is to set forth very
clearly and with all necessary fullness, the things believed and held
as vital and most important doctrines of Christianity. Beyond mere
statements, which make up the body of the work, there are arguments,
illustrations, and proofs from Scripture, by which the first are made
more definite, and the grounds upon which they rest appropriately
indicated. The design and scope of the work are such as to enable the
careful and intelligent reader to apprehend the general truths of
religion, and to know what are the grounds upon which believers build
their faith and hopes.

The advancements made within the last half century, in both
Biblical and physical learning, and the more thorough exploration of
ancient monuments and the better understanding of many things in the
history of the Jewish and neighboring nations of their period have
very largely changed some of the forms of the evidences of Christianity,
and somewhat modified the prevailing opinions of Christian scholars
respecting the methods of Biblical interpretation. But in no point
have these things changed or discredited any of the traditional
doctrines of the Church. And while these things should not be wholly
ignored by the theological teacher or author, there is always something
more than a possibility that they will be made unduly prominent. It
is not his duty to parley with every objector, nor to pause in his work
to answer the cavils of every superficial unbeliever. After a general
and comprehensive statement of the evidences upon which the Christian
system rests its claim to be believed and accepted, the business of the
theological teacher is to declare and illustrate, much more than to
defend. And since many things more or less nearly related to one's
religious opinions may be only matters of inference, or the results of
peculiar methods of considering doctrinal truths, there should be an
avoidance of all unnecessary details in the statements of doctrines.
Merely philosophical inferences should be very sparingly introduced,
and all unusual interpretations eschewed. Something is due to the
authority of the traditional faith of the Church, - the *consensus* of
the wise and good of past times; and while guarding against a slavish
conservatism, it is also highly important always to bear in mind that
the great truths of religion are not among modern discoveries, and
that whatever essentially new thing is found in the substance of a
theological system must be false.

The design of the study of theology includes much more than simply
the acquisition of knowledge, and however excellent its intellectual
lessons may be, they are of less value than the influences designed to
be effected upon the heart and life. The living truths here brought

into view, with all the force of evident convictions of their verity, on the part of him that utters them, and also enforced and vitalized by recognized personal interest in them of the writer himself, changes what would otherwise be a dry array of facts into living and quickening principles, and replaces a formal recitation by a life-giving testimony. All this will be found in these pages by those whose spiritual susceptibilities qualify them to profit by what they read, and to all such the work is commended as able to make wise, without entailing any curse.

¶   Miner Raymond.

(Taken from *Systematic Theology* (1877), I, 222-25, II, 81-89).

4. In this summary we have spoken of the Bible as history of ancient opinions and events, as a system of morals, and as a system of religion, affirming that in these respects it has claims on rational grounds superior to any other book extant among men. We come now to say that, as a revelation from God, asserting and enforcing doctrines whose rational evidence is above the powers of the human mind, it is fully and adequately authenticated. If man knows and is assured that there are three persons in one God; that in the person of Jesus Christ there were two natures, the human and the divine; that pardon is possible under the divine government only through an atonement of infinite merit; that the buried bodies of men will be raised from the dead, and that a day of judgment is appointed to be held at the end of the world, at which time eternal destinies will be awarded according to the deeds done in the body, - if man knows these things, they have been made known to him by a revelation from God. If he is assured of them, it is because he has indubitable evidence that God has declared them. The evidences authenticating the Bible as a revelation from God are: (1.) Miracles, or works wrought which no man can do except God be with him, and wrought for the declared purpose of authenticating such a revelation; and (2.) Prophecies uttered at a time and in a manner clearly evincing such a knowledge of the future as no being but God possesses, and accurately fulfilled. That the miracles and prophecies of the Scriptures do furnish full, complete, and adequate evidence that God did at sundry times, and in divers manners, speak unto the fathers by the prophets, and did also speak unto us by his Son and by the apostles, needs not be argued here; we trust that what was said when this was the special subject of discussion is sufficient to make this abundantly evident.

5. The promulgation of Bible truths has always been attended with a success, and been productive of results, which demonstrate their truthfulness, their eminent excellence, and therefore their divine origin and authority. We have strongly insisted that such a book as the Bible could never be received as true unless it were true. But if we suppose it false and yet successful, since false in matters of

427

such momentous interest, it must be in its effects injurious to a degree past computation. The Bible, if not true, must be greatly detrimental to human welfare, since its errors have respect to man's most momentous interests. But the Bible is not detrimental to human welfare, contrariwise it is highly promotive of man's greatest good; therefore, the Bible is not not true; it is rather yea, yea, and amen - a word of assurance - verily, verily I say unto you, thus saith the Lord.

6. To the venerable antiquity, historical credibility, evident truth of fundamental principles, reasonableness of leading doctrines, excellency of moral precepts, miraculous occurrences, prophetic fulfillments, wonderful successes and beneficial results, may be added the unity of purpose and harmony of principles and methods pervading the entire book. Though composed by different authors, writing at times distant from each other by centuries, and under circumstances as different as occur in human history, the principles, purposes, and methods are the same in all from Genesis to Revelation. We may also add the peculiar characteristics of style. Though each author's production exhibits a style peculiar to itself, there is yet running through all the books of the Bible a characteristic simplicity, an absence of all attempts at embellishment, so appropriate to the sublimity and momentous import of the themes discussed. Again, we may add the correspondence of allusions and references to contemporary usages and customs, to times, to places, to men, and to historic events, with whatever is known from other histories and from traditions respecting the matters to which allusions may be made. In a word, the Bible commends itself to acceptance as credible because of what it is in itself as to most of its teachings. It sustains its claim to inspiration by the indubitable proofs of miracles and prophecies. These commendations and claims are confirmed by the results of its promulgation, are corroborated by all testimonies bearing upon the case, from whatever source those testimonies come, and are demonstrated in the personal experience of all who submit to its claims.

*   *   *

Is depravity total? This question is ambiguous, and must be differently stated to be intelligently answered. By reason of heated controversy great extravagance has been indulged in speaking of the moral character of men. On the one hand, total depravity has been affirmed in terms that imply an utter destitution of all forms of good; it would seem that even automatic excellence, even in a low degree, was denied to man; he is not allowed to be good, in the sense in which brute animals or even blocks of wood or stone are said to be good; a good and faithful dog would not fairly represent him; he is a dog run mad; he is a demon incarnate. Such extravagance does not deserve sober reply. It may be reasonably questioned whether any person or thing exists in the universe of God so utterly useless and injurious as man is sometimes represented to be. On the other hand, man, even

in his lowest estate, has been affirmed to be of such high origin, of such exalted possibilities, of so dignified and noble nature, as to be deserving of the high consideration of his fellows, of angels, and of God. The question of depravity is a theological question, and has respect not to automatic excellence, but to moral desert. In respect to the former, man may be good without any merit of his own, and may be bad without deserving reproach. The question of depravity, in its theological sense, has respect to man's ability to perform by his own unaided powers, works of moral merit; or, more especially, it has respect to man's ability to save himself from the consequences of his past sins, and from the practice of sin in the future. What is the condition of man after the fall as to his power to do works of moral merit, or as to his ability to save himself from sin? Are there inhering in human nature, fallen and sinful, any recuperating forces? or any force adequate for salvation? Is a sinner, considered apart from the grace of God, and without supernatural aid, in a condition of hopeless and remediless wretchedness? To the question put in these or similar forms the Church has always, with a well-nigh unanimous voice, given answers, all of which have the same import. A sinner against God by his sin places himself in a condition from which there is no escape by any force or power within his own resources. "The condition of man after the fall of Adam is such that he can not turn and prepare himself, by his own natural strength and works, to faith, and calling upon God, wherefore we have no power to do good works pleasant and acceptable to God, without the grace of God by Christ preventing us, that we may have a goodwill, and working with us when we have that goodwill." Taking, then, the term total depravity in the sense of total helplessness, the question, "Is man totally depraved?" must be answered affirmatively. With these explanations, then, it may be said that man, apart from the grace of God, is in a condition of total depravity; but, because of the necessity of such explanations, arising as it does from the ambiguity and abuse of the term, it is, as we think, better to discard the term altogether.

But others think differently, and find use for the term in discussing the doctrine in another view of it. Do the posterity of Adam come into existence actually in a condition of utter loss, helplessness and hopelessness? and does that condition continue till regeneration? Are mankind previous to conversion in a condition of total depravity? Some affirm; we deny. We will admit, if it pleases, that man considered apart from the grace of God, if he can be so considered, is totally depraved. With such an admission our formula would be, He is totally depraved, but not totally deprived; but the admission and accompanying formula is made in accommodation to those who have a partiality for the term, in which partiality we do not at all participate. The fact, as we see it, is, that the race came into existence under grace. But for redemption the race had become extinct in the first pair, and the posterity of Adam would never have had personal, individual existence. Not only is existence secured for and posterity of Adam by the second Adam, but also justification.

From whatever of the displeasure or wrath of God, or condemnation that theoretically rested upon the race, because of corruption or guilt accruing from the first sin, they are justified through Christ. "As by the offense of one, judgment came upon all men to condemnation, even so by the righteousness of one the free gift came upon all men unto justification of life." Not only does man come to conscious being, sustaining the relation of a justified, pardoned sinner, but as such he is entitled to and actually possesses all the requisites of a fair probation. Whatever influences and agencies of the Holy Spirit are necessary to qualify him for the exercise of free moral choices are graciously vouchsafed to him.

Is it said that it is not pertinent to take into account supernatural presences and powers in a discussion concerning man's estate, since what is supernatural does not at all pertain to man? We reply, the spirit of God in the mind of man is not a by-stander, but is to the faculties and capacities of the mind an enlightening, a quickening, and an energizing power. Man is, therefore, by grace, not by his fallen nature, a moral being, capable of knowing, loving, obeying, and enjoying God. Such he is, and ever will be, if he does not frustrate the grace of God; and though he should resist and grieve the Spirit, he still, through long-suffering grace, retains a state and condition of mind in which and by which salvation is possible, until by persistent rebellion his probation terminates in a failure. When his destiny is fixed, when he is abandoned of God, when the Spirit takes a final departure, then, and not till then, is he in a condition that can properly be called a condition of total depravity. But it is objected, if this be so then is it possible for men to pass a lifetime without actual transgression, without committing voluntary sin. But no man liveth and sinneth not; all go astray from their youth. If these all, as soon as they come to years of understanding, do voluntarily transgress the law of God, this fact can be accounted for only on the supposition that their natural character renders the opposite impossible. We concede that this objection has much force, and we are aware that the asserters of total depravity are not slow to make the most of it, but we accept the difficulties of the case and maintain our position notwithstanding. We do conceive it as at least theoretically possible, that a child may be so educated, so trained in the nurture and admonition of the Lord, as that he will never knowingly and voluntarily transgress the law of God - in which case he will certainly grow up into regeneration and final salvation. To such a conception a weak objection is sometimes strongly made, that it supposes salvation by works without grace and without Christ possible - plainly a flat contradiction to the conception itself. It is grace that gives the child existence, grace that endows him with moral powers, grace that gives efficiency to his educational advantages, grace that preserves him from sin, that regenerates and saves him. And what greater grace can a creature of God have than that by which he can forever keep himself from sin? Is not prevention better than cure? Plainly, it is because the absolute prevention of sin on the part of

God is not consistent with the moral agency of man, that God does not universally do that which, were it possible, were a greater grace than to permit sin and then pardon it. Must a human being be guilty of overt rebellion against God, as the indispensable condition of experiencing divine grace? As well might it be said that man can not enjoy heaven unless he has first had an experience in hell.

But some one will say, this is only a possible conception in theory, but is never a realized fact in history; no human being ever did come to years of understanding and accountability without very soon thereafter committing actual transgressions of the law of God, knowingly and willingly. This is a statement of an historical fact, which none but the omniscient One is competent to make. Does the Bible affirm it? Let it be remembered that this discussion does not include sins of ignorance, of infirmity, short-comings, unavoidable failures, necessary want of conformity to the abstract law of righteousness; but to willful, voluntary transgressions. Those passages of Scripture which affirm that "all have gone out of the way," may be taken as universal in their import and application, including saints and sinners, including all men, and referring to the whole of their earthly life, if reference be had to imperfections, infirmities, mistakes, evil actions performed in the absence of evil intent. Experience and observation lead us to conclude, that the affirmation that "all have gone out of the way" is true in a very general sense, when reference is had to overt sin; but we affirm that the Scripture testimony does not unqualifiedly require that it be construed as universal, in respect to those sins for which the sinner is personally responsible and punishable.

When God looked down from heaven to see if there were any that did good, the looking implied an expectation and a possibility that some such could be found. Indeed, the whole doctrine of human responsibility and of divine commandment postulates in man an ability to obey God and avoid sin. Necessitated sin, taking the term sin in the sense now considered, is self-contradictory, for a necessitated act is not a sin in this sense.

Again, conversion is a restoration to the condition of childhood; a condition in which, by walking not after the flesh, man may in Christ Jesus live without condemnation. "There is, therefore, now no condemnation to them that are in Christ Jesus who walk not after the flesh, but after the Spirit." The whole economy of grace tends to purify unto God a peculiar people zealous of good works, to destroy the works of the devil, and introduce the kingdom of God, in which men shall do the will of God on earth as it is done in heaven. Total depravity, in any proper sense of the term, we discard, and also in the sense in which it is taken by those who most strenuously insist upon it as a doctrine of the Christian faith; but the doctrine of natural depravity, the corruption of our nature by sin and the total inability of man by his own unaided powers to perform good works, good works having moral

desert, we affirm.

¶   Miley on Atonement.

(Taken from John Miley, *The Atonement in Christ* (1879), 100-01,
229-40, 243-45).

In a strict or scientific sense, there are but two theories of
atonement. We have seen how many in popular enumeration are reducible
to the one theory of Moral influence. Others, as will appear in this
review, are so void of essential facts that they hold no rightful
place as theories. Nor is the scheme of Moral influence in any
strict sense a theory of atonement, because it neither answers to the
real necessity in the case nor admits an objective ground of forgiveness in the mediation of Christ.

Nor can there be more than two theories. This limitation is
determined by the law of a necessary correlation between the necessity
for an atonement, and the nature of the atonement as answering to that
necessity. This fact we have, that the vicarious sufferings of Christ
are an objective ground of the divine forgiveness. There is a necessity
for such a ground; his sufferings are an atonement only as they answer
to this necessity. Hence the nature of the atonement is determined by
the nature of its necessity. Now this necessity must lie either in the
requirement of an absolute justice which must punish sin, or in the
rectoral office of justice as an obligation to conserve the interest
of moral government. There can be no other necessity for an atonement
as an objective ground of forgiveness. Nor does any scheme of a real
atonement in Christ either represent or imply another. Thus there is
place for two theories, but only two. There is place for a theory of
Absolute Substitution, according to which the redemptive sufferings of
Christ were strictly penal, and the fulfillment of an absolute obligation of justice in the punishment of sin. This is the theory of
Satisfaction, and answers to a necessity in the first sense given.
There is also place for a theory of Conditional Substitution, according to which the redemptive sufferings of Christ were not the punishment of sin, but such a substitute for the rectoral office of penalty
as renders forgiveness, on proper conditions, consistent with the
requirements of moral government. This answers to a necessity in the
second sense given, and accords with the deeper principles of the
Governmental theory. The truth of atonement must be with the one or
the other of these theories.

*   *   *

Thus the way is open for some substitutional provision which may
replace the actual infliction of penalty upon sin. The theory of
Satisfaction, as we have seen, really leaves no place for vicarious
atonement. Its most fundamental and ever-asserted principle, that sin

432

as such must be punished, makes the punishment of the actual sinner an absolute necessity. Its own admission, and maintenance even, that sin as a personal demerit is untransferable, has this inevitable logical sequence. Nor is there any escape through a technical distinction between demerit and guilt, and an alleged transference of the latter to Christ as a sufficient ground for the just punishment of sin in him. The sin, with all its demerit, and all, therefore, that is punishable, is still left behind with the sinner himself. This fact thoroughly blanks all attempt so to escape. And the scheme of Satisfaction is inseparably bound with the logical consequence, that if sin, as such, must be punished, then it must be punished, and can only be punished, in the actual sinner. But as penalties are remissible so far as a purely retributive justice is concerned; so, having a special end in the interest of moral government, they may give place to any substitutional measure equally securing that end. Here is a place for vicarious atonement.

The nature of the atonement in the sufferings of Christ follows necessarily from the above principles. It cannot be in the nature required by the principles of the Satisfaction scheme. In asserting the absoluteness of divine justice in its purely retributive element, the theory excludes the possibility of a penal substitute in atonement for sin. And, therefore, the sufferings of Christ are not, as they cannot be, an atonement for sin by penal substitution. But while his sufferings could not take the place of penalty in the actual punishment of sin, they could, and do, take its place in its strictly rectoral ends. And the atonement is thus determined to consist in the sufferings of Christ, as a provisory substitute for penalty in the interest of moral government.

The redemptive mediation of Christ implies a necessity for it. There should be, and in scientific consistency must be, an accordance between a doctrine of atonement and the ground of its necessity.

The Moral theory finds in the ignorance and evil tendencies of man a need for higher moral truth and motive than reason affords; a need for all the higher truths and motives of the Gospel. There is such a need – very real and very urgent. And Christ has graciously supplied the help so needed. But we yet have no part of the necessity for an objective ground of forgiveness. Hence this scheme does not answer to the real necessity for an atonement.

Did the necessity arise out of an absolute justice which must punish sin, the theory of Satisfaction would be in accord with it, but without power to answer to its requirement, because such a necessity precludes substitutional atonement.

We do find the real necessity in the interests of moral government – interests which involve the divine glory and authority, and welfare of moral beings. Whatever will conserve these ends while

433

opening the way of forgiveness, answers to the real necessity in the case. Precisely this is done on the doctrine of atonement which we maintain. In the requirement of the sacrifice of Christ as the only ground of forgiveness the standard of the divine estimate of sin is exalted, and merited penalty is rendered more certain respecting all who fail of forgiveness through redemptive grace. And these are the special moral forces whereby the divine law may restrain sin, protect rights, guard innocence, and secure the common welfare. Further, the doctrine we maintain not only gives to these salutary forces the highest moral potency, but also combines with them the yet higher force of the divine love as revealed in the marvelous means of our redemption. Thus while the highest good or moral beings is secured, the divine glory receives its highest revelation. The doctrine has, therefore, not only the support derived from an answer to the real necessity for an atonement, but also the commendation of a vast increase in the moral forces of the divine government.

We are here in direct issue with the doctrine of Satisfaction: for here its advocates make special claims in its favor, and urge special objections against ours. We already have the principles and facts which must decide the question.

In their scheme, the necessity lies in an absolute obligation of justice to punish sin, simply as such, and ultimately in a divine punitive disposition. But we have previously shown that there is no such necessity. We have maintained a punitive disposition in God: but we also find in him a compassion for the very sinners whom his justice so condemns. And we may as reasonably conclude that his disposition of clemency will find its satisfaction in a gratuitous forgiveness of all as that he will not forgive any, except on the equivalent punishment of a substitute. Who can show that the punitive disposition is the stronger? We challenge the presentation of a fact in its expression that shall parallel the cross in expression of the disposition of mercy. And, with no absolute necessity for the punishment of sin, it seems clear that but for the requirements of rectoral justice, compassion would triumph over the disposition of a purely retributive justice. Hence this alleged absolute necessity for an atonement is really no necessity at all.   .   .   .

The chief rectoral value of penalty, simply as an element of law, is through the moral ideas which it conveys, and the response which it thus finds in the moral reason. As the soul answers to these ideas in the healthful activities of conscience and the profounder sense of obligation, so the governing force of penalty takes the higher form of moral excellence.   .   .   .

The same facts have the fullest application to penalty as an element of the divine law. Here its higher rectoral value will be, and can only be, through the higher revelation of God in his moral attributes as ever active in all moral administration. In its simple

retributive element, or as an expression merely of the divine wrath against sin, penalty makes its appeal only to an instinctive fear. . .

In his punitive ministries God is still love; and now, under the Gospel, the thunders of Sinai may never silence the voices of Calvary. Thus as in both his legislative and administrative justice God reveals the fullness and harmony of his moral attributes, and himself as looking out upon moral beings pre-eminently from the mount of love, and as ruling with a view to his own glory and the common good, so does he associate with penalty the highest moral ideas, which find a response in the profoundest facts of our moral nature, and give to penalty its truest, best rectoral force. Now it rules no longer through an instinctive fear, but through the profoundest ideas and motives of the moral reason.

The sufferings of Christ, as a proper substitute for punishment, must fulfill the office of penalty in the obligatory ends of moral government. The manner of fulfillment is determined by the nature of the service. As the salutary rectoral force of penalty, as an element of law, is specially through the moral ideas which it reveals, so the vicarious sufferings of Christ must reveal like moral ideas, and rule through them. Not else can they so take the place of penalty as, on its remission, to fulfill its high rectoral office. Hence the vicarious sufferings of Christ are an atonement for sin, as they reveal God in his justice, holiness, and love; in his regard for his own honor and law; in his concern for the rights and interests of moral beings; in his reprobation of sin as intrinsically evil, and utterly hostile to his own rights and to the welfare of his subjects.

Does the atonement in Christ reveal such truths? We answer, Yes. Nor do we need the impossible penal element of the scheme of Satisfaction for any part of this revelation.

God reveals his profound regard for the sacredness of his law, and for the interests which it conserves, by what he does for their support and protection. In direct legislative and administrative forms he ordains his law, with declarations of its sacredness and authority; embodies in it the weightiest sanctions of reward and penalty; reprobates in severest terms all disregard of its requirements, and all violation of the rights and interests which it would protect; visits upon transgression the fearful penalties of his retributive justice, though always at the sacrifice of his compassion. The absence of such facts would evince an indifference to the great interests concerned; while their presence evinces, in the strongest manner possible to such facts, the divine regard for these interests. These facts, with the moral ideas which they embody, give weight and salutary governing power to the divine law. The omission of the penal element would, without a proper rectoral substitution, leave the law in utter weakness.

Now let the sacrifice of Christ be substituted for the primary

435

necessity of punishment, and as the sole ground of forgiveness. But we should distinctly note what it replaces in the divine law, and wherein it may modify the divine administration. The law remains, with all its precepts and sanctions. Penalty is not annulled. There is no surrender of the divine honor and authority. Rights and interests are no less sacred, nor guarded in feebler terms. Sin has the same reprobation; penalty the same imminence and severity respecting all persistent impenitence and unbelief. The whole change in the divine economy is this - that on the sole ground of the vicarious sacrifice of Christ, all who repent and believe may be forgiven and saved. This is the divine substitution for the primary necessity of punishment. While, therefore, all the other facts in the divine legislation and administration remain the same, and in unabated expression of truths of the highest rectoral force and value, this divine sacrifice in atonement for sin replaces the lesson of a primary necessity for punishment with its own higher revelation of the same salutary truths; rather, it adds its own higher lesson to that of penalty. As penalty remains in its place, remissible, indeed, on proper conditions, yet certain of execution in all cases of unrepented sin, and, therefore, often executed in fact, the penal sanction of law still proclaims all the rectoral truth which it may utter. Hence the sacrifice of Christ in atonement for sin, and in the declaration of the divine righteousness in forgiveness, is an additonal and infinitely higher utterance of the most salutary moral truths. The cross is the highest revelation of all the truths which embody the best moral forces of the divine government.

The atonement in Christ is so original and singular in many of its fact, that it is the more difficult to find in human facts the analogies for its proper illustration. Yet there are facts not without service here.

An eminent lecturer, in a recent discussion of the atonement, has given notoriety to a measure of Bronson Alcott in the government of his school. He substituted his own chastisement for the infliction of penalty upon his offending pupil, receiving the infliction at the hand of the offender. No one can rationally think such a substitution penal, or that the sin of the pupil was expiated by the stripes which the master suffered instead. The substitution answered simply for the disciplinary ends of penalty. Without reference either to the theory of Bronson Alcott, or to the interpretation of Joseph Cook, we so state the case as most obvious in the philosophy of its own facts. Such office it might well fulfill. And we accept the report of the very salutary result, not only as certified by the most reliable authority, but also as intrinsically most credible. No one in the school, and to be ruled by its discipline, could henceforth think less gravely of any offense against its laws. No one could think, either, that the master regarded with lighter reprobation the evil of such offense, or that he was less resolved upon a rigid enforcement of obedience. All these ideas must have been intensified, and in a manner

to give them the most healthful influence. The vicarious sacrifice of the master became a potent and most salutary moral element in the government maintained. Even the actual punishment of the offender could not have so secured obedience for the sake of its own obligation and excellence.   .   .   .

5. *Only Sufficient Atonement.* - Nothing could be more fallacious than the objection that the Governmental theory is in any sense acceptilational, or intrinsically indifferent to the character of the substitute in atonement. In the inevitable logic of its deepest and most determining principles it excludes all inferior substitution as insufficient, and requires a divine sacrifice as the only sufficient atonement. Only such a substitution can give adequate expression to the great truths which may fulfill the rectoral office of penalty.   .   .

6. *True Sense of Satisfaction.* - The satisfaction of justice in atonement for sin is not peculiar to the doctrine of Satisfaction, technically so-called. It is the distinctive nature of the satisfaction that is so peculiar. The Rectoral atonement is also a doctrine of satisfaction to divine justice, and in a true sense. The narrow view which makes the retribution of sin, simply as such, an absolute obligation of justice, and then finds the fulfillment of its office in the punishment of Christ as a substitute in penalty, never can give a true sense of satisfaction. But with broader and truer views of justice, with its ends in moral government as paramount, and with penalties as the rightful means for their attainment; then the vicarious sufferings of Christ, as more effectually attaining the same ends, are the satisfaction of justice, while freely remitting its penalties. This is a true sense of satisfaction. Love also is satisfied. And a redemption of love must be in satisfaction of love as well as of justice.

Consistently with these views we may appropriate the following definition, and none the less consistently or freely because of its appropriation by Dr. Symington, although a Satisfactionist in the thorough sense of the Reformed soteriology: *"By Satisfaction, in a theological sense, we mean such act or acts as shall accomplish all the moral purposes which, to the infinite wisdom of God, appear fit and necessary under a system of rectoral holiness, and which must · otherwise have been accomplished by the exercise of retributive justice upon transgressors in their own persons.*

¶   John Miley.

(Taken from *Systematic Theology* (2 Vols. 1892, 1894), I, 39-43, 46-47, 521-22, 526-27, 528-29).

The Function of Reason in Theology. - The errors of rationalism must not discredit the offices of our rational intelligence in

questions of religion and theology. A system of Christian doctrines is no more possible without rational thought than the construction of any science within the realm of nature. There is in the two cases the same intellectual requirement in dealing with the material out of which the science is wrought. The idea of religion as a faith and practice is the idea of a person rationally endowed and acting in the deepest form of his rational agency. It is true that a religious life is impossible without the activity of the moral and religious sensibilities - just as there cannot be for us either society, or friendship, or country, or home, or a world of beauty without the appropriate feeling. But mere feeling will not answer for any of these profoundly interesting states. There must be the activity of thought as the condition and illumination of such feeling. So it is in religion: God and duty must come into thought before the heart can respond in the proper religious feeling, or the life be given to him in true obedience and worship. The religious sensibilities are natively as strong under the lowest forms of idolatry as under the highest forms of Christian theism, and should yield as lofty a service, if religion were purely a matter of feeling. The religious life and worship take their vastly higher forms under Christian theism through higher mental conceptions of God and duty. There is thus manifest a profound office of our rational intelligence in religion.

There is not a question of either natural or revealed religion that is not open to rational consideration. Even the truths of Scripture which transcend our power of comprehension must in some measure be apprehended in their doctrinal contents in order to their acceptance in a proper faith.

If we should even assume that the existence of God is an intuitive truth, or an immediate datum of the moral and religious consciousness, we must still admit that the question is open to the treatment of the logical reason. We have seen that the Scriptures fully recognize in the works of nature the proofs of the divine existence. These proofs address themselves to our logical reason, and can serve their purpose only as apprehended in our rational intelligence. When so apprehended and accepted as rationally conclusive, theism is a rational faith. Such has ever been the position of the most eminent Christian theists. They have appealed the question of the divine existence to the rational proofs furnished in the realm of nature and in the constitution and consciousness of man. Thus they have found the sure ground of their own faith and successfully repelled the assaults of atheism. The many treatises in the maintenance of theism fully recognize the profound function of our logical reason in this ground-truth of religion.

The idea of a divine revelation is the idea of a capacity in us for its reception. A divine revelation is, in the nature of it, a divine communication of truth, and especially of moral and religious truth. There can be no communication of such truth where there is no capacity for its apprehension and reception. Without such capacity

the terms of such a revelation would be meaningless. There can be no such capacity without our rational intelligence. We admit the value of our moral and religious sensibilities in our spiritual cognitions; not, however, as in themselves cognitive, but as subsidiary to the cognitive power of our rational faculties. Many of the facts and truths of revelation, as given in the Scriptures, are cognizable only in our logical reason. Hence the idea of a divine revelation assumes an important office of our reason in theology.

Are the Scriptures a revelation of truth from God? An affirmative answer must rest on rational grounds of evidence. This means that the whole question of evidence is open to rational treatment. The divine origin of the Scriptures is a question of fact. Such an origin can be rationally accepted in faith only on the ground of verifying evidence. All such evidence addresses itself to the logical reason. In experience we may reach an immediate knowledge of certain verities of religion; but all such experience is purely personal, and if it is to possess any apologetic value beyond this personal limitation, or in the mind of others, it must be treated as logical evidence of the truths alleged to be so found. Even the subjects of this experience may severally take it up into the rational intelligence and treat it as logical proof of the truths assumed to be immediately reached in experience. Beyond such experience the whole question of a divine revelation in the Scriptures is a question of rational proofs. By rational proofs we mean such facts of evidence as satisfy our logical reason. A question of fact is a question of fact, in whatever sphere it may arise. In this view the question of a divine original of the Scriptures is not different from other questions of fact within the realms of history and science. The proofs may lie in peculiar or widely different facts, but they are not other for rational thought or the logical reason. Christ openly appealed to the proofs of his Messiahship, and demanded faith on the ground of their evidence. The apostles furnished the credentials of their divine commission as the teachers of religious truth. The Scriptures demand no faith except on the ground of evidence rationally sufficient. The Church has ever recognized this function of reason respecting the divine origin of the Scriptures. Every Christian apologist, from the earliest to the latest, has appealed this question to our rational intelligence, on the assumption of proofs appropriate and sufficient as the ground of a rational faith in its truth. Such is the office of reason respecting the truth of a divine revelation.

Our position may seem to concede the logical legitimacy of the "higher criticism," with its destructive tendencies. If the Scriptures ground their claim to a divine original in rational proofs, have not all seemingly opposing facts a right to rational consideration as bearing upon that great question? Yes; and if such facts should ever be found decisively stronger than the proofs the divine origin of the Scriptures could no longer be held in a rational faith. The rights of logic must be conceded; and Christian apologetics has too long

appealed this question to our logical reason now to forbid a consideration of seemingly adverse facts in a manner logically legitimate to
its own principles and method. This is conceded in the manner of
meeting the issues of the "higher criticism." Here are such questions
as the Mosaic authorship of the Pentateuch, the unitary authorship of
Isaiah, the genuineness and prophetic character of the Book of Daniel-
questions which deeply concern the evidences of the divine original of
the Scriptures. How are the destructionists met on these and similar
issues? Not by denying their logical right to raise such questions,
but by controverting the facts which they allege and disproving the
conclusions which they reach. In these matters logic suffers many
wrongs at their hand. Nor can any legitimacy of the questions raised
free much of the "higher criticism" from the charge of an obtrusive
and destructive rationalism.

What are the contents of the Scriptures? What are the facts which
they record, with their meaning? What are their ethical and doctrinal
teachings? All these questions are open to the investigation of the
logical reason - just as the contents of other books. It is not meant
that the spiritual mood of the student is indifferent to these questions. It may be such as to blind the mental eye, or such as to give
it clearness of vision. Such is the case on many questions of the
present life. What in one's view is proper and right in another's is
wrong and base. What to one is lofty patriotism is to another the
outrage of rebellion or lawless and vindictive war. What one views
as saintly heroism another views as cunning hypocrisy or a wild
fanaticism. So much have our subjective states to do with our judgments.
But we are responsible for these states, and therefore for the judgments
which they so much influence. A proper adjustment of our mental state
to any subject in which the sensibilities are concerned is necessary
to the clearer and truer view of it. Such state, however, is not the
organ of knowledge, but a preparation for the truer judgment.
Sobriety is proper for all questions. Devoutness is the only proper
mood for the study of the questions of religion, and therefore for the
study of the contents of the Scriptures. Such a mental mood is our
duty in the study of the Scriptures, not that it is in itself cognizant
of their contents, nor that it determines the judgment, but simply that
it clears the vision of our reason and so prepares it for the discovery
of the truth. With such a mental mood it is the function of our reason
to ascertain the religious and doctrinal contents of the Scriptures.

A high function of the logical reason in systematic theology can
hardly be questioned. A system of theology is a scientific construction of doctrines. The method is determined by the laws of logic.
These laws rule all scientific work. Any violation of their order is
a departure from the scientific method. They are the same for theology
as for the sciences in the realm of nature. The method of every
science is a rational method. Science is a construction in rational
thought. A system of theology is such a science. The construction
of such a system is the function of reason in theology.

A glance at the errors of rationalism will clearly show that there is not an item of such error in the doctrine of reason above maintained. We speak of errors of rationalism with respect to its distinctions of form rather than in view of fundamental distinctions. While varying in the matters specially emphasized, it is one in determining principle. Human reason is above all necessity and authority of a divine revelation: this is rationalism.   .   .   .

The high function of reason in questions of religion and theology, as previously maintained, is entirely free from all these errors of rationalism. It is thoroughly loyal to the Scriptures as a supernatural revelation of truth from God, and submissive to their authority in questions of faith and practice. It heartily accepts the vital truths of Christianity on the ground of their divine original. This is no blind submission of our reason to mere authority. The word of God contains within itself the highest reason of its truth. Nothing is accepted with higher reason of its truth than that which God has spoken. The Scriptures ground their claim upon our acceptance in the sufficient proofs that they are the word of God. In this they duly respect our rational intelligence. Evangelical theology ever renews this tribute. It is useless to object that the authority conceded to the Scriptures in questions of religion would require the belief of things most irrational, or even contradictory to our reason, if divinely revealed. The objection is ruled out as utterly irrelevant and groundless. Such a divine revelation is unthinkable.

*   *   *

III. THE TRUE ARMINIAN DOCTRINE.

Native Depravity without Native Demerit. - We have previously shown that native depravity as a fact, and its sinfulness in a sense to deserve divine punishment, are distinct questions, and open to separate answers. The truth of the latter is no consequence of the truth of the former. We have maintained the reality of native depravity, but controverted the doctrine of its intrinsic demerit, and have no occasion to renew the discussion. The present aim is to point out the true position of Arminianism on the question of native sinfulness in the sense of penal desert, whether assumed to be grounded in a participation in the sin of Adam or in the corruption of nature inherited from him. That position, as we view it, accurately expressed in the above heading: native depravity without native demerit. Native depravity is a part of the Arminian system, and entirely consistent with its principles; native demerit is discordant and contradictory. The question may be tested by the principle of freedom in Arminianism. There is no more fundamental principle. It occupies much the same position in this system that the divine sovereignty occupies in Calvinism. As this sovereignty underlies the predestination, the monergism, the irresistibility of grace, and the final perseverance in the one; so freedom underlies the synergism,

the real conditionality of salvation, and the possibility of apostasy in the other. In Arminianism freedom must include the power of choosing the good, as the necessary ground of a responsible probation. Repentance and faith as requisite to salvation must be possible; punishable deeds must be avoidable; responsible duties must be practicable. This is the meaning of Arminianism in the maintenance of a universal grace through a universal atonement; a grace which lifts up mankind into freedom, with power to choose the good. Such freedom is the condition of moral responsibility; and without it we could be neither sinful nor punishable, because our moral life could not proceed from our own personal agency. This is the doctrine of Arminianism, always and every-where firmly maintained. But if we could not be sinful and punishable in our actual life without free personal agency, or through morally necessitated evil deeds, how can we be sinful and punishable through the sin of Adam, or on the ground of an inherited corruption of nature? Nothing could be more utterly apart from our own agency than the one or the other. Nothing could be imposed by a more absolute necessitation. Native sinfulness in the sense of punitive desert is, therefore, openly contradictory to the deepest and most determining principle of the Arminian system.

With the doctrine of native demerit there is confusion and contradiction in the Arminian treatment of original sin. This result is not from any unskillful handling of that doctrine, but from its intrinsic opposition to the ruling principles of this system. The attempted adjustment to these principles finds no resting-place until it reaches a free cancellation of that form of sin through the grace of a universal atonement. But this outcome is doctrinally much the same as the denial of original sin in the sense of demerit. It may remain in the theory, but must not be allowed to come into actuality. This is the usual outcome with Arminians who start with the doctrine of original sin in the sense of demerit. It is far better to start with the true Arminian doctrine than to reach it through so much doctrinal confusion and contradiction.

*   *   *

There is a special Arminian view of original sin which should not be passed without notice. While denying all sharing of the race in the guilt of Adam's sin, it asserts a common guilt on the ground of inherited depravity, and then covers its guilt with the cancel-ing grace of justification. This view is specially open to criticism, and for any consistency of doctrine should maintain a common infant regeneration as well as justification. If inherited depravity is intrinsically sinful, so as to involve us in guilt and condemnation, justification is impossible so long as it remains. It is the doctrine of some creeds that a portion of original sin remains in the regenerate, but that the guilt thereof is not imputed to believers. There is great perplexity even in this view. It is not claimed that this remnant of original sin is different in moral character from the

442

prior whole; rather it is declared to be of the nature of sin, just as the prior whole. How then can we be justified from the guilt of a nature, though but a modicum of the original whole, but which is intrinsically sinful and still remains within us? Let any one analyze this question and set it in the light of clear thought, and he will find the answer very perplexing. How then shall we explain the justification of infants who are born with the totality of this corrupt and sinful nature? There is no possible explanation. With such a doctrine of original sin infant regeneration must go with infant justification, for otherwise the latter is impossible. Further, if infants are born in a regenerate state, the ground of native guilt has disappeared, and there is no need of the justification. And, finally, with the disappearance of native depravity, the doctrinal outcome stands rather with Pelagius and Socinus than with Arminius and Wesley.

3. *The Requirement of a True Definition of Sin*. - There can be no true definition of sin which includes the guilt of an inherited nature. A mere nature cannot be the subject of guilt. No more can it be sinful in the sense of penal desert. Only a person can be the subject of guilt; and a person can be a responsible sinner only through his own agency. There can be no true definition of sin which omits a responsible personal agency. Arminianism can admit no definition which omits such agency or includes the guilt of an inherited corruption of nature. . . .

We add our own definition: *Sin is disobedience to a law of God, conditioned on free moral agency and opportunity of knowing the law.* In this view, law is the expression of the divine will respecting human duty, and the mode of the expression is indifferent to the principles of the definition. The disobedience may be either a transgression or an omission; in either thought or feeling, word or deed. It must be some doing or omission of doing; therefore, really some doing. An omission of duty is as really voluntary as any act of transgression. The specified free agency and opportunity of knowing the law are necessary conditions of sin. Such disobedience, and only such, is sin in the sense of penal desert. Omit any specified element, or admit any contrary element, and there can be no true definition. Therefore native depravity cannot be sin in the sense of penal desert.

443

19. WOMEN FIND A VOICE.

From the beginning women had played a vital role in the life of the church. But in a male-dominated culture they had not been widely visible in positions of leadership and the making of decisions. All that began to change in the latter part of the nineteenth century. Methodist women had an important part in this feminine renaissance.

In Methodist circles many issues were discussed and debated, but two were especially pressing: women in lay activities and in ministry, particularly ordination. These issues rose together and forced the General Conferences of the 1880's to deal with them.

The first selections pertain to the general issues. James W. Bashford, who was elected bishop in 1904, was in 1880 minister of Jamaica Plain Methodist Episcopal Church, where Anna Oliver was licensed to preach. His pamphlet, "Does the Bible Allow Women to Preach?" sought to counteract the anti-female biases of biblical conservatives. Anna Oliver herself had some strong opinions, which she gave in a rare "Test Case" pamphlet, along with testimonials from churches she had served, the alumni of Boston School of Theology, and the New England Conference.

As the General Conference of 1880 approached statements and petitions on women in ministry and church offices poured in. One came from a number of concerned women, signed by Mary L. Griffith and including Jennie H. Caldwell, Mary Bannister Willard, Frances E. Willard, and Maggie Van Cott. When that General Conference failed to open the way, a minority report of the Committee on Itineracy was signed by nineteen delegates.

The debate persisted through the 1880's and was unresolved when the General Conference of 1888 gathered to consider what to do with several lay delegates who happened to be women. The bishops deigned in their address to offer guidance.

Through it all Frances Willard of Evanston, famous as the president of the National Woman's Christian Temperance Union, participated in the efforts of women to gain recognition in their church. In her autobiography, Glimpses of Fifty Years, she reviewed her experiences with General Conferences. Her place in cultural and religious history was broad and significant. Her advanced ideas ranged from the upbringing of children and girls' clothing to peace movements, political action, labor justice, and socialism. Among her male opponents none was more vociferous than James M. Buckley, long-time editor of the New York Christian Advocate and dominating figure at several General Conferences. Her unpublished letter to Ezra Tipple takes note of him as she lists the amazing range of activities in which she was involved. Not the least of her achievements was the mastery at the age of sixty of the bicycle, an

experience which she parlayed into a perceptive philosophy of life.

In the M. E. Church, South, the drive for women's rights was much the same but delayed longer. Male prejudice, rooted in the Southern belle-delicate flower-motherhood outlook, was stronger. Belle Bennett struck blows against this resistance and for admission of women to the councils of the church. She was active in missionary, educational, and social service work. In 1910, when she addressed the General Conference in behalf of an amendment to permit participation of women in lay activities, she was elected president of the Woman's Missionary Council, a position she held for twelve years.

¶   Does the Bible Allow Women to Preach?

(Taken from pamphlet by J. W. Bashford in Garrett-Evangelical
Theological Seminary).

In 1876, the Jamaica Plain M. E. church, after a thorough
examination of one of its members, Miss Anna Oliver, licensed her as
a local preacher. She had completed the college course of Rutger's
Female College and the theological course in Boston University, with
honor, and her own convictions and the results which followed her
public testimonies clearly pointed to the ministry as her work.
After four years of trial, during which she met with remarkable
success as an evangelist, as a pastor at Passaic, N.J., and at
Brooklyn, N.Y.., the Jamaica Plain Quarterly Conference unanimously
recommended her to the Annual Conference as a suitable person to be
ordained. The committee from the New England Conference which
examines candidates for ordination reported very favorably upon her
case and moved that the Conference recommend her to the Bishop for
ordination. Bishop Andrews decided that he had no authority under
the discipline to ordain a woman and refused to put the question.
Dr. Thayer appealed from his decision to the General Conference,
which meets in Cincinnati, May 1880, and the case rests here at
present.

It should be stated, however, that the New England Conference,
by a very large majority, instructed its delegates to the General
Conference to vote and work for the removal of all sex distinctions
pertaining to the ministry. Also the alumni of the Theological
School of Boston University at their annual meeting during conference
week passed a similar resolution with but one dissenting vote; and this
action meets the hearty concurrence of the faculty of the Theological
School. A question which comes before the General Conference advocated by so large and intelligent a body of ministers as the New
England Conference and by the alumni and faculty of one of the leading theological schools in America is at least worthy a candid consideration by that body. As pastor of the church which recommended Miss
Oliver for ordination, I present some of the reasons which led the
church to this action. We are sure from the discussion of the subject thus far, that the decision at Cincinnati will largely hinge
upon the question: *Does the Bible allow women to preach?* With three
preliminary observations to clear the way, we will then consider the
Bible doctrine in regard to woman's preaching.

(1) We are told by the timid and the thoughtless that if
the barriers are once broken down, the church will soon be flooded
with female preachers. Every candidate's "gifts, grace and usefulness"
must be passed upon some dozen times by Quarterly Conferences,
committees of examination and the Annual Conference, before he is
fully ordained and admitted to the traveling connection. With recommendation after recommendation from the Quarterly Conference, with

year after year of trial, with committee after committee of examination from the Annual Conference, with two votes of the Annual Conference for ordination and two more for admission - all standing between the candidate and the ministry, it is simply absurd to speak of our barriers as broken down by this movement. Our ministry is nominally open to every young man in the land. Not one in a hundred passes these barriers and enters a Methodist pulpit. Whoever fears that emotional and voluble young women will storm this twelve-fold gate and crowd the temple of the Lord, is ignorant of the discipline and polity of the Methodist church.

(2) The Methodist church expects every woman in her fold to publicly witness for Christ. Under this rule it is not strange that some women should develop exceptional talent in our social meetings. The Quarterly Conference of any local church has the right to grant such women licenses as exhorters or local preachers, in which capacity they are authorized by the church to speak from the pulpit. Thus one of the highest functions of the ministry can be discharged without ordinations. Mrs. Van Cott, Phebe Palmer, Miss Oliver, Miss Willard and others are commended by our papers and welcomed to our pulpits as public speakers. Again, many churches employ women to assist the ministers in their pastoral work. For women to visit the sick, minister to the poor and gather children into our Sunday schools is common in all city churches. Practically then, women are now discharging the two most important functions of the minister - public speaking and pastoral work. They are only debarred from administering the sacraments and from all official recognition.

(3) If the classic passage in the 14th chapter of 1 Corinthians forbids women to preach, it forbids them to speak at all in the church. The context shows that it was a social meeting - a meeting to which one brought a psalm, another a doctrine, another a question, another an interpretation - that it was preeminently a social meeting to which Paul alludes in his command. If, then, the command is to be taken literally, it as clearly forbids women taking part in a prayer meeting as it forbids their preaching; and the universal custom of the Methodist church and the growing practice of other denominations are contrary to the plain word of God. .   .   .

I. Consider all that the writer says and does upon the question at issue, especially interpreting his precepts by his practice. We recall at once Paul's words commanding wives to obey their husbands; declaring man to be the head of the woman; ordering man to worship with uncovered head; declaring that Eve sinned first; telling Timothy that he suffered not women to teach nor to usurp authority; and ordering women to keep silent in the churches. These passages so fully confirm our traditional views that many of us have not sought further light and are hardly aware that other words and acts of Paul cannot be reconciled with the theory that these commands are universal and absolute. Notice, therefore, a little more at length the follow-

ing passages on the other side, which cannot be passed over if we are to consider all that the author says upon his subject.　.　.　.

II. What was the principle by which Paul lived and wrote and of which he made such wide and apparently contradictory applications? We think it will become plain to all who study Paul's life and writings that he tried to express, not the principle of justice, but the higher law of love.　.　.　.

III. Every deep principle is capable of wide and apparently conflicting applications. Under the same law of gravitation rain falls and mist rises. We must understand not only the abstract law but the actual circumstances which modify it, if we would know which action flows from the one and which from the other. So Paul's commands and conduct are often changed by local considerations. We need to apprehend clearly not only his ideal law of love but also the historical surroundings amidst which he applied his principle, if we would know which word or deed flowed from his central principle, and which was apparently reversed by circumstances.　.　.　.

The evangelical churches are guilty of a double injustice upon this subject. The church has had more devotion and service offered her by women than any other institution on earth. Two-thirds of her membership and much of her support comes from women. Women have been freely chosen, often without pay, to work among our hardest and vilest classes as city missionaries. Side by side with their brothers, women are trying to plant the standard of the cross in our hard and unrecognized mission fields in South America. They are trying day and night to save their Chinese sisters in San Francisco. It was a woman who saved our mission in Africa. It is women who are piercing the caste of India. Twelve girls have gone out like martyrs to the fatal mission of Liberia. For the church to hold that the Bible allows and nature and God qualify women for the hardest and most dangerous part of the Christian service and greedily accept this devotion; and then for the church to persist, while lawyers and physicians and professors are all granting women their rights, that the Bible and nature and God all forbid her to grant women the frank official recognition which she extends to her common servants, is an act of double meanness.

We expect the Methodist Church to lead the evangelical denominations in removing this disgrace: (1) Because the question is fairly before her and must be voted upon in May. (2) Because with the many guards to her ministry she can make the change without danger. (3) Because Wesley personally encouraged women as well as laymen to exhort and preach. His conference never sanctioned the step; but Sarah Crosby, Hannah Harrison, Misses Bosanquet, Horral, Barret, Newman, and others publicly taught in the churches with Wesley's knowledge and approval down to the day of his death. (4) Because for one hundred years, in the face of these verbal prohibitions of Paul and

of public ridicule by other churches, the Methodist Church has maintained the right and duty of women to publicly witness for Christ.

¶   Anna Oliver on Ordination of Women.

(Taken from "Test Case" on the Ordination of Women, pamphlet in Garrett-Evangelical Theological Seminary, [1880], copy also at Drew Theological Seminary).

Miss Anna Oliver was recommended for Deacon's Orders in the Methodist Episcopal Church at the last session of the New England Conference. The Bishop declined to submit the matter to the vote of the Conference, because, in his judgment, the law of the Church does not authorize the ordination of women. From this decision Presiding Elder Thayer took an appeal to the ensuing General Conference.

Miss Oliver asks for ordination. Ought she to be ordained?

The Church tacitly allows women to preach and labor as evangelists. For this ordination is not thought necessary. But here is a woman who believes herself called not to evangelistic work, but to the pastorate. The following are

MISS OLIVER'S REASONS FOR THIS BELIEF,

substantially as expressed before the New England Conference:

"I am sorry to trouble our dear mother Church with any perplexing questions, but it presses me also, and the Church and myself must decide something. I am so thoroughly convinced that the Lord has laid commands upon me in this direction, that it becomes with me really a question of my own soul's salvation. If the Lord commands me to just the course I am pursuing, as only they that do His commandments have right to the tree of life, I have no alternative.

Among other reasons, the following induce me to hold that I am called to pastoral and not evangelistic work:

I. I do not believe in evangelistic work as usually carried on, i.e. to warm up cold churches and *start* revivals. The legitimate sphere of an evangelist, in my understanding, is to assist an overworked minister and church, while the revival is advancing. But the only invitations I received were of the first description. I have served about two years thus, with what others call success.

II. The work of an evangelist is unsuited to women - certainly to me. It is contrary to the instincts of my nature. An evangelist has no home, is tossed from place to place. Advertisements, embracing personal descriptions are used, with other sensational methods, to

449

draw together the people. The evangelist arrives and is thrust before a crowd of strangers. As soon as she becomes a little acquainted, and forms some attachments, her time expires. She is torn away and thrust before another crowd of strangers. Women are said to be timid and shrinking, and will our good mother Church take these shrinking, delicate, modest, sensitive, home-loving, nestling, timid little things, and toss them about from Maine to California, or send them as missionaries to wild and naked barbarians, at the same time forbidding them to engage in the motherly work of the pastorate?

III. Pastoral work is adapted to women, for it is motherly work. The mother has her little group, the pastor the flock. As a mother spreads her table with food suited to the individual needs of her family, so the pastor feeds the flock. Each knows the sick ones, the weak ones, those that must be carried in the arms, and those strong enough to help others. I recognize this field as suited to my natural qualifications.

IV. My interest begins with conversions. Then an evangelist leaves. And I always felt as though a whole nursery full of my own little ones were being turned over to the care of strangers. The experience was, in a word, fearful.

V. I cannot endure to preach old sermons. I have subjects in my mind that will not let me rest until I work them up. To do so would be better for my present and future usefulness, and for my own growth in grace. But a person who is preaching every night in the week, cannot prepare new subjects.

VI. The longer I preached as an evangelist, the less interest I felt - no matter how crowded the houses, nor what the apparent success - until I became convinced that, if the pastorate were unalterably closed, the Lord had released me from preaching. But just at this point pastoral work opened to me.

VII. As a pastor my interest daily increases. I would rather toil quietly in a corner with a handful of persons, seeing believers sanctified, and families transformed, than with the greatest eclat otherwise.

VIII. In evangelistic work I always saw some harm done, even where the most good was accomplished. But in regular labor, however small the gains, there is no discount of harm.

In this connection I may mention, that as an evangelist, my own spiritual growth was hindered, and had I long continued, I am convinced I would have backslidden. On the other hand, in my present charge, and in Passaic, the Lord has visited me with wonderful mani-'festations of his presence, and I realize in myself spiritual progress.

IX. When the Lord calls one to preach, He always calls persons to hear. So in this case. Others beside myself have recognized my adaptation to the pastorate. In less than two years thirteen churches desired me for their pastor. But the ecclesiastical authorities refused to appoint a woman, *preferring in some instances to close or sell the church buildings.*

X. God sanctions my pastoral work. In proof of this I appeal to the record in Passaic, N. J., and Brooklyn, N.Y. But it may be said, notwithstanding the reasons just given, that I am

MISTAKEN

in my call. Then it is a very great pity *for myself* that I cannot be convinced that I am mistaken - a pity that I have lived in this delusion all these years. I have made almost every conceivable sacrifice to do what I believe God's will. Brought up in a conservative circle in New York City, that held it a disgrace for a woman to work, surrounded with the comforts and advantages of ample means, and trained in the Episcopal Church, I gave up home, friends and support, went counter to prejudices that had become second nature to me, worked for several years to constant exhaustion, and suffered cold, hunger, and loneliness. The things hardest for me to bear were laid upon me. For two months my own mother did not speak to me. When I entered the house she turned and walked away. When I sat at the table she did not recognize me. I have passed through tortures to which the flames of martyrdom would be nothing, for *they* would end in a day. And through all this time and to-day, I could turn off to positions of comparative ease and profit. However, I take no credit to myself for enduring these trials, because at every step it was plain to me, that I had no alternative but to go forward or renounce my Lord.

Now is it possible that I am, that I have been all these years mistaken? Is it possible that our Father would either lead or leave a child of His in such a delusion? - a child whom He knows, as He knows my heart, desires nothing else so much as to learn the Father's will *to do it.* In fact He has really given constant evidence that He sanctions my course. At every step He has met me. He opened avenues of self-support while I was pursuing my studies. When I resigned loved ones, the joy of His presence more than compensated, so that trials have been no trials, for at all times He has given me the victory. I have been enabled through all, to rejoice evermore, and in everything to give thanks. And now He has restored all my friends. My family, who once thought I disgraced them, are proud of me now. My parents love me to-day, as I am sure they would never have done had I obeyed them instead of God. Does God thus encourage fanatics or enthusiasts?

The Methodist Episcopal Church is the church of

MY CHOICE

I have no one under God with whom to advise but the Bishops and
Brethren of our Church. Therefore I ask you, Fathers and Brethren,
tell me, what would you do, were you in my place? Tell me, what
would you wish the Church to do toward you were you in my place?
Please only apply the Golden Rule, and vote in Conference accordingly.

Finally, let not the sympathies of my friends in the Conference
be taxed, imagining that I am, or under any circumstances will be,
in the least discouraged. I encourage myself in the Lord my God.

NO ONE AND NOTHING CAN HARM ME

In all I am more than conqueror through Him to whom be all the
glory. In the future, I intend in the strength of God to go forward
as in the past, *joyfully*. If helped by you, my Brothers, then God
bless you! If hindered by you, my Brothers, the Lord forgive you!
(I know He will, for I'll ask Him to.) But whether helped or hindered, with God's grace I will stand where He commands me to stand,
I will speak what He commands me to speak, because I can do no otherwise, and God takes all the responsibility.

¶   A Statement to General Conference, 1880.

(Taken from "The Position of Women in the M. E. Church",
pamphlet in Garrett-Evangelical Theological Seminary).

Our church is composed of men *and women*. Trite as this
sentence is, its truth is constantly ignored. There are at least
twice as many women as men in the average membership. In this two-
third majority resides a moral, spiritual, social, and financial
power, without which we can hardly imagine the church existing at
all; yet all through our economy, outside the higher places of
privilege, opportunity, and power for good, there is a sex-line
drawn, shutting women out. If there is friction here, who are at
fault but those who made the line? If foam breaks against the wall,
the builder is responsible, not the sea.

It is historic that women have done much for Methodism. To-day
they are doing more than ever, and yet, in the whole constitution and
organization of the church, women are ignored - not as lacking, or
being in fault, but simply as women. Churches are built and supported largely by the labors and contributions of women, yet the property
is owned and controlled by a board from which women are excluded, and
in whose election they have no choice.   .   .   .

452

The same principle runs through other matters. Women are abundant in labors, in all personal and spiritual work - in the care of the poor and sick, in supporting and encouraging the pastor; yet no woman is made steward. They have the tact and tenderness, the personal sympathy, the intense spiritual life, which should mark a good class-leader, yet very seldom does the church avail herself of such leaders. The bulk of our Sunday School work is done by women (and surely, as teachers of the young, women need no recommendation), yet the superintendency is scarcely ever filled by a woman, and it is only the "male" superintendent who is eligible to a seat in Quarterly Conference.   .   .   .

All the benevolent enterprises of the church, which are recognized and supported as such, are officered by men. Women contribute to these, as do other members of the church, but when they desire to put their hearts and brains into a plan of work, they must organize an independent society which must be supported by their own separate contributions and labors. The church is losing immeasurably by this. Methodism may well look about her in alarm, for *her women are being forced out into undenominational Unions*. The fire will burn, and if Methodism will not make a place for it, it will warm another hearth. Can we afford this loss?

So far we have confined ourselves to the consideration of women as lay members. Now, as to their being licensed and ordained as exhorters, local preachers, and ministers in regular standing. This is, perhaps, a more difficult and solemn question than any of the preceding. Certainly, a more solemn one could not be presented to any body of men. It is a question the M. E. Church must speedily settle. Women are rising up all over the land who feel moved by the Holy Ghost to preach. They are flocking into our Theological schools as fast as the doors are opened; and the Church must face their plea. You cannot quote Scripture against it; for if you claim that the restrictions laid upon ignorant, childish, Oriental women, ages ago, in a totally different state of society, were designed for the cultured, devoted, respected women of to-day, you remand us all back to vail, subjection, and silence; you hush our voices in the prayer-meeting room and Sunday-school class. We have already referred to the superior *spiritual* endowments of women. Where should the highest spirituality find its appropriate place of action if not in the pulpit - and how can the pulpit afford to deprive itself of this powerful element? It has been beautifully said, "There are truths which only a woman's heart will conceive, and only a woman's lips can teach - truths perchance, which have come to her when baby fingers have clung round her neck in the dark." Women are the *talkers* of the race. There is no trouble in having this admitted. "A woman's voice can tell a long history of sorrow in a single word." Refine and cultivate the talking gift, and you have *oratory*. We cannot afford to be blind to the drift of these things.

453

But the final test of this question lies in the *call* of women to preach. As Methodists we believe in the direct operation of the Holy Spirit on the mind. Now, numbers of women testify that they feel that burning zeal for souls, that constraining desire to tell the love of Christ, that sense of condemnation in silence, and all those other indications and impressions which in *men* are recognized as a call to preach. They are also led providentially into those paths of usefulness, they speak with that acceptability, they realize that success, they are sealed with that evident approval of God – both upon their own consciousness and in outward results – which, in a brother's case, would bring him help, encouragement, opportunities of education, and, finally, license and ordination. Have these women "gifts, grace, and usefulness"? We will risk the answer with all those who have made any considerable observation on the success of women's Gospel work; and in additional, will beg to remind you that hitherto women have worked without any special training of education, in the face of many difficulties.

To deny that many women realize the call of God to preach or speak the gospel, is to put away all faith in the conscious impressions of the Holy Spirit on the mind. Then, if God calls, how can the Church refuse to call, without coming into controversy with the Divine Master? License and ordination are merely the Church's seal of approval on what it recognizes as God's will and plan. They are right and necessary for the success and convenience of the workman. If women are called, they need these seals of approval as much as men do, and for the same reasons.

It may be said, "Women *are* permitted to speak and preach freely in the Methodist Episcopal Church; and since the work is the main thing, why ask for office and recognition?" It is true that women have great liberty with us as compared with other churches. Thank God, they are not doomed to utter silence! Our Methodism is grandly in advance, on this line, as it is on most others. We have had women preachers since Wesley's time. Probably not one who reads this will deny that women may and should deliver the gospel message in one way or another. Why deny as a Church what we admit as individuals? Why not, at least, grant the exhorter's or local preacher's license?

Is it not a solemn and fearful thing – is it not cruel beyond compare – to hinder a soul that is called of the Holy Ghost? Can the Church afford this loss? Are the fields no longer white, and are the laborers so many, that we can spurn any away, especially when the Master summons? We ask license and ordination for women because it is necessary for them and for the work. Without these, they are forced into the uncertain, exposed, wearing life of traveling evangelists without either the moral or financial support of the Church. Without these, they are left in the dubious and embarrassing position of one who goes before he is sent. The Church says, "Since you will work, go on; but we will not give our approval."

Is this fair; is this just or righteous? Nay, since the delicacy of the womanly organism is sometimes talked of - is it *chivalrous* to force them into these rough and lonely paths? We simply ask that, when a woman-worker measures up to the same standard as a brother-worker, she shall be accorded the same privileges and powers. We should not have to *ask;* for, however pure the motive - however faultless the form of request - we are, by the very fact of asking, laid open to unjust suspicion and criticism.

The Church is supposed to be founded upon *spiritual* principles. Measured by a spiritual standard, women are the equals of men. In Christ's kingdom is neither bond or free, male nor female. Does His Church on earth fairly represent that kingdom when its constitution ignores woman, and its customs shut her out of its highest places of privilege?

It rests with you, members of the General Conference, to remedy these evils, in great part, at least. You best know how it should be done. Will you not examine the Discipline and determine that this May, of 1880, shall see the end of some of these harmful distinctions?

As women we have no representatives in your midst. What can we do but appeal to your sense of truth and righteousness? Surely our blessed Methodism is too pure - the heroic age of our history too fresh upon us - to let us appeal to a lower motive.

The masculine nouns and pronouns are used, throughout the Discipline, in referring to these holding office - either lay or clerical - in the church. This is said to shut women out of all these offices. But this principle would also shut them out of church membership altogether, for the General Rules declare the church to be "a company of men." It would exclude them from the kingdom of heaven, for the Master said, "*Him* that cometh to me I will in no wise cast out."

However, in order that the matter may be clearly understood, we ask you to formulate the principle, in legal, Disciplinary enactment, that the masculine nouns and pronouns, used in the Discipline of the M. E. Church, in referring to trustees, stewards, Sunday School superintendents, class-leaders, exhorters, and preachers - itinerant and local - shall not be construed as excluding women from these offices; and, further, that the word "male" be expunged entirely from the Discipline.

We also ask that the General Conference shall recommend all our churches to devise or alter their constitutions and charters, so that the disabilities of women in all business meetings, may be removed.

Mauch Chunk, Pa.   Mrs. Mary L. Griffith.

¶   Minority Report on the Status of Women in the Church, 1880.

(Taken from manuscript in Drew Theological Seminary).

Whereas, the Majority Report on the Status of Women etc. is not according to fact in stating that the right of women to official privelieges in the church "is universally recognised among us," and

Whereas, said Majority Report favours the continuance of an unauthorised and irregular granting of official privelieges to women by individual Pastors and Presiding Elders and

Whereas, the great and growing work of "The Womans Foreign Missionary Society" devolves hortitory and didactic practices, and imposes official duties, upon women; and

Whereas, these practices, privelieges and duties ought to be authoritatively regulated; therefore

Resolved, that this General Conference does hereby interpret the Discipline concerning all offices of the laity as applying to women in the same sense and to the same extent as to men.

Presentèd May 25, 1880.

¶   Are Women Laymen?

(Taken from Episcopal Address, 1888, *Manual of the General Conference of 1888,* 18-19).

For the first time in our history several "elect ladies" appear, regularly certified from Electoral Conferences, as lay delegates to this body. In taking the action which necessitates the considera- tion of the question of their eligibility the Electoral Conferences did not consult the Bishops as to the law in the case, nor do we understand it to be our duty to define the law for these Conferences; neither does it appear that any one is authorized to decide questions of law in them. The Electoral Conferences simply assumed the law- fulness of this action, being guided, as we are informed, by a declarative resolution of the General Conference of 1872, defining the scope of the word "laymen," in answer to a question touching the classification and rights of ordained local and located ministers. Of course the language of that resolution is carried beyond its original design when applied to a subject not before the body when it was adopted, and not necessarily involved in the language itself. This also should be understood, that no definition of the word "laymen" settles the question of eligibility as to any class of per- sons, for many are classed as laymen for the purposes of lay repre- sentation, and have to do with it officially as laymen, who are

456

themselves not eligible as delegates. Even laymen who are confessedly ineligible, who are not old enough to be delegates, or have not
been members long enough, may be stewards, class-leaders, trustees,
local preachers, and exhorters, and, as such, be members of the
Quarterly Conference and vote for delegates to the Electoral Conference
without themselves being eligible.

The constitutional qualifications for eligibility cannot be modified by a resolution of the General Conference, however sweeping, nor
can the original meaning of the language be enlarged. If women were
included in the original constitutional provision for lay delegates
they are here by constitutional right. If they were not so included
it is beyond the power of this body to give them membership lawfully
except by the formal amendment of the Constitution, which cannot be
effected without the consent of the Annual Conferences. In extending to women the highest spiritual privileges, in recognizing their
gifts, and in providing for them spheres of Christian activity, as
well as in advancing them to positions of official responsibility,
ours has been a leader of the Churches, and gratefully do we
acknowledge the good results shown in their enlarged usefulness and
in the wonderful development of their power to work for God, which
we take as evidences of the divine approval of the high ground taken.
In all reformatory and benevolent enterprises, especially in the
temperance, missionary, and Sunday-school departments of church work,
their success is marvelous, and challenges our highest admiration.
Happily no question of competency or worthiness is involved in the
question of their eligibility as delegates. Hitherto the assumption
underlying the legislation of the Church has been that they were
ineligible to official positions, except by special provision of law.
In harmony with this assumption they have been made eligible, by
special enactment, to the offices of steward, class-leader, and Sunday-
school superintendent, and naturally the question arises as to
whether the necessity for special legislation, in order to their
eligibility to those specified offices, does not indicate similar
necessity for special provision in order to their eligibility as
delegates; and if so it is further to be considered that the offices
of steward, class-leader, and Sunday-school superintendent may be
created and filled by simple enactments of the General Conference
itself; but to enter the General Conference and form part of the
law-making body of the Church requires special provision in the
Constitution, and, therefore, such provision as the General Conference
alone cannot make.

¶   My Experience with General Conferences, by Frances Willard.

   (Taken from *Glimpses of Fifty Years* (1889), 615-21).

   I have seen three of these courts. The first was in Chicago in
1868, when, dressed in my spick-and-span new traveling suit for
Europe, I glanced in through the crowded door of Clark Street Church

where a tremendous debate was going on about lay delegation; but it was nearly time for my train to New York, and this glance was all I had.

The next was in 1880 in Pike's Opera House at Cincinnati. Our National W.C.T.U. had sent a message that year to all the leading ecclesiastical assemblages, respectfully asking for a friendly word from them, and suggesting that they appoint representatives who should attend our National Convention to see what we were doing and bring us words of cheer. In our simplicity, we thought it the most natural thing imaginable thus to bring the work we loved back to the church that had nurtured us and given us our inspiration, and we thoroughly believe that history will declare not only that our purpose was true and good, but that our plan was altogether reasonable. One would have thought, however, that something revolutionary had been proposed, when it was known that my friend, Miss F. Jennie Duty, of Cleveland, and myself were in the Opera House desirous of presenting this message! Grave, dignified clergymen who had always been my friends, looked curiously upon me as if I were, somehow, a little daft. "We have no precedent," they said. "How could you have?" was my answer, "the Crusade was, like the Day of Pentecost, unprecedented. The case is a new one, and your Methodist sisters earnestly believe that you will meet it on its merits."

I will not write here the names of the good Bishops, almost as dear to me as my own brothers, who passed by on the other side, not wishing to commit themselves, also not wishing to hurt my feelings at this crisis. We sought in vain for their advice. Somehow they were always busy, and never could be seen. Meantime the buzzing went on. Poor Anna Oliver, who was trying to gain recognition as a preacher, seemed hardly more of a black sheep than we two white ribbon women with our harmless little message.

The Temperance Committee, however, treated us well, invited us in to its session, and incorporated in its report a resolution that we desired about communion wine, also made kindly allusion, though not by name, to the W.C.T.U. My noble friend, Bishop Foster, consented to preside at a temperance meeting addressed by me, and stood his ground valiantly, at much cost, I have no doubt, to his prejudices. Some liberal-minded delegates, Dr. Payne, Dr. Theodore L. Flood, and Philip Gillette, a lay delegate from Illinois, flung down the gauntlet for me by introducing a resolution that I should have ten minutes in which to speak before the Conference. And now began the war of words, the opposition being headed, as a matter of course, by Dr. Buckley, who, with his faithful ally, Dr. Daniel Curry, dealt sledge-hammer blows against a man of straw. Two hours or more were expended in the debate, when the call of ayes and noes demanded by Dr. Buckley, showed that two thirds of the Conference favored giving the ten minutes. Dilatory tactics were now resorted to by the conservatives, and adjournment was secured, it being a little after

noon. In the interval, I saw that my brave friends were weakening, and they suggested that I send a note saying I would not speak, for as the matter now stood, I had the right to do so, but Dr. Buckley had declared that he would exhaust parliamentary resources to prevent it. I told them that personally I thought it would be wiser to let the question settle itself, and I was neither afraid nor ashamed to stand in my lot and place as a disturber of the peace for the sake of all that I believed was involved in the decision, but seeing that my champions strongly preferred to settle the question peaceably, I compromised the matter and wrote the following:

TUESDAY MORNING, May 18, 1880.

To The General Conference:

HONORED BRETHREN - It is the judgment of many of your members who championed the cause of woman in yesterday's debate (in which judgment I concur), that I would better state to you, with my hearty thanks for the final vote, that I decline to use the hard-earned ten minutes allotted me. Suffer me, however, to explain that, having been sent here as a fraternal visitor by our Woman's National Society, and, moreover, having so often spoken before ecclesiastical bodies upon their earnest invitation, and never having attended a General Conference before, I had no idea of the strong opposition that would be manifested, or I would not have listened to the generous friends who urged the matter on your attention.

Your sister in Christian work,
FRANCES E. WILLARD.

In October, 1887, Anna Gordon and I were at Binghamton, attending the W.C.T.U. Convention of New York State. It was a grand occasion, so many delegates being present that the large church was filled with them. We were entertained in the home of Mrs. Mather, granddaughter of Jonathan Edwards, and while sitting at the breakfast table in her pleasant home, I opened a telegram there handed to me, and read these words:

CHICAGO

I suppose you know that the Rock River Conference has chosen you one of its lay delegates to the General Conference.

A. A. KEAN.

The tears sprang to my eyes, and turning to my dignified hostess I said: "You can hardly imagine how much this means to me. The dear old Rock River Conference of which my brother was once a member, and many of whose ministers I have known from girlhood, selects me as one of its two lay delegates, and my father's business partner of twenty years ago kindly telegraphs the pleasant news. Why should I not think well of men when they can do things so magnanimous? Every one who voted for me would have given his eye teeth to have gone in my stead, yet they set to work and sent me, just out of brotherly good-will."

Much more after this sort I poured out, in my gratitude and gladness, to the quiet old lady, whose face lighted up as she "rejoiced in my joy."

No one had ever named to me the possibility of such an honor, save that Miss Phebe and Mrs. Franc Elliott (daughter and daughter-in-law of Rev. Dr. Charles Elliott, former editor of the *Central Christian Advocate*, but now deceased) had sent me a letter stating that they thought women should go to the General Conference, as they had for years helped to elect those who did go as lay delegates, and had themselves been chosen alternates, and their names placed without question on General Conference lists. I had always thought that no fair-minded person could have a doubt of their inherent right to go, since women constitute at least two thirds of the church membership, bear more than one half its burdens, and have patiently conceded to the brethren, during all generations, its emoluments and honors.

No more was known to me until, on returning West, I heard that certain lawyers of the contrary part (*i.e.*, well-known opponents of woman's larger recognition in these modern days) had said that I would never be allowed to take my seat. But my friends declared, what I fully believed, that the Discipline was so explicit, that "the wayfaring man, though a fool," could not fail to find its meaning friendly.

In the midst of the contention that came up later on in the papers of my church, I gave myself no anxiety about the subject; indeed, I hold that word, "anxiety," to be altogether atheistic, and have endeavored to weed it out of my vocabulary. "Careful for nothing, and in *everything* a giver of thanks," is what the commonest sort of a Christian is sacredly bound to be, or to become. My invitation was duly sent, my name was on all the published lists of delegates; the author of "Representative Methodists" (containing sketches and portraits of delegates), to be brought out by our official Methodist publishing house, wrote to obtain the necessary data; my Methodist friends in New York not inviting me, I had accepted the assignment to the Oriental Hotel, suggested by Gen. Clinton B. Fisk, and I went to New York a few days before the great Conference was to begin its quadrennial session as the Supreme Court of our church, representing over two millions of Methodists. By this time, Dr. Buckley had taken his position against the admission of women, the tintinnabulation of tongues had set in, and the pent-up pendulosity of pens had fairly burst forth.

I arrived in New York on the Friday previous to the Conference, and wishing to know just what was the best course for me to pursue, I went over to the Opera House where the Conference was to hold its session and inquired for General Fisk, finding him already conferring with grave dignitaries of the church and busy with his duties as

chairman of the Committee of Arrangements. He went with Mrs. Carse
and me into the Opera House and we took our seats on the platform with
the great yawning auditorium before us, empty and dark. He told me
there was going to be a vigorous fight, but he thought the women would
get in. I asked his advice about sitting with my delegation, assuring
him that I would on no account take a wrong attitude toward the
controversy. He replied, "Your moral right, there is none to dispute,
and if you are ruled out it will be on a pure technicality and not
upon the merits of the case. This being true, I advise you to be on
hand bright and early the morning that the Conference opens, and if
you like, I shall be glad to escort you along the aisle to your place
with your Rock River brethren." But there had come to me that morning a disquieting telegram from home; my dear mother had not been well
for two or three weeks, but I had received repeated notes in her
usual hand and as I knew her cheery spirit and great desire that I
should be a member of the Conference, I had gone on with my engage-
ments, knowing that she was in the very best of care, and believing
that I should be able to enter on my novel duties. However, on
receiving the morning telegram that mother was not very well and
Anna Gordon would perhaps better go to her, I telegraphed at once,
"Would it not be better for me to go?" That this made it almost a
foregone conclusion that I should return to my home, I know, for
my faithful secretaries there would hardly take the risk of telling
me not to come when I had so plainly expressed the thought and purpose of doing so. Therefore, I was prepared for the response that
soon arrived, "Do not be anxious, but come." And so on Saturday
night I took the limited express, for the first time in my life
deliberately setting out on a Sabbath day's journey. A few times,
chiefly during my travels abroad, I have been under circumstances
that seemed to me to justify taking a train on Sunday, but while I
would not conceal any such action I should wish to go on record as
having the totality of my life opposed to Sunday travel. The way
was long and dreary, but closely filled in with reading and writing,
the unfailing solace of all my years since childhood. It was on this
trip, however, that for the first time in my life of travel I had a
downright ill-mannered *vis-a-vis*.

My kindest of neighbors in the "annex", as we call the cottage
that my sister built joining our own, were at the depot in Chicago.
Helen L. Hood, that staunch white ribboner of Illinois, reached out
her strong hand to me before I left the platform of the car, and
said, "Your mother is better," I think no words were ever sweeter
of all that I have heard. Now followed a month in which I exchanged
the busy and constantly varied activities of a temperance reformer
for the sacred quiet of my mother's sick-room. I had never seen her
so ill, but she was, as always, entirely self-possessed. We had a
council of physicians and she went through the diagnosis with even
smiling cheerfulness, saying, "I think I shall get well, but I am
not at all afraid to die." Little by little she crept up again
under the skillful care of that noble women, Dr. Mary McCrillis,

461

who by day and night was with us in our trouble.

Anna Gordon arrived in New York the day I left, and remained,
at my request, until the great question was decided, sending me
constant bulletins from the Opera House box where General Fisk,
with his customary thoughtfulness, had assigned her a seat. Nothing
could exceed my surprise when I learned that our good bench of Bishops
had prejudged the entire case in their opening address. Only the cold
type of the Associated Press dispatch, giving their language, could
have made me believe this possible. Anna Gordon pictured the scene
dramatically, catching on the wing many of the bright turns and
arguments of the debaters, and seeming full of expectation that the
women would carry the day. She wrote that there was unrivaled
commotion, that our side felt confident, that friends were urgent
for my return and strongly counseled it, but without saying anything
to my mother, who is so self-sacrificing that I knew she would tell
me, "By all means go back, my child," I fully determined that I would
have nothing to do with the controversy, directly or indirectly, and
so in great quietness of spirit awaited the result. When the morning
Inter Ocean was thrown on the steps, I would refrain for some time
from going after it, and mother asked no questions. But when I read
that the lay delegates gave a majority against the admission of
women, and remembered that the vote of women, as they well knew, at
the time of the debate on the eligibility of the laity to the General
Conference, had forced open its doors to the laymen who now deliberately
voted to exclude women, I had no more spirit in me. Once more it was
a case of "Thou, too, Brutus!" That the Bishops should have "left us
lamenting," grieved me, but when the lay delegates did the same, I said
in my heart, "Once more the action of my fellow mortals weans me from
love of life, and by so doing they have doubtless helped me more than
their generosity of action could possibly have done." However, I lost
no sleep and wasted no tears over the curious transaction, and I
confidently predict that we five women, whose election was thus disavowed, will have more enviable places in history than any who opposed
us on those memorable days. Of them it will be written, while doubtless
they did not so intend, that they committed an injustice: of us, only
that in silence we endured it.

The champions of equality made a splendid record, of which they
will be prouder with each added year. They are forerunners of that
grander, because more equitable, polity that shall yet glorify our
Methodism when in her law, as in Christ's gospel, there shall be,
"Neither male nor female."

¶   Frances Willard on Raising Children.

(Taken from *Glimpses of Fifty Years* (1889), 43, 69-70, 678).

Happy the girls of the period who practice nearly every outdoor

462

sport that is open to their brothers; wear gymnastic suits in school, flee to the country as soon as vacation comes, and have almost as blessed a time as we three children had in the old days at Forest Home. It is good for boys and girls to know the same things, so that the former shall not feel and act so overwise. A boy whose sister knows all about the harness, the boat, the gymnastic exercise, will be far more modest, genial and pleasant to have about. He will cease to be a tease and learn how to be a comrade, and this is a great gain to him, his sister, and his wife that is to be.

*   *   *

No girl went through a harder experience than I, when my free, out-of-door life had to cease, and the long skirts and clubbed-up hair spiked with hair-pins had to be endured. The half of that down-heartedness has never been told and never can be. I always believed that if I had been let alone and allowed as a woman, what I had had as a girl, a free life in the country, where a human being might grow, body and soul, as a tree grows, I would have been "ten times more of a person," everyway. Mine was a nature hard to tame, and I cried long and loud when I found I could never again race and range about with freedom. I had delighted in my short hair and nice round hat, or comfortable "Shaker bonnet," but now I was to be "choked with ribbons" when I went into the open air the rest of my days. Something like the following was the "state of mind" that I revealed to my journal about this time:

This is my birthday and the date of my martyrdom. Mother insists that at last I *must* have my hair "done up woman-fashion." She says she can hardly forgive herself for letting me "run wild" so long. We've had a great time over it all, and here I sit like another Samson "shorn of my strength." That figure won't do, though, for the greatest trouble with me is that I never shall be shorn again. My "back" hair is twisted up like a corkscrew; I carry eighteen hair-pins; my head aches miserably; my feet are entangled in the skirt of my hateful new gown. I can never jump over a fence again, so long as I live. As for chasing the sheep, down in the shady pasture, it's out of the question, and to climb to my "Eagle's-nest" seat in the big burr-oak would ruin this new frock beyond repair. Altogether I recognize the fact that my "occupation's gone."

Something else that had already happened, helped to stir up my spirit into a mighty unrest. This is the story as I told it to my journal:

This is election day and my brother is twenty-one years old. How proud he seemed as he dressed up in his best Sunday clothes and drove off in the big wagon with father and the hired men to vote for John C. Frémont, like the sensible "Free-soiler" that he is. My sister and I stood at the window and looked out after them. Somehow

I felt a lump in my throat, and then I couldn't see their wagon anymore, things got so blurred. I turned to Mary, and she, dear little
innocent, seemed wonderfully sober, too. I said, "Wouldn't you like
to vote as well as Oliver? Don't you and I love the country just as
well as he, and doesn't the country need our ballots?" Then she looked scared, but answered, in a minute, "'Course we do, and 'course we
ought, - but don't you go ahead and say so, for then we would be
called strong-minded."

*   *   *

Let me, then, here and now, declare my faith more definitely:
I believe that boys and girls should be trained very much alike and
have the same toys. This will give the girls abundant outdoor
exercise, fit them out with that physical equipoise that we call
health, which means wholeness, which means happiness. It will also
develop their observing faculties, now so much less brought out than
those of boys. Perhaps the fact that a doll is so early placed in the
girl's arms may help to account for her dulled curiosity, her greater
passivity, her inferior enterprise, bravery and courage. Perhaps the
doll may help to shut out the world of wonder and surprise in which
she was meant to dwell. The ever-present doll may close her mind to
studies and observations which would develop inventors among women.
I have always believed the lack of mechanical inventions as the
fruit of woman's brain, was superinduced by a false training, and
that possibly doll-nurture had somewhat to do with it. Perhaps because my own early years were spent upon a farm, I have thought that
live dolls, that is, pets, were nobler, as they are certainly far
more frolicsome and responsive companions for children than the wax
imitations that form the "regulation pattern" toy of girls.

¶   On Social Issues.

(Taken from *Minutes of the Woman's National Christian Temperance
Union*, 1880, 18-19).

While as temperance women we keep to our own work, there are many
other philanthropic efforts which, in various localities, have been
projected by our societies. In Dover, N.H., an evening school for
employees, originating in the Union, was taken up by the proprietor
of a large manufactory, who assumed all the expenses. In Rochester,
N.Y., the Young Woman's Temperance Union give temperance lessons to
the public-school children on Friday after hours, awaiting the time
when the proper authorities shall incorporate the work into the
system of public education. In Portland, Me., the employment of a
member of our Union to attend the police-court and look after the
interests of arrested women resulted in the appointment of a woman
policeman (pardon the philanthropic paradox) by the municipal
authorities in a distant city, who were moved thereto by their know-

ledge of the Portland experiment. In Michigan, the State Woman's Christian Union last year induced the Legislature to appropriate thirty thousand dollars for a Girl's Reform School.

It has long seemed to me that our Unions, by their unsectarian character and representative aims, were fitted incidentally to furnish the incitement to noble enterprises closely related to our work, in which women who will not as yet engage in our direct temperance endeavor would gladly employ their steadily-arousing energies. In large cities we might call a meeting and do the preliminary work which would result in organizing the associated charities so beneficently operative in Philadelphia and Boston, or in the founding of an Industrial and Temporary Home like that of which the pastor of this church is the chief presiding officer; or in the inauguration of a Citizens' League in the interests of the Sabbath and the protection of children from the liquor-traffic, an enterprise which has had notable success in Chicago. We might go even beyond all this and petition municipal authorities to establish public fountains, free bathing-houses and gymnasiums, all of which, conducing directly to improved sanitary habits in the public, would accomplish much toward diminishing the feverish and unnatural thirst for stimulants. Let us not insist that all shall work with us, but rather be sedulous in the endeavor so to increase the aggregate "enthusiasm of humanity," so to glorify the sentiment of *other-hood* as opposed to the sense of *self-hood*, that all may find the secret of a happy life in working *somewhere*.

*   *   *

(Taken from *Minutes of the National W. C. T. U.*, 1888, 8-9, 10, 50-53).

PEACE

President McGill, of Swarthmore College, is the first educator to introduce the study of Peace and Arbitration. I believe he has set a noble example, and that our ethical text-books should include a careful study of these great themes.

The platform of the Prohibition party declares that "Arbitration is the Christion, wise, and economic method of settling national differences." Here, as in all things else, the Society of the White-Ribbon is in accord with the party of the White Rose. Poisonous drinks crazing the brains of legislators precipitated the Civil War; so said one of our most famous generals, never noted as a special pleader for the temperance cause. No movement means so much as ours for peace. The race brain is now so deeply leavened with gentle thoughts, that when normal and calm, the thought of shedding human blood is most repugnant to it. No evolution of work was surer than that which led to the formation of our Peace Department, with a

Secretary selected from the Society of Friends, Mrs. Hannah Bailey, of Winthrop, Maine, who has already sent out literature and speakers to acquaint our auxiliaries with our plans of work among the children and with the press. We have also a powerful friend in Mrs. Elizabeth Thompson, the philanthropist, who is devoted to the heavenly work of spreading far and wide the interest of the people in a World's Court of Arbitration as a substitute for war, and who believes that woman's hand may carry the white flag of truce between camps otherwise belligerent, and may, by wise and systematic action, help to lay firm foundations for a Universal Republic - a Brotherhood and Sisterhood wide as the world.   .   .   .

OUR WORK IN THE SCHOOLS

It has been said that "body and mind are two well-fitting halves of a perfect whole." In Greece, gymnastics and study were inseparable. Our friend William Blaikie, who speaks to us to-morrow evening on "Athletics for Young Women," writes these golden words in his book entitled "Our Children's Bodies:" "What chance has a bright and studious girl in one of our public schools to build up her health and strength? Who teaches her about either? Ambitious to stand well in her class, no matter how much work is set before her, she goes at it with determination, and willingly spends not only all her school hours, but often, as has already been seen, her hours out of school as well, in close, exacting study. Who teaches her to intersperse these with an hour or two, not of a dawdling walk at a dead-and-alive gait, but with sensible, hearty exercise and play, making her for the time wholly forget her brain work? Not only has she no guide in this direction, but her very lack of physical vigor makes her indisposed to anything like continued or even momentary muscular exertion; indeed, often she is afraid to take it, and even thinks it dangerous. Many a day passes in which she does not take one single full breath. Is it any wonder that she has small lungs, when she does nothing to expand them?"

*   *   *

THE LABOR MOVEMENT

It is in the air nowadays to live for others; it has even become "good form." Princes must be philanthropic or they are looked down upon, and the statement concerning a society woman, that "she lives for herself," sets her somewhat askew in the eyes of her associates. It is better to do good work because etiquette requires it than not to do it at all. This general drift of the fortunate class toward a study of the unfortunate, with a helpful motive as its basis, is the most hopeful feature of the times. Beside it must be placed the strongly growing tendency to study causes rather than effects, and this brings the whole labor problem into view. For the more we study causes, the more certainly we find that justice, not charity, must

be the watchword of the future. I am glad that the W. C. T. U. takes
a broad view of this question, and belongs to the newer school of
political economists represented by Prof. Ely, of Johns Hopkins
University, rather than that of Prof. Sumner, of Yale College. One
cares only for the survival of the stronger, the other would fain
help the under dog in the fight to such conditions as would develop
all his inherent powers of becoming the upper one himself. I wish
all our women would read the four essays of Ruskin entitled, "Unto
this Last," and the leaf on "Political versus Commercial Economy,"
by Dr. Ingersoll, both of which have recently been brought out by
our own publishing house under the supervision of our invaluable
editor, Mrs. Elizabeth Wheeler Andrew, and whose entrance on
another field of labor occasions to so many of us sincere regret.

For one, my study of the question convinces me, that while
prohibition of the liquor traffic would be an inestimable blessing
to the wage-workers, there is more in the labor movement than we
have perceived from our special point of view. For instance, as
our good Dr. DeCosta said recently, in Exeter Hall, England, at
the annual meeting of the White Cross Society with half a dozen
Bishops, an Earl, a Dean, and a Canon on the platform, "Starvation
wages to women are one main cause of the evil we are met to combat."
The revelations in New York, Chicago, and all our large cities, show
that the yoke on the workingman's neck rests still more heavily on
the workingwoman.

The Knights of Labor are to-day the most efficient body in this
land for the protection of women, in equal pay for equal work, and
of children from the stunting of body and mind through servitude
that is little better than slavery. The eight-hour law would increase
wages, and add one-fourth to the number of the employed, thus almost
disbanding the army of tramps. Arbitration, co-operation, state
control of all the means of public locomotion and communication, would
help to verify or refute the theory, now rapidly becoming prevalent,
that if corporate powers are good for capital, labor might appropriately
share them.   .   .   .

The climax of the Labor Movement will be reached when wage-
workers cease scoffing at the Bible, and perceive it to be above all
others the Book of Brotherhood.   .   .   .

When all is said, but three questions to-day enlist the nations
heart: The temperance, the labor, and the woman questions, and these
three are really one. The solution of any one of these in accordance
with the wishes of its friends, would mean an incalculable uplift to
the others. Total prohibition would make the world a new and blessed
place for woman, while her enfranchisement would be a death blow to
the liquor traffic; co-operative commonwealths, the final goal of the
labor agitation, would so humanize and harmonize the world that the
drink desperation would be reduced to zero; with the triumph of the

wage-worker's cause, woman's would mount to victory, since, to their
everlasting honor be it said, all laborer reformers demand equal
wages for equal work and are openly committed to equal suffrage also.
I wish every woman here would read the book by Edward Bellamy,
entitled *Looking Backward,* and see how the tyranny of "Trusts" may
perhaps be yet transformed to the boon of brotherhood, if only
"We, Us & Company," can agree to organize one great "trust" in our
own interest, whose dividends shall be declared, and whose combinations
concentrated for the greatest numbers' greatest good. Competition
has been a useful spur in cruder ages, but at last it bows before
its master, corporate control, and the bigger the corporation the
better for the corporators, because the more there are to be enriched.
Carrying out this condition of things to infinity may yet prove that
humanity is the one humane and righteous "syndicate," the only
"combination" that can be permitted to combine, the only trusted
"Trust."

But this can never be until heads are clear, hands steady, and
hearts true. Hence be it ours to work right on for the downfall of
the drink traffic, and the regnancy of home folks in Church, in State,
and everywhere.

"I have compassion on the multitude," this is the key that
Christ has set for each one's psalm of life, and deeds are the only
voices sweet enough to sing it in.

*   *   *

(Taken from *Minutes of the National W. C. T. U.*, 1895, 103-05).

In London I saw this inscription in a grimy street: "Marquis of
Westminster Buildings for the Industrial Classes." The incongruity
smote me as I gazed, for who is the Marquis of Westminster and why
should he not belong to the "industrial classes"? How much better
it would be for him if he did! Why should there be any class but the
industrial! Why should humanity be divided into grades based on the
fact that they work or that they do not work, and by what monstrosity
of delusion did it ever come to be thought that those who did not
work stood at the head, and those who worked, just in proportion to
the degree of their work, stood at the foot? I cannot bear to think
so ill of the race to which I belong as to believe that a thing so
sacred as honest toil is looked down upon for its own sake. It is
rather because under a false system of society some work so constantly
that they have not time to develop their powers, physical, mental and
moral, into that symmetry that makes admirable character and attractive deportment. But if they are unable to do this, what is the
reason? Because the work is not equalized, but certain thoughtless,
selfish, "privileged classes" have heaped the work they ought to do
upon those who had already more than was their share, and I am a
Collectivist because I believe these burdens should be distributed

according to those principles of justice which ought to teach every human being that every other has as much right as himself to life, liberty, the pursuit of happiness, the pursuit of knowledge, the pursuit of holiness. This is to my mind the whole case in a nut-shell, and the time will come when those who do not work will be drummed out of the camp and stung out of the hive, and placed by themselves as lepers are, and will learn that it is a law of God written in our members that he who will not work neither shall he eat.

But to-day we are confronted by a vegetating aristocracy on the one hand, and an agitating democracy on the other. When matters have reached this pass and the lines are more clearly drawn than in any previous age something will have to give way, and what we look for is the intersphering of the two classes as the only road to "peace with honor" for the human race.

It was well said by Froude, the historian, many years since, that the best ally of rich men in piling up their gains is the increasing tendency of drunkenness in the working classes. So long as men get drunk, they will not be politically dangerous. If the Trades Unions would make sobriety a condition of membership, they might be absolute masters of England and America to-morrow.   .   .   .

Much criticism has been expended upon me for declaring in my Third Biennial Address before the World's W. C. T. U. in June last, that as temperance people we had been in error in not recognizing the relation of poverty to intemperance, and because I stated that while from the first I had maintained that intemperance caused poverty I was now ready not only to reiterate that cardinal doctrine but to add that poverty caused intemperance. By that declaration I am ready to stand or fall. It is an axiom and will be admitted by every reasonable person; as temperance people we have not been in the habit of saying it but everybody knows that it is true. I did not say that poverty caused intemperance in the same degree that intemperance causes poverty, nor do I think it does, but as we have not been wont to recognize poverty at all among the procuring causes of intemperance it seems to me high time that we did so.

¶   Letter by Frances Willard to Ezra Tipple, 1895.

(Taken from manuscript duplicated copy at Garrett-Evangelical Theological Seminary).

Dear Brother:

Your picture is beautiful--and I am a judge! You know I am your Aunt or grand-mother as the case may be so I can say this with impunity.

469

It occurs to me to ask that you will interest yourself to see that Dr. Buckley does something like justice to our Convention, which is on all sides declared to be the best one we have ever had. 428 delegates from 45 States and territories, unusual attractiveness in the way of procession of banners, singing of its state song by each delegation, singing of Katharine Willard Baldwin etc; increase in membership and larger balance in treasury than usual; two collections taken for the Armenians; Anti-Lynching Resolution passed strong; A Y organized in the Woman's College; request to Prohibition Party to change its name to Home Protection Party; Resolution for Woman's Suffrage, on qualified educational test; strong resolutions in favor of Purity movement; department of Good Citizenship formed and of enforcement of law--there I think that you can make a first rate paragraph yourself out of these materials. What a thing it is to have a "friend at court"!

I am going to speak for you when in New York and don't you forget it. I wonder if you would not to have A. G. form an L.T.L. in your new church? She is a "master hand" at such enterprises.

Believe me,
            Every yours with high regard,
                                    Frances Willard

¶   Riding a Bicycle.

(Taken from *A Wheel in a Wheel* (1895), 21-22, 28, 38-39).

Just here let me interpolate: Learn on a low machine, but "fly high" when once you have mastered it, as you have much more power over the wheels and can get up better speed with a less expenditure of force when you are above the instrument than when you are at the back of it. And remember this is as true of the world as of the wheel.

The order of evolution was something like this: First, three young Englishmen, all strong-armed and accomplished bicyclers, held the machine in place while I climbed timidly into the saddle. Second, two well-disposed young women put in all the power they had, until they grew red in the face, offsetting each other's pressure on the cross-bar and thus maintaining the equipoise to which I was unequal. Third, one walked beside me, steadying the ark as best she could by holding the center of the deadly cross-bar, to let go whose handles meant chaos and collapse. After this I was able to hold my own if I had the moral support of my kind trainers, and it passed into a proverb among them, the short emphatic word of command I gave them at every few turns of the wheel: "Let go, but stand by." Still later everything was learned - how to sit, how to pedal, how to turn, how to dismount; but alas! how to vault into the saddle I

found not; that was the coveted power that lingered long and would not yield itself.

That which caused the many failures I had in learning the bicycle had caused me failures in life; namely, a certain fearful looking for of judgment; a too vivid realization of the uncertainty of everything about me; an underlying doubt - at once, however (and this is all that saved me), matched and overcome by the determination not to give in to it. . . .

One of the first things I learned was that unless a forward impetus were given within well-defined intervals, away we went into the gutter, rider and steed. And I said to myself: "It is the same with all reforms: sometimes they seem to lag, then they barely balance, then they begin to oscillate as if they would lose the track and tumble to one side; but all they need is a new impetus at the right moment on the right angle. . . .

We rejoiced together greatly in perceiving the impetus that this uncompromising but fascinating and illimitably capable machine would give to that blessed "woman question" to which we were both devoted; for we had earned our own bread many a year, and she, although more than twenty years my junior, had accumulated an amount of experience well-nigh as great, because she had lived in the world's heart, or the world's carbuncle (just as one chooses to regard what has been called in literary phrase the capital of humanity). We saw that the physical development of humanity's mother-half would be wonderfully advanced by that universal introduction of the bicycle sure to come about within the next few years, because it is for the interest of great commercial monopolies that this should be so, since if women patronize the wheel the number of buyers will be twice as large. If women ride they must, when riding, dress more rationally than they have been wont to do. If they do this many prejudices as to what they may be allowed to wear will melt away. Reason will gain upon precedent, and ere long the comfortable, sensible, and artistic wardrobe of the rider will make the conventional style of woman's dress absurd to the eye and unendurable to the understanding. A reform often advances most rapidly by indirection. An ounce of practice is worth a ton of theory; and the graceful and becoming costume of woman on the bicycle will convince the world that has brushed aside the theories, no matter how well constructed, and the arguments, no matter how logical, of dress-reformers.

¶   Belle Harris Bennett Advocates Lay Rights for Women in the
Southern Church.

(Taken from *Daily Christian Advocate* (M.E.S. General Conference), 20 May, 1910, 117-18). I am indebted to Carolyn L. Stapleton, Punahou School, Honolulu, for this reference).

Miss Bennett spoke as follows: Brethren, I am not unmindful of the very great courtesy you are doing me in giving me the time to speak before you here, and I believe I can convince some of you at least, that what we have asked from you in this amendment is neither unwomanly nor unreasonable.

The women who ask this of you are the same women who sit beside you in the pew every Sunday morning. They are the same women that kneel beside you at the altar to take of the body and blood of Jesus Christ. They are the same women that go out into the hard places, the lanes and by-ways of towns and cities; the very same women. I never heard one of you say that a deaconess by doing that work can become unwomanly. I never heard one of you say that these women who go out into the dark, hard places of the foreign field, who work beside the most degraded in the heathen lands, and the home lands, have become unwomanly because of the work they have done.

I stand here this morning to say that the great Church of God that you represent today needs the womanhood of the Church in the councils of the Church. Four years ago, this great body, assembled at Birmingham, helped to pass the law concerning the Woman's Home Missionary Society, which, last year, raised $264,000, a restrictive law saying that these women should not without the consent and approval of the General Board of Missions take more than $5,000 of money which they raised for buying property, etc. Men! if one woman had been on this floor, and had risen to protest against that, or to explain to you that which was hard to understand, or if there had been one woman to whom you had looked to explain this provision, you would not have done it. If there had been a woman at that time in your General Board, and could have counciled with your Missionary Committee at that time, who could have taken some control of the work in the foreign land, you would not have done that thing. It was not that you meant to do that unkind thing. At that time you passed a law that the missionary women should have two years of training in a training school, and two years of testing, before such one went out to the field, and should look to your General Board for supervision and instruction. You need us in the council of the Church.

Objection has been made that so few women want this thing. May I ask you, my brethren, when any great forward movement of the world event went forward with a majority vote. Always in the beginning of great events, or in great movements, the beginning must be with a few. This I say to you today. It is not a few who believe that the fulness of time has come. A great part of every household of men and women are feeling your sisters should sit on terms of equality in the Conference of the Church. . . .

I believe the minority report says that we do not want to put on our women this great additional work. Today I look around this house, and I see women here from all parts of the world, from far off Seattle, from San Francisco, from everywhere. Are not these the mothers of the

land, the very mothers that you say cannot leave their duties at home. I wonder if there are any babies at home today whose mothers are here, who will not accept these additional burdens.   .   .   .

I speak not for the women who sit in their parlors, with carpeted floors and curtained windows, with the tenderness of love of brethren and friends and little children around them. I do not speak in their behalf.   .   .   .

Today in Dallas, Texas, as for the last twelve years, we have had a little, though unworthy home, where the poor unfortunate girls of that section have been gathered in, and mothered. It is for the three hundred thousand such girls in the State of Texas alone, those poor fallen girls, – I stand in the councils of Church to speak for them.

And I stand here to speak for the seven millions of wage-earning women who are in this land today.

My brothers and friends, Mr. George Stuart, said to me some years ago, in speaking of these women: "I would put them all back into their homes, and let them have the comfort of their homes."

Gentlemen, if you had been in some of the homes where we have been! I stood in one of the great packing houses of Kansas City, and saw all those women; I have been in the cotton mills of all these various sections, and seen these women with their little children who had no other way of earning their living, earning their daily food, and we have these mothers whom I saw going back to their wretched homes, where they were huddled, three, five, yes, fifteen, in rooms only fifteen feet square, and I say is God pushing them out of their homes, and has the Church taken no step to protect these women by going down into the great cities and giving them sanitary homes. I do not plead for those to whom you give love and affection, and kindness, but I do ask you to let us into the councils of your Church, and bring before you the need of these women down in the hard places. Why should we not sit beside you in the Boards of Education? Seventy years ago there were less than a hundred women who taught school. Seventy years ago they had no part in higher education. Today seven-tenths of the Sunday School teachers are women, and yet you say you don't think your women ought to sit on the Boards of Education.   .   .   .

I can point out to you women in your Church who have the Doctorate conferred on them, and you cannot tell me of a woman in this whole country who has had a degree conferred upon her by a second rate university, or bought for her by money, but it is a reward of merit when a woman becomes a Doctor of Philosophy. And I give you my word that they have plenty of equipment. They are well equipped I believe to sit with you. If I could have been on the boards of education Kentucky Wesleyan would have had a better equipment. And it is true in every college to-day, if the women could have been on Conference Education Boards.

Why not sit beside the men in your Sunday School Board. You know that seven-tenths of the teachers in your Sunday School are women, and why should we not help to frame the policy of your Sunday Schools.

As I look over your arena here today, I could see that the sentiment back of you all of these years is such that you would say, "This is hardly a place for a women." But in the Conference the question is not one of the loudest voice, but it is the question of the speaker on the stand. Don't you think women could be seen as well as men if she had on a white dress, and a blue ribbon and flowers?

Now my brethren, I believe that our voices are just about as good as most of yours. I have strained my ears as I sat back there, and it is just occasionally that a man could be heard at the rear of this hall, and I believe our voices could penetrate as far as the men's do sometimes.

My brethren, this is not a matter of reason with you. You do not protest against this with your reason. It is a matter of prejudice, it is a matter of sentiment. You are burning incense to an ancestral tablet. Methodism has been doing a great deal of that.

But there are so many things I would like to say in behalf of those who stand for this. I know that there have been plenty of silly women, of gossiping women, and plenty of idle women. But you may remember what the old Yorkshireman said in Adam Bede, I believe, "God Almighty made them to match the men." I have seen many women that I thought had met more than his match.

According to the ruling of the Church, to which I listened eagerly, this matter cannot come under four years. If you put this measure on its passage, and let it go down to the Annual Conference, it must come back, and it will be eight years before some women might possibly sit in this General Conference. I do not believe you would object if there was a little corner of women over there, and I think that, if such a woman as Miss Laura Haygood sat in this body, and some question as to the foreign field came up, you would be glad to hear her. There are not a great many of our women who would sit in your Annual Conferences or General Conferences, but our contention is this, I repeat it again, you need the women in the councils of the Church, – the Church needs it, the world's evangelization needs it, and we believe that the fullness of time has come for this thing. I hope you will put this measure on its passage. If you do not, we are to have four years of education. You must have that because there are plenty of men, as well as women, who need to be educated on it. Put this act on its passage, and it will come back to another General Conference to be ratified, and even then there would not be many of you here in the Conference. A great many of us will be gone home to God. We have not done this work in our own strength. We have gone to our boarding houses to ask God to guide us. Week after week we have said we

thank Thee, O Lord, that I stand here today, after seventeen years of work guided by the same commission that brought me into the Church, and the Master has said "go." Bishop Hendrix said look at the men on this platform - one here from Asia, another from China, another from Korea, represented on this platform, and I said a woman is not considered worthy to stand on this platform.

Not yet can the women sit on the platform of the Church of Christ with her brothers. After twenty centuries we stand knocking at the door of the Church of God, saying yet, "My brothers, brothers, won't you take us in?" God made man and woman coordinate. With the co-ordination of man and woman there is no reproduction of life, no perfect government of the home. Let the father die, and the mother and the little children all along through the years miss that government. They miss in the home what makes the perfect home. Let the mother die, and again the government of that home is broken. The Church is the house of God and the mother of God's people. You need the perfect government of the man and woman in the Church. Put this measure on its passage, and let it go down to the conferences and come back to you; and eight years from now perhaps there will be one or two women in the General Conference. I thank you again, my brethren.

20. SOCIAL CONCERNS

After the Civil War American society was subjected more strongly to the pressures of the Industrial Revolution. These pressures were reflected in the attitudes of the churches and their members. Since the Methodist Episcopal Church and its Southern sibling were rapidly becoming not only well represented in all parts of the nation but also something approaching an unofficial national religion, at least insofar as this denomination was effectively Americanized, Methodist churches were widely involved in interaction with social forces.

This may be seen not only in the industrial East but also in the continuing process of the Westward Movement, illustrated by the article by T. M. Eddy (editor of the Northwestern Christian Advocate), "Influence of Methodism upon the Civilization and Education of the West," published in the Methodist Quarterly Review of 1857.

Among the early--and radical--advocates of the social application of the Christian faith was Gilbert Haven, editor of Zion's Herald, (in 1872 elected bishop). Many of his sermons carried a strong political and social message which grew out of his long-time support of abolitionism. Selections come from sermons of the 1860's, "The State a Christian Brotherhood," "The War and the Millennium" and "America's Past and Future."

A social problem of long duration was the fate of American Indians. Methodists had already confronted this problem in the removal of the Eastern tribes to lands west of the Mississippi. In the years after the War Between the States Methodist publications reacted in an interesting way to the news of Custer's defeat at the Little Big Horn in 1876 and the massacre at Wounded Knee in 1891.

Desire for peace and occasional pacifist expressions were to be found. But usually Methodists demonstrated their Americanization by active support of military ventures. This was especially true in the Spanish-American War, when President McKinley was known as a good Methodist and the promise of victory brought promise of new missionary opportunities. A. B. Leonard, secretary of the Missionary Society, was not one to let such opportunities slip by.

Illustrative of the most vigorous social attack by Methodists is the massive historical and programmatic work, The Liquor Problem in All Ages, by New England minister Daniel Dorchester. He had no reservations about his support of both total abstinence and legislative prohibition.

A crisis in labor problems was reached in the Pullman Strike of 1894. In the middle was the Methodist minister in that Chicago suburb, William H. Carwardine. Out of his hard experience came his book, The Pullman Strike. In spite of temporary opposition in his

476

own church and denomination, he persevered and was eventually vindicated in his Annual Conference. He expressed in action the principles which within a decade were formulated in the Methodist Social Creed.

Among the many published views on the Social Gospel were two in Zion's Herald, *one by Frank Mason North, the other by David H. Wheeler. Christian socialism was a new, exciting, and to some troublesome phrase, derived from an established movement in Great Britain. One who was troubled was Daniel Dorchester, the same who was so eager to press on with the temperance movement. He and others were unable to make the connection between temperance work and social Christianity, which Frances Willard made so successfully.*

As the Social Creed was formulated and made official by the General Conference of 1908, the Methodist Federation for Social Service (later Social Action) was beginning its work as an unofficial adjunct of American Methodism. One of the most active in organization was Worth M. Tippy, Indiana minister, who edited in 1909 contributed articles under the title The Socialized Church.

¶   Methodism in the Westward Movement.

(Taken from *Methodist Quarterly Review*, xxxix (1857), 284).

A full answer to this question is beyond the scope and purpose of this paper. It only designs to notice the influence of *one power*. A distinguished jurist, Judge of Supreme Court in one of the Western states, used to say, "But for the Methodist Church and the Methodist ministry, this country would have sunk into barbarism." We will not argue the truth of this sweeping declaration, but simply give it as the deliberate and repeatedly expressed opinion of an intelligent deist, familiar with the progress of the West, himself no mean part of its history. Yet how widely different from the spirit of the most who have professed to write Western history! They have usually ignored the existence of Methodism; the work of its ministry and their noble spirit of sacrifice, have found no record in their volumes. Though our denominational history has all the sparkle of poetry, all the noble earnestness of chivalry, these historiographers have made a circuit of unalleviated dullness to avoid it, preferring much stupidity to a little justice.

What we do claim is, that Methodism was second to no other visible agency in advancing the civilization and education of the West. And take, first, the peculiar type of its pioneer ministry; *it was a missionary ministry, without the aid of missionary societies or missionary appropriations*. Of the latter they had small *experience*. Their ecclesiastical organization allowed them to join a circle or chain of appointments, each in a different neighborhood, blending the whole in one pastoral charge. These different societies, though spreading over an area of many miles, they regularly visited, remaining with each long enough to preach the Gospel of the Kingdom, to administer the ordinances, and exercise proper pastoral discipline. We think we are safe in saying that no other system could have given the teachings and sacraments of the New Covenant regularly to these frontier settlements. At least no other did. Most of the men denying the validity of Methodist orders, quietly waited until the "social and moral condition of the people became congenial," ere they pressed their way to the Western frontier lines.

¶   An Early Social Prophet, Gilbert Haven.

(Taken from Gilbert Haven, *National Sermons* (1869), 352-55, 384-85, 387-88, 390, 626-27).

1. We must expunge the word "colored" from our Minutes. It ought never to have found a place there. How abominable that epithet must appear in the eyes of the Savior, by whom these His brethren were cleansed with the same blood, and perchance, at the same moment and the same altar! He does not write it in the Lamb's book of life—

the heavenly Minutes of His church. Born into His divine family, we are nearer of kin to them than brothers of a human household. And yet we shamefully degrade them. How unchristian and inhuman such conduct is, may be seen from a single example. Suppose an unfortunate dwarf should join this church, and the pastor should return three hundred full grown adults and one dwarf; or if a dozen mutes, or blind, should become members, and we should make the like distinction, how quickly should we revolt from the revelation in ourselves of the old leaven of malice and wickedness! What a torrent of indignation would be poured on our Missionary Board if they should publish in their East Indian returns their Brahmin and Pariah members in separate columns!

But the worst feature in this iniquity is, that it casts reproach on those who, by the pressure of an ungodly world, are already oppressed. The Gospel is especially tender towards the lowly and despised. We are especially cruel. It also inevitably breeds in us hardness of heart-- the extreme opposite of the new heart, whose law is to esteem others better than ourselves.

I was struck with this years ago, in a revival that occurred in a country town in the State of New York. The preacher, a godly brother, though not educated in this truth above the community in which he lived, was inviting sinners to the altar. Seeing some of his congregation urging the few of this class present to go forward, the thought dimly struck him that they were included in "all the world" whom they were singing about as being invited by Christ. So he said at the close of his invitation, "If there are any colored persons present *who have souls*, let them come forward also." To such a request no colored person who had a soul would be apt to respond. The same brother, in summing up the fruits of the revival, announced to the church that so many "had been converted, and John, Jane and Dinah, colored persons." He was unconsciously but correctly conforming to the practice of our church. .   .   .

3. We should also abolish every colored church. All should melt into each other. All ye are brethren.

4. These flourish for another and yet worse reason, which springs from the same false root. God is pleased to call some men to preach His gospel that are much nearer than we are to the complexion and lineage of Christ and His apostles. He pours grace upon their lips, so that all the world runs after them. But we call them negroes, or the more classic and more contemptuous word by which we designate this class, even if the Lord's anointed. They cannot minister to white people. They cannot associate with their not always whiter clerical brethren. We have no humility by which we love to kneel down and wash their feet, though that very deed was done by Christ, on this very night, to teach us this very lesson. It is not learned yet.

479

We compromise with conscience by setting off others of our brethren to whom they shall minister. Thus America presents a spectacle seen nowhere else in Christendom, - seen never before in Christendom, - of a body of poor believers, compelled by their brethren to worship by themselves under the ban of public infamy, and a body of God's ministers, in like manner, compelled to make full proof of their ministry under like disgrace. I say it is not seen nor known anywhere else in the world, past or to-day. James thought he had touched the bottom of sinful distinctions when he dwelt on the partialities displayed in the same church. What would he have thought had the Holy Ghost required him to give warning to Christians against pushing a portion of their brethren, and of their ministry also, into separate churches - separated for no fault of their own, for no leprosy or disease that whitened skins, but because of a heaven-daring pride on the part of their kindred.

This must be changed if we hope for the blessing of God. The ministry must lead in the change.

* * *

But the wisdom of God is wiser than men. You did not create the doctrine of human fraternity. You may have fancied that you did; that it was your patent, and could be limited and controlled at your pleasure. So did the Athenian democrats. Where are they? So have the Southern slavemongers. Where are they? God, my friends, not you, made man, of one father, that all might be brethren, that each should in honor prefer one another, esteeming others better than themselves. He is pushing us forward to His, not our, Millennium. He is using and blessing us if we choose to work with Him. If not, He is none the less using us, while also chastising, for the advancement of mankind to the same goal. He maketh our wrath or righteousness alike to praise and prosper Him. Whether gradually, and by the operation of laws that have been molding and transforming man for ages, or suddenly, and by the breaking up of the present order and institution of a new earth and new man, as some devout students of the Bible believe, whichever be the way, the end is sure and the same. The Millennium is a world of men, equal, brotherly, united, and holy. Every approach to that state now renders its violent introduction less necessary. If it can be effected by natural causes there will be no need of the supernatural. It is being effected. The divine doctrine of democracy has become choked with weeds and stones. We said, "It is true and grand, but it is only for white folks. Do you dare to say that that negro and I are of one blood, and should be one in social and civil life? that it is as much his duty to ignore my complexion as it is mine to ignore his? Horrible!" And so we stone the prophets who simply preach to us our own doctrine of democracy, rationally and divinely developed.

But God is taking vengeance on us for destroying His servants,

and is compelling us to rise to the heights of our own principles at the threat of losing all its lower developments, which we see to be our essential life. We listen, refuse, yield, and most reluctantly obey. . . .

Thus shall the millennial day break upon the world. It may be in a day. Events are hastening it forward. Every step in Europe is to emancipation, equalization, unification. There is no possibility of peace there on any other basis. Nor is there here.

Christendom thus unified, heathendom and Islamdom will soon be regenerated. Social vices will abate their violence. Liberty and unity will prevent wars and armaments, royal houses, and luxurious absorption by a few families of the people's wealth. Legitimate industry will pay the old debts of kings and crimes, and easily supply the slight demands of a popular and peaceful government. Intemperance, Sabbath-breaking, infidelity, all the fruits of crowned and Catholic Europe, will be replaced with the graces of Christianity. The Lord Jesus will be the real and recognized, if not visible, sovereign of the world. "Unto Him shall all flesh come, and every knee bow." By Him shall rulers reign, and judges decree justice. In Him shall all the world, consciously, happily, completely, live, and move, and have its being.

> "Yea, truth and justice then,
> Will down return to men,
> Orbed in a rainbow; and, like glories wearing,
> Mercy will sit between,
> Throned in celestial sheen,
> With radiant feet the tissued clouds down steering,
> And heaven, as at some festival,
> Will open wide the gates of her high palace hall."

Say not this is all a golden dream. It is scriptural,rational, inevitable. It is hardly now a prophetic vision, so much of it has been accomplished. The blindest-eyed can see,through the vista before him, the glad consummation. Compared with the dreary ages that are past, how brief, how pleasant the remnant hours! Gigantic sins can be brought low as in a moment. . . .

Let us not despair of further victories of the Lamb. This demon slain, there is no such other hydra cursing the earth. European tyrannies will fast follow it to its dishonored grave. Asiatic abominations and African savagery will feel the warm rays of the Sun of Righteousness, long held in disastrous eclipse by this horrific sin. They will wilt down at His presence, as when the melting fire burneth, the fire causeth the waters to boil.

Our own social sins, intemperance, Sabbath-breaking, infidelity, immorality, will be more easily restrained and extirpated after this

Satan among the lesser fiends is cast into the bottomless pit and chained there forever. Our prejudices, born and fostered of him, will likewise disappear, and brotherly love and unity possess all hearts.

* * *

5. But General Grant's peace opens the way for yet further victories, if any in your minds can be further. The suffrage of woman must follow that of the African. The proudest female must march behind the lowliest negro. She is a citizen already, frequently a tax-payer, always of equal intelligence, often of superior virtue to man. She is our mother; and who believes he knows more than his mother, or is better able to understand and exercise any duty? She is our wife; who that deserves a wife believes himself the superior of that wedded soul? She is our sister; and who does not know that when in school together she more frequently led him in scholarship than he her? She is of the Commonwealth, having equal rights with every other member. She is bone of our bone and flesh of our flesh. Surely, all enforced exclusion of her from her just claims is the greatest injustice. If we preeminently despise the man who strikes a woman, how should we feel toward the State who thus strikes down all its women, and robs them of all power of defense from its blows?

Above all, we need her help. Christ is seeking to establish His empire in the earth. It is an empire of peace, of unity, of righteousness, of love. It is to be established in good-willing men, in holy laws, in sacred institutions, in purified society. How can this be done except by the cooperation of the best and most numerous members of that society? Only by woman's vote can the kingdom of God be completely established. Only thus can we save the State from debauchery and utter demoralization.

That work will go forward. It is advancing everywhere; and when the next election comes may we see our sisters sitting by us, and transforming the dirty, smoky atmosphere of the voting-rooms into sweet and quiet parlors, full of pleasure and peace.

The temperance movement must go forward. It has been held back by the imperative demands of the cause of freedom. It met with a repulse from misjudging men, under wicked leaders; but it will rally and move on. It has a grand foundation laid in the convictions of every heart, the conclusions of every understanding, the decisions of courts, the statistics of jails and almshouses, the annals of crime, a generation of totally abstaining people, and the success of the experiment of prohibition. Every good and evil inure to its benefit. With the departure of the giant crime of Slavery to its own hell, the movement against its hardly inferior associate will be recommended. We have exchanged the slaveholder's ring for the whisky ring. The one elected Presidents; the other has preserved one of them in his undeserved seat. We have abolished the one; we must the other. To

482

this reform every youth should consecrate himself. In every State it should be agitated. Congress should be implored to establish it in the Territories and the District of Columbia. The new South must adopt it to save her new citizens from utter demoralization.

¶   Editorial Reaction to Custer's Defeat.

(Taken from *Western Christian Advocate*, XLIII (19 July 1876), 228).

There was fought on Sunday, June 25th, a terrible battle, between the United States forces led by General Custer on the one side, and a village of Sioux Indians on the other. The engagement took place in the eastern portion of Montana, at a point between the Yellow Stone River and the Big Horn Mountains, east of the Big Horn River, and near the banks of the Little Big Horn River. This was familiar ground to the braves. The warriors of the same tribe had fought a victorious battle nine years before near the same locality, with the United States forces under General Fetterman. But the battle of the last Sunday in June will be distinguished from all other Indian battles. The troops engaged were of high standing in the service, and were skilled in border warfare, and they fought bravely, and did all within their power but were every one sacrificed in the engagement. Fortunately the loss was not so heavy as it would have been if the reserve companies had been in the fight, for the Indians had evidently prepared to slaughter all whom they could engage. As it is, the loss is very severe. Of the five companies of the Seventh Cavalry led by the daring Custer, not a man survived. The seven companies led by Major Reno also suffered terribly in battle and retreat. The Indian loss is reported at seventy dead, among whom are many of their best chiefs.

But we have no heart to dwell on this sickening disaster. Unfortunately, as this battle did not begin, so it does not end, the cause of this Indian war. Now that we have had time to recover from the shock of this fearful calamity, and before we shall become too excited with a desire to revenge the blood of our fallen heroes to be capable of dispassionate reasoning let us reflect upon the moral questions involved in this contest. The blood of these brave men will not have been shed in vain, if the shock of defeat shall serve to induce the country to think upon the character of this warfare against the Indians. Before we give wild shouts of encouragement to a war of extermination, let us calmly look at its justice and necessity.

A leading daily newspaper says, "It is not a question of morals." If not, why not? What is it that lifts this subject out of the domain of moral questions? What are the facts about this contest for the possession of a given territory?

Assuming that these natives had no rights to the territory which they originally held, and that the country belonged to the United

States Government, it was most clearly and positively given to them by that Government in the treaty made and signed in 1868, at Fort Rice, in Dakota, Generals Harney, Terry, and Sherman, as military commissioners on the part of the United States, being present and assisting. According to that treaty the Indians were to have all the country extending from the Running Water north to fifteen miles above Heart River, east of the Missouri River, including the whole of the Black Hills country. Its terms also called for an annuity of provisions, clothing, agricultural implements, and trainers to teach such as would come down and live at the agencies the art of farming for a livelihood, as do the whites. Those who preferred to remain on their reservations were to be allowed to do so, and receive a smaller annuity. The treaty was accepted in good faith. Most of the Indians came into the different agencies. The Government showed its faith and good intentions by abandoning Forts Reno, Phil Kearney, and C. F. Smith, after as it is said, having spent more than a million dollars in establishing them. Sitting Bull was the only chief who remained hostile, and whose lead was followed by forty or fifty warriors. These natives, however, carried on against the whites no open, systematic warfare, but indulged in neighborhood depredations, occasional attacks on passing soldiers, and the occasional shooting of adventurers in the Yellowstone country. Such was the general condition of things for several years, and might have so continued, with a fair prospect of improvement, had not the United States sent an exploring expedition into this country, which had been secured to the Indians by treaty. The reports of that expedition, published broadcast, put in circulation the most romantic and exciting accounts of its attractions and richness in gold ores, and started out a class of enterprising - and, in many instances, lawless - adventurers, on the move to the Black Hills.

The Indians complained to the United States of the invasions, and asked to be protected. The Government recognized their right to protection, and forbade all parties from going into this reservation. But the Government had kindled the excitement, and the prohibition came too late. It was not now to be so easily extinguished. In fact, only a feeble show of military force was made to turn the invaders back, and then the attempt was abandoned. The President then issued his proclamation that, while the invaders had no right to enter the territory of the Sioux tribes, and were violating the treaties of the United States in doing so, yet the Indians must not molest them, nor seize any provisions in transit for them. This was a remarkable proclamation. It was, in effect, saying to all invaders, "Go on, the Government is powerless to prevent you."

The Indians were quick to understand the situation - that if their possessions were to be defended they must do it themselves. Their lands were their own, as really as any settler owns the homestead given him by the United States Government. Their only possible chance of retaining their homes for themselves and their children was by driving off these bands of intruders. In their condition would not we have

484

done the same thing? Are we to expect in the Indian a better code of procedure than we should have practiced? Through the crookedness of our dealings the Sioux were absolutely forced to defend their country, or see it overrun by lawless invaders. And yet, forsooth, in doing this they incur the displeasure of the United States. For doing for themselves what the Government had undertaken to do, and had failed to perform, the Government sends out its army under command of General Terry, the hero of Fort Fisher, to punish them. A war department that could not get an army out there to prevent lawless freebooters from overrunning the reservation, can quickly get an army there to exterminate the savages that resisted the encroachment of those invaders.

Is the course of the Government right? When was it right? In opposing the invasion, or when it opposes resistance to the invasion? Its present course is a disgraceful *repudiation* of its treaty promises. Upon the honorable observance of these treaty stipulations the security of life and property in all that region of country for years to come is depending. The honor of the nation is involved. The helplessness of the other party to the contract only makes it the more dishonorable to take advantage of them. Are there none to speak for their rights, whose voices can be heard in high places? There will be a dust-throwing effort to blind the eyes to the real moral question involved in this attack on the Sioux nation, by pointing to the flowing blood of our soldiers, and a furious outcry against the barbarous warfare of these savages will be raised, but there ought to be enough enlightened Christian sentiment in the country to stay this murderous, and wicked policy; and to settle matters in dispute according to the claims of right and law. This war has already been costly, both in treasure and blood. But its continuance, as begun, will be at a fearful expense. It is likely to swallow up many millions of dollars and hundreds more of human lives.

¶   Judgments on Wounded Knee.

(Taken from *Western Christian Advocate*, LVIII (1891), 17).

The casualties at Wounded Knee were greater than reported. The Indians who had surrendered included one hundred and twenty warriors and their squaws and papooses. Over two hundred of these are now known to have been killed, sixty-three squaws and papooses having been buried by our men. The finding of a little baby girl alive by the side of its dead mother, after three days, is a touching incident of the carnage. This little one was brought in by the burying party, and has been adopted by a wealthy New York lady.

It is gratifying that General Miles and the President insist upon humanity and justice in our dealings with the red men. A searching investigation of Wounded Knee has been ordered, pending which, the

colonel commanding, Forsythe, has been relieved. Everything indicates that it is bread, not blood, that the Indians want. There are bad Indians doubtless,who will never be good until they are dead Indians; but that they constitute the majority is denied by Generals Sherman and Miles. The unfortunate conflict of authority between the agents, with their Indian police, and the army - for Sitting Bull was killed by the Indian police - complicates the situation. In compliance with General Miles's urgent request, the President has superseded the agent at Pine Ridge by Captain Pierce of the regulars. All the agents among the Sioux, it is said, will be similarly replaced by officers detailed from the army. The latter would take the management out of politics, one great argument in its favor.

¶   Methodism and the Spanish-American War.

(Taken from A. B. Leonard, "Prospective Mission Fields," *Gospel in All Lands*, Aug. 1898, 363-64).

Startling and momentous events are transpiring in these closing days of the nineteenth century. The kingdom of Spain and the repub- lic of the United States are at war. Spain is the foremost representa- tive of political tyranny and religious intolerance among the civilized nations of the world. For centuries she has done her ut- most to block the progress of Christian civilization. Possessed at one time of vast territories, including the principal parts of two continents on this side of the Atlantic, she has, by pursuing a course of tyranny and intolerance at war with the progress of civili- zation, lost her prestige among the nations, her credit in the world's money markets, and is now on the verge of utter collapse. Had Spain pursued an enlightened policy in politics and religion toward her subjects she might now rank with Great Britain, rather than with decaying nations such as China and Turkey.

In the place of fostering intelligence among her subjects, she has kept the masses in dense ignorance and under the influence of blind superstition. In a population of eighteen millions in the kingdom of Spain all except two millions are illiterates. Of the two millions who can read and write only four hundred thousand have anything to do with the government, except to pay the enormous taxes that are levied and to go into the ranks as common soldiers in time of war.

The republic of the United States stands among the nations of the world the foremost representative of political liberty and religious toleration. Here schools are provided for all, and even compulsory education is widely enforced, while the right to freedom of worship is absolutely unchallenged.

486

Spain and the United States represent respectively mediaevalism and modern progress. The two policies have been brought face to face in Cuba, and it is not surprising that war should be the result. Spain must be permitted to go on with her policy of tyranny and intolerance, even to the annihilation of the native Cubans, or the United States must intervene.

We blamed England for allowing the unspeakable Turk to murder the Armenians, but a greater criminal, the Spaniard, by fire, sword, and starvation, was desolating, within hailing distance of our Southern borders, one of the finest islands of all the seas - the gem of the Antilles. Miss Clara Barton is reported to have said, after seeing both: "Armenia was a comedy, but Cuba is a tragedy."

There can be but one outcome of the conflict. Spain must retire from all governmental authority on this side of the Atlantic, and Cuba and Porto Rico must be free. Having broken the yoke of the oppressor, the United States will see to it that these islands shall have a stable government of their own, or, what is not unlikely, become integral parts by their own choice, as in the case of the Hawaiian Islands, of the country that has made them free.

Meanwhile an overruling Providence has thrust us out to the "uttermost parts of the earth," there also to break the power of Spanish despotism. When Admiral Dewey was ordered to proceed with his fleet of warships to the other side of the globe, he is reported to have said to a friend that he would greatly prefer to remain at home, as he anticipated war with Spain, and he would like to be here to have a hand in it. He did not know what an important part he was to play in the strife which was fast coming on. When war was declared Admiral Dewey was in the harbor at Hongkong, which belongs to Great Britain. By the neutrality laws in force he must quit British waters. Where would he go? He was worse off than Noah's dove when first it was thrust out of the ark, for though the dove found "no rest for the sole of her foot," she could and did return into the ark. The admiral, thrust out of the harbor of Hongkong, must conquer a place for the sole of his foot and a harbor in which to anchor his ships. Six hundred miles to the southeast, at Manila, was a harbor belonging to Spain, and toward that harbor he steered his course. Seven days later he entered that harbor and destroyed the Spanish fleet, without the loss of a ship or even of a sailor, and found himself in possession of a harbor all his own.

Since that time the Ladrone Islands have been taken. Sampson's fleet has annihilated the Spanish squadron under Admiral Cervera, just outside the harbor of Santiago de Cuba, and while these words are being written our army and navy are bombarding Santiago, with the certainty of its surrender or reduction. Six months ago whoever should have prophesied such results in so brief a time would have been regarded as a fanatic, if not indeed insane.

These marvelous events are now history, but no mortal ken can foretell their far-reaching influences. But we do know that great opportunities are suddenly open before the Christian Church for advancing among long-oppressed peoples the kingdom of God. The Philippines, on the other side of the world, and Cuba and Porto Rico, on this side, are by the naval and military prowess of a Christian government suddenly thrown open for evangelistic operations. The Christian Church must follow the army and occupy the territory conquered by the war power of the nation.

In this forward movement the Methodist Episcopal Church must and will do its part.

¶   An Early Argument for Prohibition.

(Taken from Daniel Dorchester, *The Liquor Problem in All Ages* (1884), 637-39).

In the carrying forward of this reform two great measures should be specified, as having been very prominent in contributing to its advancement. The first and most fundamental is *Total Abstinence*. The first societies, starting up from the low level of sentiment in their times, commenced on the platform of moderation. They raised no objection to the free use of fermented liquors. They seem not to have been thought of. It was ardent spirits, as distilled liquors were then called, from their more fiery character, that engaged attention, because of their very destructive character. New England rum, gin, whisky, and brandy were every-where freely drank, especially the first three; and it was the palpably pernicious effects of these liquors which aroused public attention to them. But the first temperance societies only pledged their members against *"the too free use of ardent spirits,"* not *wholly* excluding even these. The theory of moderation prevailed in all the early movements.

But all the early societies organized on this basis were compelled to make lamentable acknowledgments of failure. Failures were apparent on every hand, and almost all of these societies actually *"died of drunkenness."* For the benefit of some recent advocates of moderation, attention is asked to the history of this early period, in which the total and inevitable failure of the moderation theory has been fully exhibited.

After 1826 total abstinence from distilled liquors was recognized as the basis of the reform; but little objection, however, was even then made to fermented liquors. Here and there were individuals who included the latter in their pledge and protest; but few, if any, societies, however, were organized on that basis. About 1833 the principle of total abstinence from all alcoholic

liquors was quite extensively adopted; and in 1836 it was adopted by the National Temperance Convention, that met that year in Saratoga. The Washingtonians, in 1840, gave special emphasis to total abstinence.

It has been clearly brought out, in the extended sketches on preceding pages of this volume, that little progress in the work of reformation was made until the principle of total abstinence was adopted as the measure of reform. This is the unimpeachable testimony of history, one of the most palpable lessons of the past, vindicated by the clearest deductions of medical science and by volumes of experience.

The other measure which has been conspicuously connected with the best phases of the Temperance Reform has been - *the prohibition* of the sale of intoxicants as a beverage.

We entered upon this century under the license regimen, which reached back indefinitely into the colonial era. The tide of intemperance was increasing, and from 1780 to 1820 the license system was made more stringent by additional provisions, until it reached a degree of vigor not found in our more recent laws. But the evil of intemperance steadily and widely increased, the *per capita* consumption gaining more than twofold from 1790 to 1825, until it reached nearly seven and a half gallons for each inhabitant. The severe license laws did not regulate nor restrain the evil. Multitudes confessed that the license system was a failure.

About 1828 men began to protest against the license system. The agitation against it became more decided and general after 1832; and in 1835 thirteen towns in Massachusetts instructed their selectmen to withhold recommendations for licenses. Under the law licenses were then granted by county commissioners, on the recommendation of the selectmen of the towns. County commissioners were elected on that issue. In 1837 seven contiguous counties in Massachusetts granted no licenses. In 1846, in all the counties in the State except one, licenses were refused, and some of the county jails were empty. Similar movements were going forward in other States.

The term prohibition had not then come into use; but the policy of many States was against license, breaking from it partly or wholly, and verging toward what has since been known as "prohibition." From 1851 to 1856 "Maine Laws" were enacted in more than twelve States.

Under these two working measures - *total abstinence* and *prohibition* - logically germane to each other, the greatest and deepest moral reformation in respect to temperance was realized from about 1830 to 1855. The policy of the reform was clearly and unequivocally against the moderate drinking even of mild liquors, and as clearly against sanctioning the liquor traffic by licenses. If any theories have been demonstrated as utter failures, they are the theories of

moderation and license.   .   .   .

We are still in the midst of a great battle. The forces of alcohol were never before so compactly and powerfully organized either in Great Britain or in the United States as now. Their leagues are every-where. While we have much to encourage us, in the ample evidences afforded on every hand, that our labors have not been in vain, but have produced great and substantial improvement, nevertheless rose-colored views should not be entertained. The liquor traffic is not likely to soon die out from lack of drinkers. It is a moral impossibility for the drink traffic to be extinguished until it is suppressed by law, whatever may be done by moral suasion. Nevertheless, we should not intermit moral suasion efforts. They constitute the basis and afford the true moral impulse for legal suasion. That we should have so many drink shops, such large drink expenditures, and so much drunkenness and crime resulting therefrom, is certainly lamentable. No great permanent improvement in the condition of the country can be expected until government declares that the liquor traffic is an evil which must be put down in the interest of society.

¶   The Pullman Strike.

(Taken from William H. Carwardine, *The Pullman Strike* (1894), 11-14).

The Pullman strike is the greatest and most far-reaching of any strike on record in this country. It is the most unique strike ever known. When we take into account the intelligence of the employees, always the boast of the Pullman Company; the widespread advertisement of the town as a "model town," established as a solution of the industrial problem upon the basis of "mutual recognition," it is no wonder that the world was amazed, when, under such apparently favorable conditions, in the midst of a season of great financial depression, the employees laid down their tools, and, on the 11th of May, walked out of the great shops to face an unequal and apparently hopeless conflict.

After seven weeks of patient waiting, the American Railway Union, having espoused the cause of the Pullman employees, declares a boycott on the Pullman Palace Cars. This action is repulsed by the Railroad Managers' Association. The conflict is transferred at once to the arena of public commerce; organized labor and organized capital are pitted against each other; stagnation of all business interests results; the highways of trade are blocked; the great unoffending public is the innocent sufferer, riots ensue, the military are ordered out, the foundations of government are threatened; the strong arm of the law is put forth, the public demand for peace is heard, and the

crisis reached.

Now the public mind reverts to the original cause. What made these intelligent employees at Pullman strike? Were they rash and inconsiderate, or were they driven to their course by certain conditions over which they had no control, and which justified them in their action?

These and a hundred other questions are coming to me by every mail from all parts of our country. Ten days after the employees struck, I delivered a sermon from my pulpit, which created profound interest in Pullman and Chicago, and which has since been copied broadcast in newspapers all over the United States. Owing to this fact, I am accosted on all sides for information concerning the true condition of things in this model town.

For two years I have been the pastor of the Pullman M. E. Church, and closely related to the moral and social life of the town. During that time I have been a silent spectator of the life and character of the town. I have studied carefully and with much interest the Pullman system. I have had abundant opportunity to observe the town from the standpoint of a student of the industrial problem.

I wish to be fair and impartial. I have seen many things to admire as well as many to condemn. My sympathies have gone out to the striking employees. Never did men have a cause more just - never did corporation with equal pretenses grind men more unmercifully. I contend that I have a right to publicly criticise a public man or a public institution, so long as I do not depart from the path of truth or make false imputations, willfully knowing them to be such. No one has deplored this strike more than myself. I wish that it might have been averted. But so long as the employees saw fit to take this action I believe that it is the duty of all concerned to look the issue squarely in the face, without equivocation or evasion, consider the matter in its true light, and endeavor to bring about a settlement of the difficulty as speedily as possible.

I make no apology as a clergyman for discussing this theme. As ministers of the gospel we have a right to occasionally turn from the beaten path of biblical truth and consider these great questions of social, moral and economic interest. He who denies the right of the clergy to discuss these matters of great public concern has either been brought up under a government totally foreign to the free atmosphere of American institutions, or else he has failed utterly to comprehend the spirit of the age in which he lives.

Sometimes we preachers are told to mind our own business and "preach the gospel." All right; I have preached the gospel of Christ, and souls have been redeemed to a better life under the preaching of that gospel. I contend now that in the discussing of this theme I am

preaching the gospel of applied Christianity - applied to humanity -
the gospel of mutual recognition, of co-operation, of the "brotherhood of humanity." The relation existing between a man's body and
his soul are such that you can make very little headway appealing to
the soul of a thoroughly live and healthy man if he be starving for
food. Christ not only preached to the multitude, but he gave them
to eat. And I verily believe that if he came to Chicago to-day, as
indicated by the erratic yet noble Stead, he would apply the whip of
cords to the backs of some of us preachers for not performing our
full share of duty to "his poor."

> "Let not ambition mock their useful toil,
> Their homely joys, and destiny obscure;
> Nor grandeur hear with a disdainful smile
> The short and simple annals of the poor."

¶   The Social Gospel.

(Taken from *Zion's Herald*, 69 (1891), 9; 73 (1895), 562)

"SOCIALISM AND THE CHRISTIAN CHURCH"
Rev. F. M. North

What has the Church to do with Socialism? It is a belated
question. Very recently have Christian thinkers come to realize that
they should have voted urgency upon it long ago. And this clearer
perception has only come since, echoing among the vaulted arches of
great churches and disturbing the quiet of meditative theology, has
been heard from every side and in many languages that other question -

What has Socialism to Do with the Church?

In 1848 Mr. Ludlow, who had gone to Paris to study the Revolution
of that date, wrote to Maurice that he was convinced that "Socialism
was a real and very great power, which had acquired an unmistakable
hold not merely on the fancies, but on the consciences of the Parisian
workmen, and that *it must be Christianized, or it would shake Christianity to its foundation!*" How generally this was not believed by the
church of forty years ago is clear when one reads the history of the
vicious antagonism to the men whose insight and outlook created for
the generation which succeeded them a new fact and a new phrase -
Christian Socialism. In an article in the *Quarterly Review,* after a
characteristic statement of the most ultra demands of the most
absolute anarchism, a writer proceeds to say: -

"Incredible as it may appear, there is, it seems, a clique of
educated and clever but wayward-minded men, the most prominent of
them *two clergymen of the Church of England,* who from, as it seems,

a morbid craving for notoriety or a crazy straining after paradox, have taken up the unnatural and unhallowed task of preaching, in the press and from the pulpit, not indeed such open undisguised *Jacobinism and jacquerie* as we have just been quoting, but, under the name of 'Christian Socialism,' the same doctrines in a form not the less dangerous for being less honest."

And these dangerous and dishonest Jacobin doctrinaires were Frederick Denison Maurice and Charles Kingsley!

And yet this opposition was but a symptom of a wide-spread distrust of both the motives and the methods of social reformers. Indeed, the statement carries with it a fact still more fundamental and more sad - that the church does not, in the case of Socialism, for the first time confront forces which she herself should have marshaled and clothed in the uniform of the faith. For in Christianity are the creative ideas which must produce all the well-being of society, and it is a terrible indictment either of the church's perception or of her consecration when she becomes conscious of those ideas only through the teaching of "them that are without."

"METHODISM AND SOCIAL QUESTIONS'
Dr. David H. Wheeler

In common with other evangelical bodies Methodism has only

A New Testament Economic Creed.

Few of us, however, find in the New Testament any antagonism to property, either inherited or honestly gained, and no more definite doctrine of "division" than can be rationally deduced from the Golden Rule. We find all incidental applications of that Rule which are made in the Scriptures to be consistent with the custom of private ownership of worldly goods. The communism of the early church at Jerusalem consisted in helping each other by *selling* their possessions. It was a case of large-hearted benevolence; and in the case of Ananias, Peter emphatically recognizes the right of the former to keep or give, but not to lie about his giving. Our Lord sought to repress worldliness, avarice and covetousness. He declines to settle a property dispute - "who made Me a judge?" All the allusions to possessions - and they are not a few - in the New Testament recognize private property.

When we come to apply the Golden Rule, it is clear that right applications to property possession must be voluntary; there is no authority for State enforcement of that rule of action. And so most of us agree that the laws of ownership and contract are Christian, while abuses of these laws are emphatically unchristian. It follows that Methodists are not socialists in the scientific sense of that term. .

The existing social order is the work mainly of Christian men. It is less good than we would have it if we could control it. We believe its principles to be sound, and we are ready to make war upon any clearly-proved abuses side by side with anybody. All our eyes are open to the vast growth of wealth, to the dangers arising from such of this growth as is gathered into few hands; but very few of us believe that the individual freedom condensed into the law of contract is a serious menace to the well-being of the less fortunate.

The Church of the Poor.

If there has come a change, it is because Methodism has made Methodists rich. Our wealthy members were, nearly all of them, poor boys. Under a free government they have grown wealthy by ability, economy and abstinence from expensive vices. Our people pay nothing towards the seven hundred-million drink bill of the nation. The other vice bills cost fully as much and Methodists do not pay a cent to liquidate them. If these fourteen hundred million were annually saved, the saving would abolish more poverty than any social scheme.

¶   A Conservative View of Labor Unrest.

(Taken from Daniel Dorchester, *The Problem of Religious Progress*, (1900), 340-44).

The Anarchist Spirit is a dark phase in the problem of modern progress. These elements have come to us by immigration - the fruit-age of the despotism of the Old World; kindred to the spirit of the French Revolution which a century ago shook the continent of Europe. It is the most difficult and alarming problem that has confronted the citizens of the United States since the first mutterings of the civil war. The pope's encyclical on the labor question a few years ago fell powerless on his European audience, utterly failing to suppress the spirit of anarchy in its native home. The evil has overleaped the ocean and poisoned the atmosphere of the United States. Great un-rest and discontent have prevailed in many central localities, and we have had coal strikes, mining strikes, railroad strikes, armies of the unemployed marching across the land, and desperate uprisings in Pittsburg, Buffalo, and in Chicago.

If sterner and more efficient measures had been exercised in dealing with the lawless mobs who went tramping across the country, seizing railroad trains, preying upon farmers, etc., the sanguinary drama in Chicago and vicinity would not have been witnessed. It is high time for the people to be serious when they realize that men infected with anarchistic principles occupy gubernatorial chairs, and boldly share the perverse direction in which their sympathies

run. When the Governor of Illinois pardoned the anarchist murderers, he startled the country; but when he impudently stood face to face before the President of the United States and opposed his intervention to suppress the great riot, the country was startled into tumultuous rage. Severe have been the expressions of indignation; but will the people remember this evil conduct, or will they soon condone the offense? They have only themselves to blame, if they elect such men to these high offices and keep them there.

The rioters in these great tumults appear to comprise large multitudes, but the real spirits of mischief are probably comparatively few. Our great cities are unfortunate in having large numbers of desperate men who, mixing in with genuine strikers, multiply their capacity for harm, and the examples become contagious.

We cannot believe that it is our decent, well-trained American workmen who perpetrate these great offenses, though some may be tainted with the virus of the pestilence. Who would have supposed a year ago that the incomparable World's Fair would so soon be followed by these direful catastrophes, developing a spirit of evil emulous of the Parisian Commune? And yet we are told some visitors even then had ominous apprehensions of the possibility of an outbreak, as they occasionally observed clusters of scowling proletariats ripe for revolt and spoliation. It is not strange that men who project these uprisings are often shattered victims of alcoholism and Ingersollism, and that a species of demagogism among laboring men adds fuel to the flame.

Should we not reflect upon the dangers that attend that material and scientific progress of which so much strident boasting has been heard? The West has long been upheld as a marvel of enterprise, and Chicago as the wonder of the universe. One half of the population of that city is foreign. Europe and America combined there to perform prodigies of material grandeur. But was it at no cost of morals? At no sacrifice of genuine happiness? At no peril to salvation? Certainly it was the kingdom of this world and not the kingdom of God that was sought. Such a reversal of the divine edict could be attended with no real, lasting good. If we make idols of gold and worship divinities of material prosperity, the curtain will in due time be lifted, and we shall behold hideous devouring demons lurking behind the scenes. Shall our mighty cities become heaving volcanoes? What can prevent or postpone the bursting forth of the pent-up fires? Who has the wisdom to name and apply the remedy?

So far as anarchism is a spirit of madness and revenge against old-time institutions, and it is that chiefly, there is only one remedy - suppression by the civil power; but the remaining fraction will doubtless be reached by calm and thorough discussion, which will eliminate the more radical elements of the problem - the sting of the

hornet. Some of our expounders of political economy, in prominent positions, for a while stood on perilous ground, which gave comfort and encouragement to the revolutionary party. There are some indications that they are emerging from the hallucination of their extreme theorizing, retracing their steps, and are likely to become helpful to other venturesome inquirers.

The anarchistic spirit has been aggravated by certain radical and reckless discussions of unsolved economic problems. During the past twenty years or more the American people have been confronted with momentous questions closely related to the question of monopoly. Heavy allegations are made against railroad and other corporations, as so seriously grinding down and impoverishing large classes of the people as to call for interference by the State. The support of the churches, it is also claimed, should be afforded in the interest of humanity, that the offensive monopolies may be eliminated and government control be established over those large industrial operations.

The solution of this problem, some have self-confidently asserted to be easy, and two methods have been advocated, mutually dependent: First, turn over the great public functions in the industrial realm to responsible public authorities; and, secondly, civil control of those who manage these essentially public businesses, and make them so discharge their functions that they will promote the public welfare. This scheme was regarded with much favor at first by many thoughtful persons, but on maturer thought it has been judged to be impracticable and visionary. Professor Richard T. Ely has well said: "The hope of a beneficent control of private property, of the kind mentioned, is utopian. Every article, monograph, and book advocating such control should be entitled 'Utopia,' because they all rest upon hypotheses which apply only to an imaginary world."

¶   Methodist Federation for Social Service.

(Taken from Worth M. Tippy, ed., *The Socialized Church* (1909), 22-23, 27-29).

In Methodism this Federation has been formed. It is less than a year old. It has received the recognition and approval of the last General Conference of the Church. It has begun the work of publication, and also of organization in a few cities and colleges; and, while having no official standing in the Methodist Episcopal Church, South, it has hoped that cooperation in this work between the two great branches of American Methodism might be possible, and might prove another tie binding more closely together those whom no man should put asunder.

It is high time that such efforts should be made by the churches. If the German scholar was right who said, "Whosoever would contribute to the solution of the social question must have on his right hand the works of political economy, and before him must keep open the New Testament" - if he was right, then Christian men dare not turn over these difficult problems to the mere political economist with his hard laws of supply and demand, or to the idealist with his dreams that have no substance of reality. But Christian men, armed with knowledge and with love, must go out from the school of Christ into the field of daily toil prepared to apply everywhere the principles that Jesus taught and died for. They must claim every kingdom for their Master. They must make clear that religion and life are coextensive.

*   *   *

We must present not only a pure gospel for the spiritual man, but a whole gospel for the whole man, and a gospel which finds its way into our daily practices. The Son of God, the spiritual leader of the race, with but one lifetime to unfold the priceless treasure of his spiritual truth to men, spent the first thirty years in illustrating that truth in the life of the carpenter shop and of the home and of the town; then, when he came to the three brief years of his public ministry, took large sections of his precious time for curing the blind and deaf and paralytic and leprous and insane, in befriending the lonely, in comforting the sad, in training the stupid, not as though the making of sermons was the chief end of his days, and this was but incidental; but as though this was an integral and vital part of his mission. Sometimes he preached to men before he fed them, sometimes he fed them before he preached, but always the word and the deed went together. Preaching, teaching, and healing were but three parts of the one purpose. Let him that says the Church has nothing to do but to save souls go settle his contention with Jesus Christ, "who went about doing good" that *He* might save *lives*. Let him that says the Church has naught to do with lunch-rooms and work-yards and gymnasiums and strikes and labor legislation reconcile this position, if he can, with the hospital and dispensary work of his Master, with the feeding of the multitudes, with the saving of his friends from physical danger, with the mastering of the forces of nature that they might further his mission. Too often has the Church spiritualized every activity of Jesus, forgetting that what they insist on applying to the soul Jesus himself applied to the body. It has imitated but a part of his life, losing sight of the fact that the whole life of Jesus was religious, and that when he dealt with problems of doctrine and worship he was no more religious than when he cured diseases or satisifed hunger. The Church is to follow him in his *whole* life, and find that in it all the will of the Father is being done, and the kingdom of the Father is coming to earth. It is absolutely true that a revival of religion will settle all our problems, social, industrial, political, as well as personal;

497

but the religion to be revived must be the religion of the ministering Christ, the religion which has a twofold law of love, the religion which includes the Golden Rule; the religion of Paul, who made faith the first thing, but love the greatest; the religion of James, which not only kept itself unspotted from the world, but went visiting the widow and the fatherless. "Though I speak with the tongues of men and of angels, though I have all faith so as to move mountains, though I give my body to be burned, and have not love, it profiteth me nothing."

IV.

ECUMENICAL TRANSFORMATION, 1914–1980

21. GLOBAL AND ECUMENICAL DIRECTIONS AT TURN OF CENTURY

As the nineteenth century drew to a close, Americans began to look toward the new era, occasionally with anxiety but usually with great expectations. Among those filled with optimism was Charles J. Little, in 1888 professor in Syracuse University, soon to become president of Garrett Biblical Institute. His long address, excerpted here, before the General Missionary Committee of the M. E. Church in New York, 11 November 1887, rallies the church to its heady opportunity. At the turn-of-century General Conference the bishops took stock of the church's stewardship over a hundred years, and found its health very good indeed.

Dr. John F. Goucher, who delivered a paper at the Third Oecumenical Methodist Conference in City Road Chapel, London, in September 1901, was one of the most influential Methodists of his day. Founder and president of Goucher College, delegate to many General Conferences, and supporter and benefactor of world missions, he liked to view his church as one open to all persons and friendly to other denominations.

The "nitty-gritty" of negotiations for reunion of the two regional Methodisms was faced during the meetings of the Joint Commission on Unification, between 1917 and 1920. There was no way of avoiding the issue of race, which was the center of the problem. It was probably good in the long run to get it all out on the table. Even so, it was not until 1939 that a compromise settlement made possible the reunion of three branches to form The Methodist Church. David G. Downey was a minister from New York. H. H. White was a layman from Alexandria, Louisiana. R. E. Blackwell was a layman from Ashland, Virginia. Robert E. Jones was editor of the Southwestern Christian Advocate in New Orleans and, with Matthew Clair, was one of the first two black men to be elected bishop (1920).

A happier campaign was the Centenary Movement which began while World War I was still raging. John Lankford's scholarly revisiting of the campaign provides the necessary historical perspective. The less than happy outcome is equally informative on the quality of Methodism in the period between the world wars.

¶   The Place of the United States in the Conversion of the World.

(Taken from address by Charles J. Little in *Gospel in All Lands*
(1888), 64-70).

The conflict impending in America to-day is the conflict of the
moral and spiritual energies of the people with the energies of
corruption and of death, the conflict of consecrated intelligence
with a public mind thoroughly carnalized and a popular imagination
inflamed with sensual desire, impatient of restraint. Of the issue
of such a conflict we need not be afraid if we are conscious of
internal strength and of divine support; if we can in the very
agony of our trial keep alive the sense of our "manifest destiny,"
the conviction that the victory of Jesus Christ in America involves
the future and the salvation of the human race.

*   *   *

We, then, citizens of a nation whose genesis and history are
unexampled in the annals of mankind, must recognize the lien of
Almighty God upon our national life. We no more than Israel or
Rome, Germany or England, exist for private or political reasons.
To assume that we have been established only that we may reveal to
posterity a marvelous display of energy devoted to purely material
aims; that our institutions, our political systems have no higher
destiny than to afford free play and increasing power to vast
multitudes who shall be destitute of any ideals but those of sense
and of the passing moment is to involve the sure and swift decay of
our organic life.

In that case the catastrophe of the twentieth century will be
as terrible as the progress of the nineteenth has been stupendous;
we shall be turned into hell with the nations that forgot God,
punished not for what we have done but for what we shall have failed to do.

But for this audience I may assume the belief that the world is
to be converted sometime and that it is to be converted by human
co-operation with almighty energy. For it is the life-thought of
Christianity, that humanity is to be redeemed by humanity, Christ
Himself becoming man in order to redeem him.

*   *   *

Here we are a Protestant people possessed of a domain not only
separate from whilst intermediate between the other worlds, but a
domain so rich and so fertile that we are absolutely independent ef
the rest of the earth.

A thousand millions may live in comfort upon the productions of our soil; every form of energy may here find material for its display; the quickening atmosphere which sweeps across our prairies and down our mountain slopes inspires our people to strive their utmost up and on. Room and riches, energy and opportunity, freedom and power, faith in God and faith in individual possibility, the constructive influence of law, and the diversifying influence of interblending races, never met together on this wise in all the cycles of terrestrial history.

No wonder that a candid statesman like Mr. Gladstone admits that we are soon to displace England as the chief servant in the household of nations; no wonder that less generous spectators wish for some mighty confusion to arrest us in the upholding of our colossal empire.

To the one who thinks of us, a missionary nation radiant with beneficent activity, illuminating the ends of the earth with the outstreamings of the Holy Ghost, the prospect of our greatness is a thought of joy.

*   *   *

Wonderful as is the century now closing – and anything so wonderful is not to be found in earthly chronicles – we are confronted with a situation far more appalling and inspiring. To master such a situation requires a sagacity, a comprehensive intelligence, an inspiration, a faith of almost superhuman character.

Nay it will require an ideal of national life, a motive for national endeavor, a source of national enthusiasm which are not to be found in any of the impulses which usually feed a nation's life.

Sometimes the mere rush of energy carries a people forward to its destiny; sometimes a passion for plunder or for glory makes them the willing instrument to individual greed; sometimes a wild, un-reasoning, half-noble, half-brutal enthusiasm sweeps them, as in the crusades, to peril, to hardship, and to death.

But problems such as are now confronting us are of quite another kind. These demand intelligence, not vehemence; unfalter-ing trust in God, not mad belief in some man's star; unconquerable devotion to man as man, invincible belief in human possibilities, not despair of human freedom and distrust of human conscience. Now whence are these to come?

Where are we to find the ideal of national existence vast enough, divine enough, to stir us to that expression of our energies

which shall save us to ourselves?

Let me answer in the words of a member of the Massachusetts Legislature spoken during the discussion of the charter of the American Board. "Mr. Speaker," said this wise man, in answer to those who pleaded that the money and the energy of Christian people were needed most at home. "Mr. Speaker, religion is a curious commodity, the more of it you export, the more you have at home!"

In that one phrase lies the clue to our national salvation. God in his infinite wisdom has so bound the nations together, that the intelligence and wealth, the prosperity and spiritual growth of each is involved in the redemption of them all. The very nature of the missionary enterprise is such as to develop in the participating nations the qualities which are essential to a vigorous and splendid life. And that because God has appointed that no nation shall live merely to itself.

All other problems are included in the problem of the world's conversion. The intelligence, the courage, the truth, the self-devotion equal to its vast proportions are equal to any difficulty and to any emergency which our future history may bring. God, I maintain, has so ordained it, that we without the others, may not be perfect.

*   *   *

There are times when certain careless words clothe themselves with strange solemnity. So has it come to pass with the old extravagance about the boundaries of our country:

Bounded on the East by the Rising Sun, on the North by the Aurora Borealis, on the South by the Precession of the Equinoxes, and on the West by the Day of Judgment.

Yes, the old jest is now dead earnest, terribly portentously true!

For when our nation appeared among men it was like the rising of the sun to thousands who had watched and waited for the morning. The burdened of the earth rejoiced and their gladness filled them with new strength, for they beheld a land where all men are brothers, where love was the light of the people and liberty clasped hands with law.

Bounded on the North by the Aurora Borealis, for as the flashing fires of the North are but the witness of the overflowing electric energy which enwraps the earth, so the exhibitions of our strength that have already taken shape upon the firmament of history,

are but the witness of a power without a parallel in human chronicle.

But the great laws of God which determine the seasons and hold the planets to their course hold us also to His purpose and His will. Irrevocable and relentless, irrepealable for no world, no man, no nation; destructive to the false and disobedient; a transcendent pledge of life to all that are true to the Eternal and Invisible.

And beyond us on the West looms up the Day of Judgment. For yonder on our vast frontiers where gathered multitudes shall weave for America in the twentieth century either a garment of glory or a shroud; yonder across the blue Pacific where China stands sullen but slowly yielding to the light, where Japan is thrilling with new purpose and new experience; where India verges swiftly to some great surprise, *there* is our Day of Judgment.

¶   Progress.

(Taken from Episcopal Address, M. E. General Conference, 1900).

A CENTURY OF METHODIST LIFE.

From such conditions we turn with wonder and thankfulness to those now existing. Our reference is not chiefly to national progress; to the advancement of the Republic in territory, in population, and in influence; to its material, intellectual, and social development; nor to liberty and order, so far in its history happily conjoined. Such topics might befit this occasion, but must not detain us. Nor may we dwell upon the growth and present vigor of the American Churches under the voluntary principle, though with profound gratitude we accept the computations by which it appears that in the Protestant Churches of the United States the ratio of communicants to the whole population has advanced during the century from one in fourteen to one in five.

Our topic is more specific. During the century the various Methodist Churches in the United States, all being derivatives from the one Church of 1800, have increased from sixty-one thousand communicants to nearly six million; that is, in a population which has increased fourteenfold the Methodist Churches have increased more than ninety-sevenfold. Commensurate with this, or even beyond it, has been the increase of the Ministry, of Churches and Church property, and of Church literature. The Church school, which had no existence in 1800, has been founded, and in its various grades is now numbered by the hundreds. Meantime the great benevolences of the Church have been successively organized. Our mission fields are on all continents, and God grants gracious increase among many races. New philanthropies, exponents of the grace of Him who went about doing

good, have risen in all our chief cities. The successive additions to the Republic, from the Louisiana purchase to the islands and island groups recently acquired from Spain, have all been occupied by our vast itinerant system.

But it is the interior and spiritual view of the century of Church life which profoundly moves the thoughtful soul. Spiritual results, indeed, admit no arithmetical measurement. We cannot even approximately estimate them. What multitudes for whom Christ died have through this ministration been saved from sin, and enriched and ennobled for the service of this present life! What comforts of patience, sweetness, and hope have been conveyed to innumerable weary and saddened souls! How have earthly homes been purified and exalted into the image of the heavenly! How many dull and narrow intellects have been enlightened and enlarged for world-wide uses by the ministry of the pulpit, the school, and the press! What quickening and aid have been brought to other Churches through freer and truer interpretation of the Christian scheme! What contributions have been made by a Church coeval with the Republic to civic virtue and order! And what uncounted companies of "our translated friends" now before the throne are triumphant witnesses for the work of the hundred years which now end!

¶   Methodist Openness. Address by Dr. John F. Goucher.

(Taken from *Proceedings of the Third Oecumenical Methodist Conference* (1901), 69-73).

At its inception Methodism did not propose to affect any man's ecclesiastical relations. Its one purpose was to have established in human experience the consciousness of personal acceptance with God. It protested against subordinating experience or its expression to tradition, creed, or ritual, and insisted that "everyone must give an account of himself to God." Theoretical acceptance of truth and perfunctory service could not satisfy its demands. Its persistent inquiry was, "Have ye received the Holy Ghost since ye believed?" It claimed the logical results of the doctrines revealed by Christ and preached by Paul, re-stated in modern phrase the old theology, and proclaimed man to be the beneficiary and objective of God's government. With this vital relation to God realised in the human consciousness there had to be freedom for growth and variety of experience, the narration of which became the dominant subject of conversation with those whom it brought into fellowship. Like the early disciples, they could but speak the things which they had seen and heard. Thus awakened and thus related, a doctrine of Christian perfection was consequential, and striving for it was a necessity.

The authority of American Methodism to teach, admonish, and console is not derived from a creed or polity formulated in some ecclesiastical Jerusalem or sacerdotal Rome. An itinerant Pentecost has burned

506

in our valleys and on our mountain sides, along our frontiers, and in our cities, bringing conversion and the commission to witness simultaneously to all who accepted salvation. The musty records of Councils, embodying a theoretical orthodoxy, have never been a procrustean conservator of its spiritual life; but its spiritual life has conserved its orthodoxy, and that, too, notwithstanding the untempered zeal and untutored condition of many of its evangelists. "From the effective appeal to sanctified heroism by lofty example came the development and perpetuation of holy daring and conquering energy." Its changing environment and its passion for the largest usefulness account for its varying forms. . . .

Methodism is in no sense a proselytising movement, and has given many times more converts to the various Protestant Churches than it has received from them, yet its enrolment includes more than 32 per cent, or nearly one-third of all the evangelical communicants, and from 1800 to 1900 its communicants increased two and two-tenth times faster than all the other Evangelical Churches. About one-third of all the people in the United States look to Methodism for their religious instruction and Christian ministries. In divine relations the necessary is coterminous with the possible, and numbers do not gauge efficiency. They are only an element of power, and indicate responsibility.

Methodism is rich in ministries, both personal and organised. Service is its life; for this it was born, by this it is justified. It was the first Church in America to commence the systematic publication of religious literature, and one branch has published more than all other Churches combined. Its establishment and maintenance of Schools and Colleges, Orphanages, Homes for the Aged, Hospitals, Training Schools and Homes for Deaconesses, Missions foreign and domestic, Boards, Societies and Auxiliaries for systematising its benevolences, Publishing Houses and Periodicals, Churches and Parsonages, the supervision of its preachers, the care of its young, and the organised co-operation of its laity have kept pace with its numerical increase, and gave it a material equipment and a completeness of organised agencies unexcelled for varied and efficient Church work. The personal initiative and genius for invention of the average American suggest a tendency to over-production of machinery and a need to guard against sub-divisions and the substitution of mechanical activities in an institutional Church for the initiative energy of an inspirational Church. The strategic point of society is at the centre, not on the periphery; with the individual, not with classes. Christian character and not organisations is the largest contribution any Church can make to the Kingdom. . . .

Its pulpit is not occupied with negations, dissent, or novelties. It is loyal to, and, in the main, preaches with apostolic simplicity, the doctrine once delivered to the saints. The siren songs of pleasure, the allurements of worldliness, and the pride of position have taken the place of open antagonism, controversy, and ostracism. The days of

polemics and apologetics seem to have passed. The class meeting, with its educative and constructive converse, is becoming occasional where it was universal. Doctrinal discourses are less frequent, and the lines are less sharply defined; there is less persecution and more fellowship, less theology and more religion; liberty of conscience is conceded, and knowledge of the Scriptures is more general; but it is a serious question whether the membership, recruited largely from the Sunday School, possesses as discriminative and sturdy a faith as formerly. It has not been fully demonstrated whether the Young People's organisation will prove to be a conserver of doctrine and discipline, or a spiritual dissipation. The commendable desire to make Sunday School and Church services interesting to the young shows a tendency to yield their direction to the inexperienced, and, in exceptional places, to so modify music, sermon, and service as to mar their simplicity, directness, and power. The personal attitude of some members and preachers toward Sunday observance and amusements which tend to frivolity and sensuousness awakens apprehension for their spiritual life, but the Churches generally are loyal to those things which make for righteousness, and the members bear the likeness of the King. Never has there been more thorough nor more comprehensive work, nor a more religious spirit in its schools and colleges. Its students have never shown greater interest in, or devotion to, missionary work. It is the only Church which has a surplus of young men offering for its ministry, and its influence through Bible exposition, godly living, unselfish ministries, unceasing effort, is diffused, potential, cumulative.

The conditions of the problem confronting Christianity change continually. At the present time the frontiers of our civilisation are in the great cities. With the masses character is largely a product of environment, and crime a question of opportunity. The congested tenement house is less accessible than scattered cabins. The peculations of commerce are more destructive of the moral sense than seclusion. Aggregation breeds vice of more subtle and more blatant forms than isolation. But sin, entrenched or deployed, secret or manifest, is enmity against God, from which the only salvation is the all-conquering Love of Jesus, working through human ministries. John Wesley won his victories, spiritual and social, amid worse conditions than obtain in our most homeless cities. The only power which can complete social regeneration is the Holy Spirit. Under His guidance American Methodism is prosecuting its high calling, focussing the love of the devout, the experience of the spiritual, the counsel of the mature, the money of the wealthy, the enthusiasm of the young, the heart power and special gift of each, whatever it may be, to safeguard the humblest in the exercise of conscience, intellectual freedom, and the development of Christian manhood.   .   .   .

So in America the actinic rays of Methodist influence have worked with subtle power beyond the general spectrum of the Methodist Church.

The deep religious truths and experience voiced in its hymns have been
sung into the creeds and conduct of our Christendom, till in words of
ancient form, but used with a modified meaning, old churches are proclaiming the Gospel of Love and Life. The doctrines it protested against,
such as limited atonement, and absolute or unavoidable reprobation, are
no longer emphasised, and rarely preached. The truths it has always
kept to the fore, and which were almost universally attacked, are
emphasised in every Evangelical pulpit. The Methodist conception of
sanctification, illustrated by a "Happy Holiness and a Holy Happiness,"
has given other Churches their ideas of saintliness, and some of them
rival it in their possession of the experience and their insistence upon
the doctrine. Its lay service, utilising woman, "the mourner and comforter of the race," as well as man, has been contagious, and in
Christian Associations, Endeavour Societies, Guilds, and others forms
of lay Evangelical work, is established in all the Churches. Methodism
has made its way by the inherent vitality of its doctrines and the
transformed lives of its followers till "the despised is respected and
welcomed by every communion, sweetening, modifying, and vitalising,
and mobilising wherever it goes." If some of its Sister Churches were
to return the ministers and converts who have overflowed into their
communions it would seriously deplete their ranks and limit their
activities.

Standing for liberty without license, purity without prudishness,
conscience without persecution, Methodism has been a devoted and
staunch friend of temperance and all other social reforms from the
beginning. Whether considered in relation to the leaders it has prepared, the doctrines it has promulgated, or the vigorous administration
it has maintained, its influence for morality and manhood has been
beyond computation.

While Methodism is in no sense a political organization, its
numerical strength and the vital character of its teachings, quickening
the perceptions and conscience of its members, purifying morals,
diffusing education, determining ideals, and developing character, have
made it the most constructive force in our great Republic. The Chief
Executive, President McKinley, is a communicant in the Methodist
Church; so are many United States Senators and Representatives, the
Governors of a number of States, and in some States a majority of both
Houses of Assembly. America and Methodism are two developing world
powers so inter-related that to discuss either philosophically requires
a discussion of the other.

¶   Debate on Status of the Negro, 1918.

(Taken from *Proceedings of the Joint Commission on Unification*
(1920), II, 100-03, 128-131, 136-41, 162-75).

REPORT OF THE COMMITTEE ON THE STATUS OF THE NEGRO
IN THE REORGANIZED CHURCH.

The Committee on the Negro met at the close of the meeting of the
Joint Commission in Traverse City, Mich., July 3, 1917, and appointed
a subcommittee of two members from each Commission. The subcommittee
made the following preferential and alternative reports. The committee
herewith presents these two reports as submitted to it to the Joint
Commission, without recommendation.

REPORT OF SUBCOMMITTEE.

Your committee have found it impossible to present their conclusions
as to what should be the status of the negro membership in the reorganized and unified Church without stating the same in form which relates
this subject to questions already reported upon or to be reported upon
by coordinate committees and tentatively adopted by the Joint Commission.
We present as our preferential report the following, which places the
negro membership in a Sub-Regional Jurisdiction of the kind and powers
herein indicated:

Associate Regional Conferences.

Section I. There shall be the following Associate Regional
Jurisdictions, each having its own Associate Regional Conference:

(1) The Afro-American, which shall embrace within its jurisdiction
all Annual Conferences, Mission Conferences, and Missions composed of
persons of African descent in the United States and in the Continent of
Africa.

(2) The Latin-American, which shall embrace within its juris-
diction all Annual Conferences, Mission Conferences, and Missions in
Latin-American countries, including Porto Rico, Cuba, Mexico, Central
America, and South America.

(3) The European, which shall embrace within its jurisdiction all
Annual Conferences, Mission Conferences, and Missions in the countries
of Europe, Northern Africa, and the Madeira Islands.

(4) The Eastern Asiatic, which shall embrace within its jurisdiction all the Annual Conferences, Mission Conferences, and Missions in
China, Korea, Philippine Islands, and Malaysia.

(5) The Southern Asiatic, which shall embrace within its jurisdiction all the Annual Conferences, Mission Conferences, and Missions in
India and Burma.   .   .   .

510

ALTERNATIVE REPORT.

We present as an alternative report the following, which places the negro in an Associate General Conference:

1. Create an Associate General Conference which shall comprise within its jurisdiction the negro membership of the Church in the United States and Africa, and which shall have complete legislative, judicial, and executive powers in the ecclesiastical government of said negro membership in harmony with and subject to the Constitution of the unified Church. Said Associate General Conference shall have the power to elect the bishops, constitute the boards, and elect their general administrative officers, for the said negro Conferences and membership.

2. Create a Judicial Council for and out of the said negro membership, whose duties and prerogatives shall be the same or similar to those of the other membership and jurisdiction of the unified Church, represented by the General Conference.

3. Create a Constitutional Council, to which shall be referred all and only questions as relate to and affect the Constitution of the unified Church and which demand consideration and determination. Said Consitutional Council shall be constituted of representatives of each of the jurisdictions in proportion to the Church membership represented by the respective General Conferences.

4. Provide for the representation of each jurisdiction in the connectional administrative boards in proportion to the Church membership and interests involved.

          *   *   *

Dr. Downey: I suppose somebody has to begin the afternoon session, and possibly I might as well say what is in my heart to say now as at any other time. It must, I think, be evident to every Commissioner that we have come to the point when the decisions made will cause us to go either backward or forward. I desire to speak as one who has a forward look and who earnestly and prayerfully and hopefully desires that we may reach conclusions that shall help us forward. I trust that I may be kept, both by good sense and God's grace, from saying anything that would in any way make for either a backward look or a backward movement. . . . the essential parts of a brief letter . . .

[the letter states that some Northern Methodists want unification on any terms, more want full unification without any terms, and others want unification on equitable terms]. . . .

Now, as to the immediate question which is before us: The negroes in the Methodist Church have a certain position. They are in the

511

Church. Quite naturally our preference is that they be continued in
the relation in which they now are. We do not see any very good
reason for a change. It ought, however, to be clearly in mind as
to just what the *status quo* is and what it implies. It does not imply
social equality. This is not a matter that is at all before us.
Social equality is something that takes care of itself. It is really
hardly a matter to be considered by thoughtful men who are handling
Church matters. Again, the *status quo* does not mean mixed Churches
or mixed Conferences. Of course, there will be sporadic instances
in which there may be a few negro members in some Churches of the
South as well as of the North. Indeed, from what I have heard, I
imagine you have far more of these sporadic instances than we have.
I think we should bear these matters clearly in our thought. It is
not a question of mixed Churches, it is not a question of social
equality, it is not a question of mixed races. These things are not
at all in our thought. They are not in the mind or conscience of the
M. E. Church. It simply means ecclesiastical equality. That is all.
Now, it has been said here and said, I believe, with a good deal of
truth, that the color line is already drawn in the M. E. Church.
This is unquestionably true. We have colored Churches, we have
colored Conferences, and we have colored ministers in our Annual
Conferences, ministering only and always to colored congregations.
But we do not need to be misled by this. This is largely just the
same color line that you have here. But there is no color line in
the M. E. Church on the manhood rights of the negro in the Church.
That is the point – that is the main point in our Church. He has
all the rights of a minister. He has his judicial rights– his
legislative rights, his right to appointment, his right to appeal,
and everything of that sort. It is not a color line on the question
of his manhood rights and his manhood standing, and I do not think
the M. E. Church would be willing to write into the Constitution of
the reorganized Church anything that would be a discrimination upon
the manhood rights of any man in the reorganized Church. There is
no discrimination against the rights of the negro in the Constitution
of the United States. There is no discrimination on his manhood
rights, I take it, in the various States. I do not believe that you
would expect that we should write into the Constitution of the reorganized Church of Jesus Christ what is not written into the
constitutions of the States and the Nation. A good deal has been said
about the necessity of setting the colored brother apart in an associated or independent General Conference in order that he may have
racial development. It is easily possible, brothers, in these days
to overstrain the matter of racial development. The fact is, the
world to-day is suffering from an excess of racialism – from an
exaggerated sense of racialism – and we shall do well to be on our
guard lest we go too far in that direction. I suppose what is meant
is that he should have an opportunity for self-development; but I
call attention to the fact that in the M. E. Church at the present time
he has autonomy in the local Church. Nobody interferes with his

development in the local Church or with the management of his affairs
in the local Church; nobody interferes seriously with his management
of affairs in the Annual Conference. Indeed, I think it would have
been better if we had given a little more attention to him in his
management of affairs in his Annual Conference. But the fact is that
he has been allowed pretty much to have his own way. He controls his
Annual Conference; he carries on the business of his Annual Conference.
It has been my privilege as a connectional officer to visit a number
of our colored Conferences. I have listened to reports of their
district superintendents. I have listened to their discussions and
their debates, and I make bold to say that they do not seem to suffer
because of any pressure that was put upon them by the bishop who
happened to be presiding. I make bold to say that they gave evidence
of development and of wisdom and of careful thought and ability in
their discussions. I have heard white men who have made no better
presentations of their causes than many of these black man. They
have a good deal of autonomy in their affairs at present. They
control a great many educational institutions that do really high
and serviceable work. Now, we are asked to believe that an independent General Conference, meeting once in four years, will be the
capstone to all that I have mentioned. I beg leave to differ with
that. I believe his presence in the General Conference as now
constituted is just the one thing he needs to give him ideals and
suggestions and helpful inspirations which he can take down to his
educational institutions, to the Annual and District Conferences,
and to his local Church. I am perfectly confident that meeting once
in four years cannot by any possibility do for him in an educational
way or in an inspirational way what his association with men who have
had a much longer and finer chance for civilization than he has had
can do for him. . . .

We have before us the preferential plan, and it occurs to me
that that preferential plan may be the middle ground on which we
can agree. It is not all we would like it to be. There are certain
things in it that I certainly hope will be changed. But as I look it
over, taking all the elements into consideration, it seems to me that
it points in the right direction, and that it might be perfectly
possible with a reasonable amount of sacrifice and of compromise to
come to unity on something akin to that preferential plan.

*   *   *

[H. H. White:] I do not know that the views which I shall express
will meet the approbation of many who are present, and I am sure they
will not deserve in any sense the high encomiums which have been placed
on the episcopal addresses and what have been referred to as ministerial
addresses by others to-day. However, I feel that perhaps the best
thing I can do at this time is to lay before you gentlemen of the
Commission my views on this, as I consider it, the greatest question

513

which will come before this body. I do not desire to strike any note which will be out of harmony with almost everything else that has been said. I do not consider it necessary for every member of this Commission to proclaim his loyalty to the purposes which caused this Commission to meet, or his friendship and devotion to the brethren who are here. I shall simply say that the association which I have had at Baltimore and Traverse City and here with the members of the Commission on both sides has been very pleasant and sweet. I now ask your permission to do something I have never done before on any occasion that I can recall, and that is to read the remarks which I desire to make. I do this perhaps because of the danger of mis-interpretation of the sentiment of the section from which I have come. The views expressed are my own views, but so far as my observation goes they represent and reflect very accurately the sentiment of a very large body of the M. E. Church, South. With your permission I shall now read:

THE NEGRO QUESTION AS RELATED TO THE PROPOSED UNION OF THE METHODIST EPISCOPAL CHURCHES, NORTH AND SOUTH.

Brethren: Pretermitting any discussion as to the desirability or feasibility of union of our two great Churches, were all other causes for division removed or satisfactorily adjusted, I shall address myself to a short discussion of the proposition as related to what should be the proper status of the negro Methodists, either in or out of the proposed united Churches.

This question should be viewed from the standpoints of desirability and of feasibility, taking account both of ethical and of practical considerations.

The time and place are met when in Christian brotherhood frank statements should be made, and the exact status of both thought and feeling should be made known.

We raise no question here as to the relative superiority of races, nor as to whether such racial differences as exist are due to education or to nature; but, speaking from what the South believes in its heart of hearts to be true, both from the teachings of ethnology and from the instincts of six thousand years, the question must be considered to be one of race and not of caste, and one of the mass and not one of the individual.

Leaving argument to biologists, ethnologists, philosophers, and theologians, I shall state what I believe the South and the Southern Church will stand for, and will regard as a *sine qua non*. What I state may sound brutally frank, but it is stated in kindness and in brotherhood, in order that we may see each other "face to face" and not as "through a glass, darkly."

514

I believe that our position may be condensed into the following statement:

The South and our grand division of the Methodist Church believe:
(a) That the color line must be drawn firmly and unflinchingly, in State, Church, and society, without any deviation whatever; and no matter what the virtues, abilities, or accomplishments of individuals may be, there must be absolute separation of social relations. If the color line is disregarded in relations so intimate as those necessitated by the equal status theory, demanded, as I understand it, by the strongest negro members of the Methodist Church, North, it will be impossible long to continue the fixed status of separation in affairs governmental, civic, and social.

(b) We further believe that in this matter the South is but fighting the preliminary battle of the North, and is but now further advanced along the path which the North has already entered and will unfalteringly follow. At any rate, to use the language of another: "But he who supposes that the South will ever waver a hair's breadth from her position of uncompromising hostility to any and every form of social equality between the races, deceives himself only less than that other who mistakes her race instinct, the palladium of her future, for an ignorant prejudice and who fails to perceive that her resolution to maintain white racial supremacy within her borders is deepest rooted and most immutable precisely where her civic virtue, her intelligence, and her refinement are at their highest and best." Of course, that highest and best of civic virtue and intelligence and refinement is found in her Churches.

We further believe that the leaders of Southern thought and policy should keep step in Church and in State; and it is but well-known history to state that for forty years the South struggled, with an eagerness surpassing that of war, to throw off and to keep off the burden and the shadow of negro influence in political affairs; and only now are the labors of the men who led in that struggle being crowned with a moderate degree of success. It was only yesterday that constitutional provisions, such as the understanding clause in Mississippi and the grandfather clause in Louisiana, took the place of harsher and more dangerous means of correcting the evils turned loose upon the South by the adoption of the fourteenth and fifteenth amendments.

But why has the South demanded and endured the storm and stress of reconstruction? We answer that it was to attain and maintain Caucasian supremacy, unadulterated and untainted in political and civic affairs.

But can the South, or what we fondly consider its leading Church, admit negroes on the plane of perfect equality in its religious councils and lawmaking or interpreting bodies, while it denies, or

515

helps to deny, correlative rights and privileges in those so much less intimate relations of official and legislative life?

There is no use to blink the question: Until we are ready to admit that we and our fathers have perpetrated and assisted to perpetrate civil wrong in the reestablishment of purely Caucasion government in the South, we cannot permit the admission of any tincture into the pure Caucasian control of our ecclesiastical council and Conferences or courts.

But our Northern brethren now propose that there shall be only a modicum of negro representation in our Conferences; or that the negroes shall be set off into some special or Regional Conference where they will have a quasi territorial form of government.

Again, let us not blink the facts. All such propositions are subterfuges, to fool "the brother in black" - to amuse him with the shadow of equality while the substance is denied him. The grandfather clause of the Louisiana Constitution is a paragon of frankness and clarity, as compared with such schemes. And nobody knows this better than the negro. Witness the prompt, energetic, and unanswerable reply of Dr. Jones to Dr. Blake's proposition that for the sake of harmony the negro surrender some portion of his present rights and privileges.

If I understand the position of the negro members of the Methodist Episcopal Church, as voiced by their press and by Dr. Jones and Dr. Penn of this Commission, they claim as a vested right the full *pro rata* share for each member of power, influence, opportunity for advancement, office and property, with every other member - Caucasian, Mongol, or Malay.   .   .   .

I take the liberty of trying to draw some general conclusions from the foregoing statements, which, while they have been presented in the form of conclusions, could in my opinion be supported by sound argument. Among those conclusions are these:

1. That the Southern Church will not be willing to go into any arrangement by virtue of which the colored delegates sit either in a General Conference or Supreme Court, and take part in their deliberations, on any basis whatever.

2. That the colored ministry and congregations of the Northern Methodist Church would resent very determinedly and even bitterly any proposition to assign them any sort of a minimum or modified representation in the General Conference. They are demanding, as I understand, full, absolute, and unqualified equality as members of the Church with all other members. This view on their part has been recently expressed very forcibly by Dr. Jones, who is on this committee which is meet-

ing here, and who edits the leading *Advocate* for the colored Methodists in the Southwest, published at New Orleans.

3. The Southern Methodist Church would not feel justified in going into a union which would take care of, say, three hundred and fifty thousand colored members, now belonging to the Northern Church, but would not fully and adequately take care of or provide for the other, say, million and a half or two million negro Methodists belonging to other organizations, as the African Methodist C.M.E., and others.

4. The only way in which a union of the Northern and Southern Churches can be brought about will be by the immediate or gradual elimination of the negro membership and in good faith attempt on the part of both Churches, North and South, to cause all negro Methodists to unite in one great body, which should be brought, in so far as may be, under the tutorship, and which would receive the encouragement of the white Church. . . .

I have thought over and studied these matters for something like thirty years, was a member of the Constitutional Convention of Louisiana which gave to the white people of the State the right to control the State, without the necessity of resort to force or fraud against the negroes. I am satisfied that the best men of the negro race really in their hearts look forward to and cherish the hope that some day what Professor Dubois refers to as the "veil which separates the white and the colored races" shall be removed.

I belong to the class of white men who believe that the relations of the races should be governed, and are occasioned, by race differences rather than by matters of artificial caste. I champion negro education and the safeguarding of the rights of the negroes both as to property and person, but I have not been able to persuade myself that they ought to have been admitted into partnership in the political government of the country, or that it would be wise to give them such position in the Church as we feel we must withhold from them in the realm of politics.

R. E. Blackwell: I feel that we are discussing a subject that is the most momentous that has ever been discussed by any Church assembly on this continent. It is a question that concerns not merely the Northern and Southern Churches: the whole Christian world is looking at us to-day. When it was announced that I was on this Commission, I got letters from men of various denominations expressing the hope that we would show Protestantism how to get together. It is not a question, therefore, that concerns us alone. If we refuse to unite because of an almost negligible number of negroes in the General Conference, I believe it will go down in ecclesiastical history as "the great refusal." The most pathetic spectacle in history is the negro. He

517

was brought here against his will. We Southern people have profited by him. I stand here as one who has profited by him. As far back as the records of two Virginia counties go, my ancestors were slave owners. I was helped in getting my education with money that was mine through my mother's slaves. I owe him a debt. I have not paid it. Many of my fellow Southerners have not paid the debt they owe the negro. We Southern Methodists were paying it at one time. I think we wanted to pay it. My heart beats with noble emotion when I think of what Bishop Capers did for the negroes. I think we are all proud of it. I am not proud of anything my Church has done for the negroes since they were set up for themselves.   .   .   .

We have hardly more concern about the negroes of the Colored M. E. Church than we have about Presbyterians or Episcopalians. Our people did not intend that it should be so, but it came as the result of putting the negroes off to themselves. But, as has been said here to-day, we are getting a new conscience on the subject of the negro. The young men who are to be leaders of the country are studying this problem at all Southern universities. Every State University in the South has a fund at its disposal to be expended on the study of this problem; and men of our own Methodist institutions have said to me that the relation between the negroes and the white people in the unified Church must be made closer than the relation that exists between us and the colored M. E. Church.

*   *   *

Robert E. Jones: When I spoke to you at Baltimore, I uttered the conviction that as one man I would do everything I could for the consummation of the union of these two great Churches. I am of that opinion to-day, but I speak this morning with just a little misgiving and some personal embarrassment. I do not like to be the occasion of all this.

E. C. Reeves: You cannot help it.

Robert E. Jones: If anybody knows my intense feeling, if he knows something of my inner life, if he knows something of the policy of aloofness I have pursued, he will understand that personally I would rather be elsewhere. I am in favor of the union of these two Churches. I am absolutely sure it ought to come. Dr. Bishop, I am sure that it will come. I do not know that I say with others that it ought to come to-day; God grant it may. I do not believe that if it does not come to-day it is not coming. I do not believe that you can stop it. I do not believe we ought to take that position at all. I think as Commissioners we are here as custodians of an idea, that it is not necessarily our task to frame a plan that will pass. I rather think it is our task to frame a plan that will meet our own judgment and that will be a working ideal for

518

the Church. But be that as it may, that is absolutely on the side. I had a great experience yesterday. As a negro, yesterday was a revelation to me and a real joy. I enjoyed Judge White's speech, really I did. There is no camouflage in that at all. I did not agree with all he said – of course, I did not – but I enjoyed the speech. I enjoyed its frankness. I think when men can come together in the beautiful spirit in which we talked yesterday there is hope for the future. . . .

God knows that for twenty-one years in New Orleans I have been doing everything that I knew how to do that there might be peace and good will. I have preached to my people over and over again that it made no difference what a man should do to me or what a race of men should do to me, I should hate no man. God is my judge that I have pursued that in my private life and in my daily life. And how sad I was when the whole question of migration came up and 600,000 of my people moved into the North, some too soon, some who knew not where they were going. An old negro woman went to an agent of one of the railroad companies and laid down $25 and said, "I want a ticket." "Where to?" asked the ticket agent. She said, "That is none of your white folks' business. Give me a ticket; I want to go." . . . .

Do you think we want social equality? If you do, I will underwrite a contract with you and I will split my veins and sign it in my own blood and we will build a wall so high that no negro can get over it, and so thick that no white man can go through it. I was down in Georgia the other night soon after Dr. Steel had made that statement in the *New Orleans Advocate* about the intermixture of the races, and I said to them that we should drive from our midst any negro woman who sells her virtue to a white man and that sort of thing should cease. I put it with a sort of emphasis, and for five minutes I could not go on with my speech. The people jumped over the benches, and one man who was a cripple left his crutches and picked me up and carried me about on the platform. You don't understand us, brothers. We have our own social life. When I married, I married a woman of darker skin than my own. I said before God that my children should know who they were. I am not responsible for what I am. You cannot blame me. I have always pursued that same policy; and if there is any man here to-day talking about social equality, don't think that I want it – don't think that the negro wants it. . . .

Bishop Mouzon said yesterday that every man should have a chance. That is all I want. I do not want anything else but simply a man's chance. I want a square deal and fair play, and I want the cards dealt fairly so that I can have a man's chance in the game of life. Now, you will indulge me, I am sure, just a minute. It is so easy for a man to trump up a position at a time like this. That you may quite understand me this morning, let me read where I stand on this

matter, and this speech was delivered at Evanston and recorded a
year or so ago when I had no thought of ever being on a Commission
such as this:

Now I state in a sentence the program: The largest possible
contact of the negro with the white man with the largest possible
independence of the negro. Both sides of the proposition are for
the good of the negro, contact for inspiration and for ideals,
independence for growth and for development. The weak grow by
doing. A man ought not to do for another what the other man can
do for himself. A man ought not to permit another to do for him
that which he can do for himself. The day is passing when the white
man is to work over the negro. Maybe the day is waning when the
white man is to work among us, but the day is at sunrise when the
white man is to work through the negro for the uplift of millions,
and this latter program for stimulating the ideals of civilization
can be carried forward just as effectively and even more effectively
than by former methods.

With a selection made and with absolute recall upon this
selection, the Church can work more effectively through the chosen
men, preserve its ideals, carry forward its program, infuse and
diffuse its spirit, and at the same time more assuredly keep the
esprit de corps of the negro people and thus advance the kingdom of
Jesus Christ. That is where I stood then; that is where I stand
now.   .   .   .

There is no servile blood in me. If I thought I had one drop
of it, I would open my veins and let it out. I hope, however, that
every drop is thoroughly saturated with the humility of Jesus Christ.
And in this spirit I try to live a humble, devout, God-fearing man.
I do not know how much I have done, but I have tried to do my level
best every day of my life to develop among my people a love for our
section, for its industries, for our neighbors, and for all that
would make for peace and happiness.   .   .   .

Maybe you ask the question, Why don't you people withdraw from
the Church? Do you stay here for office? God forbid. I do not want
any office, men. Principle is above preferment with me, and whatever
office I have to-day was not given to me by my people. It was given
to me by the vote of an assembly eight-ninths of which was white,
and can be taken away to-morrow as easily as it was given. You know
it and I know it. Is it for money? There are men in the Church who
have made generous offers to us in the way of money if we go out.
They have said, "If you will go out, you can have your property."
Why, we would be the richest negro Church in the world. Is it money?
I don't want any price put on my head, my heart, or my convictions,
whether it be ten dollars or ten million dollars. I want to be somewhere that I will be above money, above place, and above preferment.

520

I have already answered the question as to social equality, that it is not for social equality. "Then why do you cause all this confusion, why do you remain?" I am asked. First, I believe it promotes the best interests of my people. I think it is best for my people to be somewhere close to a large Church with great ideals. I have been able to do things for my people, I have been able to say things in correction of their lives and to give to them ideals that I never could have done if I did not have a strong organization behind me standing for those ideals. Then, you will excuse me: to give you a concrete example, I stood before a Conference the other day and lambasted those negro preachers about not paying a debt, and I did it straight from the shoulder - and I have to have the suffrage of those men. But I did not care for that. I was standing by the principles of my Church. Second, I stay in the Methodist Episcopal Church because I believe it is a Church founded on a New Testament basis and American democracy. I believe it is New Testament teaching for the Church to take into it all people and I do not believe I should run at the first fire of a gun. Third, Bishop Mouzon said the other day that he loves his Church as he does his life. Well, I love my Church, I honestly do, with all my heart. I was born in it and was brought up in it. My grandfather was brought up in it and it has done much for me. But I love it beyond what it has done for me. I actually love my Church beyond and above all other Churches. Then I stay in my Church, the Methodist Episcopal Church, because I believe a large part of my Church desires me to stay; and whenever the time comes when any large part of the people in the Methodist Episcopal Church does not want me in its communion, whether it is for convenience or organic union or otherwise, I shall not stay in that Church. If I believed to-day that I were unacceptable to any considerable number of the members of the Methodist Episcopal Church, I would step down and out. Self-respect would work automatically. I believe in my Church because it has made it better for the South.   .   .   .

Now, there are just two or three other things I want to say. Much has been said about the negro Church coming under; and so, to pursue some of the methods used by you and your friends, I thought I would get in touch with some of these negro bishops to find out if it were actually true that they were looking forward to us to bring them all together. So on Saturday night before I left home, I dictated a letter to all the negro bishops and I inclosed the proposition of the Rev. Dr. Blake and of that *Zion's Herald* up there in Boston, and I said: "Tell me frankly if it is true - maybe I don't quite understand - if it is true that you men are now going to come under the Black proposition." And I will read two or three of the letters.

[Here followed extensive quotations from 8 letters, all saying not interested]   .   .   .

Now, what do we want? You will be interested in that. First

of all, we do not want any caste written in the Constitution. That
is fundamental. We do not do that in Louisiana, and we do not do
it in the nation, and we should not do it in the Church. Second, we
do not want any offensive name in whatever arrangement you make. We
want to be "Samuel" and not "Sambo." We want some sort of dignified
name to whatever arrangement you may make. And it is fundamental
that we should ask for representation in the General Conference. We
will agree to the formation of our membership from one end of the
country to the other in a centralized Conference. The Supreme Court
of the United States has wiped out the Segregation Ordinances, and
it was a unanimous court that did it and there were Southern men on
the Supreme Court bench. Segregation in temporal affairs has been
wiped out; and the only segregation that ought to obtain is segregation by the choice of the people, and there is a good deal of that.
We don't have any trouble over that in Louisiana - we don't have
any trouble in New Orleans. We will agree to show you our spirit.
I don't think it is fair and I don't think it is democratic, but
we will agree on a basis of non-self-support. Mark you, Dr. Goucher,
the Church, the white Church, did not give the negro $500,000 a year.

    John F. Goucher: I would like it if it would.

    Robert E. Jones: We negroes are a part of the Church that does
that. Now, as to our representation in the General Conference,
Wisconsin has eight delegates, with 28,000 members. The South
Carolina Conference has eight delegates and 55,000— There are no
small Conferences that have a membership between 900 and 1,000 among
us - these are white Conferences; the smallest Conference we have is
5,000. But be that as it may, we are just as dead in earnest as you
are. We will agree to a largely reduced representation in the General
Conference. By the way, before the war three-fifths of an ignorant,
helpless negro down on the plantation in the South was the basis of
representation in Congress. A negro was three-fifths of a man.
Five thousand counted for three thousand then. And in this new day
I am at least four-fifths of a man, but to show that I am square I
will agree to a reduced representation in the General Conference; I
will not agree to elimination. I want the right of the initiative
and referendum. I want to do just as I do in Louisiana: vote on
constitutional questions. I do. Judge White, you referred to
Louisiana and a conventional amendment on suffrage. You will have to
have another constitutional convention soon. You have 20,000 negroes
who can register and vote, no matter what terms you fix. Whatever
terms for suffrage you fix, we are going to qualify, if it requires
a bachelor's degree. We want the right of initiative and referendum
so that whenever you want to change the constitution, whether we
count for little or for large, we will have the right to pass on it.
The question of the bishops does not concern us. We will agree to
our bishops having jurisdiction within our territory - that is, that
by some process they shall be limited to our people, so that there

will not be any fear that any of our bishops shall ever preside over a white Conference.

Bishop Leete: What is the concession you are making on that?

R. E. Jones: I said we will agree to a reduced proportionate representation in the General Conference, and we will agree that our bishops shall be limited to our jurisdictions. I think that is all. O brothers, let us not think the task is hopeless. Don't make us prevent reunion. Don't put upon me and upon my people any more burdens than we have, don't make us the scapegoat – we cannot stand it. Don't let us go out and have it said that these two Churches did not unite because the negro was not willing to do his share. We are. We don't want to stand in your way. Appreciate how we are situated, and God give us grace and wisdom to reach a final conclusion.

¶   The Centenary Campaign.

(Taken from John Lankford in *Methodist History*, II (Oct. 1963), 27-37).

During the third week in September, 1917, one hundred ministers and laymen of the Methodist Episcopal Church met at Niagara Falls to plan for the celebration of the centennial of the Missionary Society. After three days of discussion this assembly adopted "a World Program which if carried out to its full conclusions will reach and stir with its inspiring appeal the last church and the last man in Methodism and should result in a revived and reconsecrated church at home and a church abroad adequately equipped, manned and munitioned for the conquest of the 150 millions whose evangelization is the accepted task of Methodism." John R. Mott, Methodist layman and long-time leader in the American foreign missionary movement, addressed the meeting and urged upon the Methodist Church a plan of "enduring work." Mott warned the delegates, "Everywhere the age-old institutions are slipping. Their foundations are shifting sands. What alone can stand the strain such as it is now upon the world?" .   .   .

The September 1917 meeting issued a list of recommendations to the Methodist Episcopal Church. These recommendations included a vigorous affirmation of the foreign missionary work and the suggestion that $8,000,000 a year for five years be secured to cover the expanded undertaking in this realm. Further, the group suggested that during the years 1918-1919 a full-scale campaign be undertaken "by means of press, picture and pulpit" and that "a vital missionary organization be carried from Area, Conference and District, down to the last church" in Methodism. To complement the emphasis on missionary activity, the Niagara Conference stressed the necessity for

"teaching of stewardship of life, character and possessions (the tithe) ... as fundamental to Christianity." The 1918-1919 drive was to culminate in a grand denomination-wide celebration at the State Fair grounds at Columbus, Ohio, in June 1919. In conclusion the meeting voted to lay the program before the Board of Bishops.

The administrative structure which emerged from the work of the Niagara Conference comprised, on the national level, a Commission directed by S. Earl Taylor. This organization functioned through a series of ten departments and interested itself in almost all aspects of Church life. Its departments were concerned with such problems as education, spiritual resources, Christian stewardship, and publicity. . . .

Although the apparent impetus for the Centenary came from the northern wing of American Methodism, the Methodist Episcopal Church, South, was involved from the beginning. Cooperation between the two denominations was formalized at a meeting held in Memphis in March 1918. W. B. Beauchamp served as Director General of the Centenary in the southern Church until elected Bishop in May 1922. He was succeeded as Director by his assistant, W. G. Cram. Generally, the same administrative structure served both branches of the Church and became in 1918 the Joint Centenary Commission. Plans and strategy were interchangeable and the national fund raising advisers served both denominations. The Southerners aimed at the same range of goals as did their northern counterparts. Missions, missionary education, the cultivation of stewardship and tithing, and a national campaign to solicit pledges for $35,000,000 to be used in carrying out the aims of the Centenary program - all these, plus cooperation with the Northern Church for the Columbus Celebration in 1919, made up the program for the southern branch of American Methodism. . .

Following the general organizational principles used by Charles S. Ward in his earlier campaigns, American Methodism divided itself into units, groups and sub-groups with teams and leaders. These teams were to be responsible for the actual gathering of subscriptions. According to a writer in the New York *World*, "No such publicity campaign was ever undertaken by a church organization. Not only the church press, but the secular press and the labor and trade journals will be utilized." The editorial continued by analyzing the sources from which the Methodists got their ideas and promotional techniques. "Liberty Loan drives gave them their cue. Billboards, posters, motion pictures, special rallies indoors and out - no way of letting the great American public know that the drive for worldwide Christian democracy is on will be overlooked." The Methodists adopted the Minute Men, a technique used during the Liberty Loan campaigns, to serve as publicity agents for the Centenary. It was reported by the New York *World* that an army of 100,000 such Methodist Minute Men had been recruited, "largely from the very men who did

similar service for Uncle Sam in his war for democracy."   .   .   .

The promotional methods employed by the Joint Centenary Commission, including sermons, a veritable flood of articles, advertisements and pamphlets, and the work of the Methodist Minute Men, brought results. Who could refuse to pledge to the Centenary Fund under such pressure as the Nashville *Christian Advocate* (Feb. 7, 1919) exerted? "What Would John Wesley Say?" asked one full-page advertisement. "Let Us Have No Slackers," it continued. "It Is The Duty Of Every Methodist To 'Carry On,' If The World Shall Be Won For Christ." Other writers urged the wartime custom of wheatless and meatless days during the Centenary canvass, suggesting that the money thus saved be pledged to the cause. *Men and Money* offered its readers a list of ten points to keep in mind during the coming financial campaign. These ranged from the purely spiritual to the purely financial and were couched in the extreme promotional jargon of the day:

1) CELEBRATING. Sure, all of us! Great time we've had – 100 years past. Frontiers gone. Uncle Sam a teetotaler. Germany gone Democratic.

2) AWAKENING. Time to settle down, come to ourselves, get a good job with big wages and lots of work. We need 'em. Begin to save now. Pass the thrift stamps.

3) SURVEYING. What do we want? "Thy Kingdom come." That's our goal. "On earth" – you understand. Right here – now.

4) DETERMINING. We're going to stick to this. Our word is given. Cluttered old world must be cleaned up. Somebody must do it. We're somebody. Our hat's in the ring. Here goes.

5) PAYING. Well – yes, we'll pay,too. Bills must be met. $100,000,000 is a lot of money. By H.C.L. [High Cost of Living] we feel poor. But it's 9 for me and 1 for Him. Sounds stingy. Wonder if they'd accept more.

6) ACKNOWLEDGING. That's where the tithe comes in. Proves we mean business with all we have. Established credit with Father. He backs His boys. Competition stiff after war. Watch your credit.

7) ADMINISTERING. Who's a tightwad? The covetous. "By *their* works" – not by Father's. "He gave" (John 3:16). *Pay* your acknowledgment. You can't *say* it.

8) PERSONALITY.is self-directing. Volunteer! Enlist! Shout, if you 're hurt, or can't help it. Fight, if you're fit. Form a fighting front. Life enlistments, good wages – pensions.

9) PRAYER. Keep in touch with headquarters. No absence without leave. Orders direct from Commander. Use the wireless– Pray.

10) STEWARDSHIP. Your firm and your profits. Work
because you want to. Obey orders same way. Don't
forget the council meetings. Get busy.

Both branches of American Methodism "went over the top" in
their drives. The Southern Church received a total of $35,787,338
in subscriptions and the northern branch received $113,741,455 in
subscriptions. The Methodist Episcopal Church far exceeded its
original goal during the campaign.

Both branches joined in a gala celebration held in Columbus,
Ohio, during June and July 1919. It must have been a poor man's
World's Fair. Exhibits showing the work of American Methodism
in the mission fields served as the main attraction. There were
pavilions devoted to China, India, the South Seas, Africa and
South America. Whole Indian villages were set up and young people
modeled native costumes. Revivals and prayer meetings were a
daily occurrence, in addition to such nationally known speakers as
William Jennings Bryan. A special pageant took place each evening
depicting the historical development of Methodism in both Great
Britain and the United States. As one turns the pages of *The
Centenary Bulletin* and examines the list of events and the pictures,
the impression is gained that the Joint Centenary celebration must
truly have lived up to its slogan, "The World at Columbus." . . .

The fate of the Joint Centenary Movement is typical of the circumstances which befell the other great drives undertaken by American
Protestant denominations between 1917-1920. It must be remembered
that the Joint Centenary Movement took pledges and subscriptions to
be paid over a five year period. Although the drives "went over
the top" as far as promises to pay at a future date were concerned,
the denominations were not assured of actually collecting the sums
pledged. The intensive campaign was merely the first step toward
fulfilling the financial goals set by the national Church leadership and subscribed to by American Methodists. However, the directors of the missionary boards adjusted their plans to fit a
radically increased income and undertook new work on the basis
of the prospect of full payment of pledges and subscriptions during
the five year period. . . .

In the fall of 1920 the missionary boards of the Methodist
Episcopal Church issued an "emergency appeal." This appeal assured
churchmen that "This is no frenzied appeal of regulation form. It
is a calm statement of actual facts soberly considered. Unless
measures are taken and a general response is made, the Board of
Foreign Missions and the Board of Home Missions and Church Extension...
will be under the necessity of reducing the appropriations for 1922
...10 to 25 per cent. The Council of Boards of Benevolence
announced that in view of shrinking pledge payments there were two
alternatives: to cut the administrative staffs of the various

boards and reduce salaries, or to summon the Church "to a great
and holy crusade to get subscriptions from all members...to the
full sum which we have advertised to the world has been laid on
the altar by Methodist people."

The sharp but short-lived post-war economic recession did not
help the situation. Just as church members had earlier thrilled at
watching the big clock-like device used by C. S. Ward to chart the
progress of subscriptions, so now they viewed with sorrow and regret
the unwinding of that same clock as the payments fell farther and
farther behind the levels at which they ought to have been in terms
of monies pledged. Homer C. Stuntz, bishop in the Northern Church,
lamented "the tragedy of a shortage in Centenary collections," because "it puts the honor of the Church in pawn! And this is on a
world-wide scale." .   .   .

In the fall of 1922 the Northern Church resorted to a special
drive. Noting that the Board of Missions was faced with a deficit
of approximately $2,000,000, the leaders organized the "I Will
Maintain Fund." The fund was aimed at strictly cash support and
church members were asked to take up blocks of the debt at $100 per
share. Even with this device, the total giving on Centenary pledges
was $2,000,000 below the giving of the previous year.

Southern Methodist Bishop Warren A. Candler warned that if
the Centenary Movement failed, it would "bring backsliding at
home and dishonor abroad." The editor of the Nashville *Christian
Advocate* (July 29, 1921), reviewing the adverse conditions which
hampered collection of the Centenary pledges, felt that economic
recession was no excuse for the situation which confronted Southern
Methodism. He suggested that if giving in good times was a blessing,
giving in times of hardship would be even more of a blessing. "We
must meet the pledges already made," he concluded, for "great
enterprises of the Kingdom await the payment of these sacred obligations." .   .   .

Southern Methodist leaders were of two minds in their evaluation
of the Centenary. Elmer T. Clark, director of much of the promotional work of the Church, viewed the closing out of the Centenary
Movement as "one of the most serious tragedies ever encountered by
the Methodist Episcopal Church, South." He sorely lamented the new
work which was entered into in the expectation of higher standards of
support and which now had to be abandoned. Further, Clark saw the
end of the Centenary as a "retreat." He cried, "Our morale is broken.
Once admit defeat, and we may never - certainly not in this generation -
regain the ground we give up. We suffer shamefully in our prestige,
influence, and self-esteem." Clark concluded, "Few worse calamities
could befall us. In the history of Christianity God's favor has
never rested on any Church which has failed in its missionary obliga-

tion." E. H. Rawlings, Foreign Secretary of the Board of Missions, took a more optimistic view. He considered the $20,000,000 in new money raised during the five year period as "no small thing." Before the Centenary, "It was difficult to get as much as $100,000 or $50,000 outside of regular collections." Further, Rawlings pointed to the example set by the Methodist Joint Centenary Movement and noted how other Protestant denominations borrowed the idea.

After the "I Will Maintain Fund" the benevolent income of the Northern Methodists continued to fall behind expectations, and the boards were driven first into debt and then to an over-all reduction in their work. A note of desperation was sounded when the editor of the New York *Christian Advocate* (June 26, 1924) suggested that the men of the denomination give their gold watches to save the mission boards from further debt. By this point the foreign work was over $2,000,000 in the red. It was suggested that the Foreign Missions Board issue bonds against its debt and that these bonds be sold to churchmen. The leaders rejected this scheme.

At the end of the five years through which the Centenary collections had run, it was reported that 70 per cent of the subscriptions had been paid. Considering the nature of the American economy during these years, probably 70 per cent was a good showing. American economic life never fully or uniformly recovered from the sharp post-World War One recession.

However, the real damage was psychological. The hopes of many members and of the missionary leaders were far too high. Plans were implemented which never received financial support from the Church at large. In spite of the large sums collected, debts and demoralization followed in both branches of the American Methodist Church. Finally, missionaries were called home from the fields. Undaunted by all this, the editor of the New York *Christian Advocate* (March 26, 1925) declared in answer to those who saw the Centenary as a complete failure:

> The Church made a tremendous Centenary effort in 1919 –
> why belittle it by reckoning the per capita giving? – and
> fairly kept the faith. Not many pledges were defaulted.
> The shrinkage was no larger than was to have been expected
> in a subscription extending over a five-year period and
> written by optimists, who rashly multiplied by five every
> pledge, though positively signed up for but a single year.

The failure of the Joint Centenary Movement, like the failures of the other drives undertaken by major Protestant denominations at the end of the first World War, was more apparent than real. Substantial monies were collected and churchmen moved toward new conceptions of world-wide responsibility. Further, the Centenary

528

brought with it the need for an overhauling of the administrative machinery of the denominations. This was especially true in the case of the Methodist Episcopal Church and the final result was the creation in 1924 of the World Service Commission, which replaced the Council of Boards of Benevolence. This created a new administrative approach to the problem of raising funds for the philanthropic work of the denomination and, in the long run, this method was adopted by the unified Methodist Church after 1939.

22. NEW LIBERALISM AND NEW REFORMATION

When Frederick Carl Eiselen wrote his The Christian View of the Old Testament, *he had been for ten years professor of Old Testament at Garrett Biblical Institute and had weathered already some of the storms of criticism that swirled around biblical scholarship in those days. His thorough grounding in historical and scientific study of the Bible, combined with his abiding and articulately expressed Christian faith, brought him recognition throughout the church. He was a natural choice to serve as general editor of the* Abingdon Bible Commentary *of 1928, which won enduring use in the Methodist Episcopal Church and beyond. His approach to disputed issues was forthright but not pugnacious.*

Solomon Gamertsfelder, professor and president of Evangelical Theological Seminary in Naperville, Illinois, was the outstanding theologian of the Evangelical tradition. His interpretation of the central doctrine of sanctification set a moderate but firm position in maintaining the Evangelical view of Wesley's emphasis.

One of Eiselen's colleagues, who spent his long teaching career in and out of many debates over theology and social witness, was Harris Franklin Rall. He took on resurgent premillennialism as one face of conservative and fundamentalist reaction to the liberal theology for which he was a vigorous spokesman. As if theology did not provide sufficient debatable material, he was an active member of the Methodist Federation for Social Service.

Rall was inevitably on Harold Paul Sloan's list of persons suspected of infidelity to Methodist (and Christian) faith. Sloan was a redoubtable opponent of the growing spirit of liberalism in the church, and occupied many positions of influence as a leading minister of the New Jersey Conference, delegate to many General Conferences, and editor of the New York Christian Advocate. *The passage quoted from his work of 1922 was directed specifically against the books designated for the General Conference Course of Study--in those days the principal means of acquiring a theological education for entry into Methodist ministry.*

In a Southern church that, in spite of some courageous voices for change in a new day, remained conservative, Wilbur Fisk Tillett, of Vanderbilt University in Nashville, was probably the most important theologian. His cautious consideration of recent forms of biblical and theological scholarship maintained a moderate position.

In New England, where Boston University School of Theology was entering one of its greatest eras, Edgar S. Brightman stood forth

*as a persuasive interpreter of Christian faith for the new liberal
day. In many books, including the three quoted here, he spoke
effectively on such matters as the rationality of the universe as a
reflection of a reasonable God, personal experience as a means of
understanding a personal God, and, not least, the concept of a
limited God.*

*One of his contemporaries was Edwin Lewis of Drew Theological
Seminary. Lewis had developed in the prevailing liberal tradition.
But in 1933 and 1934 he dropped a bombshell with his seemingly sudden
change of direction under the influence of the Continental theology
associated with Karl Barth. Some of his liberal friends thought of
this transformation as apostasy; but Lewis went on to defend the
delayed but potent forces of Reformation theology. A Christian
Manifesto was a dramatic and effective proclamation of his own
reformation.*

¶ A Modern Understanding of the Bible.

(Taken from Frederick Carl Eiselsen, *The Christian View of
the Old Testament* (1912), 56-58, 75-78, 85-89).

One thing is quite certain, namely, that the Bible makes not
the slightest claim of being a scientific treatise complete and
up-to-date. It is equally true that it does not deny being such
a treatise, hence the inquirer is thrown back upon a study of the
facts presented in the Bible; and upon the basis of these he must
determine whether or not there is reason for believing that
scientific knowledge comes within the scope of inspiration. Now,
the abstract possibility of God communicating to man a knowledge of
exact scientific facts in a prescientific age need not be denied.
It is, however, a question whether God could have communicated such
facts to man three thousand years ago without robbing him of his
personality and changing him into a mechanism. So far as the ways of
God are known from experience, observation, history, and other sources,
he has always treated with respect and consideration the powers and
faculties of his chief creature.   .   .   .

This is not an arbitrary limitation of the scope of inspiration;
it is a conclusion based upon a careful consideration of the facts
of science and of the Bible, which seem to furnish sufficient
evidence that the biblical writers were not in any marked degree in
advance of their age in the knowledge of physical facts or laws. In
other words, the Bible is primarily a book of religion; hence religion, and not science, is to be looked for in its pages.
Altogether too much time has been spent in an effort to find in it
scientific truth in a scientific form. Such attempts clearly disregard the purpose of the biblical writers as interpreted in the
New Testament.   .   .   .

First of all, it may be well to define, if possible, the term
"higher criticism." It is too often assumed by those who should know
better, that the adjective "higher" exhibits the arrogance of those
using it, who claim thereby an unwarranted precedence for their
methods. This assumption is erroneous, for the adjective is used
simply to distinguish this kind of criticism from the lower or
textual criticism, which, since its purpose is to fix the exact text
of a book, necessarily precedes the application of the processes of
the higher criticism. The designation may be unfortunate, but thus
far no clearer or less objectionable substitute has been found. But
what is higher criticism? Higher criticism may be defined as a process of scientific investigation for the purpose of determining the
origin, original form, and intended value of literary productions.
It cannot be emphasized too strongly that higher criticism is nothing
more than a process of study or investigation. It is not a set of
conclusions respecting the books of the Bible; it is not a philosophical principle underlying the investigation; it is not a certain

attitude of mind toward the Bible; it is not a theory of inspiration nor a denial of inspiration. Higher criticism is none of these things. It is simply a process of study to determine certain truths concerning literary productions.   .   .   .

Once more: the higher criticism as such is not opposed to traditional views. In the words of Professor Zenos: "Its relation to the old and the new views respectively is one of indifference. It may result in the confirmation of the old, or in the substitution of the new for the old...It is no respecter of antiquity or novelty; its aim is to discover and verify the truth, to bring facts to light whether these validate or invalidate previously held opinions." It is a grave mistake, therefore, to attribute to higher criticism an essentially destructive purpose. In reality, it has confirmed traditional views at least as often as it has shown them to be untenable. It does not approach its investigations even with a suspicion of the correctness of tradition; it starts out with the tradition, it accepts it as correct until the process of investigation has brought to light facts and indications which cannot be harmonized with tradition. In such a case criticism believes itself bound to supply a satisfactory explanation of the facts, though such explanation may be contrary to the claims of tradition. Any student who approaches the inquiry in a spirit different from that here indicated introduces into his investigation elements that are not a part of higher criticism as such, and the latter cannot and should not be held accountable for them.   .   .   .

It is not necessary to enlarge upon the views of the traditional class of critics, for theirs are the views with which most Christians now living have been familiar since their childhood. In order to understand, however, the bearing of the nontraditional criticism upon the Christian view of the Old Testament it is necessary to consider the most important conclusions of the nontraditional class of evangelical criticism; and to these conclusions we may now turn our attention.

1. Modern criticism has placed into clearer light the progressive character of Old Testament revelation. God is the same yesterday, today, and forever, but man has taken many advance steps; and as he advanced his spiritual capacities and powers of apprehension increased. This growth enabled him to secure, from generation to generation and from century to century, during the Old Testament dispensation, an ever-broadening and deepening conception of the nature and character of God and of his will. The Old Testament books, says Kent, are "the harmonious and many-sided record of ten centuries of strenuous human endeavor to know and to do the will of God, and of his full and gracious response to that effort.

2. Formerly the beginning of the Old Testament canon was traced

533

to Moses. He was thought not only to have written the books of the
Pentateuch but to have given to them official sanction as canonical
books. To these books were gradually added the other sacred writings
of the Old Testament on the authority of the divinely chosen
successors of Moses, like Joshua, Samuel, and the prophets. The
close of the canon was ascribed to Ezra, who, according to later
views, had to share the honor with the men of the Great Synagogue.
Modern criticism assigns new dates to some of the Old Testament
books; it believes that the exile was a period of great spiritual
and intellectual activity, and a number of books are placed subsequent to Ezra and Nehemiah, which in itself would imply a denial of
the view that the canon was finally closed in the days of Ezra.
The modern critical view is that the Old Testament books were canon-
ized - whatever the dates of their writing - gradually and at a
comparatively late period. The canonization of the Law is placed at
about B. C. 400, that of the Prophets between B. C. 250 and B. C.
180, while the third division of the Jewish canon, the Writings, is
believed to have acquired canonical authority during the second and
first centuries B. C.

3. Formerly the order of the Old Testament books determined
largely the view of the development of Hebrew religion. Just as
in the New Testament the Gospels occupy first place, the Epistles
being expositions of the principles laid down in the Gospels, so it
was thought that the Law of the Pentateuch, coming from the hands
of Moses, served as the basis of the religious development of the
Hebrews during subsequent centuries. The prophets were looked upon
chiefly as expounders and interpreters of this Law. Modern
criticism has introduced a change of viewpoint. It does not deny
the pre-exilic existence of all law, or of sacrifice, or of a
ceremonial, or of other priestly elements, but it believes that in
the religious development of Israel, the pre-exilic period was
preeminently the period of the prophets, while the religious life
during the post-exilic period was dominated by the priests, the
priestly type of religion finding literary expression in the
ceremonial system embodied in the Pentateuch.

4. According to modern criticism, compilation had a prominent
place in the production of Old Testament books. The composite
character of the Pentateuch is touched upon in the next paragraph,
but, in addition, it is believed that there is sufficient evidence
to establish the composite character of practically all the other
historical books. McFadyen accurately represents the modern viewpoint when he says, "In the light of all these facts the general
possibility, if not the practical certainly, of the compositeness of
the historical books may be conceded," Evidences of compilation are
seen also in several of the prophetic books. The assignment of
Isaiah and Zechariah to more than one author each furnishes perhaps
the best known examples, but other prophetic books are similarly

534

divided.

5. The Pentateuch is no longer assigned in its entirety to Moses; it is thought, rather, to contain material selected from four different sources, which the compiler had before him in writing. These documents did not reach their final form until some time subsequent to Moses, but all of them contained ancient material, much of it going back to the time of Moses, some of it even to pre-Mosaic days. Among the contents of the Pentateuch special attention is called to three legal codes - the Book of the Covenant, the Deuteronomic Code, and the Priestly Code - belonging to different periods in Hebrew history, and reflecting different stages in the religious and social development of the nation. The Deuteronomic Code, in some form, is believed to have been the basis of the reforms instituted by Josiah and to have been written most probably during the early part of the seventh century. On these general questions respecting the Pentateuch there seems to be general agreement among critical scholars; on the other hand, there is wide divergence of opinion concerning points of detail, such as the chronological order in which the several documents reached their final form, their exact dates, the manner and time of their compilation, the detailed distribution of the material among the several sources, etc. The differences of opinion on these points are due to the fact that the data upon the basis of which the problems must be solved are not sufficiently numerous or decisive.

6. Doubt is thrown upon the authorship of a number of Old Testament books, or parts of books, which have been assigned to certain authors by both Jewish and Christian tradition.

¶   Sanctification in the Evangelical Church.

(Taken from S. J. Gamertsfelder, *Systematic Theology* (1913), 508-09, 516).

Under the preceding subject we have endeavored to set forth the Christian life as progressing from regeneration to the end of natural life. Entire sanctification must not be thought of as simply identical with, nor the acme of progressive sanctification. But we should rather look on entire sanctification as a definite state of Christian experience, a stage that has been preceded by a progressive Christian life, and that continues simultaneous with other new attainments in the Divine life of the soul.

By essential element we mean, that particular constituent ingredient, or form of activity, without which the attainment, whatever it may be, can not be properly called entire sanctification. Like all other stages of the Christian life entire sanctification, or perfect

535

love, can not be bounded as to details by the same lines for all believers. In regeneration the vigor of the spiritual life imparted
to one may vary greatly from the vigor imparted to another, although
the persons may have been brought up in the same environment and
under the same religious instruction. So also in the experience of
perfect love; the higher Christian life of one person may differ
widely from that of another as to details. Notwithstanding all this
diversity, there is a unity in essential element that justifies a
doctrinal statement of this stage of Christian experience. The
essential element of entire sanctification is the removal of certain
carnal remains that occasionally becloud the consciousness of being
a child of God, or weaken the disposition of holy love implanted
in regeneration.

*   *   *

The carnality that must be removed in entire sanctification is
not material substance. It can not be weighed nor measured, nor
handled with hands nor moved with a derrick. It is some form of
moral or ethical activity; it is evil tendencies and desires. The
only way to eradicate these evil tendencies and desires is to fill
the soul with good tendencies and desires. When these new affections
completely fill the soul and engage all its powers, there will be no
room for any evil affection to arise in the mind. That degree of
holy love which is sufficiently strong in present and enduring force
to drive out all evil tendencies and desires, is perfect love. When
that disposition of holy love which became the dominant power at the
new birth, has been made sufficiently strong by the Holy Spirit
to drive out all evil tendencies and desires, then the soul is made
perfect in love. One who has attained such an experience has the
victory over every sin inwardly and outwardly, and is so firmly
rooted and grounded in God that all selfishness is eradicated, and
he is perfectly resigned to the will of God.

¶   Harris Franklin Rall on Liberal Christianity and Premillennialism.

(Taken from *Modern Premillennialism and the Christian Hope* (1920),
219-24).

The method of God with man is that of freedom. There is one
rule over servants; there is another over sons. The servant yields
so much of time and toil; the son gives love and trust and all of
life in inner loyalty. But the deed of a son is a free deed. Here
is the transformation of religion, seen from afar by a Jeremiah (31.
33), set forth in word and life by Jesus, championed in his own way
by Paul in his fight against legalism and his great teaching of the
freedom of faith. The freedom of the Christian man is the freedom
of faith, an obedience that springs from inner conviction; and that

is but the human side that corresponds to God's method of appeal through the truth. And the freedom of the Christian man is the freedom of an inner life, whose obedience is the compulsion of his own spirit of love and loyalty; and this corresponds to the doctrine of the indwelling Spirit. That doctrine we must look at a moment again, for there is a misleading dualism which is always setting divine and human over against each other in mutual exclusion. This is the great truth about the Christian doctrine of the Spirit, that for the man who receives God the Spirit in him ceases to be an Other and becomes his own self. Paul struggles with the paradox: "I live...I no longer live...Christ liveth...I live" (Gal. 2.19, 20). The Spirit of God does not sweep away consciousness, thought, will; it is not the repression of the human but its realization. As never before a man can say, "I live." He knows that this new life is God's gift, but he knows equally that it is his own life. And so it is the life of freedom, the only free life; it is the expression of what is within, not the submission to something without.

The method of growth or development follows necessarily from what has preceded. God reaches man through the truth; no other way is possible with a moral being. But truth is always gradually apprehended. What we can perceive depends upon what we already have. The Bible as a whole shows this growth in clearest fashion. The most confirmed literalist will not take his ethics from Joshua or Judges. The method of God is that of education. To contrast education and regeneration is to put asunder what God has joined together. Education is the development of life through the truth. The truth is not the life but it is the door of entrance for it. Education is life-giving, not simply imparting facts and developing skill; but it gives the life through the truth. If the Spirit of God is to work in man ethically (as Holy Spirit) and not as bare force, then it must work this way (John 14.17, 26; 16. 13,14). And truth and grace thus come together, and both by growth (2 Pet. 3.18). Similarly, God's method in bringing the kingdom is one of growth because the kingdom is a matter of life.

The method of conflict and crisis has been too often overlooked by those who have emphasized the method of growth. There is a shallow optimism which talks as though the nature of all things were essentially good and some inner and necessary power were moving us all on to better days. That this is false any man may know who looks into his own heart or out upon the world. Goodness is not a drift; it is a choice and a struggle. The doctrine of the kingdom must deal with the fact of evil. There is a realm of evil that stands opposed to the kingdom of the good and of God. It is not necessary to share the elaborate demonologies of Jewish apocalyptics, but we must do justice to this fact. Three elements may be distinguished here:

1. There is the evil tendency of human nature which any man knows who seeks to serve the good. What constant struggle it takes to overcome the lure of the sensual, the tug of selfish desire, the swift onset of passion, or the dead weight of indifference and inertia!

2. There is the rule of false ideas and false ideals in the world, exercising their sway in wildest extent over individual and group. We note the delusion that the possession of things is the key of life. We think of the false goals that have lured whole nations to the ways of destruction. Looking out to-day, we see that the fall of Germany has not taught the peoples their lesson. There is the same dependence upon force, the same grasping after national advantage. Shantung and Fiume and the Saar Valley and Persia all have a word to say here, nor is the systematic effort to embroil the United States with Mexico without its meaning.

3. There is an intrenchment of evil in institutions and associations. Such embodiments of evil were once found in individuals; in Daniel it is Antiochus Epiphanes, in Revelation it is Nero. To-day no individual could play such a role. In Russia a corrupt bureaucracy was stronger than the Czar. The fateful force in Germany was not Kaiser Wilhelm; it was a combination of the Junkers, the militaristic group, and the jingoistic party of expansion. Economic exploitation, organized in many different forms, is perhaps the greatest single force obstructing the way of justice and freedom.

The opposition of evil means not only conflict but crisis, and sometimes revolution. The dammed-up waters of a swollen stream simply increase their power of pressure with resistance until they sweep everything before them. We are in the midst of such an epochal change; the World War was but an aspect of it, and the end is not yet in sight. The autocracy of economic privilege is doomed as truly as the autocracy of government, and it may be that the day has come for the passing of that long period in which strong peoples have exploited the weak, parceling the kingdoms of earth among themselves. Whether the new day will come through gradual change or with terrific and destructive revolution is not yet clear. History has known many such a crisis of deepest importance to the progress of the kingdom of God. Social organization is necessary for human life in every part, religious as well as political and economic. But history repeats the same story over and over again of institutions that cease to be instruments and become obstacles to humanity and to God. Deterioration, stagnation, petrifaction, appropriation by the few for selfish ends – these all occur to the institutions of society or to its organized social life, and revolution may have to solve the problem which does not yield to vital change. History has illustrations in abundance: Jerusalem and its temple, Roman empire, mediaeval church, the old French empire before the Revolution, and outstanding

instances of recent years whose tale may not yet be full. And quite aside from all this there are great crises when a day marks a change in the tide or brings forth forces whose work long generations will not exhaust.

Certain facts, however, must yet be noted. Revolution and crisis are always an organic part of history, related to what precedes and follows. God does not work from outside. The greatest event of human history, the coming of Jesus into the world, best illustrates this. Further, revolution itself may sweep aside obstruction, it cannot build up. And, finally, every day of great change, like this day, is a tremendous summons to faith and service. To-day old institutions are crumbling, life is in a flux, in places the stagnation of generations has yielded to mobility that responds to a touch. But all this of itself does not mean a new day. We look at international life and see governments that seem to be settling back into the old ways of selfish alliance, diplomatic intrigue, and the scramble for concessions and spheres of influence, while in the economic world the cries are being raised on both sides that range group against group with little sense of the larger life and larger justice for the while. Revolution is an opportunity, not a solution.

We are all agreed that the goal of God is social both for this world and the next. Whether we talk of the kingdom of God, of a new world, a new humanity, or a redeemed race, we are using social figures just as he does who speaks of a coming brotherhood. But the social goal can come only through social means. The social goal is a way of living together that involves love and truth and justice and patience and good will and cooperation. These are not abstract ideals. They can be learned only by practice, and only through long practice can they be built up in the relations of life and the institutions which embody them. Justice means justice learned and illustrated in industry. Love means a definite spirit and practice bodied forth in home and community. It is one of the childish superficialities of premillennialism that it overleaps such facts and steps at once from individual regeneration to a perfect social order.

¶   Sloan's Index.

(Taken from Harold Paul Sloan, *Historic Christianity and the New Theology* (1922), 30-31).

The Course of Study as at present constituted contains twenty-four books to be studied, and twenty-three to be read. Of the books to be studied, seven do not come up to the standard required by the law; and of those to be read, six do not.

The books provided for study that are defective are:

1. New Testament History, by Dr. Rall, of Garrett.
2. The Pupil and the Teacher, by Dr. Weigle.
3. The Graded Sunday School, by Dr. Meyer.
4. History of the Christian Church, by Dr. Walker, professor of Church History at Yale.
5. The Christian Pastor, by the late Dr. Gladden.
6. Introduction to the Study of Sociology, by Dr. Hayes, a professor in Illinois State University.
7. The Five Great Philosophies of Life, by Dr. Hyde, of Bowdoin College.

Not all of these books are to be criticised in equal degree, but we will not stop at this point with details. The books in the reading courses that are clearly out of accord with our standards, and so do not fulfil the law are:

1. The Main Points, by President Brown of Yale School of Religion.
2. How to Teach Religion, by Professor Betts of Northwestern.
3. Life of Luther, by President McGiffert, of Union.
4. Studies in Christianity, by Professor Bowne, late of Boston University.
5. Modern Pre-Millennialism, by Professor Rall, of Garrett.
6. Outline of Christian Theology, by Dr. Clarke, late of Colgate.

Here again the measure of failure, and even its character differs widely, but again we will pass by details for the present.

It will be immediately noticed that no books in the critical field are included in these lists. The explanation is that in our judgment no book in the courses is for critical reasons discordant with the constitutional standards of Methodism. There are several books the critical views of which do not appeal to this writer personally. But personal views are in no measure the basis of this criticism. The constitutional standards of Methodism define the headlands of faith as it has obtained in the Church from the beginning. Those headlands of belief are adequate to determine the essential Christian quality of any man's thought. Beyond this general outline is the sphere of private judgment. In these matters men can differ and remain properly Christian thinkers. Doubtless in this sphere of private judgment opinions will be proposed, that, when they have been developed and correlated will be found to be out of accord with the fixed headlands of Historic Christianity. When this appears, then these opinions must be surrendered.

One of the things our times needs to discover is how to relate liberty and orderliness. It is quite possible our earth is every day moving through spaces never traversed by it before, that it is every day exploring new vastnesses; yet its relation to the sun is constant. And is not this the analogy of our Christian faith of God Incarnate? Our relation to him, as fallen, lost men, whom he has redeemed by the Atonement of his cross; to whom we are united by faith and the inworking of his supernatural powers; whose salvation is forever a relationship of justification from the guilt of sin through his finished work, - this relationship is constant. This is the gospel he gave us through the apostles. This relationship, and those several truths that define it must be constant. An opinion that sacrifices this central relation, or any of the truths that define and secure it is not Christianity, and cannot honestly be called by its name. In this body of faith the Bible must be preserved as God's supernatural revelation, and a conception of that revelation must be held that secures the Messianic hope and all its great moral, spiritual and redemptive values; but the mechanics, if we might so speak, of this great revelational movement may be variously conceived.

¶   A Moderate Southern Voice.

(Taken from Wilbur F. Tillett, *The Paths That Lead to God* (1924), 63-65).

Theistic thought has undergone a change in recent years in its interpretation of God's relation to and government of the world. Traditional theology in its conception of God had much in common with deism. It conceived of the world as created by a personal God and placed under the reign of natural laws as "secondary causes," after which God removed himself, so to speak, to his dwelling place, which was separate and apart, and more or less distant, from the world. So far traditional theology was in accord with deism. But it differed with and from deism in saying that God was not only an observant and ever-interested spectator of what was going on in the world, but held himself ready to "come down" from heaven, his dwelling place, in answer to the prayers of men - or whenever, in the observing of human affairs, he found it wise to interfere with the ordinary operations of nature's laws and work miracles or "special providences." These special miraculous interventions of his power in the realm of natural law, and in the realm of human free agency in the form of answers to prayer and special providences, were looked upon as necessary in order to prove his existence and his presence and power in the government of the world. And these special visitations were thought to be more significant and impressive by the fact that he "came down" from a more or less distant dwelling place in the heavens to accomplish these displays of his power on the earth. This

541

traditional anthropomorphic type of theism placed its chief emphasis upon the transcendence of God - upon his separateness from our world, his aloofness, his "above-ness" - and might not improperly be designated as deistic theism.

Wherein now, let us ask, does modern Christian theism, as represented by its best interpreters and exponents, differ from this deistic theism of traditional theology? We answer, by transferring the whole emphasis in its conception of God's relation to the world from the transcendence to the immanence of the divine Power that not only created the world but sustains it by a relationship so essential and ceaseless that the world could no more continue without God than it could have begun to be without him. This transference of the emphasis from the transcendence to the immanence of God could not fail to result in a reinterpretation of God and of nature and the supernatural.

Seeing that much depends upon our understanding this doctrine of the Divine Immanence, if we are going to view God and nature with the eye of a modern Christian theist, it is necessary that we keep clearly in mind the points wherein pantheism, deism and deistic theism differ from this modern form of theism. It will be recalled, therefore, that pantheism affirms God's immanence, but denies his transcendence, while deism affirms his transcendence, but denies his immanence. But Christian theism teaches that God is both transcendent and immanent. By the term transcendence, when applied to God, is meant that the Divine Being is a person, separate and distinct from nature and above nature - "nature" being used here in its largest significance as including all created things. By the Divine Immanence is meant that God is in nature as well as over nature, and that the continuance of nature is as directly and immediately dependent upon him as is the origin of nature - indeed, by some, God's preservation of the created universe is defined as an act of "continuous creation." By the Divine Immanence is meant something more than omnipresence, which term, in itself alone, does not affirm any causal relation between God and the thing to which he is present, whereas the term immanence does affirm such causal relation.

By asserting the Divine Immanence, therefore, as expressing the mode of God's providential efficiency, we affirm that all created things are dependent upon him for continued existence, that the laws of nature have no efficiency apart from their Creator and Preserver, that God is to be sought and seen in all forms and phases of creaturely existence, in the natural as well as the supernatural and miraculous, that he is not only omnipresent but always and everywhere active both in the natural and the spiritual world, and that without him neither the material atom, nor the living organism, nor the rational soul, nor the vast universe of worlds, could have any being. He not only created all things, but "by him all things consist," that

is, by him all things are preserved in being. God's existence is not
dependent upon the existence of anything else; but everything that
exists is dependent upon him not only for its origin but for its
continuance in being. "In him we live and move and have our being" -
and in him, in some true sense, all things have their being.

¶   Edgar S. Brightman's God.

(Taken from *The Problem of God* (1930), 148-9; *The Finding of
God* (1931), 55-56, 114-16; *Is God a Person?* (1932), 55-58).

Let us first consider the evidence of the rationality of the
universe. Whatever shows the universe to be rational shows it to be
what one would expect from the handiwork of a Supreme Mind. It is
true that rationality is a very general term, and it does not
necessarily follow that a rational order in the universe implies such
a God as religion worships; but an irrational universe would exclude
the possibility of a God, and we must show the universe to be rational
if there is to be a God. An irrational God would be an untrust-
worthy God, that is, no God at all.

Is the universe rational? Does it embody laws and meanings
which mind can discover? It seems like a vast and proud assumption
of human reason to assert that the entire universe, past, present,
and future, conforms to a reason in some way akin to the human.
Yet human reason is a real part of the universe and must partake of
the nature of the whole in some measure. When we object to thinking
of the universe as in any way anthropomorphic, we forget that man is
to some extent cosmomorphic; the same laws are everywhere. Yet can
we be sure that the same laws are everywhere? Do we know with absolute certainty that the universe is not a lawless chaos? We know in
part. All knowledge of what extends beyond the present moment of
experience rests on faith in reason. If we accept this faith in
reason, we build up an ever-increasing body of scientific knowledge,
of moral law, and of religious insight. By distrusting reason, we
can undermine science or morality or religion. But if we distrust
reason, we have taken away the basis from skepticism itself; for
doubt which rests on no reason is meaningless. It is both logically
and practically necessary for us to trust reason and to assume the
rationality of the universe. It is only on the basis of this
assumption that science can lay claim to having found any laws which
extend at all beyond the data that have actually been examined.

*   *   *

First of all, there is one respect in which religion plainly needs
reason, namely, in the very idea of God. If there is a God at all, he
must be reasonable. To be reasonable means ideally to be self-con-

543

sistent and coherent, to take everything into account and to perceive the interrelations of all things. If the Supreme Being were to be thought of as self-contradictory or incoherent or as failing to observe some of the facts and relations in the universe, such a Being could not be regarded as a God. Irrationality or ignorance would disqualify him as an object of worship. If he cannot be trusted to understand, he cannot be trusted to save, and only a Savior-God can be worshiped.

It would seem to follow that, if there is a reasonable God, reason must be a road to him. Of course God must be thought of as far above man. But that is true in every respect and not as regards reason alone. Some seek to discredit reason, yet to save some other approach to the divine, such as intuition or emotion. But if reason be rejected because human reason is inferior to divine reason, then there is equally good ground for rejecting every human approach to God on the ground that every human experience is inferior to divine experience. It is difficult to escape the suspicion that the way of reason is avoided because it involves hard thinking rather than because God's reason is so superior to man's.

History shows that many who have sought God by reason have found him. Plato and Aristotle, St. Thomas and Bishop Berkeley, Leibniz and Hegel, and many others, actually reached conviction about God through reason. It is not the task of the present Chapter to point out the details of the arguments or the ways by which reason may find God. The present author has shown how his own thought moves in *The Problem of God*. But each individual must wrestle with the rational approach to God in such fashion as his own mind requires. We are now concerned, not to trace the stages of thought in its intellectual fight for divine truth, but rather to interpret the religious value of reason.

*   *   *

In the second place, experience shows that if man acts on the hypothesis that there is a God, he finds that there is a power operative in himself and in the world which is able to save him from the real evil of his situation. That power does not, it is true, save him from all suffering or from the weakness of humanity, its frailty and the death of the body. It does not give him all, or nearly all, that his heart desires. But it does for him the central thing: it saves him from the misery of despair and self-condemnation. The divine power works in no magic way. Its relation to man is personal; that is, in so far as man seeks for that power by every avenue of his own personality, he finds it reenforcing his thought, his feeling, and his will. And religious experience feels this power to be good — a power of love and forgiveness, as well as a source of strength.

What sort of God, then, is the God to whom religious experience leads? In the nature of the case, it must be a finite God. No possible experience could reveal unlimited and absolute power. The God who has worked throughout man's religious history has been sufficient to save those that called upon him; but he could not demonstrate omnipotence if he would. Every demonstration to a finite being like man must assume a finite form. The God revealed in experience, then, is a God powerful enough to lead the world toward higher and higher levels, yet, if we are to believe the evidence of experience, not powerful enough to do it without great difficulty; for, just as the higher forms of biological life are achieved slowly and with pain and loss in the evolutionary process, so the higher forms of spiritual life are also developed gradually and under great difficulties.

The God suggested by religious experience, then, is a spirit contending against obstacles. The obstacles cause pain and delay but not defeat or frustration. There is no adequate basis for the fear that the good spirit of God is so weak that sometime he will cease to struggle. "He will not fail or be discouraged." Every reason for any belief in God is a reason for belief that he controls both matter and spirit (whatever "matter" and "spirit" may be) as instruments through which his purposes are eventually realized. Yet the same evidence which indicates a spirit at work in nature also indicates the presence of mysterious obstacles to the fulfillment of spiritual ends.

*   *   *

If the attacks on the personality of God have failed, it is still possible that faith in a personal God may also fail, and that we shall be left in utter skepticism. Yet there is no virtue in a skeptical conclusion unless we are driven to it by intelligence.

Let us, then, ask what a personal God means in terms of the actual experiences of today. What I am about to say is not intended as an argument. It is simply a statement of the meaning of the idea of God for experience.

To call God personal is to hold that the functions of conscious personality are present in him to the highest possible degree. Those functions are feeling, thought, and will. If we approach God through feeling, he is our comfort. If we approach him through thought, he implies a criticism of our entire civilization. If we approach him through will, he is the principle of cosmic progress.

In so far as we think of God as a feeling person, as was just said, we think of him as a source of comfort. This is not all that his feeling means to us, and certainly not all that it means to him; but it is the central meaning. It is interesting to speculate as to

what would happen in the modern world if mankind were to become convinced that God actually feels love for his world. Is there anything that the world needs more than such comfort? If every human being were to experience the hope and joy that would grow out of such a love, it is impossible to predict the changes that would come over individuals, homes, and nations. The despair of the world would be at an end as soon as men could believe that the supreme power of the universe is a loving person. The hope that would spring up on that basis would be no groundless optimism, for it might well perceive that the love of God was also a suffering love, symbolized by a cross. If God is love, as well as power, no suffering in the whole universe is meaningless, no situation is hopeless. God is the power that cannot be defeated, and his love means that permanent defeat is impossible for anyone who truly loves him and works with him.

The comfort that comes from faith in God, however, is at bottom spiritual in nature, and is not always what is called "creature comfort," that is, material comfort. God is no agent of what we Americans call prosperity. He does not promise health and wealth and success to all who love him. The curses of the twenty-eighth chapter of Deuteronomy do, indeed, declare that pestilence, consumption, fever, inflammation, fiery heat, the sword, blasting, and mildew, will all come upon the unfaithful, whereas believers will be blessed and preserved. But the deeper insight of Jesus teaches that material consequences do not thus follow upon spiritual qualities, for the sun shines and the rain falls on the just and the unjust alike. The loving God has no interest in bribing us to love him, or in making spiritual devotion a mere means to material prosperity. His love has our true and permanent welfare at heart far more than our doctor's bills or our bank account. We experience his comfort only when we long to become like him, not when we demand that he shall be like us.

There is another restriction, besides the one just mentioned, on the spiritual comfort which we can derive from the love of God: that is, that we can find spiritual comfort for our life of feeling only when we can believe in God sincerely with our intellect. This does not mean that every believer must be a philosopher or a theologian; to demand that would be nonsense. It does mean, however, that every believer must be intellectually honest. No religious value is derived from a pious fraud or a sacrifice of the intellect; there is no comfort in an emotional uplift which is based on ideas that the intelligence must reject. The idea of divine personality does not mean merely that there is a vast reservoir of cosmic emotion; it means also that there is a cosmic reason, a mind with rational ideas and ideals.

¶ Edwin Lewis Drops a Bombshell.

(Taken from "The Fatal Apostasy of the Modern Church," *Religion in Life*, II (1933), 483-92).

Modern theological liberalism undoubtedly rendered the church an important service. It helped to break the strangle-hold of terms and phrases which had become in all too many cases merely empty shibboleths. It re-established, after the fashion of the thirteenth century, the rights of the intellect in the evaluation of the things of the spirit. It garnered for the use of the church the rich harvest of scholarship in many fields - biblical, historical, sociological, psychological. It served notice to a world too often skeptical that a man could believe in Jesus and at the same time be fully aware of all the amazing kaleidoscopic changes occurring in contemporary life. For such a service we cannot but be grateful. Nevertheless, all is not well with us. Liberalism has not brought us to the Promised Land. We may have gained a battle, but the campaign is still on, and there is more than a suspicion that the gain made at one point involved a serious loss elsewhere. We yielded positions whose strategic significance is becoming more and more manifest. We so stressed the Bible as coming to us in "the words of men" that the sense in which it is also "the word of God" has become increasingly vague. We so freely allowed the influence of contemporary forces in the development of doctrine as to have endangered the continuity of that living core of truth and reality for which contemporary forces were but the *milieu*. We exposed all the delicate nuances of spiritual experience to the cold dispassionate gaze of psychology, until it has become a question whether psychology of religion is not in danger of destroying the very thing it lives by. And in particular we were so determined to recover for the church "the human Jesus" that we lost sight of the fact that the church is the creation of "the divine Christ," or at least of faith in Christ as divine. Have we sown the wind, and is the whirlwind now upon us?

*　　　*　　　*

THE ORIGINAL CHRISTIAN MESSAGE

The Christian "facts" are not to be limited to what fell between Bethlehem and Calvary. What was then said and done was but part of a larger whole - of a movement taking place within the very being of God. Men believed that this was implied in the indubitable historical and experiential facts. They therefore wrought out the idea of "pre-existence" as applied to their Lord, identified him as the permanently active occasion of that life of fellowship in which the church as they knew it was constituted, and from this were led on step by step to formulate finally the doctrine of the Trinity. It is easy enough to complain that this was to transform "the simple Gospel" into a *Weltanschauung*, yet we have no evidence that the so-called simple Gospel was ever preached, even at the beginning, apart from at least

547

some of the elements of this philosophy. Not that unlettered apostles suddenly found themselves possessed of a full-blown philosophy that answered all questions in the world and out of it. But they were making affirmations of such an astounding character as that inevitably before long took to themselves coherence, and the original Christocentric religion became a Christocentric philosophy.

As to this, the New Testament is the evidence, and the New Testament reflects the life and faith of the primitive church. Here we read of a God who had an eternal purpose respecting mankind, a purpose that had to do specifically with delivering men from the power of sin and bringing them to holiness. We read that such a deliverance could not be an arbitrary act upon the part of God, since in all that he does he must be true to the demand of his own holy nature. We read that God himself was so constituted that he could enter in the most intimate and personal way into the stream of human life both to experience all its limitations and struggles and to establish within the stream the principle of its purification, and that the point of this entry was the man Jesus, who would never have existed at all but for the eternal purpose of God. We read that the ensuing intimacy of relationship between the Eternal God and this human life was such that the experience of the man thereupon became the experience of God - which makes it actually true to say that the Infinite knows finitude, that the All-Holy knows moral trial, that the Creator knows creatureliness, that the Deathless knows death. We read that therefore something has "happened" to God which makes his relation to men different from what it would have been had this *not* "happened." And we read that henceforth in speaking of God men may speak of him as One who was in Christ reconciling the world unto himself: therefore the Christian God is God suffused with all the qualities men saw in Jesus, and a God so suffused and transformed is also that divine Christ who is the very source and center of the life of the redeemed.

What then is the object of Christian faith? Not a man who once lived and died, but a Contemporary Reality, a God whose awful holiness is "covered" by one who is both our representative and his, so that it is "our flesh that we see in the Godhead," that "flesh" which was historically Jesus of Nazareth but is eternally the divine Christ whose disclosure and apprehension Jesus lived and died to make possible. I do not deny for a single moment that this overwhelming conception lent itself to all sorts of crudities of expression, impossible analogies, and gross materialisms. But he is blind indeed who cannot see what the New Testament is trying to say. Though language were not adequate to the thought, we can see what the thought aimed to be. It was that thought that created and sustained the church, and the church languishes to-day because it has substituted that thought with one of lesser power as it is of lesser

power as it is of lesser truth.

THE REPUDIATION OF CHRISTIANITY

Many reasons are alleged for the modern turning away from Christianity as thus understood. Not one of these reasons can touch its intrinsic credibility. A philosophical view that precludes it is quite possible. A philosophical view that allows for it is equally possible. Why is the first view so generally accepted? Because Christianity, with the view of things it necessarily calls for, makes such a terrific onslaught upon human pride. We would fain be self-sufficient, and this means that we are not. We would fain be the masters of our fate and the captains of our souls, and this says that our fate is in another's hands and that our souls are not our own but have been bought with a price. We do not like Christianity, not because it is intrinsically incredible but because it is so vastly humiliating. We do not *want* it to be true that "the Son of Man came to give himself a ransom for many," and so we find "critical" reasons for doubting that the words were ever spoken - as though by proving that Jesus did not say them we should prove that they were not true! We do not *want* it to be true that "the Word became flesh and dwelt among us": therefore we get rid of one of the most profound, heart-searching, and revolutionary truths ever uttered - the truth which must always be the touchstone of any proposed Christology - by the simple device of labeling it "Platonism." We do not *want* it to be true that "through one act of righteousness the free gift came unto all men to justification of life": this being so, we ask by what right Paul "distorted" the simple Gospel of brotherhood and service and good will by introducing into it misleading analogies from temple and law-court.

No; we do not like Christianity. We do not like its cosmic audacity. We do not like its moral pessimism. We do not like the way it smashes the beautiful orderliness of our metaphysical systems. We do not like its uncompromising insistence on the possibility of our being damned souls, whose only hope is in the sovereign grace of God - a God who voluntarily endured self-immolation as the cost of his own graciousness. We be *men* - men whose prerogative it is to stand before God, face him without a tremor, and *demand*; not slaves whose duty it is to kneel before him with covered face, humbly and reverently and gratefully to *accept*. Away with this doctrine of grace! Away with this whole mythology of Incarnation! Away with this outworn notion of Atonement! Make way for emancipated man!

THE PLIGHT OF THE CHURCH

But in this pride lies our shame, our weakness, and our defeat. What has it done for us? What has it done for the church - at least, for evangelical Protestantism? How far have we gotten with our various

substitutes? Look over our churches: they are full of people who, brought up on these substitutes, are strangers to those deeper experiences without which there had been no New Testament and no Church of Christ. Thousands of clergymen will go into their pulpits next Sunday morning, but not as prophets. There will be no burning fire shut up in their bones, by reason of which they cannot forbear to speak. Those who come to listen will not be brought face to face with eternal verities. Hungry sheep will look up, but will not be fed. Men harassed with a thousand problems and seeking not inexpert advice on how to solve them but the sense of another world in whose light they can see this one and find strength to cope with it and remold it nearer to the heart's desire, will go away as impotent as they came for anything the preacher has to say. Grievous is the hurt of the daughter of God's people, and slight is the proffered healing. They go to Gilead, and there is no balm. They go to the fountain of waters, and they find there a broken cistern. They cry for bread, and behold a stone.

And to a large extent, this plight of the church is traceable to a weakening of its dogmatic basis. Whether the phrase, "humanitarian Christology," is defensible or not is a question. Unless Christ is conceived as one who "stands on the divine side of causality in effecting redemption," it is difficult to see why we need a doctrine of him at all. If Jesus is not specifically related to God's eternal purpose to enter sacrificially the stream of our humanity, to the end that he might thereby change its direction and set it flowing toward himself, then we no more need a doctrine of Jesus than we need a doctrine of Jeremiah or a doctrine of Paul. There is no permanent resting-place between *some form* of the Logos Christology and a "humanitarian Christology" (allowing the phrase) which in effect surrenders the whole idea of direct divine sacrificial saving activity. And what we mean theologically by a Logos Christology we mean practically by a Christ-centered religion rather than a "religion of Jesus." If the emulation of "the religion of Jesus" were presented as the possible end of a Christ-centered faith, that would be different. What we are actually doing, however, is supposing that unregenerate men can be "like Jesus"! Even a casual acquaintance with great sections of modern Protestantism makes it evident that it has departed very widely from the Christocentric emphasis. We must recover that emphasis, or perish. The divine Christ saved the human Jesus from disappearing, and if the human Jesus is to continue to mean for men all that he should, it must still be through the divine Christ. Christ must continue to save Jesus!

It is not that men cannot live "the good life" without faith in the divine Christ. It is not that there cannot be a profound appreciation of the character of Jesus without it. But Christianity does not consist simply in the good life and in moral appreciation and endeavor. It *is* this, of course. One of the incredible

suppositions of our day is that the only persons who are interested in the wellbeing of their fellows are the so-called "humanists." No one who really knows what Christianity has done for the world could possibly make that supposition. . . .

Yes; Christocentric religion means human devotion carried to its ultimate issue - say a Damien with a crucifix on his breast the while he dresses the rotting stumps of a leper, a Damien who, as R. L. Stevenson says in his noble defense of the man, "shut to with his own hand the doors of his own sepulcher." But it means an "experience" as well - an experience falling within that "unleaguerable fortress" of the innermost soul "whose keys are at the cincture hung of God," and which is something one can better know for oneself than describe to another. And this experience, whence comes it? It comes of *belief*. If we are going to psychologize religion, well and good; but by what imaginable psychological process can there be "spiritual experience" completely independent of all intellectual assent? It were absurd to say that Christianity is *only* credal; to say that it is in no sense credal would be equally false. And to say that "it does not matter what one believes" so long as one "lives the good life" and "has a religious experience" reveals rather an amazing *naiveté* than any profound insight into the life-movement.

But what *does* the modern church believe? The church is becoming creedless as rapidly as the innovators can have their way. The "Confession of Faith" - what is happening to it? Or what about the "new" confessions that one sees and hears - suitable enough, one imagines, for, say, a fraternal order. And as for the Apostles' Creed - "our people will not say it any more": the Virgin Birth and the resurrection of the body, have elected the easy way of believing in nothing at all - certainly not in "the Holy Catholic Church." So we are going to allow them to be satisfied with "The Social Creed of the Churches," quite forgetful of the fact that unless the church has a "religious" creed besides a "social" creed the church as such will cease to exist long before it has had time to make its "social" creed effective in the life of the world. "But the social creed *is* religious." Yes; but has its religion proved dynamic enough, impelling enough, to maintain itself at the high point - the Himalayanly high point - necessary to make its creed effective? The church has set itself to do more at the very time that it is lessening its power to do anything.

"WHAT MUST WE DO TO BE SAVED?"

The church, especially the American evangelical churches, must re-enthrone Christ, the divine Christ, in the life and thought of the people, or cease to exist. Not that the church merely as an institution is the necessary desideratum. But the church in the

high New Testament sense of "the body of Christ" - this *must* be saved for the sake of the world. Here is the world's one redeeming force because here is the world's one redeeming message - if the message be *complete*. It is that completeness whose lack is the secret of our impotence. Can we recover it? Nay rather, do we here highly resolve that we *will* recover it? Let us be done with compromise, and let us affirm - affirm magnificently, affirm audaciously. Let us affirm God - his unchanging love for men, his unchanging hatred of sin, his sacrificial presence in all the life and work of Jesus. Let us affirm Christ - Christ as the meaning of God, Christ as what God *is* in virtue of that mysterious "kenosis" by which he made himself one with a human life, and at the same time that he was doing the utmost he could do for men endured the worst - a Cross - that men could do against him. Let us affirm the Spirit - the divine concern to bring to bear upon the hearts and consciences of men the impact of what God in Christ has done and is forever doing on their behalf, to the end that they may be moved to repentance, to that faith which ensures forgiveness, to that love which brings moral empowerment, and to that surrender of the will which makes God's purposes their purposes. Let us affirm the church - the community of the redeemed, those who in all their life seek the regnancy of the spirit of Jesus, carrying on and extending the mystery of the Incarnation against that day when God, the Christ-God, shall be all and in all. Let us affirm the Kingdom - the Christianizing of life everywhere, children with straight backs and happy faces, women released from drudgery and set free for creative living, industry conducted for the good of all, war and kindred evils done away, racial antipathies lost in a universal brotherhood, the rich heritage of culture made available to the last man. O there is no limit to the affirmations, and better still, no limit to the dynamic needful to make them effective, once we grasp the profound structural coherence of Christianity, the wide sweep of its thought, the absoluteness of its demands, the revolutionary results of its consistent application. "That in all things he, who is the image of the invisible God, might have the pre-eminence."

"O Church of Rome, would that thy creed were sound!" So cried Newman, distracted, uncertain, seeking a light amid the encircling gloom. But his lament was too narrow in its reference. O Church of Christ *everywhere*, on the avenue, down the side-street, in the town-square, at the country cross-roads, would that thou believedst as thou should! For of believing comes feeling, and of feeling comes being, and of being comes doing.

Not willingly does one write what has here been written. It may be so easily misunderstood, by friend and by foe alike. If there be any extenuation, it is in the prophet's simile: "The lion hath roared: who will not fear? The Lord Jehovah hath spoken: who can but prophesy?"

Edwin Lewis and Back to Basics.

(Taken from A *Christian Manifesto* (1934), 199-201, 215-16).

I would not presume to be critical of the church in general as
respects matters such as these, but I may perhaps be conceded the
right to speak frankly of the particular church to which I happen to
belong. Concerning that church at least, I am sure I am not wrong
when I say that we have too generally abandoned the passion which
was once our glory and which had no great difficulty in finding
appropriate avenues of expression: we have abandoned this passion for
carefully worked-out programs which had "efficiency" written all
over them, but which have been strangely futile in keeping the fires
burning on the altars of the church and in bringing the gospel to
bear in an overwhelming way on the life of the world. I have what
I believe is a justly grounded pride in the history and achievements
of Methodism, the church in which I was cradled and to which I have
given my life. It has written a great chapter in the story of
Christian conquest. It has done a work for Jesus Christ second to
none done by any other branch of Protestantism. In the Old World
and in the New, and in the lands beyond the seas, it has borne a
valiant and successful testimony to the power of the Evangel in the
transformation of human lives and in the creation of social institutions which seek the good of men. It can be only a question of time
before the Methodist Church as such must cease to exist as a separate
entity and be gathered up into a reunited Protestantism - dare one
say even a reunited Christendom? But its contribution when that
day comes will be of value in proportion to its continued loyalty to
the spirit and the faith and the purpose in which it had its origin.
And what we have seen in recent years all along the line has been a
weakening of that loyalty because we have fallen victim to the lure
of grandiose schemes whose counterparts in the secular world are the
hundred-story skyscraper, the vast corporation whose energies head up
at the cash register, the advertising "drive" aimed to reach "the
last man" by whatever means may be. Anyone who knows the life of our
church for the last twenty years or so knows that under the goading
of the "experts" we have adopted scheme after scheme, participated in
drive after drive, set ourselves even the impossible task of making
America "dry" by legislation, and the total result of the prodigious
efforts - what is it? That there is some gain in the total need not
be denied, but there has certainly been much more of loss. We have
created in the minds of many a totally false conception of the nature
and the function of the Christian Church.

*   *   *

There is nothing for us to do, when we find ourselves in a blind
alley, but to go back. And go back the church must, or go down. I
do not mean go back in the sense of surrendering all our new and

improved technique of instruction and action and service. Not for nothing is the new psychology. Not for nothing is historical criticism. Not for nothing is better church architecture. Not for nothing is the demand for more reverent worship. Not for nothing is the awakened social conscience. If anyone supposes that what I have here written implies indifference to things such as these, then either I have written very carelessly, or he has so read. The church has a right to commandeer for its purpose the best that we can find. When, therefore, I say, go back, I do not mean back to a primitivism of method and of expression. But I do mean go back to the message of original Christianity - the message of God's atoning and redeeming love for a lost world, the message that puts a new value on every human soul and gives to it a new meaning, the message that transforms a fallen and sin-doomed creature into a potential son of God, a potentiality that becomes actualized according as by faith Christ is formed anew in the believer's life. It is to the proclamation of that message that the church is called to return - and, let it be added, to an incarnation of the message in such forms as we wish. We may bring to our assistance every bit of psychological insight that we can muster. But if we want to see a redeemed world, this is the only way by which it can come to pass. It cannot come by buildings and programs and drives and machinery of one sort and another. These things have their rightful place, but only as instruments - and not altogether indispensable instruments even at that. When you bring a man to the place where Jesus Christ is the ruling power in his life, you have done something for him for which there is no substitute; you have caused a new center to be set up from which will flow into the life of the world healing and light.

¶   Francis J. McConnell Reviews *A Christian Manifesto*.

(Taken from *Religion in Life*, III (1934), 614-18).

It has been in order for some time for somebody to do something of the sort which Professor Lewis has done in *A Christian Manifesto*. The book is a vigorous, not to say passionate reaffirmation of the truths which Doctor Lewis thinks essential in Christianity. In more than one prominent theological school in our country to-day some teachers of systematic theology have given up theism altogether; others have watered the idea of God down into an impersonal process and others seem afraid even to use the word God. As long as we have a situation like this it is just as well for men like Doctor Lewis to speak up. Protests like *A Christian Manifesto* help clear the air.

I do not think I have ever seen a stronger or better statement of the fundamental trustworthiness of the scriptural revelation with a franker recognition of the fallibility and error of the human

channels through which such a revelation must come. The book is not afraid of the critical, historical, scientific scrutiny of every detail of the scriptures: in fact, it would go farther than most of us would in accepting the results of all such investigations. The implications of many things Doctor Lewis says are not for the intellectually panicky. The timid soul who, having heard that this book is orthodox, expects to find in it re-enforcement of such dogmas as scriptural infallibility, for example, will get the scare of his life. Yet the book is the best statement I have ever seen of the position that a doctrine like that of the divinity, or, if you prefer, of the deity of Christ, can be made credible and faith-compelling by erring and faulty human utterance. Again, the book is irresistible in its insistence that the strength of the church has always lain in its acceptance of this view of Christ as divine.

Through incessant practice Doctor Lewis has wrought out a fine style for religious utterance. There is a swing about it which carries us along. Speaking for myself, however, I find the style of this book interfered with by the author's constant reference to his consciousness that what he is saying is not in line with current, popular theological discussion. He feels that the modernists will criticize him - that he has said things hard to be accepted by liberals - that he will appear as inconsistent with previous utterances of his own. All of which gets annoying after a time. Professor Lewis has made his own way - and won an assured position as a thinker in his own right. Even if the modernists, so-called, do not accept it, the book has to be reckoned with.

With my full agreement with the need of a book like this, and with hearty thanks for the greatness of the service rendered in the main points of the treatment, may I call attention to some suggestions which seem to me important. To begin with there is over-exact statement of some truths - or shadowing-forths of truths which are better hinted at than definitely stated. For example, Doctor Lewis takes direct issue with the claim that children are by birth citizens of the kingdom of God, and need chiefly Christian nurture. Children, it seems, are born under the divine wrath and have to be saved by a virtually miraculous operation of grace. All I wish to say about this particular item of theology is that to one who knows Doctor Lewis it is not nearly as terrifying as it sounds. Let no one think that our author is on the path back to the belief that hell is paved with infants' skulls. What we have here is a sturdy belief in the righteousness of God - with perhaps not quite so thorough-going a belief in the divine grace. Now when a writer says that God creates human souls in wrath, we get that stiff idea in our heads. When we have to wait till the next chapter or even till the next sentence to hear about a grace that will go to the last limit to save men from wrath, we have two qualities - or attributes - or forces - or somethings - set over against each other in the

divine nature. The Christian truth is that God is a person. He is righteous and he is loving - terms which taken as descriptions give us no particular trouble, for we see human beings who are at the same time measurably righteous and loving. Now let me talk sharply of wrath and then of love, and the abstractions take the field - with the Divine Person the stage where the abstractions do whatever the logical, dogmatic, over-confident intellect calls for. Doctor Lewis says in this book that he wants more iron in theology. Quite right, if we are to use the iron as a tonic. We do not, however, need any more cast-iron, after the fashion of a rigid frame in which divine qualities are to be set.

Again, *A Christian Manifesto* seems to me to over-emphasize the divine sovereignty. The God of Lewis is a fairly gritty Being. Upon occasion, we are told, he can do quite a bit of smashing. Here again it was time that somebody said this - or something like it. Doctor Lewis does not have overmuch to say about the Fatherhood of God. I am not sure that I wonder at this, for I recognize the force of somebody's jibe that in our soft day the preaching of the divine fatherhood has become the preaching of the divine grandfatherhood - with all the suggestiveness of a grandfather's doddering inability to mark sharp distinctions between right and wrong - and to treat right and wrong differently. Still, if we are going to use terms like sovereignty, we may well consider more carefully the obligations of sovereignty. Doctor Lewis says repeatedly that God has a right to create - I suppose a right to create in wrath but I let this "suppose" pass as a quibble, if the reader chooses. Now has God a right to create? If I may speak as confidently about cosmic and divine ethics as this book does, I say he has no right whatever to create, *unless he is willing to undertake and discharge the obligations thereby assumed.* Obligations to whom? Obligations to those whom he has created. That ought to be enough. There are other obligations, I should think - obligations to the creator's own self-respect, and to the moral approval of any intelligences anywhere. Professor Lewis uses in quotation marks an expression that I have been fond of using - though I do not flatter myself that he knew that the expression is a favorite of mine - the frontiersman's protest against the Calvinistic statement of divine sovereignty to the effect that "the people won't stand it," The Lewis comment is that the people will have to stand it. We are likewise informed that Christianity does not declare to men the alternative of yielding or not but says "Yield."

Surely this is the real thing in dogmatism. Nevertheless, situations like this cannot be solved by emphasis. The historic fact is that the people have not stood for some statements of divine sovereignty. If we left out of the history of the church recognition of those who would not yield to statements of arbitrary divine sovereignty no stronger than those of this book, we should have some

notable omissions - especially when we count in those who would not bow down to the abominable, privileged and established orders which always flourish in the shelter of these stern statements of divine sovereignty. Professor Lewis's predecessor, Dr. Olin A. Curtis, used to like to quote from Mark Twain's *Huckleberry Finn*. Perhaps with such a Drew precedent before me, I may be permitted to refer to the same classic. At one crisis in the book, Huck Finn is in terrible inner torment because he is helping "Nigger Jim" to escape from slavery. He feels that he will go to hell if he keeps on in such a nefarious course. At last Huck rises to the heroic with the avowal: "All right, then, I'll go to hell." Whereupon his soul was filled with peace. In other like crises, others of mightier historic significance than Huck have found peace in the same way.

Again, *A Christian Manifesto* rather makes light of the statement that we human beings are in this world not of our own choice. Well - the statement happens to state a fact. It is the attitude toward such statements which makes me wonder whether Professor Lewis knows what is back of the widespread distrust of such doctrines of divine sovereignty as his to-day. The truth is that the thinking of hosts upon hosts of honest and earnest people who have lost their hold on Christianity - or on whom Christianity has lost its hold - starts just there, that we are here not of our own choice. They will not share in Doctor Lewis's preference to be damned for the glory of the most old-fashioned Calvinistic notion of God rather than for the glory of whatever bit of material is man's ancestor, in the materialistic basis. They will not accept the Calvinistic God in any case. They may look on themselves as the outcomes of the play of blind forces but they do not necessarily hate those forces. They accept things as they are, things in a desperateness of condition which Doctor Lewis has himself most eloquently stated elsewhere. Men have been on the earth a long time and the majority of them have not up to date found the conditions of proper human existence. The logic of the denial of God would seem to call for frank materialism in conduct - which is what we do not find in persons of the type I have in mind; persons who labor with an undying zeal for the help of their fellows; persons who do not ask how the good and true and beautiful got before us in this strange existence but who accept these as impressive values now that they are here. Moreover, the devotion of some of these mistaken persons to human welfare is so great that in opposition to war, for illustration, they do go to prison and are willing to go to death. They cannot accept an arbitrary sovereign without hating him. They can accept a primordial atom ancestor without hate. It is all illogical, but we have the warrant of this book itself for the idea that in the deeper spiritual crises logic is not the final arbiter. Of course, sovereignty conceived of as the relation of the Father of our Lord Jesus Christ to his children is another matter. In that sovereignty, Doctor Lewis himself believes and works. What he says about smashing, and having

to stand it, and divine condemnation, and all similar matters has to be qualified by the whole trend of his system, in which we can find plenty of grace and mercy. The trouble is that Doctor Lewis is so much more eloquent when he is talking about smashing than when he is talking about grace, that we remember the smashing longer. In one place or another the reader can find passages which will answer every criticism that can be urged against *A Christian Manifesto*. In a long burst of almost furious eloquence, we have an invective against the church for its apostasy in this, that, and the other. Then a little later we discover that the author is in favor of all these things - except possibly legislative prohibition and legislative socialism. Of course, there is no sense in being too exacting when an author becomes eloquent. In spite, however, of the passionate burst against apostasy by the church, one can hardly keep one's face straight to hear the prohibitionist classified with the apostates. All the section inveighing against the recent large-program activities of Methodism is oratory - good oratory - but oratory just the same. Methodists all can make the proper discount. One form of our apostasy was the attempt to get so much more for grandiose schemes, which was admittedly a mistake. Inasmuch, however, as it was all conceived in good faith, and carried on as far as possible in good faith, and represented the honest self-sacrifices of millions of people, the word "apostasy" seems to be merely one of those terms which a man grabs at when he is making a speech. If I may say so without being intentionally unfair, a good deal of our most famous and most successful campaigning - our Centenary - aimed at aiding our theological schools. If that is apostasy, let us make the most of it.

Well, so much for "sovereignty and apostasy!" All that to one side, there are superb passages in *A Christian Manifesto*. Whether we agree with all the author's conclusions or not at disputed points, we may be confident that we shall never find them better stated. Nobody that I know of has ever phrased better the significance of the Atonement for God Himself. Moreover, whatever we think about the Trinity, I believe we shall have to admit that the following putting is about perfect of its kind - in profundity, in comprehensiveness, in perspective: "In essence, the Trinity means that the Eternal God is the subject of a necessary process of self-differentiation, which he can no more prevent than he can prevent his own existence, and which results in his containing within himself all the elements of a complete personal experience."

23. DENOMINATIONAL DEVELOPMENT

In the midst of global change and theological upheaval the three main branches of Methodism continued their institutional movement into the twentieth century. Many of the issues they faced were inherited from the previous century. Among them was the role of the historic itinerant ministry in a society increasingly inhospitable to this roving form of witness. The bishops of the Methodist Episcopal Church took rueful note of this problem in their address before General Conference in 1912. One of those bishops was Edwin Holt Hughes, who began thirty-two active years in that office in 1908. In his winsome autobiography he recalls the particular qualities of some of his fellow bishops.

One of the important developments in the place of women in the new century was the Wesleyan Service Guild, an organization which early recognized the significance of working women in the life of the church. It began in 1920 and continued until the formation of United Methodist Women as a result of the merger with the Evangelical United Brethren.

Southern Methodism retained its special character through the early years of the new century. The gradual changes which made possible the reunion of 1939 are succinctly summarized by Robert W. Sledge in his doctoral research, which was published as the Jesse Lee Prize in 1975.

Painful memories of the debates over reunion of North and South during the years of World War I were revived as the three branches struggled toward formation of The Methodist Church. Much of that pain came into the open at the General Conference of the M. E. Church in 1936, where the plan of union was approved by a heavy margin. Lewis O. Hartman was then in the midst of his twenty-four years as editor of Zion's Herald. E. F. Tittle was nationally renowned as pastor of First M. E. Church in Evanston, Illinois, and a persistent spokesman for pacifism. He and Lynn Harold Hough were both durable delegates to many General Conferences. The latter was a minister and prolific author who served on the faculties of Garrett and Drew and as dean of the latter. David D. Jones and Matthew S. Davage filled the difficult and delicate position as representatives of black Methodists in negotiations which led to establishment of the Central Jurisdiction, a continuing form of racial segregation which had the merit of giving an assured voice to Negroes in the new denomination.

Views of Southern Methodists and Methodist Protestants are reflected in the selections from the General Conference of the M. E. Church, South, in 1938, the historical review by Bishop John M. Moore, who played a crucial role in the process of reunion, and the manuscript

559

*reminiscences of James H. Straughn addressing the same General
Conference and his "Valedictory" published in the* Methodist Protestant Recorder. *Thus the seeds planted in the Cape May Conference
in 1876 came to final, long delayed, and typically human mixed
harvest in 1939. Finally a hopeful yet apprehensive "greeting" was
prepared for the Bicentennial of 1966 by the Bicentennial Committee
and the Association of Methodist Historical Societies for inclusion
in the Time Capsule which rests in Mt. Olivet Cemetery in Baltimore,
Maryland*

¶   The Itineracy.

(Taken from The Episcopal Address (1912), pamphlet, 18-23).

Whatever befalls our Methodism, this will ever remain a glorious
tradition - that as the eagle by the life within itself grows the
wings that bear it undaunted through sunshine or storm wherever its
vision leads, so once the eagle souls of men grew wings that bore
them as flying evangels in quest of souls, abandoning themselves to
God as utterly as the eagle abandons itself to the air. For the
more effectual functioning of the God-life in their souls the fathers
grew the itinerancy. Let no sons of theirs declare their type out-
grown by the Church they created. It is far more likely that the wings
of the fathers are too large for their sons. If we still aspire to be
eagles, let us beware of imitation wings. The best substitute for
life-grown wings that men have yet devised has by its uncertain
mechanical heartbeat dropped many an adventurer to his death. For the
typical itinerant, consecration meant a whole offering on the altar.
His test was God's answer by fire. Then he was ready to "die daily"
or on the instant. That was the beginning of our heroic age.

Such a ministry gathered people of like spirit. United they
sang their way through persecution and pioneer tribulations. The
people asked God for the right preacher. When he came he was their
answer to prayer. There was no preliminary bargaining, no discretion-
ary refusing, in the system. Does any modernized Methodist ask why
preachers and people should enter into such a compact? The answer is,
to serve the Kingdom of God. It was the only way by which a continent
might be speedily won, and it is the only plan that does not leave a
large percentage of preachers idle and a corresponding number of
churches vacant, sometimes for months, sometimes for years. Thus the
itinerancy is sane from the standpoint of common sense as well as
apostolic in type and spirit. Un-American? Only in print. Who
established the system? The preachers who were to be governed by it.
Who re-ordained it by a free vote only twelve years ago? Both
preachers and laity after a hundred years' experience of its working.
Granted that it is military in its movement. Is not enlistment
voluntary, and continued service optional? A militant company compactly organized will win a dozen victories while a town-meeting is
wrangling about the choice of a leader.

After all the academic criticism visited upon the itinerancy
the outstanding record proves that its operation and product have
been essentially democratic. It has not created class distinctions
in its worshipping congregations, but has rebuked such. It has
stood for open churches and free seats. It has sought out the poor
and welcomed the outcast. It has banished "the election of grace"
by its "whosoever will may come." It has always administered the
sacraments without charge. It has made of the communion it has

established the freest spiritual democracy on earth. It has fought and won more battles for the highest ideals of democratic citizenship than any other system, because its pulpits have been set up in every hamlet and countryside, and every pulpit has been a free forum for fearless men who were to answer for their utterances to God only, and not to the political or commercial interests represented in the pews.

"SALARY" OR "SUPPORT"

If anywhere this itinerant ministry has fallen short of these aims and their achievement, it is where it has dealt like Esau and sold its birthright. The self-proclaimed apostolic successors of St. Peter may have forgotten the lesson he once taught another Simon, but the heirs to the apostleship of John Wesley and Francis Asbury should never forget that a Methodist preacher's consecration means no less than this: All I am God made me; all I have God gave me; all I need my Savior has bought for me; all I hope for He has promised me; therefore all my years and all my powers are His while life endures. I have nothing left to see, but everything to give away that love can yield. Here flames passion for souls. Here rules the love that vaunteth not itself, that is not puffed up, and doth not behave itself unseemly.

For such heroic consecration it is profane to quote money values. The eloquence that may be hired, the learning that may be subsidized, the pulpit style that may be paid for in coin, cannot be of this type, and is spiritually impotent. Hence to typical Methodists the word "salary" was from the beginning offensive. Once it crept in from the world vocabulary, but was promptly expelled a hundred years ago, because it did not savor of consecration, and carries a perverted conception of the gospel ministry. The Christian ministry is not a profession. Nothing can be more inimical to the spirit of a God-called ministry, nothing more utterly subversive of the sacredness of the pastoral office, than to place soul-winning and soul-shepherding on the secular basis of compensation. No prophet of God ever prophesied for wages. No apostle ever sold his inspiration to the highest bidder. Methodist preachers are "supported," not hired. The difference is vital. A "support" is the sum estimated, *for a pastor already appointed,* by an authorized committee after consultation with the pastor, as sufficient to furnish himself and family a comfortable livelihood. Under this plan consecration is not compromised, and the preacher's message may weigh its full gospel value.

"Salary," on the other hand, implies a stated stipend proposed as compensation for services to be rendered, fixed before the service begins and as a condition to its beginning at all. We shall write the tragedies of the altar diamonds that glowed with holy fire when first discovered by exploring Church committees, but which quickly turned

562

to glass in the setting to which they were transferred, thus telling that the glow was in the altar fire, not in the polished stone?

NEGOTIATIONS COMPROMISE PULPIT FREEDOM

"A comfortable support" is the sacred claim of every man of God who in city or country is doing the work of God on the basis of God's call and covenant. But his contract is not with the Official Board or Quarterly Conference. It is an altar covenant with God alone, who in His own way will hold the stewards of His substance to answer to Him for an honest estimate and for faithful fulfillment of their acknowledged obligation. This is our inherited Scriptural conception of the gospel ministry and its support. Only at their peril and the peril of souls do our ministers depart from it. Crippling inconsistencies and humiliating entanglements attend every preliminary negotiation between our preachers and Churches. That blunt layman who said "the preacher is our hired man and must do as we tell him," was brutally business-like; but, to be candid, he was only giving the thumbscrew of commercial logic an extra turn, if the pastor had agreed to serve in that capacity for an offered and accepted consideration. Many a faithful servant of God has been unwittingly lured from his apostolic freedom into a galling pulpit serfdom, at once abject and pitiable, as the result of a commercial bargain.

Nor must the fact be overlooked that the bargaining process implies that the two parties thereto have the legal right to negotiate with each other and to carry out the agreement made. But as between a Methodist preacher and a Methodist society neither of these implications is valid, because both parties are bound by previous obligations, voluntarily entered into with other parties, with which older obligations the new is inconsistent. When nineteen thousand other Methodist preachers and as many Churches rise up in protest, it does not meet the case if the respondents confidently point to a parenthetical proviso in their agreement, which declares in substance that this call and its acceptance are to become binding - *"the bishop consenting."* Of course; it could not be otherwise. But that does not restore the forgotten vows, nor mend the Discipline, nor reunite the broken covenant circle of 19,000 preachers and three millions of Methodist people, nor give back the apostolic note to that preacher's message, nor redeem that pulpit from the taint of commercialism, nor heal the hurt done to the spirit of our itinerancy.

ITINERANCY ENDANGERED

As for the bishop concerned, he is left to choose between so many involved alternatives, usually hazardous, that in most cases he is unduly pressed to give legal sanction to the arrangements illegally initiated. But in its legal essence his part in the transaction is a travesty upon his high office. Every Methodist knows this; every

563

bishop feels it. It can not be that our brethren who have lapsed into this practice have measured the far-reaching purport of their action. Will they be patient, for our motive's sake, while we speak further?

No system which involves the rights and destinies of men can endure unless conceived in justice and administered with equity. To its last demand does this principle apply to constitutional government. More inexorably still is impartial administration essential in a constitutional system created by voluntary mutual covenants, individually assumed in a spirit of self-renunciation for the advancement of a sacred cause.

Thus it becomes manifest that the Episcopacy and the Itinerancy, which took life from the same heartbeat, also breathe through the same lungs. The Itinerant ministry created our Itinerant General Superintendency, and hedged it about with constitutional safeguards, so that the spirit of the Itinerancy should perpetuate itself in the appointing power. To secure as far as possible the indispensable element of impartiality in administration, and for no other purpose, they protected the appointing power from the temptations that beset candidacy for re-election by leaving its incumbency without a time limit. So Itinerant Episcopacy exists for the Itinerancy, not for itself. It was not created a high office to tempt human ambition, but to preserve the Itinerant system in our ministry.

Let us now face fairly the question, What yet remains of the system? As we review the outstanding features of Itinerancy in its days of glorious conquest, we freely confess that the physical hardships and deprivations of our ministry to-day, except on the frontier, are much less than formerly. The time limit is gone, and almost every charge has its comfortable parsonage. Very few pastors go to new appointments without some knowledge of what their support will be - so much less therefore the excuse for preliminary negotiations. Appointments are still made and read at the Conference. But there is not the same call for the *daring*, the *venture* of faith, the high courage that tells of *heroic* sacrifice, save in the one remaining significant vow of obedience to the appointing power. There are still noble examples of this, but its spirit is constantly impaired by the growing practice of preliminary negotiations. . . .

VITAL QUESTIONS ASKED

All this is the more deplorable because in the long run neither the Churches nor the preachers directly involved in calls and negotiations have gained by the innovation. There was and is a lawful method by which all interests, even those local and personal, would have been better cared for without jeopardizing the general welfare. We earnestly urge upon your most prayful consideration these questions:

564

1. Can the Itinerancy continue unless equitably applied to all who owe it allegiance?

2. Can the appointing power hold the confidence of preachers and Churches unless absolutely impartial in its administration?

If any one answers that it is for the bishops to regulate this entire matter, then we respectfully ask a third question:

3. Will the General Conference and the Church uphold the bishops in refusing to consummate any arrangement involving a preliminary "call" or understanding in violation of the common rights and common interests of all the preachers and all the Churches? If not, then the time has fully come for a legal modification of the Itinerant system, and a *new* order which shall be of universal application.

¶   What Bishops Are Like.

(Taken from Edwin H. Hughes, *I Was Made a Minister* (1943), 184-86).

The men who have had the closer knowledge of that line have been the chief admirers. Of the bishops in the old Methodist Episcopal group I have personally known all but twenty. I have been associated in the Board with every bishop beginning with Henry White Warren, who was numbered thirty - except the eight who died prior to 1908.

The first bishop I met was the sixteenth - Bishop Matthew Simpson, a parsonage hero for whom my older brother was, in part, named. When I was eleven years of age he put his hands on my head and gave me his benediction. How little could I have dreamed that I would be one of his successors in the presidency of DePauw University, and in the episcopacy!

The first bishop that I heard preach was Randolph S. Foster. I slept for more than an hour. Then the enthusiastic West Virginia preachers interrupted my slumbers. When the sermon began I was twelve years old; when it ended I was two hours and twenty minutes older.

The first missionary bishop that I encountered was William Taylor of Africa - a fair duplicate of Michelangelo's "Moses." He wore an astounding beard. In dealing with him a cannibal would have had to be selective. One of the most marvelous sermons I ever heard was delivered by Bishop James M. Thoburn, of India. Of our seventeen missionary bishops I have known all but two, and I have met in close range all of our Central Conference bishops.

I have greeted all but seventeen of the fifty-eight bishops in the former Methodist Episcopal Church, South, group. Alpheus W.

Wilson was a wonderful preacher. Elijah Embree Hoss was a sparkling person, especially when scornful or semi-angry. John J. Tigert was massive in appearance, in thought, in utterance. Walter R. Lambuth was a glorious, gentle soul, with a missionary passion. Eugene R. Hendrix was a courtly gentleman, who escaped from sectional feeling and willingly took some blows as an advocate of Methodist union. Warren A. Candler had a gift of drawling wit, coupled with a background of mind and a foreground of fervor that made his utterances unforgettable. Atticus G. Haygood, by his book *Our Brother in Black,* made millions of hearts tender toward the Negro and introduced the sable hosts as candidates for sainthood and service. Charles B. Galloway had unassuming majesty, a musical voice, a restrained emotion, and an alert intellect that classified him with the very great speakers.

On the Northern side the best-informed bishop was John M. Walden. Bishop Goodsell made a fine phrase when he said, "Our Brother Walden has a noble avarice for work." I depart from my rule by mentioning a grand bishop still living, and saying that tributes for wise industry belong as well to Thomas Nicholson.

The most symmetrical bishop was Edward G. Andrews. The best ecclesiastical lawyers were Stephen M. Merrill, Charles W. Smith, and Luther B. Wilson. The best financial promoters were Charles C. McCabe, Willard F. Mallalieu, and John W. Hamilton. The best-known builder of a popular institution was John H. Vincent. The most constructive in European missionary work was William Burt. The most ornate and melodious in public address was Robert McIntyre. The one most scintillating in his use of words was William A. Quayle - converted in a little room as he prophetically knelt at an unabridged dictionary converted into an altar. The largest in size was Bishop Peck; his name should have stood for a larger measure. Over the continent he scattered a procession of broken chairs and beds. Daniel A. Goodsell, too, would receive notice for his avoirdupois. He was sensitive about his size, and unaware that his felicitous use of English, his charm in personal conversation, his ventriloqual play with parsonage children, all removed him from oddity and made love reduce him to normal stature. The wittiest bishop was Naphtali Luccock. The best platformer was Homer C. Stuntz. The most distinctive in manner and speech was William Fraser McDowell. The most strenuously energetic was Theodore S. Henderson. The most prophetical in educational and missionary outlook was James W. Bashford. The most torrential in a grand, old-fashioned oratory was Frank M. Bristol. The most patient in the carrying of great burdens was Wilson S. Lewis, who once diffidently told me that he would not be represented by a race horse that sped to the tape, but by an ox that pulled heavy loads over rocky ways. The most persistent in his advocacy of the reunion of Methodism was Earl Cranston. John L. Nuelsen had a sadly exceptional career in his office. After a brief

residence in America he was assigned to the Zurich Area, which included Germany. His remaining active years were spent in Europe -
years that were soon involved in the first World War and that closed
in the awful tragedy of the second. Amid all the seasons of storm
he played a wise and noble part.

¶   The Wesleyan Service Guild.

(Taken from duplicated essay by Florence L. Norwood, 1973).

        Historians say that an idea finds its time! Between 1915 and
1921 the idea of a business women's group associated with the local
church and the mission program of the total church was catching on.
In different places in this country without any knowledge of each
other such groups were taking form. Some of the places we know
about were Fort Wayne, Indiana; Anderson, Indiana; Battle Creek,
Michigan; and Chicago, Illinois. The midwest saw the beginnings
of these groups before the rest of the country.

        In 1920 at a meeting of the Northwestern Branch of the Woman's
Foreign Missionary Society, Mrs. Franklin Clapp, superintendent of
Young People's Work for W. F. M. S., asked a young business woman
named Marion Lela Norris if a business women's group might be organized. Hence the conversation was begun. Mrs. Daniel Stecker,
associate secretary of the Department of Young People's Work of the
Woman's Home Missionary Society, was approached and became a quick
convert to the idea. These three women are ones to remember as
"first thinkers and workers" toward the Wesleyan Service Guild
organization.

        Let's take a look at the idea which was taking form and indeed
growing quickly. The Woman's Foreign and Woman's Home Missionary
Societies were well established by this time. They had about 50
years of existence and a fine program at home and abroad to their
credit. Both organizations, however, were planned on the local
level and to a lesser extent on the national level to involve the
wife and mother who was not employed outside the home. Meetings
were in the daytime almost exclusively, and all other plans of the
groups were directed toward that lifestyle. Employed women—some
married and some not, some older and some younger—were equally
concerned about the mission of the church at home and abroad and
wanted to share their time and talents in a meaningful program. They
admired the work of the two existing women's organizations, but meeting schedules made participation impossible. Reports on what
happened are a bit hazy, but this seems to be the gist of it.

        In March 1921 an informal Central Committee including two
national officers of the Woman's Foreign Missionary Society, two of

the Woman's Home Missionary Society and two employed women was formed to study the place the employed woman might fill in the church.
A name for such a group was chosen--*Wesleyan Service Guild*. *Wesleyan*
designated it as Methodist. *Service* showed its objective, and *Guild*
was the name applied to groups coming together for a common purpose.
Spiritual Life, Missionary Service at home and abroad, and Christian
Citizenship were adopted as that common purpose. This first planning
meeting was held at First Methodist Church in Evanston, Illinois. An
excellent beginning for an unofficial group!

There were now fourteen units in the midwest and the Evanston
meeting had given them new courage. At this time, therefore, they
asked the two missionary societies if they might join them as one
union(foreign and home) society of business women. The answer was
no. They were disappointed but not discouraged, and so they did
what minority groups do so often--set to work to prove their worth!
They undertook a foreign project for employed women in China and a
home project for Negro children in a settlement in Indiana. At the
end of the first year, the fourteen units turned over to the W.F.M.S.
over one thousand dollars, and the same amount to the W.H.M.S.--a
per capita giving of over seven dollars from each Guilder. Miss
Norris said, "Though unwilling to adopt our young organization, they
did accept our money."

The Central Committee was still at work, and so after the "no"
vote an alternate idea arose. In 1921 pilot Guilds were given the
green light in four states--Illinois, Indiana, Michigan, and Wisconsin.
Miss Helen Wesp, the leader of the first business women's group in
Anderson, Indiana, was a guiding force during this trial period.
Mrs. Stecker refers to Miss Wesp as the co-founder of the Guild.
The trial period proved successful and soon boundary restrictions
were removed. Units sprang up across the country proving a need
and an interest. Between 1921 and 1924 they met, studied and
pledged their money--many tithed. Finally in 1924 the Wesleyan
Service Guild attained the status of a separate department in the
Woman's Foreign and Woman's Home Missionary Societies. Here in
this group of employed women we see the beginning of the Women's
Society of Christian Service as it brought together the two mission
groups in 1940.

Administration of the new organization progressed smoothly.
Division of funds was no problem. Fifty percent was to be credited
to and administered by the Foreign Society and 45% by the Home
Society. Five percent was to be administered by the local unit for
Christian Citizenship and personal service--really a part of home
missions. Funds went through the regular channels. .   .   .

Marion Lela Norris was chairman of the Central Committee and
national secretary of the Wesleyan Service Guild from its beginning

until 1928. This young business woman volunteered her time on Sundays, evenings, and vacations for Guild work. In 1922 she started a news sheet, *World Service Greetings*.

The new organization was on its way! By February, 1925 there were 52 units in seventeen states. In those early years its growth was at the rate of 40 to 60% annually in units, memberships, tithes and money. As the Guild grew in numbers so it grew in its concerns. In addition to the China and Indiana projects already mentioned there was a pledge to help industrial girls in Japan at Ai Kei Gakuin Settlement under the direction of a Guild missionary, Mildred Paine, and then there was work with foreign children at Campbell Settlement in Gary, Indiana. . . .

Growth in membership and financial giving of any organization cannot be considered apart from the leadership which gave the direction and inspiration. The Guild can be justly proud of its leadership through its 50 years, and Northern Illinois Conference can be proud of the many women from this area who were those dedicated leaders. The Guild was born here, and so its leaders came from our churches. After Miss Norris resigned in 1928 as secretary and chairman, Mrs. Merle English of Evanston became the secretary. In 1935 a central committee office was opened at 1630 Hinman Avenue, Evanston and the first paid secretary was Miss Marian Thayer of Wilmette. In 1938 she left for missionary service in Japan and was followed by Mrs. Adella Langill. In 1937 Miss Lillian Williams became editor of the official magazine.

There are other women who may not have been early leaders in the Guild but who received their concern for the mission of the church through membership in that organization and went from there into leadership positions in the Women's Division. Among those we can name Eunice Harrington, Doris Handy, Florence Little and Gene Maxwell. Local leaders whose names will be familiar to many are Sarah English, Freda Nurse, Adair Myer, Lucille McCormick, Retha Sadler, Gladys Cook, Daphne Swartz and Nadine Van Sant. These are only a few.

In 1940 the Standing Committee of the Woman's Society of Christian Service adopted the three-fold program division of the Wesleyan Service Guild: Spiritual Life, Missionary Service and Christian Social Relations (Christian Citizenship). The Guild was thrilled! Their idea had proven its worth and found its time. . .

As we look forward to 1973 toward the uniting of the Women's Society of Christian Service and the Wesleyan Service Guild into a new organization called United Methodist Women, we can all look with pride at our past accomplishments. For 50 years we have worked together in our Christian witness as women in the church,

associated with the Women's Division, and thus responding to God's love and the world's needs. Times and places of meetings have varied but the mission has been the same.

In 1931 the Guild adopted a slogan, "Christian business women for a Christian business world." Employed or not employed, young or old, living in the country or city, black or white, we United Methodist Women might well make this motto "our business."

¶　　　　　The Change in Southern Methodism, 1918-1939.

(Taken from Robert W. Sledge, *Hands on the Ark* (1975), 242-43).

The denomination that entered unification in 1939 was markedly different from the Church that went to Atlanta for General Conference in 1918. In one sense this is not surprising, for the M.E. Church, South was always fairly well attuned to its cultural milieu, and the South itself had changed substantially over the two decades. The completeness of the change was an effective measure of the extent of the victory of the progressive point of view in the M.E. Church,South.

The Church in 1918 was conservative. Its theology was based on biblical literalism and stressed objectifiable tenets of doctrine as the standard for orthodoxy. It believed that a person became a Christian in an instantaneous, emotional conversion experience and that the most effective technique for inducing such an experience was the revival. The chief task of the Church was evangelism aimed at conversion. The body tended to be intolerant of newly-raised theological points of view. While admitting that modern Biblical scholarship had value, they felt it had far exceeded its mandates and raised more doubts than it had enhanced faith. Modernism was a heresy to be combatted.

In 1939, the theology of the denomination was different. It still appealed to its Biblical and Wesleyan roots but was far more willing to interpret those standards to meet existing conditions. Instead of insisting on an orthodoxy of doctrine, it more and more insisted on a personal, subjective faith and an orthodoxy, if any, of conduct. Persons became Christians, in the new view, as much by slow growth in grace as by instantaneous conversion. This growth was best fostered by an improved apparatus of Christian education. The Church still had the task of evangelism, but it also had other tasks that were important, too. Further, the denomination had by 1939 given up much of its old dogmatic certitude in favor of a more humble latitudinarianism in the area of doctrine, though it still spoke with authority when the occasion demanded it. "Modernism" was embraced as a useful ally, leading persons to a more informed and mature faith.

The bases of power within Church polity shifted considerably in the twenty-year period. In 1918, power was concentrated mainly in the hands of a group of authoritarian bishops. Those bishops acted as executive, judicial and sometimes legislative officials. As executives, they had a high degree of autonomy, cooperating with the Boards and agencies of the Church only when it suited them. The bishops even helped set the policies of those boards through their membership on them. These powerful men were virtually unchecked in their administration of their Annual Conferences, choosing the same sets of presiding elders over and over, and making appointments with a minimum of consultation in the closed cabinet system.

In 1939, the bishops exercised only limited powers. The Judicial Council now decided matters of constitutional law, the Commission on Courses of Study set educational standards, the appointing power was restricted. As executives, the bishops found themselves increasingly cast in the role of promoters of programs planned by the boards and agencies. The Centenary was the beginning of this development. The bishops initiated less and less policy. The Church, like big business, had discovered that the one-man-show was no longer possible, and the powerful single executive was giving way to a corps of bureaucratic technicians. The power that once was vested by law, by tradition and by personality in the bishops, was now spread to other agencies and people. This was the fruition of the democratization movement.

The Church in 1939 found itself with a new relationship to the world. The old Church-as-spiritual image of 1918 was badly shattered. In 1918, the denomination still felt that the Church's role was in the realm of the spirit and that the Church had little to do with the political, racial and economic orders of life, save perhaps to give general support to the status quo. The Church of 1939 was far more willing to question the society on all those issues. It was less racist, less fearful of criticizing the economic structures and less committed to the Democratic Party. Above all, it had a different definition of sin. In 1918 sin was personal and individual, and the remedy was personal repentance. In 1939, sin had another dimension, being also, in the eyes of churchmen, corporate and institutionalized. The remedy was a reordering of the social, political and economic structures of the culture.

Statistically, the Church of 1939 was considerably larger than it had been in 1918, having jumped from 2,183,974 members to 2,965,381, an increase of over 35 percent in two decades. Only in two years of that period was there a membership decline. The ranks of the travelling ministry did not expand as rapidly, being retarded by the depression and higher educational standards. There were 7,671 ordained ministers in 1918 and 7,976 at unification in 1939. Despite the depression, the denomination's finances increased during the two decades. Church

property valuations jumped from $65,438,232 to $177,615,962. Other fiscal yardsticks showed similar increases, the lone exception being missionary giving. The 1918 figure for missionary outreach reflected the opening phases of the Centenary campaign and the Church's optimism about world evangelism. The 1939 total for missions was still down from the depression and also reflected a more cautious valuation of evangelism.

The M.E. Church, South looked in 1918 to its past. It represented the attitudes of the nineteenth century in theology, polity and social stance, and it glorified those attitudes. It saw its task to be one of preserving those hallowed and time-tested patterns as a solid rock in a changing world. The progressive Church of 1939 looked to its future, asking what new patterns might be needed in order to help it bear its witness most effectively. It established the pattern of denominational life for the next three decades. It embraced change with the optimism that it could meet future challenges with appropriate measures.

¶   Debate over Central Jurisdiction, 1936.

(Taken from *The Daily Christian Advocate,* May 5, 86-88).

L. O. Hartman: We are in a very critical hour. It is possible to unite and pile up a great total of millions of members and yet lose our spiritual power.

Fellow delegates, I cannot bring myself to endorse unification at the price of the Negro. In recent months, moreover, this conviction has deepened with the discovery that very many of the rank and file of our Negro brethren, both ministers and laymen, are looking with sad disapproval upon the plan here under consideration, though it should be said in fairness that not a few of their leaders endorse it. I have also heard inklings that ultimately our Negro friends will go out from us if the plan is finally adopted by the three churches. I hope not. I trust they will not under any circumstances leave their old home. They need us; but in an even deeper sense of the word, we need them.

Just one hundred years ago the General Conference, meeting at Cincinnati in one of its sessions, rebuked with a stinging resolution its two delegates from New Hampshire for advocating the abolition of human slavery at a meeting held the previous evening. God grant that this General Conference, as it faces another and later phase of the Negro question, may make no mistake.

I intend to vote against this report but with no abatement of love and respect in my heart for those who differ from me on this

572

most important issue.　　.　　.　　.

Ernest F. Tittle: I may truthfully say that never in my life have I wanted so much as now to support an organizational plan before the church in which it has been my privilege to serve for more than a quarter of a century. Bishop William F. McDowell, utterly sincere in his belief that this plan if adopted would create a church which the living Christ may use as perhaps he may use no other now in existence; I just as sincere, however, in my belief that this plan which does, I think, undeniedly make a concession to race prejudice, would, if adopted, present a church which the Christ could not use without considerable embarrassment.　　.　　.　　.

Loss Is Greater Than Gain

To be sure, by segregating Negroes in a Negro Conference we give them political opportunities which they would not possess as minority groups within our white conferences; but we take away from them the experience of Christian brotherhood which, in my judgment, is far more important than is political opportunity.

I am very much afraid of the effect of this plan, if adopted, upon the younger people of our churches – black and white – who are to constitute the church of tomorrow.　　.　　.　　.

I am fearful, also, of its effect upon the thinking of colored peoples in mission lands and indeed, the world around. In India today are sixty million outcasts looking for a spiritual homes in which they may enjoy the elementary human right – to live as men, as sons of God. If this plan is adopted, will that large group look sympathetically in our direction?

For every other feature of the plan I am prepared to vote. I wish it were not necessary to vote "yea" or "nay." If we could make this one reservation I would be voting with all my mind and all my heart. As it is, my belief is that we should wait another quadrennium, if necessary two quadrenniums, when I fully believe we can have union without compromise; and in that case we will have a church which the living Christ can use, I profoundly believe as he may use no other now in existence.

Lynn Harold Hough:. . . I think the time has come when it is necessary for us to speak very frankly. The Utopian, sir, who substitutes an undisciplined and uncritical idealism for a cool and clear analysis of the practical elements of a situation has been for centuries, without desiring or meaning to do so, the greatest foe of the on-going of the Kingdom of God. It is, sir, when, we ask what in a particular situation we cannot have; instead of being content to take a step, with the other steps to be taken when the

proper time comes. It is precisely by doing that that century after century the really on-going movement of the Kingdom of God has been made practically impossible.

Let us look at this situation. What, sir, would give all of us the right? No, I would say, what would impose upon us the responsibility of voting against this plan if in any way this committee had given a report which closed the door, fastening us in such a situation that no forward movement was possible, saying to men of particular color – not the color of some of us – in all the future, by this structural plan we are adopting, you must stay at the point of the adoption of this plan? Had that been so, I would have been making a speech, provided I had gotten the floor, against the adoption of the report.

What have we done? In every way we have left the future free to follow the guidance of the spirit of the living God just as rapidly as with wholesome majority we can go. It is true now that a vote against this report is a vote of want of confidence in the members of this United Church which is to be.

That is the thing we ought all to remember. I want to say this, too, that, after all, the success of this plan is not going to depend upon any formula. It will depend upon the men and women who belong to the church; and if our preliminary attitude is that we are afraid to trust them, what a curiously cynical attitude that is.

I want to remind you and the members of the Conference that this report does go as far as the Methodist Episcopal Church has gone in seventy years, when it has regarded itself as the particular guide and philosopher and friend of those who are in our thought this morning. To say that we will not adopt the report, unless it goes farther than we have cared to go – when we ourselves possessed a majority at every point to say that – is to ask something incredible of those who are anxious to meet us, and go forward with us. . .

David D. Jones: I realize the situation in which I am when all of the heavy artillery, the finest munitions in the world, are aimed at a little nation, and one ragged Ethiopian runs out and pulls a pop gun; but I am here because I cannot do otherwise, God help me. I am here because my brethren bid me speak, not that I chose to speak. In our meeting last night, there were forty-four Negroes. Thirty-three of them put up their hands and wrote their names and said to me, "Protest in a mild, but manly, way against this Plan of Unification."

Why do we protest? In the first place, there has been a good bit of specious argument about this Plan. Everyone knows the Plan is segregation, and segregation in the ugliest way, because it is

574

couched in such pious terms. My friends, what does segregation do for a people? It sets them aside, it labels them, it says that they are not fit to be treated as other people are treated. My friends, you have that privilege of saying that to us, but surely you will expect us to be men enough not to say it ourselves. This Plan turns its back on the historic attitude of the Methodist Episcopal Church. All through the years we have had inter-racial fellowship. Some people are good enough to say that the Negroes have made more progress than any other race so situated. I say to you if we have made progress it has been in a measure due to the kind of fellowship and the kind of leadership we have had. Do you ask us today to turn our backs on those men who have come and labored with us? Do you ask us to turn our backs on Hartzell, on Mary Haven Thirkield, on people who have come and given their lives to us? We cannot do it.

.   .   .In conclusion, you may adopt this plan. We are power-less to prevent it, absolutely powerless. All we can do is to appeal to time. That is all we can do: appeal to time; but maybe in the years that are to come we can paraphrase Edwin Markham's poem, the poem of Brotherhood, and say

> Ye drew a circle to shut me out,
>   Heretic, rebel, a thing to flout,
> But love and we had the wit to win,
>   We drew a circle which took you in.

Matthew S. Davage: I am for it.

The proposed Plan of Unification is not something that was ruthlessly thrust upon us. Two of the ablest men of our group (one a bishop, the other the president of a theological seminary), men of mature judgment, of skill in leadership and of exceptional experience in ecclesiastical statesmanship, helped to formulate this Plan, and the whole commission unanimously concurred in it before it was submitted to the church.

Granted that it is not a perfect instrument - and that it does not wholly satisfy the desires of any single group - in making our decisions this day we are not called upon to agree that the thing proposed is perfect, but to decide whether or not this endeavor to bridge the gap between this ultimate ideal and the immediately possible real is a step in the direction of the attainment of the ultimate goal of one fold and one Shepherd.

I have no word of censure for those who disagree. I know their fears and their anguish of heart. Because of inadequate information and lack of faith they fancy themselves mourners at the grave of a dead ideal; but, watchmen of the night who look carefully toward the past through westward windows and mourn the deepness of the shadows

marking the departure of a dying day, turn you about and face with me
toward the east, and you will discover that already the dawn herald-
ing the beginning of a new and better day has appeared, a day of enlarged opportunity and of increased responsibility.

> Ye fearful saints, fresh courage take;
> The clouds ye so much dread
> Are big with mercy, and shall break
> In blessings on your head.

After all of these years the Methodist Episcopal Church has been
our unfailing friend, she has never failed us, and I do not believe
she will fail us now.

Negro Rights Are Guaranteed

May I say - and I may be pardoned to humbly follow the example
of the Episcopal Address in the momentous General Conference of 1936 -
concerning the proposed Plan of Unification future historians will
find this question: "Are the rights of the Negro members of the
Methodist Episcopal Church adequately protected and completely and
constitutionally guaranteed?" The answer is: "Indeed they are."

Paradoxical as it may seem, the very thing which more than
anything else guarantees this right is the very thing which is the
occasion of our fears and the object of our bitterness and attacks,
namely, the Jurisdictional Conference. This guarantees as a
minority group we shall always have proportionate representation
at the General Conference, that we shall have fair representation on
the boards, that we shall have bishops - and they will be bishops of
our own choosing. We shall not lose anything, but we shall gain
much.

¶ Southern Bishops Look at Race Relations, 1938.

(Taken from Episcopal Address, Journal of General Conference,
245-47).

A Great Mission Field at Our Door

No survey of our missionary obligation would be complete without
some statement of our responsibility for the Negro that is at our
doors. The ten million Negroes of the United States, three-fourths
of whom are in the territory of the Methodist Episcopal Church, South,
constitute at once our greatest mission field and the major racial
problem of American life and one that affects our Christian approach
to every one of the backward peoples of the world.

576

Our own Church laid foundations for the civilization of the race when it sent many of its best-qualified ministers to work among the Negroes during the years of that feudal dynasty that was terminated by the Civil War. Many a Southern mistress taught the Negro children, along with her own, the principles of the Christian religion. Southern Methodism will never cease to be proud of the fact that "Founder of Missions to the Slaves" is inscribed upon the tomb of one of her greatest bishops, William Capers of South Carolina. Out of such effort, 207,000 Negroes were enrolled in the membership of our Church - nearly one-third of the total - before the outbreak of the Civil War. It is a matter of profound gratitude that nearly 400,000 Negroes now find their religious home in the Colored Methodist Episcopal Church, which was created, and is still fostered, by the Methodist Episcopal Church, South. Such a background has had much to do with the progress of the race - a progress that is greater than ever marked any other minority and subject people in the previous history of the world.

But after all is asserted that can be justly claimed, it must be conceded that the white race has not given the American Negro the full Christian consideration that is his due. Whatever may be the sins of others and whatever may be pleaded in extenuation of our own short-comings, a large bulk of omission needs to be rectified in the course of our future relations with our brother in black. The Negro wants good wages, good schools, better housing, wholesome recreation, police protection, justice in and out of the courts, a larger share of civic improvements, and a chance to make the most of himself and the same things for his children. This is nothing more than, as a human being and an American citizen, he has the right to expect. For the most part, however, he has lived since the manifest of his freedom under an economic and political system that has not always fostered his best development.

The Negro is restricted throughout the nation in the class of work that is available to him, because he is a Negro, and there is still a general indisposition to pay him equal wages for equal work and equal efficiency. His housing conditions, which he is usually helpless to improve for himself, are generally congested, frequently without proper regard for sanitation and often a menace to the community health. Justice is not always ministered with an even hand by the controlling race in the economic arrangements of his life or in the processes of the law. Public utilities, such as schools, sewers, water connections, sidewalks, parks and playgrounds, are very inadequately supplied to the Negro districts in our cities, while the appropriations for public health and other welfare service are by no means administered on any basis of general need. The fact that the white man pays most of the tax is no sufficient justification for such a vast difference in the distribution of its benefits. The whole theory of our taxing system, whether federal or state, is that

577

the revenues of government should be administered for the service of
the whole people and according to their need.

There are certain elementary things that civilization owes the
Negro in our midst. We owe him an assured justice in the broad
world of economic life and at the courthouse door. We owe him
protection against any extra-legal attack upon his person or property. We owe his children a fairly equal opportunity for education
and self-realization. We owe him better housing and a fairer
distribution of the welfare services that are maintained for the
public good. We owe him the privileges and responsibilities of a
citizen, for his own good and ours, as he may be able to qualify
under any proper standards of citizenship. We owe him the salvation
and enrichment of life that come through the gospel of Jesus Christ
and the opportunity to express that life in an unhampered field.

The South needs to face these issues afresh. The fundamental
question of human rights and relationships in a Christian civilization profoundly concerns us all, and its solution will not only bring
the largest good to 10,000,000 Negroes that are among us by no choice
of their own, but will insure to the largest moral and economic benefit of the whole South. No repressive measures will furnish the
solution. The masses of our Southland, living side by side with the
Negro, owe to themselves as well as to him an outstretched hand of
helpfulness. It is as certain as the sequence of day and night that
the application of the principles of the Sermon on the Mount to this
whole problem will bring immeasurable blessedness to both. The
Church of Jesus Christ must lead the way in the inculcation of justice and righteousness in all racial relationships. The evangelistic passion of William Capers and his colleagues toward this great
mission field that is at our doors is a challenge to Southern Methodism, and its adequate occupation will bring the approval of God and
the benedictions of all good men.

¶   Jurisdictional Conference in Methodist Union.

(Taken from John M. Moore, *The Long Road to Methodist Union*
(1943), 226-30).

The plan and purpose of union contemplate an expanded and ex-
panding horizon of a great new American Methodist Church. That
Church must fit into every nook and corner of this country, into
every class and classification of people, and into every type of
regional and community thought and civilization. The United States
has a great variety of thinking, feeling, willing, and action, and
the Church that satisfies and serves such a population and citizenship must find many and varied ways of domesticating itself among the
people. Back of the Jurisdictional Conference System of interest and

institutions, administration and promotion, boards and agencies, is a very sound philosophy which churchmen more and more are recognizing.

There is still a North and a South in this country, and there is an East and a West, and they are not merely geographical. They are social, economic, ethnic, cultural, civilizational, ideological: To be sure, they are not so extremely so as to be divisional, but they are sufficiently distinct to create varied human characteristics and values. Each of these great sections has produced values that should be conserved and promoted. New England is a storehouse of great American treasures. From its western border through a half-dozen great states lie the major industrial regions with immense populations with continental European backgrounds, ideas, and ideals. Then there is the Middle West, largely agricultural, with a commercial outlook, and with ideas and attitudes of its own. The vast Northwest, reaching to the Pacific Ocean, has another very different outlook on life. Then there is the Old South extending from Virginia to the Gulf and out to the Mississippi with a marvelous homogeneity, and a civilization that is rooted in settled thought and fine culture that defy the ravages of change, and with a proud people who are devoted to their history and traditions and loyal to their country and its fundamental idealism. Then comes the broad Southwest of independent thought and action, progressive in spirit and creative of a new civilization. The Church that wins and serves these great sections must fit into them and must have respect and regard for them and their distinctive social, political, economic, and cultural views. Not to do so is to invite gradual deterioration and decay of the Church.

In producing an ecclesiastical structure for an American Methodism that would establish an acceptable and binding unity of all these sections it was necessary to provide for variety in expression in administration and in promotion. The Plan of Union was built with that in view. Provision was made to protect and promote regional rights, regional thought, regional ingenuity and resourcefulness, regional distribution, regional cultivation, regional responsibility, regional control, and the development of regional interest, loyalty, and action. That is the meaning and purpose of the Jurisdictional Conference. Its possibilities for the stimulation, development, aggressiveness, and growth of Methodism are immeasurable.

The early and old contention that six strong, vigorous, well-organized Jurisdictional Conferences would make six Churches instead of one now has little standing with those who have thought the matter through and know the durability and power of the constitutional connectional bonds of this Methodist union. To hold such a contention is to discount and discredit the General Conference,

having as it does the only connectional legislative powers, the constitutionally intrenched general superintendency, the common ministry, common membership, common doctrine, ritual, spirit, purpose, and procedure in the entire Church, as bonds of permanence and power. The Jurisdictional Conference has no voice on any of these unifying bonds, nor even a vote on any connectional legislative or constitutional question and alteration. When it is seen how impregnable is the solidarity of congregationally governed and diocesanly administered denominations, the fear of a strong, vigorous Jurisdictional Conference can be forever banished.   .   .   .

The Jurisdictional Conference has to win its standing against several obstacles before coming into full recognition, cordial appreciation, and loyal support from a great part of the Church's constituency. In the first place, it is new, a new administrative and promotional unit in American Methodism; and new measures are generally received with suspicion, or at least with hesitancy. This has been so with the Jurisdictional Conference. It is feared by some almost as much as a divider of the Church into sections as embraced by others as the only safe and sane bond of substantial union. In the second place, instead of being accepted as a coordinate, which it is, it is being regarded by many as a subordinate, which it is not. The General Conference, constituted as formerly, very naturally could be inclined, because of its history, to assume the right to dictate to the Jurisdictional Conference what it should do, and how it should do it, in the fields of responsibility which have been assigned constitutionally to the Jurisdictional Conference.

In the third place, if the General Boards are allowed or ordered by General Conference action to monopolize all the funds raised in the general budget, the Jurisdictional Conference will be denied the necessary resources for carrying on the work of its constitutionally required Boards. If after that the Jurisdictional Conferences are encouraged, if not instructed, not to lay an assessment of their own, the breakdown of the plan of union as it relates to the Jurisdictional Conference is inevitable. Death by starvation would be inescapable.

This creates a state of centralization in the Church which the Jurisdictional Conference was constituted to prevent. The promotional work of the Church in all departments was meant to be done by the Jurisdictional Conference Board and not by the General Boards. The responsibility of the Jurisdictional Conference for the "interests and institutions within its own boundaries" requires that the administration of these matters shall not be in some far-away General Board, but in the Jurisdictional Conference Board which will observe the policies of the General Board.

In the fourth place, those who were reared in the atmosphere and thought of a supreme General Conference, who have always thought

of centralization as indispensable to unification, who have considered
distribution of power as disparaging if not destructive to unity, who
have regarded the Jurisdictional Conference as a temporary expedient
for getting union and not as the permanent and essential basis for an
indissoluble union, will be inclined to allow it to become ineffective,
and to be drawn more and more under the influence and control of the
General Conference and the General Boards. This attitude is very
hurtful.

¶   Methodist Protestants Face Union.

(Taken from typed manuscript in G-ETS, *Articles and Addresses by
James H. Straughn,* (1) "Methodist Union and the Methodist Protes-
tant Churches," fraternal address to General Conference, M. E.
Church, South, 29 Apr. 1938; (2) "Valedictory," published in
Methodist Protestant Recorder, 20 Sep. 1940).

In gospel and government Methodism is the layman's church and
apart from the layman's participation Methodism loses its meaning and
fields of widest usefulness. We see lay influence today in particular
fashion in the Oxford Group movement, and you see it highly developed
if you please in Christian Science. The Methodist Protestant Church,
recognizing as it does and did this lay value feels that it has been
continuing the principle most apparent in the Christmas conference,
that the Methodist Episcopal Church in America was organized by a body
every one of which was a layman, not one in orders, admitting that Coke
was an outsider, which he really was. It is also true that the
Methodist Protestant Church has not altogether found fullest employment of the layman but he has been in our midst a singular force for
brotherhood and fellowship, a constant reminder of the church's dependence upon his loyalty and support, of his right to participate in all
of the church's affairs, and that he is the natural demonstration or
visualization of the church itself at work and participating in the
councils of the church. Into the Plan of Union for the Methodist
Church goes this principle of lay rights.

While the church of which I happen to be a member has had for its
distinctive economy such privileges, I do not hold that the recognition
accorded the laity in the Plan of Union was done as a concession to our
church nor as a vindication of our contention, although it is just that.
I feel that it is the natural outcome of the spirit and character of
Methodism itself, it just had to be, and it arrived when the two major
Methodisms were ready for it. And, on the other hand, while the
Methodist Protestant Church has held with the utmost tenacity to the
lay principle it also, in its hundred years of life, has had the
opportunity to sense the values of authoritative administration, what
you call the Episcopacy. Despite the common notion, the contention of
the Fathers of our church was not so much against Episcopacy as against

the unrestricted powers of the Episcopacy and which they felt could be corrected by the introduction of lay powers within the church. But now, it is manifest that all three Methodisms, parties to this Union, have been converging on each other and each has grown in the recognition of the characteristic principles of the others.

The hope of the evangelical movement is in the laity and there is no way for Methodism to continue save as it seeks to inspire in its people, its laity if you please, the possibility of enlarging responsibility and service. It is possible to have a church wherein the ministry accepts and directs its entire destiny. It is not so, however, in a church which makes of its people free agents, people whose spirits have been liberated by the power of the Spirit of God and who owe to the Church only such loyalty and allegiance as the Church may make possible to them. This Church 'body' must indeed be a fit dwelling for the Spirit that is to live within, even as our bodies must be fit temples of the Holy Ghost. A church at last is simply the grouping of likeminded persons and must conform always to the fullest expression of their religious needs. In our day Methodism with its gospel of everlasting release of spirit, must and will make provision for the widest exercise of these spiritual gifts. It involves the character of our organized structure; it involves the nature of our services; it involves the form of our architecture; it involves our World Service; it involves our social application; it involves the conception of what is the Kingdom of God as revealed in the message of Christ.

*   *   *

The old order changeth -- farewell and hail! Methodist union, mechanically, is almost complete -- the new House is about finished and the three bodies have moved in. The honeymoon is over and we are settling down to the sterner matters of housekeeping and of learning how to live with each other. In all probability -- now that the sentimental phases of the union are over -- the practicalities of the merger will be more and more revealing. Some of the things we did not know about each other will become apparent and in all likelihood we'll run into some situations we will not enjoy. But the faith we've had in each other through the formative years of the union will without doubt be confirmed in the years ahead. For myself, on every retrospection, I am amazed, not that we have had some irritation, but that the union has produced so little disappointment and disturbance.

Other than the completion of the union, and the fact that we have been able to bring practically all of our people into it without serious loss of members, the new Church has yet to vindicate itself. By which I mean we are yet to prove that living together will not produce friction; that organizations of great importance and resources can be dismembered and put together into new forms without hurt; that

great leaders can suffer readjustment of position with courage and loyalty; that the confidence and faith with which we began will last; that the overstrains and tensions of new alignments will in no way interrupt the release of spiritual resources all of us have felt so important and vital to the values of genuine union --. Will we accomplish a spiritual equivalent comparable to the material structrue with its vast investments! We may be able to raise more money for benevolent purposes and spend less in administration than before, as many of us believe, but even that is yet to be known. But our faith remains. Nothing yet has happened of such serious character as to disillusion us or invite repentance. We will believe that Methodist union has fully justified itself to date and that the future can only make more positive our first confidence.

Into this has gone everything the Methodist Protestant Church has had, without regret, without hesitation. Neither of the other two churches could do any more. We have played our part with great fidelity and our people have demonstrated their sincerity through all that has taken place. Denominationally we could have wished for certain recognitions which did not come but all along we have known that the major issues of union were between the Northern and Southern churches, and still are. Our minority position, spread out as we were over such wide territory, put us at a very serious disadvantage, apparent for the most part when the ratios of early representation were dissolved. But we realize as well that along with these major issues between the larger church goes the major part of the responsibility for the success of the union. But we are in. We have made our contribution and will continue to make it. For our people have loved Methodism, and they have loved God, and today we are thankful for the privilege which came to us in helping to heal the wounds of a broken church. In remembrance of another great captain of our church -- "Ephraim and Judah have joined ranks in the establishment of a new kingdom and little Benjamin has carried the flag and beat the drum for these marching hosts of God."

The Methodist Protestant Church has had an honorable history. It offers no apologies for having been. It fought a good fight and ran a good race. Its trophies do not bulk large, it may be, but its garlands and tokens of victorious devotion are everywhere apparent. Like the other two of this new household it ended its separate existence when the occasion of separation has ended. There is more of what was the Methodist Protestant Church written into the texture of the new Church than many persons realize. We still live!

It fell to my lot to be the last president of the General Conference, charged with the responsilility of union administration. How well or how poorly I may have gone through with my part of it is now a matter of history and cannot be recalled. And the ties which bound me fast to the traditions of my fathers, to the fellowship of dear and present friends, to the hallowed associations of almost forty

years of ministry -- these, officially, are at an end. Fragments of
duty yet remain. But the closing of the office of the general
treasurer, Mr. Staley - one of God's finest servants and one of
the most devoted laymen we have had, and they are many -- and my own
relocation to my new home and the Pittsburgh area, -- these bring
vividly to realization a stern sense of the new order. And to that
new order, with the rest of you, I consecrate myself -- that these
remaining years may be lived in genuine usefulness and worth. To all
of you I give my sincere love and appreciation. No man ever had finer
loyalty and cooperation, and for all of you I will be grateful for the
rest of my days.

The old order changeth -- farewell and hail!

¶   A Response and Greeting from 1966 to 1866 and 2066.

(Taken from typescript of statement in Time Capsule, Mt. Olivet
Cemetery, Baltimore, Maryland, 1966).

In addressing a greeting to you, Methodists of A.D. 2066, the
Methodists of 1966, upon the occasion of the observance of the bicentennial of the planting of Methodism in America, wish first of all
to acknowledge with appreciation the greeting extended to us one hundred years ago by Abel Stevens. In his centennial volume of 1866 he
explained that his generation would raise a symbolic educational monu-
ment which

> shall be witnessed by the eyes of our posterity, when
> on the anniversary morning of . . . 1966 they shall
> throng in redoubled hosts to their temples, and res-
> pond back over our graves to this anniversary epoch,
> and send forward to the next the anthems of our jubilee.
> God grant that the hymns of that morning may resound
> not only over this, but over both American continents,
> from Labrador to Tierra del Fuego, and that the missions
> of Methodism may respond to them from all the ends of
> the earth!

Even as the thunders of the Civil War subsided, he wrote with
confidence and optimism. We today are glad to witness the fulfillment
of much of his glorious dream, and to express our deep sense of indebt-
edness to him and the devoted Methodists of his century. Our strength
today is largely the strength of their sinews. We are their spiritual
children, ten million of us. In this we rejoice with thanks to God for
his many blessings.

Some of us would like to repeat this message of great expectations
in this our greeting to you of 2066. We, too, yearn for the kingdom of
God so far as it may be realized on earth. We, too, hope for a worthy

place in that kingdom. But we are sobered by the realization that our world is not that of Dr. Stevens. We are acutely aware that another landmark in world history was passed on July 16, 1945, when an awesome burst of atomic energy first exploded in the desert of New Mexico. We are aware that the course of world history is moving faster and faster in smaller and smaller circles, as we and our fellow human beings struggle with the multiple problems of this new global world of rapidly increasing population, automation, and communication. We are fearful that the era which will witness man's exploration of the solar system may also witness the destruction of his ancient home, earth.

The America of Abel Stevens still offered the promise of the frontier and the broad horizon of wide open spaces. Methodists, along with most Americans, were intent on entering and possessing their manifest destiny. Our America has lost the old frontier and filled up the open spaces. Our worldly destiny is not at all manifest. Our theological perspective is out of focus. Nevertheless, even in this radical shaking of the foundations, we express anew our gratitude for the "kingdom that cannot be shaken" (Hebrews 12:28). The Christian hope is our hope.

What can we offer to you, Methodist Christians of 2066, in place of heady optimism and ambitious advance? First, we place in your hands the treasure we have received in the Methodist church -- the heritage of John Wesley and Francis Asbury. We trust that this treasure may prove as bright for you as it always has been for us. Second, we give you what we have of abiding Christian faith. We are determined that our time also shall witness that reformation which is always a sign of life in the community of faith. May it never be said of the Methodist Church of 1966 that it settled down, stopped growing, and therefore died. *Ecclesia semper reformanda est.* Third, we accept the obligation laid on our generation to seek and find a solution to the old problem that has so vexed Methodists and in this day comes to a crucial issue -- the oneness of all men in Christ in utter defiance of differences of race. We pray that, by the grace of God in Christ, we may present to you a church free from bias drawn from the color of a man's skin. And last, we offer up our Methodist church in endowment of the highest dream of our generation -- the achieving, at long last, of the fullness of unity with all our Christian brethren, confessing that we have "one Lord, one faith, one baptism, one God and Father of us all" (Ephesians 4:5).

This is our hope for you, Methodist brethren of 2066: That our common heritage in Wesley may, as he himself always recommended, be placed, in "catholic spirit", at the service of all Christians. If the Methodist church in a hundred years matures into union with a larger ecumenical family, we rejoice in this fulfillment of our heritage. In this way the Wesleyan spirit shall enliven the whole.

24. THE SOCIAL GOSPEL IN THE TWENTIETH CENTURY

Along with the optimistic belief in progress at the beginning of the twentieth century came awareness of deep malaise in the economic and social fabric. Strikes and industrial violence in the 1880's and 1890's brought this malaise to the surface. A major result in Methodism was the formulation of the Social Creed, which then became a widely accepted document throughout Protestantism. Another major result was organization of the Methodist Federation for Social Service.

Many of the bishops of the M. E. Church were active supporters of social witness. The General Conference which approved the Social Creed heard a clarion call in the Episcopal Address of 1908. Among the leaders of this social movement none was more energetic and influential than Harry F. Ward, Methodist minister, theological professor, and long-time secretary of the Federation. Two selections from a book edited by him about the time of the adoption of the Social Creed illustrate the active social conscience in and out of the Federation. Frank Mason North was another of the charter leaders in the Federation.

One of the most socially active bishops was Francis J. McConnell, who won national fame as arbitrator of the great Steel Strike of 1919. His readable autobiography, By the Way, covers the exciting episode thoroughly. Another Methodist bishop, equally involved in social issues but on an entirely different level, was James Cannon, Jr., of the M. E. Church, South. As he explains in his somewhat defensive autobiography, he was embroiled deeply in the political controversy which swirled around Alfred E. Smith as presidential candidate in 1928. The center of the trouble was the inseparable connection between two conflicts over Governor Smith: his opposition to the constitutional amendment which prohibited manufacture, sale, and possession of liquor, and his Roman Catholicism. Bishop Cannon found it impossible to oppose the "wet" candidate without opposing the Roman Catholic candidate-- although he insisted he was concerned only with the former issue until the Catholic Church itself broke out the religious issue. Reconciliation was not the guiding principle of the principals in that campaign.

One of the persons who studied the garment workers' strike in Passaic, New Jersey, in 1926, was Winifred L. Chappell, who identified with the working women. After fifteen years at Chicago Training School she joined the staff of the Methodist Federation for Social Service, where she served as research secretary and editor. Her article in the Christian Century shows her deep involvement in the social gospel.

One of the most durable pacifists between the two world wars was Ernest Frement Tittle of First Church, Evanston, Illinois. Throughout the 1920's, when Red Scares and ardent patriots tried to flush out

586

disloyalty and slackerism, he had maintained a firm commitment to Christian pacifism. This carried over into the thirties, when the threat of military power loomed with the rise of Nazi Germany. Tittle did not waver, although many of his contemporaries, including the influential theologian Reinhold Niebuhr, insisted that the Nazi threat must be opposed by justified force. Tittle's Lyman Beecher Lectures of 1932 reaffirmed his position. In the ensuing struggle in Evanston, the Official Board of his church issued a forthright and courageous declaration of support for their beloved pastor. The women's organization wanted their names added to the official list. The first signature in the list, which included some of the most noted leaders in Chicago business and Garrett and Northwestern education, was that of the president of the Chicago and Northwestern Railway Co., a man whose own political beliefs were quite conservative but whose commitment to the pastoral leadership of Tittle was unqualified.

Under repeated charges of "communist sympathies" and "radicalism" from ultra-conservative leaders the faculty of Garrett Biblical Institute (now Garrett-Evangelical Theological Seminary), under the leadership of Murray H. Leiffer, prepared a carefully reasoned and balanced comparison and contrast between "Christianity and Communism, an Analysis," which was widely distributed and well received over several years, eventually passing the 200,000 mark. Given here in full except for title page and bibliography, the leaflet served well to clarify the issues and avoid the most blatant and emotional outbursts.

In the midst of all this social turmoil, and part of it, came the Great Depression of the 1930's. The Episcopal Address of 1936 exposes the raw nerves of pain engendered by the universal economic distress, not only among individual church members but also in the whole fabric of the churches themselves.

Through it all the Methodist Federation for Social Service continued unremitting critique of American society in the interests of Christian social justice. It was in the eye of the storm during the "red-baiting" of the mid thirties, as reported by Winifred Chappell, who, along with Harry F. Ward, was very visible in the Federation. Identification of this piece as Chappell's is clearly proved by Miriam J. Crist, minister of the United Methodist Church of East Quogue and Flanders in New York. Some of the many concerns were reported at the Annual Meeting of the Federation in Evanston, Illinois 4-6 May 1937.

¶ The Social Gospel Has Status.

(Taken from Episcopal Address, 1908, pamphlet, 14-17).

THE CRY OF THE CHILD

While in many states the law now protects children from severe
and continued labor, at the expense of health, growth, and education,
it is yet true that, in some states, the legislation is inadequate in
that the age at which the child may be employed in mines, mills,
factories, stores, and other places is too low, and the penalty on
parents for misrepresentation as to age too slight. When industrial
plants have invaded the mountain regions, or have come near them, it
is not uncommon to see the father and mother in middle life supported
entirely by the labor of their children in the mills. Any changes
from these conditions is resisted, not only by those whose children
are thus employed, but by owners who often reside in states where
the laws against child labor are ample. In the name of Jesus Christ
we protest against the sacrifice of childhood on the altar of mammon,
whether it be by the sloth of parents or the greed of proprieters.

We demand from legislators such laws as will, in securing freedom to children from exhausting toil, contribute to the vitality, the
growth and the mental power and moral sense of all youthful employees.

PEACE

We have noticed with delight the great advance made since we last
met toward a peaceful settlement, by Christian methods, of international
disputes. We rejoice in the honor which came to Theodore Roosevelt, the
President of the United States, on account of his successful efforts
to bring the Russo-Japanese war to an end. It is a notable fact, also,
that an American citizen, Andrew Carnegie, is building a home for the
peace tribunals which are to meet at The Hague, and which have been
created by the International Conference.

Distant as the day seems, when "they shall beat their swords into plowshares, and their spears into pruninghooks: nation shall not
lift up a sword against nation, neither shall they learn war anymore,"
it is yet evident by the creation of the Hague Tribunal and by the
revision of the laws of war, that the consciences of the nations are
more sensitive as to the wickedness of war than at any other time;
that strong efforts are being made to diminish its evils, both on sea
and on land, and that the spread of democratic ideas is such that very
soon rulers will not be able to go to war without the consent of those
whose bodies must pay the cost in labor, wounds, and death. Questions
of national honor are withheld from the jurisdiction of the Hague
Tribunal. This reservation greatly delays the day of abiding peace.
It permits sudden passion, under real or supposed insult, to drive one

nation to attack another, without waiting for the calm which comes
by time and investigation. In the middle ages, and since, there were
courts of honor for individuals. We can see no good reason, except
despair of human nature, why there might not be a court of honor for
nations to which such questions should be referred, and which should
decide as to the fact and intent of the supposed insult, and as to the
measure of the apology due.

WORKINGMEN AND THE CHURCH

For those who labor with their hands, and whose reward is a wage,
the Church has great sympathy. Their share of the profits of business
is often such that, if they have families, they can have no hope of
saving a competence for old age. In many trades the earning value of
a mechanic almost ceases at forty-five. Unless promoted to supervision
he must descend at old age to the wage of watchman and the day laborer.
The freight trainmen seem to have nothing so surely before them as
maimed hands, missing feet, and a dollar a day at grade crossings,
and in old age not that. To those of us who are secured from accident
by the nature of our employment, it seems as if it would be difficult
to find men to meet the dangers of railway work. Information direct
from the Interstate Commerce Commission shows that in the quarter
covered by the latest accessible bulletin, 519 employes were killed
and 8,273 injured. Making large allowance for the penalty of
individual recklessness, we shudder at the cost in life and limb of
our railroad transportation.

The case is as bad, if not worse, among those who provide the
fuel for our homes and factories. Men die by hundreds in one ex-
plosion. A poorly ventilated mine, from which a wicked economy fails
to drive out the explosive gas, has, in some cases, permitted an
ignorant and careless miner to open his safety lamp and blow into
eternity the working force of the entire village. So far as greed
makes such things possible the Master whom we serve demands from us
the protest of his Church, and for the sufferers the tenderest
sympathy. The love we owe our brother man warrants and compels us to
plead for greater protection against accident and greater mercy and
justice even to care, in old age, for the wounded and crippled from
the industrial battlefields.

While perceiving the dangers to American civilization and
especially to the wages of the laboring classes, if the immense populations of Eastern Asia were free to enter this country with habits
of living which are hardly possible to the last extremity of American
poverty, we claim for the immigrants from Eastern Asia who are already
here, and for those who lawfully come, the most just and equitable
treatment. Especially do we insist upon protection for them from the
mob spirit, so often inspired and led by those who are themselves new
arrivals on our shores. We deplore the unwisdom of those journals and
agitators who fan the fire of the war spirit and of race prejudice,

and fail to recall the fairness, the intelligence, and the deference to public opinion which guide the counsels of the Chinese and Japanese governments in their response to our exclusion acts, and to the difficulties which our national government finds under our constitution in rectifying the wrongs done against the immigrants from Eastern Asia and from all other countries.

TRADES UNIONS AND THE CHURCH

It is impossible that the Methodist Episcopal Church, under the command to love and serve all men, and appealing throughout her history to the masses and composed as it is in large measure of workingmen, can be opposed to the working classes. We hold the right of those workingmen who desire to do so, to form labor unions for the advancement of their interests, as we hold the right of individual laborers, who prefer to do so, to keep the control of their own labor.

We are confident that a closer and unprejudiced study on the part of labor unions of the aims and principles of the Church will convince those who exalt Jesus at the expense of his Church that the difference in America between the Master and his disciples is much less than they have been taught to believe. The Church and the trades unions should seek each other's help for the uplift of mankind.

There is one point especially in which the labor unions, as commonly voiced, mistake the Church. The Church is not a museum of perfected specimens. It is a workshop to which all who are willing to "work out their own salvation with fear and trembling" must be admitted. The Church cannot refuse its help and countenance to anyone who professes to accept its principles and to seek a better life, be he either capitalist or laborer. By so much as a capitalist is selfish, miserly, exacting, oppressive, the Church has business with him. She cannot throw him off and away until the last day of his desiccated and shrunken life brings him before God. She must hold before him the image of the unselfish Christ in the hope that in its light he will see how far he is from the kingdom of God.

Just so the Church must love, embrace, care for, and welcome those whose chief capital is their mechanical skill and muscular strength. If ignorant, she must teach them; if drunken, she must sober them; if improvident, she must bring them to Christian thrift. She can ignore no soul. Whatever the future may promise of a different system, or the dreams of social philosophers may prophesy, the present system is likely to outlast our day and we must permeate it with the Christ spirit on both sides, or leave the employer in an insecurity which paralyzes and the workman in a helplessness which degrades.

590

Some labor critics of the Church have said that the Church is a closed shop, and only those who comply with certain obligations are admitted to be foremen and workmen therein. The Church is certainly not a closed shop in the sense intended by these critics. It is no more closed as to its foremen than is necessary to ascertain their fitness to lead. The Protestant church does not attempt to interrupt the labors of those who do not work in their way, nor forbid the individual Christian worker from doing what good he can. Nor does it shut away from its most sacred ordinances those who belong to another church, nor exclude the seeking soul which does not belong to any. It does not hold down the labor of the most successful Christian to the level of the least successful, or prescribe how much or little any servant of Christ shall do. Nor does it socially or financially boycott those who do not think as it does, nor exclude the poorest unbeliever from its worship or its benevolent service. The obligation which the Church recognizes is to all souls.

¶   Labor and Religion.

(Taken from Harry F. Ward in Harry F. Ward, ed., *Social Ministry* (1910), 125-26, 128-29).

It remains now to ask what this movement means for religion; for, separated though it is by mutual misunderstanding from the forces of organized religious work, it yet is liberating spiritual forces that are destined to bulk large in the religion of the future.

The religious value of the Labor Movement appears first in its fundamental effort to make the wage-earner more independent. This, as we have seen, is essentially an effort to free the soul from the domination of things, to set free and express personality, and whatever does this makes for the advancement of religion, for religion can progress only through free, intelligent personality. In the day when religion itself is in danger of sharing the common subjection to the bondage of things, through her need to use them for her own extension, she may well be thankful for the aid of any movement that aims to put the goods of life beneath the feet of man instead of about his neck.

It must never be forgotten, the smoke and dust of current struggle must never blind our eyes to the fact, that the real aim of this movement is a spiritual aim. It is not a call to the disinherited to rise up and possess the fat of the land, it is an appeal to them to share in the higher possibilities of life. Of necessity it must first take the form of a struggle for higher wages and shorter hours, for upon leisure and freedom from grinding care, health, culture, and even religion, largely depend. When men are forced to work to the point of exhaustion and live like beasts, how shall they

rise above the animal life? The shortened span of life, schools
that need no teachers for the upper grades, empty churches and full
saloons, a population soddened with dull animalism and spiritual
apathy - these are the inevitable results of the denial of leisure
and a sufficient income. Starved bodies and starved souls are twins,
and the struggle to be rid of one is also a struggle to be rid of the
other.   .   .   .

This means that the Labor Movement is one of the strongest
religious forces in the modern world, because of its idealism. It
is alive with a passionate faith in a new and divine social order.
It believes that men are capable of nobler and more unselfish living.
It preaches the regeneration of society, and this appeal to the
instinctive ideals of men, and not its program or its philosophy, is
the reason for its success. The proclamation and realization of the
ideal is the essential business of religion, but in times of great
material prosperity there is danger that religion become entirely
concerned with the things that are instead of the things that ought
to be. Then, left without vision, the people perish in the sloth of
fat contentment. So that it must be counted as an achievement for
religion that the Labor Movement has roused with the vision of an
ideal a large mass of the population that was apathetic to organized
religion, and has set it to struggle against the soul-destroying
barbarism of material prosperity.

Last and greatest of the influences which the Labor Movement
is exerting for the progress of religion is its cultivation of
brotherhood, both as a sentiment and a practice.

¶   The Gospel in the City.

(Taken from Frank Mason North in Ward, ed., *Social Ministry*
(1910), 305-06, 308-09).

All institutions of society, government, church, school, state,
commerce, literature, will be brought to the test of the intention of
Jesus concerning the Kingdom of God. All progress in the individual
or in society is the unfolding of his purpose. The permanent elements
in human history are fundamental in his aims. The intention of Jesus
is our measure of duty and our interpretation of life. It is not final
when we ask of institutions of society their relation to theories of
the social order. We reach the final query only when we ask how they
relate themselves to the intention of Jesus. Do they promote his plan?
Are they the ministers of his will?

To this test comes the modern city. As a phenomenon it excites
the world's wonder. In the economic equation it enters as a prime
factor. No formulae of social science or of government are complete

without it. The philosophy of life reckons with it. Art and poetry are sensitive to its allurement, and its mysterious influence is everywhere permeating literature. Philanthropists find in it their largest opportunity. Its demand has broadened education upon new and wide levels. Upon the moral order it has brought an unparalleled strain. In language and in history central to civilization, the city brings to that civilization its supreme problem.

But what has the city to do with the Kingdom of God? . . .

The way to the Kingdom is not over the ruins of the city, but through its streets. It is an infamy to utter the cry of old, "Carthago delenda est," over the city of our own age. The gospel will conquer the city, not destroy it. Its conquest evokes the very powers essential to the Kingdom. It is not innocence for which that Kingdom asks; it is virtue. The symbol of victorious purity is not the garden of paradise, but the city of God. Humanity will come to its own through conflict. There are realms, the highest and the broadest, which cannot come by gift; they are the reward of struggle.

If, then, the Kingdom is to be won, if the qualifications for it in the individual character and in the social order are those most surely wrought out in the complex conditions of a community life, the place of the city in the age-long processes of God becomes strikingly significant. The "social joys" in that city of God are the fruit of the social struggle in these cities of men. The equipment for the ultimate service will be the product of the present effort. The communion of saints there is conditioned upon the community of interest here. It is precisely to this end that the city, rightly interpreted and used, moves - the perfection of character and the completion of a true social order.

Thus the city is a final discipline for personal character.

¶   Arbitrating the Steel Strike, 1919.

(Taken from Francis J. McConnell, *By the Way* (1952), 214-18).

The steel strike of 1919 came just about the time the Inter-church World Movement was getting under way. A meeting of one hundred ministers was called for the consideration of the general social situation after the strike had started. The meeting was held in 1919 while the strike was still on. The ministers assembled in Pennsylvania Hotel in New York, and I was asked to preside. In the course of the discussions frequent reference was made to the strike, and the sentiment grew in the assembly to ask the Industrial Relations Department of the Interchurch Movement to investigate the strike and report. Fred B. Fisher, who first raised the question as to an investigation,

chairman of the Industrial Department, was asked if in his judgment such an investigation was feasible. He replied that he thought it was, and the meeting of one hundred voted a request for the investigation. I was in the chair at the time and put through the motion, which was carried, as I now recall, without a dissenting vote. The Industrial Committee proceeded at once to set up a special committee to carry the project through. There was some difficulty in finding anyone willing to assume the active chairmanship of that special committee. A number of prominent churchmen were asked to undertake the task, but none would accept. Two very prominent progressives whose names, even if the men did no work, would have added weight to the task, declined, for no important reasons that I could see. Finally, though this is only my own guess, I was asked as a last resort.

The other members of the commission were Daniel A. Poling, editor of the *Christian Herald;* George W. Coleman, of Ford Hall Forum; Mrs. Fred Bennett, of the Presbyterian Home Missionary Society; Alva W. Taylor, an expert in social problems; Bishop William M. Bell, of the United Brethren Church; Nicholas Van Der Pyl of Oberlin College; Bishop Charles D. Williams, of the Episcopal Church in Michigan; and John McDowell, of the Presbyterian Board of Home Missions.

All the committee agreed that the actual investigations of technical matters were to be in the hands of expert social workers, and especially were the economic phases to be handled by men skilled in such inquiries. Fred Fisher secured the co-operation of an economic bureau of which Robert Bruere was the head, and Bruere in turn secured the services of Heber Blankenhorn, extraordinarily keen and conscientious in such inquiries, caring supremely for facts and facts only. The report never could have made the impression upon the public that it did if the committee had not had the mass of information that Blankenhorn secured. With the special committee started on its work the Interchurch Committee gave it a free hand, stipulating only that when the report was finally completed, the Interchurch Committee on Industrial Relations was to have the sole right of saying whether or not it should be published. The two committees kept out of each other's way.

The difficulties before the special committee were largely in the attitudes of the directors of the industry. We held meeting after meeting with these men, and we did not meet any discourtesy. As far as I could see, the feeling of the steel leaders was at first somewhat of amusement, changing to surprise that the committee should think itself qualified to ask any questions, and at last pain at being questioned. They could not see that the committee was trying to find out human situations, and that it was not concerned with technical processes except as they affected the men involved in them.

As chairman of the special committee I had to do a lot of the questioning. One day a leading steel man was telling me about the close intimacy between himself and his laborers. From some things he said it was clear that he was talking of situations long past, and I asked him how far in the past that condition was. It was a long time earlier, and the number of men whom he looked after carefully was about thirty. Then he admitted that at the moment of my question the number was several hundred, a situation in which he personally could not do what he had done in the earlier days.

On some broad questions of human welfare the United States Steel Corporation was beyond cricicism. In the days of my youth the old adage was: "There are too many one-legged men around a steel mill." That was not true at the time of our inquiry. The severest critic of the steel industry who came before us of his own initiative made the statement that the laborers could not find any fault with the safety equipment in the United States Steel Corporation.

In one city in Pennsylvania the president of a steel company asked to see me when I was there on church business. I told him I should be glad to see him. When he arrived at the hotel, he had two assistants with him. In a polite way he said he had come to tell me what a dreadful mistake I had made in getting mixed up in the steel investigation. He conceded that I was a good enough fellow as long as I stuck to my own field, but that in dealing with wage scales and similar matters I could not possibly know what I was talking about. Then he told me about the generosity of the wages in a certain department of his mill. Finally I said, "Mr. So-and-so, I want you to get full credit for your wage scale. In fact the hourly wage in that department is ten cents higher than you have said." He replied, "I have the wage scale right here, and I'll show you." One of the men with him handed him a sheet, and I was right. That figure had struck me as generous when I saw it, and I remembered it. I don't know that I could have recalled any other scale so accurately. In as much as his whole argument was based on the assumption that I didn't know anything, there wasn't much use in prolonging the conversation. That steel man was a good sport; when he left, he expressed appreciation of the sermon he had heard me preach the day before.

The most surprising phase of our effort was the significance the steel group placed on their spy reports. There were about six hundred of such reports in one plant - reports on the laborers' attendance upon street meetings where all descriptions of radical speeches were made. Probably there was a lot of wild stuff being said at these meetings, but it was reported in such a way that we could hardly make anything of it. This was because the mills used so many policemen to gather the reports. I have no doubt that these policemen were excellent in their way, but their way was not in

595

reporting social doctrines. The steel people never could understand why we didn't take the spy stuff more seriously. There were a good many changes going on in public life at that time that some who stood closest to them could not see. I remember a conversation with an employer of labor who could not find words strong enough to express his rage at trade unions, at their agreements to stand by one another and their profiting by the strength that came just out of union itself. Later he told me of agreements among employers in a business in which he was an important factor, how he and his fellow, controlling officials in about all the factories in that business stood together in loyalty one to another, and how much of a privilege it was to be associated with such men. This man was a worthy Methodist, in good standing among us.

Dan A. Poling and John McDowell, both members of the special committee, had to undertake more of the questioning than I did, because they were in New York and I was somewhat at a distance. Poling had direct personal contacts with the men who felt they had been more unjustly treated than any of the others. An amusing incident occurred involving Poling. He is like Job's war horse. He sniffs the battle from afar. I don't know any man outside the actual fighting ranks who faced more danger in both world wars in attempts to help the soldiers than did he. One day of severe fighting on the western front in the First World War a barrage was laid down by the Germans which cut off a group of American boys who were far out in front. Poling crawled through that barrage, got up to the group, and found one man in bad shape. How under fire he got that wounded soldier back to a place of safety, I cannot imagine. Naturally the soldier who had thus been aided was grateful. After the war when the special committee was working on its report to the interchurch officials, Poling received from his former soldier a copy of a spy document dealing with the members of the special committee, chiefly Poling and me. This paper had been given the soldier by some defender of the steel group who was probably distributing such papers as widely as he could. It dealt mostly with me. The writer seems to have been troubled by a bishop's having any connection with the committee. Before we began our conference, the steel official who had received us said that before we spoke, he wished to take up with us certain points about the chairman of the committee. He felt in his pockets for his copy of the paper and couldn't find it. He sent for his "welfare" man, and he couldn't find it. Poling had given his copy to me. Then I said, "Please take my copy," and he did, but that took all the spirit out of this approach, and the conversation died out. I learned later that this steel official, who outside of a committee room dealing with strikes was a most estimable gentleman, had been shocked at what he called my "unethical conduct in the use of a confidential document," It happened to be a document largely about me!

596

There is no use of my going into much further detail about this matter. The report attracted wide attention both here and in England. The feature that attracted special notice in circles not closely familiar with American industry was that the twelve-hour day, the seven-day week, and the twenty-four-hour shift were still largely essentials of a labor policy among us. This meant that mighty as the Steel Corporation was largely in its business aspects, it was still behind the times in its labor relationships.

¶   Bishop Cannon on Election of 1928.

(Taken from James Cannon, Jr., *Bishop Cannon's Own Story*
(1955), 389-91, 394).

My address at the Virginia Conference was published exactly as it was delivered by the Richmond *Times-Dispatch* under the headline, "All Candidates of Wet Tendencies Are Banned by Bishop Cannon in Vigorous Statement at Danville." ...

The New York *Times* gave about a column to the address under the heading: "Bishop Cannon Puts Smith Out as a Wet. He Urges Virginia Methodist to Cut Party Ties to Elect a Dry. See Issue as Paramount."...

There was not the slightest intimation in the newspaper reports of the Danville address but that my appeal for action against wet candidates was based upon the paramount importance of the prohibition issue. No news report or comment which I saw had any reference to bigotry or religious intolerance.

On December 7 I delivered an address before the Anti-Saloon League Convention in Washington, D.C., with the title, "Shall Dry America Elect a Cocktail President?" In addition to the statements made before the Virginia Conference, I called attention to an article in the issue of the *Nation* of November 30 by the editor, Mr. Oswald Garrison Villard. As my statements on this matter in the 1928 campaign were misrepresented, I give here the statement which I made on December 7, 1927:

Continuing his discussion of presidential possibilities, Mr. Villard discussed Governor Alfred E. Smith. Mr. Villard said: "Do you believe in electing to the presidency a man who drinks too much for his own good, and is politically a rampant wet? Does Al drink, and does he drink too much? I am reliably informed that he drinks every day, and the number of his cocktails and his highballs is variously estimated at from four to eight. It is positively denied that he is ever intoxicated, much gossip to the contrary notwithstanding. He is wet and he lives up to it, and for that consistency he is to be praised. One may regret with all his heart, as does the

writer of these lines,that being in an exalted position he cannot set
an example of abstinence to the millions whose state he governs, but
at least one knows where he stands."

There was never any denial from any source of the statement made
by Mr. Villard as quoted above. In discussing Mr. Villard's declaration I raised the question as to how a President of the United States
who drank from four to eight cocktails a day could manage to secure
and to have intoxicants legally. To do so it would be necessary to
transport a stock of intoxicants from his private residence to the
White House, which intoxicants had been purchased before 1920, or he
would be obliged to indulge his appetite by visiting friends in
Washington who might have stocked their liquors before 1920, or
finally he would be obliged to purchase such intoxicants from persons
who in selling to him would be violating the Constitution, which he,
as President, had solemnly sworn to uphold.

I asked the question:

Would not any nation which should elect such a "cocktail
President" to uphold the Constitution, and to execute the laws pertaining to prohibition, be properly the object of the amazement, the
ridicule, indeed the contempt, of the other nations of the world?
What justification can be offered for such a course? On what
ground should it be seriously contended that a "cocktail President"
should be elected for dry America? The only basis for such a contention is that political party loyalty is more important, takes
precedence, overwhelms, blots out loyalty to moral, conscientious
convictions. To the question, "Should the United States of America
elect a wet 'Cocktail President,'" the moral forces must give a
positive, emphatic, thundering NO.   .   .   .

There was nothing in the newspaper reports, or editorial
comments, on my Washington address which intimated that there was
any consideration on my part of anything but the prohibition issue.
Nothing whatever did I say concerning bigotry or religious intolerance.

But on January 6, 1928, the issue of religious bigotry and
intolerance was brought before the whole world by an "Encyclical
Letter on Fostering True Religious Union, of our Most Holy Lord,
Pius the XI, by Divine Providence Pope to his Venerable Brethren,
the Patriarchs, Primates, Arch-bishops, and other Local Ordinaries
in Peace and Communion with the Apostolic See."

*   *   *

It is quite remarkable that very shortly after this bigoted,
intolerant encyclical was printed in full, the first intimation

598

appeared from the Smith supporters that the religious question would be made an issue in the campaign. Certainly, I never made the religious question an issue of the campaign until after Raskob and Smith had deliberately openly injected it as an important and, as Smith said later, a paramount issue.

¶ A Methodist Woman Writes on the Strike.

(Taken from Winifred L. Chappell, "Women of Passaic," *Christian Century*, 6 May 1926, 582-83).

Every observer of the present strike in Passaic and the neighboring textile towns notices and comments on the women. Not the girls who flutter in and out of strike headquarters, busily helping with the distribution of relief funds, or bantering with the young men strikers - like other girls the world around. . . .

But what of the women mothers of children-some of them leading kiddies by the hand or even trundling baby carriages in the picket line; middle-aged women; elderly women? They are of the European peasant type; many of them must within the decade have changed their old country life for the textile mills of New Jersey. So obviously they are not the sort who would be class-conscious. Yet so very obviously they are becoming class-conscious. Their faces attract one in the strike meetings, more than the faces of the girls who flutter in and out of the halls, or the young men who stand on the side lines; more even than the faces of the middle-aged men, peasants also from the fields of Europe, husbands of the women.

No word escapes these listening women. One of the speakers is asking a question and answering it. "When the bosses wanted to cut your wages, did they talk it over with you? No, they put up a sign saying that wages would be reduced." Peasant woman looks at neighbor peasant woman nodding vigorously, and receives a vigorous nod in return. "Why yes, that is the way it was," the nods say. . .

There is something of religious atmosphere in the meetings. It reminds a Methodist observer of a revival meeting. An elderly man with saintly face is pleading with the strikers to join the new union. "If there is a single person in this house who is not a member of the union, let him not go to sleep tonight until he has taken out membership." . . .

It is when the meetings become most intense that one becomes most aware of the women. Someone reports that a striker was viciously beaten by the police and died from the blows - the sort of rumor that gains easy credence in the tense strike atmosphere. Through the woman part of the audience ripples the tch! tch! tch!

with which women through the ages have expressed sympathetic horror.
A speaker ventures to turn his criticism on the Catholic church.
"Over in Garfield the halls have been closed. Someone asked the
priest for the church house and he refused. He, a priest, sided
with the bosses. Why should he side with the bosses? The priest
belongs with the oppressed people. If priests refuse the church
houses, use them anyway. Who pays to support the church? You do."
It is an audacious thing to say. How will these peasant women, the
very backbone of the church, respond? They waver a minute. They
seek support in each other's eyes and in the eyes of the men. Their
old religious emotions are struggling with their new emotions of
group solidarity, of class consciousness. But the young men on the
side lines are leading with the hand-clapping; presently the women
join the applause.

So is it with their Americanism. America , they must have been
taught, is the land of the free. Their communist leaders, but no
less the speakers from outside-socialists, trade union folks, students from theological seminaries, preachers, are helping them to see
that when the constitutional rights of freedom of assembly, including
picketing, collide with intrenched business interests, the former, as
Walter Rauschenbusch once put it, "go down with sickening regularity."
The speakers, though, would talk against the tide as far as the
women are concerned but for the fact that those women have seen in
action fire-hose and tear bombs and police clubs; that they have been
terrorized neighbors fleeing-have themselves joined in the flight-as
officers on motorcycles have ridden into the picket lines.

When, in 1920, the Consumers league investigators interviewed
one hundred night-working women of Passaic, picked after the manner
of statistical sampling, they reported: "Take almost any house in the
non-resident section, knock at almost any door, and you will find a
weary, tousled woman, half-dressed, doing her housework, or trying
to snatch an hour or two of sleep after her long night of work in the
mill." Much water has gone under the bridge that spans the stream of
American industrial life in these six years. But the women of
Passaic and the other textile towns still work at night, and by day
care for babies and get meals and wash and mend clothes, snatching
sleep as they can. But it is not chiefly pity that one feels as one
looks into their faces. Chiefly one feels admiration. For when their
families needed much more than their men's wages provided, they themselves went into the mills-and they chose night work instead of day
work, because their families needed them by day. And they have not
been done to death by this cruel experience of double work. They have
sufficient spunk left so that when in January a ten per cent cut of
wages already unendurably small was announced, they walked out of the
mills with their men and their young folk. For three months now they
have been living on meagre strike funds. And their spirits are still
undaunted. Go back to work? Not a bit of it. Not till everybody

goes. "Me no scab," they say. "Solidarity forever" is the new battle-cry not only of the vigorous and spirited youth but of the working women of Passaic.

¶   Ernest Fremont Tittle Perseveres in Pacifism.

(Taken from *Jesus After Nineteen Centuries* (1932), 103-07).

The method of dealing with evil which Jesus did advocate would, by many persons, be pronounced "idealistic"; that is, impractical and absurd. But in view of the tragic failure of other methods, surely one may venture to urge that his method should to-day be given a fresh consideration. There are some even still who suppose that in respect of evil Jesus counseled absolute nonresistance. A man should make no attempt to defend himself; no, nor his wife nor his child nor his country nor anything else that is dear to him. Whatever happens or threatens to happen, he should stand by and do nothing. In the face of triumphant or impending evil he should remain inactive and quiescent. But Jesus himself, when confronted by evil, did not look on and do nothing. Not, to be sure, with physical weapons, but with carefully chosen spiritual weapons he boldly attacked evil. He "went after" men who were selfishly neglecting their fellows, or taking some mean advantage of them, or making life needlessly hard for them. In the face of evil Jesus did not remain nonresistant; nor did he advise his disciples to do so. If they were struck in the face, they were not to do nothing; they were to turn the other cheek! If they were dragged into court and by unjust, although legal, processes robbed of a coat, they were not tamely to submit to such injustice; they were to give to the robber their cloak also! If they were compelled to go one mile, they were not to offer no resistance to forced labor; they were to go two miles!

Now, one may, if he choose, label this teaching strange, fantastic, quixotic; but he will be blind indeed if he fails to see that, taken even literally, what it recommends is not nonresistance but a new kind of resistance—a spiritual assault upon anger and hate, upon greed and pride and the ethical pretensions of imperialism; a laying bare of the adversary's own weakness, the fact that he is in the wrong; the awakening in him of a feeling of penitence, "a burning sense of shame," and, therefore, a desire to right the wrong that has been committed. Jesus sanctions no use of violence in dealing with evil, no employment of guns or of gas; but, far from recommending non-resistance, he recommends a kind of resistance which may, after all, be far more effective than violence has ever proved to be.

And now, surely, the time has come for us to lay aside another misconception of the method of Jesus, namely, that it is devised for the weak, not for the strong; for what someone has recently called

"gentle, womanly souls, not aggressive, pugnacious males." It certainly will be conceded that Jesus himself was in no sense a weakling; even Nietzsche conceded that. Must it not also be conceded that his method of dealing with evil requires at once more intelligence and more courage than are required by any violent method now in use? An irritated father or mother whipping a child; an infuriated warden ordering an unarmed criminal to be beaten into unconsciousness; angry employers or bitter labor unions hiring thugs to do their fighting for them; frightened nations acknowledging the colossal expense and the awful menace of competition in armaments, yet refusing to disarm – are these Class A examples of superior intelligence or of superior courage? Whatever view we may feel obliged to take as to the efficacy of the method advocated by Jesus, let us at least have enough grace to acknowledge that his method is designed, not for the weak, but, rather, and only, for the strong. It is not, as Nietzsche and others have supposed, the weapon of a cringing slave; it is the weapon of a man who has enough intelligence to recognize the futility of violence and who has enough moral courage to pit reason, right, and good will against all this world's stupidity, injustice, and hate.

When Jesus advocated his nonviolent method of dealing with evil, was he thinking only of individuals, not of groups? It has long been thought easy to say that he was, for, beyond dispute, Jesus was mainly concerned with individuals. But in this case it is important to remember that his countrymen felt toward the Roman Empire very much as to-day Gandhi's countrymen feel toward the British Empire. The year of his birth witnessed a Jewish insurrection which the Romans put down in blood. Forty years after he was crucified, Jerusalem was in ashes as the result of another insurrection which proved to be fatal. Is it not difficult and, indeed, impossible, to suppose that, living at such a time, Jesus was unaware of the political situation or unconcerned about it? What is the meaning of that oft-quoted lament over Jerusalem: "Would that you too knew even to-day on what your peace depends! But no, it is hidden from you! A time is coming for you when your enemies will throw up ramparts round you and encircle you and besiege you on every side and raze you and your children within you to the ground, leaving not one stone upon another within you." And consider also the reference of the saying, "If anyone compel thee to go with him one mile, go with him two": clearly, that saying refers to forced labor exacted by the state–the Roman state. Is it, after all, entirely clear that when Jesus advocated nonviolent resistance to evil, he was thinking only of wrongs done to individuals? Is it not at least conceivable that he was thinking also of a nation suffering oppression? In any case, his plea for nonviolent resistance to evil admits of the very widest of applications, as in our time Gandhi has made abundantly clear.

¶   First Church Evanston Stands Behind Tittle.

(Taken from typed manuscript in Tittle Papers, Garrett-
Evangelical Theological Seminary, dated 6 Mar. 1933, quoted
in R. M. Miller, *How Shall They Hear Without a Preacher?* (1971)).

For some time a campaign of insinuation, misrepresentation, and
slander, much of it anonymous, has been directed against our pastor,
Dr. Ernest F. Tittle. We believe that we owe it to him and to our
church and to this community to assert unmistakably our loyalty to
him and our protest against such un-American and un-Christian procedure.

After fourteen years of intimate association with Dr. Tittle
as our minister, we would express our absolute confidence in his
Christian character and his deep and unselfish devotion to his country,
to the church, and to humanity. He is unalterably opposed to the
methods of violence advocated by communism, and steadfastly committed
to the orderly processes of democratic government.

We stand for a free pulpit and a free church. We do not expect
or desire a minister simply to echo the opinions of the congregation,
and we do not assert our individual agreement with all of our minister's utterances. But we vigorously resent the effort of outside
organizations to dictate to the church or to prescribe its message.

We hold it peculiarly important in this day that the church
should stand apart from all appeals to passion, prejudice, and
partisanship, and that our nation should have in the Christian church
a clear, strong voice rising above all divisions, speaking in the
name of God for justice, mutual understanding, and good will. This
statement is authorized by the governing board of the First Methodist
Episcopal Church of Evanston. It is personally endorsed by those
whose names appear below.

Fred W. Sargent, B. J. Denman, M. H. MacLean, Arthur Andersen,
William A. Dyche, Charles W. Spofford, A. D. Bruce, James F. Oates,
Wilbur Helm, William KixMiller, Joseph H. Beek, H. L. David, Earl J.
Cooper, Chester D. Tripp, Annie H. Price, E. S. Mills, Andrew H.
Phelps, R. C. Wieboldt, Thomas F. Holgate, W. H. Dunham, Harris
Franklin Rall, James A. James, Frank M. McKibben, Harold A. Smith,
Walter E. Schwind, Robert C. Teare, Edward S. Price, S. P. Whiteside,
C. B. Carter, M. J. Newell, D. E. Winter, James G. Carr, Carrie H.
Wilson, Marie V. Swanson, Jeane Haskins Colwell, Alec R. Allenson,
and Bruce H. Corzine.

¶   Methodists Think About Communism.

(Taken from leaflet edited by Murray H. Leiffer, Garrett
Biblical Institute).

CHRISTIANITY AND COMMUNISM,
An analysis by members of the faculty of Garrett Biblical Institute.

Communism is one of the most acute issues of our day. It claims
to be the one way of salvation for human society but stands opposed
to Christianity at essential points. Here in America the suspicions
and fears which it has engendered have been the occasion of serious
threats to the civil liberties which are fundamental to our democracy.
For these reasons we, as teachers charged with the task of training
leaders for the church, have deemed it important to undertake this
study of communism and to compare its principles with those of
Christianity.

By Christianity we mean not only that way of faith and life
which we find in Jesus Christ, but also the significance of this in
and for society today. By communism we mean not only the theory
proposed by Marx and his followers, but the expression of this in
the Soviet Union, its satellites, and the Communist parties around
the world, in their policies and practices.

These two ways have some points in common. Communism asserts
the equality of all men irrespective of race and color. From its
beginning Christianity has asserted that God made of one blood all
men to dwell on the face of the whole earth. Communism is concerned
with economic welfare and the accessibility of the goods of life to
all men. Christ came to preach good tidings to the poor, release
for the captives, liberty for the oppressed, and the coming of a new
world of justice and righteousness.

Christendom has failed to embody in its institutions and practice
the full gospel of Christ, and this has afforded an opportunity to
communism to make its appeal. Christians are called upon not only to
set forth the principles of Christ but also to apply them to the
whole social life of man.

A Christian Analysis of Communism -

Although Christianity and communism have some goals in common,
there are radical differences alike in aims and in methods of their
attainment. (The following are representative and not all-inclusive.)

1. As to criticisms of the existing order:

COMMUNISM CONDEMNS

a) Private ownership of property, except for a few types of consumer goods, asserting that private property results in the exploitation of the masses (the proletariat or "working class").

b) Inequalities in opportunity and power, resulting from capitalism, which must be removed by concentrating economic control in the state.

c) Emphasis on individualism and unrestrained self-expression. All should work for the promotion of "the cause," according to a plan.

d) Middle-class bourgeois morality as expressed in traditional standards of marriage and the family. These are sanctioned only insofar as they fulfill a function for the state.

CHRISTIANITY CONDEMNS

Selfish use of property, as all property, private and public, is a trust from God. "The earth is the Lord's." (for communism the crucial matter is the ownership of property; for Christianity, its use.)

Concentration of power, in the state or other agency, which endangers the liberties of the people. It also condemns the inequitable distribution and the irresponsible use of power.

Depersonalizing of the individual through the control of large impersonal organizations or the state. It also condemns emphasis on selfish individualism.

Attitudes of irreverence and irresponsibility toward sex and family life. (For example, for the Christian, marriage vows are not a mere legal contract, but also a pledge of love and loyalty made before God.)

2. As to the character of a just social order:

COMMUNISM PROCLAIMS

a) The supremacy of the proletariat, in which the individual's significance derives from his membership in the class.

b) A classless society, which is to be secured by eliminating all but one class.

c) Economic security as the supreme concern (secured, however, by the sacrifice of human freedoms, as we understand that term).

d) No racial discrimination (but other types of discrimination are deliberately used).

CHRISTIANITY PROCLAIMS

Supremacy of the person, who is conceived of as a child of God and an object of inherent worth.

The brotherhood of man, in which all individuals and groups work for the common good.

Security with freedom. Economic security, while imperative, is not the sole or even the supreme good. Genuine security requires intelligent self-restraint and uncoerced concern for the general welfare.

Equality before God, which means all men of all races and classes are entitled to justice and freedom from discrimination.

3. As to the methods of effecting social change:

COMMUNISM INVOLVES

a) Dictatorship of the proletariat, actually exercised by small disciplined groups. Beyond the proletariat there is no higher authority.

b) Elimination of dissenting minorities as a threat to the new order.

c) Violent revolution, as the indispensable way for the redistribution of political and economic power.

d) The doctrine that the end justifies the means: any means are justified that secure the desired ends as determined by the aims of the Party.

CHRISTIANITY INVOLVES

Government founded on the consent of the governed, who are children of God and therefore worthy to have a voice in their own rule. All political power is a trust from God.

Protection of dissenting minorities in the exercise of constitutional freedoms of assembly, speech and petition.

Peaceful change, through education, persuasion and reconciliation. "Be not overcome of evil, but overcome evil with good."

Christian character development, which cannot be achieved by means that deny or are in conflict with the ends sought.

4. As to the meaning of life:

COMMUNISM TEACHES

a) Atheism. Religion is a product of fear and a flight into fantasy. "Religion is the opiate of the people," used as a control device by capitalism.

b) Social derivation of all values. The only significant standards and values are those which arise out of society; these are derived from the interaction of economic forces.

c) A utopian view of history. Human existence will find fulfilment on earth in a progressively improved social order, through the operation of economic laws and by means of the class struggle.

d) The subordination of individual personality. The interests of the individual must be subordinate to the communist system (and must be sacrificed if necessary as a means to victory in the class struggle).

e) The restricted nature of community. Fellowship, though potentially world-wide, is earth-bound and is restricted to those holding the communist philosophy.

CHRISTIANITY TEACHES

Theism. An all-righteous, all-loving God is the source of man's existence and his only final deliverance from sin and evil. Service to Him is man's primary motivation in continuing personal and social reconstruction of life.

All moral and spiritual values founded in the character of God. The good life is achieved through responsible obedience to His will.

The Kingdom of God. The meaning of human existence must be understood in terms not only of the processes of history but also of God's purposes for man's life now and in eternity. If men will obey the will of God, justice and peace will increasingly prevail in history.

The supreme worth and dignity of persons. Every individual is

of infinite worth in the eyes of God and must always be regarded by his fellows not as a means to an end, but as an end in himself.

A universal and eternal fellowship. Men are made by God for fellowship with himself and with one another, in time and eternity, within a community transcending all barriers of nation, race, class or political opinion.

Christian Principles for Action –

We believe that the church should:

1. Continue to declare that above all human authorities there is the supreme authority of the just, righteous, and loving will of God. This declaration requires the honest recognition that no existing economic or political system can be identified with the perfect will of God; that all are limited and warped by human ignorance, pride and selfishness. The will of the majority is not necessarily the will of God.

2. Teach that all men share a common humanity and have essentially the same physical and spiritual needs.

3. Voice continuous and creative criticism of social institutions and practices which violate the requirements of the Kingdom of God: love, justice, and universal brotherhood.

4. Practice a ministry of reconciliation, both within and outside the church, between conflicting groups of men, whether they be divided by race, creed, political belief, nationality or economic status.

These principles need to be applied to the whole range of life – political, economic and social – including the life of the organized church. Christian men will differ as to the specific procedures by which these principles are to be implemented. However, the following commend themselves to us as appropriate actions.

a) Resist all individual and group practices which restrict or threaten constitutional human rights. This involves the condemnation of every type of totalitarianism, whether it be political, economic or religious.

b) Support efforts to extend civil liberties to individuals or minority groups now denied them.

c) Provide more adequate and equitable educational facilities and services throughout the country.

d) Develop a broad program of health protection, to secure reasonably satisfactory medical care for all, regardless of location or economic condition.

e) Work for a comprehensive housing program, realistically planned and executed so as to make possible wholesome home life.

f) Advocate opportunity for regular work for persons desiring it without regard to race, religion or national origin, with provision for adequate compensation and protection against occupational hazards, illness, and involuntary unemployment, and with assurance that such employment shall promote the dignity of human labor.

g) Warn against the threat of mounting militarization in America and elsewhere; advocate world disarmament; strengthen the civil functions of government.

h) Insist upon the more efficient use of United States government funds to reconstruct the peacetime economies of the nations.

i) Advocate government by law on a world basis and support constructive movements in that direction.

j) Encourage and support private humanitarian agencies such as the world service organizations of the churches, CARE, and Citizens' Committee on Displaced Persons, for whose programs there is abundant need beyond all the government agencies can perform.

k) Appeal directly through press, radio, and where possible, personal contacts to Russians and other peoples, showing our Christian concern for the establishment of peace with justice throughout the world.

l) Work toward the achievement of these objectives through local voluntary organizations - economic, educational, political and religious - and counsel others to do likewise.

Communism is not simply an economic program. It is a total theory of life, which is radically in conflict with Christianity, especially in its methods, but also in its goals and its attitudes toward persons. Communism itself recognizes this in its opposition to religion and the church. Our failure to apply consistently the basic Christian principles of justice and freedom and equal opportunity for all, our failure to rectify the common wrongs of exploitation and the common ills of poverty - this is what has given opportunity for the specious appeals not only of communism but also of fascism. As long as there is poverty, insecurity, fear, oppression, there will be a fruitful field for such false messiahs as have led peoples astray in this last generation. No campaign

against communism can succeed unless it also attacks these evils and proceeds toward the realization of a just and Christian society.

¶   The Great Depression and Social Reform.

(Taken from Episcopal Address, 1936, pamphlet, 28-30).

8. While we work for improvements in the present order of our society, we must not overlook the social obligations laid upon us by current conditions. We have good reason to doubt the ardor of conscience in those who postpone generous sacrifice, waiting for a regime that may not come until they themselves pass from earthly life. We are in the seventh year of the most devastating depression of modern times. More than twenty millions of the world's workers are unemployed, many of them walking the streets seeking vainly for work, often dependent upon public and private charity, and filled with nameless anxiety for nearly eight millions of children. It is an appalling social disaster. The Church of Christ cannot be silent in the face of this catastrophe, involving defenseless multitudes. While we have no specific program to propose, we do insist that the solution of this problem is not beyond our power. Surely the nation has resources, wisdom, leadership, and inherent goodness of heart for correcting these fearful conditions. The opportunity is here for generous sharing; for merciful aid; for persons and corporations to assist the government in reducing the army of enforced idleness; and for bringing in such economic readjustments as will give every willing person a chance not merely for a bare livelihood, but for meeting the financial and cultural necessities of himself and his beloved family. We feel that we can pledge the Methodist Episcopal Church to co-operation in meeting this need; and to this assuredly Christian challenge, with an immediate demand in its very nature, we summon all our constituencies.

9. There is needed, also, a caution for all parties gravely concerned. Some have been thrown into fright by the revolutions in several lands. The indisputable statement that Christian principles should be applied to industry is nervously met by the charge that the speaker has become a radical. Directly good men are so obsessed by an imaginary menace that they cannot see the obvious faults of the social and financial system. The critic is regarded as an enemy, whereas he may really be the long-run friend. So it occasionally happens that some of the best men are represented as the country's foes, while commercial representatives who take millions in unearned salaries or in subsidies for watered subsidiaries receive no stern condemnation. Without now debating the merit or the demerit of the so-called capitalistic system, it may still be said with assurance that the best way to preserve it for its claimed service is to make an honest endeavor to purge it of its

wrongs and excesses. Great wealth does make for great temptations. Modern reformers are not the originators of the warning based on the figure of the camel and the needle's eye; neither are they the first utterers of the slogan that "the love of money is the root of all evil." We do well to give heed to Jesus, and to Paul, and to the emphatic lessons in the sweep of the Bible about the insidious perils of riches. An English clergyman has pointed out that in the parable of Christ the avaricious man is stigmatized not as "Thou thief!" but as "Thou fool!" We should earnestly pray that we may be saved from yielding to folly — the temptation of Lot, or Gehazi, or Demetrius, or Simon Magus. It will require a tremendous faith in our faith if we truly proclaim its power to sanctify all material means to holy ends. Pleaders for social changes should themselves be on guard against unbalanced and fierce presentations of their views. This is particularly true of those who are in forms of service that deal with all aspects of religious life. These are charged with the duty of presenting proportionately the varied phases of Christian devotion and practice. We have among us many preachers who, being most earnest in declaring the social gospel, keep themselves free from epithets and from harsh utterances and so avoid needless irritations and cleavages. Some of their equally sincere comrades could well afford to study the kindly methods of these men who combine passion with wisdom and who work toward distant goals with a commendable patience. We should strive to maintain the spirit of Christ not only in fixing our goals but also in our efforts to reach them. If the Gospel of our Lord is equal to producing a society of redemption, it is also equal to producing individuals who live under untoward conditions in the mood of redemption. We do not further our holy faith by hurling epithets or by cultivating schismatic souls. Like Moses we may be compelled to say to quarrelling partisans, - "Ye be brethren." But it will be well not to kill too many taskmasters lest our deeds drive us to mountains too lonely for social accomplishments! We may be assured that as we learn to follow Jesus to the Temple, we shall duly learn, as well, how to follow Him to the Carpenter Shop. Our Gospel is so great that it has many phases: but the phases are not foes. The personal applications and the social applications abide, and are certainly so big and meaningful as to give us programs whose difficulties are their challenge and their glory. The closet of prayer and the room of work may be united in the service of Christ, until Markham's prophecy is fulfilled and men shall emerge from the altar's quiet and the labor's hum to say in "glad, quick cries": "The King who loves the lilies, He has come."

¶   Red-baiting Methodists.

(Taken from "The Red-Baiters and the Methodists" by Winifred L. Chappell, in *The Social Questions Bulletin*, May 1936).

611

The Red-baiters have recently been laying down a heavy barrage against "the Methodist Reds."

THE ATTACK FROM WITHOUT

The Hearst Press. Last summer William Randolph Hearst syndicated a series of articles by Rev. George Donald Pierce, a Protestant Episcopal preacher, to the effect that the "Reds" were using the clergy in a drive to destroy the institutions of the United States. He followed these by another series, "Rid the M. E. Church of 'Red' Incubus." For this drive he used Ralph M. Easley, of the National Civic Federation. Easley has for many years been attacking the social movement in the churches, especially in the Methodist Church (along with collective bargaining, minimum wage laws, old age pensions, social security legislation, etc.) Now his eye is on General Conference. He hopes that that body "will deal with the McConnell-Ward-Chappell radical aggregation without gloves." . . .

[Reports follow on attacks by the *Philadelphia Enquirer*, the newspapers of Los Angeles, and Coal and Lumber associations] .

THE ATTACK FROM WITHIN

Here and there groups of Methodist laymen are taking a hand in heading off "radicalism" in their church.

The Conference of Methodist Laymen. On July 29th, 35 Methodist laymen from several central states met at the Union League Club, Chicago, and organized the Conference of Methodist Laymen - "for renewed emphasis on the spiritual phase of the life and work of the church." Its chairman is Henry S. Henschen. He was president of the Chicago Bank of Commerce which closed June 24, 1932. The secretary is Wilbur Helm, also a Chicago banker and president of the Illinois Society of the Sons of the American Revolution.

Its Position. The Conference has issued two pronouncements, two pamphlets and an address by one of its members; also a statement to the Methodist press which summarizes "the essential points" in the principles adopted. These are: The building of Christian character is the fundamental object of our church. Its message is personal, individual. For its influence on social and economic conditions true Christianity relies upon the work of Christian individuals. There is essential and inevitable conflict between the personal philosophy of Christianity and the philosophy of economic determinism, which relates all human happiness to economic reward. Therefore when pulpit and religious press substitute economic and social systems for the Christian ideal of individual responsibility and freedom of choice they are losing sight of their fundamental

objectives. Methodist ministers and laymen are called to join in the study of the problems growing out of the conflict between these opposing philosophies.

What It Means. Here is first a purely personal religion - as though the social meaning and imperative of the Christian religion had never been realized or taught. Next is the assumption that any view of life which goes beyond this is based on "economic determinism." Thus the exponents of a religion to be worked out in the organized as well as the personal aspect of life are classed with the advocates of materialism. This magician's trick is completed by declaring that economic and social systems are "mechanistic in character, impersonal in operation"; by asserting that the ills of the world will not be cured by "more materialism"; and by charging that "certain minorities in Protestant organizations...would substitute the external compulsion of artificial and materialistic systems for the motivation from within..." The facts, of course, are exactly opposite to this strange mixture of ideas. It is these "minorities" who challenge the present social order who are waging a spiritual warfare, theoretically and practically, with economic determinism and materialism. Their judgment upon our present economic method rests upon its dependence upon selfishness and greed, upon its impersonal and mechanistic nature. They seek a more spiritual way of life for organized mankind as well as for the individual.

Further Meaning. This these Methodist laymen cannot see because their underlying purpose is the defense of the present order. The first meeting assembled "for the purpose of discussing 'the growing radical propaganda and hostile attitude toward business and the established order which are being disseminated and proclaimed in the name of the Methodist Episcopal Church'..." One of their pamphlets proclaims that "the economic system has done an amazingly creditable job of maintaining employment..."; that the profit motive "is the mainspring of economic progress..." The author sees "not the slightest proof that the economic system has failed in its essential service to society."

An Offensive! This defense of the existing order becomes an offensive in press statements of the officers of the Conference: "We are going to demand settlement of the status of the Communist-influenced Methodist Federation for Social Service, and of clergymen and church officials who use their positions to preach Socialism and Communism...The campaign is being planned with thoroughness..." Educational policies of the church together with its institutions, such as schools, colleges, charities and missions, may fall within the range of the movement's careful scrutiny." "Many laymen, we believe, are of the opinion that pastors and editors should speak only as citizens until the church is ready to pronounce..." From

these and other similar statements quoted in the *Chicago Tribune*
and the Hearst press it becomes clear what "renewed emphasis upon the
spiritual phase of the life and work of the church" means in fact.
It means control over and limitation of the utterances of preachers,
editors, educators, board executives and voluntary groups. The
specific and immediate objectives are the Board of Education and the
M.F.S.S.

California Laymen. In the Southern California Conference a
Methodist Laymen's Committee, with 100 names on its letterhead, has
set itself the job of getting the General Conference to "take
definite action to correct the existing situation by adopting such
measures as will eradicate those sinister influences that have in-
sinuated themselves into the church..." with special reference to
the Methodist agencies that have to do with the training of youth.

A Memorial. It has prepared a General Conference Memorial to
the effect that the General Conference statements on the economic
order have been followed by annual conferences and have encouraged
preachers to over-emphasize the social gospel at the expense of
its "personal and more spiritual aspects," thus creating the
impression that Methodism is not loyal to American institutions;
that some of those responsible for the education of the church youth
are misleading them on this matter. It petitions the Conference
to correct this situation, especially by "removing from office"
such leadership and to provide that youth be "grounded in the
fundamentals" in such a way as to be fortified against "insidious
propaganda." It reminds the General Conference, "We lay members
have held or are now holding important offices in the church and
through the years have supported it with our services and our means..."

In Personal Terms. These organizations and their locals do
not stop with counsel and denunciation. They continually snipe at
individuals whose voices are raised against the profit system or
against war, or in behalf of social justice in concrete cases.
Methodist leaders come in for their share of this sniping. A few
illustrations from many: The U. S. Chamber of Commerce ordered its
research assistant to write an article on "Communism's Threat to
Academic Freedom," which was aimed especially at President G. Bromley
Oxnam of DePauw. (The research man resigned rather than write the
article.) Dr. E. F. Tittle has for years been under attack by the
"patriots" because of his stand against war. When a young Chicago
Methodist preacher went with others to the Police Commissioner to
get permission for an unemployed demonstration, the American Vigilant
Intelligence Federation sent a letter implying that he was a
Communist to the preacher's community newspaper, the Chief of Police,
neighboring preachers, the district superintendent and bishop and
the local Legion post.

THE REAL LINEUP

The lineup is not, as some sections of the church press have indicated, laymen vs. preachers.

Laymen vs. Laymen. Many laymen are questioning the present social order. Some of them are organizing to say so. A Laymen's Religious Movement (Methodist Episcopal, unofficial, not affiliated with any other group), was started in Chicago in January. H. C. Snyder, of Madison, Wis., is chairman and John C. Lazenby of Milwaukee is secretary. Over 200 laymen from 30 states have endorsed the Movement. Quotations from a press statement show its position: "...in every age religion has been quickened and revived by active participation in the great group social movements which have arisen from the ever-changing conditions of human living." Then faithfulness to religious ideas "makes it impossible to be silent regarding the 'unchristian, unethical and anti-social' aspects of present-day civilization which everyone recognizes." "The present leadership of the Methodist Church is standing true to the spirit of the Gospel ..." "The summons, therefore, is for our laymen to establish the way of Christ in the changing social order of our generation." This group thinks that there is "a large and somewhat inarticulate group of laity which believes in the indivisibility of the personal and social gospel."

Preachers vs. Preachers. There is a lineup also among preachers. It showed itself in the east when Bishop Leonard instructed the Pittsburgh social service commission last fall not to sponsor the M. F. S. S. conference held in that city, and issued an open letter directed against the M. F. S. S. and its secretaries. And this spring when he and district superintendents wrote Erie Conference preachers discouraging attendance at a meeting at Meadville called by Federation members. It showed itself in the west when Adna Leonard of the Southern California Conference, sent out a letter warning against a "political machine" which he said certain preachers – whom he named – "known for their extreme ideas on social and economic theories" were setting up to get themselves elected to General Conference. (Bishop Herbert Welch, on the organizers of the M. F. S. S., now looks upon it "with some concern." He notes "current reports" that the executives have "denounced the profit motive as utterly unchristian, renounced the capitalist system... proposed the complete overturning of the present order..."

The Issue. Within the church the issue then is between those, both preachers and laymen, who want a purely personal "regeneration of the heart" gospel, leaving economic and social matters alone, and those who seek the Christian way of life in organized society as well as in personal behavior. This is also the division between those who find that the Christian way of life and the needs of humanity now

615

require the transforming of the present economic order and those whose interests are best served by its continuance in its present form and who therefore want religion to keep its hands off.

How did the prophets and Jesus, the apostles, the Church Fathers, John Wesley, hear the voice of God and find the course of a regenerating religion? By listening to the needs of the poor or to the desires of the powerful?

¶ What the Methodist Federation for Social Service Was Thinking and Doing.

(Taken from *The Social Questions Bulletin*, Vol. 27, No. 6, June 1937).

In Evanston, this past month, one hundred and twenty-six members and friends of the Federation gathered to hear and act on policy-forming reports, to exchange experiences of both success and failure in our efforts as Christians to help change the mind-set of our communities toward a more realistic and ethical social consciousness, to survey the world scene and analyze the crisis confronting our civilization, to plan for further advance: in short to recharge our spirits for more courageous and effective service to the cause which we deem vital.

Four paragraphs from Dr. [Harry F.] Ward's report clearly indicate the scope of the discussion.

Reaction in the Denomination. "The struggle against reaction in the denomination should be helped by the growing interdenominational action in the same direction. Since our last meeting there has been formed the United Christian Council for Democracy, a federation of nationally organized unofficial denominational units with a platform similar to our own. The Executive Committee includes representatives of nine denominational units and one interdenominational (in the South). Several local units have been formed containing the local members of the national denominational groups. Members should initiate and support these local organizations in order that a united voice may be heard on crucial occasions."

Our Apparent Recovery. "The issues that confront us increasingly challenge our capacities. Our apparent recovery will undoubtedly change the psychology of many. Those who know it cannot last must enlighten those who are deceived. They must point out that the basis of the present price and profit boom is the buying of metals for armament; that the 'recovery' will not only be short-lived, it will be deadly. We must make it clear that our opposition to the profit system rests not simply upon its inefficiency, but upon the

evil in its very nature."

Preserve Democracy! "The combined approach of war and Fascism challenges us. We see the British Rearmament Program placing the economy of the world on a war base. We see our Industrial Mobilization Plan decreeing Fascist controls when war is declared. It becomes our duty to resist the plans of the warmakers, to ward off fascist enroachments upon our liberties. We must proclaim with increasing clarity the truth that the preservation and extension of the democratic process is the only road to the progressive organization of peace."

Governmental Action. "In the field of governmental action we are faced with the concrete questions of the Supreme Court, the rights of labor, and the needed changes in our concepts of property rights brought to light by the sitdown strikes and the soil conservation program. We must recognize not merely the public interest in, but the social nature of, both our industrial plant and our natural resources. Our position in these matters must be worked out in discussion and in action under the guidance of our basic principles of the necessity of replacing the struggle for profit with the mutual cooperation of social economic planning, resting upon social ownership and carried on under increasingly democratic controls."

The struggle against reaction in the denomination was emphasized by Charles Webber's report from the field.

New Units. "In several of the Conferences I found that the Conference Social Service Committee had been merged in a Conference Commission on Citizenship, Temperance, and Public Morals and had become conservative in the process or else had been devitalized by the newly appointed ministers and laymen. In such cases, I urged the formation of an independent M. F. S. S. unit to carry on an educational and action program - a program calling for the radicalization of the formal Social Service Committee or Commission report, the development of open forums and discussion groups in the churches, the promotion of social ownership by the people organized as citizens and consumers, cooperation with the trade unions and the organized unemployed, and for active participation in anti-war demonstrations and in non-violent coercive measures in defense of civil and religious liberties. Such Federation units are now in existence in the Erie, Ohio, Indiana and Rock River Conferences, and other units are in the process of formation."

Economic Ties. "In community after community, I found that our local churches and ministers are bound by economic ties to the beneficiaries of our capitalistic system. These ties are restricting our ministers' freedom of action. Several ministers have kept silent on economic issues for fear of what might happen to their

families. Other ministers have allowed persons on their Official Board, their District Superintendent or their Bishop, to curb the freedom of their pulpit, out of consideration for what has been called the 'Unity of the Church.'"

Unity? "The question arose time and time again, 'Is the unity of the church, on a basis acceptable to the beneficiaries of the present economic system, of such value as to warrant a minister's sacrificing the preaching of the gospel in relation to economic issues?'"

As touching the training of ministers who shall be able to understand and withstand the forces of reaction brought to bear upon the pulpit, a theological student, present at the meetings, writes as follows:

"Our liberal seminaries are giving courses that have a definite bearing on contemporary problems. Despite this, the very way in which the subjects are taught, coupled with the emphasis on being as 'sociologically objective' as possible, has enabled many theologs still to be neither socially conscious nor interested in social Christianity. . . . Many ministers lack the training and insight necessary to deal with the problems of the contemporary world, not to mention the problems of the individual in modern society. It is more convenient to stress the deepening of the religious experience, emphasize liturgics and 'comfort' preaching than to take hold of life where it is 'hot.' Minority group membership is shunned by many 'career' men. . . . True religion stands with collectivism over against Fascism. Though many of the clergy see this, to implement their convictions is another matter."

Interdenominational Agency. A spirited discussion of cases of interference with freedom of the pulpit resulted in a motion requesting the American Civil Liberties Union to initiate an inter-denominational agency to act as the American Association of University Professors does in relation to academic freedom. (The Civil Liberties Union has responded favorably.) Also a letter was sent to the Board of Bishops, then in session, calling their attention to the situation. (A sympathetic reply, informing us of their discussion of the issue, has been received.)

Even Clergymen. Under the caption "Another Hearst Expose'" the *St. Louis Post-Dispatch* holds up to ridicule the *Chicago Herald-Examiner's* attack upon the Federation for endorsing the action of the A. C. L. U. at this point. "The A. C. L. U. is a non-partisan organization, representing all factions of political thought, devoted solely to defense of civil liberties. It is just as likely to go to the bat for Ogden Mills as for Earl Browder, and has, in fact, done both...As to the specific action: It turns out to be

approval of a resolution demanding freedom of speech for all clergymen. So it has become a sign of Red affiliation to demand free
speech! Americans had always thought that was guaranteed by the Bill
of Rights, even to clergymen, so the Hearst interpretation is a
definitely novel view."

The alarming approach of war was analyzed by Dr. Charles F.
Boss, Secretary of the Peace Commission of our Church:

"We are moving rapidly toward war. It is all but inevitable.
Clear evidence is found in the breakdown of the economic order, the
rearmament of the nations, and the threat of the Fascist nations
driven by lack of gold, lack of raw materials and lack of markets
for the sale of their goods. Is there any way to stop or postpone
the coming war?

"The United States, France, Great Britain, with others, should
take immediate steps enabling the Fascist nations to obtain: (1) Raw
materials, (2) Markets by which to make payments in goods since they
have practically no gold, (3) Favorable trade agreements through a
more rapid and generous application of the Reciprocal Trade Agreement
Act.

"Furthermore, the United States, France and Great Britain should
lay down a genuine proposal for complete disarmament."

Postpone the War! "Such steps would postpone the coming war.
Precious time might be gained for continued education for social
change – for economic justice and cooperative planning, for a peaceful world order, for the preservation of the democratic method as
the road to a new social order.

"There is a high degree of probability that all efforts to postpone or stop war will fail. What then? We set ourselves to the further steps of educating and organizing our people to meet the war
when it comes."

Write Your Congressman! "In the interim we are opposed to the
Industrial Mobilization Plan, the Hill-Sheppard Bill; to the militarization of the Philippines; and to the increases in army and navy.
We support the Nye-Kvale Bill, the repeal of the Asiatic Exclusion
Act, and the Ludlow Bill calling for an Amendment which would require
a popular referendum before men could be conscripted for service in
foreign lands or waters."

The following resolutions were presented and adopted:

Committee for Industrial Organization. "The members of the
M. F. S. S. re-affirm their historic demand that labor be accorded

the right to bargain collectively through representatives of their own choosing. In our opinion, the nature of the organization to which labor should turn must be dictated by the conditions under which men must work.

"Large sections of our industrial order are organized on a mass production basis. This is especially true of the basic industries like steel, oil and automobiles. For workers engaged in such industries, industrial rather than craft unions are most practical.

"Therefore, while recognizing the historic value of craft unions, we urge persons engaged in mass industry to join in the movement toward industrial organization which is being pushed forward with such energy by Mr. John L. Lewis and his Committee for Industrial Organization. We commend the efforts of Mr. Lewis and his committee in attempting to provide the great mass of workers a form of collective bargaining which best meets their needs for effective unionization."

Compulsory Arbitration. "We are opposed to legislation requiring compulsory arbitration of industrial disputes as being incompatible with democratic procedure between representatives of capital and labor, unless provision is made, as in Mexico, for the complete suspension of production, by authority of the government, pending the full settlement of the dispute. Without such safeguards compulsory arbitration tends toward progressive denial of the right to strike, which is labor's hard won and most effective weapon, and thus it would constitute another step toward a Fascist order."

Incorporation of Unions. "We hold that social justice will not be advanced by yielding to the current cry for the incorporation of labor unions. Incorporation of unions is unnecessary as a means of insuring responsibility either in case of destruction of property or violation of contract, and such action would make possible and probable an undue judicial interference with recognized union activities.

"In case such a law should be enacted, there should be an immediate demand for the incorporation, and publicizing of the financial affairs, of all employers' organizations related to collective bargaining with employees."

Sit-down Strike. "We support the use of the sit-down strike against employers who refuse to adjust differences, through collective bargaining, with representatives of their employees' own independent choosing. Our endorsement is justified by at least two considerations. First, the sit-down is less provocative of violence than any other form of strike yet generally adopted, and when violence does occur its responsibility is readily determined. Second, it symbolizes the worker's vested right in his job under scales of

wages and working conditions to be democratically determined.

"We are confronted with another human situation in which legal enactment has not yet kept pace with moral insight and essential justice. Only yesterday, collective bargaining, the right to strike, and to picket, were held inconsistent with the private property rights of employers. Just as these rights are now widely recognized by law, so we believe that enlightened public opinion will soon compel legal recognition of the worker's vested right in his job as symbolized in the sit-down.

"In the interim, we hold the use of private or civil force to eject sit-downers to be subversive of essential justice and wholly incompatible with democratic principles."

25.   MINORITY ASPECTS

In the twentieth century both an ebb and a flow took place in expression of minority interests in the church. Racial problems, although a part of the social gospel movement, had to share attention with many other issues. The older ethnic groups, such as Germans and Scandinavians, who had enjoyed annual conference structures of their own, merged into the English-speaking geographical Annual Conferences and gradually lost separate identity. Before that happened, however, the German Methodists suffered a traumatic shock under the super-patriotic pressures of World War I. This is poignantly illustrated by the fate of the German-language Advocate, Der Christliche Apologete.

Another exception to the submergence of ethnic presence was the Spanish-speaking Hispanics of the Southwest. Alfredo Nañez gives an excellent account of the persistence of Hispanic Methodism into the Rio Grande Conference, in a recent article in Methodist History.

But the race issue involving black Methodists simply would not go away. Many articles and editorials in the Advocates, *illustrated here by three, show the strength and the depth of feeling long after the failure of the wartime negotiations to solve the problem. I. Garland Penn was a black layman, field secretary of the Board of Education for Negroes. Robert E. Jones had been editor of the* Southwestern Christian Advocate, *and in 1920 was elected one of the first two Negro bishops in the M. E. Church. A later black bishop, Willis J. King, summarized in an article the role of the Negro members of The Methodist Church as it became the United Methodist Church.*

One of the most significant developments in the recent history of the United Methodist Church is the formation of Black Methodists for Church Renewal, a sort of architype for ethnic and racial minority voices. Some of the sources of Methodist black power are illustrated in the seminal efforts of the Black Caucus of the Northern Illinois Conference.

Another aspect of minority Methodism is found in the holiness churches, most of them offshoots of Episcopal Methodism. Donald Dayton in a recent article in the Christian Century *reviews their history and present prospects.*

¶   *Der Christliche Apologete* Under Pressure, 1918.

(Taken from *Northwestern Christian Advocate*, 30 January 1918, 122).

IMPORTANT STATEMENT BY THE PUBLISHING AGENTS

The Methodist Episcopal Church in the United States is un-equivocally against the Central Powers of Europe and whole-heartedly with the United States and her Allies in the present war for freedom, democracy, and humanity.

The officers and members of the Church desire to put the total force of the Church behind the Government now, as in all our previous wars. We cannot be dumb, nor sound a doubtful or uncertain note.

Since the United States declared War with Germany, the Publishing Agents have felt that the policy of the editor of *Der Christliche Apologete* was not in full harmony with the spirit of the Church and the country.

The attention of the editor has been called to this condition without the desired result in a change of editorial policy. Under the law, the Publishing Agents are responsible to the Government for the utterances of a paper which has the use of the mail service, and circulates among the people of the United States and other countries.

The Agents distinctly and sincerely regret that the *Apologete* has not been outspoken in its support of the United States and our Allies - Great Britain, France, Italy, and the other nations, and in its opposition to the war spirit, the war conduct, the broken treaties and the unspeakable atrocities of Germany and the other Central Powers; that it has not rung clear for the victory of the Allied nations over the Prussianized autocracy that has broken the peace and threatened to destroy the liberty of the world.

There can be but one attitude consistent with the American and Methodist spirit. In what it has said as a whole, in what it has refrained from saying, in the spirit and atmosphere it has created, the *Apologete* has not contributed, as it should in our judgment, either to the best interests of the Germans themselves, or to the cause of the United States and her Allies.

The Agents have therefore felt obliged to make such arrangement for the editorial conduct of *Der Christliche Apologete* as will relieve it of all the criticism of its patriotism. Henceforth it will sound a clear note for the utter defeat of Germany, and its despotic military system and rulers, together with the other Central Powers, and for the complete victory of the United States and France and Italy and Great Britain, and the other nations joined with them.

There shall be no half-hearted or divided allegiance.

The Publishers firmly believe this to be the best for our German Methodists themselves. We can understand the affection of the German-born for the Germany of which they dream, but neither we nor they can have two countries. We have but one, the United States, and to that we are committed heart and soul. And, in the name of our Master and our common country, we ask and expect our German brethren to accept the new arrangements with heartiness, and to unite with us to make the honored and historic old *Apologete* a new advocate of democracy and humanity against tyranny, despotism, and military autocracy.

In order that all these conditions shall be fully met, we have arranged for the appointment of an associate editor for the *Apologete*, who shall have entire charge of all matter appearing touching the war in editorial, history, or comment, relieving the present editors from that department of the paper. The name of this associate editor will be announced soon.

In reaching the above conclusions, we are under obligations to the Local Committee at Cincinnati, and three of our bishops, who were with us at the meeting and who have greatly aided us by their advice and counsel.

> H. C. JENNINGS,
> EDWIN R. GRAHAM,
> JOHN H. RACE,
> Publishing Agents.

We, the undersigned, the editor and assistant editor, heartily subscribe to the above as a correct statement of the situation occupied by *Der Christliche Apologete* in the past, and agree to abide by the policy as here set forth by the terms which are to govern *Der Christliche Apologete* in the future.

> ALBERT J. NAST, Editor,
> FRANK T. ENDERIS, Assistant
> Editor.

¶ The Transition from Anglo to Mexican-American Leadership in the Rio Grande Conference.

(Taken from article by Alfredo Náñez in *Methodist History*, XVI (1978), 67-74).

This paper will deal with the transition from Anglo leadership to Spanish-speaking leadership and with the effort of the conference

624

over a long period of time to be recognized as a full annual conference, free from the domination of individuals or agencies. Because of the nature of its work and of its dependence, financial and otherwise, upon the church in general, the conference had not received this recognition in the past. The church and its agencies should give an annual conference its full recognition of the rights, privileges and responsibilities that are specified in the Constitution, whether financially, numerically or otherwise an annual conference is large or small, strong or weak. . . .

Due to the Mexican Revolution and other circumstances, the work in the United States had to be separated from the work in Mexico. In 1914 two missions were organized in our country: the Texas Mexican Mission covering the territory east of the Pecos River in Texas and the Pacific Mexican Mission west of the Pecos River. This latter one did include a few appointments in Mexico. In 1918 it became the Western Mexican Mission.

Throughout the history of these two missions, from their organization in 1914 to 1930, their superintendents were Anglo missionaries: Frank S. Onderdonk for the Texas Mexican Mission, J. F. Corbin, J. A. Phillips, J. P. Lancaster, Joseph Thacker, Lawrence Reynolds, and R. J. Parker for the Western Mexican Mission, which had two districts and the presiding elders acted as superintendents.

In these missions the dominance of the Anglo missionaries was complete. The only sign of dissatisfaction can be detected in the 1917 meeting of the Texas Mexican Mission when on the first ballot for delegates to the General Conference, a Spanish-speaking clergyman, E. B. Vargas, was elected. Due to a technicality, he was disqualified and F. S. Onderdonk was elected instead.

In 1929 the missions sent memorials to the General Conference requesting that they be elevated to the status of Annual Conferences. The memorials were accepted and in 1930 two new conferences were organized: the Texas Mexican Conference and the Western Mexican Conference. . . .

Frank S. Onderdonk, the great missionary leader who did so much to extend the Spanish-speaking work, passed away in 1936. Immediately upon his death, several missionaries from other conferences made application to fill his place. But since Onderdonk had been the only missionary working within the Texas Mexican Conference at the time, the presiding bishop, Hiram A. Boaz, did not deem it wise to bring in an outsider for the leadership position. He appointed Frank Ramos, who had earlier served as presiding elder, to take Onderdonk's place. So for the first time in the history of the conference the leadership was placed in the hands of Mexican-Americans.

In 1938 both Spanish-speaking conferences elected Spanish-speaking clerical delegates to the United Methodist General Conference which met in Kansas City and for the last time the lay delegates were wives of missionaries, Mrs. F. S. Onderdonk and Mrs. R. J. Parker.

The unification of Methodism in 1939 started a new chapter in the work of the Methodist Church among the Spanish-speaking people in Texas and New Mexico.

Representatives from the Texas Mexican Conference, the Western Mexican Conference and what was left of the work of the Methodist Episcopal Church in New Mexico and El Paso, Texas, met in Dallas, November 2-5, 1939, to reorganize the work in the two states into a single conference.

The new annual conference was organized November 3, under the name of Southwest Mexican Conference. It was to embrace all the Spanish-speaking work in the states of Texas and New Mexico. It was divided into three districts, the El Paso, Northern and Southern districts with N. B. Stump, Frank Ramos and José Espino as superintendents respectively.

In 1940 the Southwest Mexican Conference sent to the General Conference two memorials which clearly show the yearning of the group to be on the same footing with the other annual conferences of The Methodist Church.

One of the memorials dealt with the elimination of the exception for the term of service of the district superintendents in the Spanish-speaking work. The second memorial requested that the special provision specified in the *Discipline* for membership for ministers in the Spanish-speaking annual conferences be eliminated. They wanted the requirements to be the same as those of the church in general.

These two memorials were accepted and the Southwest Mexican Conference became a part of the Methodist connection without any exceptions or limitations.

The territory covered by the new conference overlapped all or part of six English-speaking conferences of the South Central Jurisdiction and two of the Central Jurisdiction.

The constituency in this vast territory was heterogeneous. In the El Paso District the majority of the people were descendents of the original Spanish settlers who had come to that section during the sixteenth, seventeenth and eighteenth centuries. The wave of immigrants in the first quarter of the twentieth century did not go to New Mexico.

In Texas, although many of the Spanish-speaking inhabitants were descendents of the original Spanish settlers, the majority were only first or second generation Americans of Mexican parentage. To be able to bring a sense of unity in the conference from such a diversity of people was no easy task.

The very name of the conference, because it contained the word "Mexican," became a source of dissension from the very beginning. The word had been used in all the names which had been given to the Spanish-speaking work in Texas: Mexican Border Mission District, Mexican Border Conference, Northwest Mexican Conference, Pacific Mexican Mission, Texas Mexican Mission, Western Mexican Mission, Texas Mexican Conference and Western Mexican Conference.

In New Mexico the Methodist Episcopal Church in naming the organizations working among the Spanish-speaking people never used the word "Mexican." The names used were: Spanish-speaking District, Spanish Mission, Southwest Spanish Mission, Latin American Provisional Conference.

Finally, the annual conference of 1947 asked the Jurisdictional Conference to change the name. This was done in El Paso, Texas in 1948 and it became the Rio Grande Annual Conference.

In the efforts to become an annual conference, not only legally but also in practice, some serious problems were encountered. One was the support of the district superintendents who in the past had been missionaries. Covering such a large geographical area, the conference was first divided into three districts, later into four, although the membership per district is relatively small.

Another problem has been the adequate support of the ministry. This problem has lingered because of the nature of the constituency and the small size of the congregations. Related to the support of the ministry has been the development of a pension program. In 1940 the amount of $395.70 was raised for the support of five retired ministers and widows of ministers. By 1975 the conference had some $100,000, which made it possible to pay sixty dollars per year of service to its retired clergy.

In spite of its limitations, the Rio Grande Conference has always accepted and paid one hundred per cent of its share of World Service and has contributed gladly to every cause the Church has sponsored.

During the forties, as Missionary Secretary and Executive Secretary for the Board of Education, this writer kept pressing for recognition of the importance of the Spanish-speaking work by the National Division of the Board of Missions. These efforts were

finally heeded and in 1948 a director for Spanish-speaking work was appointed with residence in San Antonio. The appointment was timely and the work benefitted from it. Unfortunately the National Division did not make a job description for the position, particularly in regard to the director's administrative relationship to the Rio Grande Conference. The director was left on his own with promotional, administrative and financial responsibilities. The paternalistic approach to the work created from the beginning resentments, friction and misunderstandings between the leadership of the conference and that office.

Because of these conflicts, Edward Carothers, the new Associate General Secretary for the National Division, called a meeting in 1965 at Southern Methodist University to consider these matters. Out of that meeting came the suggestion that upon the retirement of the director for Spanish-speaking work, the new appointee should serve under the Joint Commission of Education and Cultivation of the Board of Missions with no administrative responsibilities in the conference. The suggestion was accepted by the Board of Missions and in May, when the Rio Grande Conference met in annual session in Albuquerque, New Mexico, the new policy was announced by Dr. Carothers and Miss Mary Lou Barnwell, Assistant General Secretary of Home Fields. They both stated that the new director for Spanish-speaking work would serve under the Joint Commission of Education and Cultivation rather than the National Division and that he was not to have any administrative responsibilities in the conference. The responsibility of the new appointee was to be in the field of promotion and interpretation. They also announced that the Conference Board of Missions was to be the body to make decisions about the minimum salaries for pastors receiving mission aid and for church extension projects, as well as all recommendations related to the conference board's responsibilities to the National Division.

This new policy was reiterated by Harry Komuro and Darwin Andrus, executives of the National Division, when they met with the Board of Missions of the Rio Grande Conference on April 22, 1966, in Houston, Texas. Dr. Komuro introduced the Rev. William Cheyne, the new director for Spanish-speaking work, to the Rev. Roy D. Barton, chairman, and members of the conference board. Quoting Dr. Komuro in part:

> The active administration of the mission aid program
> and related services is the responsibility of the
> National Division working through this Board of
> Missions of the Rio Grande Annual Conference. This
> means that the Board of Missions of the Rio Grande
> Conference has the responsibility of determining the
> actual askings for the various items needed for
> salary support, administrative costs, church

extension loans, grants, etc.

With the official announcement of this new policy, the relationship of the conference to the National Division of the General Board of Missions was clarified and another new day was started for the Rio Grande Conference. The conference was to be trusted by the National Division like any other conference in Methodism, regardless of its numerical or financial limitations. With the declaration of this new policy plus the earlier end of the double standard of the ministry, the Rio Grande Conference came of age.

¶ Shall There Be a General Superintendent of African Descent?

(Taken from editorial, *Christian Advocate*, Apr. 21, 1912, 571-72).

After the Methodist Episcopal Church, South, was established under that name in 1844-1845 - its constituency at the time being thirteen Southern Conferences - there was little access for the Methodist Episcopal Church to the Negroes of the South. There was, however, a large membership of the Negroes in the thirteen Conferences.

I

At the close of the Civil War the emancipated slaves were in great need, from every point of view, and the Methodist Episcopal Church considered itself bound to assist in the development of the freedmen. By 1876 the Methodist Episcopal Church registered 150,000 members of African descent, the very large proportion being in the States in which slavery had existed.

In that year, memorials from five of the Conferences which had been established in the interim, were presented to the General Conference asking for the election of a colored man to the Episcopacy. The Conference took cognizance of the petitions and passed the following:

> We reiterate the declaration of the General Conference of 1872 touching the election of a man of African descent to our episcopal office, and assert that race, nationality, color or previous condition is no bar to the election of any man to the episcopal office in our Church, nor to any other elective office to be filled by the General Conference.

The same Conference received a number of petitions for and against a separation, under certain circumstances, of a Conference made up of persons of Caucasian and persons of African descent.

629

The report of the committee was long and luminous. Certain facts were brought forward, such as: *"There is not a single church of white members* with a colored preacher; nor a single district of churches of white members with *a colored presiding elder."* Further it stated that there were, in all, nineteen Conferences "where the white and colored are mixed, or being separate *occupy the same territory"*; that there were three Conferences exclusively colored — the Delaware, the Washington and the Lexington; that they had been decidedly prosperous, and that there were five Conferences that were "almost, though not exclusively, composed of colored members." Finally, the following was passed:

Resolved, 1. That where it is the general desire of the members of an Annual Conference that there should be no division of such Conference into two or more Conferences in the same territory; and where it is not clearly to be seen that such division would favor or improve the state of the work in any Conference; and where the interests and usefulness of even a minority of the members of such Conference, and of the members of churches in such Conference, might be damaged or imperiled by division, it is the opinion of this General Conference that such division should not be made.

Resolved, 2. That whenever it shall be requested by a majority of the white members, and also a majority of the colored members of any Annual Conference that it be divided, then it is the opinion of this General Conference that such division should be made, and in that case the Bishop presiding is hereby authorized to organize the new Conference or Conferences.

This report was adopted by more than two thirds, in a very heavy vote.

In 1896 the Committee on Episcopacy reported, and the General Conference adopted, the following:

In the election of Bishops there should be no discrimination on account of race or color, but men should be chosen because of their worth and fitness for the position.

In the presence of this statement, often reiterated by various *bodies of our Church, we believe the time has come when the General Conference may safely and wisely choose a Bishop from among our seventeen hundred ministers of African descent.*

On the first ballot in the election for Bishops at that General Conference, J. W. E. Bowen, a colored man notable for learning and eloquence, received 147 votes for the Episcopacy; C. C. McCabe, 141, and Earl Cranston, 115. On the second ballot C. C. McCabe received 218 votes, J. W. E. Bowen, 175, and Earl Cranston, 164. For two more ballots Professor Bowen's vote was above 100, but in the end Chaplain McCabe and Earl Cranston were elected.

II

The present situation of our brethren of African descent, who are members of the Methodist Episcopal Church, and feel the need of a Bishop of their own race, is unusual, and to many painful. They now number about 325,000. They say that the Church has heard the appeal of its constituents in foreign lands – namely, South America, Europe, China, India and Africa. In response to a petition of these foreigners the Church has granted them ten Bishops, six as missionary Bishops and four as General Superintendents.

They maintain that there are conditions in the South which they deprecate, and which cannot be changed all in a moment, that make it embarrassing for our Bishops of Caucasian descent to administer our work in many sections and that at times cause no little embarrassment to themselves. They declare that there are 6,000,000 unchurched Negroes in this country; that the increase of the Negro population in the State of Mississippi alone during the last ten years was 100,000, and that the fact that for nearly fifty years they have not had a Bishop of their race has caused them to be taunted by many Negroes of other denominations.

A large number who belong to our Church have been growing in intelligence and learning for several decades; and to approximate their wishes the General Conference in 1904 voted for a change in the Constitution which would alter the third Restrictive Rule so as to make it read as follows:

The General Conference shall not change nor alter any part or rule of our government so as to do away Episcopacy, nor destroy the plan of our itinerant General Superintendency; but *may elect a Bishop or Bishops for work among particular races and languages, or for any of our foreign Missions, limiting their episcopal jurisdiction to the same respectively.*

When it was put to vote, the number in favor of the amendment as proposed in the report was 517 and those who were opposed to the Constitutional amendment 27. This was an honest attempt to make it possible to elect Bishops for our colored brethren in this country without placing it under the title Missionary Bishop.　.　.　.

631

To elect to the General Superintendency an elder who is in good standing in his Conference, whatever his race or nation, is unquestionably constitutional.

To elect a Bishop exclusively for the colored Conferences is plainly unconstitutional.

For the Bishops to confine the jurisdiction of a General Superintendent to his own race exclusively would involve a perversion of the Constitution.

But to do so chiefly, *assigning him occasionally to other Conferences,* would be supported by previous cases.

Our correspondence reveals the fact that some of our brethren of African descent do not desire the election of one of their race to the Episcopacy, believing that the time for that has not yet come.

The coming General Conference should give to this subject much and serious consideration, for the present condition of our brethren of African descent is one of perplexity and uncertainty.

¶   "A New Departure for Our Freedman's Aid Society"

(Taken from I. Garland Penn in *Western Christian Advocate,* 25 Mar, 1914, 369).

For the first time in the history of the Freedman's Aid Society the twenty-two presidents and principals of our schools met at the headquarters in Cincinnati, Ohio, from February 17th to 20th, for their annual meeting in joint session with the Board of Managers. Such a meeting was deemed wise for several reasons.

No such joint meeting having ever been held, it could but be profitable to the presidents and members of the Board to know one another. A survey of the work being done, and results accomplished by those doing it, would be information of inestimable value for the Board.

The report of the Commission of Educators recently on a tour of inspection of the schools was to be made to the Board. This report vitally concerned the presidents and principals of the schools. To consider the report in joint session could save time and beget results in the formulation of plans and remedies for meeting conditions and needs arising from modern-day educational methods as applied to our schools.

Again, if the Jubilee sum of $500,000, ordered by the General Conference of 1912, is to be realized this quadrennium, to say nothing of the still larger sum of one million dollars suggested by the commission as the amount necessary to provide for the proper doing of the work and to meet the actual needs of the case, then our presidents must get under the lead with the officers of the society.

As is usual in such meetings, much profit came which could not be foreseen.

The meetings commenced on Monday morning, February 16th, the presidents being given the right of way for introduction and presentation of their work before the Cincinnati Preachers' Meeting.

Monday afternoon the presidents and principals went into their first formal session, with Dr. J. S. Hill as president and Dr. A. P. Camphor, secretary.

The joint session of the Board of Managers and presidents began formally Tuesday, at 10 A. M., Bishop W. F. Anderson in the chair. Reports from the treasurer, Dr. John H. Race; from Corresponding Secretaries Maveety and Penn, and Inspector Bennett, with some routine business, were quickly gotten out of the way so that the report of the Commission of Educators could be heard.   .   .   .

The most important of the recommendations which required the larger consideration was that referring to a constructive policy for the future development of the schools, involving name and curriculum, thus eliminating the wide use of the word "university," and the standardizing of the schools to meet needs and adaptation of communities and people to be served. After the most searching inquiry into all phases of the question, and hearing from the president and principal of each institution, the final action of the Board on the commission's recommendation was as follows:

1st. Only one institution of the twenty-two will bear the name of university.

2d. Two of the institutions are definitely located as colleges without limitation, in addition to the one university, and they will carry college courses of four years. Increased appropriations to these for laboratory equipment, etc., were made as far as funds were available.

3d. Five others of the institutions will bear the name "college" carrying college courses of four years with conditions. These conditions relate to the number of students taking college courses, also equipment and endowment, the same to be met within a given time to justify the continuance of any one of them as

colleges with a four years' course after the prescribed time.

4th. The remaining ten schools are to be called academies or institutes, and are to do normal and academic work.

5th. The strongest emphasis was put upon industrial work at all the schools, and as fast as possible these departments are to be strengthened and enlarged.

Great attention was given Meharry Medical College, for it is one of the two medical schools most prominent in the country in the training of Negro physicians. The college now graduates annually more of these physicians than any medical school in the world. Attention was called to the fact that a large sum of money will be needed this year to meet the requirements of the American Medical Association if Meharry is to continue in the front rank of medical schools. The surprising information came to the surface that at the last examination of the Tennessee Medical Examining Board, fifty-five of Meharry graduates were examined, fifty-two of whom passed and three failed, giving an average of 5.5% of the failures.

There is only enough space left for us to refer to one other outstanding feature of the report. It is quoted verbatim:

"We found the schools generally well located and filling a useful place. Their influence and product, the special development of industrial training at some points, the creditable quality of most of the teaching, the long periods of sacrificial service given by some engaged in this work, all left their pleasing impression. There is as noble missionary spirit here as on the foreign field. When the difficulties are considered which have had to be overcome, and the limited resources available for the work, the results are both gratifying and surprising. We are persuaded that in spite of the better rural schools now being provided for the Negroes, in spite of some growth in normal school and high school accommodations, the work of the Freedmen's Aid Society is still an urgent need of the South. So far from sounding any retreat, we of the Church should make a great advance, provide a large endowment, give more adequate facilities, pay better salaries, and, in general, strengthen the institutions we have established. They are needed to train a Christian leadership for the colored race, and while they can touch but a few out of the Negro millions, they can do, as they have already done, great things through these selected leaders."

It is confidently hoped that such non-partisan commendation of the work being done from so eminent a source will focus the interest of the Church in this work anew. The commendation is followed with a recommendation as follows:

"We heartily commend the Jubilee Fund Movement. A million dollars for additional buildings and endowment would be none too much at the present juncture."

¶ Bishop Jones Speaks for Black Methodists.

(Taken from *Northwestern Christian Advocate*, 21 May 1924, 543).

Sunday Morning Session

Although on Sunday morning notable visiting ministers occupied nearly all the evangelical and several liberal pulpits in Springfield and vicinity, the vast auditorium was the center of interest for twenty-five hundred men. The service of worship was in charge of Judge Henry Wade Rogers of New York. The Rev. C. Oscar Ford, superintendent Springfield District, led in prayer.

Bishop Robert E. Jones spoke on "Inter-racial Adjustments." His message was a very frank and comprehensive analysis of the race problem in America. Again and again his most unpleasant statements were greeted with enthusiastic applause.

Bishop Jones gained the close attention of the audience when he began, by saying, "We face one of the most difficult problems of our national and international life. I wish to respectfully remind you, you white men, that you are not all of it. There are many others in the world, yellow men and black men."

"Your cry of white supremacy," he declared, "gives us no concern. I want to point out to you that the Negro has waked up. It is a matter of impossibility to keep us where we once were. You white men would never stand for a moment what we go through. We get along remarkably well. Thank God for the sweet brotherly communion we have had during this Conference."

Then Bishop Jones named a number of disturbing conditions between the 12,000,000 Negroes in this country and the white people. "Brethren," he warned, "the red lights are out. The Germans tried to get Negro sympathy during the war. Red propaganda is on. I regret that the happy, smiling, singing Negro is being transformed so that he now burns, in a measure, with hate. You talk about Anglo-Saxon supremacy over the black man. To make the race worth while we must have the same show to make the thing a race."

Undermining Negroes

"I can get more applause in an audience of my people," he said, "by saying something drastic against you white men than by anything else. The Negro is thoroughly Protestant, but there is a body at

work, calling itself one hundred per cent American, that is under-
mining one of the most thoroughgoing of Protestant churches."

Negroes will continue to come North in search of economic
independence, he prophesied, declaring that the coming of the
Negro from Mississippi to the Boston Common "makes some difference"
in the viewpoint with which they are thought of.

Speaking of the bloc of 12,000,000 Negroes, he said, "you want
to break up that bloc somehow," declaring that if it is kept
absolutely apart great mischief may be done. Love is the remedy for
all possible misunderstandings, he said. He praised a movement among
the whites of the South to give justice to the Negroes. "And we will
be satisfied with nothing less," he added.

¶   The Role of the Central Jurisdiction.

(Taken from article by Willis J. King in *Methodist History*, VII
(Apr. 1969), 40-42).

The vigorous educational and evangelistic program carried forward by the Methodist Episcopal Church among the Negroes, especially
in the South, from the close of the Civil War until 1939, when the
Plan of Union was adopted, had both its advantages and disadvantages
to those interested in Methodist unification. To those who believed
in the possibility of the evangelization of people of all racial and
national origins, and their inclusion in the same church, the plan of
the Northern Church, while not ideal, had proven that the idea could
be made to work. For those with the other point of view, namely,
that the two racial groups should remain in separate denominations,
on the basis of race, the Negro membership in the Methodist Episcopal
Church was a definite obstacle to Methodist unification. The fact
that the Negro membership in the church numbered more than 300,000
did not make the problem any easier.

One of the major issues in the negotiations on Methodist unification from 1916, when the active discussions on the subject began, until
1939, when the Plan of Union was adopted, was the status of the Negro
membership in the reorganized church. To appreciate the total problem, we must see the issue from the standpoint of all the groups concerned: the Methodist Episcopal Church, South; the white membership
of the Methodist Episcopal Church; and the Negro membership of the
Methodist Episcopal Church.

From the standpoint of the Southern Church, with its history
and social background since the division in 1844, and its definitive
action in 1870, in which it set up its Negro membership into an independent denomination, the logical status of the Negro in any plan

for the reorganized church seemed to be the establishment of the
Negro group into a separate denomination, either alone or with other
Negro church groups, with no organic relation to the white membership of the church. Leaders of the Southern Church supported that
position for many years during the period of negotiations.

In the case of the Methodist Episcopal Church, whatever might
have been the individual preferences and even practices of many of
its members and local congregations, the church officially had a
long tradition in welcoming (theoretically at least) all groups into
its fellowship. There were still fresh memories among the older
members of the church of the vigorous educational and evangelistic
programs which had been carried forward among the freedmen since the
Civil War, and there were thousands of Methodists who were committed
to that program. Then there was the legal fact that the Negro membership was as definitely a part of the church as was any other group
and could not be eliminated from its membership except by their own
choice.

Finally, the Negro membership (although a minority group both
numerically and in standing in the church) was conscious of its rights
and prerogatives in the church and was not disposed to relinquish
those claims. More important to them, however, than rights was the
instinctive conviction, evident from their earliest connection with
"the people called Methodists," that this fellowship represented a
communion that was seriously seeking to build a brotherhood among
all men. They believed that their membership in such a fellowship
would help in the achievement of world brotherhood.

It was these varying views over the period of nearly a quarter
of a century of negotiations which had to be resolved before a
Plan of Union satisfactory to a majority of Methodists could be
agreed upon. This meant compromises on all sides. For the Methodist
Episcopal Church, South it meant giving up the insistence on a
separate and independent church. For the Methodist Episcopal Church
it meant giving up the concept of a strongly centralized General
Conference and (theoretically at least) open membership for all races
in favor of a regionally-structured church. To the Negro membership
it meant accepting an arrangement by which the annual conferences of
the Negro group would be set up as a regional group, or Jurisdiction,
on a racial basis rather than geographical as was true for the white
membership.

Many of us can remember the bitter debates that went on in the
Negro conferences and among Negro leaders prior to the adoption of
the Plan of Union. The Plan failed to carry in the majority of Negro
annual conferences, although it was approved by a majority of the
white conferences.

What was the basic objection to the Central Jurisdiction? The fact that it was a separate racial structure and that it wrote into the Constitution of a Christian denomination a definite segregated arrangement. On the other hand, it did offer manifest advantages, "such as proportionate representation on all of the Boards of the church, membership in its highest councils, with members of its group being eligible to hold the highest posts in the church, without discrimination as to salaries and other prerequisites." More important than these material benefits was the fact that the Central Jurisdiction made possible the beginning of the full-fledged brotherhood which is now evolving, not only in Methodism but among Christians of every denominational persuasion, both Protestant and Catholic.

That is what M. S. Davage, speaker at the Uniting Conference in 1939, had in mind when he said, "We want to be a Church which embraces all mankind, and *is big enough for God.*"

The Central Jurisdiction was the beginning of an experiment among Methodists, North and South, white and Negro, which sought to embrace all mankind, and to be big enough for God. It was because the Negro membership of the church had faith in the goodwill of their fellow-Methodists and in the leadership of the Holy Spirit in the Church of Jesus Christ that they became a part of this experiment in Christian fellowship.

THE CHALLENGE OF THE NEW
STRUCTURAL ARRANGEMENT

The question logically arises as to the possible effect of the new structural arrangement of the United Methodist Church on the total program of the church and particularly on the attitudes of its membership, both to the majority and minority groups. To those who are inclined to be cynical and call themselves realists, there are still grave questions as to the wisdom of the change in the structure. To optimists and men of faith who believe in the power of the Holy Spirit to give leadership in adventures in the area of human brotherhood, there are definite values in the new structure and hope for its potentialities in promoting Christian brotherhood:

1. It recognizes the fact of "change" in the political, social and spiritual climate of our world in the last two decades. It was Prime Minister MacMillan of Great Britain who coined the phrase, "the winds of change," in his warning address some years ago to the minority group of white leaders who still rule the Commonwealth of Rhodesia. And how marked is that change! More than 30 new nations in Asia and Africa have achieved political independence since the close of World War II. While most of them are having terrific political, economic, and social problems, the old order is gone forever.

638

2. It means that the Christian church - all Christian churches, both Protestant and Catholic - must sense this need for change and must be able and willing to accommodate its structure and institutional life to the needs of the new day.

No church organization has given more evidence of its determination to restudy and reform its own huge structure than has the Roman Catholic Church, which was begun under the leadership of Pope John XXIII and has been continued under his successor, Pope Paul VI. The United Methodist Church, one of the largest Protestant churches in the nation, has by its action in eliminating the Central Jurisdiction shown its willingness to make this venture of faith.

3. This action places a responsibility on both the white and Negro members of the church to seek to deal constructively with the new developments in the racial situation.

¶   Sources of Methodist Black Power.

(Taken from mimeographed copy of address by Philip Harley at Northern Illinois Conference, 1977).

During the fall of 1966, in the wake of exploding cities across the land, the restlessness of so-called "indigenous groups" - gangs violence; the ineptness of the church to speak the healing word; the rising fear of Black and White citizens in our cities; the sense of impotency of our leaders in the face of Black youths challenging threats; disgracefully inadequate salaries and unimaginative and irrelevant church planning; several Black United Methodist clergy (Harley, Ammons, Gibson, Pembroke) met at St. James to talk over the nature of the crises and the necessity for us as United Methodist clergy to seize the initiative of leadership and confront and challenge the Northern Illinois Conference if we were to survive career-wise, literally.

The urban crisis was a clear challenge to the Black church leadership. We clearly understood our people calling us to professional accountability and responsibility for new styles of ministries and mission. Through the office of Edsel Ammons we sent out a call to all "the brothers," who responded to a man. We met again at St. James and the challenge to unite was heavy upon us. There was consensus in our reading the signs of the times, hesitancy and anxiety over the unorthodoxy of our proposed action, but the hour had come, the Black Caucus was born. After long hours of historical and theological reflection and review, we developed a distinctive logos and prophetic stance. We identified and heralded the arrival of a new day for the black church. Our identity was sure. We were Black people first, children of God by adoption, United Methodist by choice and church persons by calling.

Two events capture this moment:

1. At the home of Dr. H. B. Gibson, Superintendent,
   Western District, Oak Park, in the fall of 1967,
   we hammered out the first two position papers
   that became the foundational statement for the
   yet unborn Black Methodists for Church Renewal:

   (a) Black Power
   (b) Black Power and the Itinerancy

2. Later in the same year, in the wake of the Detroit
   rebellion, at a called meeting of all United Methodist clergy, in the Chicago Temple, over 100
   Methodist clergy responded to a call to minister
   to the burgeoning urban crises. After long and
   heated debate, with primary leadership from the
   Black Caucus, they voted unanimously to raise
   and turn over $250,000.00 to the Black Caucus to
   develop an urban ministry. This was the first time
   and the first evidence of White churchmen recognizing
   and affirming the leadership potential and integrity
   of Black churchmen in Northern Illinois Conference.
   The die was cast.

"A HISTORICAL MOMENT"

On December 13, 1969, at a special called session of Northern
Illinois Conference meeting in Naperville, Illinois, the Black Caucus
became a recognized program area and obliquely an agency of Northern
Illinois Conference.

December 13, 1969 was a challenge by Black United Methodists for
self-determination, self-empowerment and leadership opportunities within the United Methodist Church and Northern Illinois Conference in
particular.

December 13, 1969 was a challenge to Black United Methodist
church people to develop and strengthen the Black church in the city,
especially United Methodist churches, and to provide a more authentic
and radical leadership in all areas of the life of the church engaged
in the liberation struggle, (the ideological construct being "Strong
Centers") and the raising of the recognition of the imperative of
Black ecumenicity.

¶   The Black Paper of Northern Illinois Conference Black Caucus.

(Taken from mimeo statement, Chicago, 1967).

I. OUR CONFESSION

We, a group of Black Methodists in America are deeply disturbed about the crisis of <u>racism in America</u>. We are equally concerned about the failure of a number of Black people, including Black Methodists to respond appropriately to racism and the current Black Revolution.

We as Black Methodists want to first respond in a state of confession because it is only as we confront our selves that we are able to deal with the evils and forces which seek to deny our humanity.

We confess our failure to be reconciled with ourselves as Blackmen. We have too often denied our blackness (our hair texture, our color and other God-given physical characteristics) rather than embrace it in all its black beauty.

We confess that we have not always been relevant in our service and ministry to our Black Brothers. And in so doing we have alienated ourselves from many of our Brothers.

We confess that we have not always been honest with ourselves and with our white brothers. For we have not encountered them with truth but often with deception. We have not said in bold language and forceful action that "you have used white power inside and outside of the church to keep us in a subordinated position."

We have failed to tell them "like it is," but rather as we thought they would like to hear it.

We confess that we have not become significantly involved in the Black Revolution because for the most part white men have defined it as "bad." And for the other, we have been too comfortable in our "little world," and too pleased with our lot as second-class citizens and second-class Methodists.

We confess that we have accepted the philosophy of racism too long which has created a kind of relationship in which white people have always defined the "terms" and in fact defined when and how we exist.

We confess that we have accepted a "false kind of integration" in which all power remained in the hands of white men.

II. THE BLACK REVOLUTION

The Black Revolution is a fact! It is a call for black people throughout the nation and the world to stand on their feet and declare their independence from white domination and exploitation.

The mood of the day is for black people to throw off the old crippling myths of white superiority and black inferiority. The old myths are being replaced by black pride, self development, self awareness, self respect, black solidarity and black self determination. We are becoming new men--the "old" man (the nigger) is dead! The "boy" is now a man! We stand as proud black men prepared to embrace our blackness and committed to addressing ourselves unequivocally and forcefully to racism wherever we find it, in and outside the church.

III. BLACK POWER

How then do we respond forcefully and responsibly to racism in America and racism in The Methodist Church? We unashamedly reply-- Black Power!

"It is abundantly clear to many Americans that power is basic to all human dynamics. The fundamental distortion facing us in a controversy between 'black power' is rooted in a gross imbalance of power and conscience between Negroes and White Americans. It is this distortion, mainly, which is responsible for the widespread though often inarticulate assumption that white people are justified in getting what they want through the use of power, but that Negro Americans must, either by nature or by circumstances, make their appeal only through conscience. As a result, the power of white men and the conscience of black men have both been corrupted."

Black Power provides the means by which black people do for themselves that which no other group may do for it.

Black Power speaks to the need for black people to move from the stand of humble and dependent and impotent beggars to the stature of men who will take again into their hands, as all men must, the fashioning of their own destiny for their own growth into self-development and self-respect.

Black Power is a call for people in this country to unite, to recognize their heritage, to build a sense of community. It is a call for us to take the initiative, to build a kind of community which crosses all class lines and geographical lines, in order that the resources and leadership of all black people may be used.

Black Power means the development and utilization of the gifts of black men for the good of black men and the whole nation.

Finally, it is a call for us to respond to God's action in history which is to make and keep human life human.

IV.   BLACK POWER AND THE METHODIST CHURCH

We as Black Methodists affirm the search for Black Power. When we affirm and embrace our Blackness we are acknowledging what God has done and no longer wear our blackness as a stigma, but as a blessing.

"In religious terms, a God of power, of majesty and of might, who has made man to be in His own image and likeness, must will that His creation reflect in the immediacies of life His power, His majesty and His might. Black Power raises, for the healing of humanity and for the renewal of commitment to the creative religious purpose of growth, the far too long overlooked need for power, if life is to become what in the mind of its Creator it is destined to be."

Therefore, as Black Methodists if we are obedient to God's creation we have a responsibility to ourselves, the white community and to Methodists who are white, to relate from a position of power.

The Methodist Church has failed institutionally and spiritually to be the Church. It has refused to take its mission to redeem mankind seriously. It has denied the black man's right to self determination because it has frustrated his quest for self realization. It has failed in every respect to see the black man as a child of God. The reality has been that the black man is denied full membership in the institutional church.

We as Black Methodists reaffirm our belief in God and his Church. We believe that all men are brothers and that God is our Father. However, we see the possibility that "white" Christians in general, and white Methodists in particular, may not be seriously committed to the church or the concept of the Brotherhood of man under the Fatherhood of God. We therefore have a responsibility under God to bring about renewal in the church at all levels of its existence. The thrust of "black Power" in this context are to awaken black and white Methodists so they might come to see and carry out the mission of the church as it relates to all men. The Methodist Church ought to be sensitive to every segment of society and need to minister realistically and effectively to the total needs of man, especially those who have been dispossessed by society and the church. "Black Power" seeks to be the moving force behind the black man's effort to get the church to see and recognize him. A second aim of "Black Power" in the Methodist Church is to help the dispossessed, especially the black man, to establish his selfhood in society and the church.

To do this we propose the Black Methodists across the country mobilize their spiritual, intellectual, economic, social and political resources in order to exert the necessary influence and/or pressure upon the power structure of the Methodist Church on all levels to

bring about change and renewal in order that it might unconditionally include all Methodists in its total life. At the same time we propose to preach the Gospel of the "somebodies" of the black man so that those who have not "identified" themselves as men, might find that identity and exert their manhood.

We hope that this can be done within the existing framework of the Methodist Church. As Black Methodists, we are determined to serve God by redeeming our brothers, which in turn redeems us.

¶   Black Power and the Itineracy

(Taken from mimeographed statement of Northern Illinois Conference Black Caucus, 1967).

The need for the Church of Jesus Christ to relate sensitively and sensibly to the changing shape of life in the city is no longer seriously questioned. There is considerable dispute, however, over the development of strategies which the mission-task demands. This is the case not only with the Methodist Church, but with the entire religious community. New occasions have indeed made "ancient good uncouth." If there is any one thing that can be said of all of us, it is that none of us can be certain that even our best efforts will be either wise or sufficient.

This is especially true as we rethink our ministries in the face of the black-white crisis. Every presupposition or working assumption bears examining afresh so that we design our ministries around the kinds of issues that are realistic and needs that are current. Very practically, for Methodism this means, (1) reordering of priorities, (2) new use of our resources, (3) redesign of structures, in order to get the most out of our labors. It is out of this context of concern, in fact, that we lift up for reappraisal the question of itinerancy as it has to do with the appointment of black pastors to all white churches.

Having agonized over the nature of the imperatives confronting the Church and the options open to us, the Black Clergy of the Rock River Conference are now persuaded that Methodism in black communities ought to be under black leadership. We fully realize that in view of the severe shortage of black clergy in our Conference (and in the seminaries, as well) this implies that for the foreseeable future we may need to discontinue the attempt to appoint black pastors to white churches. We realize, too, that the racists in our Conference will surely take great comfort in this decision on our part; will accept it as confirmation of their own opposition to open itinerancy. Nevertheless, we take this position at this time convinced that our motives will be evident to those who are concerned to understand.

However, we wish to make it clear that we stand firmly in support of inclusiveness in the church as an unimpeachable Christian principle.

Part of the role of the itinerant system at this point in history is that of bringing in and through the church the rich cultural heritage of Black folk. The black community is part and parcel of the American community, the church has a responsibility to this troubled black community. It is believed that this can best be done under the leadership of black clergy.

Our decision grows out of our determination to take seriously what the black power movement is saying to our day and to exploit, as fully as possible, its positive values. We believe that the very nature of our nation's racist history renders the average white pastor incapable of the depth of sensitivity and knowledgeability which are requisite to leadership today in critical black communities. We readily admit to some noteworthy exceptions and would agree perhaps that where strategy, carefully considered, commends it, the appointment of a white pastor to a black congregation deserves to be considered. We would still have to say, however, that we do believe that in this period of "interim" reappraisal and readjustment of our relations around the issue of race it would seem wise to adopt the principle of black _pastors_ for black churches.

As a matter of strategy, the need is to appoint competent black ministerial leadership to churches in the black community. Furthermore, it becomes the function of the church and the white community to support that ministry - emotionally, administratively and financially that it might be effective wherever it is. The hierarachy of the church must discover ways and means to develop black interest in the ministry by opening and broadening the opportunities of ministerial expression, promotion and financial increments. We must develop ministries for black men, aside from pastoral. Our great goal in the Church is to erase from our purview any need to refer to race, color, or nationality. We know that where this exists there is an over amount of sin. The goal further of the Church is to overcome racism, which is sin, wherever it exists.

¶   How Black Methodists for Church Renewal Got Started and Why.

(Taken from pamphlet owned by Maceo D. Pembroke, June, 1978).

BMCR came into being as a result of the combined action of a few dedicated black churchpersons within The United Methodist Church who recognized the need for the kind of renewal within the church which would insure total inclusiveness in the fellowship of the church structure as well as a church at work in the world, dedicated to serve mankind. This group (an ad hoc committee of more than 100) issued a call to

other concerned United Methodists (259 of whom responded) to attend a conference in Cincinnati, Ohio, February 6-9, 1968. During this meeting the National Conference of Negro Methodists assessed the church as a whole, and as a result, developed the "Findings of Black Methodists for Church Renewal," later referred to as "The Findings."

It should be noted that this group came, as did participants in the 1962 Central Jurisdiction Study Conference, against a background of more than 175 years of continuous effort on the part of Negroes to achieve full, free and unrestricted participation in the total life of The United Methodist Church in America. The National Conference of Negro Methodists, later to become incorporated as Black Methodists for Church Renewal, was interested in developing a life of power and unity in the "new" United Methodist Church. The group came together to look at the situation before us in The Methodist Church; to explore strategies for helping The United Methodist Church to really become effective on the local level, through annual conferences, boards and agencies, jurisdictional conferences, and the General Conference; to consider the recruitment and itinerancy of Negro pastors; to lift up the distinctive mission that the black church can and must carry into the "new" church; to propose urgent priority missions for the cities where we live; to suggest new forms for the life of the local congregation; and to precipitate creative motives for the kind of unity among Negro Methodists that can mean a vigorous, faithful Methodism.

Accepting the responsibility under God to bring renewal in the church at all levels of its existence; to awaken black and white United Methodists so that they might come to see and carry out the mission of the church as it relates to all persons, and adopting the identity of "an agitating conscience," we have engaged in a variety of forms of activity in trying to achieve our goals. All of our activities have been performed in the Spirit of Christ; of course, as the scriptures reveal, so often man does not recognize Christ when he sees Him.

In 1968 BMCR witnessed at The United Methodist General Conference. As a result of effective lobbying, conference delegates: (1) approved formation of the Commission on Religion and Race; (2) ordered an investigation of employment practices of The Methodist Publishing House; and (3) adopted a $20 million quadrennial fund - The Fund for Reconciliation - to finance community action projects in the inner cities.

We published our first newsletter, *Now*, in July, 1968. This was several mimeographed pages which principally contained news in Methodism. In the Spring of 1971 we published our first printed newspaper which contained printed news plus accompanying photographs, a much more attractive arrangement. In January, 1978 BMCR began publishing *Now* monthly. The paper is now a 12-20 page tabloid.

The General Conference-ordered investigation of The Methodist Publishing House exposed discriminatory hiring practices. BMCR staged a demonstration on April 11, 1968 around the Methodist Publishing House to dramatize its demand that the Methodist Publishing House join Project Equality as a sponsor-member.

Beginning in 1969 regional caucuses began to be formed, later to be followed by annual conference caucuses and local caucuses. Some very significant events have taken place at these levels of organization.

Some of the history of the organization represents events which many of our constituents could not accept or understand. We trust by this date we have grown enough through experience to at least understand the strategy behind some of the events.

In May, 1969 our former executive director actively participated in the May take-over at the Board of Missions (475 Riverside Drive, New York City) in response to the Black Manifesto. The tactics were questioned by some members and caused considerable concern among many of our black staff members of the Board of Missions, now the Board of Global Ministries.

In August, 1969 BMCR engaged in confrontations with the Boards of Evangelism and Education of The United Methodist Church in Nashville, Tennessee.

On December 10, 1969 one of our past National Chairpersons was arrested in Memphis, Tennessee on charges related to his involvement in the strike by black union workers at St. Joseph's Hospital.

On March 4, 1970, board member Phil Lawson was issued a subpoena to testify in Washington, D. C. on parish relationships with Kansas City Black Panthers.

We must not overlook the fact that BMCR played an important role in the sponsorship of the Black Community Developers program and the establishment of a Mass Communications Center at Clark College in Atlanta, Georgia.

At the 1970 Special Session of the General Conference, BMCR youth confronted the Council of Bishops. This confrontation resulted in temporary funding of the Black Youth and Young Adult Action Task Force.

BMCR as a whole also made a presentation to the 1970 Special Session of the General Conference in St. Louis. It proved to be a significant gesture and was supported by a cross section of community groups and organizations as well as members of several races and

647

ethnic minorities within our church. BMCR made several demands which were referred to several different committees in the usual tradition where they were curtailed greatly or got lost in the shuffle altogether. All in all, General Conference legislation resulted in the adoption of resolutions as follows: (1) allocated $2 million annually for fiscal year 1971 and 1972 to the Commission on Religion and Race for Minority Group Economic Empowerment; (2) established annual goal of $4 million for Race Relations Sunday on behalf of the twelve Black Colleges; and (3) established a million dollar scholarship fund for minority group college students to be administered by the Board of Education.

In 1971 BMCR attempted to sponsor a drug after-care center in Atlanta, but insufficient funding caused this program to terminate.

BMCR presently sponsors Enterprises Now, Incorporated, a Minority Enterprise Small Business Investment Company (MESBIC) which is an arm of the Small Business Administration. This program is designed to assist minority entreprenuers in the development of business enterprises. Limited funding has limited our progress in this venture. We are still struggling to survive.

BMCR spent much time in study and preparation of petitions for entry into the legislative channels at General Conference in April, 1972. There were seventeen petitions and nine resolutions submitted to General Conference. Some petitions were given favorable consideration; others fell by the wayside via nonconcurrence. These petitions covered a multitude of BMCR concerns. They were titled as follows: (1) Social Consciousness in Investment Policy; (2) The Structure Study Commission; (3) Politics as Social Concern; (4) Church Property Use; (5) Prison Reform; (6) Homes and Residences; (7) Annual Conference Mergers; (8) The Social Creed; (9) A Uniform Standard for Pensions; (10) A Uniform Standard for Salaries; (11) Involuntary Location; (12) Project Equality; (13) Black Community Developers Program; (14) Black Colleges; (15) University Senate; (16) Black College Trustees; and (17) Church Publications. (See BMCR 1972 General Conference Handbook for contents of petitions.)

¶   The Holiness Churches: A Significant Ethical Tradition.

(Taken from article by Donald W. Dayton in *Christian Century*, 26 Feb. 1975, 197-201).

To many outsiders, the world of "conservative" Christianity no doubt seems an undifferentiated mass. But the uniformity and agreement often claimed by advocates of "evangelicalism" are to great extent a myth. The groups that compose conservative Christendom are marked by distinctive theological stances and sociological dynamics

as significant as those that distinguish other church traditions or those that separate evangelical groups from mainline denominations.

For example, the major ecumenical body in conservative circles, the National Association of Evangelicals (NAE), comprises more than 30 member denominations, which fall into three natural groupings. About one-third are "Pentecostal"; these denominations have become better known since the rise of the "charismatic movement." A second third are the sort of "evangelicals" represented by *Christianity Today* and the dominant conservative seminaries. The third group, the "Holiness" churches, is the one least noticed or understood by those outside the conservative tradition. . . .

Holiness churches claim to stand in the direct succession of John Wesley and "original" Methodism. But the movement is perhaps best viewed as a synthesis of Methodism with the revivalism of Charles G. Finney, as it found expression in pre-Civil War America in a reaffirmation of the doctrine of "Christian perfection."

The major concern of the "mainline" or CHA Holiness churches has been the doctrine of "Christian perfection" or "entire sanctification." This doctrine encourages the seeking of a "higher Christian life" of "victory over" or "cleansing from" intentional or voluntary sin. This is usually achieved in a "second blessing" or a crisis experience subsequent to conversion. In the more classically Wesleyan expressions of the doctrine, this crisis is embedded in a gradual process of santification or growth. In the late 19th century such an experience was called the "baptism of the Holy Ghost," a terminology still preserved in such groups as the Church of the Nazarene. It was this development that eventually led to Pentecostalism, but most Holiness churches have shied away from this "Pentecostal" language for fear of identification with glossolalia movements. (Interestingly, in view of their own history, ethos and theology, the Holiness people are among the strongest critics of classical Pentecostalism.)

The ethos of Holiness churches reflects American revivalism and the spirit of the camp meeting – though attenuated, of course, over the years. There has been an affinity for the "gospel song," combined with a tradition of classical Wesleyan hymnody and Methodist ritual. The movement has produced some 200 colleges, at least half of which are still in existence. Two small 100,000 member denominations, the Wesleyan Church and the Free Methodist Church, each support half a dozen colleges, including such thriving institutions as Houghton College (New York) and Seattle Pacific College. Four seminaries (Asbury in Kentucky, Anderson School of Theology in Indiana, Nazarene in Kansas City, and Western Evangelical in Portland) serve the movement.

The Holiness movement differs from fundamentalism and evangelicalism in that it is more oriented to ethics and the spiritual life than to a defense of doctrinal orthodoxy. Indeed, one of the distinctive features of the Holiness traditions is that they have tended to raise ethics to the status that fundamentalists have accorded doctrine. This theme was certainly explicit in the early abolitionist controversies and has consistently re-emerged since. The emphasis given the doctrine of sanctification has led naturally in this direction.

The Holiness ethic has been described as the "revivalist" ethic of "no smoking, no drinking, no cardplaying, no theatergoing." Such themes have, of course, characterized the Holiness movement - as have large doses of anti-Catholicism and anti-Masonry. Some of these concerns are still worth some defense, but the Holiness churches have been slandered by observers who fail to penetrate beneath these themes.

The earliest issue of the Holiness movement was abolitionism. The early editors of the *Guide to Holiness* were abolitionists. . . .

Just as in the 1960s, in Haven's time agitation on the race issue led to concern for the role of women. In addition to erasing the color line, Oberlin College became the first to attempt coeducation; the school graduated a number of the most vigorous and radical feminists of the era. The first women's rights convention was held in the Wesleyan Methodist Church of Seneca Falls, New York. Antoinette Brown, the first woman to be ordained in an American church, was a graduate of Oberlin, and at her ordination Wesleyan Methodist minister Luther Lee preached on "Woman's Right to Preach the Gospel" (1853). Wesleyans themselves began to experiment with the ordination of women in the 1860s. Catherine Booth, who with her husband, William, was cofounder of the Salvation Army, was also an ardent feminist; she insisted on radical equality for women in the new organization. In a book published in 1891, B. T. Roberts, founder of the Free Methodists, argued in favor of *Ordaining Women* though his denomination did not capitulate until 1974.

Phoebe Palmer defended the right of women to preach in *The Promise of the Father* (1859). Her book became the fountainhead of innumerable writings that argued that "Pentecost laid the axe at the root of social injustice." Acts 2, relying on a prophecy in the book of Joel, affirms that "in the latter days...your sons and your *daughters* shall prophesy." By the turn of the century this Scripture passage constituted the standard Holiness defense of the practice. An early constitution of the Church of the Nazarene specifically provided for the ministry of women. Seth Cook Rees, a founder of the Pilgrim Holiness Church, insisted that "nothing but jealousy, prejudice, bigotry, and a stingy love for bossing in men have prevented women's public recognition by the church." Alma White, founder of the Pillar of Fire, claimed to be the first female bishop in the

history of Christianity. For years her denomination published a periodical, *Women's Chains*, which fought for the right to vote, advocated total participation of women in society (including Congress and the White House), and suggested imprisonment for the inventors of the high-heeled shoe.

Another recurrent theme in Holiness churches has been involvement with and ministry to the "poor and oppressed." Early abolitionist literature has striking parallels to today's "liberation theology." The "free" in Free Methodist also stood for opposition to church pew rentals, which served to exclude the poor. . . .

Somewhat ironic - in view of this history - is the fact that the past generation or so has seen great dilution of these values - and this just at a time when many of these values were receiving wider vindication in the larger cultural and church life! Prevailing social forces, a generation or two of "progressive" leadership, and a desire on the part of many to avoid identification with the caricatures of the movement have effected profound changes. Many contemporary Holiness leaders have come to think of their tradition as a variety of "evangelicalism" with a slightly different belief structure. The result has been the development of patterns of church life much like those against which the founders originally rebelled.

But the earlier ethos remains subliminally present and is breaking out again, especially among the younger generation. Those working with college students report that students from Holiness colleges respond more quickly to "discipleship" demands than some "evangelicals" who are more conditioned to responding with verbalization or doctrinal formulation. As an officer of the NAE Social Action Commission recently put it, "Holiness people still have an ear for ethical issues."

Current stirrings of social concern among conservative Christians have found reception in the Christian Holiness Association. June 1973 saw an ecumenical conference on issues of war and peace under the auspices of the CHA. Though the National Association of Evangelicals would not touch it, the 1974 CHA annual convention endorsed the "Chicago Declaration of Evangelical Social Concern" without hesitation (though one member of the resolutions committee feared that endorsement would imply that CHA had not held these values all along). Ron Sider, though he has worked primarily among the "evangelicals," is from a CHA church; he was the major force behind the "Chicago Declaration" and the earlier "Evangelicals for McGovern." Senator McGovern himself was the product of a Wesleyan Methodist parsonage. And Free Methodist Gilbert James of Asbury Theological Seminary has been one of the strongest voices for social conscience within conservative Christendom. Over a quarter of a century ago he was editing a paper on race relations and social legislation. More recently he has

created Chicago's "Urban Ministries Program for Seminarians," which provides "urban action training" for a coalition of seven midwestern conservative seminaries.

Also worth noting is the Holiness attitude toward ecumenism. This is a curious dialectic of "schismatic" and "unitive" tendencies. Early Holiness leaders delighted in the "nonsectarian" and inter-denominational character of their meetings. Some even hoped that the new movement would produce unity in Christendom. Such hopes were, of course, doomed to failure; what resulted was more a redrawing of denominational lines as the Holiness movement spread beyond Methodism.

But the main thrust of the formation of Holiness churches has been "unitive." Turn-of-the-century Holiness churches were formed by the gradual coalescing of missions and local organizations. The Church of the Nazarene and the Pilgrim Holiness Church brought to-gether perhaps 30 antecedent organizations. These forces are still at work. The year 1969 saw the emergence of the Missionary Church in the Mennonite wing of the Holiness movement. In 1966 the Wesley-an Methodists absorbed the Reformed Baptists and two years later merged with the Pilgrim Holiness Church to form the Wesleyan Church. The merging General Conference voted to begin negotiations with the Free Methodists (these are still in progress). The Christian Holiness Association even attempted "confederation" in the mid-1960s but had to settle for a more loosely organized program of "cooperative ministries" in such areas as publishing and evangelism. It is still possible that we will see the merging of these groups into a major denomination.

Reaction to all these currents has left the "mainline" Holiness churches somewhat at sea as they struggle for new ways to express an updated identity. The process has been complicated by a new intellectual and theological maturity. Seminary programs expanded rapidly in the 1960s. The founding about ten years ago of a Wesleyan Theological Society (it now has about 700 members) and an associated academic journal has been another force. During the 1960s a sizable number of Holiness students entered the most prestigious graduate schools in the country. Unlike an earlier generation of students, most of these are retaining identification with the movement.

This new generation of theological teachers is faced with two major theological problems. The first of these is to re-express the distinctive doctrine of the Holiness movement with some fidelity to Scripture and history in a manner that speaks to the modern age. This is no easy task. In some parts of the movement the doctrine has fallen into disuse. Such persons often tend to move toward the style and ethos of the *Christianity Today* constituency. Others have moved in the direction of the Keswick Movement and a doctrine of a "victorious Christian life." Even those who have remained most

652

faithful to the doctrine have modified some of the cruder forms of the "second blessing" theology by reaffirmation of the more subtle classical Wesleyanism, with its themes of growth and process in sanctification. But new interpretations are beginning to appear. Recent years have seen the emergence of existential, relational, phenomenological, and even process interpretations of Holiness theology! The most recent of these has been *Love, the Dynamic of Wesleyanism* (Beacon Hill Press of Kansas City, 1972), by Mildred Bangs Wynkoop, immediate past president of the Wesleyan Theological Society.

The other theological problem that leaders and theologians of the Holiness movement face is the sorting out of the relationship between the Holiness movement and modern fundamentalism. Holiness bodies were deeply influenced by fundamentalism during the fundamentalist modernist controvery. Lacking a developed apologetic and a theologically sophisticated intellectual tradition, many Holiness leaders adopted the fundamentalist apologetic and doctrine of Scripture. The CHA was reorganized and the Wesleyan Theological Society formed in the wake of the emergence of NAE and the Evangelical Theological Society. Early CHA and WTS doctrinal statements were modeled on NAE and ETS counterparts. Such men as Stephen Paine, until recently president of Houghton College, brought NAE motifs into Holiness bodies. Under Paine's influence, for example, the Wesleyan Methodist Church rewrote its articles of religion in the 1950s to incorporate the fundamentalist doctrine of Scripture.

But the Wesleyans were the only body to go that far. The larger CHA bodies prefer to see themselves as "conservative" rather than "fundamentalist" or "evangelical." Remnants of earlier reformist "post-millenialism" kept many from complete capitulation to fundamentalist chiliasm. Restrained forms of biblical criticism have found acceptance among Holiness scholars - so much so that many do not find themselves at home in the Evangelical Theological Society. Recent years have seen struggles to move to a more inclusive doctrinal statement. Both the CHA and WTA creeds have recently been reformulated with the express purpose of avoiding the characteristic expressions of the "evangelical" doctrine of Scripture, as well as the endless specification of particular doctrines.

What will finally come out of all these currents remains to be seen. But there is little doubt that we are witnessing the emergence into wider dialogue of what will prove to be an increasingly important theological and ecclesiastical tradition.

26. UNITED METHODISM

As Methodists in the 1960s gasped from one crisis to another, along with the rest of the country and the world, the Evangelical United Brethren, a denomination which had been formed in 1946 from the United Brethren in Christ and the Evangelical Church, entered more directly into discussions of possible merger with the larger body. These negotiations came to fruition in 1968 with the formation of the United Methodist Church. Some of the ecumenical backgrounds of the United Brethren are discussed by K. James Stein in an article in **Methodist History.**

Before the merger could be achieved, some thorny problems had to be overcome. Although many parts of the respective traditions were similar if not identical, including a high regard for Wesleyan theological roots and the spirit of the Evangelical Revival, some difficulties raised questions in "A Critical Appraisal" of the proposed union. Even more recalcitrant were the issues surrounding the Central Jurisdiction, a racially motivated compromise inherited from formation of The Methodist Church in 1939. Persistent efforts to get rid of that left-over from a segregated past were very important in the debate on May 3 in the Uniting Conference of 1968. Almost all were agreed on the goal. The issue was the method of achieving it. Much celebration accompanied this union. "A Union . . . and Much More" described the process and prospects for the United Methodist Church, printed in the popular church magazine, Together.

But mergers do not solve problems. They only transfer, perpetuate, and create them. Hence the new united church inherited and faced up to the continuing issue of equal rights for women, both in and out of the church. A new commission came into being. Not a new problem, but one complicated by new factors, was that of doctrinal standards. John and Charles Wesley had been rather clear on the need for broad latitude in interpretation of the Christian faith. Union in 1968 brought the matter to a head as two similar but different theological and doctrinal traditions were brought into juxtaposition. A Theological Study Commission struggled to find ways toward consensus.

In 1979 a further step toward ecumenical fellowship in the Methodist "family" was taken in a Consultation of Methodist Bishops in Atlanta, Georgia. A.M.E., A.M.E.Z., C.M.E., and U.M. bishops spent two days together and issued to the various Methodist people a Message which appropriately brings this collection of readings to anuend.

654

¶ United Brethren Seek Friends.

(Taken from article by K. James Stein in *Methodist History*, V
(Oct. 1966), 50-59).

The Tripartite Union

In August, 1902 the *Religious Telescope* printed a letter signed
by twenty-two United Brethren laymen, pastors, and denominational
executives in the Dayton, Ohio area urging their bishops to initiate
union conversations with "churches similar to ours in polity and
doctrine." Of the denominations approached, only the Methodist
Protestants were interested. Prior conversations with the Congrega-
tionalist churches caused leaders of that denomination to declare an
interest in the United Brethren proposal. A three-way union was
planned.

The plot of the Tripartite Union can be divided into three acts.
First there was an attempt at federation in anticipation of organic
union. . . .

The second stage in the Tripartite Union proceedings began at
the meeting of the first provisional General Council in Dayton, Ohio
in February, 1906 where a concentrated effort at organic union was
launched. Here with little difficulty the council adopted a common
creed of six articles. A meeting a year later in Chicago drew up
an *Act of Union* which included the creed and eight *Articles of Agreement*. . . .

The enthusiasm of the commissioners for the *Act of Union* was not
sustained by their respective denominations. . . .

The third stage of the Tripartite Union was the effort of the
United Brethren and the Methodist Protestants to unite. Negotiations
began in 1912. A *Syllabus of Union* was drawn up in April, 1913. It
proposed the creation of "the United Protestant Church" with an
eight-article *Confession of Faith*. The Methodist Protestants accepted administrative and connectional oversight, while the United
Brethren agreed that the new church would have "general superintendents" instead of bishops. . . .

The proposed union failed for non-theological reasons. The
Methodist Protestants were divided over whether to join the United
Brethren or to work for a re-united American Methodism. The United
Brethren did not favor being merged with a united Methodism. Moreover, they were doubtful about the success of a union with a group
as badly divided as the Methodist Protestants seemed to be. The
failure of the negotiations was a defeat for the major ecumenical
theme of the United Brethren.

The next serious church union negotiations entered upon by the United Brethren came unsolicited by them. In April, 1928, in response to an overture from the Reformed Church in the United States, the United Brethren began to discuss the possibilities of organic union. The fact that the United Brethren were increasingly emphasizing an educational approach to evangelism and adopting more traditionally churchly ways of worship, while the Reformed Church was mounting an accelerated program of evangelism made it appear that the era of antagonistic relations between the two denominations was about to end. The proposed union became trilateral when the Evangelical Synod of North America, a denomination centered in Missouri and other midwestern states, and one which included in its make-up both Lutheran and Reformed elements, accepted an invitation to join the deliberations. The Evangelical Church took part in negotiations for several months and then voluntarily withdrew. The commissioners of the three denominations unanimously adopted a *Plan of Union* on February 7, 1929. . . .

But the months immediately following dispelled the optimism. The United Brethren General Conference in May, 1929 ordered its new Commission on Church Union to study the plan for an additional quadrennium. The General Synod of the Reformed Church, and the General Conference of the Evangelical Synod resolved that same year, if need be, to proceed without the United Brethren. During 1930, however, anti-union sentiment in the Reformed Church became vocative. . . .

The Church of the United Brethren in Christ formally united with the Evangelical Church at Johnstown, Pennsylvania on November 16, 1946. Their union was eminently successful in that it was effected without the loss of a single pastor or congregation. Success was attributable to a number of factors. Some were external-the witness of the wider ecumenical movement, the fear that the future held no place for the small denomination, the desire to avoid wasteful competition, and a concern to unite the church for the sake of her mission in the world.

Other factors which made the union possible were internal. Never before had the United Brethren found a denomination that so fitted the demands of its major ecumenical theme. Both denominations were American born, the fathers of both were of the same teutonic blood, both emerged out of the evangelical revival at the turn of the nineteenth century, both emphasized the same evangelical truths, particularly the necessity of the conversion experience, and both had amazingly similar doctrinal systems and governmental policies. The Evangelical Church, founded by Jacob Albright (Albrecht) (1759-1808) along the lines shaped by his own religious experience and Methodist relationships, had come into being in Pennsylvania at the very time the Otterbein-Boehm fellowship was being created. It too experienced parallel periods of denominational formation and growing

maturity. Furthermore, it had made a healthy response to the ecumenical movement in the twentieth century.

Historically, the mutual Evangelical and United Brethren courtship manifested itself in four different stages over a period of a century and more. First, there was the cross-fertilization era of primitive beginnings when, for example, Albright experienced conversion at the home of Adam Riegel, a United Brethren lay-preacher. Second, there was the "Social Conference" in 1817 between representatives of the two communions when unsuccessful negotiations toward union were held. Third, for a century there was a series of fraternal exchanges at General Conferences and occasional services, in which there were fruitless overtures toward union. Fourth, in 1924 the delegations of the two Churches in attendance at the meeting of the Federal Council of Churches in Atlanta, held informal conversations which led in 1933 to the beginning of formal negotiations toward union. In the next 13 years, the commissioners prepared a plan of union which the Evangelical General Conference approved by a vote of 226 to 6 in 1942 and which its United Brethren counterpart adopted in 1945 by an almost identical majority - 224 to 2. Subsequent votes at the annual conferences of the two churches and in a popular referendum among the United Brethren produced an equally overwhelming acceptance of a movement that culminated in the historic session at Johnstown, Pennsylvania in 1946.

The pilgrimage to union, however, was not smooth. Despite the affinities enjoyed by the two churches, their different theological emphases occasioned a certain resistance to change. The Evangelical Church had adhered more closely to the doctrine of Christian perfection than had the United Brethren. The United Brethren had a sizable constituency which favored believer's baptism. The commissioners, however, found no essential difference in the confession of faith of the two denominations and inserted them side by side in the new *Discipline*. They likewise resolved the baptismal difficulty by making provision for the dedication of infants in the new denomination. Discrepancy in the licensure and ordination of ministers also raised problems. The *Plan of Union* provided that the United Brethren relinquish their practice of licensing men at the quarterly (local) conference level and of making appeal from pastoral assignments. The Evangelicals were called upon to surrender their diaconate. Further administrative adjustments in denominational structures at the general level were necessary. Evangelicals accepted the United Brethren Council of Administration which at several levels of church government served as an interim body between the regularly held conferences. United Brethren agreed to unite all missionary enterprises under a single board.

The greatest single obstacle to the union was financial. While the depression of the 1930's had taken its toll in both churches, the United Brethren especially faced staggering institutional debts.

Their earnest desire for union was partially typified by their heroic reduction by 1945 of a debt of $1,988,228 on their publishing interests and an additional obligation of $650,000 against Bonebrake Theological Seminary. They likewise raised over $1,000,000 between 1937 and 1946 in order to endow their ministerial pension fund in a manner commensurate with that of the Evangelical Church. Union for the United Brethren was costly.

Four trends can be observed in the creation of the Evangelical United Brethren Church.

First, was the pragmatic character of the negotiations. Since the theological differences between the two churches were not great, major attention was given to practical problems. The two churches were harmonized into one with as few institutional changes as possible.

Second, was the anticipation of church renewal in connection with the union. Whether this was anticipated through a return to the merging denominations' common past or through the dynamics unleashed by the uniting of the two bodies themselves, there seems to be unquestioned evidence that new vigor emerged as a result of union at congregational and institutional levels. Cherished hopes that this new life would express itself in a denominational social conscience that would call for a full-time secretariat of Christian Social Action went unheeded, however. A dominantly conservative social ethic remained entrenched. Not all was clear gain.

A third factor in the process of union was the comprehensive and deliberate way in which it was effected. Full cognizance was taken of all the knotty questions of power distribution and staff relationships and of the need to keep the rank and file of the two churches informed and involved in the union procedures. Above all, painstaking effort went into the creation of a *Discipline* of over 500 pages in order that the proposed purpose and structure of the new body might be available to all who would vote upon it. Such diligence drew considerable praise from other churchmen in America.

However, there was a consciousness of incompleteness about the union. The new *Discipline* ordered the creation of a permanent Commission on Church Federation and Union in order to deepen the denomination's sense of fellowship with other communions and to forward its efforts on behalf of greater unity in the church. Subsequent Evangelical United Brethren informal discussions with representatives of several denominations, and the formal negotiations with The Methodist Church, which incidentally have brought them into the current eight-denomination Consultation on Church Union, indicate the new church's serious intention to explore the possibilities of further church union.

¶   A Critical Appraisal of the Proposed EUB-Methodist Union.

(Taken from article by Paul F. Blankenship in *The Garrett Tower*, 42 (Mar. 1967), 13-21).

There was a time when Methodists could admit a lack of familiarity with the Evangelical United Brethren without feeling embarrassed, but that time is no more. Since the General Conferences of both denominations have approved a Plan of Union and passed it on to their annual conferences for a straight yes or no vote, the proposed union must now be faced squarely by at least every pastor and lay delegate.

The issues involved are not necessarily so simple as the distinctly favorable Methodist vote (749 to 40) implies. The closer EUB vote (325 to 88; only 15 more than was necessary) may present a more accurate picture of the situation that confronts us. At any rate, the issues need to be analyzed further, and this is what I propose to do. Taking for granted that you have heard several times about the common heritage of these two churches and the reasons for uniting, I will attempt to give a concise survey of the present negotiations and suggest why the prospects for a union based upon the present Plan are still questionable.

First of all, it seems advisable to point out some negative factors in the history of EUB-Methodist relations which are generally overlooked, since these have a direct bearing on the presently proposed union.

I.   *Some Negative Factors in Our Common Heritage.*

1.   The Evangelical United Brethren and their predecessors were never Methodists. Their founders were people mainly of Reformed, Lutheran, or Mennonite backgrounds who were deeply influenced by German Pietism and who were preaching so-called "awakened Christianity" before the first Methodists landed in America. They later adopted some Methodist methods, but the main similarity of the two groups and the thing that drew them together in the first place is their common heritage in German Pietism. It is true that some early American Methodists referred to the predecessors of the EUBs as "German Methodists," but it is also true that they (especially Christian Newcomer) just as casually referred to the Methodists as "English Brethren."

Therefore, the presently proposed union is not a Methodist family reunion - unless Methodism be falsely equated with Pietism - and if we look upon it in this manner we are unfair to the EUBs as well as to the facts, and we make union sound too easy.

2. A second negative and neglected factor in our common history is the fact that the language difference is not the primary reason why Methodists and EUBs did not unite in the early days. Furthermore, Bishop Asbury did not oppose the use of German in worship services; he only opposed using German exclusively. The booklet, "Our Churches Face Union" (pp. 7-8), is mistaken in dealing with this matter and the present negotiations have proceeded on a false assumption. . . .

From the beginning the most bothersome difference between EUBs and Methodists was not language, but rather organization and polity. The EUBs were much slower to organize than the Methodists. This was especially true of the Church of the United Brethren in Christ. Then and now the EUB power structure has been focused from the annual conference down to the local church, whereas the Methodist power structure has been focused from the annual conference up to the General Conference, Judicial Council, and the bishops. Consequently, EUB annual conferences and local churches are more powerful than ours, but our General Conference and bishops are more powerful than theirs.

This, rather than language, was in the beginning and is now perhaps the most dominant difference between Methodists and Evangelical United Brethren.

3. Although Francis Asbury had a friendly relationship with Philip Otterbein, Martin Boehm, and some of the leaders of the "Albright People," it is important to see that, on several occasions - even at Martin Boehm's funeral - he expressed serious doubts about the effectiveness of both the United Brethren and the Albright People. . . .

With these negative but (I think) necessary thoughts out of the way we can get on with the present negotiations themselves. . . .

III. *Toward Solving Five Major Problems.*

1. From the beginning of the negotiations it has been taken for granted that the main problem to be resolved was the difference in size - the EUB Church having a little under 800,000 members and the Methodist Church something over 10,000,000 members. Therefore, a concerted effort has been made to insure that the EUBs will not merely be absorbed by the Methodist Church.

Late in 1957 and early in 1958, some of the Methodist negotiators suggested that the EUBs might come into the Methodist Church as a special temporary jurisdiction or division (like the Dhevrolet Division of General Motors), but by late 1960 the EUBs let it be known that they did not particularly care to be segregated in a jurisdiction, and this idea seems to have been put aside. A

few months later it was generally agreed that some sort of guaranteed representation for the EUBs should be included in the *Discipline* of the united church for at least a few quadrenniums. The first draft of a Constitution (September, 1963) included a provision for double EUB representation on the General, Jurisdictional, and Annual(boards and agencies only) Conference levels for the first three quadrenniums following union. The second draft of the Constitution added a provision which would allow former EUB annual conferences to retain their names and boundaries, if desired, and to continue their present methods of electing conference (district) superintendents and delegates to Jurisdictional and General Conferences (ministers and laymen voting together rather than by orders) for a period of three quadrenniums following union. Both of these provisions were retained in the final draft of the Constitution and represent together the main concession of Methodists to EUBs. While the 1966 Methodist General Conference was considering this matter, Mr. Charles Parlin (secretary of the *ad hoc* committee) explained that it was necessary to grant these concessions to the EUBs in order to persuade them to accept our method of selecting superintendents – commenting that the people who were giving the most resistance on the superintendent issue were people who were "not personally interested in the issue after twelve years." (*Daily Christian Advocate,* p. 928)

Whether this is enough – since it is only temporary – remains to be seen. Some critics have suggested that this indicates that we are not ready for union.

2. The name of the united church was not a live issue at the beginning of negotiations because the Methodist Commission let it be known in December, 1957, that it would be practically impossible to change the name of the Methodist Church and the EUBs raised no strong objections; the Methodist Commission reported as much to their 1960 General Conference. But a change in the Methodist attitude on this matter was indicated in April, 1961, when a Methodist negotiator said that "The Methodist Evangelical Church" might be suitable.

In October, 1961, a survey (of themselves) by the joint study committee on the name of the united church showed that there was support for such names as "Methodist Brethren," "Evangelical Methodist," "Methodist Evangelical" and "United Methodist" as well as significant bi-partisan support for "The Methodist Church."   .   .   .

3. Several problems are centered in the episcopal office because the EUBs elect their bishops for terms of four years and install (instead of consecrate) them, while Methodists elect their bishops for life tenure and consecrate them. Both churches agree that the episcopacy is an office rather than an order, and the EUBs have rarely failed to re-elect their bishops until retirement.

The Methodist commission let it be known early in the negotiations that it would be extremely difficult to give up the system of consecration and life tenure of bishops. The main concern of the EUB commission on this issue has been to guard against allowing excessive power to bishops. After being assured that each Methodist bishop gets a thorough examination from a Jurisdictional Committee on Episcopacy every four years - supposedly more rigorous than the examination undergone by the EUB bishops - the EUB Commission indicated a willingness to change their position. The resultant move was to raise the Methodist provision for a Jurisdictional Committee on Episcopacy from the status of a disciplinary requirement (which can be changed by any General Conference) to a constitutional provision which can only be changed by amendment. This change was incorporated in the second draft of the proposed constitution and remains in the final edition, as approved by the 1966 General Conferences.

As far as the question of episcopal life tenure was concerned, the commissions discovered that life tenure was not guaranteed in the Methodist Constitution or *Discipline,* but that it had been taken for granted through the years. Therefore, they included a provision in the proposed constitution which guaranteed life tenure to those who are Methodist or EUB bishops at the time of union, and, in the final edition of the constitution, which was approved by the recent General Conferences, they included a provision for life tenure of all bishops in the united church.

4. In the words of a Methodist negotiator, Mr. Charles Parlin, "The most troublesome item which confronted the joint commission was the manner of selecting district (or conference) superintendents." This is another problem which centers on the episcopacy, because Methodist district superintendents are appointed by the bishop for a six-year term (no more than six out of any nine years) while EUB conference superintendents are elected by the annual conferences for four-year terms without limitations on re-election.

Agreement on this point was very difficult because the EUB commissioners doubted that their annual conferences would be willing to give up their right of electing superintendents, while the Methodist commissioners felt that they could not accept the elective plan. Their contention was that election by annual conferences might be acceptable for small conferences, but not for large conferences - assuming that most Methodist conferences are large. It must also be noted that the Methodist bishops involved in the negotiations have been generally the most consistent and insistent opponents of any provision that would diminish the power of the episcopal office.   .   .

The proposed constitution which was presented to the 1966 General Conferences included a provision for episcopal appointment of district superintendents and ministers. Neither of these have

been constitutional provisions for Methodists before (only disciplinary provisions) and this change seems to have appeared to the EUBs to be a further entrenchment of episcopal power. During the General Conferences, at the request of the EUBs, the constitutional provision for appointment of district superintendents was deleted, leaving it to be a disciplinary matter.

5. The difference in the number of Methodist (two-deacon and elder) and EUB (one-elder) ministerial orders has not proved as bothersome, thus far, as these other matters.   .   .   .

3. During the last few months there has been increasing criticism of the Plan of Union because no doctrinal statement has been worked out for the united church. Instead, the doctrinal and ethical standards of both denominations have been printed in the Plan of Union with a provision that common statements will be developed after the proposed union is approved.

It seems rather certain, after reading the booklet "Our Churches Face Union" and the other documents produced during the negotiations, that there has been a lack of clear theological reflection within and concerning the negotiations. This may have been because of the negotiators' assumption that there were no theological differences between their two denominations (since both are "Arminians"), or because, until 1964, there were few (if any) trained theologians on either commission, or perhaps because Methodists are not inclined to get involved in theological reflection if they can avoid it.

However, even if this deficiency were not present, it seems unrealistic to expect our two denominations to come up with a common doctrinal standard this soon. This means expecting two over-worked commissions or their sub-committees to do something within a few years that the Methodist Church in the United States has never done - for we have no accurate doctrinal standard. Our "official" Articles of Religion have never been a positive statement of Wesleyan theology and were never intended by John Wesley as a single doctrinal standard. Furthermore, we have dropped Wesley's Doctrinal Minutes, Standard Sermons, and Notes on the New Testament, and have not taken our General Rules seriously for almost a century. Therefore, we have no doctrinal standard that was intended as such, and our Social Creed probably comes closer to being this sort of thing than anything else that we have. Strangely enough, the new EUB Confession of Faith is more Wesleyan than anything that we have currently in use.

4. During the past two years, since the "Kirk Amendment" was approved by the 1964 General Conference, the question of racial segregation in the united church has probably been discussed more widely than any other issue related to the negotiations, and it seems likely to provoke opposition to the proposed union in the annual

conferences for varying reasons.

The deliberations of the 1966 Methodist General Conference were permeated with the racial issue and the final result was the establishment of 1972 as a non-mandatory "target" date for racial integration on the annual conference level. Anti-discriminatory statements were added to the enabling legislation and the Constitution of the Plan of Union, but a decision of the Judicial Council ruled that these provisions would not strictly prohibit racially segregated annual conferences during the twelve-year transition period in the united church. Thus, segregated annual conferences could be eliminated sooner in the united church if the Plan of Union did not allow EUB (and Methodist) annual conferences to remain as they are for twelve years following union.

This so-called "compromise" decision on the racial question is more like a victory for conservative forces within the Southeastern Jurisdiction who have always fought against any kind of mandatory deadline, and this fact will elicit negative votes on the union in some annual conferences. But still others will vote "no" because they always think negatively on any issue that is even vaguely related to racial integration in any form or fashion.

The effect of the racial "compromise" upon the EUB vote in the annual conferences is impossible to calculate at this point, but it may not have a drastic effect, since the Central Jurisdiction racial issue has been and still is an intra-Methodist squabble - in which some EUBs have expressed an interest.   .   .   .

7. The whole question of episcopal power is especially important, because it has an even more far-reaching significance than our proposed union with the EUBs. If we are ever to unite with anyone else (especially Presbyterians, Episcopalians, United Church of Christ, Disciples of Christ, etc.) our episcopal power will have to be trimmed down a bit because Methodist bishops are probably the most powerful denominational officials in main-line Protestantism (maybe even including Roman Catholic bishops) today. This is the issue that we have been most sensitive about in negotiating with other denominations - both with the EUBs and in the Consultation on Church Union. The Plan of Union does not alter our episcopal power except to strengthen it slightly by placing, for the first time, provisions for episcopal life tenure and episcopal appointment of ministers in the Constitution. Our victory on this point in the proposed union with the EUBs is likely to make us less willing to compromise here in any future negotiations (especially in the Consultation on Church Union) and thus less likely to unite - unless, of course, some denomination is willing to meet our terms.

¶   End of the Central Jurisdiction.

(Taken from *Daily Christian Advocate*, May 6, 1968, pp. 754-55).

LEONARD SLUTZ: Mr. Chairman, I speak on behalf of the majority on the Committee on Conferences and also as chairman of the Commission on Interjurisdictional Relations, the report of which was before you previously and which does bear also on this same subject. We are most regretful and frustrated that we have had all this hassle and haggle for the last hour because we have tried very hard to present this matter to you squarely and directly and simply and without legal technicalities or parliamentary maneuvers. We felt that we had an opportunity to do that, this is the first time this General Conference has had a majority report and a minority report, so that both sides are presented to you.

We think we have a simple issue where you should not be able to find ways to amend and to substitute but rather to decide for or against because we are dealing here with a very simple basic issue and we should get it in front of you and you should decide it. I want to read very briefly that statement of the majority which is summarized on page 527. The majority of 54 as opposed to the minority of 24, we moved non-concurrence on a constitutional amendment because we believe the entire church has unmistakeably expressed determination to end all remaining racial structure not later than the Jurisdictional Conference of 1972.

It is working expeditiously and in good faith and will reach that goal. We believe adoption of compulsory legislation at this time would tend to delay and hinder plans now in progress and more importantly, much more importantly, seriously jeopardize the spirit of good will and understanding so necessary to make structural changes a significant step toward the much greater objective of genuine brotherhood and an inclusive church.

I ask you to think back just 17 months to the General Conference of the Methodist Church in Chicago. At that time the Commission on Interjurisdictional Relations came before the conference and presented a plan. .   .   .

finally the plan was adopted by better than 95 percent of the general conference.

The plan was submitted to the EUB General Conference which was meeting across the hall and that General Conference agreed to the insertion of the language in the Enabling Legislation which was read to you a little while ago. That resolution was then adopted unanimously. It was adopted unanimously by every College of Bishops. It was voted on by every annual conference just about a year ago, last May

and June, it was approved by a vote of 93.6 percent across the South Central Jurisdiction, 67.7 percent in the Southeastern Jurisdiction and 76 percent in the Central Jurisdiction.

The effect of that vote was, we then transferred from the Central Jurisdiction all but three conferences. We would have then ended and abolished Central Jurisdiction except that the resolution did not get a two-thirds vote in one of the Central Jurisdiction Conferences and was voted negatively in two others. . . .

Far more important, far more important than these transfers and these mergers that have taken place and even in the abolition of the Central Jurisdiction, because that is only structure. Far more important, it was an acceptance of a challenge and pledge, to move forward together in good faith and harmony, to complete the plan that we all believe in and want to see finished. Now, we are here, our commission again has earnestly studied the developments of the past year, we are convinced that there is good faith, we are convinced that there is intent to accomplish this goal. Therefore, we again recommend no compulsive legislation but we did attempt to facilitate and to further the progress.

We presented legislation which you have adopted to give financial aid to make these mergers more possible and you have created a great new Commission on Race and Religion. You have given it considerable budget and staff so that that commission can go forward with what we have been trying to do. It can try to merge conferences and encourage them and persuade them and lead them and help them just as we have tried to do with the preceeding commission.

Now, we have presented a constitutional amendment, what would it do? Would it speed up the process? Would it get these conferences merged any sooner? We sincerely submit that it would not. It would in some cases, at least, delay and obstruct and would mean that if constitutional amendment were passed, some of these mergers would be deferred until 1972 that are ready to be voted on this year, within the next month if we don't upset the apple cart. Would this constitutional amendment, and this is far more important, far more important in the long run, would it promote harmony, would it promote good will, would it promote brotherhood so that over the long period the church would move forward together? That is the principal reason that we are opposing a constitutional amendment. We are convinced that it would endanger such harmony.

¶   A Union...And Much More.

(Taken from editorial in *Together*, July 1968, 5-6).

New Church Born in Dallas

Largest Religious Merger in U. S. History

United Methodists Plan For Future

So said the April 23 headlines in hundreds of newspapers across
the United States, as a nationwide television audience watched the
historic uniting ceremony in the Texas city. Inside the mammoth
Dallas Memorial Auditorium, a capacity throng of 10,000 witnessed the
formal rite which joined The Methodist Church and The Evangelical
United Brethren Church in a new denomination with 11 million members
in the U. S. and a million more in 50 other countries around the world.

The events climaxed many months' preparation and, in fact, nine
years of Methodist-EUB negotiation. And almost from the opening gavel
of the first business session, it was clear that this was not to be a
conference like any other which delegates from either church had seen
before.

There is risk, in describing the historic Dallas meeting, that
the word "new" will come to sound like a cliché. Out of it came *new*
programs, *new* leadership, *new* stances, *new* structures, *new* willingness to meet controversy squarely, and, more impressive than anything
else, *new* daring to ask 12 million United Methodists to make new
sacrifices as a Christian community in confrontation with a not-so-
new but changing, incredibly complex, and conflict-wracked modern
society.

Surprisingly, perhaps, the feeling of unity engendered by the
union ceremony was not dissipated in the subsequent days of sometimes
heated debate. Lines of separation, when they appeared, were rarely
along the lines of former Methodists versus former EUBs, but rather
between progressives and conservatives from both groups.

Far more decisive than any lingering sense of Methodist and
EUB denominationalism in shaping the conference's direction was the
activity of two close-knit church "renewal" groups - both on and off
the conference floor. Methodists for Church Renewal (MCR), an organization formed prior to the 1964 Methodist General Conference,
was represented by spokesmen in important Uniting Conference roles
and its members were influential debaters on key issues.

The second group, Black Methodists for Church Renewal (BMCR),
was formed early this year, and its leaders, too, were vocal and
effective, indicating for some other delegates, perhaps, what black
churchmen mean when they use the phrase "black power,"

MCR and BMCR, using carefully prepared strategy, affected the

conference's action far out of proportion to their numbers, and few of the measures they championed were defeated. But they could not take sole credit. Their causes, it turned out, were causes which a majority of the delegates were predisposed to favor.

The conference, particularly its first week, was packed with electric moments of high emotion and excitement. But toward its close it became abundantly clear that such two-week sessions put a severe strain on the nerves, stamina, and goodwill of all concerned. The final Uniting Conference session, a marathon which held forth until nearly 12:30 a.m., very nearly collapsed into parliamentary chaos when the delegates could not agree on how to handle matters which had not yet been debated.

Acting finally in near desperation, the conference adopted without debate all material which had been approved by its Legislative Committees for inclusion in the new United Methodist *Discipline*. The Joint Commissions on Union were authorized to work with the *Discipline's* editors to harmonize any conflicts adopted unknowingly.

Publication of the *Discipline* is not expected until early 1969, but a separate printing of new legislation regarding local-church organizational precedures is planned this fall.

Recognizing the need for an early review of the work done in Dallas, the Uniting Conference called a special General Conference session to be held April 20-24, 1970, in Baltimore, Md. This five-day meeting, it was emphasized, will be a working session "without pageantry and pomp." Its cost was estimated at about $500,000. The next regular session will be held April 16-30, 1972, in Atlanta, Ga.

Reflecting on the Dallas meeting at its close, Bishop Eugene M. Frank of St. Louis, first president of the United Methodist Council of Bishops, said, "Mission has constantly taken precedence over structure...There has been a very obvious mood to shape this small part of the Body of Christ so that it would be best equipped and prepared to make real in our society the love of God for all men, his forgiveness and grace, his demand for justice and humanity.

"The shape of this new church will please some and displease others. But we can live with what we have done here if each local congregation is also determined to make real the mission of Christ in the world."

¶   Equal Rights for Women.

(Taken from "The Status and Role of Women in Program and Policy
Making Channels of the United Methodist Church" (1972), 21-
24, 37-38).

GOALS FOR THE UNITED METHODIST CHURCH IN RELATION
TO THE PARTICIPATION OF WOMEN

The issue of the participation of women in the life and work of
the denomination cannot be considered in isolation from the entire
issue of the role of women in society and in all of life. Part of
the genesis of the issue which is currently manifest within the
organizational patterns and structures of the church is found in the
lack of concern indicated by society in general and the Christian
community in particular for the enablement of all peoples. The
affirmation of the personhood of the individual must be more than
just an affirmation. It must be translated into action.

It is in this context of affirmation as a prior condition to
action that the Study Commission gave considerable time and thought
to a discussion of goals for The United Methodist Church in the area
of the enablement of women as persons, in their involvement in the
Christian community and in their participation in the organized
structures of the denomination. The goals which were formulated are
presented so that a sense of concerned purpose and direction can be
developed by the denomination. This statement of goals is to serve
as the starting point for rechanneling of attention, concern,
energies and resources to enhance the God-given potential of each
person regardless of sex. These goals speak to the specific concerns
which were placed before this Study Commission by the General
Conference. These goals are recommended to the 1972 General Conference
of The United Methodist Church for its consideration, discussion and
adoption.

The United Methodist Church in serious consideration of
the issue of the role of women in the Christian community
and their participation in the life and work of The United
Methodist Church believes that it should direct its energies
and resources:

1) To move toward the liberation of all persons so that
   all may achieve full humanity;
2) To bring about attitudinal changes in relation to (a)
   theological, philosophical and Biblical interpretations
   and understandings of the role of women and (b) expectations for achievement and contributions of women;

669

3) To make all United Methodists sensitive to the issues involved in the rights of women;
4) To overcome rigid sex-role distinctions which have traditionally characterized church structures and society;
5) To eliminate all discriminatory language, images and practices in the life and work of The United Methodist Church;
6) To create an openness and receptivity for women in the professional ministry of The United Methodist Church;
7) To utilize the full potential of both men and women in elections and appointments at all levels in The United Methodist Church;
8) To establish a process for evaluation of the performance of The United Methodist Church regarding the role and participation of women in its life and work.

RECOMMENDATIONS FOR THE ENHANCEMENT OF THE PARTICIPATION OF WOMEN

In the light of the above stated goals the Study Commission affirms that specific actions are needed to assist in the movement of the denomination toward the realization of these goals. Therefore, the Study Commission on the Participation of Women in Program and Policy Making Channels of The United Methodist Church requests the General Conference to approve the following recommendations for action and to commend and refer these to the appropriate bodies for implementation. The Study Commission recommends:

1) that every programming agency in the denomination give serious attention to developing new avenues of participation for younger adult members of the denomination, particularly women in the 20-35 age range, and further that this attention be in the form of staff time and financial resources needed to explore varied styles of family life, that alternative life styles by considered, and that new styles (i.e., single women, employed women) be made more acceptable in the overall church population; and

2) that, inasmuch as the Study Commission has been preoccupied with the study of the problems of women's roles in general, to the exclusion of the particular problems of women in racial and ethnic groups, the study should be continued with special attention given to the roles of women of minority racial groups and ethnic groups within The United Methodist Church; and

3) that experimental ministries be developed to and by women, in order to increase awareness of roles and potential of women through consciousness-raising, counseling, education and political action; and

4) that the media-development agencies of the church produce and disseminate materials which would aid a sensitization process concerning the role of women with consideration being given to all forms of media presentation; and

5) that there be a development of curriculum which would help United Methodists avoid sustaining an inadequate image of male and female roles and understand how our rigidly-held sexual roles deprive us of our full humanity, and which would assist in the exploration and development of new and alternative life styles; and;

6) that careful consideration be given to the professional ministry, beginning with the traditional practices of entering the profession and continuing through recruitment and acceptance at the schools of theology, the educational programs for women in the schools of theology, the processes and attitudes of annual conference boards of ministry and of local congregations toward women clergy; and

7) that the Theological Study Commission on Doctrine and Doctrinal Standards be requested to study and report on the role of women from a theological and doctrinal perspective; and

8) that all nominating committees in local churches, annual, jurisdictional and general conferences give attention to the nomination of women for membership on committees, commissions, boards, councils and other organizations, so that women are included in all of these units in significant numbers (bearing in mind that at least 50% of the membership of The United Methodist Church is women; and

9) that the General Conference take whatever action is necessary to
   (a) assure an increased proportion of women in all levels of professional staff in general boards and agencies, and
   (b) create a more favorable setting for the recruitment, education and appointment of women clergy, and
   (c) encourage local churches to be open to the acceptance of women as clergy (senior ministers, associate ministers and ministers in special appointments) and as lay employees; and

10) that the General Conference establish a Commission
on the Role of Women in The United Methodist Church
to foster an ongoing awareness of the problems and
issues relating to the status of women and to
stimulate progress reports on these issues from
the various boards and agencies.

¶ The Problem of Doctrine and Doctrinal Standards in The United
Methodist Church.

(Taken from "Interim Report" of Theological Study Commission on
Doctrine and Doctrinal Standards).

1. Our Rootage in the Christian Tradition

In the triple lineage (former Methodist, Evangelical, and United
Brethren) of the United Methodist Church, whatever continuity and
integrity we have managed to maintain in doctrine has come at least
as much from informal consensus as from deliberate attention to
creedal and confessional standards. From the first we have tended
to assume that all who rightly bear the Christian name share in the
mind of Christ and, therefore, possess the premises from which sound
doctrine is developed. Our forefathers in the faith were self-
consciously rooted in the deep subsoil of historic Christianity. They
understood themselves as neither imitators nor innovators but, rather,
as renewalists in polity and doctrine. Their zeal for souls inspired
new modes of evangelism and new structures within the churches. But
their doctrinal instincts were conservative. They were convinced
that the Christian message is perennially valid, that the resources
of the Christian tradition are ample and relevant for every new
situation.   .   .   .

Wesley, Albright and Otterbein were all aware of the tragic
failures of the fierce struggles of the 16th and 17th centuries
between rival systems of "pure doctrine," and had been persuaded
that "dogmatism" as a method of theology was counter-productive.
This led them to affirm the new spirit of theological pluralism,
within the limits of an old, familiar distinction between the
actual "essentials" of the Gospel and allowable variations in
doctrinal interpretation.   .   .   .

And yet, if tolerance is a theological virtue of great merit,
it is not an absolute. Wesley's insistence that there is a "marrow
of Christian truth" was as firm as his willingness to allow for
differing opinions was sincere. This essential core he found in the
common teaching of all the Christian churches. His avowed formal
doctrines were self-consciously orthodox and none of his own
opinions was original. Even his doctrine of "assurance," charged

against him under the label of "palpable inspiration," was not original. But what was unique was his selection and synthesis of themes from this common tradition: faith *and* good works, Scripture *and* tradition, God's sovereignty *and* man's freedom, universal redemption *and* conditional election, original sin *and* Christian perfection. This marked off Wesleyan thought from the typical Anglican, Lutheran and Calvinist versions of the Christian message. The only "opinions" he ever condemned were those that seemed to him to threaten the vital balance between "law" and "gospel" (e.g. "the German stillness"), or else those "opinions" that were pressed upon the faithful as "essentials" (e.g. predestination).

Wesley was sensitive to the demand for credible authority and he tested his own teaching, and that of others, within a four-element compound of interdependent norms. The cornerstone, of course, was Scripture. Here Wesley never faltered, first or last. . . .

God's self-disclosure in Scripture, interpreted by tradition, received in personal faith may be taken as epiphanies of his redemptive love. When any of this is conceptualized, however, it becomes subject to the critical strictures of *reason*, which for Wesley meant something like *logical cogency*. Reason is man's God-given capacity to appraise the meaning of propositions, including the incurably imprecise language of theology. Wesley never doubted "the reasonableness of Christianity." Its deepest insights arise from levels below and beyond the range of reason, but they become credible only as they are rendered intelligible by reflection (Wesley's version of Anselm's famous *fides quaerens intellectum* [faith seeking understanding].

In this quadrilateral of "standards," Scripture stands foremost without a rival. Tradition is the distillate of the formative experiences of the People of God in their wrestlings with the problems of biblical interpretation. "Experience" ("the inner witness of the Spirit") is the name for that vital transit from the objective focus of faith to its subjective center - from "dead faith" (correct belief) to "living faith" that justifies and saves. And reason is the referee of the terms in which all this is expressed. Any insight, therefore, that is a disclosure from Scripture, illumined by tradition, realized in experience and confirmed by reason is as fully authoritative as men may hope for in this life.

As a safeguard against confusion and eccentricity, Wesley borrowed a leaf from the ancient history of councils in the church and adapted it to the needs of the Methodist movement. He called it a "conference." It was chiefly a device for developing and maintaining *dynamic consensus by means of open consultation*. . . .

Wesley then conceived the idea of supplementing the conference progress with a collection of exemplary sermonic essays in which he

673

attempted to sum up *all* the "essentials" of his doctrine and most of
his "opinions," putting his written word in place of his personal
presence. In 1746, he published the first of our volumes of *Sermons
on Several Occasions* in which he sets forth his basic method of
theologizing and suggests, indirectly, that the *sermons* are a more
nearly adequate medium for doctrinal teaching than "confessions,"
on the one hand, or formal theological treatises, on the other!

This unprecedented pattern of *sermons as doctrinal guidelines*
turned out to be useful in many ways. In the first place, the
biblical text gives the hearer an equal access to the preacher's own
acknowledged authority. In the second place, a sermon allows for
more originality and latitude in its interpretation than the sacral
aura of a liturgy, the attempted precision of a "confession" or the
technical demands of a doctrinal treatise. Thirdly, sermons are
more apt to stimulate their hearers (readers) to personal theological
discussion and reaction than confessions usually do. Finally,
sermons are more readily adapted to a mass movement that does not
require a high level of sophistication in the rank and file.

However, if doctrinal teaching is to be truly "biblical," then
preachers and hearers need guidelines for their exegesis and interpretation of Scripture; therefore, Wesley undertook to provide them
with yet a third standard reference: his *Explanatory Notes Upon the
New Testament* (first edition, 1755; four other editions in his
lifetime). As with the *Sermons*, the *Notes* illustrate Wesley's twin
principles of exegetical precision and hermeneutical freedom
(precision in studying the text and freedom in interpreting it).
They show Scripture and tradition interacting in search of a dynamic
harmony of objective exegesis and personal faith!

*   *   *

5. Doctrinal Standards in American Methodism

The Methodists in America rejected Wesley's direct control over
them (1784) but retained their traditional loyalties to his three-
fold *magisterium* of the Conference, the *Sermons* and the *Notes*. Thus,
when the Constitution of The Methodist Episcopal Church and its first
"Restrictive Rule" were adopted (1808), the meaning of the phrase,
"our present existing and established standards of doctrine," was
self-evident to those present. What had to be added was an explicit
reference to the "Articles of Religion." These Articles had come to
the American Methodists as an *appendix* to Wesley's *Sunday Service*,
his hastily abridged version of the 1662 *Book of Common Prayer*. The
original Thirty-Nine Articles had never functioned as a "confession"
in the Church of England nor had Wesley ever regarded them as such.
Hence, in the earliest American *Disciplines*, they also appeared as
appendices. It was only in 1792 that somebody moved them forward to

their present position - without formal authorization (much in the same way that we lost "descended into hell" from our version of the Apostles' Creed). Therefore, as the memories of later generations dimmed, the Articles were left in the front of the *Discipline*, looking for all the world like the Methodists' "confession." There they have remained, unchanged, unchallenged - and largely disregarded.

Methodists have gone on theologizing, of course, but the development of doctrine among us has been rather more piecemeal and accidental than guided by commonly consented standards.   .   .   .

6. The Evangelicals and United Brethren

Along with its roots in the Wesleyan-Anglican tradition, the United Methodist Church is also grateful heir to the spiritual and doctrinal legacies of Jacob Albright and Phillip Otterbein. Their traditions have run parallel with those of Methodism but with significant differences that deserve more attention than they have thus far received. Both the Albright Evangelicals and the Otterbein United Brethren sprang from a transplanted German pietism - with its Lutheran roots in Arndt, Spener and Francke - and yet also with strong affiliations with the *Heidelberg Catechism* and its interpreters. In the "Dutch" communities of America, however, these men were more intently preoccupied with the communication of the Gospel than with doctrinal reflection upon it. Their common stress was on "conversion" (regeneration, "new birth"), justification by faith attested by "sensible assurance," the priesthood of all (converted!) believers, and Christian perfection as the crown and goal of Christian experience.

In both traditions, the primal font of Christian truth was God's Word in Scripture. Otterbein's dictum, "to be careful to preach no other doctrine than what is plainly laid down in the Bible" was generally taken for granted. A class member was expected "to confess that he received the Bible as the Word of God." Ordinands declared their acceptance of the authority of Scripture "without reserve." In John Dreisbach's *Catechism* (1809) every question was answered by a biblical quotation, with no added comment. In authorizing its first official church paper (*Der Christliche Botschafter*, 1835), the General Conference of the Evangelical Association specified that its first aim should be "to impart the divine truths of Holy Writ in their unadulterated purity and in such a manner as can be plainly understood by the common people."

But (converted) Pietists read Scripture with a specific "Christian consciousness," and here all distinctions between learned and unlearned fall away. The "converted" are instructed by the Holy Spirit in their understanding of the living truth, and their insights are

675

likely to be more valid than the abstruse dicta of theologians –
emphatically if the theologian is unconverted.

7. The Evangelical "Articles"

Even if this attitude left historical theology unstressed, it was
equally unconfined by anything resembling "confessionalism" in
doctrine. Jacob Albright and George Miller utilized a German translation of the Methodist "Articles" and added one of their own –
"Of the Last Judgment." This is a paraphrase of Article XVII of the
Augsburg Confession and clearly different, on this point, from
Chapter XXXIII of the *Westminster Confession*. It is interesting that
this doctrine had been omitted from the Thirty-Nine Articles and from
the majority of the Protestant confessions as well. In any case,
amongst the Evangelicals, the function and use of these confessional
Articles was conditioned by their undogmatic temper and also by the
general climate of American pietism.   .   .   .

In the 1870s, a flurry of debate was touched off by a proposal
of Theophilus G. Clewell that the Articles be extensively revised –
Clewell called them "Iron Jackets." The Conference of 1875 rejected
this move. Dr. S. P. Spreng spoke for the majority in *The Evangelical Messenger:* The old faith is the safest and best...Saving truth
must not change, lest it have no longer saving power." Thereafter,
the Articles remained unchanged and were brought intact into the EUB
union of 1946.

8. The United Brethren "Confession"

In the earliest years of the United Brethren, there was no great
urgency for a creedal statement. In their first General Conference
(1815), however, they adopted a "Confession of Faith" (drafted by
Christian Newcomer and Christopher Grosh) amounting to seven short
paragraphs chiefly in paraphrase of the Apostles' Creed (with an
interesting echo from the so-called "Athanasian Creed"). In 1841,
the UB General Conference decreed no further changes in the Confession.
But there was agitation for change and in 1885 a commission was appointed
to undertake a revision. Their resulting proposals for a new Confession
of Faith and Constitution were duly submitted to the Annual Conferences
and finally placed before the General Conference of 1889 by the commission.
They were adopted with a formal "Proclamation." It was generally agreed,
however, that the new doctrinal standards had not altered the substance
of the old ones, either by design or implication. This action was, however,
viewed by a minority as a violation of the rule of 1841 – and became one
of the warrants for a resulting schism ("The United Brethren Church[Old
Constitution]").

The Confession of 1889 had an explicit article on "Sanctification,"
deliberately open to both the Wesleyan-Evangelical emphasis on the
expectation of holiness in this life as the crown of faith and the

Lutheran-Calvinist nuances about sanctification by imputation in conjunction with justification itself.

9. The EUB Confession

In the union of 1946, the Evangelical Articles and the United Brethren Confession were both printed unchanged in the new *Discipline*, in deference to the Evangelicals' rule against change (1839). The General Conference of 1958, however, authorized the Board of Bishops of the new church to provide them with a new Confession of Faith. This was undertaken with extensive consultation throughout the denomination. The new Confession was submitted to the General Conference of 1962 and was adopted without amendment. It was declared to supplant both former Confessions - and was brought over intact into the Constitution of the United Methodist Church. Its most striking difference from the Methodist Articles, or its own EUB antecedents, is the long article on "Sanctification and Christian Perfection." This is all the more interesting in that this Confession adds a unique *Wesleyan* doctrinal emphasis - something that episcopal Methodism had never done with its own Articles.

One of the more obvious conclusions from this sketch of a very complicated history is that both the Evangelicals and United Brethren have maintained a more effective corporate doctrinal continuity than their Methodist cousins, especially over the last 100 years. Their conference process served them as their central and chief *magisterium*. This was all the more important since neither the Evangelicals nor the United Brethren had anything comparable to the Wesleyan "standards" of "Sermons" and "Notes." Thus, they have never forfeited any major fraction of their inheritance as the Methodists have done.

10. Doctrinal Standards in the United Methodist Church

The architects of the Plan of Union of 1968 consciously avoided the difficulties of doctrinal decision: the line of least theological disturbance seemed also the line of least ecumenical resistance. The "Preface" (*Discipline*, pp. 35-37) was a reluctant afterthought and refers chiefly to the problem of standards as it then stood in the Methodist Church. The Methodist Articles and the EUB Confession are printed back to back in the new *Discipline*: they are "deemed congruent if not identical in their doctrinal perspectives, and not in conflict." And yet their differences are important enough to raise a host of questions, not only with respect to the problem of their being "harmonized" but also with respect to the larger question as to how "doctrinal standards" should be understood in The United Methodist Church and how they could be put to profitable use. Neither of these questions has an easy answer.

For one thing, as we have seen, the Methodist Articles are not, and never have been, distinctively *Wesleyan*. They hark back to the high-water mark of Reformed influence in Anglican theology (1543-63) and they are the nearest thing to a "confession" the Church of England has ever had. Wesley filtered out as much of their Calvinism as he could; he left their other biases intact. He undoubtedly subscribed to their doctrinal substance, but they were not his own prime reference for theologizing and not preeminent in his own doctrinal standards and norms. American Methodism gave them more formal status than he did, chiefly as they came to neglect what he regarded as more important (i.e., the *Sermons* and *Notes* understood as "guidelines" and negative limits). By the same token, the EUB articles and confessions have functioned rather less as primary doctrinal determinants than as boundaries. The attention they have received was always in the context of their conciliar *magisterium* as it sought to coordinate doctrinal impulses from many quarters - colleges, seminaries, denominational periodicals, etc.

Yet, again, both the Articles and the Confession as they now stand can all too easily be dismissed, or at least denigrated, as "pre-modern." In the current bedlam of theological denial, affirmation and invention, there are not many disputed questions that could be settled by direct appeal to either the Articles or Confession, or both together. This is not to disparage their essential validity but only to raise a question as to their efficacy in the present circumstances.

Finally, it is painfully plain that the present "moment" is inauspicious for the production of new creeds and confessions, as both the United Church of Christ and the United Presbyterians have discovered - and Paul VI as well. It is also worth noting the difficulties experienced by the Consultation on Church Union in connection with the problem of doctrinal standards and a "Confession" for the proposed "Church of Christ Uniting."

11. Anomalies and Confusion in the UMC

In the acute and deepening crisis of authority in the churches, our sense of tradition (such as it ever was!) has been gravely weakened and with it has come a drastic erosion of force of external standards of every kind. On the other side, there is an escalation of contrariety and discord in the contemporary theological debate, with no dominant perspective in sight or prospect. There is a widening chasm between clergy and clergy and between clergy and laity, with respect to theological "opinions" - and essentials too! The primacy of Scripture can no longer be taken for granted; the pietistic appeal to "Christian experience" has undergone existentialist mutations; the rule of reason is under protest. Activism is "in";

678

tradition is "out." And in every case, the inevitable tension between any bid for consensus and the priceless values of intellectual and spiritual freedom is more tightly drawn than before. Truth can neither be established nor maintained by majority vote or the imposition of official "standards." And all this poses a double threat to *any* new "creedal statement" that might claim enforceable authority. It would take a miracle to turn out one that was fully *representative* and, besides, it would take yet another miracle to produce one that was actually relevant. The likelier fate for any less miraculous "statement" would be that it would either be rejected or more probably ignored.

And yet, our present theological predicament as a church – a church newly united, wracked by the travails of renewal, committed to the ecumenical enterprise and yet, also insecure in its own self-confidence – is quite literally untenable. We can scarcely identify ourselves to ourselves; we baffle our separated brethren. Our Wesleyan heritage goes largely unclaimed; the mingling of Methodist and EUB traditions has barely begun. Our doctrinal norms are ill-defined and anomalous. We have a *Discipline* that is generally clear on questions of administrative polity, but blandly vague with respect to doctrine and doctrinal standards. The simplest proof of this is the frequent mention of *"our* doctrines," with no definition of what the phrase refers to. It is as if, once upon a time, an earlier generation understood it all and then forgot to tell their children – who never asked.

Our first two Restrictive Rules (¶ 16) place formidable barriers against any change of "our Articles of Religion," "our Confession of Faith" or "our present, existing and established standards of doctrine." But what does this prohibition mean or amount to? Besides, what is the constitutional status of the historical *Preface* (Part II) and how is it to be interpreted? It is impossible to decide from the text of the *Discipline*.   .   .   .

12. The Recovery of our "Common History"

What, then, is the wisest course in so ambiguous a situation? Your Commission has no formulary answer and no delusions about its present or prospective influence in the church. Its hope and confidence rest, rather, in the possibility that if the Methodist people were somehow aroused to the challenges and dangers of this crisis and were enlisted in the cause of *doctrinal renewal* as a re-inforcement to all our other commitments, there still remains in our present resources the potential for renewal and progress. And so we turn to the church at large for counsel and aid, inviting all interested parties to count themselves our allies in this endeavor.

There is an obvious, and relatively easy, first step toward any rebirth of consensus amongst us. It is simply that we must get to know each other better and our several traditions. It does us no credit that most former Methodists know even less about EUB history than about their own; that many former EUBs are just beginning to be aware of their Methodist inheritance. Even the veterans on both sides have much to learn from this "new history" of our *united* church; many of the young might find it more relevant to their future than they now suspect.   .   .   .

13. The Problem of Updating Our Doctrinal Heritage

But what more than this? There would be no great difficulty in producing a "new confession" in place of the two we now have. *That* would be a conventional assignment in "ecumenical drafting." But what useful purpose would such a statement serve? A new confession in the old rhetoric would not necessarily reflect the Wesleyan vision nor would it express the spirit of perennial reform. A new confession in the new rhetoric would be promptly outdated. It would be far more fruitful for the theological enterprise if we could recover the dynamics of our Methodist and EUB conciliar traditions: annual conferences devoted to the current issues, but also with a conscious concern about "our standards of doctrine"; a renaissance of interest in the Wesleyan *Sermons* and *Notes* (and their EUB analogues); a new self-consciousness and a new authority in our ecumenical outreach and negotiations. Are such things beyond our reach - or resolution?

This brings us to a crucial and touchy question not yet fully faced: how is doctrinal consensus rightly sought? Should a new creedal statement reflect an even partial consensus - and if so, which part? Or, should it anticipate such a consensus and attempt to bring it off? In the latter case, how could we agree on the appropriate "standards"; or, is such a thing necessary?

There are other possibilities. Our Roman Catholic brethren, after the counter-productive episode of their new "Creed of the People of God" supplied them by Pope Paul (1968), have had considerable success with new collective doctrinal essays (e.g. "the Dutch Catechism," their new "directories" on the ecumenism, on the Jews, their project called *Concilium*, etc.). United Methodists issue megatons of religious literature of various sorts, reflecting varying degrees of doctrinal self-consciousness. How could this flood be made responsive to the question of doctrinal "standards?" We have, besides, study-programs almost in surfeit: local churches, WSCS, Pastors! *Schools*, "continuing education," etc. These are natural resources for supporting any purposeful effort to renew our theological self-identity as a church. And such a renewal would amount to a new chapter in our theological history.

680

Is there a recognizable Methodist "style" for the guidance of our official teachers (clerical and academic), that would be significant in the development of doctrine within the United Methodist Church, in the ecumenical dialogue and in the widening discussions with partisans of the gospels of secular humanism? If so, can this style be characterized in ways that we and others can understand?

In our deepening frustrations over the hindrances to church renewal, is theological renewal an actual precondition of authentic reform in other aspects of our life and mission as a church? If so, what sort of re-formulation of "doctrinal standards" would best serve this larger cause? In short, is it conceivable that the United Methodist Church can move into the difficult future that is pelting down upon us with any lively hope, apart from some sort of conscious reconnection with her own past and that of the larger Christian past of which we have been a part? It is our concern for positive answers to such questions as these - our quest for a *usable past on behalf of a viable future* - that will shape the further efforts of your Commission.

¶   Message to People Called Methodist.

(Taken from Proceedings of the Consultation of Methodist Bishops, March 15-16, 1979, Atlanta, Georgia, pp. 82-86).

For two days from March 15-16, 1979, we, the bishops of the African Methodist Episcopal Church, the African Methodist Episcopal Zion Church, the Christian Methodist Episcopal Church, and the United Methodist Church, have been meeting together in Atlanta, Georgia, for fellowship and for discussion of mutual concerns. The meeting was called by the episcopal bodies of all four of our churches.

For well over a century bishops of the four churches have served as fraternal messengers to our respective General Conferences. Some of us have sat together often in meetings of the National Council of Churches, the World Council of Churches, the World Methodist Council, and the Consultation on Church Union. All of us have had occasional contact with our counterparts in the same geographic area. But here in Atlanta for these two days the bishops of all the four churches have met together for the first time in history.

In our deliberations four papers were presented on the following themes, each prepared by one bishop from each church: We Share a Common Faith and Discipline, We Share a Common Witness, We Share a Common Ministry and Episcopacy, We Share a Common Commitment. Each presentation was followed by three reactors, one each from the other three churches, and plenary discussion. In addition five small groups continued the discussion in a more intimate way.

1. Out of our meeting together we would remind our people of our common heritage as the spiritual children of John Wesley. We share one faith; we exalt the same emphasis upon personal and social redemption; we sing together the Wesleyan hymns; we share the same general pattern of church organization; we cherish the same goal for the individual of perfection in love; and together we dream the same dream of a new world wherein dwelleth righteousness. Above all, we see ourselves together with all true believers as the sons and daughters of the Almighty. Our sessions have enabled us as bishops to get to know one another better. Yet we need to go even further in our mutual understanding of our separate histories and traditions and reciprocally to honor them. We would mention, for example, that in the present United Methodist Church our heritage has been enriched by the union in 1968 with the Evangelical and United Brethren traditions.

2. Out of our meeting together we would remind our people of the gains that the years have brought to our respective churches. All of them have grown in numbers, in resources and, we trust, in influence for good and in service for God and humanity. Not only have they grown as churches counting their converts by the hundreds of thousands and helping their members to develop spiritually, but also growing out of their concern schools, colleges, universities, hospitals, homes and other institutions have been established, the full story of whose ministry to humanity can be known only to God.

3. Out of our meeting together, on the other hand, we are forced to remind our people that these gains have largely been made separately. There have been scattered instances of all working together on some particular project but by and large each of our four churches has gone its own way, operating generally unto itself. On occasion we have even been in competition. One cannot help wondering what further gains might have been made had all of us taken more notice of each other.

4. Out of our meeting together we would call attention of our people to the gains which recent years have registered particularly for the black church and the black community with the coming of desegregation, the passage of civil rights legislation and a general acceptance of new patterns of social behavior. These gains have come all too slowly and have been purchased at great price. All too often they have been resisted by some persons while, on the other hand, they have not only been heartily welcomed but also eagerly worked for by others.

5. Out of our meeting together we would remind our people that there are other gains which still need to be made. There are yet millions of people outside the church who need to be won for Christ. There are children to be taught and loved into the Kingdom.

There are thousands of persons whose names are on church rolls who have become inactive and are now only nominal members who need to be restored to a living, vital relationship with their Lord. And all our people need to be further built up in the faith and to come to yet a fuller understanding of what is actually required for living the life that becometh the Gospel. Effective evangelism is a part of the very lifeblood of each and all of our churches.

There are social gains yet to be made if, in accordance with the prayer of our Lord, His Kingdom is to "come *upon* earth." Racism, poverty, exploitation, unemployment, inadequate housing, inferior education, insufficient health care, injustice and rights of women, children and the elderly remain problems for American society as a whole. They are particularly acute for much of the black and other ethnic minority communities and for the poorer section of the white community. If our churches called Methodist were now to take these issues with the utmost seriousness, we who are called to social holiness in our collective strength might effect the drastic remedies our society cries for in America, Africa--particularly southern Africa--, Asia and the isles of the sea.

Thousands of our local churches need to become far more effective than they are today. They need to experience a fresh call to ministry and to come to a fuller appreciation of what effective ministry involves. The importance of their becoming such effective local churches can scarcely be overemphasized because life for thousands of our people centers largely around them.

6. Out of our meeting together and the rich, shared experiences of these days, we would dare to suggest to our respective General Conferences, as a first step at least, that some formal arrangement be developed for the regular consulting together by these four churches which have so much in common. It could be that such regular consultation might lead eventually to arrangements for mutual planning and working together and, in time perhaps, to further steps. Meanwhile we can find ways of acting together on a regional basis. We can exchange speakers at annual conferences. We can share significant documents and other information. We can plan further meetings such as this one. We can in many ways move forward together.

In 1984 Methodism in the United States will celebrate its 200th anniversary. All of our churches look to a common American foundation in the Christmas Conference of 1784, held in Baltimore, Maryland. As bishops of the African Methodist Episcopal Church, the African Methodist Episcopal Zion Church, the Christian Methodist Episcopal Church, and the United Methodist Church, we would call our four churches and all our people to a fresh examination of our common heritage and a new commitment to world mission and to the goal voiced by our predecessors to "reform the continent"--and the very world itself--and "to spread scriptural holiness throughout the land"--and other lands as well.